International Money and Finance

Third Edition

International Money and Finance

Third Edition

C. Paul Hallwood, *University of Connecticut*
Ronald MacDonald, *University of Strathclyde*

Blackwell
Publishing

BLACKWELL PUBLISHING
350 Main Street, Malden, MA 02148-5020, USA
108 Cowley Road, Oxford OX4 1JF, UK
550 Swanston Street, Carlton, Victoria 3053, Australia

First published 1986
Second edition 1994
Third edition published 2000

11 2009

Library of Congress Cataloging-in-Publication Data

Hallwood, C. Paul
    International money and finance / C. Paul Hallwood and Ronald
    MacDonald — 3rd ed.
        p.   cm.
    ISBN 978-0-631-20461-9 (hbk : alk. paper) — ISBN 978-0-631-20462-6 (pbk : alk. paper)
    1. International finance.   I. MacDonald, Ronald.   II. Title.

    HG3881.H255   2000
    332.4'5 — dc21   99–053308

A catalogue record for this title is available from the British Library.

For further information on
Blackwell Publishing, visit our website:
www.blackwellpublishing.com

Contents

Figures

Tables

Preface

The subject of international finance continues to develop as fast or faster than any other field in economics. During the course of the last three decades, and especially in the last decade of the twentieth century, the degree of international financial integration has increased enormously. All major country groups – OECD, developing country and, newest of all, the transition economies (from central planning) – are experiencing vastly increased cross-border flows of money and capital. Today the value of *daily* foreign exchange trading is more than one-hundred times the value of *annual* international trade in goods and services. Almost as rapidly growing is the mass of scientific literature on international finance. This literature can be broadly divided four ways: into theory, evidence, institutions, and policy. All of these are subjects of investigation in *International Money and Finance*. Important new developments have appeared in diverse areas such as theoretical innovations in the general equilibrium theory of exchange rate determination; explanations for the relative immobility of long-term capital alongside, apparently, highly mobile short-term capital; the behavior of exchange rates within an exchange rate fluctuation band (or, target zone); theories of the best course of financial integration by countries previously largely divorced from the international circuit of capital; explanations for why real exchange rates wander away for long periods from purchasing power parity – so disturbing real economic activity; how misinformed speculation and speculative bubbles cause floating exchange rates to be unstable and largely unpredictable; a reconsideration of the performance of the gold standard in the nineteenth century and its role as a causal factor in the Great Depression; and on how best to reform the international monetary system.

We have tried hard to keep abreast of the literature in all the main fields of international finance – as a glance at the long bibliography will attest. We believe that scholarship requires the scholar to know the sources of ideas – every idea having its own author – and we have not spared the student the bother of knowing about how research and the generation of ideas is progressing. We reject the idea that a textbook should present just what is accepted, for so often in economics what is accepted is not necessarily accepted for very long nor by everybody in a field – as witness the current state of macroeconomics.

In this third edition of *International Money and Finance* we have added four new chapters to those that appeared in the second edition. They are: the general equilibrium monetary approach to the exchange rate and exchange rate regime volatility (chapter 10); currency crises and speculative attack (chapter 14); target zones and dirty floating (chapter 15); and one on the international gold standard (chapter 16). So now we offer two chapters on the history of the international monetary system that deploy state-of-the-art economic and econometric analysis. The chapters on transition economies (22) and the one on monetary union (18) have both been entirely rewritten so as to reflect recent theoretical and empirical work in their respective subfields. Furthermore, for the same reasons, scattered throughout the book, nine new sections have been added, or, existing ones entirely rewritten. These are those on the current account and intertemporal utility maximization, and the equilibrium real exchange rate (both of these appearing in chapter 4); the empirical validity of purchasing power parity (chapter 7); the development of a *successful* short-term exchange rate forecasting model (chapter 9) – for anybody familiar with the field of finance your eyes should be popping out at this one; foreign exchange micro-structure (chapter 13); the East Asian dollar standard (chapter 17); long-term capital flows (chapter 19); and developing country economic policy and the real exchange rate, and the IMF and financial distress (both in chapter 20).

The emphasis of our endeavor continues to be to describe the most significant modern theoretical and institutional developments in the field and to examine the most important policy and empirical research. We emphasize accessibility of the material to students with moderate levels of mathematics – intuitive, but nevertheless often quite rigorous, explanations appear alongside mathematical arguments. We also make an important feature of *International Money and Finance* an emphasis on the application of econometrics to the study of international finance. We realize that many students and teachers will not wish to get into so much econometric detail as we offer. For this reason the more advanced, indeed, quite often "state-of-the-art," econometrics has been separated into *starred* sections. Specialists in econometrics should find the *starred* sections a useful insight as to how econometrics is being used in international finance today. Those offering/ studying courses of a less quantitative-empirical nature may simply ignore them. We also hope, in fact we know from the feedback that we have received, that graduate students embarking on their first empirical investigations in the area of international finance will find the *starred* sections useful points of departure for their own research.

The book is aimed at second- and third-year undergraduate and graduate courses in International Economics or International Finance. It is also suited as a companion text to courses in Development Economics. If needed chapter 1 could be used as an introduction to basic concepts, and there are three chapters highly relevant to the study of developing countries: those on, respectively, developing country balance of payments, choice of exchange rate regime and the IMF (chapter 20); the order of liberalization (chapter 21); and international debt (chapter 23).

C. Paul Hallwood
Department of Economics U-63
University of Connecticut
Storrs, CT 06289
USA

e-mail
hallwood@uconnvm.uconn.edu

Ronald MacDonald
Department of Economics
Strathclyde University
100 Cathedral Street
Glasgow G4 0LN, Scotland

e-mail
r.r.macdonald@strath.ac.uk

April 2000

1

Introduction

In this book we build the tools (balance of payments and exchange rate theory) needed to understand international money and finance. These are then applied to a wide selection of issues – including money and macroeconomics in an open economy; the efficiency or otherwise of foreign exchange markets; the modeling and measurement of short- and long-term capital flows; international macroeconomic policy coordination; the history and future of the international monetary system; international financial features of economic and financial reform in both transition economies and in developing countries; the economics of monetary union, pegged exchange rates, dollarization, currency crises and speculative attack; the international debt crisis; and the functioning of international institutions such as the IMF, the EMS, and international banking.

In this, the third edition, we have added whole new chapters on the general equilibrium monetary approach to the exchange rate and exchange rate regime volatility, currency crises and speculative attack, target zones and dirty floating, and the international gold standard. Two chapters have been completely revised – that on transition economies and that on monetary union.

We have also added or revised sections in several other chapters to reflect recent theoretical or empirical research on the current account and intertemporal utility maximization, the equilibrium real exchange rate (both in chapter 4), purchasing power parity (chapter 7), *successful* short-term exchange rate forecasting (chapter 9), foreign exchange micro-structure (chapter 13), the East Asian dollar standard (chapter 17), long-term capital flows (chapter 19), and the IMF and financial distress (chapter 20).

One of our objectives is to describe the richness of the subject matter of international finance – a field which is undergoing considerable development in both theoretical and empirical methods. Both of these aspects are reflected in this edition of *International Money and Finance*. As we also emphasize topics on economic policy and institutional development, we hope that the reader will gain a good grasp of the subject matter of international money and finance across its four main dimensions: theory, evidence, policy, and institutions.

It is also worth noting that *International Money and Finance* is not just a book on open economy macroeconomics, although whole chapters (5, 6 and, arguably, 8 and 10) and several sections of other chapters are devoted to this important topic. The field of international finance is in fact broader than just open economy macroeconomics and it should properly include examination of topics such as exchange market efficiency, the rationality of agents in exchange markets, the choice of international monetary system, the economics of monetary union, and international finance in transition and developing countries.

We also believe that it is a great advantage of this book that it explicitly reflects the work over many decades of a great number of talented researchers. We do not think that it is a good academic exercise to offer the student of international money and finance the subject distilled into a single point of view. This is partly because this can hardly be fair to all research agendas – being both neoKeynesian and neoclassical at the same time; and more especially, we believe that students should be presented with the intellectual challenge of deciding for themselves. Intellectual challenge is also the reason why we have not ended each chapter with a Further Readings section. Readings are in fact cited time and again throughout each chapter and we leave it to the student and to the instructor which ones to pursue further. We would like to think that this book is more than just a textbook as it attempts to point the student in the direction of further research. Perhaps this is no more evident than in the many *starred sections* where the econometric evidence is broached.

The Chapters

Chapters 2, 3, and 4 provide an introduction to basic concepts in international money and finance including, in chapter 2, definitions of the balance of payments and the exchange rate, and testimony against floating exchange rates; in chapter 3, amongst other things, the elasticities view of exchange rate determination and discussion of the important concepts of covered and uncovered interest parity; and in chapter 4 the absorption approach to the balance of payments, current account disequilibria as a result of intertemporal utility maximization and an elementary discussion of international macroeconomic policy coordination.

Chapter 5 discusses the topic of macroeconomic management in an open economy. It is shown that opening an economy to international trade and capital flows changes the nature of the constraints on policy makers. With mobile international capital flows, depending upon whether exchange rates are pegged or floating, the effectiveness of monetary or fiscal policy is compromised as an instrument of macroeconomic policy. But this is not say that one or other instrument necessarily becomes a broken reed for, depending upon the assumptions made about the macroeconomy, it does not.

Chapter 6 is very much related to chapter 5 in that it discusses international macroeconomic policy coordination. With macroeconomic spillover effects from one country to another it is shown that countries may gain from international cooperation. This point is returned to again in chapter 17 on monetary unions where, fiscal policy externalities between members could be managed to the benefit of the union as a whole.

Chapter 7 discusses the topic of purchasing power parity (PPP). This concept is important because it plays a central role in several theories of the determination of the exchange rate and of the balance of payments. While theoretically PPP ought to hold, if not from moment to moment then at least in the "long-run," for a couple of decades or so empirical evidence seemed to show that it did not. However, research using econometric techniques not previously available now shows that deviations from PPP are not as persistent as once thought: estimates now are for a half-life of deviations of about 3 to 4 years.

Chapter 8 sets out the venerable and important subject of the monetary approach to the balance of payments – dating from at least the days of the eighteenth-century Scottish philosopher David Hume. Through this theory we gain an understanding of the causes and persistence of balance of payments deficits. Mastery of the model also throws light on to a wide range of subjects, e.g. why balance of payments deficits persist, fundamental causes of the international debt crisis, and why no open economy economic liberalization is likely to be successful until domestic monetary conditions are stabilized. The model also provides justification for various conditionality clauses included by the IMF on borrowers.

In its modern form, the monetary approach to the balance of payments was mainly developed in the 1960s – when it largely superseded the elasticities approach, developed in the 1930s, and the absorption approach which grew out of closed economy Keynesian economics in the 1950s. With simple modifications the monetary approach to the balance of payments is turned into the monetary approach to the exchange rate. More recently, the monetary approach has been reset within a new general equilibrium theoretical framework.

Chapters 9–13 present the core theories of exchange rate determination. Although we discuss a number of theories in these chapters a key element in our discussion concerns trying to explain the volatility of exchange rates, which has been such a feature of the recent floating experience (see section 2.5). Modern exchange rate theory views foreign exchange as an asset that is priced in an asset market (rather in the same manner as are stocks and bonds), and an exchange rate is the price of one asset (currency) in terms of another. In chapter 9 three theories are presented that model the exchange rate as determined solely as an asset price in the capital account of the balance of payments – with the current account playing virtually no part. Marked differences show up between the flexible-price and sticky-price versions of exchange rate determination. In the former, dramatic exchange rate movements are associated with agents' collapsing their expectations of future events into the current exchange rate, whilst in the latter asymmetrical adjustment speeds in goods and asset markets lead to the phenomenon of exchange rate overshooting. As we shall see, sticky prices and floating exchange rates have proved to be an especially unhappy combination for many countries because it results in sharp movements in real exchange rates which can have damaging effects on economies.

Currency substitution is the third exchange rate model investigated in chapter 9. Its contribution is to show how the reallocation of currency portfolios by international transactors – such as multinational corporations – affects the exchange rate and, by extension, the stability of the international monetary system in an era of highly liquid international money flows. Currency substitution renders the demand for money unstable and so questions the case for monetary targeting. An additional topic addressed in chapter 9 is the fashionable concept of speculative bubbles.

Chapter 10 discusses two further applications of the monetary model. The first considers real shocks in a general equilibrium model. This asserts that the empirical regularity of a near perfect positive correlation between nominal and real exchange rates can be explained by real shocks (as in real business cycle theory) rather than nominal shocks (as in exchange rate overshooting models). After reviewing the empirical evidence we conclude that the real shock hypothesis receives little support. The other main topic in chapter 10 is exchange regime volatility. We point out that after the move to floating exchange rates in 1973 exchange rates became much more volatile while macroeconomic fundamentals did not. This casts doubt on macroeconomic models of exchange rate determination and sets off a search for other explanations of exchange rate determination which we investigate in later chapters – especially chapter 13.

The portfolio balance model of the exchange rate, the subject of chapter 11, drops the assumption that domestic and foreign bonds are perfect substitutes, so enriching the portfolio adjustment characteristics of exchange rate determination. Uncovered interest parity is not assumed to hold; it is also recognized that ignoring the current account of the balance of payments overlooks important wealth effects which feedback onto the exchange rate. Such wealth effects are shown to be a central part of the process of adjustment to monetary or fiscal shocks. Moreover, monetary shocks are shown to be non-neutral in the portfolio balance model – so destroying the classical dichotomy.

Traditionally asset prices have been thought to be determined in efficient markets. Indeed, the efficient market hypothesis (EMH) was for many years taken to be the industry paradigm in the financial markets literature (i.e. that on stock markets). That paradigm has now been called into question and there currently seems to be a shift away from the EMH toward alternatives like the noise-trader approach. The abandonment of the EMH has largely been due to its rejection when confronted by the data. However, it is crucial to recognize, and this is something emphasized in chapters 10 and 12, that the EMH is a *joint hypothesis* consisting of some view about how the equilibrium price of the asset is determined along with the concept, which many people equate with the EMH, that agents efficiently exploit all available information (which is often understood to mean that agents process their expectations rationally). Therefore, an empirical rejection of the EMH may reflect an inefficient information process or it may simply reflect the fact that the researcher has chosen the wrong equilibrium model.

Applied to the foreign exchange market, we demonstrate in chapter 12 that the popular definition of the EMH, which implies that the forward exchange rate should be an optimal predictor of the future spot rate, is overwhelmingly rejected by the data. Because of the jointness of the hypothesis being tested, the interpretation placed on this rejection in many ways depends on a researcher's prejudices. Many researchers have interpreted the rejection as prima facie evidence of a foreign exchange risk premium (rather then inefficient information processing) and such an interpretation is considered in some detail in chapter 12.

In chapter 13 we discuss the alternative interpretation, that it is something to do with failure of agents' expectations formation (which, as we shall see, need not mean that agents are actually inefficient information processors). More specifically, in chapter 13 we discuss peso effects, chartism, market microstructure, noise trading, and deterministic chaos. A recently emerging literature uses survey data on exchange rate expectations to try to determine which component of the joint EMH is responsible for rejection. The survey-based literature is also used to motivate the market microstructure view of the foreign exchange market.

Another implication of the efficient markets theory is that if a prediction is made at time t for the exchange rate at time $t + 1$, the prediction will probably turn out to be wrong if new information turns up. In foreign exchange markets new information is constantly turning up and, empirically, this has had the expected effect on the accuracy of exchange rate prediction made at time t. That is, although unbiased, the forward rate at time t between pairs of major currencies such as the dollar, yen and DM, is not a good predictor of future $(t + 1)$ spot rates. This is discussed formally in chapter 13.

Consider one important implication of this latter observation: even though the forward rate is the best guess that well-informed transactors can make, it turns out that they are not much good at guessing where an exchange rate is heading next month, or in six months, let alone next year or in five years. Exchange rate prediction it seems had become a game of blindman's bluff with the players not having much of a clue about the actual direction of future changes in exchange rates. It was not like this during the days of the international gold standard or even for much of the two decades ending in 1971 when the exchange rates of important international trading countries were more or less reliably fixed.

The predictability of exchange rates matters because many real economic decisions require knowledge about future exchange rates, especially long-term real investment in traded goods sectors, and the present situation compares unfavorably with earlier years. Moreover, the unpredictability of exchange rates, and the deviation of real exchange rates from levels that balance the current account, may be increased if rational speculative bubbles occur. A bubble can in theory push the nominal exchange rate far away from purchasing power parity. However, economists are still searching for convincing examples, but the suspicion remains.

Still another problem with the predictability of exchange rate movements concerns the lack of a nominal anchor on which to base exchange rate expectations. Empirical tests indicate that published models of the exchange rate are not particularly good at predicting exchange rates out of sample. The implication of this would seem to be (i) either that economists have not yet discovered the fundamental factors which drive exchange rates; or (ii) that interactions between fundamentals and the exchange rate are far more complicated than once thought (and recent empirical work would seem to support this contention); or (iii) that exchange rates are not driven by fundamentals, rather by catastrophic changes in loosely held and uncertain expectations.

Chapters 14 and 15 examine some topics which are best understood by combining the theoretical insights gained in earlier chapters on the monetary approach to the balance of payments and to the exchange rate. In chapter 14 we discuss currency crises and speculative attack, outlining a popular model. In this model exchange rate theory is used for the calculation of a *shadow* floating exchange rate – which motivates speculation if the shadow rate diverges from the actual rate. The monetary approach to the balance of payments is also utilized to calculate how foreign exchange reserves will eventually be exhausted when the rate of domestic credit expansion is excessive. The chapter then proceeds to examine the problems of forecasting speculative attack, and the policy choices open to emerging market governments that were so shaken by currency attacks in 1997 and earlier years.

The main topic in chapter 15 is an examination of exchange rate behavior in a target zone (i.e. a pegged rate fluctuation band). Within the zone the exchange rate may float, being determined by fundamentals; but at its edges intervention may be necessary so that foreign exchange reserves will change. The target zone model has been used extensively in the examination of pegged exchange rate systems from the nineteenth-century gold standard through the Bretton Woods system to the European Monetary System – the findings of which we reflect in chapters 16 and 17. We also examine "dirty floating" in chapter 15 using the so-called exchange market pressure model which indicates how in an environment of floating a government may use foreign exchange reserves to nudge the exchange rate in a preferred direction.

Chapters 16 and 17 consider important historical aspects of the international monetary system. In chapter 16 the main (but not the only) subject of interest is the credibility of commitments to both the classical nineteenth-century gold standard and the reconstituted interwar gold standard. We find that in both periods financial markets generally believed the major national players' commitments to a fixed price of gold. The UK, France, and Germany were always secure on the classical standard – although the USA in the 1890s was not. In the 1925–31 period the French franc and the dollar were thought to be secure, as was the pound until almost the end. A remarkable fact about this period – generally regarded as being one of economic turmoil – is that the gold standard worked much better at stabilizing exchange rates than did the European Monetary System during the 1980s, and this despite a virtual absence of exchange restrictions in the former period. As far as the USA's suspension of the gold standard in 1933 is concerned we point out that the gold standard was connected with both the US bank failures and the Great Depression in that country.

Chapter 17 reviews the history of international monetary arrangements in the post-World War II period. The key argument is that for 50 years the international monetary system can be characterized as a dollar standard. The switch to floating exchange rates in the early 1970s only marking a switch from the prior relative stable system to the current volatile system. Political economy, not pure economics, explains why pegged rates were abandoned. First, the asymmetry in monetary leadership that came to exist under the Bretton Woods system – between the USA, as leader, and the other, mainly OECD, countries – was no longer accepted by the latter countries. Secondly, the USA itself found the burden of leadership becoming too great. In particular, the USA was no longer satisfied with having to accept that it could not independently adjust the external value of dollar, even though the dollar became over-valued – causing a growing current account deficit and the export of US jobs by US multinational corporations to Europe where exchange rates were undervalued. The US was thrust into this situation as a facet of having the dollar play the so-called "n^{th} currency" role where everybody else chose their exchange rate against the dollar and America practiced "benign neglect."

The result of this general dissatisfaction was that pegged exchange rates against the dollar were abandoned in 1973 and major currencies were freed to float.

With the fall of the gold-exchange standard, the European Community scrambled to find an arrangement to paste their exchange rates together – an effort that proved to be too costly for Britain, France, and Italy – but the European currency snake, the proto deutschmark zone and the precursor of the European Monetary System, was brought into existence.

Meanwhile, the international monetary system became evermore unstable with the severing of the link between commodity production and liquidity creation. That is, an albeit loose link had existed under both the international gold standard and the gold-exchange standard (ended in August 1971) between the creation of credit money and the growth of real commodity production. The function of the "golden" anchor was to discipline monetary authorities to regulate the rate of monetary creation and, as the records of the 1870–1914 and 1945–71 periods show, secular inflation as a widespread international phenomenon was held in check. Moreover, during these periods the exchange rates of countries adhering to these standards were stable. It is the severing of the link between credit creation and the rate of real economic activity that ushered in the unprecedented international inflation of the 1970s (vestiges of which are still with us), highly variable and largely unpredictable exchange rates and the international debt crisis.

The creation of the EMS in 1979 was a reaction to the failings of the international monetary system as well as a step on the road to a united states of Europe. It was created as a "zone of monetary stability." It also aimed for symmetry between the members – it was a lack of symmetry in balance of payments and economic policy adjustment that had brought down the Bretton Woods system and had made the European currency snake unattractive to some EEC countries, including the French. Ironically, the EMS quite quickly became a deutschmark zone, in some ways similar to the manner in which the Bretton Woods system turned into a dollar standard. That is, it was never planned that either the US dollar or the DM would become the central currencies of an international monetary system, yet it happened just the same. During the 1980s and for most of the 1990s it fell to Germany to provide stable monetary conditions for the EMS as a whole. Unfortunately, following the reunification of that country, German nominal and real interest rates increased sharply, so straining the exchange rate mechanism (ERM) of the EMS and, in 1992, forcing Britain and Italy out of it and causing Ireland and Spain to reintroduce foreign exchange controls. Then in the summer of 1993 the French were embarrassed into asking for the modification of EMS rules so that the franc could be devalued without actually leaving the system. Even earlier, some EU members came to resent German monetary hegemony and sought a means to create symmetry in European monetary affairs. The Delors Committee Report (1989) and the Maastricht Treaty (1991) were expressions of the desire to correct these fault lines in the EMS. A political economy consequence of the introduction of the euro managed by the European Central bank under the management of EU central bankers is the removal of Germany from monetary hegemony in Europe – or, so it seems at this time.

In chapter 18 we set out the theoretical case for monetary union starting off with seminal ideas developed in the 1960s and leading on to the modern theoretical statements of the 1990s. Chapter 18 applies these theories not only to monetary union proper (in which a single currency and single central bank – the latter possibly de facto rather than de jure – effectively replaces all others) but also to the choice between exchange rate pegging, currency boards, and dollarization. As modern monetary union theory stresses the importance of shocks – asymmetric versus symmetric (with the latter favoring monetary union) – we briefly review the empirical evidence with respect to the EU in this chapter. Broadly speaking this evidence suggests that monetary union might be workable for many, but not necessarily all, EU members.

Chapter 19 begins by describing the large scale of international capital flows and investigates them in some detail. One argument is that while eurobanks are an important conduit for international capital they have little scope to create money and thereby undermine the stability of the international monetary system. The explanation for the enormous growth in Eurobank assets and liabilities is shown to reside in the failure of the international monetary system to impose balance of payments discipline. As eurobanks and other international financial intermediaries have a tendency toward under-capitalization owing to the public good nature of bank equity capital – international bank failures may result with potential contagion effects undermining the international monetary system (as well as national banking systems). It is necessary, therefore, to examine bank regulation under the Basle Capital Accord. We also assess the degree of mobility of international capital, arguing that perhaps short-term capital is rather less mobile than conventional wisdom seems to believe; but we reaffirm, using a different modeling technique, the famous Feldstein–Horioka finding that long-term capital is rather immobile. The chapter signs off by examining the growth of international bond markets.

Chapters 20 and 21 are on developing countries in the international monetary system. Chapter 20 discusses their relationships with the IMF and the issues raised by the "new structuralists" on the desirability of IMF loan conditionality as applied to developing country borrowers. Under weight of criticism during the last decade or so, the IMF has relented somewhat and now allows developing country borrowers more generous loan terms. Empirical evidence on the effects of IMF loan conditionality, though mixed, does lend some support to its desirability.

Chapter 21 considers the subject of the "order of liberalization" in developing countries as they pass through a process of moving from being highly regulated to being much less so. Early hurried attempts at liberalization in the southern cone of Latin America had led to financial chaos. It turns out that the order in which markets are liberalized does matter and this includes the positioning in the sequence of the liberalization of the foreign exchange market.

The newest group of national actors on the stage of international finance are the formerly centrally planned or so-called transition economies (TEs) – examined in chapter 22. Here we offer a simple integrated microeconomic–macroeconomic model in which the various economic reform processes may be understood. We also examine exchange rate overshooting in TEs, offering a simple economic model and a review of some empirical evidence.

Chapter 23 returns to the issue of international debt first broached in chapter 14 on currency crises and speculative attack. Topics of discussion include the debt "problem," its causes, capital flight, the lenders' trap, and some debt relief policies.

Finally, in chapter 24 we discuss the matter of international monetary reform. The principles upon which the design of an international monetary system must be based are laid out. We assess the costs and benefits of flexible exchange rates, McKinnon's plan for international financial stability, and Williamson's "extended target zone" proposal. Finally, it is worth noting that at various points throughout this book we have referred to the idea that any viable international monetary system has to rest on the foundation of sound *domestic* financial systems, something that Eichengreen (1999) has referred to as the "international financial architecture." Thus it was that crumbling domestic banking systems were at least in part responsible for bringing down the East Asian dollar standard in 1997, and were in part responsible for the ejection of both the USA and Belgium from the interwar gold standard.

2

Some Basic Concepts
in International Finance

In this chapter we start out on the study of international finance by introducing some basic concepts. Section 2.1 introduces the familiar concept of the exchange rate and explains the difference between spot and forward exchange rates and foreign currency futures and options. Section 2.2 describes the balance of payments accounts and mentions the link that exists between a country's balance of payments and underlying monetary conditions. Section 2.3 describes the concepts of purchasing power parity and the real exchange rate. In section 2.4 we compare the case for floating exchange rates with the disappointing experience with them over the last two and a half decades. In the final section exchange rate volatility is defined and described.

2.1 The Exchange Rate

A convertible currency can legally be exchanged for another convertible currency at a *rate of exchange*. Inconvertible currencies may also be exchanged, but illegally on a "black market." A currency could be partially convertible – as when it can legally be used to purchase foreign exchange to finance only certain transactions (e.g. current account but not some capital account transactions – so-called dual exchange rates).

The foreign exchange rate measures the price of one currency in terms of another (see table 2.1). We use the letter S to represent the home currency price of a unit of foreign exchange – the first two columns of numbers in table 2.1 which has the US dollar as the "home" currency; and E to represent the amount of foreign currency per unit of domestic currency – the last two columns. In other words S and E are reciprocals of each other. If S increases the home currency depreciates.

Table 2.1 Exchange rates, Friday, March 26, 1999
The New York foreign exchange mid-range rates below apply to trading among banks in amounts of $1 million and more, as quoted at 4 p.m. Eastern time by Telerate and other sources. Retail transactions provide fewer units of foreign currency per dollar. Rates for the 11 Euro currency countries are derived from the latest dollar-euro rate using the exchange ratios set January 1, 1999.

Country	US$ equiv.		Currency per US$	
	Fri	Thu	Fri	Thu
Britain (Pound)	1.6226	1.6235	.6163	.6160
1-month forward	1.6220	1.6229	.6165	.6162
3-months forward	1.6216	1.6225	.6167	.6163
6-months forward	1.6219	1.6229	.6166	.6162
Canada (Dollar)	.6607	.6633	1.5135	1.5075
1-month forward	.6607	.6633	1.5136	1.5076
3-months forward	.6607	.6633	1.5135	1.5075
6-months forward	.6610	.6637	1.5128	1.5067
Germany (Mark)	.5506	.5540	1.8163	1.8051
1-month forward	.5515	.5549	1.8133	1.8022
3-months forward	.5533	.5568	1.8072	1.7961
6-months forward	.5563	.5592	1.7976	1.7883
Japan (Yen)	.008314	.008463	120.28	118.16
1-month forward	.008348	.008499	119.80	117.67
3-months forward	.008415	.008567	118.83	116.73
6-months forward	.008520	.008673	117.37	115.31
Mexico (Peso)				
Floating rate	.1044	.1037	9.5800	9.6390
Netherland (Guilder)	.4886	.4917	2.0465	2.0339
New Zealand (Dollar)	.5346	.5384	1.8706	1.8574
Sweden (Krona)	.1203	.1208	8.3118	8.2758
SDR	1.3615	1.3677	.7345	.7311
Euro	1.0768	1.0835	.9287	.9229

Special Drawing Rights (SDR) are based on exchange rates for the US, German, British, French, and Japanese currencies.
Source: International Monetary Fund.

Source: *Wall Street Journal*, March 29, 1999

2.1.1 Spot and forward exchange rates

Table 2.1 also shows quotations against various currencies for 30, 60, and 90 days *forward* as well as the *spot* exchange rates that have already been referred to. Spot exchange rates are quoted for delivery of the currency purchased within two days. *The forward exchange rate quotations are for prices agreed today for delivery at one of the future days* – 30, 60, or 90 days ahead. These quotations are usually made by commercial banks and other "customized" maturities may be negotiated.

Foreign currencies are bought spot for many reasons, e.g. to finance the purchase of imports, to buy foreign assets such as bonds and real estate, or to finance holidays and business trips.

Forward markets for foreign exchange are used for three main classes of activity: hedging, arbitrage, and speculation. Consider each of these in turn. *Hedging* is used when, for example, an importer – buying foreign goods denominated in foreign currency – would be hurt by a rise in the spot exchange rate. Usually there are lags between the delivery of goods and their actual payment, and under a flexible exchange rate system exporters and importers may wish to guard against the risk of exchange rate changes during this period by hedging in the foreign exchange market. For example, an importer may take delivery today of goods which require payment in 30 days. To avoid the exchange risk inherent in such a transaction, the importer will often use the forward exchange market to sell domestic currency for foreign currency in 30 days at a price agreed now. Since the importer holds a foreign currency asset (the foreign currency due in 30 days) and an equal offsetting foreign currency liability, his position is classified as being "closed."

Forward markets are also used for *arbitrage* when, for example, a foreign currency is simultaneously bought spot and sold forward. The objective of interest arbitrage is to allocate funds between financial centres in order to realize the highest possible rate of return, whilst at the same time avoiding exchange rate risk. Thus, say a UK individual had £100 to invest for 90 days. She may consider buying a UK treasury bill yielding 8 percent interest (annualized). Alternatively the funds could be invested in a similar US treasury bill at a 10 percent interest rate. On the face of it we would expect the investor to put her funds into the US investment since it appears to offer the higher return. Thus she would sell £100 at the spot exchange rate and obtain $142.86, assuming the exchange rate is £0.70/$1. At the end of the 90 days the dollar value of her investment would be $157.14 (i.e. $142.86 (1 + 0.10)) and if the exchange rate remains at £0.70/$1 the pound value would be £110, which is clearly greater than the amount she would have obtained had the funds been invested in the UK treasury bill (£108).

Note that so far in this example, and indeed in a real world decision, the investor is certain today about (i) how many pounds she may obtain in three months; (ii) how many dollars she can obtain in three months and, if the pound–dollar exchange rate remains fixed throughout the investment period, (iii) the pound value of the dollar investment.

However, if exchange rates are free to float only the remotest chance would have given the same exchange rate at the time the investment was made and on the maturity date. Rather, the exchange rate would in all probability differ and may on maturity be, say, £0.69/$1 which would still make the dollar investment worth more than keeping the funds in the UK (£108.43). If, however, the exchange rate fell to £0.65/$1 the US investment would be worth less than the UK strategy (i.e. only £102.14). If the exchange rates are flexible the pound value of the dollar investment is in fact uncertain. The interest arbitrageur is assumed to be risk averse and in order to avoid this exchange risk the arbitrageur, at the time of her sale of pounds, will simultaneously sell the expected dollar proceeds of her investment (buy forward pounds) at the current 90-day forward exchange rate. In this way the arbitrageur can avoid foreign exchange risk and make the pound value of the dollar investment certain, even though exchange rates are flexible. This type of foreign exchange transaction is known as *covered interest arbitrage*.

Speculation is the third activity that occurs on forward markets: here the objective is to make profits by taking on risk. Thus, for example, if a speculator expects a currency to appreciate it can be bought spot and held (in the form of a treasury bill perhaps), later being resold at the higher price if the appreciation does actually occur. However, this method of speculation does involve tying up funds. Another method, which has only a margin requirement, is to buy the currency on the forward exchange market. Then, when the forward contract matures, and assuming that the currency did in the meantime appreciate, it can be sold at a profit.

To illustrate how speculation on the forward exchange market works, suppose that the 90-day forward rate today, 1 January, is $1.75 = £1, and that a speculator's expected spot exchange rate for 31 March is $1.80 = £1. The speculator will expect to profit by, today, selling dollars for pounds on the 90-day forward market. When the 90 days are up, on 31 March, the forward contracts will come due and the speculator will collect the pounds that were bought on 1 January. Supposing that the spot pound does indeed move to $1.80, each pound can then be resold at a profit of $0.05. Because an expected profit occurs whenever a matched pair of forward and expected spot rates are not equal, if there are plenty of speculative funds, the forward exchange rate will approximate the market's expectation of the future *spot* rate. If this was not so, speculators would continue to buy a currency until the difference was more or less eliminated. (It will be entirely eliminated only if speculators are risk neutral.) In our example, the buying pressure on the forward pound would raise its forward price until it equalled the expected future spot exchange rate (i.e. the forward pound rose from $1.75 to $1.80).

2.1.2 Foreign currency futures and options

Foreign currency futures are financial instruments that obligate a holder at a future settlement date to buy (if long) or sell (if short) a specified amount of a given foreign currency. However, transactors usually close open positions before the due settlement date by creating an offsetting position, e.g. balancing a long position with a short position. To buy a foreign currency futures contract is to bet that the currency will rise in value (the opposite when "shorting" a currency). Settlement is on a "mark-to-market" basis with daily gains (or losses) being added to (deducted from) the buyer's margin account with its broker. Foreign currency futures can be used for the purpose of hedging. For example, a bank in Liechtenstein, holding spot dollars, may hedge the risk of a fall in the value of the dollar by selling dollars on the futures market. Supposing that at the settlement date the spot dollar has indeed fallen in value, the loss will be offset by the profit on the sale of dollars on the futures market.[1]

Foreign currency futures markets are operated by market-makers, e.g. on the Chicago International Money Market, the London International Financial Futures Exchange and in a few other centers. Market-makers set futures prices so as to balance the flow of long and short orders. As there are some differences between foreign currency forward and futures contracts, will their prices be equivalent? It turns out that the differences between the contracts are small enough, and arbitrage between the two markets great enough, to drive the two prices very close together. Specifically, Cornell and Reinganum (1981) found that the difference between forward and futures rates was less than the bid–ask spread on the forward contract.

Another way of hedging in foreign exchange is through *foreign currency options* – a type of derivative financial instrument that works rather like an insurance policy. To get an idea of how currency options can be used as a means of hedging suppose that a French bank holds US dollars as an asset. It wishes to hedge the risk of a fall in the value of the dollar *vis-à-vis* the franc. The bank may hedge by buying a foreign currency *put option* on the London interbank market.[2] This gives the bank the right but not the obligation to sell its dollars within a given time-frame at a strike price agreed that day. Thus, if the spot dollar does fall in value the bank can sell its dollars at the previously agreed strike price. If the dollar does not fall in value below the strike price the bank need not exercise its option – in effect, the purchase of the option has worked like an insurance policy guaranteeing that the bank's dollars are worth at least the strike price (less the premium as the cost of the insurance).

Although both foreign currency futures and foreign currency options offer a useful way of hedging (or speculating) in foreign currency, trading in these instruments is relatively unimportant compared with that in foreign currency forward contracts. Thus, in the world's largest centre for trading foreign currencies and foreign currency instruments – London – in 1992 trading in futures and options totalled only 3 percent of the market while trading in forward contracts amounted to 47 percent. The other 50 percent was trading in spot currencies.[3] The dominance of spot and forward trading over futures, options and other types of foreign currency trading (such as foreign currency swaps), together with the belief that arbitrage between the different markets is quite effective in establishing similar prices, justifies the concentration in this book on the study of spot and forward markets. Another justification is that the overwhelming volume of research, theoretical and empirical, has concentrated on the latter markets.

2.2 The Balance of Payments Accounts

A typical layout for a country's balance of payments is shown in table 2.2. In the balance of payments accounts all credit items – i.e. those that earn foreign exchange – enter with a plus sign while all debit items enter with a negative sign. Thus, *sales* to foreigners of goods and services (i.e. exports) earn foreign currency

Table 2.2 Balance of payments accounts

---

1 Exports of goods and services (+)
   Merchandise
   Services
     Travel, insurance, banking etc.
     Income from assets held abroad: interest, dividends etc.
2 Imports of goods and services (−)
   Merchandise
   Services
     Travel, insurance, banking etc.
     Foreign investors' income from assets in the reporting country: interest,
       dividends etc.
3 Unilateral transfers ((−) = net outflow)
4 Current account (= 1 + 2 + 3)
5 Private assets abroad, net (increase = capital outflow (−))
   Direct investment
   Portfolio investment
6 Private *foreign* assets in reporting country, net (increase = capital inflow (+))
   Direct investment
   Portfolio investment
7 Capital account (5 + 6)
8 Change in foreign exchange reserves (4 + 7, increase = (−))
9 Statistical discrepancy (+ or −)
10 Allocation of special drawing rights (+)

---

as does capital *in*flow. The latter is the counterpart of the *sale* by domestic residents or the home government of claims on domestically owned assets such as corporate notes, bonds or equity, or similarly with public sector liabilities. A domestic bank also "sells" a liability to a foreign depositor when it accepts a deposit denominated in local currency and this is also a capital inflow. Liabilities sold to a foreign entity with less than one year to maturity are classified as short-term capital inflows and those with over one year long-term capital inflows. Direct investment is in the form of acquisitions that give managerial control of investments overseas (e.g. as when a multinational corporation purchases control of a subsidiary in a foreign country); and portfolio investment is investment in foreign financial assets such as bonds and bank accounts – control is not a defining characteristic in this case.

Correspondingly, purchases from foreigners of their goods and services (i.e. imports) or claims on their assets (i.e. capital *out*flow) are debit items on, respectively, the current and capital accounts.

A common mistake is often made with respect to interest payments: these are current account items – payment of interest to foreigners is a type of invisible import and the converse with interest income from abroad. This particular detail is important at various points in the book and especially in chapter 11 where the portfolio model of exchange rate adjustment is discussed.

Table 2.3 Balance of payments accounts: 1997, billion US dollars

	USA	UK	Germany	Japan	Sweden
Current account	-155	10	-3	94	7
Capital account	256	-13	-3	-122	-12
Errors and omissions	-100	-1	2	34	-2
Official settlement balance	-1	4	4	-6	7

Note: Official settlements balance: + means decrease in reserves.
Source: IMF, *International Financial Statistics*, February 1999

A third major component of the balance of payments accounts is the official settlements balance – "change in foreign exchange reserves" in table 2.2 – also known as the balance of official financing. This shows the change in foreign exchange reserves held by a country's central bank. Foreign exchange reserves are used for intervention in the foreign exchange market so as to influence the exchange rate. The central bank buys or sells foreign currency in exchange for domestic currency for this purpose. Such intervention is necessary only if, at some desired level of the exchange rate, there is either an excess supply or an excess demand on the foreign exchange market for domestic currency. If there is an excess supply, the central bank mops it up by purchasing with foreign currency drawn from its reserves. Conversely, if there is an excess demand for domestic currency on the foreign exchange market, the central bank increases its supply by buying foreign exchange – paying for it with domestic currency.

If a country chose to let its exchange rate float cleanly – allowing the market to determine the foreign exchange rate – foreign exchange reserves would not be needed. Thus, the use of foreign exchange reserves implies that a government is not prepared to accept the prices set in the foreign exchange market.

So far it has been assumed that the statistical discrepancy (or, "errors and omissions") is zero. In practice it is sometimes rather large and has to be added back in order to balance the accounts. The statistical discrepancy arises as a result of the non-recording by the relevant statistical departments of some items that should not have been omitted. Some possible sources of error are random variations in data collection, smuggling and unrecorded capital inflow. Table 2.3 shows the balance of payments accounts for five leading trading nations. It is evident that to make the balance of payments balance use has been made of the statistical discrepancy.

At this juncture it is also worth mentioning three other definitions pertaining to the balance of payments accounts. The *basic balance* is the sum of the current account plus long-term capital movements. It is sometimes regarded as a measure of a country's "underlying" or "fundamental" balance of payments: it is the amount requiring real exchange rate adjustment in the long run. A *below the line* item is anything which comes after item 7 in table 2.2. Correspondingly, an *above the line* item is anything above item 8 in the balance of payments records in table 2.2.

Given that at any point in time the balance of payments must balance, i.e. the sum of debt and credit items is zero or, equivalently, on the foreign exchange market excess demand is zero, we can write

$$CA + CAP + OSB = 0 \qquad (2.1)$$

when the terms are, respectively, the current account, the capital account and the official settlements balance. On rearranging

$$CA + CAP = -OSB \qquad (2.2)$$

Suppose that the left-hand side is negative, implying that on private transactions there is an excess supply of domestic currency (excess demand for foreign currency) on the foreign exchange market. This is made possible if the official settlements balance is positive: the central bank mops up the excess supply of domestic currency by selling foreign exchange. Hence, a sale of foreign exchange balances the foreign exchange market. Notice that, somewhat confusingly, a reduction in foreign exchange reserves shows up as a positive official settlements balance. Correspondingly, if the left-hand side of equation (2.2) is positive, the official settlements balance must be negative (two negatives making a positive). Thus, an increase in reserves shows up as a negative change, i.e. a supply of domestic currency.

If the central bank refrained from intervention in the foreign exchange market we can write:

$$CA = -CAP \qquad (2.3)$$

So a current account deficit is balanced by a positive capital account, i.e. by capital inflow; and a current account surplus by capital outflow. Here the private sector's supply and demand for currency is balanced at every instant of time. This is possible if the exchange rate is allowed to float. Thus, if a current account deficit appears, the exchange rate must move to the level at which foreign lenders are prepared to finance it through capital inflow. Such exchange rate movements may be very large and sudden as will be shown in later chapters. It can also be argued that, in the long run, the current account must move to that level which will be willingly financed by foreign lenders. This level is not necessarily zero as the country in question may offer irresistible investment prospects.

2.2.1 The balance of payments and the money supply

It was understood by David Hume as long ago as the middle of the eighteenth century that, if a country operates with a fixed exchange rate, it loses control of its money supply – the money supply becomes endogenous. We shall discuss this matter in much greater detail in chapter 8 on the monetary approach to the balance of payments, but the point can be readily understood using equation (2.2).

Suppose that the central bank increases the domestic money supply through open market purchases of domestic bonds. The effect is probably to raise the domestic prices of goods and assets, and this will induce current and capital account deficits as residents turn to foreign markets where these things are now relatively cheaper. To support the fixed exchange rate the central bank will have to sell foreign exchange reserves for domestic currency. Thus, while the effect of open market operations is to increase the money supply, the sale of foreign exchange will reduce it. Under certain assumptions, spelled out in chapter 8, after the adjustment process has worked itself out, the domestic money supply will be back where it started and the central bank will have ended up swapping foreign exchange for domestic bonds.

◈ 2.3 Purchasing Power Parity

Purchasing power parity is an important and recurrent concept in international finance. Several theories of the balance of payments and of the exchange rate deploy it in one way or an other and the whole of chapter 7 is devoted to an examination of it. Here a brief description of the concept is presented.

The theory of purchasing power parity says that the same goods or basket of goods should sell for the same price in different countries when measured in a common currency. Thus, letting P and P* stand, respectively, for home and foreign prices (or price indexes) we can write

$$P = SP^* \tag{2.4}$$

where S is the exchange rate.

Purchasing power parity has been used as a theory of the price level: if the exchange rate is fixed and the home country is small, foreign prices P*, will determine domestic prices. Alternatively, purchasing power parity has been widely used as a theory of the exchange rate, where on rearranging equation (2.4) $S = P/P^*$. One version of the "monetary approach to the exchange rate" (see chapter 9) keys a theory of the price level, derived from the demand for money function and the money market equilibrium condition, onto purchasing power parity and so derives a monetary theory of the exchange rate.

Variants of these models assume that purchasing power parity holds either at all moments of time or only in the long run. The flexible price monetary model is an example that uses the former assumption; while sticky-price models (e.g. Dornbusch's "overshooting" model) deploy purchasing power parity only as a long-run concept.

2.3.1 The real exchange rate

A change in the nominal exchange rate may not give a complete picture of how much a country's international competitiveness is changing. For example, if the rate of nominal currency depreciation is less than the rate at which the price level is rising relative to that of another country, the country's international competitiveness could be declining despite the depreciation of the nominal exchange rate. The concept of the real exchange rate is used to cope with this type of problem. The real exchange rate Q is calculated as

$$Q = S(P^*/P) \tag{2.5}$$

That is, the real exchange rate is the nominal exchange rate weighted by the relative price levels (various measures of the latter may be used, including relative wage levels). Thus, if inflation is faster in the home country, the nominal exchange rate will have to rise just to stabilize the real exchange rate. Notice that a fall in Q is a real exchange rate appreciation which reduces international competitiveness, while a rise in Q increases competitiveness.

2.4 Floating Exchange Rates: Prospect and Retrospect

For many years during the so-called Bretton Woods pegged-but-adjustable exchange rate era (ca. 1945–73) several leading monetary economists argued that exchange rates should be allowed to float. Their main claims will be examined in a moment. What quickly became apparent when exchange rates were allowed to float in 1973 was that the predictions about the greater efficacy of a regime of floating exchange rates were quite simply wrong. And they were so because exchange rate theory was in too rudimentary a state to base robust predictions on it. In this book the broad outlines and some details of the development of exchange rate theory will be laid out. Sadly, it will be shown that even today, after a further two decades or so of research, no single exchange rate theory provides a satisfactory – empirically consistent – theory of the exchange rate. We shall lay out the currently popular theories of the exchange rate, show how well they have performed in statistical tests, and try to explain the various weaknesses as they have revealed themselves.

Six main claims were made in favor of flexible exchange rates (Friedman, 1953; Sohmen, 1961; Johnson, 1970). We briefly list what they were and how they have stood the test of time.

1   As we saw when discussing the real exchange rate, changes in the nominal exchange rate can offset the effect on a country's international competitiveness of differences in national inflation rates. If S is fixed, a rise in P relative to P^* appreciates the real exchange rate and reduces the country's degree of international competitiveness (leaving aside differential rates of productivity growth). Serious real economic effects could follow as the country passes through a period of deflation in order to restore the real exchange rate – output and employment both probably falling. But with flexible exchange rates, a depreciation of the exchange rate (rise in S) would in principle offset the higher rate of domestic inflation, so avoiding

the deleterious real economic effects. Thus, it was claimed that if exchange rates were allowed to float, and abstracting from other factors that can affect international competitiveness, the real exchange rate should be more or less constant.

After two decades of floating exchange rates the empirical evidence contradicts this rosy expectation. Real exchange rates have been far from constant in the short term as figures 7.3, 7.4, and 7.5 show. And, in the long term, even allowing for international differences in rates of productivity growth, according to De Grauwe (1989) the real exchange rates of important trading nations have shown little or no tendency to return to levels that would establish viable current accounts.

2   It turned out that pegged-but-adjustable exchange rates were changed in big jumps only once in a while and usually in a situation of "crisis" (e.g. the 1967 devaluation of sterling). By contrast, proponents of floating exchange rates claimed that, with no central bank to hold them back, flexible exchange rates would change *slowly, smoothly*, and *predictably*.

But, again, this hopeful expectation has been dashed. Table 2.4 shows that between 1973, when the yen–dollar exchange rate was allowed to float, and 1999 *large* exchange rate changes occurred on average almost once a year. For example, in 1998 there was a large swing in the yen–dollar exchange rate: in the three-month period prior to the October of that year the yen *appreciated* 19 percent against the US dollar; this followed a 13.2 percent *depreciation* in the six months prior the July of the same year.

Nor have exchange rate changes been predictable. As was pointed out on page 16, speculators will tend to push the forward rate to equal their expectation of the future *spot* exchange rate because, if they do not, they will be leaving profitable opportunities untapped. But, as figures 12.1–12.4 (pp. 251–2) show, the forward exchange rate has been a rather poor predictor of the future spot rate. That is, very few actual major currency exchange rate changes have been expected. Put another way, most of a given percentage change in the actual exchange rate has come as a complete surprise, and sometimes the market has even failed to predict the correct direction of actual changes (i.e. they thought that it would go up when it actually went down, and vice versa). There will be a deeper examination of these matters in chapters 12 and 13.

3   Floating exchange rates were expected to insulate an economy from shocks emanating from abroad, e.g. a fall in foreign income and import demand. In this case the exchange rate would depreciate and stabilize the volume of exports. However, the correlation of gross domestic product growth rates in major industrial economies has tended to increase, rather than decline, in the period since 1973 – when exchange rates were allowed to float. Several explanations of this phenomenon are possible, including the oil shocks of 1973–4, 1979–80 and 1985–6 which similarly impacted most industrial nations. But there is also a monetary–exchange rate explanation: interest rate movements have turned out not to be independent as countries are not indifferent to their real exchange rates. Thus, for example, in 1980–1 US interest rates moved sharply upwards closely followed by European interest rates: unless European countries had also raised their interest rates their real exchange rates would have depreciated (as capital flowed more

Table 2.4 Large[a] six-month percentage changes in the Yen–Dollar exchange rate since the breakup of Bretton Woods in 1973, ranked by size of change

Ending date	Size of change[b]
February 1986	−27.8
October 1978	−23.6
April 1979	21.6
October 1998	−19.0
August 1995	18.2
March 1978	−17.7
December 1987	−17.4
October 1982	16.5
September 1980	−16.3
May 1989	15.9
April 1983	−15.7
July 1981	15.7
September 1986	−15.6
October 1990	−15.4
April 1987	−14.6
May 1993	−14.6
April 1995	−13.7
July 1998	13.2
January 1997	13.0
January 1974	12.7
February 1980	12.7
March 1999	12.3
September 1992	−10.5

[a] Defined as exceeding 10 percent.
[b] Positive values indicate depreciation of the yen. End of month exchange rate data were used.
Source: Federal Reserve Bank of Atlanta, *Economic Review*, September–October 1990, p. 11; and IMF, *International Financial Statistics*

strongly to the USA) with inflationary consequences. Similarly, with falling interest rates in the USA, Europe's real exchange rates would appreciate causing recession in Europe.

4   Floating exchange rates were expected by proponents of the system to allow a country to pursue an independent monetary policy. Floating the exchange rate relieves the central bank of the need to intervene in the foreign exchange market, so leaving it with complete control over its assets and liabilities and therefore over the domestic money supply. (This leaves aside exogenous changes in central bank liabilities to domestic commercial banks – such as changes in float and in the components of the money multiplier.)

However, as pointed out above, national monetary policies have turned out not to be completely independent. Changes in foreign money supplies can cause massive incipient international capital flows and sharp nominal and real exchange rate movements. Because the real exchange rate is such an important variable (perhaps the most important "price" in any even moderately open economy) governments and central banks have not been prepared to allow the market unfettered to set this price. Thus, to prevent wide and damaging fluctuations in the real exchange rate, a country's monetary policy has had to accommodate exogenous pressures on the real exchange rate. For example, foreign monetary expansion may have to be matched by domestic monetary expansion in order to stop the real exchange rate from appreciating.

5   Floating exchange rates would always balance the balance of payments without central bank intervention, so removing pressures for tariffs, quotes and other forms of international trade restraint. In fact, current account imbalances were bigger in the 1980s and 1990s than at any other time in the post-war period and, as the proliferation of "voluntary' export restraints and banana "wars" indicate, progress in trade policy has not been given a noticeable boost by the move to floating exchange rates.

6   It was also thought in the period before exchange rates were allowed to float that, as foreign exchange reserves could be done away with when a floating system was adopted, large social savings would result. The foreign exchange reserves could be invested in real capital assets (or spent on consumption). But, yet again, the expectation has been frustrated – foreign exchange reserves are today, even in real terms, larger than they were in the period of fixed exchange rates.

2.5 Exchange Rate Volatility

As we have indicated, one of the key features of the recent floating exchange rate experience has been the volatility of exchange rates and, in particular, their volatility *relative* to some form of bench-mark: to some commentators they have in fact been *excessively* volatile (although as we shall see in later chapters this is not an uncontentious issue). Since we shall refer to such volatility on a number of occasions throughout the book, it is worth defining at the outset what we understand by it. The recent volatility of exchange rates may be viewed from four perspectives.

First, exchange rates have been volatile on a *historical* basis. For example, the volatility of the Group of 7 bilateral US dollar currencies increased, on a monthly average basis, from 0.20 percent in 1961–70 (part of the Bretton Woods period) to 1.18 percent in 1974–83 (see MacDonald, 1990b).

Second, exchange rates have been volatile relative to their so-called *fundamental determinants*, such as money supplies, income levels, price levels and current account balances (see MacDonald, 1988b), and this is illustrated in table 2.5. For example, in table 2.5 the coefficients of variation of a number of US dollar bilateral exchange rates are recorded alongside the coefficients of variation of a number of variables which we shall see in succeeding chapters are regarded as the fundamental determinants of exchange rates. The striking feature of this table is that exchange rates have been considerably more volatile than fundamentals such as commodity prices and money supplies (and this is true regardless of the

Table 2.5 Coefficients of variation[a] of three bilateral dollar exchange rates and some "fundamentals"

German consumer price index	1.00	German money supply (M1)	5.11
Japanese consumer price index	1.80	Japanese money supply (M1)	5.97
UK consumer price index	0.94	UK money supply (M1)	2.08
US consumer price index	0.69	US money supply (M1)	3.08
German mark–US dollar	14.15	German treasury bill	23.99
Japanese yen–US dollar	9.47	Japanese treasury bill	70.18
UK pound–US dollar	16.05	UK treasury bill	22.04
		US treasury bill	33.42

[a] The coefficients of variation relate to the logarithmic monthly change of the relevant variable over the period March 1973 to December 1992 (in absolute terms).

commodity price or money supply measure chosen), but have exhibited a similar order of magnitude of volatility to the prices of other financial assets such as government debt (this is picked up in the table by the coefficients of variation of the treasury bill rates which, to a crude approximation, may be thought of as the reciprocal of the price of the bill). The latter phenomenon is in fact a central theme of chapters 9 to 11.

Finally, exchange rates have been volatile relative to the change predicted by the forward foreign exchange rate premium. Why this should be indicative of excess volatility will be explained in some detail in chapters 10–12. At this stage we may note, however, that the forward premium is often taken to be the markets' consensus of what it expects the exchange rate to be in some future period. However, a plot of the forward premium against the actual change in the exchange rate reveals that the premium is roughly constant (around zero), whereas the actual change in the exchange rate is highly volatile: a large component of exchange rate changes is therefore unpredictable (this seems to be true regardless of the currency chosen) (see, for example, figures 12.3 and 12.4 on p. 252).

NOTES

1 There are several differences between foreign currency futures and forward contracts including the following: (i) on the forward market future price is agreed, but not so on a futures contract; (ii) there is no mark-to-market settle on forward contracts; (iii) futures contracts are for standardized amounts, whereas this need not be the case with a forward contract; (iv) futures contracts are for standardized periods with expiration dates usually in March, June, September and December, whilst expiration dates for forward contracts can be negotiated; (v) a futures position can be "killed" by taking out an offsetting position with the clearing-house but forward contracts virtually cannot, i.e. forward contracts usually run their course and are executed.
2 It could also use the interbank markets set up for this purpose in New York or Tokyo.
3 These figures are for April 1992 (Bank of England, quoted by *The Economist*, December 12, 1992, p. 116).

3

Spot and Forward Exchange Rates: Some More Basic Ideas

This chapter extends our discussion of the basic concepts used in the study of international money and finance. Section 3.1 discusses the elasticities approach to the determination of the balance of payments and/or the exchange rate. In section 3.2 attention turns to the determination of the forward exchange rate and several new concepts are introduced: covered and uncovered interest arbitrage, the Fisher "open" condition, the simultaneous determination of spot and forward exchange rates, and risk premiums on currency exchange rates. Sections 3.3, 3.4 and 3.5 present empirical evidence of the validity of the theoretical relationships.

 ## 3.1 The Elasticities View of the Exchange Rate

In the elasticities view the exchange rate is determined by the *flow* of currency through the foreign exchange market. The focus of attention is on the trade account mainly because, when the theory was developed, capital flows were restricted enough not to enter as an argument. Capital flows are treated as exogenous shocks rather than as being endogenous to the model. This approach is very different from the modern *asset view of the exchange rate* where the exchange rate is treated as the price of an asset (or, more particularly, as the relative price of two monies). In the asset price models the exchange rate is determined at that

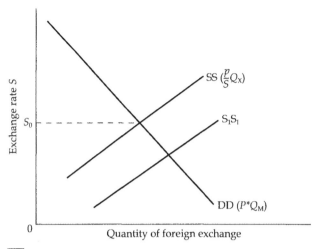

Figure 3.1 Elasticities view of exchange rate determination

level where wealth-holders with internationally diversified portfolios are willing to hold the outstanding *stocks* of monies.

The latter approach, which gives much greater emphasis to the capital account – sometimes to the exclusion of the trade account – is considered in chapters 9–13 but, for the moment, we concentrate on the older theory. The elasticities theory remains relevant today because some economies, especially those of less developed countries in Africa, still attract little by way of private international capital flows – the trade account continues to dominate their balance of payments accounts. Also, it is now recognized that a comprehensive theory of the exchange rate must include the trade account – for example, see chapter 11 on the portfolio balance model.

Figure 3.1 shows the exchange rate S determined by the supply and demand for foreign currency. It is assumed that home and foreign exporters are paid in their respective domestic currencies. Exports of the home goods give rise to a supply of foreign exchange as foreigners buy domestic currency in order to make payments to the home country's exporters. Imports by the home country give rise to a demand for foreign exchange so as to be able to pay the foreign country's exporters in the exporters' own currency.

The demand for foreign exchange is calculated as P^*Q_M, where it is assumed that the foreign currency price P^* is fixed and the quantity of imports into the home country, Q_M, is a negative function of the domestic currency price of imports. DD is downward sloping because as S falls, for the given P^*, the home currency price P_M of the foreign good falls (given that $P_M = P^*S$).

The supply of foreign exchange is calculated as $(P/S)Q_X$, where it is assumed that the home currency supply price P is fixed and the quantity of exports, Q_X, is a negative function of $P^*(= P/S)$: a rise in S lowers the price of the home country's exports in the foreign country. The slope of SS in figure 3.1 depends upon the elasticity of demand for the home country's exports in the foreign country. If it is elastic, total expenditure, measured in foreign currency, increases and SS is upward sloping as shown. But if this demand elasticity is less than unity (in absolute terms), the SS function will be backward sloping.

As drawn in figure 3.1, the foreign exchange market is stable as a rise in the exchange rate above the equilibrium rate S_0, leads to an excess supply of foreign exchange and a fall in its price. Below S_0 there is an excess demand for foreign exchange and its price will rise.

Capital flows can be brought into this model as shift parameters on the SS or DD functions. For example, higher interest rates in the home country can be expected, *ceteris paribus*, to attract capital inflow (see the discussion of interest arbitrage in chapter 2) and to shift the SS curve to the right to S_1S_1. Thus, in the elasticities (or "balance of payments") approach to the exchange rate, an increase in the rate of interest leads to an appreciation of the exchange rate (i.e. S falls). Conversely, higher interest rates in the foreign country will, *ceteris paribus*, shift the DD function to the right (not shown) – so depreciating the exchange rate. These conclusions on the relationship between changes in interest rates and exchange rates are in stark contrast to those derived from the asset approach models of the exchange rate – see especially chapter 9 – where entirely the opposite conclusions are drawn.

Pegging the exchange rate

If the authorities peg the exchange rate at S_0 (figure 3.2) they may have to intervene in the foreign exchange market using their foreign exchange reserves. Thus, if the demand for foreign exchange rises, shifting DD to D_1D_1, the exchange rate can be maintained at S_0 only if the central bank supplies cp of foreign exchange.

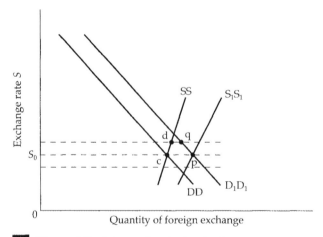

Figure 3.2 Intervention in the foreign exchange market

Similarly, if the supply of foreign exchange rises, shifting SS to S_1S_1, the exchange rate can be prevented from appreciating if the central bank buys foreign exchange in the amount cp. In practice, though, even when exchange rates have been pegged (such as in the Bretton Woods system) they have been allowed to float within narrow margins around the peg. In terms of figure 3.2 these margins are indicated by broken lines. The authorities would only need to supply dq of foreign exchange reserves as a result of the change in demand.

3.1.1 Unstable exchange rates

The foreign exchange market as drawn in figures 3.1 and 3.2 is stable. However, if foreign demand for the home country's goods was strongly inelastic the SS function could be so sharply backward bending that its slope would be more negative than the DD curve. In that case the foreign exchange market would be unstable: a depreciation of the exchange rate would cause further depreciation.

An important question therefore is what determines whether the exchange rate will be stable? Clearly, the answer must have something to do with the elasticity of demand for goods in foreign trade: according to the Marshall–Lerner condition, the foreign exchange market is stable if the sum of the export elasticities of demand (home and foreign) is greater than unity. (The Marshall–Lerner condition is due to Marshall (1923) and Lerner (1944); see also Robinson (1937) and Haberler (1949).) If the Marshall–Lerner condition holds, then there is excess demand for foreign exchange when the exchange rate is below the equilibrium value and excess supply when it is above the equilibrium rate, as in figure 3.1 for example. Under these conditions the exchange rate will move to its equilibrium value and the market will be cleared.

Friedman (1953) went further, arguing that exchange rates would be stable in relation to their underlying fundamental determinants (i.e. the long-run supply and demand curves) because speculation in currency markets would be price-stabilizing. That is, even if an exchange rate did have a tendency to be unstable in the short run relative to the long-run fundamentals, the action of speculators would tend to stabilize it near its expected long-run value. For example, if the price of foreign exchange fell below the long-run *expected* rate, speculators would be tempted to buy foreign exchange and would thereby support its price (i.e. speculators may be characterized as having regressive expectations – see chapter 5 for a discussion). This would prevent a runaway appreciation of the home currency. Moreover, while Friedman recognized the possibility of destabilizing speculation (e.g. selling on a falling market), he argued that such speculators would be driven from the market as such speculative activity is unprofitable.

We shall return to the question of speculation and the stability of the foreign exchange market in chapter 9. It will be argued that, even though exchange rates have fluctuated a lot in recent years, this is consistent with the existence of stabilizing speculation. Indeed, we will see that speculation can be defined as "stabilizing" if it hastens the movement of an exchange rate to the level consistent with its fundamental determinants.

3.1.2 The Marshall–Lerner condition

Consider a devaluation by the home country in a two-country, two-good model where supply is perfectly elastic. The goods are "exports" sent abroad by the home country, and "imports" bought abroad and consumed in the home country. A proof of the Marshall–Lerner conditions is as follows: write B, the balance of payments, as

$$B = P_x.X(S) - P_m^*.S.M(S) \tag{3.1}$$

i.e. B is measured in domestic currency and is defined as the value of exports minus domestic currency spending on imports. Assuming that $P_x = P_m^* = 1$ then:

$$B = X(S) - S.M(S) \tag{3.2}$$

$$dB/dS = dX/dS - S.dM/dS - M \tag{3.3}$$

Define $s_m = -(dM/dS)\,(S/M)$ as home import demand elasticity, and $s_x = (dX/dS)\,(S/X)$ as foreign demand elasticity for the home country's exports. Devaluation improves the payments balance, $dB/dS > 0$, if the right hand side of equation 3.3 is greater than zero. To find the Marshall–Lerner condition first and set $dB/dS = 0$, then multiply the right-hand side through by $1/M$ and multiply the first term there by SX/SX. Upon simplification the right-hand side becomes:

$$(X/SM)s_x + s_m - 1 > 0$$

If trade is balanced, $X/SM = 1$, so the trade balance improves if $s_x + s_m - 1 > 0$, which is the Marshall–Lerner condition. If devaluation occurs in the presence of an existing payments deficit, $X/SM < 1$, $s_x + s_m$ must be correspondingly bigger if devaluation is to improve the trade balance.

Supply elasticities

Most attention in the literature has focused on the Marshall–Lerner case of infinite supply elasticities. But the formula can be generalized to derive the conditions for trade balance improvement when supply elasticities are less than infinite. Assuming that trade is balanced to begin with, following Stern (1973, pp. 64–7) devaluation will improve the payments balance and the foreign exchange market is stable if

$$\frac{s_x(d_x - 1)}{s_x + s_m} + \frac{d_m(s_m + 1)}{d_m + s_m} > 0 \tag{3.4}$$

where s_x and s_m are, respectively, the home and foreign export supply elasticities and d_m and d_x are, respectively, the absolute values of the home and foreign import demand elasticities. The first term measures the proportionate increase in the devaluing country's export earnings and the second term measures the increase in spending on imports.

According to the first term in equation (3.4), if the foreign country's import demand elasticity d_x is elastic, then the *more* elastic is the domestic supply of exports, the greater will be the improvement in export earnings and the payments balance following a devaluation.

If the demand for exports (d_x) is *in*elastic, which it may very well be in the short run, then devaluation reduces export earnings more the more elastic is domestic supply. This possibility has been used as an argument against devaluation by primary commodity exporting nations faced with payments deficits. These countries may well face inelastic foreign demand and, if excess capacity exists in the export industries or if output can be easily switched from home to foreign markets, devaluation will reduce export earnings.

Also of interest is the case of the small country where s_m and d_x are both equal to infinity. Then equation (3.4) is positive and devaluation must improve the payments balance.

3.1.3 The J curve

The elasticities approach ignores time in its analysis, but one of the lessons of experience has been that, while exchange rates may adjust instantaneously, the prices of goods and demand change only after a lag. Thus, if the country is running a trade deficit the first effect of a devaluation at time t may be to make the deficit larger, as is shown in figure 3.3 where the time path of the trade balance does look like the letter J.

Following a devaluation, if imports are bought at world prices and home demand is price inelastic, there will be little change in foreign currency expenditure in response to higher prices in terms of domestic currency. Export receipts

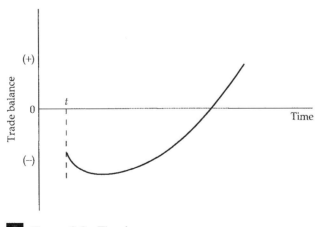

Figure 3.3 The J curve

Table 3.1 Representative elasticity estimates[a]: USA

	Imports	Exports
Median long-run price elasticity	1.1	0.8
Median lag from exchange rate, change to initial trade volume response (years)	0.6	0.8
Median exchange rate effect on price	0.9	0.2
Median income elasticity	1.8	1.2

[a] Averaged from six independent econometric models.
Source: Krugman, 1991a

in foreign currency on the other hand may drop unless the home currency price of exports is raised by the full extent of the devaluation. Failing such a price adjustment, the price of exports in foreign currency will fall and, if foreign demand is inelastic – which it may very well be on impact – receipts of foreign currency will indeed fall. This combination of changes in expenditures and receipts following a devaluation will cause the trade balance to deteriorate. It is estimated (Cairncross and Eichengreen, 1983, and similarly Artus, 1975) that over the first two years after the British devaluation of 1967 there was no net gain in export earnings, since the loss through lower export prices (in foreign currency) was only offset by increased volume in the second year.[1]

A very interesting J curve episode followed the decline in the dollar from early 1985. In fact, the US current account deficit, rather than declining, continued to grow (both in dollars and as a percentage of GNP) through 1987. Is this evidence that the traditional adjustment mechanism no longer worked? On the basis of the evidence of the data in table 3.1 Krugman (1991a) argued that it worked pretty well as expected, but with a rather long lag. The average *long-run* price elasticity of US import demand is estimated to be 1.1 and that of exports to be 0.8. As these sum to more than unity, they are sufficient to ensure that devaluation, "other things equal," should work to correct a current account deficit.

However, the corresponding short-run elasticities are much lower. As the second line of table 3.1 shows, it takes seven months for import volumes to begin to respond and even longer for export volumes. Moreover, as the third line of the table indicates, measured in dollars, import prices tend to rise by about the full amount of a devaluation while export prices hardly rise at all. This combination of price and volume effects, in the short run, serves to raise spending on imports more than dollar export earnings rise and accounts for some of the J curve effect. Indeed, simulation of a 20 percent dollar devaluation shows that the US current account would worsen in the following year, and that it takes more than two years for most of the effect to come through (but after five years the current account improves by 1.45 percent of GNP).

Several other factors also contributed to the J curve of 1985–7. First, "other things" were not "equal": during the period GNP in the USA grew at least as fast as in Germany and Japan which, given the income elasticities reported on the final line of table 3.1, served to worsen the USA's current account deficit. Second, with the value of US imports greatly exceeding the value of exports, devaluation had to raise the growth rate of exports significantly more than the rate at which imports were growing. Third, the dollar had sharply appreciated in the prior years and some lag effect would be spilling over from this into the 1985–7 period. Fourth, there is some weak evidence that exporters to the USA were "pricing to market" – in effect setting export prices in terms of the dollar rather than their local currencies – and this too would have delayed the adjustment process.

3.1.4 Devaluation and the terms of trade

Changes in a country's terms of trade can affect welfare (as is well known to those who have studied the pure theory of international trade). In the simplest case, when imports are the only consumption good and exports are the only production good,

$$Y = ZT \tag{3.5}$$

where Y is real income, Z is output and T is the terms of trade, i.e. *the ratio of export to import price*. Hence, a rise in export price relative to import price raises T and real income.

However, the effect of devaluation on a country's terms of trade (more generally the ratio of an index of export prices to an index of import prices measured in a common currency) cannot be settled *a priori*. Recall from chapter 2 that the real exchange rate Q is SP^*/P. If all goods are traded goods then P and SP^* represent a country's index of export and import prices respectively. Hence, in this case, the terms of trade are measured as the inverse of the real exchange rate, $1/Q$.[2]

The effect of a devaluation on the terms of trade depends on the independent effects of devaluation on export and import prices. If a country faces a downward-sloping demand curve for its exports but is "unimportant" in its import markets (i.e. faces perfectly elastic foreign supply curves in terms of foreign currency) devaluation will worsen the devaluing country's terms of trade: export prices will fall relative to import prices measured in foreign currency. Meade (1951) has shown that the terms of trade will deteriorate if the product of home and foreign supply elasticities is greater than the product of demand elasticities. In practice, it seems likely that the terms of trade will deteriorate with a devaluation because, as Michaely (1962) has shown, countries are more important in their export markets (increased exports lowering prices) than in their import markets. But if a country is a price-taker in both its import and export markets devaluation cannot affect the terms of trade, e.g. a 10 percent devaluation will raise both prices also by 10 percent.

Looking again at the third line of table 3.1 we can see that devaluation of the dollar will worsen the USA's terms of trade as, following a devaluation, dollar import prices rise more than export prices. In fact, given the import and export price effects of 0.9 and 0.2 respectively, a 10 percent dollar devaluation worsens the USA's terms of trade by about 6.4 percent. Furthermore, as internationally traded goods and services account for about 12 percent of US GNP, this devaluation would cause US real income to fall by about 0.8 percent.

■ 3.2 The Forward Exchange Rate, Arbitrage, and Pure Speculation

So far in this chapter it has been assumed that the exchange rate is determined as a result of currency transactions in the spot market to finance international trade, and no mention has been made of the forward exchange rate. Yet the forward exchange rate is important because, as was pointed out in chapter 2, three main classes of transactors use the forward exchange market: international traders (of goods and services) may use the forward market for hedging; portfolio managers who practice covered interest arbitrage to earn a rate of return which is free of exchange risk; and other portfolio managers who accept risk to speculate by taking open positions in foreign currencies. In the next section it will be shown how these three classes of transactor come together *simultaneously* to determine the spot and forward exchange rates. Before that we will deepen our understanding of the concepts of arbitrage and speculation.

Crucial to the following analysis is *covered interest arbitrage* and *covered interest parity*. This may be expressed succinctly in the following way: an investor is indifferent between placing an extra £1 into home or foreign treasury bills when the rates of return on them are equal and risk free, i.e. when £1 invested in home treasury bills yields the same return as £1 converted at the spot exchange rate into the foreign currency (which we will take to be dollars) and the proceeds expected when the treasury bill matures (i.e. principal plus interest) are simultaneously sold at the forward rate F for the appropriate maturity date:

$$1 + i = \frac{F(1 + i^*)}{S} \tag{3.6}$$

where i and i^* are respectively the home and foreign interest rates on the treasury bills expressed at an annual rate, S is the spot exchange rate and F is the forward exchange rate (both exchange rates stated as the home currency price of one unit of foreign currency). Upon rearrangement:[3]

$$i = i^* + \frac{F - S}{S} \tag{3.7}$$

where the term $(F - S)/S$ is understood to be the *forward premium p*, also known as "the cost of covering". Thus, if $i < i^*$ the forward dollar will go to a discount (i.e. $(F - S)/S$ becomes negative). This is indeed likely to happen as covered arbitrage funds will be flowing through the spot market to the USA -- in order to buy the US treasury bills – and this will tend to raise the price of the dollar in the spot market, i.e. S rises, while, in the forward market, the selling of the forward dollar ("to bring the funds home") will strengthen the forward pound, i.e. *reduce F*. With S rising while F is falling it is to be expected that the forward premium on the dollar will become negative – the dollar is at a discount (or the pound is at a premium). This premium on the pound is "the cost of covering." It is expected that arbitrage will ensure that equation (3.7) and covered interest parity holds continuously. This is because, if it does not, arbitrage funds will continue to flow and persist to pressure the forward discount on the dollar.

Equation (3.7) can be rearranged to show the covered interest differential CD:

$$CD = i - i^* - p \qquad (3.7a)$$

If CD > 0 there will be UK capital inflow as the return in the foreign country inclusive of the cost of covering is less than the return in the home country. If CD < 0 there will be capital outflow, whilst portfolios are in equilibrium if CD = 0.

Speculation in foreign exchange can take various forms. One of them is *"pure" speculation*, which takes place in the forward market. This has the attractive feature that a foreign currency does not have to be bought and held, so tying up funds. (In practice the speculator will be required to make a margin requirement.) Equilibrium for pure speculation (i.e. an additional forward contract will not be bought or sold) is when

$$F = S^e \qquad (3.8)$$

where S^e is the expected spot exchange rate for a future date and F is the forward rate for the same future date. If $F < S^e$, speculators will buy – at the price F – foreign currency forward because they expect to be able to sell the foreign currency that they will eventually get at the higher expected spot price S^e.

If the inequality runs the other way, $F > S^e$, speculators will buy the home country's currency in the forward market hoping to sell it at a profit when the forward contract comes due.

If "pure" speculators are risk neutral, buying pressure in the forward exchange market will force the equality (3.8). But, if "pure" speculators are risk averse, they will not force the equality: expected profit on the *last* contract bought remains positive.

There are other types of speculation in foreign currency which are worth mentioning. One type is *leads and lags*, which is often important when a country's capital account is blocked for residents by foreign exchange controls – such as the UK's before 1979 or many developing countries' today. Thus an importer with an outstanding foreign currency obligation, who expects depreciation of the home currency, will lead paying off the debt to "beat" the depreciation. An exporter holding a similar expectation will lag transmission home of foreign earnings so as to benefit from the expected higher value of foreign currency. In both cases speculation is occurring because a "bet" is being made on the outcome that the domestic currency will depreciate. Leads and lags may at times severely distort flows through foreign currency markets and can be a problem for authorities that are managing the exchange rate.

Banks may speculate in foreign currency simply by not covering with their correspondents any net foreign currency sales that they may have made during the course of a trading day. That is, a bank may choose to hold an open position in foreign exchange.

More esoteric forms of currency speculation have opened up with the recent development of foreign currency options where an investor can pay a premium to have the option to buy (or sell) a foreign currency. If the currency moves in the expected direction the option can either be sold at a higher price or the foreign currency can be collected and resold on the spot market.

Then, of course, there is always the possibility of holding foreign currency under the mattress – spending it the next time that you go for your two-week holiday in the sun.

3.2.1 Determination of the forward exchange rate by arbitrageurs and speculators

The classic work on this is Tsiang (1959). To simplify matters it is assumed that the spot exchange rate between two currencies, the dollar and the pound ($/£), is at the level A in figure 3.4. It is maintained at this level by central bank intervention whenever there is an excess demand for one of the currencies on the spot market. The following argument has the pound as foreign currency and the dollar as the home currency.

Given that A is the current spot exchange rate and with US interest rates above UK interest rates, the covered interest arbitrage forward exchange rate for the pound will be at a premium at B (with the percentage premium being

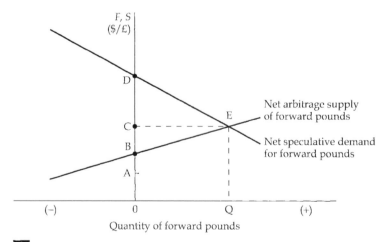

Figure 3.4 Determining the forward exchange rate

AB/0A). At this forward exchange rate the covered interest differential CD = 0, and the net demand for forward pounds is zero. However, if the forward cost of the pound is above B (i.e. the premium on the forward pound is increased), CD < 0 and arbitrage funds flow out of the USA to be invested in UK treasury bills. Covering of the expected sterling proceeds will set up a supply of forward pounds. If the forward rate was below B then CD > 0 and funds will flow into the USA. The sale of expected dollar proceeds by arbitrageurs sets up a demand for the forward pound. Thus, the net arbitrage supply curve slopes upwards to the right – it would be horizontal through B if there was an infinite supply of arbitrage funds and arbitrageurs had no fear of sovereign default or counter-party risk.

Speculators form a view of what they expect the spot rate to be at a future date. Suppose that the expected future spot rate is D in figure 3.4. From equation (3.8), if $F = S^e$ equals the value at D, net speculative demand for the forward pound is zero. But if the forward rate for the relevant future date is less than the expected spot rate, $F < S^e$, speculators will buy the forward pound as the spot pound is expected to rise relative to the forward rate. In figure 3.4 the net speculative demand function is drawn with a negative slope to reflect speculators' risk aversion – with risk neutrality this function will be horizontal through D.

The intersection of the two schedules at E in figure 3.4 establishes the equilib-rium forward rate C, with arbitrageurs supplying 0Q forward pounds to meet the speculators' demand at this price. In this case arbitrageurs are moving funds to the lower interest rate country, the UK, and covering themselves forward by supplying pounds, with the forward premium on the pound being such as to off-set the lower interest rate.[4]

3.2.2 Risk premiums

Equation (3.8) implies that the forward rate is an unbiased predictor of the future spot rate, but this implicitly assumes that speculators are risk neutral. If they are then we can look at the forward rate and take it as the market's expectation of the future spot rate. But look again at figure 3.4: the forward rate (at C) is not equal to the expected future spot rate (at D). Thus, the forward rate is not an unbiased predictor of the future spot rate. It is a biased predictor for the same reason that the speculative demand curve slopes downward in figure 3.4 – i.e. because of risk aversion on the part of speculators. (If speculators were risk neutral the speculative demand function would be perfectly elastic through S^e equal to the value at D.) In general, $S^e - F$ (or DC in figure 3.4) can be regarded as a measure of the risk premium.

Estimates of average risk premiums on several currencies against the US dollar have been made (Isard, 1987). Direct observations of *expected* future spot exchange rates for the period 1981–5 were taken from survey data gathered by American Express Bank and *The Economist*. With risk neutrality the forward rate for the relevant dates should have been equal to the market's expectation, i.e. $S^e = F$ (equation (3.8)). However, Isard found that the expected rate S^e consistently

Table 3.2 Some estimates of risk premiums

	Expected depreciation of the dollar (%)	Forward premium on non-dollar currency (%)	Risk premium $(S^e - F$, DC in figure 3.4) (%)
Pound	3.92	0.39	3.53
French franc	4.60	−5.44	10.04
Deutschmark	12.81	4.82	8.53
Swiss franc	12.35	5.87	6.48
Yen	12.71	5.16	7.55

Source: Isard, 1987

exceeded the forward rate F and he took this as a measure of the risk premium demanded by speculators to hold non-dollar currencies. The extents of the risk premium on each of five currencies are shown in table 3.2.

The numbers in the first column are all positive which indicates that the dollar price of these currencies was expected to rise. The second column gives actual forward premiums in the foreign exchange markets. The third column indicates the risk premium as the difference between the expected depreciation of the dollar and the forward premium for each currency. The premiums appear to be quite large relative to the size of the expected depreciation of the dollar. For example, the Swiss franc was expected to appreciate by about 12 percent, but speculators appeared to want a further 6 percent profit (from appreciation of the Swiss franc above its premium) just to hold the Swiss franc rather than the US dollar.[5]

3.2.3 Uncovered interest arbitrage

Another form of speculation is uncovered interest arbitrage. Here an investor holds a foreign treasury bill (or it could be some other foreign financial asset such as a bank account) without covering in the forward market. A risk-neutral investor will be indifferent to where an extra £1 is invested and uncovered interest parity holds when

$$1 + i_t = \frac{(1 + i_t^*)S_{t+k}^e}{S_t} \tag{3.9}$$

where the i_ts are again the interest rates, S_t is the current spot exchange rate and S_{t+k}^e is the spot exchange rate expected to prevail in period $t + k$. The term on the left-hand side of (3.9) is the per period return earned investing in UK treasury bills, and the right-hand side states the expected per period return investing in the foreign financial instrument. Foreign currency is bought today at the exchange rate S_t. The proceeds (principal plus interest) are expected to be sold at the future spot exchange rate S_{t+k}^e.

Equation (3.9) can be rearranged as

$$i_t = i_t^* + \frac{S_{t+k}^e - S_t}{S_t}$$

(3.9a)

or as

$$i_t = i_t^* + \Delta s_{t+k}^e$$

(3.9b)

where in equation (3.9a) the term $(S_{t+k}^e - S_t)/S_t$ is the expected proportionate appreciation of the foreign currency (if it is negative it is the expected proportionate depreciation of the foreign currency) and in equation (3.9b) the term Δs_{t+k}^e is the natural logarithm of $(S_{t+k}^e - S_t)/S_t$ (recall that a change in a log value is a *proportionate* change). In later chapters we shall find that it is most convenient to use equation (3.9b).

Equation (3.9b) can be rearranged to show the uncovered interest differential (UD):

$$UD_t = i_t - i_t^* - \Delta s_{t+k}^e$$

(3.10)

If $UD_t > 0$ the home country will experience capital inflow – the expected rate of return on home assets is higher than on foreign assets; there is capital outflow if $UD_t < 0$ as now the expected rate of return is lower than on foreign assets; and, if $UD_t = 0$, asset portfolios are in equilibrium and there will be no international flow of capital between a pair of countries.

If wealth-holders are risk neutral equation (3.10) (and (3.8), (3.9a) and (3.9b)) will strictly hold (i.e. speculators consider only the mathematical expectation of S_{t+k}^e and not its subjective variance). Alternatively, a risk-averse investor will not necessarily move funds when an inequality in equation (3.10) exists. Such an investor will require the expected return on the foreign treasury bills to be larger – depending on the degree of risk aversion – than the risk-free return on domestic treasury bills.

3.2.4 *Ex ante* purchasing power parity

Equations (3.9) imply that the expected change in the exchange rate is equal to the interest rate differential, i.e.

$$\Delta s_{t+k}^e = i_t - i_t^*$$

(3.11)

A very interesting result can be derived using the so-called "Fisher open relationship" where the expected rate of change of the exchange rate, Δs^e, depends on the relative rates of expected price inflation. Thus, the nominal interest rate in each country may be decomposed into a real interest rate component and an expected inflation component:

$$i_t = r_t + \Delta p^e \tag{3.12}$$

$$i_t^* = r_t^* + \Delta p^{e*} \tag{3.13}$$

where r denotes the real interest rate and Δp^e denotes the expected rate of inflation. By assuming that the real rates of interest are equalized across two countries (by international arbitrage of real capital) and substituting (3.12) and (3.13) into (3.11) it follows that

$$\Delta s_{t+k}^e = \Delta p_{t+1}^e - \Delta p_{t+1}^{e*} \tag{3.14}$$

That is, the expected rate of change in the exchange rate is shown to depend on the expected inflation differential. Equation (3.14) is sometimes referred to as the Fisher open or *ex ante* purchasing power parity condition, and it will be used in later chapters.

 ## 3.3 Covered Interest Rate Parity – Empirical Evidence

How well supported is the covered interest rate parity (CIP) relationship considered above? Perhaps the best known study concerning the validity of CIP is that by Frenkel and Levich (FL) (1975), and their approach can be motivated around figure 3.5. In figure 3.5, the 45° line, labelled CIP, denotes combinations of the interest rate differential and the forward premium which ensure that CIP holds *exactly*. Points above the CIP line are consistent with $CD_t(= (i - i)_t - P_t)$ being regative and therefore represent a potential capital outflow, whilst points below the CIP line indicate positive values of CD_t and therefore represent a potential

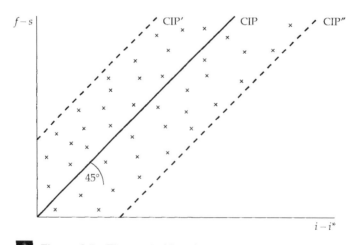

Figure 3.5 The neutral band

capital inflow. FL use three-month treasury bills for the UK and the USA and for Canada and the USA to compute whether the covered differential CD_t is equal to zero or not. In fact FL report that there were many observations which give a non-zero value for CD_t. In terms of figure 3.5 this may be captured by the crosses around the 45° line. How may these deviations be rationalized and, in particular, do they reflect an important market inefficiency? FL suggest not. First, it must be borne in mind that all of our discussion so far has ignored the potential costs facing an investor who engages in a covered position. FL distinguish four types of transactions costs associated with a covered position (outflow): the transactions costs involved in selling a domestic security; the transactions costs associated with the purchase of spot foreign currency; the transactions costs of buying the foreign security; the transactions costs of forward cover.[6] In figure 3.5 these costs mean that the true CIP line along which CD_t, adjusted for transactions costs, is zero will be given by a line such as CIP′, a kind of upper bound for CIP deviations to fall within whilst still being consistent with market efficiency. A similar set of costs associated with a covered inflow defines a lower bound, CIP″. The area bounded by CIP′ and CIP″ is commonly referred to as the neutral band and any non-zero CD_ts which occur within this band are not inconsistent with CIP adjusted for transactions costs.[7] In their study, which covers the period from January 1962 through November 1967, FL report that over 80 percent of their reported deviations lie within the neutral band. What about the remaining 15 percent of the deviations? Are they potentially exploitable? To answer this question we need to consider the kinds of assets FL use in their study.

As we noted, FL use treasury bill rates in their computation of CIP. However, Aliber (1973b) has argued that these kinds of assets are not appropriate for such a computation because they are liable to sovereign or political risk. Such risk arises because of the potential for the foreign government to default on its loan or renege on its interest payments (which seems unlikely for the countries considered by FL) or more realistically because of the potential for the foreign country to introduce some form of exchange control which would prevent the investor from retrieving his or her funds. This type of risk, however, may be avoided if the investor uses domestic and foreign financial instruments, such as Euro dollar bonds, which are issued in the same financial centre (i.e. within the same political jurisdiction). In fact when FL recompute their CD_t estimates with Euro-bills they find that all the deviations from the CIP line lie within the neutral band (i.e. the 15 percent of deviations reported above must be due to political risk).

In a further paper, FL (1977) apply the analysis of the neutral band to three different time periods which they categorize as "the tranquil pegged exchange rate period" (1962–7), "the turbulent pegged exchange rate period" (1968–9) and "the managed float period" (1973–5). They show that for the tranquil and managed float periods over 80 percent of the deviations for the treasury bills considered lie within the neutral band and almost 100 percent for the Euro-bills; however, for the turbulent period a much smaller percentage of the deviations is explained in terms of transactions costs and this is interpreted as a reflection of the financial uncertainty in the period.

A number of researchers, however, have questioned the quality of the data used by FL. This point relates to whether the spot and forward rates and the relevant interest rates were recorded contemporaneously; i.e. does the CD deviation generated by the interest combination and forward premium used by FL represent a value that a trader could actually have traded at or is it simply a mongrel variable representing the mismatched timing of the underlying variables.[8] For example, in order to provide a true test of CIP it is important that data on the appropriate exchange and interest rates be recorded at the same instant at which a dealer could have dealt.

A second method for testing the validity of CIP is the use of regression analysis. Thus, if CIP holds, and in the absence of transactions costs, estimation of

$$f_t - s_t = \alpha + \beta(i - i^*)_t + u_t \tag{3.15}$$

should result in estimates of α and β differing insignificantly from zero and unity, respectively, and a non-autocorrelated error. Equation (3.12) has been tested by researchers for a variety of currencies and time periods (e.g. see Marston (1976), Cosandier and Laing (1981) and Fratianni and Wakeman (1982)). Broadly speaking, CIP is supported; although there were significant deviations of α from zero (reflecting perhaps non-zero transactions costs), the estimates of β differed insignificantly from unity in the majority of cases. However, it is not clear what regression-based analyses of CIP are actually testing. For example, it may be that the hypothesis that $\alpha = 0$ and $\beta = 1$ in equation (3.12) cannot be rejected, but that the fitted residuals themselves represent substantial arbitrage opportunities. Put another way, such a test may strongly suggest that CIP held *on average* over a period, when in fact it did not hold at *any instant* during the period. Thus, although regression-based tests may be useful for testing the broad stylized fact of CIP (which may be of interest, for example, in exchange rate modeling), they can say virtually nothing about market efficiency. In spite of this caveat, we summarize the above evidence as suggesting that CIP does appear to be strongly supported by the data, especially if Eurodeposit interest rates are considered.

■ 3.4 Uncovered Interest Rate Parity – Empirical Evidence

In order to test uncovered interest rate parity (UIP), some assumption must be made about the formation of expectations. Two approaches are common in the literature. Most researchers assume that agents' expectations are formed rationally and that therefore

$$\Delta s_{t+k} = \Delta s_{t+k}^e + \varphi_{t+k} \tag{3.16}$$

where φ_{t+k} is a random forecast error. Substituting this expression into (3.9b) we obtain

$$\Delta s_{t+k} = (i - i^*)_t + \varphi_{t+k} \tag{3.17}$$

One way of testing the validity of (3.17) – which consists of the *joint* hypothesis of rationality and UIP – would be to estimate a regression equation of the form

$$s_t = \beta_0 s_{t-k} + \beta_1 (i - i^*)_{t-k} + \zeta_t \tag{3.18}$$

and test whether β_0 and β_1 equal -1 and 1, respectively, and whether ζ_t is uncorrelated with information widely available in period t (which it should be if agents are indeed rational – this concept is discussed in some detail in chapters 9 to 11). Equation (3.18), or variants thereof, has been tested by, *inter alia*, Hacche and Townend (1981), Cumby and Obstfeld (1981), Davidson (1985), and and Loopesko (1984); in all instances, UIP was rejected very strongly. Since UIP is predicated on the assumption that the forward exchange rate is equal to the expected spot rate, and therefore there is no risk premium, the most common interpretation of this rejection is that there is, in fact, a time-varying risk premium separating the forward rate from the expected future spot rate. However, this can only be an interpretation since it could reflect some problem with the expectations component of the joint hypothesis subsumed in (3.16) (as we shall see in chapters 9 and 11, where these kinds of issues are discussed in detail, this need not necessarily be synonymous with irrationality).

The second approach to empirically implementing (3.18) has been to take an agnostic stand about the formation of agents' expectations and to use a direct measure of the expected change in the exchange rate as provided by a number of financial services institutions, such as Money Market Services (MMS). This is the approach adopted by MacDonald and Torrance (1990) (for the dollar–mark, dollar–yen, dollar–pound and dollar–Swiss franc exchange rates) and they demonstrate, *inter alia*, that rejection of the joint UIP hypothesis was caused by both a time-varying risk premium element and expectations factors (the use of survey data in expectational tests is also discussed in some detail in chapters 9 and 11).

3.5 Real Interest Rate Parity – Empirical Evidence

Another international parity condition that has received attention in the literature is real interest rate parity. This may be derived using UIP (equation (3.9b)), *ex ante* purchasing power parity (equation (3.14)) and Fisher closed conditions for the home and foreign country (equations (3.20) and (3.21)) below:

$$\Delta s_{t+k}^e = \Delta p_{t+k}^e - \Delta p_{t+k}^{*e} \tag{3.19}$$

$$r_t = i_t - \Delta p_{t+k}^e \tag{3.20}$$

$$r_t^* = i_t^* - \Delta p_{t+k}^{*e} \tag{3.21}$$

where r denotes the real interest rate, i is the nominal interest rate and p is the logarithm of the price level. Combining these three equations yields

$$r_t = r_t^* \tag{3.22}$$

Thus, given the stated assumptions, real interest rates must be equalized across countries, and the scope for the policymaker to alter real economic activity by changing the real interest rate is limited. Is condition (3.22) supported empirically? The real interest rate parity condition has been tested by a number of researchers for the USA against other OECD countries (see, for example, Cumby and Obstfeld (1984) and MacDonald and Taylor (1990)). For example, Cumby and Obstfeld empirically implement (3.22) by running the following regression:

$$\Delta p_{t+1} - \Delta p_{t+1}^* = \alpha + \beta(i - i^*)_t + v_{t+1} \tag{3.23}$$

which is obtained by using equations (3.18) and (3.19) in (3.20) and by assuming that expected inflation rates are formed rationally. A test of $\alpha = 0$, $\beta = 1$ (the null hypothesis) is a test of the equality of expected real interest rates. A sample of Cumby and Obstfeld's results is reported here:

$$\Delta p_{t+1} - \Delta p_{t+1}^* = 0.028 + 0.503(i - i^*)_t \tag{3.24}$$
$$\quad\quad\quad (0.01) \quad\;\; (0.23)$$

USA–Germany   January 1976–September 1981

where standard errors are in parentheses, the price terms are consumer price indexes and the interest rates are Eurodeposit interest rates. For this equation, and for others reported by Cumby and Obstfeld, the null hypothesis of *ex ante* real interest rate parity is easily rejected.

NOTES

1 For studies of trade elasticities covering different countries and time periods see Houthakker and Magee (1969), Junz and Rhomberg (1973), Spitaller (1980), Gylfason (1987) and Dunaway (1988).

2 $1/Q$ is not the terms of trade if some goods are non-traded. Their prices must be included in the national price indexes and this is likely to make some difference – see equation (7.21).

3 The required manipulation is as follows: the forward premium is defined as $p = (F - S)/S$ and upon rearrangement $p + 1 = F/S$. Substitute the latter expression into equation (3.6) to give $1 + i = (p + 1)(1 + i^*)$. Now, multipling through and solving for i gives $i = i^* + p + pi^*$. The last term is usually very small and is ignored, whereupon $i = i^* + p$, which is equation (3.7).

4 Funds could flow to the country with the lower interest rate if speculators were expecting the dollar to depreciate and bought pounds on the forward exchange market – so raising the dollar cost of the pound above B in figure 3.4.

5 One criticism of using survey data to estimate risk premiums is that it may not be reliable. Responders to a questionnaire may be less careful in their assessments of the prospect for a currency than if they were actually moving funds.

6 Clinton (1988) has demonstrated that deviation from CIP should be no greater than the minimum transaction costs in one of three markets: the two underlying deposit markets (e.g. Europounds and Eurodollars) and the foreign exchange swap market (i.e. the market in which a currency can be simultaneously bought and sold forward against another currency).

7 In their 1975 paper Frenkel and Levich estimate the neutral band to be an average (for the three currencies considered) of ±0.147 percent.

8 McCormack (1979) questioned the quality of the data used by FL to calculate their trans-actions costs. In particular, he noted that FL's method of using two exchange rates, the dollar–pound and the dollar–mark, to calculate the exchange rate transactions costs of a US–UK interest arbitrage transaction resulted in a much higher estimate of such costs because the two rates were quoted at different times in the day. Using exchange rates quoted at the same point in time, McCormick found that the neutral band was dra-matically narrowed – in the most extreme case only 27 percent of observations fell within the band.

4

Income and the
Balance of Payments

A problem with the elasticities approach is that it assumes that income levels are unchanged. On reflection, and deploying a little knowledge about the Keynesian income–expenditure model, this assumption is not valid if either or both exports and imports are related to the level of income. However, a trade deficit (surplus) will have a negative (positive) effect on national income via the foreign trade multiplier. Then, as income changes, the import (and/or export) functions in figure 3.1 (p. 25) will shift. Thus, it is now time to investigate some elementary applications of Keynesian economics to the open economy. Section 4.1 outlines the concept of the foreign trade multiplier. Section 4.2 discusses the concept of the equilibrium real exchange rate. "Targets" and "instruments" are addressed in section 4.3; and section 4.4 discusses the assignment problem, also known as the "principle of effective market classification." Section 4.5 describes the absorption approach to the balance of payments and the concepts of expenditure reduction and expenditure switching to manage an economy toward internal and external balance. In section 4.6 current account imbalances are analyzed as a result of intertemporal utility maximization. The next section, 4.7, discusses the USA's problems with its so-called "twin deficits" which persisted through much of the 1980s and to 1998 when the federal budget moved into balance. Section 4.8 weighs macroeconomic repercussions between large trading nations.

■ 4.1 The Foreign Trade Multiplier

How does an autonomous change in exports or imports affect (i) national income, and (ii) the trade balance? To answer these questions consider a simple Keynesian model without a government sector

$$E = C + I + G + X - M \qquad (4.1)$$

$$C = a + b(Y - T) \qquad (4.2)$$

$$T = tY \qquad (4.3)$$

$$I = \bar{I} \qquad (4.4)$$

$$G = \bar{G} \qquad (4.5)$$

$$X = \bar{X} \qquad (4.6)$$

$$M = N + mY \qquad (4.7)$$

$$E = Y \qquad (4.8)$$

where E is expenditure on domestic produced goods and services by both residents and foreigners, C is consumption, $\bar{I}$ is investment (assumed autonomous), $\bar{G}$ is autonomous government expenditure, T is T revenue, and t the tax rate, $\bar{X}$ is exports (also assumed autonomous), M is imports, b is the marginal propensity to consume, and m the marginal propensity to import.

Substitution into equation 4.1 and rearranging gives

$$Y = (a + \bar{I} + \bar{G} + \bar{X} - N) \, [1/(s + m + bt)] \qquad (4.9)$$

where $s = 1 - b$, the marginal propensity to save. If we differentiate equation (4.9) with respect to $\bar{X}$ and N (i.e. autonomous exports and imports, respectively) we find the foreign trade multiplier for exports, $dY/dX = 1/(s + m + bt)$; and for imports, $dY/dN = -1/(s + m + bt)$. In principle, the foreign trade multiplier is no different to any other expenditure multiplier – being determined by the marginal propensity for income to leak away from spending on domestically produced goods and services.

4.1.1 The trade balance

Defining the trade balance, TB, as $X - M$ and using equations (4.1)–(4.8) we find that

$$\Delta TB = \Delta X[1 - m/(s + m + bt)] \qquad (4.10)$$

which says that the change in the trade balance is less than a change in exports for usual values of m, s, and t less than unity. This is because of the foreign trade multiplier effect of changing income on imports where the foreign trade multiplier is the term in [ ] in equation (4.10). Thus, if exports fall, income falls too as will the level of imports, and the worsening of the trade deficit will be mitigated to some extent: it still worsens but by less than if imports had not changed.[1]

4.2 The Equilibrium Real Exchange Rate

The literature on real exchange rate determination is divided into that part which sees it as determined by macroeconomic balance, and that which sees it as determined as the relative price of traded and non-traded goods in microeconomic equilibrium. The macroeconomic part is usually used when developed countries are being discussed, while the other part is often applied to transition economies and emerging markets. As in this book we are interested in both cases we show how the equilibrium real exchange rate is determined in simultaneous macroeconomic–microeconomic equilibrium.

Different writers have given the equilibrium real exchange rate different names, Williamson (1983, 1994) calls it the FEER (fundamental equilibrium real exchange rate), and Allen and Stein (1991) the NATREX (the natural real exchange rate). Apart from details of econometric estimation, these really amount to the same thing – the equilibrium real exchange rate is determined at that level which gives simultaneous internal and external balance and an optimal allocation of resources between the traded and non-traded goods sectors.

Recall from section 2.3 that the real exchange rate, Q, is:

$$Q = S(P^*/P) \tag{4.11}$$

where S is the foreign currency price of a unit of domestic currency, the Ps are price levels and the asterisk denotes the foreign country. Thus, an increase in Q, a depreciation, increases the home country's international competitiveness.

The real exchange rate also measures the relative price of traded (T) to non-traded goods (N) in the home country:

$$Q = P_T/P_N \tag{4.12}$$

This is found by assuming that the domestic price level is Cobb–Douglas ($P = P_N^a P_T^{1-a}$), purchasing power parity holds for traded goods, and the foreign price level is normalized to unity. Thus: equation 4.11 becomes $Q = S/P_N^a S^{1-a}$, which simplifies to equation 4.12.

4.2.1 Macroeconomic balance

For macroeconomic balance we use the model due to Swan (1955), Salter (1959) and Corden and Neary (1982). When internal and external balance occur together

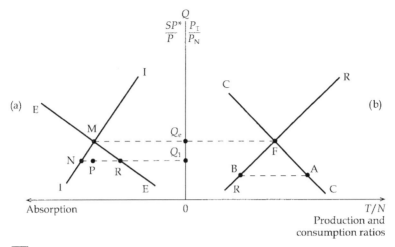

Figure 4.1 Internal and external balance in macroeconomic and microeconomic equilibrium

an economy is in macroeconomic equilibrium. Thus, assuming some price-stickiness and the possibility of Keynesian unemployment equilibria,

$$Y = Y(A, Q) \qquad Y_A > 0, Y_Q > 0 \qquad (4.13)$$

for internal balance, where Y is real GDP, A is spending (or "absorption" as defined in section 4.4 as $C + I + G$), and Q is the real exchange rate. Also,

$$TB = TB(A, Q) \qquad TB_A < 0, TB_Q > 0 \qquad (4.14)$$

where TB is the trade balance, which $= 0$ if there are no "sustainable" capital flows, otherwise it differs from zero.

In figure 4.1a II is the internal balance function which slopes downward because, given full employment, an increase in domestic absorption requires a real exchange rate appreciation to divert some domestic and foreign spending away from domestic goods, otherwise spending would exceed full employment output, so disturbing internal balance. To the left of II there is excess demand, as absorption is too great at any Q. Inflation and a negative wealth effect, or, nominal exchange rate appreciation, may be presumed to adjust the real exchange to give internal balance. II is drawn for some given equilibrium rate of unemployment and it will shift if the equilibrium rate of unemployment changes – a feature that is especially relevant to transition and emerging economies as they undertake economic reforms.

The EE function slopes upward because an increase in absorption reduces net exports, so requiring a real depreciation to switch some demand towards domestic goods. To the left of the EE function there is a trade deficit which, in the absence of a nominal depreciation of S, will eventually correct itself as absorption falls due to either a fall in the real money supply and/or a fall in real wealth as international indebtedness increases.[2]

Factors which affect the sustainable trade balance at any given real exchange rate will shift the EE function. An increase in sustainable capital inflow will shift it to the left. A reduction in import tariffs, licenses or quotas will shift it to the right as the increased domestic demand for traded goods must be balanced by reduced absorption at any Q.[3]

4.2.2 Microeconomic balance

As the real exchange rate is the relative price of traded and non-traded goods we need to combine this microeconomic aspect of internal–external balance with the macroeconomic aspect already considered.

In figure 4.1b, RR is the ratio of traded to non-traded goods in domestic production (R_T/R_N). This ratio is an increasing function of the real exchange rate, as depreciation (higher Q) increases profits in the traded goods sector relative to those in the non-traded sector.[4]

The CC function in figure 4.1b traces out the ratio of traded to non-traded goods in domestic consumption (C_T/C_N), and it is a decreasing function of the real exchange rate. Thus, a real depreciation increases the relative price of traded goods, so reducing C_T/C_N.[5]

At F in figure 4.1b the share of traded goods in production and consumption are equal and the traded account is balanced.[6] Notice that on II at M there is trade balance, and that moving down II the trade deficit grows.

The more responsive are the shares of traded goods in production and consumption to a change in Q (i.e. the flatter are RR and CC) the flatter will be the EE function.[7] Similarly with II: the more sensitive are CC and RR to a change in Q, the flatter is II – as a given increase in Q causes a larger trade deficit which needs to be offset by a larger increase in absorption to maintain internal balance.

If the EE and II functions are steep neither macro- nor micro-disequilibria will be all that great for a non-equilibrium real exchange rate reasonably close to the equilibrium rate such as Q_1. For example, if the economy was at P neither the payments deficit nor the unemployment rate would be all that great, and need not be of great concern to a government. Steep EE and II functions are likely to be a short-run feature as microeconomic price elasticities are often low in this time period.

This observation seems to be the basis of Williamson's (1983, 1994) preference for international monetary reform in the direction of a wide-band nominal exchange rate target zone. Variations in the nominal and, therefore, the real, exchange rate do not matter so much as both resource allocation and the macroeconomy are quite unresponsive in the short run. But such a wide band would work only if the nominal rate mean reverted because in the long run the EE and II functions are likely to flatten out as resource allocation has time work.

4.2.3 A comment on purchasing power parity

A further comment concerns the use by some practitioners of the purchasing power parity doctrine to determine a country's equilibrium nominal exchange rate. This doctrine – as described in chapter 7 – asserts that a country's nominal exchange rate is determined by relative price levels. If this is true, the real exchange rate would be constant over time, with the nominal exchange rate changing in proportion to the ratio of relative price levels. However, in this section we have seen that the equilibrium real exchange rate changes if the EE function shifts (which it will if the RR or CC functions shift), or if the II function shifts (which it will if the equilibrium level of unemployment changes). In either case, a change in relative price levels does not necessarily cause a proportional change in the equilibrium nominal exchange rate as the change in relative price levels may just be the means through which the real exchange rate is moving to its equilibrium level. Or, the real exchange rate could be altered via a changing nominal exchange rate with no necessity for the latter to be caused by changes in relative price levels. Given these observations, the purchasing power parity doctrine may only be true when a country suffers from a large shock to its price level, for then the change in relative prices may dominate the other factors which influence a country's real exchange rate.

 ## 4.3 An Early View of Economic Management

Governments have several acknowledged economic goals, e.g. price stability, full employment, economic growth, balance in foreign payments and an equitable distribution of income, and one of the lessons of the theory of economic policy (see Tinbergen, 1952) is that as a general rule each policy objective requires a corresponding policy weapon or instrument. If there are more policy goals than there are instruments, simultaneous attainment of all goals can occur only by chance. The problem can be illustrated on the assumption of two goals, namely full employment and balance on foreign trade, as set out in figure 4.1a.

Suppose that an economy with a fixed exchange rate found itself at P, where neither objective is being attained. There is a balance of payments deficit (because of the lack of international competitiveness for the given level of domestic real expenditure), and high unemployment (because for the given level of international competitiveness there is inadequate domestic expenditure). Suppose that, at least in the short run, international competitiveness cannot be changed – due to a fixed exchange rate and sticky prices. To achieve internal equilibrium would require an increase of domestic expenditure of PN at the level of competitiveness corresponding to Q_1. To restore external balance would require a reduction in domestic expenditure of PR, which would lead to increased unemployment. One goal can be achieved only if the other is relinquished to an even greater extent. Britain's "stop-go" policies of the 1960s correspond somewhat to this model. Each "go" (i.e. increased domestic real expenditure) to reduce unemployment was shortly followed by a "stop" imposed by the balance of payments constraint.

In figure 4.1a, the adoption of a second policy-instrument makes possible the attainment of simultaneous internal and external balance. Thus, from point P, the policy-combination of devaluation (moving the economy vertically above P) and reduced domestic real expenditure ultimately moves the economy to M. But as Mundell (1962) demonstrated, this analysis makes no allowance for the differential impacts of monetary and fiscal policy – see chapter 5.

■ 4.4 The Assignment Problem

The assignment problem is an application of the "principle of effective market classification," which asserts that policies should be paired with the objectives on which they have most influence. If macroeconomic policies are incorrectly assigned they may destabilize economic activity. Mundell (1962) argued that the proper assignment is of monetary (interest rate) policy to external balance and fiscal policy to internal balance. This is because interest rates have relatively greater effect on the balance of payments – through international capital flows – than on the domestic economy, while the reverse is true of fiscal policy. Figure 4.2 lays out the assignment problem.

The vertical axis measures the budget surplus (moving down the axis aggregate demand is rising), and the rate of interest is measured on the horizontal axis. The EE schedule shows external balance – reducing the budget surplus increases aggregate demand which would worsen the balance of payments if interest rates are not allowed to rise in order to attract capital inflow. (Note, therefore, that moving down EE the current account is moving into increasing deficit and the capital account into increasing surplus.) The II schedule shows internal balance at full employment. It too is negatively sloped because a rise in aggregate demand caused by a smaller budget surplus needs to be offset by higher interest rates.[8]

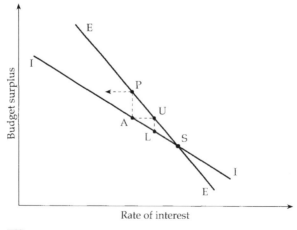

■ **Figure 4.2** Wrong pairing of monetary and fiscal policy

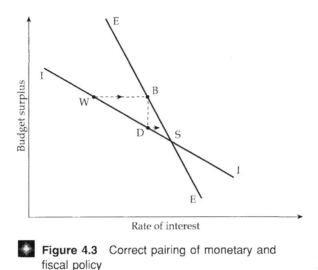

Figure 4.3 Correct pairing of monetary and fiscal policy

Wrong pairing would be budgetary policy for external equilibrium and monetary policy for internal equilibrium. To see this suppose that the economy is initially at L in figure 4.2 enjoying internal equilibrium but with a balance of payments deficit (international reserves are falling). The assignment of a larger budget surplus to cope with balance of payments deficit could move the economy to U, but now the economy is off the II schedule with unemployment having increased. If monetary policy is assigned to achieve internal equilibrium, interest rates are lowered and the economy moves to point A. But now the economy is even further away from simultaneous internal and external balance than it was at point L. A further bout of fiscal tightening – to achieve external balance – moves the economy to point P and a further step away from equilibrium at S.

Correct pairing is shown in figure 4.3, where monetary policy is targeted to external equilibrium and fiscal policy to internal equilibrium. Thus, beginning at W, there is internal equilibrium with a balance of payments deficit. Higher interest rates, aimed at attracting increased capital inflow, moves the economy to B. But at B the budget surplus is too large and unemployment has increased. Now fiscal policy should be used to achieve internal equilibrium. A smaller budget deficit moves the economy from B to D. Ultimately, with this correct pairing of monetary policy to the external balance and fiscal policy to internal balance, the economy will achieve equilibrium at S.

It may be objected that the treasury and the central bank should get together to simultaneously adjust monetary and fiscal policy to move directly from point L to S in figure 4.2 or from W to S in figure 4.3. This is, of course, desirable. However, the assignment problem remains relevant to cases where, for some reason (e.g. forecast government expenditure) multipliers turn out to be incorrect. Under these circumstances initial economic policy objectives are not achieved.

◆ 4.5 The Absorption Approach

From the national income accounting identities

$$Y = C + I + G + (X - M) \tag{4.15}$$

Domestic absorption (a term due to Alexander, 1952, 1961, see also Black, 1959, and Johnson, 1961) is defined as

$$A = C + I + G. \tag{4.16}$$

Defining the current account balance, B, as:

$$B = X - M \tag{4.17}$$

gives 4.15 as

$$Y = A + B, \tag{4.18}$$

and upon rearrangement,

$$B = Y - A = -I_f. \tag{4.19}$$

Equation 4.19 shows that a current account surplus arises if gross domestic product is greater than absorption and that the difference shows up as capital outflow, $-I_f$. Alternatively, a payments deficit is due to domestic absorption being greater than gross domestic product – the difference financed by capital inflow, I_f.

The absorption approach can also be spelled out using the leakage–injection terminology. Thus,

$$S + M + T = I + X + G \tag{4.20}$$

and on rearrangement

$$(S - I) + (T - G) = (X - M) \tag{4.21}$$

i.e. net national saving (i.e. private net saving plus the budget surplus) equals the current account surplus.

Thus, to tie the aggregate spending and leakages and injections approaches to together, from 4.19 and 4.21 we get

$$B = Y - A = \text{net national saving} = -I_f \tag{4.22}$$

so that a current account surplus occurs when gross domestic product is greater than absorption, net national saving is positive, and this financial surplus is used to purchase foreign assets.

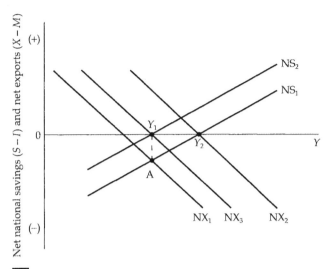

Figure 4.4 Equilibrium national income in an open economy: NS, net national saving; NX, net exports

4.5.1 Some policy considerations

Equilibrium national income in an open economy can be shown using equation 4.21 as in figure 4.4. Net national saving, or *hoarding* (usually defined as the flow demand for money, i.e. the change in the aggregate holding of real money balances), is a positive function of income because of the assumption that saving and taxes rise with income while investment and government spending are autonomous. Net exports $(X - M)$ are a negative function of income because imports rise with income while exports are autonomous.

As shown in figure 4.4 equilibrium national income occurs at point A with income Y_1 and there is balance of trade deficit. Foreign investors will not finance this deficit indefinitely: what economic policies can be adopted to correct the deficit?

To answer this question suppose that:

$$X = \bar{X} \tag{4.23}$$

$$M = M(Y, Q) \qquad dM/dY > 0, \quad dM/dQ < 0 \tag{4.24}$$

where $Q = SP^*/P$, the real exchange rate. Thus, currency devaluation, for given price levels, will raise exports and lower imports. In figure 4.4 the net export function shifts NX_2 assuming that the Marshall–Lerner condition holds. If Y_2 is the full employment level of income then both *external* and *internal balance* hold.

However, suppose that full employment income is Y_1 where the economy's aggregate supply curve starts to slope upwards; then the devaluation will cause excess demand and the price level, P, will rise, reducing competitiveness and shifting the NX_2 function to the left. Rising prices will bring the *real balance effect* into play so shifting the net saving function, NS_1, to the left as wealth-holders cut spending in an effort to restore real balances. In the long run the NX and NS functions may intersect through Y_1. In a sense this effect is analogous to the closed economy Pigou effect. Thus, price level movements are all that are required to get the economy back to equilibrium – activist fiscal–monetary policy is therefore not required (aside from the devaluation of course).

Alexander (1951) devoted most attention to the real balance effect of a devaluation – higher prices increase hoarding, thereby reducing absorption and improving the balance of trade. The emphasis on maintaining real cash balances anticipates the arguments of the monetarist protagonists – as will be seen in chapters 8 and 9. It has been pointed out (Johnson, 1976) that the absorption approach is quite schizophrenic in its treatment of the real balance effect. It recognizes the need to rebuild real balances in the face of the price rises after a devaluation, but it ignores the reduction in the money supply which is the counterpart of the deficit which caused the devaluation.

However, the real balance effect is likely to take some time to have its effect. In practice if a government wants to correct a trade deficit and avoid inflation it should adopt a combination of *expenditure switching* and *expenditure reduction* policies (Johnson, 1961). Expenditure switching switches demand toward home produced goods. Devaluation is the best policy but import tariffs and quotas could also be used. Expenditure reduction policies reduce the level of domestic absorption. This can be achieved through higher interest rates and higher taxes or lower government spending.

In figure 4.4 expenditure switching will shift the NX_1 function directly to NX_3, while expenditure reduction shifts NS_1 directly to NS_2. Full employment with balanced trade is achieved without inflation.

Laursen–Metzler effect

Laursen and Metzler (1950) argued that after a real currency depreciation and consequent worsening of a country's terms of trade, real income would fall. Real income they said should be measured as nominal income deflated by an appropriately weighted domestic price index (i.e. where the weights reflect the proportions of home and foreign goods in consumption). But in figure 4.4 real income, on the horizontal axis, is measured as the value of domestic output in domestic prices, and the NS_1 function represents net saving out of real income measured in this way. As the average propensity to save is a positive function of real income calculated using the correctly weighted price index, a change in import prices will affect the level of net saving. Thus, in figure 4.5, depreciation of the real exchange rate lowers saving at each income level, so shifting NS_1 downward. One effect of this is that currency depreciation is less effective improving the trade balance. That is, there are positive correlations both between the terms of trade and real income and between a worsening of the terms of trade and a worsening trade balance. In effect, in the face of falling real income, residents borrow abroad in order to sustain the level of real consumption. Empirical support for these two

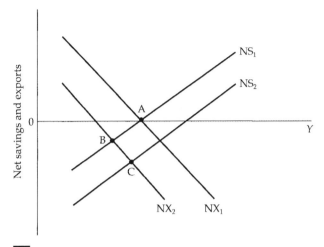

Figure 4.5 Import prices and the balance of trade

proposition for G7 countries over the 1960–89 period is found in Mendoza (1992, table 1).

The Laursen–Metzler effect can be used to show the effect of higher import prices, as with the oil shocks of 1973 and 1979/80. Increased import prices lower net exports and shifts NX_1 downward to NX_2 in figure 4.5. The economy's equilibrium would move from point A to point B. But as higher oil prices significantly reduced real income in many oil-importing nations, the net saving schedule is also shifted downward. Thus, the new equilibrium is at point C. Notice that because of the Laursen–Metzler effect, the trade deficit is larger than at point B, but that domestic income is greater due to the increase in domestic spending.

Laursen–Metzler argued that the real income consequences of changes in nominal and real exchange rates meant that a floating exchange rate would not insulate a country from the effects of shocks to foreign income. Thus, if the rest of the world experiences a recession, the home country's exports will fall and its nominal and real exchange rates will depreciate. Again, the home country's net saving function will shift downward, worsening the trade deficit and causing domestic income to *increase*.[9]

There were two main defects in the balance of payments analysis derived in this Keynesian tradition, defects shared also by the elasticities approach. These are that the analysis applies only to the current account of the balance of payments – it virtually ignores capital account transactions; and, secondly, the analysis ignores the monetary consequences of payments imbalance. The former defect can be explained in that most of the analysis was developed in a period when international capital flows were subject to severe controls (McKinnon, 1981). As these controls were relaxed in the 1960s, new models were developed to take account of international capital flows (Mundell 1963, Fleming 1962 – see chapter 5) and they also showed the implications of the free flow of capital for policies to attain internal and external equilibrium.

The second defect – the failure correctly to model the monetary consequences of payments deficits – was dealt with by the development of monetary models, to be discussed in later chapters.

◼ 4.6 Intertemporal Utility Maximization and the Current Account

In this section we discuss the current account in a simple intertemporal two period ($t = 1$, $t = 2$) model of consumption allocation. Apart from its intrinsic interest in "explaining" some current account deficits, we will use it again in section 12.4 and 19.4 in an assessment of the general failure of forward exchange rates to predict future spot rates. The idea is that a representative consumer has a known time-profile of real income, Y_1, Y_2, which, together with the real interest rate, r, defines an intertemporal budget constraint. This is combined with a utility function, $U = f(C_1, C_2)$, which has the usual characteristics of being concave, twice differentiable, and is time separable. This utility function is explicitly defined in section 12.4 (equation 12.12) where we investigate time-varying risk premia; here we get by with a statement below of the first-order utility maximizing condition.

The general rule for maximizing utility given a budget constraint is, of course, that the (subjective) marginal rate of substitution equals the (objective) price ratio.

The MRS is measured as the ratio between the discounted present value of the marginal utility of an extra unit of $t = 2$ consumption, $\beta u_2'$, and the value of one unit less of $t = 1$ consumption, u_1'. The term β is the time preference discount factor ($= 1/[1 + \alpha]$ where α is the rate of time preference). Hence, The MRS of present goods for future goods is $\beta u_2'/u_1'$, and its absolute value measures the increase in the present value of utility gained from moving one unit of consumption from $t = 1$ to $t = 2$.

The objective price ratio between present and future goods depends on the real rate of interest, r. Thus, saving one unit of the present endowment, Y_1, and lending it out returns $1 + r$ units of future goods. We could say that $1 + r$ is the "price" of present consumption because this much of future goods is given up. Moreover, the reciprocal, $1/(1 + r)$ measures the price of future consumption in terms of present consumption; this amount of present goods is given up in exchange for one unit of future goods.

Intertemporal welfare is maximized, therefore, when

$$\beta u_2'/u_1' = 1/(1 + r). \tag{4.25}$$

If this equality did not hold reshuffling consumption between time periods would increase welfare. For instance, suppose that the equality held but then the real rate of interest fell – so that the inequality ran <. The price of future goods has increased (present goods fallen). To reestablish the equality, the LHS of equation (4.25) must also increase. This is accomplished by increasing present consumption at the expense of future consumption – which reduces u_1' and increases $\beta u_2'$.

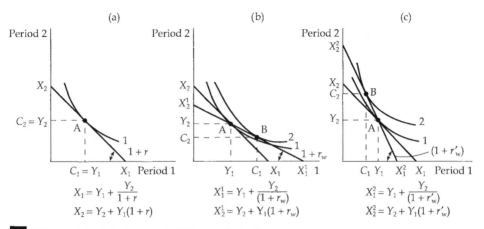

Figure 4.6 Intertemporal utility maximization

Suppose initially that the economy is closed to international trade and that the domestic real rate of interest is r, the representative consumer satisfies equation (4.25) at A in figure 4.6a. To makes things as simple as possible we shall assume that $C_1 = Y_1$ and $C_2 = Y_2$ so that the representative consumer sets saving to zero in both time periods.

If this economy is now opened to international trade in goods and financial assets, and the world rate of interest, r_w, differs from r a welfare gain can be had from *intertemporal international trade*.

Thus, if $r_w < r$ the budget constraint flattens – as shown in figure 4.6b – and consumption moves to point B. Here $C_1 > Y_1$, which is possible if the country runs a current account deficit, $CA_1 = Y_1 - C_1$. What has happened is that the potential to borrow at the lower world rate of interest reduces the price of present goods and the representative consumer substitutes into them. This CA_1 deficit is financed by issuing securities to foreign lenders which, in this two-period model, are retired through a current account surplus in period 2. In figure 4.6b, $CA_2 = Y_2 - C_2$.

Which countries are likely to choose a welfare maximizing CA_1 deficit? Developing countries are a case in point as their closed economy real interest rate would be higher than the world rate given their need to invest at rates in excess of current savings. Rich countries such as the USA and the UK, with relatively low investment rates by world standards, have also run current account deficits during the 1990s. This may be explained by a high rate of time preference, α, and large discount factor, β. Taken by itself this reduces the value on the LHS of equation (4.25), which is increased back to the welfare maximizing equality by increasing current consumption (so reducing u_1') and reducing future consumption (so increasing u_2').

Alternatively, if $r_w' > r$ the budget constraint steepens as in figure 4.6c. The price of present consumption has increased and the representative consumer substitutes out of present goods into future goods. To do so a current account surplus is run in period 1, $CA_1 = Y_1 - C_1$, foreign financial assets being accumulated. A current account deficit occurs in period 2, financed by running off foreign assets. See Obstfeld and Rogoff (1998) for a comprehensive treatment of intertemporal macroeconomic models.

A country with a high period 1 saving rate with expected dissaving in period 2 would fit into this category. Japan with an aging population is a case in point.

4.7 Twin Deficits

From equation (4.21) a current account deficit arises if a budget deficit, $T - G < 0$, is not offset by an excess of private saving over investment. To put it another way, a payments deficit arises if net national saving is insufficient to purchase all of the net increase in the volume of bills/bonds being issued by the government to finance its deficit.

The term "twin deficits" was used to describe the concurrent US budget and trade deficits, ca. 1981–1998 – both of which having reached record levels. Other OECD countries in part of this period face twin deficits, for example, Australia and, from a later date, the UK and Germany following unification. If private sector saving and investment are broadly in balance then equation (4.21) indicates that a budget deficit and a trade deficit will be found together (empirical support for this proposition is found in Miller, 1988). Which way causality runs cannot be determined from (4.21) because, strictly speaking, it is an identity. However, there is broad agreement in the literature that the budget deficit *caused* the trade deficit (e.g. see Bergsten and Cline 1985; Marris 1985; Feldstein 1986; Darby 1987; and, especially, Hooper and Mann 1989). In the UK the twin deficit phenomenon, and particularly the idea of causality running from the budget deficit to the trade deficit, has become synonymous with the Cambridge tradition of macro-policy prescription.

Hooper and Mann (1989) identified macroeconomic factors as the main cause of the growth and persistence of the US current account deficit during the 1980s. In their model, the exchange rate, income, saving, investment, imports and exports are all endogenous and are driven by fiscal and monetary policy. The fall in US net domestic savings (mainly caused by the rise, beginning in the early 1980s, of the budget deficit and, also, the fall in the private rate of saving), is estimated to have caused almost a third of the increase in the current account deficit. Tight monetary policy was also important because without it, fiscal expansion would have probably caused the exchange rate to depreciate, so helping the current account to improve. However, in the circumstances, tight monetary policy in the USA (beginning in 1979 and sustained for several years) led to a sharp rise in nominal and real interest rates, capital inflow, and an abrupt appreciation of the dollar on foreign exchange markets. Hooper and Mann (1989) attribute almost two-thirds of the rise in the American current account deficit to this mix of loose fiscal and tight monetary policy. The rest of the rise in the payments deficit was attributed to *ad hoc* factors: mainly, lost US exports due to the international debt crisis; and containment of price increases by foreign suppliers even as the dollar appreciated due to the acceptance of lower profit margins and increased rates of productivity growth (e.g. in business machines).

But then why did dollar depreciation beginning in 1985 *not* strongly improve the current account deficit? The main reasons it seems were: the persistence of the loose fiscal stance (the nominal budget deficit continued to increase, though falling from 6 percent of GDP in 1983 to 3 percent in 1989, and rising again to 4.9 percent in 1992); faster GDP growth in America than in other industrial countries; and "J" curve effects caused by lagged responses of trade flows to exchange rate changes.[10]

But as the US budget deficit fell during the 1990s, eventually becoming a surplus in 1999, large current account deficits persisted. From equation (4.21) this has to be associated with a fall in US private saving rate. The latter itself perhaps stimulated by a strong wealth effect stemming from the long US stock market boom and lower goods prices caused by the Asian economic crisis and a strong dollar.

 ## 4.8 Foreign Repercussions with no Capital Mobility

If a country is small its payments position will have an insignificant impact on the world economy. But what if a country is large? What are the foreign repercussions of its payments imbalances? After all, if a large "home" country runs a payments deficit the rest of the world, which we will call the foreign country, must be experiencing a payments surplus. The payments surplus will, via the foreign trade multiplier raise income and imports in the foreign country. Suppose that the home country starts from a position of trade balance but then there is an autonomous increase in imports. Natural questions to ask are what will be the ultimate effect on the home and foreign income levels, and will the foreign repercussions be enough to restore the trade balance to zero in the home country?[11]

In what follows the capital account is closed, so foreign repercussions are affected only through the current account. We drop this restrictive assumption in chapter 6 – on international policy cooperation – where international capital flows are assumed to be large.

Here, to simplify matters further, assume that the world is composed of only two large countries: the USA and Japan. In figure 4.7 (with the exchange rate equal to unity and home and foreign price levels fixed) the axes measure Japanese and American real incomes in a common currency.

To construct the UU function, which shows American income levels for different levels of Japanese income, begin by replacing $X = \bar{X}$ in equation 4.6 with

$$X = c + m^*Y^* \tag{4.6a}$$

where m^* and Y^* are, respectively, the Japanese average (equal to marginal) import propensity and income level, and c is autonomous US exports (reflecting US competitiveness and tastes etc.). Solving equations 4.1 to 4.8, but replacing 4.6 with 4.6a, for American income, Y, gives

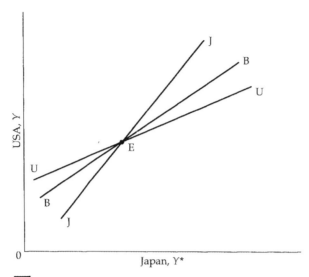

Figure 4.7 American and Japanese trade balance and income interdependence

$$Y = \frac{Z + m^*Y^*}{s + m + bt} \tag{4.26}$$

where Z is the sum of US domestic autonomous items $(a + \bar{I} + \bar{G} + c - N)$. Hence if m^*Y^* is given Y is determined. To find how American income depends on Japanese income, i.e. the UU function, differentiate equation 4.26 with respect to Japanese income:

$$\frac{dY}{dY^*} = \frac{m^*}{s + m + bt} < 1 \tag{4.27}$$

as long as the respective import propensities are not too dissimilar. Notice from equation 4.26 that UU will shift upward (i.e. higher American income at given Japanese income) if Z or m^* increase or if s or m decrease.

To find how Japanese income depends upon American income – i.e. the JJ curve in figure 4.7 – equation 4.26 should be rewritten for Japan's equilibrium income as

$$Y^* = \frac{Z^* + mY}{s^* + m^* + b^*t^*} \tag{4.28}$$

where mY is American imports (equal to Japanese exports) and the asterisks denote Japanese values. Differentiating 4.28 yields

$$\frac{dY^*}{dY} = \frac{m}{s^* + m^* + b^*t^*} < 1 \qquad (4.29)$$

for not too dissimilar values of Japanese and American imports.

The BB curve is drawn for payments balance in both countries. Thus, if American income rises, sucking in imports, so must Japanese income, if payments balance is to be maintained. The slope of BB is m^*/m.[12] In figure 4.7 BB has been positioned so that at the initial equilibrium, E, the balance of trade is zero. To the left and above BB the US trade balance is in deficit (Japanese in surplus) as, for a given Y, Y^* is too low to induce sufficient Japanese imports. To the right and below BB the US balance of trade is in surplus (Japanese deficit) – for, at a given Y, Japan's income is too high for BOT = 0.

4.8.1 Effect of an autonomous increase in US expenditure

A rise in US autonomous expenditure moves UU upwards and parallel to U^1U^1 in figure 4.8. (Upwards because in equation 4.27 the Z factor has increased, and parallel because the slope factor is unchanged.) If there was no impact on Japanese income, US income rises only from Y_0 to Y_1. But US income growth does impact Japanese income. At point F, where Japan's income has not yet risen, Japan has a balance of trade surplus which sets off its foreign trade multiplier and Japan's income rises to Y_1^*. This induced Japanese income growth in turn impacts American income which rises even further to Y_2. The new "equilibrium" is at E_2 – the US has a payments deficit as E_2 is above the BB function.

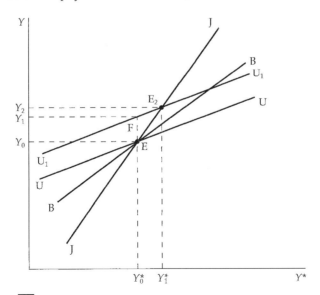

Figure 4.8 An autonomous increase in US expenditure

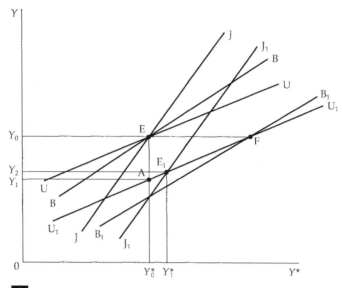

Figure 4.9 An autonomous switch in expenditure from home to foreign goods

4.8.2 Autonomous switch in US expenditure to Japanese exports

An autonomous increase in US expenditure on Japanese goods means that, for a given Y^*, Y falls. This is because in equations 4.9 and 4.26 N (autonomous imports) enters with a negative sign. Thus the UU function shifts down and parallel in figure 4.9 (parallel because its slope, $m^*/(s + m + bt)$, is unchanged). There is a fall in demand for US goods at every level of Japanese income.

At the same time BB shifts parallel[13] downward – as the rise in US demand for Japanese goods puts the US balance of payments into deficit at the initial income level Y_0, so either Y must fall or Y^* must increase. B_1B_1 cuts U_1U_1 perpendicular to Y_0. This is because a rise in Japanese income by EF will reduce the US deficit to zero if US income were to remain at Y_0.

Furthermore, JJ shifts upward to J_1J_1 because the increased American spending on Japanese goods raises Japanese income at every level of American income. J_1J_1 cuts B_1B_1 at the original Japanese income level Y_0^*. The reasoning here is similar to the last argument: to remove the Japanese payments surplus a fall in US income is needed.

The new equilibrium is at E_1 in figure 4.9. The outcome of the adjustment process is that:

1 Japanese income has increase to Y_1^*;
2 US income is higher at Y_2 compared with the case where Japanese income had not increased leaving US income at Y_1, and

3   The US deficit is smaller than it otherwise would have been had Japanese income not increased – that is, E_1 is closer to B_1B_1 than is A.

4.8.3 Cooperative and "locomotive" expansion to end a world recession

Assume that the world economy is in a deep recession with all major countries (just two of them in our model) facing a balance of payments deficit. The situation could be that of 1974–5 or 1980–1 following the sharp increase in oil prices. Figure 4.10 shows the initial situation with the US and Japanese income levels at Y_0 and Y_0^*, respectively, corresponding to high levels of *un*employment in both countries but balanced trade between them – shown in figure 4.10. (However, each country is presumed to have a large overall deficit when oil imports from OPEC are included.)

If the US alone expands autonomous expenditure – shifting UU to U_1U_1 – it faces a trade deficit at E_1. The US may feel constrained by this increase in its trade deficit and so refrain from expanding autonomous expenditure in the first place. As things stand, the same story may hold for Japan. Thus, with neither country taking steps to expand their economies the world will remain stuck in a recession.

The world recession may be resolved if the US and Japan expand autonomous expenditure *cooperatively*. Then UU and JJ shift to the right, expanding Y and Y*, and if they gauge things correctly leaving the balance of trade between them equal to zero. This is the case at E_2.

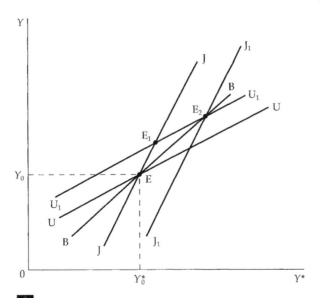

Figure 4.10 Cooperative economic expansion to end a recession

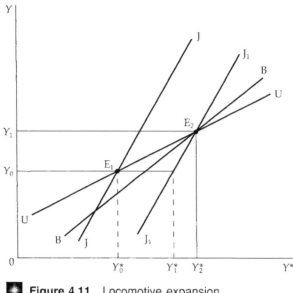

Figure 4.11 Locomotive expansion

A "*locomotive*" expansion could be used in somewhat different circumstances: both countries are again in deep recession but one of them, Japan, has a trade surplus. This situation is described in figure 4.11: E_1 is the initial equilibrium but it is above the BB function – which means that Japan has a trade surplus and the US a trade deficit. US economic leadership out of the recession may have to be aborted because of the trade constraint. However, Japan is not so constrained and is free to act as a locomotive – expanding its economy to pull the world out of recession.[14]

An increase in Japanese autonomous expenditure shifts JJ to J_1J_1. This raises Japanese income, initially to Y_1^*, and sets off economic expansion in the USA as American exports to Japan increase. Taking into account the feedback of the latter on Japan's income, equilibrium is eventually achieved at E_2 where world income is higher and the payments imbalance has been cured.

NOTES

1 The implication is that in figure 3.1, as the autonomous fall in exports – which will shift the SS curve to the left – sets off a fall in income and imports which shifts the DD curve to the left. At the initial exchange rate the deficit is smaller than when income effects are ignored. But, as equation 4.10 shows, the deficit is not entirely eliminated. As we may assume that there are no capital flows in this model we may wonder how can the country sustain the trade deficit? The simple elasticities model must be incomplete in some way. Both Keynesian and monetary models of the balance of payments try to put this right.

2 Notice that the absolute slope of EE is flatter than II as a given ΔA needs less adjustment, via ΔQ, of net exports for external balance than is the case for internal balance.

Thus, suppose that $\Delta A = 100$ and that the induced $\Delta X = -25$. To restore external balance Q may need to depreciate by, say, 10 percent. But to restore internal balance, the fall in net exports must equal -100, and this will need a larger depreciation of Q.

3 Other factors connected to the adoption of economic reforms in transition and emerging economies may also cause the EE function to shift – see chapter 22.

4 The RR function is derived from a country's production possibility frontier between traded and non-traded goods. Thus, RR traces the combinations of the price ratio P_T/P_N and the associated production ratio R_T/R_N. In transition and emerging economies, where factor mobility is not yet highly developed, the production possibility frontier is degenerate (i.e. not rounded out) and the associated RR function is relatively steep. The implication being that resource allocation between traded and nontraded goods is not very responsive to changes in the real exchange rate.

5 If we simplify by assuming that changes in a country's real exchange rate do not have income effects, the CC function is copied over from a community indifference curve. As the real exchange rate increases (i.e. the relative price of traded goods rises) the desired ratio of traded to non-traded goods in consumption falls.

6 A minus B is a measure of the trade deficit at any given Q. To see that $A - B$ measures the trade deficit define
$$A - B = (C_T/C_N) - (R_T/R_N)$$
$$= (C_T - R_T)/R_N$$
as, by definition, $C_N = R_N$
Thus, $(A - B)R_N = C_T - R_T =$ the trade deficit measured in non-traded goods.

7 More formally writing $C_T/C_N = f(Q)$, $f' < 0$; and $R_T/R_N = g(Q)$, $g' > 0$. Forming $f(Q) - g(Q)$ defines excess demand for traded goods. Differentiating shows that excess demand is a negative function of Q; and excess demand will be greater the more sensitive are the consumption and production ratios to a change in Q, i.e. the greater are f and g in absolute value. To maintain external balance, as Q appreciates, a reduction in domestic absorption is needed to reduce C_T relative to R_T, so restoring external balance.

8 EE is absolutely steeper than II for the following reason. With no international capital flows EE lies on top of II. Suppose that exports are autonomous and imports are positively related to income. But income is constant (at the full employment level) along II, so the current account too is constant $= 0$. Thus, the more mobile is international capital the absolutely steeper is EE.

9 It is only domestic demand for domestic goods which determines domestic output and employment since, with a floating exchange rate and assuming that the capital account is closed, $X = M$ at all times.

10 Some recent research indicates that, in long-run equilibrium, net foreign assets depend not only on international differences in public indebtedness but also on demographic factors which independently influence rates of private saving (Heller 1989, Kremers 1989, Horne, Kremers and Masson 1989). On this view, American net indebtedness to the Japanese – the USA's largest creditor – is likely to reverse itself as the aging Japanese population begins to draw down its savings sometime during the years 2010–2020. This is consistent with the intertemporal utility maximizing model of section 4.6.

11 The following discussion draws on Stern (1973) and Kenen (1985).

12 To show this the US balance of trade (BOT) is defined as:
$$BOT = X - M$$
and as before,
$$X = c + m^*Y^*$$
$$M = N + mY$$

therefore,

BOT $= c + m^*Y^* - N - mY$

dBOT $= m^*dY^* - mdY$

But on the BB function dBOT $= 0$ (and BOT $= 0$), therefore, set the last equation $= 0$ and rearrange to find $dY/dY = m^*/m$ That is, the slope of BB depends on the relative marginal propensities to import.

13 Parallel because m^*/m is unchanged.

14 The argument in this paragraph does not reckon with capital flows financing trade deficits for years on end. As it turned out in the 1980s, if anything the USA was the locomotive country and it ran up huge trade deficits being so. But this is not to say that the argument in the text is wrong, only that it leaves capital flows out of account. This may be the correct approach for countries other than the USA that are not able to finance big trade deficits for a upwards of a decade. Besides, in the early 1980s, as the US trade deficit grew, few economists, would have said that the USA should not be the locomotive country for the world economy.

5

Macroeconomics in an Open Economy: The Mundell–Fleming Model and Some Extensions

In this chapter we examine a model which has had a fundamental influence on international monetary economics, namely the Mundell–Fleming (MF) model (see, *inter alia*, Fleming, 1962; Mundell, 1963, 1968; Sohmen, 1967). This model is particularly useful for analyzing the effectiveness of monetary and fiscal policy in an open economy setting and also, as we shall see in chapter 9, forms the basis of recent models of the determination of the exchange rate. The focal point of what we refer to as the base-line, or basic, MF model is a small open economy with unemployed resources, a perfectly elastic aggregate supply curve, static exchange rate expectations (i.e. the exchange rate is not expected to change from its current level) and perfect capital mobility. Given such assumptions it can be demonstrated that with flexible exchange rates monetary policy is extremely powerful in altering real output and fiscal policy is completely impotent. The inefficacy of fiscal policy under floating exchange rates has been one of the most widely accepted conclusions in international economics. However, this conclusion is crucially dependent on the underlying assumptions of the MF model; relaxing such assumptions results in both fiscal and monetary policy having an effect on output. In this chapter the basic MF model is analyzed, its properties are outlined and some of its underlying assumptions are questioned.

More specifically, the basic MF model is outlined in section 5.1. The so-called large country case is discussed in section 5.2. The insulation properties of a floating exchange rate in the context of the small country MF model are considered in section 5.3. In section 5.4 the assumption of perfect capital mobility is relaxed and it is demonstrated, *inter alia*, that fiscal policy does have some power in increasing domestic output. Consideration to expectations is given in section 5.5 and in section 5.6 an interesting critique of the MF model by Niehans (1975) and Dornbusch (1976b) is also discussed. The role of wealth effects in disturbing the basic MF equilibrium is considered in section 5.7. Finally, in section 5.8 the MF assumption of a fixed price level is relaxed and the consequences for real money balances and aggregate supply are considered.

 ## 5.1 The "Base-line" Mundell–Fleming Model

The base-line MF model is a model of a small open economy facing a given world interest rate and a perfectly elastic supply of imports at a given price in terms of foreign currency.

More specifically, in the basic MF model there are assumed to be four assets: a domestic and a foreign bond, each having an identical maturity, and a domestic and a foreign money. The bonds are assumed to be perfect substitutes while monies are assumed to be non-substitutable and thus only held in the country of issue (models in which domestic and foreign residents are allowed to hold both currencies are termed currency substitution models – such models are discussed in chapter 9). Expectations are assumed to be static (i.e. the expected change in the exchange rate is equal to zero, $\Delta S^e = 0$) and arbitrage is assumed to ensure that bond yields are continually equalized. The above assumptions imply that the domestic rate of interest must continually equal the foreign rate (unless otherwise stated, all variables in this chapter relate to the current period t):

$$i = i^* \tag{5.1}$$

which, with static exchange rate expectations, denotes the uncovered interest rate parity condition and, as we saw in chapter 3, is a representation of perfect capital mobility.

Money market equilibrium

Equilibrium in the domestic money market occurs when the demand for money equals the supply of money. The demand for money is given by

$$\frac{M^D}{P} = L = L(i, Y) \qquad L_i < 0, \quad L_Y > 0 \tag{5.2}$$

where M^D is the demand for nominal money balances, P is the price of domestic output (which is assumed constant – see the discussion surrounding equation (5.4) and L is the corresponding real demand for money, which is assumed to depend upon the domestic rate of interest i and domestic real income Y. The assumed responsiveness of the demand for money is given by the partial derivatives L_i and L_Y, which have the conventional signs.

The supply of money M is given as

$$M = D + F \tag{5.3}$$

where D is the domestic component of the money stock and F denotes the volume of foreign exchange reserves, expressed in domestic currency. Changes in the supply of money will be driven by changes in the D and F components:

$$\Delta M = \Delta D + \Delta F \tag{5.3a}$$

where Δ is the first difference operator. Since ΔF, as we shall see below, is the balance of payments, balance of payments disequilibria can have important consequences for the money supply (equation (5.3) is central to the monetary approach to the balance of payments – see chapter 8). Money market equilibrium is defined as a situation where the demand for real money balances, given by (5.2), is equal to the real supply of money balances given by (5.3):

$$L = \frac{M}{P} \tag{5.4}$$

Equation (5.4) is the conventional LM relationship.

Underlying the condition for goods market equilibrium in the basic MF model are the assumptions of unemployed resources, constant returns to scale and fixed money wages resulting in a typically Keynesian "deep depression" aggregate supply schedule (i.e. perfectly elastic).

Equilibrium in the goods market is given by

$$Y = D = A(i, Y) + T(Q, Y) + G \tag{5.5}$$

where $A_i < 0$, $1 > A_Y > 0$, $T_Q > 0$ and $T_Y < 0$, Thus Y, domestic output, is determined by aggregate demand D, where the components of demand are A, domestic absorption or spending, which is a negative function of the rate of interest (via investment and also perhaps consumption) and a positive function of income (note that the marginal propensity to absorb, or spend, lies between zero and unity); and T, the trade balance, or net exports, which depends upon income and the competitiveness term Q (= SP^*/P). Since we assume for the time being that the domestic price level is fixed, and the foreign level is constant by the small country assumption, we may normalize P and P^* to be unity and therefore competitiveness is simply determined by the nominal exchange rate. The assumption that T_Q is positive reflects the fact that the Marshall–Lerner condition is assumed to

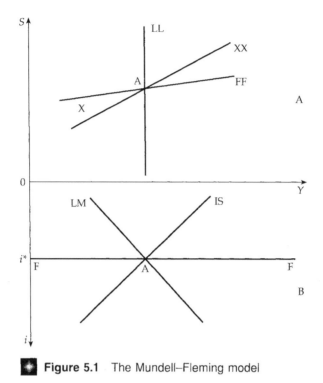

Figure 5.1 The Mundell–Fleming model

hold (see chapter 3) continuously in this model. Relationship (5.5) represents the open economy IS relationship.

The balance of payments equilibrium condition in the MF model is given by

$$B = T(Q, Y) + C(i) \tag{5.6}$$

where $T_Y < 0$, $T_Q > 0$, $C_i = \infty$ and B equals the change in reserves, ΔF, which, with a flexible exchange rate, will be zero. The small country assumption combined with the assumption that expectations are static implies that only the domestic rate of interest enters our capital flow function, which is written here in a general form. The value of the partial derivative C_i reflects the perfect mobility of capital assumption.

The workings of the MF model are illustrated in figure 5.1. In quadrant A, the schedule XX represents the locus of points of exchange rates and income levels along which there is equilibrium in the goods market. It has an upward slope because a higher level of output, with a marginal propensity to spend of less than unity, will lead to an excess supply of goods which necessitates an exchange rate depreciation (a rise in S) to maintain goods market equilibrium (the rising exchange rate improves the trade balance – given that the Marshall–Lerner condition holds – diverting demand towards domestic goods). Above the XX schedule there is excess demand for domestic goods and below it there is excess supply.

The LL schedule represents the locus of S and Y consistent with money market equilibrium: for a given rate of interest (equation (5.1)) there will be only one income level at which the money market clears (remember the price level is constant). To the right of LL income must fall to equilibrate the money market, while it must rise if income is temporarily less than LL.

In quadrant B the curve IS represents the locus of interest rates and income along which there is equilibrium in the goods market. The curve LM is the locus of i and Y consistent with equilibrium in the money market. We assume that the reader is already familiar with the derivation of these schedules (see any intermediate macro text).[1]

The FF schedule represents combinations of i and Y consistent with equilibrium in the balance of payments. In quadrant B, the perfectly elastic external balance schedule reflects the assumption of perfect capital mobility. Thus the balance of payments can only be in equilibrium when the domestic interest rate i equals the foreign interest rate i^*; if for some reason i was above i^* the net capital inflow would be potentially infinite and swamp the current account (trade balance). The FF schedule in S–Y space is upward sloping since an increase in income, by causing the current balance to deteriorate, requires an increase in S (depreciation) to maintain equilibrium in the balance of payments. The FF curve in S–Y space is drawn for the initial rate of flow of capital imports. Above the FF schedule there is a balance of payments surplus, below it a deficit. If net capital outflow increases, the FF schedule in S–Y space shifts upward – so that an improved trade balance is able to finance the deteriorated capital account. That the XX schedule is drawn steeper than the FF schedule reflects the assumed stability of the system. Thus in quadrant A of figure 5.1, at point X there is both a balance of payments deficit and excess demand for domestic goods – both of which will be "cured" by a rise in domestic production. But if FF were drawn steeper than XX and the economy was at a disequilibrium point such as X, movements in S and Y would push the system away from equilibrium point A. That is, there would be a payments surplus and an excess supply of goods. The existence of the latter would tend to cause income to fall further away from the equilibrium of the system. Initially equilibrium pertains at point A. We shall now consider two types of shock: an increase in the money supply and an expansionary fiscal policy.

A monetary expansion in the Mundell–Fleming model

With *flexible exchange rates* an expansionary monetary policy, conducted by an open market purchase of bonds by the central bank in exchange for increased domestic credit D, shifts the money market equilibrium schedule in figure 5.2 from LM to LM'. At the initial levels of income and interest rate the expansionary monetary policy must imply an excess of liquidity. With the domestic interest rate effectively fixed at the world level (equation (5.1)), and prices assumed constant, the only way money market equilibrium can be restored is via an increase in income from Y_1 to Y_2. The latter will occur because the expansionary monetary policy leads to an *incipient* decline in the domestic interest rate which, in turn, leads

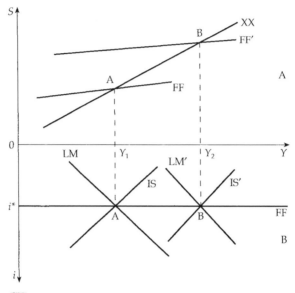

Figure 5.2 Monetary expansion in the Mundell–Fleming model

to a capital outflow and exchange rate depreciation. The rising price of foreign exchange will result, via the Marshall–Lerner condition, in an improved trade balance and will have an expansionary effect on income as demand is switched from foreign goods to home goods; income will continue rising, and IS will shift rightwards, until money market equilibrium has been restored at point B. Since the marginal propensity to spend in our model is less than unity, the current account must be in surplus at B and the capital account in deficit; the capital deficit implies that FF shifts upwards to FF'.

The effects of monetary policy on income and the exchange rate may be affirmed by deriving the following money multipliers from the system (5.1)–(5.6) (see the appendix):

$$\left.\frac{dY}{dM}\right|_{dB=0} = \frac{1}{L_Y} > 0 \tag{5.7}$$

where L_Y is the sensitivity of the real demand for money to a change in income;

$$\left.\frac{dS}{dM}\right|_{dB=0} = \frac{1 - A_Y - T_Y}{L_Y T_S} > 0 \tag{5.8}$$

where the partial derivatives are the responsiveness to changes in income of absorption A, trade balance T and money demand L. Since capital is perfectly mobile ($C_i = \infty$), both multipliers will be positive.[2]

With *fixed exchange rates* the conclusion that monetary policy has a powerful effect on income is reversed. Thus the monetary expansion of LM to LM' results in an incipient fall in the interest rate and capital outflow, which does not in this case have any beneficial effect on income since the exchange rate does not change. Indeed the fixity of the exchange rate implies that the authorities must be losing reserves. As they intervene to support the currency the money supply will fall (assuming no sterilization) and the LM schedule will shift back to intersect IS at A, since only at the initial equilibrium will there be no incipient change in the interest rate. From the system in the appendix, the policy multiplier is therefore

$$\left.\frac{dY}{dM}\right|_{dS=0} = 0 \tag{5.9}$$

An expansionary fiscal policy

Consider now an increase in government spending, financed purely by issuing bonds, which shifts the XX and IS curves to XX' and IS' in quadrant A and quadrant B, respectively, of figure 5.3. With a *fixed exchange rate* an increase in government spending which shifted IS to IS' would be effective in raising income. For example, an increase in G caused by raising income would increase the demand for money and the rate of interest. The latter would attract a potentially infinite inflow of capital, resulting in a change in reserves in (5.3a) shifting the LM schedule rightwards and increasing income by the full multiplier. Since the interest rate is jammed at the world level and the exchange rate is fixed we have

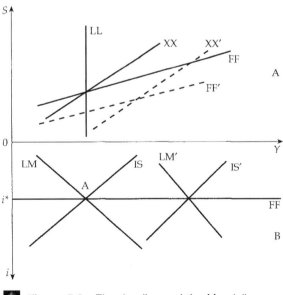

Figure 5.3 Fiscal policy and the Mundell–Fleming model

an expansion of income analogous to the expansionary effects of fiscal policy in the textbook Keynesian liquidity trap case.

However, with *floating exchange rates* the increased rate of interest leads to an exchange rate appreciation which worsens the trade balance by crowding out exports and sucking in imports, pushing the IS' curve back to IS. In the top quadrant the FF curve shifts to FF' with no change in output.[3] An alternative way to see this result is to consider the effect of the fiscal shock on the velocity of money. Since fiscal policy cannot alter the domestic interest rate, it cannot alter the velocity of circulation (Y/M) and hence there is only one level of output (the initial level) which can be supported by the given money supply.

The effects of a change in government spending on income and the exchange rate, with a floating rate and perfect capital mobility, are neatly captured by the following multipliers, derived from equations (5.1)–(5.6):

$$\frac{dY}{dG}\bigg|_{dB=0} = 0 \tag{5.10}$$

$$\frac{dS}{dG}\bigg|_{dB=0} = \frac{-1}{T_S} < 0 \tag{5.11}$$

With *fixed rates* the corresponding income multiplier is

$$\frac{dY}{dG}\bigg|_{dS=0} = \frac{1}{1 - A_Y - T_Y} > 0 \tag{5.12}$$

5.1.1 The principle of effective market classification and the assignment problem

In chapter 4 we mentioned the Tinbergen rule of economic policymaking, that the policymaker should have one policy instrument for each policy target. Mundell (1962) proposed that this rule be complemented by what he called the *principle of effective market classification*, which concerns the *pairing* of instruments with targets. He argued that policies should be paired with the objectives on which they have the most influence. Failure to observe this rule would lead, he believed, to a cyclical approach to equilibrium or to instability. In terms of our analysis above of a small country with fixed exchange rates and perfect capital mobility, fiscal policy should be paired with the goal of internal equilibrium.

While the principle of effective market classification is still relevant, one of the corollaries of the analysis above is that it is not possible to allocate one policy instrument unequivocally to one policy target, since the effectiveness of a policy instrument varies according to the regime in which it operates, While it is correct to pair fiscal policy and internal equilibrium under a fixed exchange rate, the pairing is inappropriate under a flexible exchange rate. This dilemma associated with the pairing of instruments is called the *assignment problem*: it is not possible to assign one instrument in all cases to one target.

 ## 5.2 The Large Country Case

The conclusions of this analysis have to be modified in the case of a large open economy such as the USA, for even with a fixed exchange rate US monetary policy can have some domestic effectiveness. A rise in US money supply reduces the rate of interest in the USA and leads to a monetary outflow of a size significant to the rest of the world, whose money supply is increased and rate of interest reduced. Thus the increase in money supply in the USA reduces rates of interest throughout the world and expands output in both the USA and abroad. In terms of quadrant B of figure 5.2 the USA has the power via monetary expansion to shift the FF schedule towards the Y axis, so that equilibrium is possible on IS to the northeast of A. When the country is large monetary policy is no longer ineffective in a fixed exchange rate regime.

The conclusion that a flexible exchange rate renders a fiscal expansion impotent also needs to be amended. The initial effect of such an expansion in the USA would cause a rise in the US interest rate and an inflow of capital from abroad. The size of this flow in relation to foreign capital markets would raise interest rates abroad. The FF schedule in quadrant B of figure 5.3 would shift down, away from the Y axis, producing a new equilibrium southeast of A, so that in the case of a large country the expansionary effects of a fiscal stimulus would not all flow abroad but would be shared between the large country and the rest of the world.

On the other hand the effectiveness of the correctly paired instruments and targets, fiscal policy for a fixed exchange rate and monetary policy for a flexible exchange rate, is diminished. A fiscal expansion with a fixed rate will pull up interest rates both in the USA and abroad and induce a smaller capital inflow, and consequent increase in the money supply, than is the case with a small country, so that the expansion would be less proportionately for the USA than for a small country. In addition the rest of the world may suffer a fall in income as a result of the rise in interest rates, unless the USA takes from it an extra quantity of imports which offsets this.

In the case of a monetary expansion with a flexible rate the rate of interest will decline leading to a monetary outflow. This will reduce interest rates abroad and cause a movement of FF towards the Y axis in quadrant A of figure 5.2. The payments deficit for the USA will be reduced with a lower required depreciation of the exchange rate. IS will move less far to the right than IS' in figure 5.2 and the expansion of income will be correspondingly less.

In short, the results differ for a large country in that it is a price-maker and not a price-taker with regard to the interest rate. As fiscal policy and monetary policy affect interest rates under both exchange rate regimes, they are both effective to some degree under both regimes.[3]

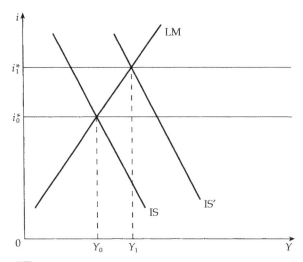

Figure 5.4 The insulation properties of the Mundell–Fleming model with respect to a foreign interest rate shock

■ 5.3 Insulation and the Mundell–Fleming Model

Hitherto in our discussion of the MF model only shocks emanating from the domestic economy have been considered. But how well does a flexible exchange rate insulate the domestic economy, or in terms of the stabilization of income, dampen the effects of shocks emanating from the rest of the world? In this section two 'foreign' shocks are considered in the context of the small country MF model: a foreign interest rate shock and a shock to the trade balance. The insulation properties of fixed and flexible exchange rates is considered in some detail in the next chapter in the context of a two-country model.

An increase in the foreign rate of interest is illustrated in figure 5.4, with the foreign interest rate rising from i_0^* to i_1^*. (The higher foreign interest rate results in agents reallocating their portfolios and switching from domestic to foreign bonds, pulling up the domestic interest rate until it equals the foreign rate (equation (5.1)). The arbitrage process will also result in an exchange rate depreciation. Both the higher interest rate and the depreciated exchange rate will have offsetting effects on income, with the higher price for foreign currency boosting income through the trade account and the higher interest rate curtailing the income expansion. Which effect dominates? In the ensuing equilibrium, with a given money supply the higher interest rate implies excess money balances which can only be absorbed by a rise in income. IS moves to IS′ in figure 5.4 and income expands from Y_0 to Y_1. Thus a flexible exchange rate with perfect capital mobility does not insulate the small country from a foreign interest rate shock. Under fixed rates a rise in i^* also leads to a capital outflow, a fall in the money supply and an equal rise in i which induces a *fall* in the equilibrium level of income.

The insulation properties of a floating exchange rate can also be considered with respect to *an exogenous change in the demand for the home country's exports*. Say, for example, that there is a world recession and a fall in the demand for home country exports. The export fall will induce an exchange rate depreciation which in turn results in a fall in imports and a rise in the exchange-rate-related component of exports. With perfect capital mobility the interest rate remains at i_0^* and for a given stock of money so too must the level of income: the exchange rate moves to stabilize income in the case of an export shock. However, if the world recession is accompanied by a fall in i^*, which is highly likely, i will fall. The fall in i will raise the demand for money and, with the domestic nominal money stock fixed, domestic income must fall to equilibrate the money market.

Under fixed exchange rates the export shock is transmitted to the domestic economy: both the IS and LM curves are shifted to the left to find a new equilibrium at a lower income level. The fall in net exports is responsible for the shift in the IS curve while the LM curve shifts to the left as foreign exchange reserves (and the money supply) are reduced to support the fixed exchange rate.

So a flexible exchange rate in the context of the simple MF model only insulates the home economy from a shock to net exports. The high degree of capital mobility ensures that the effects of a foreign interest rate shock are transmitted to the domestic economy.

The MF model presented in this and the previous section is based on a number of crucial assumptions which a number of researchers have questioned. However, despite this, we believe that the basic MF model is insightful and, of course, one cannot understand more sophisticated versions of the model until the basics have been mastered. We now investigate versions of the MF model which incorporate more sophisticated assumptions regarding, for example, the formation of expectations and the determination of the price level. Rather than move immediately to a version of the MF model which incorporates all the modifications proposed in the literature, we proceed in a sequential fashion considering versions of the model which modify one assumption at a time.

5.4 Imperfect Capital Mobility and the Mundell–Fleming Model

With perfect capital mobility and flexible exchange rates the MF model suggests that monetary policy is extremely powerful and fiscal policy is completely impotent. If, however, capital is less than perfectly mobile (i.e. $C_i < \infty$) it can be demonstrated that both monetary *and* fiscal policy are efficacious with floating exchange rates (although the former policy will now be less effective). Thus the policy multipliers dY/dG and dY/dM are both positive. The effect of less-than-perfect capital mobility on our MF diagrams is to render the slope of the FF curve less than perfectly elastic, since a small rise in the domestic interest rate no longer leads to a massive capital inflow, swamping the trade balance; the trade account is no longer a mere appendage to the balance of payments, as it is when capital is perfectly mobile.

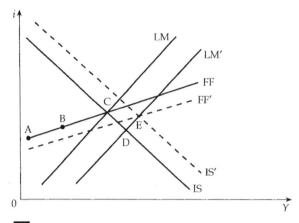

Figure 5.5 Monetary expansion and imperfect capital mobility

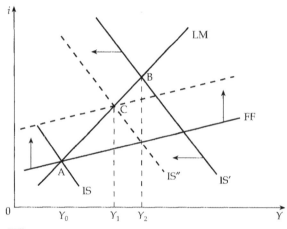

Figure 5.6 Fiscal expansion and imperfect capital mobility

In figures 5.5 and 5.6 FF is the locus of i and Y consistent with equilibrium in the balance of payments and its slope can be understood by considering points A and B in figure 5.5 and an initially fixed exchange rate. At point B, income is relatively high and thus the trade balance deficit will be greater than at point A; to keep the overall balance of payments in equilibrium we require a relatively large capital account surplus at B and thus a relative higher interest rate. FF has been drawn with a flatter slope than the LM schedule implying that, even with imperfect mobility, capital flows are more elastic than money demand to the rate of interest (i.e. $C_i > L_i$).[5] Points above the FF schedule represent points of balance of payments surplus with fixed exchange rates and an appreciated exchange rate with floating rates. Points below the FF schedule represent a balance of payments deficit with fixed exchange rates and a depreciated exchange rate with floating exchange rates.

In figures 5.5 and 5.6 we consider the two policy shocks discussed earlier for the perfect capital mobility case, namely an increase in the money supply and a fiscal expansion.

From an initial equilibrium at C in figure 5.5, monetary expansion shifts the LM curve rightwards. A new equilibrium could be thought of at D where both the domestic goods and money markets are in equilibrium. However, for a given exchange rate, D is not consistent with balance of payments equilibrium since it implies a balance of payments deficit. Hence the exchange rate must depreciate, which will push the IS curve rightwards, but with less than perfectly mobile capital this will also push the FF schedule downwards (i.e. the trade balance improves). A new long-run equilibrium is given at E where income is higher, the interest rate is lower and the trade balance has improved. The position of the final equilibrium will clearly depend upon the relative elasticities of the schedules.

A fiscal expansion from an equilibrium of A in figure 5.6 leads, as in the perfect capital mobility case, to a rightward shift in the IS schedule. At the intersection of the IS' and LM curves at B we have a tendency for the exchange rate to appreciate. The latter, via its effect on the trade balance, shifts the FF schedule upwards and the IS schedule back from IS' to, say, IS". Point C is suggestive of the system's final equilibrium, with an expansionary fiscal policy having generated higher income, an appreciation of the exchange rate and a current account deficit which is offset by the effect of a higher interest rate on the net capital inflow. As in the perfect capital mobility case, some of the extra government spending is offset by a fall in private expenditure – the move from Y_2 to Y_1 – but the offset is *not* complete. Clearly then, the effectiveness of monetary and fiscal policy with flexible exchange rates depends crucially on the mobility of capital.

Before leaving the topic of imperfect capital mobility, it is worth considering the polar opposite assumption to perfect capital mobility, namely completely immobile capital. Such a situation may be regarded as representative of many countries in the 1940s and 1950s, before the removal of capital controls. In terms of the model above, it implies that C_i is zero and therefore the balance of payments equilibrium condition consists only of the T term in equation (5.6). The diagrammatic representation of this scenario is presented in figure 5.7(a) and it can be seen that its effect is to render the FF schedule completely inelastic. Equilibrium (i.e. internal and external balance) is initially at A.

Consider now a disturbance which upsets the equilibrium at A. More specifically, assume that the rest of the world suffers from a recession and this leads to a drop in domestic exports. The effect of this on domestic aggregate demand will work through the trade account and this is represented in figure 5.7(b) by a leftward shift in the IS schedule to IS'. Although point B is consistent with internal balance it is clearly not consistent with external balance; at B the balance of payments will be in deficit. This is so because if we were to separate the import multiplier from the export multiplier in equation (5.6) the latter would be larger than the former, in absolute terms, and so importers' demand for foreign exchange reserves will be unambiguously greater than the supply of such

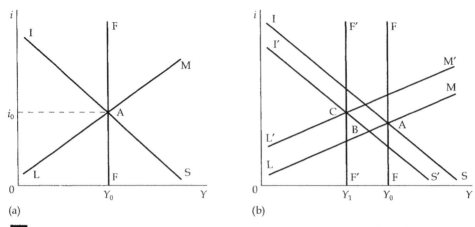

Figure 5.7 Completely immobile capital: (a) open economy equilibrium with constrained capital flow; (b) adjustment with constrained capital flow

reserves from exporters. The combined effect of this will be to reduce the domestic money supply -- see equation (5.3) -- pushing the LM schedule leftwards until a new equilibrium is achieved at C (i.e. the higher domestic interest rate is required to choke off domestic demand for imported goods). The reader is referred back to chapter 4 for a discussion of how the policy-maker, unhappy with the new equilibrium at C, can attempt to move the economy back to A.

■ 5.5 Regressive Expectations and Monetary–Fiscal Policy

The assumption concerning exchange rate expectations in the MF model is particularly odd. With the exchange rate freely floating, it presumably must be changing on a day-to-day basis in response to a policy change, yet foreign exchange market participants regard each day's exchange rate as essentially fixed and have no anticipation of any future change. Thus the foreign exchange market fails to predict either the monetary expansion or its subsequent effects.

Following Argy and Porter (1972), let us now relax the assumption that $\Delta S^e = 0$ and instead assume that exchange rate expectations are inelastic, or regressive, in the short term (the expected exchange rate is assumed to relate to some future period, say $t + k$). Regressive exchange rate expectations are captured by the following schema:

$$\Delta S^e = \theta(\bar{S} - S) \qquad 0 < \theta < 1 \qquad (5.13)$$

where, in the context of our present discussion, $\bar{S}$ is the "old" equilibrium exchange rate, S is the exchange rate that *will be* established after a shock such as a non-reversed monetary expansion – also referred to below as the market rate

– and θ is the proportionate adjustment that is made to the expected exchange rate in successive time intervals.

If $\theta = 1$ the expected exchange rate immediately changes by as much as the change in the current exchange rate so that the expected and current rates coincide. If $\theta = 0$ expectations are static and the expected exchange rate remains unchanged (this is the assumption invoked in the basic MF model considered in sections 5.1 and 5.2). And if θ lies between these extremes, the expected exchange rate is adjusted fractionally in successive time periods towards the market rate S.

Regressive expectations may be justified in a world where economic agents have insufficient information to make a point estimate of the new equilibrium exchange rate so that some inertia enters into their calculation of that exchange rate. Or, this could perhaps be due to agents being unsure of which economic model to use to determine the equilibrium future exchange rate. Or, agents may be thought to have some notion of the "normal" exchange rate as in the Keynesian liquidity preference function.

It is important to notice that during the period while expectations are being adjusted S^e will differ from S.

When ΔS^e is not equal to zero we have to modify the relationship given in (5.1) to the more general form of uncovered interest parity (see chapter 3):

$$i = i^* + \frac{S^e - S}{S} \tag{5.14}$$

If the currency is expected to appreciate the last term is negative and the home country's interest rate i can fall relative to the foreign interest rate i^*. Portfolio returns are equalized because of the expected appreciation of the home country's exchange rate.

The existence of regressive expectations modifies the macroeconomic effects of monetary and fiscal policy in a world of floating exchange rates and perfect capital mobility (where it will be recalled that with static expectations monetary policy has an immediate magnified effect on income while fiscal policy is powerless).

The short-run effectiveness – the "impact" multiplier – of *monetary* policy is reduced as can be seen from the money market equilibrium condition (5.4), restated here:

$$\frac{M}{P} = L(i, Y) \tag{5.15}$$

With static expectations ($\theta = 0$) $i = i^*$ and the money market must be equilibrated by a sufficiently large rise in real income Y, as the interest rate is fixed. But with regressive expectation i falls and plays a role in equilibrating the money market as the demand for money will increase. Hence, the rise in Y necessary to clear the money market will not be as large as with static expectations. In figure 5.8(a)

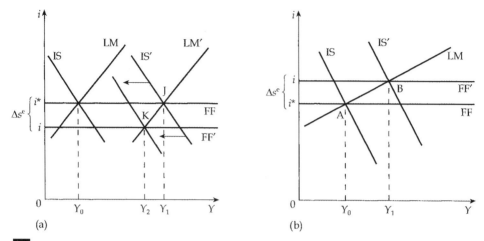

Figure 5.8 Monetary and fiscal policy and regressive expectations

this is represented as the move to a point such as K (the static expectations case referred to already is represented by J).

However, over time (i.e. as equation (5.13) passes through a number of iterations) the expected and actual exchange rates will move closer together. Thus, in equation (5.14) i will move closer to i^* until equality between them is established. Now, with i rising, the demand for money will be falling and to take up the slack in the money market Y must increase. Ultimately, in the "long run" monetary policy is just as effective as with static expectations (i.e. we ultimately move to J in figure 5.8(a)). The only difference is that it takes more time for the full effects to work themselves through.

Fiscal policy

With static expectation it will be recalled that fiscal policy is powerless. This can be seen in equation (5.15) where with M, P and $i = i^*$ all fixed so too must real income be fixed. However, with regressive expectations, in the short run i can differ from i^* and fiscal policy can have some effect on real income.

An increase in government expenditure appreciates the exchange rate and, with regressive expectations, currency *depreciation* will be expected. For portfolio equilibrium with uncovered interest parity, i must rise above i^*. But the rise in i reduces the demand for money and the money market will be in disequilibrium unless real income increases. So fiscal policy has some effectiveness in the short run. In figure 5.8(b) this is represented by the move to point B (the case of static expectations is given by A).

However, over time, S^e will approach S and i will fall to again equal i^*. The change in real income will also reverse itself until income reaches its original level. In the long run fiscal policy is again shown to be ineffective – the economy returns to A.

Inelastic exchange rate expectations also modify the short-run insulation properties of a flexible exchange rate system. In the case of an increase in exports (see p. 76–7 above) and static expectations, the exchange rate appreciates to maintain equilibrium in the trade balance. With inelastic expectations the exchange rate appreciation gives the expectation of a future depreciation, thus allowing the domestic interest rate to be above the foreign rate. For a given money stock the latter implies an excess supply of money which can only be eliminated in this model by a rise in income. In contrast, for the case of a foreign interest rate shock, the insulation properties of a flexible exchange rate system are improved by the introduction of inelastic expectations. Thus although the foreign interest rate shock results in an exchange rate depreciation (see page 76), the depreciation will be attenuated since via (5.13) it will result in the expectation of an appreciation in the future. However, and following on from our discussion of monetary–fiscal policy with regressive expectations, these effects will only exist in the short run; in the long run the insulation properties discussed in section 5.3 will prevail.

The modification in this section of the policy results derived earlier is a consequence of the fact that inelastic expectations drive a wedge between the home and foreign interest rates. As in the imperfect capital mobility case the two rates are not inextricably linked together – at least in the short run – allowing, for example, an expansionary fiscal policy to have some purchase on output.

5.6 The J Curve Effect and Regressive Expectations

As has been demonstrated the efficacy of various policy shocks depends upon a number of crucial assumptions. One particular assumption which underlies the MF model is that there is no J curve effect: either there are no lags or the price elasticities of exports and imports are highly elastic throughout the adjustment process so that an exchange rate change leads to an *instantaneous* improvement in the trade balance. However, as discussed in chapter 3, it is more than likely that in the short run the demand for imports and exports will be inelastic and thus the immediate impact of an exchange rate depreciation is to worsen the current account. Under floating exchange rates a current account deficit must have as its counterpart a capital account surplus; the country requires a capital inflow and not an outflow as suggested by the MF model. Thus the powerful MF result that an expansionary monetary policy has its effect via a trade balance surplus is countered with an inelastic demand for imports and exports – the trade balance will be initially weakened. Clearly the "perverse" J curve effect will not last forever, and eventually an expansionary monetary policy will have the predicted MF effect. But how can the foreign exchange market clear in the short run with a deficit on the trade and capital accounts? The two deficits can be explained by means of equation (5.13).

An expansionary monetary policy leads to a capital outflow and an exchange rate depreciation which in turn allows the domestic interest rate to fall, via (5.13), below the world level. The fall in the domestic interest rate is not an incipient fall but an actual fall, and will have an expansionary effect on the economy. Although this sequence of events will give short-run money market equilibrium in the presence of a J curve effect, we require a net capital inflow for balance of payments equilibrium. In the short run this can be achieved by the current exchange rate falling further than in the absence of the J curve effect; the exchange rate must overshoot its equilibrium value and depreciate by more than is required for money market equilibrium. Hence even with the domestic interest rate below the world rate, the expectation of an exchange rate appreciation in the future gives speculators an incentive to hold domestic bonds. Although the introduction of regressive expectations allows a country to operate an expansionary monetary policy in the presence of a J curve, Niehans (1975) has argued that monetary policy is often reversed before the demand elasticities become sufficiently elastic to give the "normal" trade balance effect.

A further interesting twist to the above story, noted by Dornbusch (1976b), is that even if the Marshall–Lerner condition holds continuously the introduction of regressive expectations can in itself result in a monetary expansion having a deleterious effect on the trade balance. Thus with regressive expectations a monetary expansion lowers the domestic interest rate which will stimulate aggregate demand and increase imports, and this in turn may offset the increase in exports, worsening the trade balance. Thus it is possible for the trade balance to worsen even if the Marshall–Lerner condition holds. Whether or not the trade balance does worsen will depend, *inter alia*, upon the interest response of aggregate demand and the elasticity of expectations.

 ## 5.7 Wealth Effects

One important omission from the basic MF model is the role of wealth effects and, in particular, their effect in undermining the monetary/fiscal results discussed above. Such effects may arise from two sources: from an unbalanced government budget and/or via the current account. Here we concentrate on the latter route. For example, consider again a monetary expansion with flexible exchange rates.

In figure 5.2 a monetary expansion moved the economy from point A to point B. At B remember that the domestic country is running a current account surplus. This implies that domestic residents will be accumulating foreign assets and their level of wealth will be rising. To the extent that there are positive wealth effects in the demand for money and expenditure functions it follows that point B cannot be a final equilibrium. For example, with a positive wealth effect on the domestic money demand function the rising level of wealth will increase the demand for money and, for a given supply of money, this must imply that the LM schedule is shifted back from LM'. This, in turn, will result in an incipient rise in the domestic interest rate which attracts a capital inflow, appreciates the exchange rate and shifts the IS schedule back from IS' towards its original level. Indeed, if the current account was originally in balance at A the IS–LM schedules must shift back until A is restored since otherwise wealth will be changing and there will be a remaining disequilibrium.[6] In chapter 11 we consider such wealth effects in greater detail in the context of the portfolio balance model of the determination of the exchange rate.

 ## 5.8 Aggregate Supply, the Real Balance Effect, and the Exchange Rate in the Mundell–Fleming Model

One particularly unappealing feature of the MF model is the assumed constancy of the price level. For example, in the model the price measure used is the price of domestic output. Such a price will be relevant to domestic firms which are likely to base their output and labour input decisions on the basis of the price their goods command in the domestic market. However, in an open economy a more general price index such as the consumer price index, since it includes both domestic and foreign prices, can change as a consequence of an exchange rate change. Further, such an overall price index is the relevant one for workers in their money-holding, consumption and labour supply decisions.[7] The introduction of this dichotomy between price levels into the MF model has some interesting policy implications which are now discussed.

The use of a price index which includes both a domestic and a foreign component and can therefore be affected by exchange rate changes has basically two implications for the MF model (see Argy and Salop (1979) and Branson and Buiter (1983) for a further discussion). First, if the general price index is used to deflate money balances in equation (5.2) then exchange rate changes will result in real balance effects: this can have, as is demonstrated below, important implications for the operation of fiscal policy. Second, if, as suggested above, firms and households use different price indexes then this may have considerable implications for aggregate supply and the efficacy of monetary and fiscal policy. Let us consider each of these factors in turn.

First, the real balance effect. Rewrite equation (5.2) as

$$\frac{M}{P_c(S)} = L(i, Y) \tag{5.16}$$

where P_c is the consumer price index assumed to be a function of the exchange rate (i.e. $P_c = P_c(S)$ where $0 < P_c < 1$).

Consider again the case of an expansionary fiscal policy in a flexible rate regime with equation (5.16) used instead of equation (5.2). In terms of figure 5.9 the increase in G shifts IS to IS'. As before, however, the consequent exchange rate appreciation will push IS' back over time to IS since it has a deleterious effect on the trade balance. However, the appreciating exchange rate will be reducing the home currency price of foreign goods, P_c will be falling and real money balances will be rising, pushing the LM curve to the right to LM' with a new equilibrium at point B. Thus the government spending multiplier, dY/dG, is

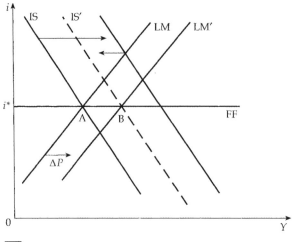

Figure 5.9 Fiscal expansion and the general price index

no longer zero even under conditions of perfect capital mobility and flexible exchange rates.

The relative efficacy of monetary and fiscal policy in the MF model also depends crucially on the responsiveness of wages to exchange-rate-induced price changes. In the basic MF model it is implicitly assumed that workers are interested only in their nominal wage and not their real wage (of course, with prices constant this distinction is not crucial). But a number of researchers (see, for example, Branson and Rotemberg, 1980) have empirically demonstrated that workers in a number of industrial countries (UK, Japan, West Germany, and Italy) have real wage targets: changes in the general price level induced, say, by exchange rate changes result in corresponding changes in nominal wages. If firms base their hiring and firing of labour on nominal wages deflated by the price of domestic output, interesting supply-side effects may be induced as a result of monetary and fiscal policy. We now consider a version of the MF model extended to incorporate *supply-side factors*.

At the heart of the supply side considered here (and also in the next chapter) is the kind of wage targets workers have. This may be discussed by considering

$$W = W_0 P_c^\lambda \tag{5.17}$$

where W is the nominal wage rate, P_c is a general, or consumer, price index to be distinguished from P which is the price of domestic value added. If the parameter $\lambda = 0$ then (5.17) says that workers have a target for nominal wages equal to W_0. Thus although the general price index may be changing this has no effect on workers' wage demands: workers suffer from money illusion. If alternatively $\lambda = 1$, workers have a real wage target, fixed at W_0, and therefore do not suffer from money illusion. Branson and Rotemberg (1980), for example, have empirically shown that for the UK, Japan, Germany, and Italy the real wage model is appropriate, whilst for the USA the nominal wage model is relevant. This has crucial implications for the effectiveness of macroeconomic policy.

Following Argy and Salop (1979) we assume that the domestic economy produces a good which is both consumed at home and exported abroad. Since a different good is imported from abroad, the law of one price need not hold. This has the important implication that the general price level P_c is a function of the price of both domestic goods and foreign import goods, as in

$$P_c = f(P, SP^*) \qquad f_1 > 0, \quad f_2 > 0 \tag{5.18}$$

Thus from (5.18) it is clear that the domestic price level and consumer price levels can in general differ: this equation captures the direct effect of the exchange rate on the consumer price index. The supply of domestic output is given by a simple production function:

$$Y = y(N, K) \tag{5.19}$$

where $y_N > 0$, $y_{NN} < 0$, $y_K > 0$, $y_{NK} < 0$ and the partial derivatives have their usual textbook interpretation (i.e. the production function is characterized by diminishing marginal productivity). Assuming that firms operate in competitive markets and take the price of their domestic output P as given, the usual profit maximizing condition will be that the marginal product of labour equals the real wage:

$$y_N = \frac{W}{P} \tag{5.20}$$

Thus equation (5.20) is our demand for labor equation, and since equation (5.17) will determine the quantity of labor supplied, it represents our labor supply equation. Notice that the price term entering the real wage in (5.17) and (5.20) differs: it is the domestic price of output which is of interest to firms and the consumer price index which is of interest to households. Notice also that equation (5.20) may be rearranged as

$$P = \frac{W}{y_N} \tag{5.20a}$$

and therefore, for a given marginal productivity, an increase in W increases P.

Equations (5.17)–(5.20a) describe the supply side of the model. The model's demand side is given by a version of equation (5.5), namely

$$PY = P_c A(Y, i) + PX(Q) - SP^*M(Q, A) \tag{5.21}$$

where $A_y > 0$, $X_Q > 0$, $M_Q < 0$, $A_i < 0$ and $M_A > 0$. Equation (5.21) simply states that the nominal value of domestic output must equal the nominal value of aggregate demand for domestic output. The functional forms of the components

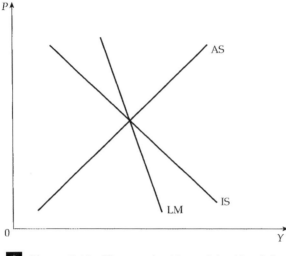

Figure 5.10 The supply side and the Mundell–Fleming model

of aggregate demand should be clear from our earlier discussion. The money market expression is given by

$$\frac{M}{P_c} = (i, Y) \tag{5.22}$$

where notice, following our discussion above, that the consumer price index is used to deflate nominal money balances (P is used to deflate nominal domestic value added). Finally capital is perfectly mobile and, for simplicity, expectations are static, and therefore equation (5.1) holds:

$$i = i^* \tag{5.23}$$

The equilibrium in the money, goods and labour market is represented diagrammatically in figure 5.10. The slopes of the various schedules may be explained in the following way. The AS curve must be upward sloping since, from an initial equilibrium, an increase in income can only be induced by an increase in P which, for a given W, lowers producers' real labor costs. The IS curve must be downward sloping since, from an initial equilibrium, an increase in income can only be induced, given the other parameters of the model, by a decline in P which switches demand from foreign goods towards home goods. The LM schedule is also downward sloping because an increase in Y from a position on the LM curve can only be consistent with money market equilibrium if P falls, thus allowing real money balances to support the higher level of income (given the interest rate).

The three schedules depicted in figure 5.10 will shift as a consequence of exchange rate changes. Hence an exchange rate depreciation will shift the IS curve rightwards since the improved competitiveness of home goods relative to foreign goods shifts demand towards the home good and this will result in increased income for a given value of P. The LM curve will shift leftwards as a consequence of an exchange rate depreciation since the increase in S by reducing real money balances (refer to equation (5.22)), and for given values of i (remember i is continuously equal to i^*) and P, requires a lower level of income for money market equilibrium. Shifts of the AS curve depend on the degree of money illusion as characterized by equation (5.17). Thus if there is no money illusion, $\lambda = 1$, an exchange appreciation will decrease P_c which in turn will result in wage bargainers demanding a lower nominal wage. For a given P, real labor costs will fall and producers will supply more output: the AS curve shifts rightwards for an appreciation (and conversely leftwards following a depreciation). If there is money illusion, as is assumed in the MF model, AS will *remain unchanged*; i.e. neither appreciations nor depreciations result in wage changes and therefore for a given price of domestic output the real wage facing employers, W/P, does not change and consequently output does not change.

Fiscal policy again

Consider now, in the context of the above model, an expansionary fiscal policy which shifts the IS curve from IS to IS' in figure 5.11. In contrast to the consideration of the same shock in the MF model we here assume no money illusion, $\lambda = 1$. The resulting effect of the excess demand in income increases the demand for money which, by inducing an incipient rise in the home interest rate, results in a capital inflow and an exchange rate appreciation. As we have seen, the latter effect will shift the AS curve rightwards from AS to AS', the IS curve back

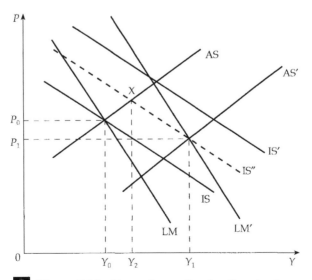

Figure 5.11 Expansionary fiscal policy, $\lambda = 1$

from IS′ to say IS″, and the LM curve rightwards to LM′. The initial fiscal expansion has therefore resulted in a rise in income from Y_0 to Y_1 and a fall in the price level from P_0 to P_1 (the more money illusion in the system, the smaller will be the shift in the AS schedule, and the more likely it is that P will have risen in the new equilibrium).

In contrast to the simple MF result, the fiscal expansion is efficacious in affecting output for two reasons: first, the effect of the appreciating exchange rate on the LM curve and, second, the supply-side effects due to the incorporation of a wage-price nexus into the model and the assumed asymmetry of prices used by wage bargainers and producers. When workers have a nominal wage target, and therefore complete money illusion ($\lambda = 0$), only the real balance effect prevails as a result of the exchange rate appreciation and we move to a point such as X, with an income of Y_2.

Monetary policy again

For given values of P and i, an expansionary monetary policy shifts the LM curve to LM′ in figure 5.12. The effect on output and prices is again seen to depend on the degree of money illusion in the system. If workers have a nominal wage target, and thus money illusion, the consequent exchange rate depreciation will leave the AS curve unchanged and shift the IS curve to IS′; the new equilibrium will be at a point such as X, where output and the price level have clearly risen from the situation prior to the money supply shock. In the case of a real wage target and no money illusion the AS curve shifts leftwards in figure 5.13 to AS′ and the domestic price level and the exchange rate increase by the same percentage as the money supply increases, output remaining at Y_0. This must be the case, since with no money illusion labour costs will not have altered for producers and therefore they will not attempt to expand output. A given output level from the

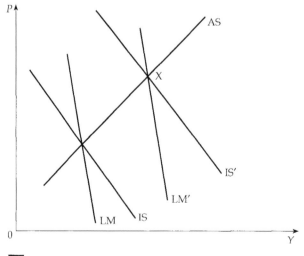

Figure 5.12 Expansionary monetary policy, $\lambda = 0$

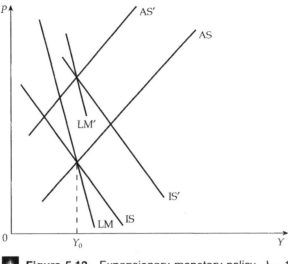

Figure 5.13 Expansionary monetary policy, $\lambda = 1$

Table 5.1 Effect of policy shocks on Y and P

		dY/dG	dP/dG	dY/dM	dP/dM
Money illusion	$\lambda = 0$	+	+	+	+
No money illusion	$\lambda = 1$	+ +	+ +	0	+ +

+, only the liquidity effect is operative; + +, both the liquidity effect and the supply-side effect are operative.

production side necessitates that the overall price level (and P) must rise in proportion to the money supply increase for money market equilibrium. With P and S increasing by the same amount, there will be no change in real aggregate demand.

The effects of monetary and fiscal policy on income and the domestic price level are summarized in table 5.1 for the two extreme cases of money illusion and no money illusion.

5.9 Summary and Conclusions

In this chapter we have demonstrated that the basic perfect capital mobility version of the MF model implies that monetary policy has no effect on output with fixed exchange rates, but has a powerful effect with flexible rates. In contrast, fiscal policy has a powerful effect on output under fixed rates and no effect under flexible rates. However, these conclusions have to be modified somewhat when some of the rather restrictive assumptions which underpin the model are relaxed. Thus open economy macroeconomic policymaking depends crucially on the degree of capital mobility, the formation of exchange rate expectations, the importance of wealth effects and the flexibility of the price level. In the next chapter we use a two-country version of the model developed in this chapter in order to discuss the issue of policy coordination.

◈ Appendix

In order to derive the various policy multipliers discussed in the text we totally differentiate equations (5.5), (5.4) and (5.6) to obtain

$$dY - A_Y dY - A_i di - T_Y dY - T_S dS - dG = 0 \qquad (A5.1)$$

$$dM - L_Y dY - L_i di = 0 \qquad (A5.2)$$

$$dB - T_Y dY - C_i d_i - T_S dS = 0 \qquad (A5.3)$$

On rearranging equations (A5.1)–(A5.3) in matrix form we obtain

$$\begin{bmatrix} (1 - A_Y - T_Y) & -A_i & -T_S & 0 \\ -L_Y & -L_i & 0 & 0 \\ -T_Y & C_i & -T_S & 1 \end{bmatrix} \begin{bmatrix} dY \\ di \\ dS \\ dB \end{bmatrix} = \begin{bmatrix} dG \\ -dM \\ 0 \end{bmatrix} \qquad (A5.4)$$

With flexible exchange rates the dB term can be set equal to zero and, additionally, the last column of the first matrix vanishes, whilst, with fixed rates, $dS = 0$ and the third column of the first matrix vanishes. The various policy multipliers in the text may then be computed using Cramer's rule and by additionally assuming that capital is perfectly mobile (i.e. $C_i \to \infty$).

NOTES

1 In this section we use the two-sector diagram given in figure 5.1 because it neatly illustrates the joint determination of the exchange rate, income and the rate of interest. In the remaining section of this chapter we only use the bottom sector of this figure. Versions of the top sector will be used in chapter 9.
2 See Cushman and Zha (1997) for empirical support of these kinds of effects in a vector autoregression model.
3 The fiscal-policy-induced shift in the IS curve with flexible exchange rates is conducted purely for pedagogic reasons, since with perfect capital mobility the domestic interest rate is continually tied to the foreign rate and thus the IS curve cannot shift.
4 The results in this section anticipate those in the next chapter concerning the macroeconomic interdependences of countries.
5 From equation (A5.4) it can be demonstrated that the slopes of the FF and LM schedules are given by di/dY and hence, the more responsive are capital flows, *ceteris paribus*, to the interest rate relative to the interest responsiveness of the demand for money, the flatter will be FF relative to LM.

6 In fact the story is not quite so simple. Because domestic residents have been accumulating foreign assets during the adjustment period, their interest earnings will have risen and at the final equilibrium it is possible to have a trade deficit offset by foreign interest earnings (remember that the current account is the sum of the trade balance and net foreign interest receipts; hence a zero current balance is consistent with a deficit on the trade account). This means that it may not be necessary to return to the original level of income. This idea is discussed in more detail in chapter 11. Also, of course in reality the sequence of events would be somewhat different from that portrayed in the text. Thus it is unlikely that the system would move mechanistically from A to B and then back again. It is more likely that as soon as the current account surplus developed there would be a tendency for the system to return back to A.

7 The appropriateness of a general price index for consumers and a more limited price index for producers is discussed by Salop (1974).

6

International Policy Coordination

The purpose of this chapter is to consider two important topics, namely the macroeconomic interdependence of national economies and the potential benefits that might arise when national governments decide to coordinate their macroeconomic policies. The former topic has already been discussed on a number of occasions in the book. In particular, in chapter 4 we examined the interdependences of national economies using a simple Keynesian open economy macro model. Although that analysis was insightful it did have its limitations in so far as it ignored the capital account of the balance of payments. Since, as we saw in chapter 5, the capital account can have an important bearing on how well a small open economy is insulated from shocks emanating in the rest of the world, it seems important to discuss international interdependence with explicit recognition of the capital account. This is especially important given that world capital markets are much more closely integrated than goods markets (and also, of course, that the capital account for many countries is, in value terms, of a similar order of magnitude to the current account). Although we also discussed the potential benefits of policy coordination in chapter 4, our discussion was relatively brief. In particular, we did not discuss the theoretical underpinnings of policy cooperation, nor did we discuss the empirical evidence which seeks to quantify the merits of such cooperation. In this chapter both of these issues are also addressed.

In section 6.1 we exploit the Mundell–Fleming (MF) model, introduced in chapter 5, to analyse macroeconomic interdependences and, especially, to illustrate the spillovers that occur when a country alters its macroeconomic mix. In particular, we introduce a two-country version of the MF model, consisting of a home and a foreign country, in which the countries no longer take variables (like interest rates) as being determined parametrically in world markets. It seems intuitively obvious that since we live in a world of many countries the "first-best" type of analysis would be one in which multilateral interactions were considered. Unfortunately, the level of analytical techniques assumed for this book precludes such an analysis. However, we do discuss a multilateral simulation model below, due to McKibben and Sachs (1991), which suggests that the two-country MF results go through in a more complex multilateral setting (a multilateral interpretation may be given to the two-country model by interpreting the foreign country as the rest of the world).[1] The MF model is especially useful for considering macro interdependence since it can be analyzed with a variety of assumptions about the degree of capital mobility and also it can be extended to allow for wage–price interactions.

Having demonstrated the potential spillovers from macro-policy making in section 6.1, we move on in section 6.2 to an examination of a variety of issues relating to the potential benefits from policy coordination. We examine, for example, the potential gains from coordination in a game-theoretic framework; the empirical literature which seeks to quantify the gains from coordination; and potential impediments to the successful implementation of coordinated policies.

6.1 The Two-Country Mundell–Fleming Model and Macroeconomic Interdependence

The model we consider in this section is due to Cooper (1968), Mundell (1968), Mussa (1979b) and McKibben and Sachs (1991).[2] The model consists of two symmetric countries,[3] each producing a traded good which is an imperfect substitute for the foreign equivalent and each facing perfect capital mobility. The model is summarized in table 6.1. Equations (6.1) and (6.2) are simply the money market equilibrium conditions and aggregate demand relationships for the home and foreign country discussed in chapter 5; the partial derivatives were also discussed in that chapter. We initially assume perfect capital mobility and static exchange

Table 6.1 The two-country Mundell–Fleming model

$M/P = L(i, Y)$	(6.1)
$M^*/P^* = L^*(i^*, Y^*)$	(6.1a)
$Y = D = A(i, Y) + T(Q, Y, Y^*) + G$	(6.2)
$Y^* = D^* = A^*(i^*, Y^*) + T^*(1/Q, Y^*, Y) + G^*$	(6.2a)
$i = i^*$	(6.3)
$P = W/MP_l$	(6.4)
$P^* = W^*/MP_l^*$	(6.4a)
$W = W_0 P_c^\lambda$	(6.5)
$W^* = W_0^* P_c^{*\lambda^*}$	(6.5a)
$P_c = f(P, SP^*)$	(6.6)
$P_c^* = f^*[P^*, (1/S)P]$	(6.6a)

rate expectations and this may be represented by condition (6.3) (again, see chapter 5 for a discussion of this interest rate parity condition). Equations (6.4)–(6.6) denote the wage–price sector of the model and were also discussed in chapter 5.

Before turning to the model, however, it is worth highlighting the three key transmission mechanisms whereby macroeconomic events in one country can spill over to other countries. First, there is the income–expenditure effect resulting from the trade account of the balance of payments: the higher the proportion of a country's trade relative to its GNP, the more important is this linkage likely to be. Since most economies, and blocks of economies (such as the European Union (EU)), have important trading links in goods, this mechanism is likely to be very important. Second, monetary impulses in one country may be transmitted internationally via their effect on interest rates and the capital account of the balance of payments. This effect will depend on the degree of integration between an economy's real and monetary sectors and the degree of capital mobility. Since the latter is likely to be close to perfect for most developed countries, this mechanism is also likely to be an extremely important conduit. Finally, relative price adjustments will spill over from one country to another through movements in the terms of trade. The speed of such adjustments will depend on the degree of price flexibility and on a country's wage–price nexus.

For pedagogic purposes, we analyze each shock in three stages, each of these capturing the three key elements of transmission and interaction between nations noted above, namely income (trade), monetary (capital flows) and prices. In the first stage, the interdependences of the two countries emanate solely from the implications of a policy change for the current account of the balance of payments and, in particular, the income repercussions of trade flows. Further, in this stage, much as in the standard closed economy discussion of the Keynesian model, interest rate changes are realized (instead of being incipient as they are in the small country MF model). In the second stage, the capital account ramifications of the policy change are incorporated (in this second stage there may also be further current account repercussions of the policy change). Finally, we examine the final outcome of each shock under constant and flexible price scenarios, with differing assumptions about wage indexation. We believe that this three-stage discussion should be helpful in highlighting the international transmission of macroeconomic policy and should lead naturally into more complex models of international transmission, considered below.

6.1.1 Floating exchange rates

Monetary, or beggar-thy-neighbor, policy

Consider an expansionary monetary policy, induced by a change in domestic credit expansion, which shifts LM to LM_1 in figure 6.1(a). As in the small country case, discussed in chapter 5, the immediate effect of this policy expansion is to put downward pressure on the domestic interest rate. This fall, in turn, generates an expansion of domestic output and this may be illustrated by the move

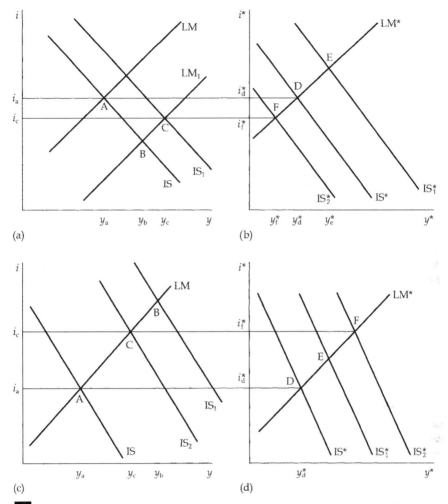

Figure 6.1 Floating exchange rates and the two-country Mundell–Fleming model: (a) monetary policy for the home country; (b) monetary policy for the foreign country; (c) fiscal policy for the home country; (d) fiscal policy for the foreign country

from A to B in figure 6.1(a). The expansion of domestic output, through the marginal propensity to import, will lead to an expansion of foreign output and a rise in the foreign interest rate; this is represented by the move from D to E in figure 6.1(b), and the corresponding shift from IS* to IS$_1^*$.

However, neither equilibrium B nor equilibrium E for the home and foreign country will be final. This is because although the IS/LM shifts are determined in each country, the world interest rate change will be determined by the inter-action of both countries. In the home country there will be a capital outflow, an incipient balance of payments deficit at B (incipient, because with a flexible exchange rate the overall balance of payments must balance) necessitating an exchange rate depreciation, whilst in the foreign country there is an incipient balance of payments surplus requiring an exchange rate appreciation. In the home country, the currency depreciation will stimulate exports and curtail imports, and this will generate a further expansion of output, captured by the move of the IS schedule from IS to IS_1. Output in the foreign country will, in turn, fall because the change in relative prices, implied by the devaluation, results in both domestic and foreign residents substituting away from foreign goods towards home goods. This is illustrated by the shift in IS_1^* to IS_2^* in figure 6.1(b). These subsequent exchange rate movements will generate final equilibria of C and F in the home and foreign countries, respectively. The expansion of domestic credit considered here is usually regarded as a classic example of a "beggar-thy-neighbor" policy because it results in an expansion of domestic output at the expense of foreign output.

So far, we have ignored the wage–price implications of the monetary expansion – we have implicitly assumed that $\lambda = 0$. In the home country, the exchange rate depreciation will push up consumer prices and this in turn (via (6.5)) will result in an increase in domestic wages. If $\lambda = 1$ – i.e. we have full indexation – there will be no output implications of the monetary expansion in either country. This is because wages and prices will rise in proportion to the money supply increase, therefore giving companies no incentive to expand output, and with equiproportionate changes in M and P real money balances cannot change and therefore the interest rate cannot change either.

Perhaps a more interesting indexation example is where the domestic country has no indexation ($\lambda = 0$), but the foreign country has full indexation ($\lambda^* = 1$). Such a scenario could be interpreted as a characterization of labor market conditions in, respectively, the USA and Europe. Thus, Branson and Rotemberg (1980) have empirically demonstrated that workers in the UK, West Germany and Italy have real wage targets, whereas workers in the USA have nominal wage targets (i.e. there is little, or no, indexation in the USA). As we saw above, with no indexation in either country an expansionary monetary policy in the home country is a beggar-thy-neighbor policy because the currency appreciation in the foreign country crowds out net exports by an amount which offsets the stimulative effect of the lower interest rate. However, with foreign indexation the appreciation of the foreign currency will result in an equivalent fall in wages and prices and therefore competitiveness will be maintained (although competitiveness will not be maintained in the domestic country since it does not have indexation). This, in turn, means that the only implication of the monetary expansion in the domestic country for the foreign country will be the lower interest rate. Hence output expands in both countries, although by slightly less in the home country than the non-indexation scenario (because it no longer benefits from a change in the competitiveness of the foreign country).

Fiscal policy

As we saw in chapter 5, the key implication for a small open economy with flexible exchange rates and perfect capital mobility is that domestic fiscal policy is completely ineffective in stimulating real output. Does this result change in a two-country setting and what are the implications for the foreign country? Again we adopt a two-step procedure to analyze the fiscal change. A fiscal expansion in the home country is represented in figure 6.1(c) by a shift in the IS schedule from IS to IS_1. This in turn implies an output expansion and an increased interest rate, represented by the move from A to B (the "closed economy" case). In the foreign country, the increased expansion of output in the other country, through the foreign expenditure multiplier, will have an expansionary effect on the foreign country's output and interest rate, as represented by the move from D to E (figure 6.1(d)).

The relative change in interest rates which occurs in stage 1 will imply an incipient net capital inflow toward the domestic country and an outflow from the foreign country. This, in turn, means that the domestic country has an incipient balance of payments surplus whilst the foreign country has an incipient deficit. These disequilibria require an appreciation of the home currency price of a unit of the foreign currency. The implications of this appreciation will be to shift the IS schedules in both countries to IS_2 and IS_2^*, respectively, giving a net final expansion of output in both countries.

Assuming flexible prices, the currency appreciation in the home country will mean, as in the small country model, that fiscal policy has less of an inflationary impact than monetary policy because the price of foreign goods priced in domestic currency will fall. The ultimate effect of this on output in the two countries will depend on the form of wage indexation employed. If there is no indexation in the domestic country and full indexation in the foreign country (which, as we have suggested, could be interpreted as the situation in the USA (the home country) and Europe (the foreign country)) foreign output can actually fall. This is because the nominal appreciation of the home currency will raise foreign prices and wages and this offsets the improvement in foreign competitiveness which occurs when $\lambda = 0$; the foreign country suffers a higher interest rate and little or no change in competitiveness. With full indexation in both countries' real wages, real interest rates and the real exchange rate do not change and so fiscal policy has no effect.

6.1.2 Fixed exchange rates

Monetary policy

With fixed rates, the efficacy of monetary policy depends very much on which country is responsible for pegging the exchange rate. If the monetary expansion emanates in the domestic country and if, additionally, it is responsible for maintaining the peg, monetary policy has no effect. This is simply because the initial expansion of domestic credit puts downward pressure on the domestic interest rate, generating an incipient capital outflow and incipient exchange rate depreciation. The latter is prevented from being an actual depreciation by the central bank selling foreign exchange reserves in an amount exactly equal, and opposite, to the initial domestic credit expansion.

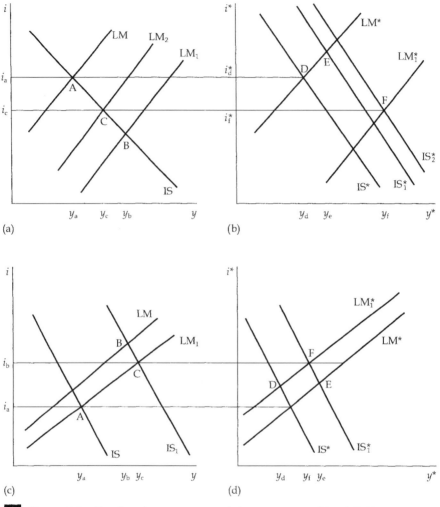

Figure 6.2 Fixed exchange rates and the two-country Mundell–Fleming model: (a) monetary policy for the home country; (b) monetary policy for the foreign country; (c) fiscal policy for the home country; (d) fiscal policy for the foreign country

When the foreign country is responsible for maintaining the peg, the domestic monetary expansion results in an increase in the foreign money supply as well (the foreign central bank buys foreign exchange, thereby increasing the F component of its money supply). We again use our three-stage analysis to interpret this. The initial monetary expansion is illustrated in figure 6.2 as a move in the domestic LM schedule from LM to LM_1, which decreases the domestic interest rate and generates an income stimulus. The latter, through the propensity to import, will increase foreign income (IS* moves to IS_1^*) and the foreign interest rate.

The domestic interest rate fall corresponding to this change results in a (realized) capital outflow and an increase in the foreign money supply represented by the move from LM* to LM$^*_1$: at B the domestic country will be running an overall balance of payments deficit and this, because it implies a loss of reserves, will push the LM schedule back somewhat from LM_1 (to, say, LM_2) and also, because it implies an increased demand for foreign exports, will push the IS* curve further rightwards. A possible final joint equilibrium is illustrated in figures 6.2(a) and 6.2(b) by points C and F for the home and foreign country, respectively. If the price level is allowed to vary this will increase as a result of the global expansion of the world money supply and this, in turn, will attenuate the global output expansion.

Fiscal policy

A domestic fiscal expansion, represented in figure 6.2(c) as the shift from IS to IS_1, will increase output and the interest rate to, say, B. This output expansion will, in turn, increase the demand for foreign exports, thereby shifting the foreign IS curve to, say, IS^*_1.

The policy change will, though, have further balance of payments implications in that the upward pressure on the domestic interest rate attracts a capital inflow. If both countries are responsible for pegging the exchange rate this inflow will increase the domestic money supply (to the extent that the stance of domestic credit remains unchanged) and reduce the foreign money supply, represented in figures 6.2(c) and 6.2(d) by the shifts in the LM schedules to LM_1 and LM^*_1. Final equilibrium is represented by C and F for the home and foreign country, respectively, with output having risen in both countries and the world interest rate also having increased. The effects will be more ambiguous if responsibility for pegging the currency is left to one of the two countries. If, for example, the foreign country is responsible for pegging the exchange rate and the domestic country engineers a fiscal expansion, output in the foreign country may actually fall. This is because with the foreign country pegging the exchange rate it loses reserves and suffers a monetary contraction which may offset the expansionary impetus, via the current account, of the domestic fiscal stimulus.

With a flexible price level, and both countries responsible for pegging the exchange rate, the overall output expansion will be less than in the fixed price case because of the rising price level in both countries. With full foreign indexation the foreign price level rises by more than the domestic price level, thereby increasing the real exchange rate (competitiveness) and giving domestic output a further stimulus. Conversely, full home indexation results in a worsening of domestic competitiveness and this will attenuate the initial output expansion.

The purpose of the above discussion has been to illustrate that macro-policy making in one country will have spillover effects for its trading partners. It is possible that such repercussions will be viewed as desirable adjuncts to foreign policy, but this seems unlikely. For example, it is doubtful that the beggar-thy-neighbor implications of a domestic monetary expansion would be welcomed in the rest of the world unless, of course, the domestic country's trading partners were suffering from overheated economies. Similarly, a domestic stimulus, such as a domestic fiscal expansion, would have unwelcome consequences in the rest of the world if the country's trading partners were pursuing counter inflationary measures. Further spillover effects are implicit in the above analytical examples and may help to illustrate the potential benefits of international policy coordination.[4] In a worldwide recession, as we pointed out in section 4.6, a government on its own may be reluctant to engage in an expansionary policy because of the unfavourable balance of payments/exchange rate implications of its actions. However, if it knew other countries would match its expansion in a coordinated fashion such reluctance might disappear. Second, governments often have objectives for their current account positions[5] and if they all attempt to achieve such objectives in an uncoordinated way this may have extremely disruptive consequences for the functioning of the international economy. Third, if governments unilaterally attempt to implement disinflation policies which consists of tight monetary policy, and by implication an appreciated exchange rate, combined with an expansionary fiscal policy to stabilize output, the result will be unnecessarily high interest rates and an inappropriate monetary–fiscal policy mix.

6.1.3 Imperfect capital mobility

As in the original Mundell paper, perfect capital mobility was not taken as the bench-mark although it has become so in much subsequent writing. Although in practice perfect capital mobility is often a good working assumption, for countries with capital controls the case of imperfect capital mobility may be more realistic. What difference then does imperfect capital mobility have for the inter-relatedness of economies? If we go to the opposite extreme of zero capital mobility then all of the transmission of macro-policy will occur through the current account and we are effectively back to the model considered in section 4.6. The policy conclusions may be summarized as follows. With a flexible exchange rate home country expansions of monetary and fiscal policy will be effective in stimulating output and the price level in the home country but because the exchange rate moves to ensure the current account is always balanced there will be no output implications for the foreign country (although the foreign consumer price level will fall due to the exchange rate change).

6.1.4 Further extensions to the two-country model of interdependence: the McKibben–Sachs model

Although the basic two-country MF model discussed above has extremely useful insights into macroeconomic interdependences, it does have a number of limitations, not least with respect to some of the assumptions employed. Since we have already presented a critique of these assumptions, as they relate to the small country MF model, in chapter 5, we merely list them here. The model discussed in the previous section assumes only static expectations, a rather restrictive assumption especially when the exchange rate is flexible. The model ignores any dynamics arising from the issuance of government debt (through the government budget constraint) and the accumulation or decumulation of foreign assets through the current account of the balance of payments (see chapter 11 for an exposition of the portfolio balance model in which stock–flow dynamics emanating from the current account are appropriately dealt with). Also the supply side of the MF model has only been dealt with in a rather rudimentary way in this section. In particular, the shocks considered have all emanated from the demand side. An alternative portrayal of the international transmission of shocks stems from the "real business cycle" literature which emphasizes supply-side shocks to the exclusion of demand-side shocks (see, *inter alia*, Dellas, 1986; Barro, 1989).[6] Unfortunately, an attempt to incorporate all of the above extensions into the MF model would make the model analytically intractable. One could proceed by changing one assumption at a time and holding all other assumptions the same, in much the same way as we did in chapter 5. However, one would never know if the results so obtained would be robust with respect to modifications of the other assumptions.

Rather than build an analytical extension of the MF model incorporating the above factors, McKibben and Sachs (1991) have proposed a numerical simulation exercise in order to provide tractable solutions.[7] This model has become known as the McKibben–Sachs global (MSG) model; the current version is referred to as MSG2. Other models in this genre are the IMF's Multimod and the OECD's Interlink. The MSG model was specifically developed in order to try to understand the large external imbalances that arose in the 1980s, particularly between the USA and Germany and Japan, and as a result to try to offer policy measures which would generate an appropriate adjustment of such imbalances. For example, their model may be used to answer the following type of question: what would the effect be on the USA and on the rest of the world economy of a dramatic cut in the US fiscal deficit? Further the model may be used to shed light on the usefulness of international policy coordination (a topic considered in section 6.2). Before discussing the MSG approach, however, a quote from their book highlights the usefulness of the basic two-country MF model outlined above:

> the short-run multipliers that we found from the basic, static Mundell Fleming model (given wage setting and exchange rate regimes) are remarkably robust to the inclusion of dynamics, expectations and aggregate supply considerations. The intuition provided by this basic model is therefore very useful, even for understanding the complete simulation model. (p. 40)

The MSG model is one which blends recent developments in macroeconomic theory[8] in which rational agents attempt to maximize intertemporal objective functions – households maximize an intertemporal utility function (like equation (11.12) on page 222) and firms maximize the value of output, with standard macroeconomic relationships describing adjustment in financial markets (such as the condition of uncovered interest rate parity). Although the optimizing behaviour of agents is emphasized, markets do not continuously clear[9] and so the model

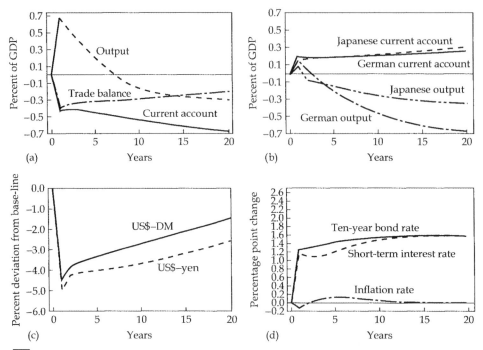

Figure 6.3 Effects of a US fiscal expansion in the McKibben–Sachs model:
(a) US output and foreign trade; (b) non-US output and trade; (c) nominal
exchange rates; (d) US inflation and interest rates
Source: McKibben and Sachs, 1991

may be regarded as neoKeynesian. The model is in fact described by McKibben
and Sachs as a dynamic general equilibrium model of a multiregion world economy. The countries and regions modelled are the USA, Japan, Germany, the
rest of the European Monetary System (REMS), the rest of the OECD countries
(ROECD), non-oil developing countries (LDCs) and the OPEC countries. Given
assumptions about the form of utility and production functions, parameter values
are, in general, calculated so that the model replicates the actual data found in
the base period (1980);[10] i.e. the parameters are not estimated using econometric
techniques as is common in most macroeconometric models. Once calibrated, the
model is then used to analyze various monetary and fiscal shocks emanating in
the different countries.

The big advantage of models like MSG or the IMF's multimod is that they facilitate an evaluation of the *net* effect of the three links (income, monetary and price)
referred to in our discussion of the MF model in section 6.1. Thus, in a theoretical model like the MF model, one can only sign the partial derivatives of each
of the linkages on its own (i.e. income links imply positive spillovers, monetary
links negative spillovers), but not the net effect of their combination. This can
only be achieved with an empirically based model which weights the positive
and negative spillovers.

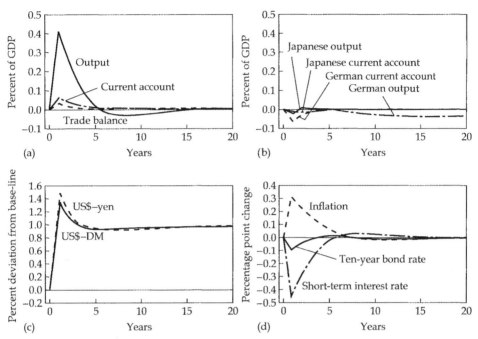

Figure 6.4 Effects of a US monetary expansion in the McKibben–Sachs model: (a) US output and foreign trade; (b) non-US output and trade; (c) nominal exchange rates; (d) US inflation and interest rates
Source: McKibben and Sachs, 1991

We consider here two of the policy shocks analyzed by McKibben and Sachs, namely a permanent US fiscal expansion and a permanent US monetary expansion. For both shocks the exchange rate is assumed to be flexible. The former expansion consists of an unanticipated rise in the level of US government expenditure.[11] In figure 6.3 the time profiles which result for the fiscal expansion for output, the trade balance, the current account, interest rates, inflation and two exchange rates are portrayed. As in the MF model, output expands (by 0.6 percentage points in the first year) and the exchange rate appreciates (by 5 percent against the yen and 4.5 percent against the deutschmark) as a result of the fiscal expansion. The effect on foreign output (Germany and Japan), illustrated in figure 6.3, is initially positive; however, as wages adjust to rising prices the output effect becomes negative and this is the dominant effect for the time profile.[12]

In figure 6.4, the US and foreign output and exchange rate responses to a sustained 1 percent rise in US money balances are recorded. Again, as predicted by the MF model, this results in a rise in US output (of 0.42 percent) and a US exchange rate depreciation. Interestingly, in the first year the exchange rate is seen to overshoot its long-run value by 1 percent and this is attributed to relatively sticky US commodity prices (see our discussion of the sticky-price monetary model, due to Dornbusch (1976a), in chapter 9). On balance, the expansionary US monetary policy has a negative effect on foreign outputs, although as figure 6.4 illustrates this is very small in magnitude. Notice also that the policy has very little impact on the current/trade balances in either the domestic or foreign country.[13] The monetary policy simulation would seem to have important implications for the kind of locomotive policy described in section 4.6. Thus the lesson here is that an expansionary monetary stimulus conducted in the USA will have very little effect on output in the rest of the world; US monetary policy is insulated by the flexibility of the exchange rate. We return to the MSG model in the next section.

6.2 The Potential Gains from Policy Coordination

In section 6.1 we have demonstrated, *inter alia*, that once we move away from a small country setting, domestic macroeconomic policy changes can have important spillover effects for other countries, the extent of such spillovers depending crucially on the type of exchange rate regime, the degree of capital mobility and the wage–price mechanism. Under certain circumstances a policy designed to expand domestic output can have a deleterious effect on output in the rest of the world – the beggar-thy-neighbor policy being a classic example of this. Also, of course, even domestic policies which result in an expansion of foreign output may not be desirable from the point of view of the foreign economy if it is already at, or close to, a full employment level. In both these examples, the foreign country could, of course, react to the policy changes emanating from the domestic country by altering its macro-mix accordingly and this, in turn, would have spillover effects for the domestic country which may not be to the domestic policy-makers' liking. This therefore raises the question of whether it would not be more efficient, or optimal, for the two countries, or more generally all countries, to coordinate their macro-policies in some way. This is the issue we address in this section.

Cooper (1968) has expressed the central issue of international economic cooperation rather nicely as the answer to the question "how to keep the manifold benefits of extensive international intercourse free of crippling restrictions, while at the same time preserving a maximum degree of freedom for each nation to pursue its legitimate economic objectives" (p. 15). However, as with marriage, he argues, the benefits of closer cooperation may be enjoyed only at the expense of relinquishing a certain amount of independence. Of course, in practice, the degree of independence or freedom that a country has is likely to be greatly compromised anyway, because of the important linkages we referred to above, and therefore what the country is relinquishing by coordination may in fact be more apparent than real. Indeed, by coordinating the country can attempt to optimize what remains of its freedom. In other words, the only independence lost by coordinating is the ability to achieve what cannot in fact be obtained! Policy coordination can therefore be seen as a way of restoring, or increasing, the policy effectiveness which non-cooperation, or failing to optimize, reduces, and this really is the baseline reason for coordination.

In a model consisting of two symmetrically dependent economies (with fixed exchange rates and prices) Cooper (1969b) examines the issue of policy design and the dynamics of policy adjustments.[14] In this context, three specific policy regimes are considered:

1 no coordination, where domestic instruments are assigned to domestic targets with a one-to-one pairing *à la* the Mundellian assignment;
2 internal coordination, where no account is taken of foreign targets and domestic instruments are used simultaneously to achieve domestic targets;
3 full coordination, where domestic and foreign instruments are used jointly to achieve the set of all domestic *and* foreign targets.

The second and third regimes represent scenarios which are externally non-cooperative and cooperative, respectively, whilst the first regime represents decentralization both internally and externally. Numerical experiments are used to draw conclusions from Cooper's model across the different policy regimes. The effectiveness of macro-policy is revealed in the *size* of intervention required to restore targets to their desired values and the *speed* with which targets approach those values.

For example, with no coordination target overshooting and oscillations can be removed by a one-to-one targeting, but such a policy ignores the side-effects on the targets to which it is not assigned. Increasing the degree of coordination (for a given level of interdependence) damps out the transitory effects of shocks more rapidly, whilst increasing the degree of interdependence (for a given policy stance) increases the magnitude and duration of the target disturbances. These examples lead to the important conclusion that policy coordination increases the power of policy interventions, whilst interdependence reduces the effectiveness of policy.

The benefits of cooperation are confirmed by, for example, De Bruyne (1979), who demonstrates that a necessary condition for non-cooperative decisions to be Pareto efficient is that the aims and priorities for the union of targets must be identical for all countries. Since we know that countries pursue national rather than international objectives this condition will be violated and another decision rule must dominate in the Paretian sense. Thus, when a collective agreement has been reached regarding objectives, all countries may gain by solving one global policy problem.

A very general definition of international economic policy coordination, in that it covers a broad range of alternatives from the very narrow to the more ambitious, is that given as a statement by the Group of 30 countries in 1988: "countries modify their economic policies in what is intended to be a mutually beneficial manner, taking account of international economic linkages." Currie (1990) suggests that at the more ambitious end of the policy coordination spectrum is something like the view emanating from the Bonn economic summit of 1978, at which the Group of Seven countries agreed to a comprehensive package of coordination measures. A more limited measure of coordination was that supplied by the International Monetary Fund (IMF) in terms of its multilateral surveillance process for the Bretton Woods system and the more recently established exchange rate surveillance of the Group of Seven countries. Somewhere in between these two extremes, perhaps, lie the Plaza and Louvre Accords which were attempts at coordinating exchange rates.

6.2.1 The prisoner's dilemma

The benefits of coordination can be illustrated at a basic level using the famous prisoner's dilemma game (Luce and Raiffa, 1957), familiar from the oligopoly literature. This game is described as static in nature because in the current context the game relates to the domestic country and foreign country each trying to set the optimal level of their monetary policy in response to an inflationary shock (see Okun, 1965). The effect of this shock and the corresponding monetary response could be measured using the so-called misery index, the sum of unemployment and inflation.[15] In table 6.2 the payoff matrix for the two countries is given, each cell containing a measure of misery in response to the type of monetary policy pursued by each country. For example, cell (ii) indicates the loss to the home country (–8) and foreign country (–11) of the home country pursuing a tight monetary policy, whilst the foreign country pursues a loose monetary policy. Smaller absolute values are more desirable.

In the context of the configuration portrayed in table 6.2 what happens if each country pursues a monetary policy which minimizes its misery value (or maximizes its pay-off) *whilst assuming that the other country's policy remains unchanged*? Given the construction of the payoff matrix, if the foreign country adopts either a tight or a loose monetary policy it will always be in the interests of the home country to pursue a tight money policy because only this policy minimizes its losses in each case (to –8 and –10, respectively). By symmetry it turns out that the foreign country will end up pursuing the same strategy and hence the equilibrium in this case will be cell (iv). This equilibrium is unique and is referred to as the Nash equilibrium (it is the solution which occurs in the traditional prisoner's dilemma when both prisoners confess).

Notice, however, that (iv) is not the optimal solution for the two countries; a Pareto improvement would be achieved if the countries could somehow get to cell (i). Given the assumed strategy of both countries this solution is impossible. However, if the two countries decide to cooperate, or collude in the parlance of

Table 6.2 The prisoner's dilemma and the Nash–Cournot equilibrium

		Foreign country	
		Easy money	Tight money
Home country	Easy money	–9, –9 (i)	–11, –8 (iii)
	Tight money	–8, –11 (ii)	–10, –10 (iv)

oligopoly, they could move to cell (i). But for (i) to be a lasting or permanent equilibrium the two countries have to enter into a binding commitment; otherwise there is an incentive for the countries to cheat (i.e. if the home country believes that the foreign country will maintain the loose policy given by cell (i) it has an incentive to tighten its monetary policy and therefore reduce its misery value by moving to cell (ii)). This is a familiar problem in oligopoly theory, and it was the reason given by Milton Friedman and others for the inevitable collapse of the OPEC oil price cartel.[16] The Nash equilibrium is referred to as the non-cooperative outcome, whilst cell (i) may be regarded as the cooperative outcome. As the vigilant reader may discern, the above example is rather contrived; there may in fact not be a Nash outcome or even if there is it may not be the most efficient solution.

6.2.2 The Hamada diagram – targets and instruments revisited

The issues brought out in the prisoner's dilemma example above are illustrated in this section using a diagram developed by Hamada (1979).[17] Before turning to this diagram, it is worth briefly noting its antecedents as they have a bearing on an understanding of the coordination issue. Essentially Hamada's work represents an extension of the Tinbergen–Mundell instruments and targets approach (see chapter 3) as developed by Cooper (1969b) and Niehans (1968). One of Tinbergen's key contributions to the macro-policy debate was to stress the inefficiency (i.e. inferior outcomes) that arises from one-to-one policy assignments (essentially because they ignore the side-effects of an instrument on the targets to which they have not been assigned) – hence his advocacy that the number of instruments should be at least as great as the number of targets. Cooper (1969b) demonstrates that the inefficiency is reflected in poor average outcomes for macroeconomics objectives due, in turn, to increased oscillations and overshooting in the targets (see the discussion above).

The latter authors were concerned with two limitations of the pairing of targets with instruments in an open economy setting. First, in practice a one-to-one pairing of targets to instruments (even this follows Mundell's effective classification) will not be sufficient because in most instances "an optimal mix of degree or strength of economic targets is needed in order to achieve an efficient realization of conflicting goals" (Hamada, 1979). Second, although a country may attempt to pair targets with objectives for the achievements of its own ends, it will not have incentives to take into account the effects its pairing may have on other countries. The first weakness may be dealt with by adopting what Niehans (1968) describes as an *optimizing approach*, which involves maximizing a social welfare function subject to the feasible region of target objectives. The second weakness may be dealt with by adopting a *strategic approach* (Hamada, 1979), i.e. an approach which is based on the joint reactions and counteractions of each country. Indeed Niehans (1984) suggests that the strategic approach is a natural outcome from applying the optimizing approach to a two-country model (i.e. once

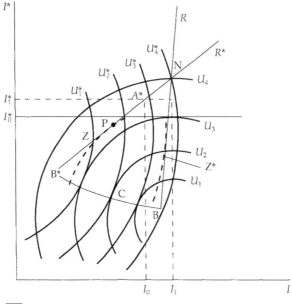

Figure 6.5 The Hamada diagram

we apply the latter approach to a two, or more, country setting the behaviour of each country will depend on what it expects the other country(s) to do). Such extensions to the targets-instruments model may be seen in the following way. Assume, as in our previous discussion, that we are operating in a two-country world. Each country is assumed to have a national welfare, or utility, function which it seeks to maximize and which is of the form

$$W = W(V)$$

where W represents national welfare and V denotes a vector of targets such as, perhaps, full employment and a low inflation rate. This equation may be thought of as summarizing the ultimate objective of economic policy and these objectives are achieved by the manipulation of the intermediate objectives of policy, namely the policy instruments. In the original Hamada model there is only one instrument and that is monetary policy. Here we do not take a stand on what this instrument is; we merely assume that the government of the country has at its disposal at least one instrument.

The welfare functions of each country define a set of indifference curves and these are illustrated in figure 6.5 as ellipses in I and I^* space, where I denotes the policy instrument (again an asterisk denotes a foreign magnitude). The points of highest utility are denoted B and B* – the bliss points – and as we move out from these points we move to lower levels of utility. The indifference curves have their particular shape because of the potential spillovers from country 1 to country 2. It is worth noting that the key reason that countries can generate outcomes which enable them to get to their bliss points is that they both have the same number of instruments as they have targets. Complete policy independence for the two countries is represented in figure 6.5 by vertical straight line indifference curve for the home country and the horizontal straight line for the foreign country (neither shown). Such policy independence could arise, most obviously, if there are no policy interactions between the two countries. In this case each country could simply manipulate its policy instrument, with no regard to the policies pursued in the foreign country, in order to get to the bliss point. There are, additionally, a number of other justifications for vertical and horizontal reaction functions: when the number of targets is less than or equal to the number of instruments, if the countries are "small" or if the countries have equal preferences (i.e. the non-cooperative outcome is socially optimal).

The points at which the indifference curves are tangential will represent the efficient, or optimal, policies for the two countries, and all such points are represented on the diagram by the contract curve which joins all combinations of bliss points. Since welfare of one country clearly worsens as we move along the contract curve, the points must represent Pareto-optimal policies. Consider now uncoordinated policies conducted by the two countries. Will such policies enable us to get onto the contract curve? Uncoordinated policies in the Hamada diagram may be illustrated using reaction schedules.

The reaction functions may be developed in the following way. If the home country takes the monetary policy of the foreign country as given, represented, say, by the horizontal line at I_0^*, it will set its policy to ensure a tangency between its indifference map and I_0^*. This process will be repeated for each new level of I^* and this will map out a reaction function, R. A similar reaction function may be mapped out for the foreign country for different choices of I, and this is labelled R^* in figure 6.5. Where will the two countries end up on these schedules if they adopt uncoordinated policies? With such policies the countries must in fact end up at the intersection of the two reaction functions. This point represents the uncoordinated equilibrium point, since at this point each country is doing the best it can, assuming that each country operates on the basis that the other country does not react to its policy. This may be seen in the following way. If the home country adjusts it instrument to I_0, the optimal policy for the foreign country will be to choose I_1^*. However, given the foreign country's choice of point A* it will now be optimal for the home country to choose I_1, and so on. This interaction of each country setting its policy on the basis of the other country's policy remaining unchanged will eventually result in point N being achieved.

Point N in figure 6.5 is the analogous Nash point to that discussed in the prisoner's dilemma example above. A different non-cooperative equilibrium would emerge if one of the countries adopted a leadership stance. In this scenario the leader would recognize the effect its policies would have on the other country and take this into account in its actions. If one of the countries were to adopt a leadership stance then it would attempt to get onto its highest possible indifference curve, subject to the reaction function of the other country. Thus if the home country were the leader it would move to point Z, whereas if the foreign country were the leader it would manipulate its instrument to achieve Z*.

These points are optimal for the leader because they are the best attainable, given the range of reactions facing the leader. Maintaining the terminology from the theory of interdependence with oligopoly, points Z and Z* are referred to as Stackelberg non-cooperative equilibria. One recent example of Stackelberg behaviour is the experience of the operation of the exchange rate mechanism (ERM) in the 1980s and 1990s. Thus, Germany was throughout this period prepared to accept leadership of the ERM and this had a profound impact as a result (especially in the events surrounding "Black Wednesday" in 1992). However, this has not led to a proper Stackelberg equilibrium since the follower ERM countries have adopted a very simple (fixed) following rule, rather than optimizing along their reaction functions.

Both the Nash and Stackelberg equilibria are clearly inferior to either of the bliss points and also Pareto inferior to at least some of the coordinated policies lying on the contract curve. Hence the case for policy coordination: by co-operating, at least one of the countries can become better off without the other country becoming worse off.[18] The exact point the two countries end up at on the contract curve depends on the relative bargaining strengths, subject to incentive compatibility. It is worth noting that a full solution of the coordination problem requires a formal bargaining model to determine the optimal bargain (or bargaining strength parameter) endogenously as part of the solution. In the coordination literature it is usual to use a Nash bargaining framework, although there are many other alternatives available in the game theory literature (for example, Hansayni, Kalai–Smorodinski, Rubinstein and Thomson). The relative inferiority of non-cooperative policies has been made in a more general context by Da Cuhna and Polak (1967). In particular, they formally demonstrate that non-cooperation is Pareto inferior to cooperation (provided that incentive compatibility is honored).

A point worth noting regarding the coordination of policies represented by the contract curve is that they do *not* require governments to have the same objectives (Currie, 1990). Indeed, this is captured in the Hamada diagram by the different bliss points (if the two governments had the same objectives they would end up at the same bliss point). More generally, the cooperation does not require governments to have the same preferences (as distinct from objectives).

6.2.3 Policy regimes

Before leaving static game theory models, mention should be made of a model due to Canzoneri and Gray (1985) which highlights how different policy regimes arise as a result of the way the international linkages referred to earlier operate between countries. This model helps to clarify a key element in the coordination literature, namely that the scope for coordination, and the kind of policies required to achieve coordination, depend crucially on the kind of regime in place.

The Canzoneri–Gray model is one consisting of two identical economies with a single (monetary) spillover channel between them and a static decision-making framework.[19] The economies are subject to supply-side shocks and the governments in each country seek to maintain output at full employment levels without increasing inflation. The model may be captured using the equations

$$\hat{y} = \rho_1 \dot{m} + \rho_2 \dot{m}^* + \rho_3 q^* \tag{6.7}$$

$$\hat{y}^* = \rho_1^* \dot{m}^* + \rho_2^* \dot{m} + \rho_3^* q \tag{6.8}$$

where $\hat{y}$ denotes the deviation of output from its full employment level, $\dot{m}$ denotes the change in money supply growth, q is a supply-side shock and an asterisk denotes a foreign variable. If the two domestic money multipliers ρ_1 and ρ_1^* are assumed to be positive, different policy regimes will be determined by the spillover multipliers ρ_2 and ρ_2^*. Three possibilities are considered by Canzoneri and Gray. First, if a monetary expansion in each country has the same negative effect on output in the foreign country (i.e. $\rho_2 = \rho_2^* < 0$) we have the "beggar-thy-neighbor" case referred to earlier in the context of the extended MF model. Second, where the money supply expansion has the same positive effect on output in the other country (i.e. $\rho_2 = \rho_2^* > 0$) we have the "locomotive" case referred to in chapter 4. Third, where monetary spillovers have different signs (i.e. $\rho_2 < 0$, $\rho_2^* > 0$, or $\rho_2 > 0$, $\rho_2^* < 0$) we have the "asymmetric" case. The regimes which we actually observe will clearly be an empirical issue, although little empirical work has been conducted on the signs of spillovers between countries.

■ 6.3 Dynamic Games, and the Sustainability and Reputation Credibility of International Cooperation

As we indicated earlier, the kind of games portrayed in section 6.2 are static in nature; they do not, in particular, capture the intertemporal dimension of policy making and interdependences. In order to capture such aspects, and in particular to highlight the benefits of cooperation, the focus of research in this area has shifted away from static towards dynamic games (see, for example, the papers contained in the volume by Buiter and Marston, 1985). One of the key elements of such games is that they introduce the important issue of time consistency (introduced by Kydland and Prescott, 1977). Time-consistent policies are optimal policies provided that they are actually followed in the future. In contrast, a time inconsistent policy is one which the authorities have an incentive to renege on at some point in the future. The concept may be illustrated in the following way.[20] Consider a government which embarks on a disinflationary macroeconomic policy by tightening monetary policy in the current period and announcing a declining profile of monetary growth rates for a number of periods in the future (much as many OECD governments did in the 1970s – in the UK, the Conservative government's medium-term financial strategy is a classic example). Such a policy may aid the formulation of inflationary expectations on the part of the private sector. For example, if the policy is believed agents may revise their inflationary expectations downwards and the economy may very rapidly move to a new low inflation equilibrium, at very low cost in terms of unemployment (i.e. the economy moves directly down its long-run Phillips curve, rather than initially moving to the right along a short-run Phillips curve). However, at some point in the future, say before an election, the government may be tempted to cheat and depart from its pre-announced monetary reduction and engineer a boom – i.e. to adopt a *time-inconsistent* policy. If the public realizes that the government has an incentive to cheat on the prior announced policy, it may not believe the policy to begin with. Thus the government may have a problem with credibility. In general, lack of credibility will lead to Pareto inferior outcomes. Essentially the intertemporal dimension arises because private sector agents are forward looking (i.e. they have rational expectations, rather than the simple static expectations invoked in the two country MF model).

It is worth emphasizing the distinction between the cheating referred to in the previous paragraph – which may be referred to as time-domain cheating – and the form of cheating referred to earlier in the context of static game theory – player-domain cheating. There is a crucial difference between these two forms of cheating in that with the former the player (the relevant government) gets locked into a particular policy and cannot retaliate once it is cheated against, whilst with the latter the government can retaliate at any stage to cheating. The former type of cheating has a Stackelberg nature because of the lack of a retaliatory instrument after time zero, whilst the latter is a Nash-type problem in player space. Both types of cheating are problems covered by the general concept of reputation and, from a policy coordination perspective, player-domain cheating is likely to be the most important component of reputation.

The issues of time consistency and the reputation of policymakers has particular relevance with respect to the *sustainability* of coordinated policies. Thus in terms of the Hamada diagram, once the countries have agreed on a point on the contract curve there will then be an incentive for one of the countries to renege or cheat on the contract – in other words, to pursue time-inconsistent policies. For example, if, say, the home country believes the other country will maintain its instrument at C (a coordinated equilibrium on the contract curve) it would be in the interests of the home country to move to its reaction function and so obtain a higher level of utility – in this instance the gains from coordination will not be reliable. In order to ensure the coordinated policy is time consistent some method of punishment – either implicit or explicit – has to be devised in order to prevent either country reneging on its commitment to C. This may simply involve each of the countries threatening to revert to the Nash equilibrium if the other country reneges on its promise. In practice, however, it may be the case that one or other of the countries is unable or unwilling to carry out the threat of punishment. More generally this may be seen by means of an example.[21]

If one of the "countries" on the Hamada diagram is Europe, the other being the USA, then in the days of the ERM Europe may find it impossible to threaten the USA. This is because of the desire of EU governments to maintain their currencies within European Monetary System (EMS) bands, which in practice meant that these currencies had targeted the Deutschmark and made their monetary and fiscal polices subservient to this end. Given that German monetary policy had traditionally been geared to a very low inflation rate, and that German fiscal policy (at least until the reunification measures) had been highly constrained by constitutional and other restraints, meant that there were in practice very few degrees of freedom for the European monetary–fiscal mix. Thus with the European monetary-fiscal mix set at C, the USA will perceive Europe's capacity for punishment as being rather limited and so will have an incentive to move to P which gives it a higher level of utility. However, P is clearly Pareto inefficient because it is dominated by the set of efficient points on the arc connecting B and B*.[22]

The issue of reputation may also have an important role to play in negating the potential benefits of cooperation (this point is due to Rogoff, 1985). For example, in an open economy a government without credibility/reputation may be discouraged from engineering positive monetary surprises (as it would be in a closed economy) because of the potential for the exchange rate to depreciate (perhaps dramatically so, if it overshoots), thus rapidly communicating to agents the government's inflationary intentions. Coordination on the part of countries to peg their exchange rates means that this obstacle to monetary expansion is removed and countries could embark on, say, a joint monetary expansion. However, rational private sector wage bargainers will incorporate this extra inflation risk into their decisions (i.e. wage bargaining) and so the average inflation rate will actually rise with cooperation compared with the non-cooperation scenario. Rogoff has suggested that one way of improving the credibility of the authorities in the coordination scenario would be to alter the institutional framework within which they operate (e.g. make the central bank an independent institution responsible for maintaining a zero or very low inflation rate).

An interesting twist to the Rogoff story has been provided by Levine and Currie (1987) and Currie et al. (1987) who demonstrate that, in the absence of coordination, policies which rely on reputation may be undesirable. This is because coordination failures (especially those relating to the exchange rate) that arise from the non-coordination of policies are more likely to be increased when a government has reputation (because it can more readily affect market expectations).

■ 6.4 Some Evidence on the Potential Benefits of Coordination

We have so far discussed the benefits from international policy coordination from a theoretical perspective. In this section we summarize some of the evidence which seeks to quantify whether, in fact, coordinated policies are more desirable than unco-ordinated policies.[23] One of the best known attempts at such quantification is the study by Oudiz and Sachs (1985). They demonstrated, in a static game context, that if the USA, Japan, and Germany had complete coordination of their macroeconomic polices for the period 1984–6, they would have gained one-half of 1 percent of their gross domestic products – a rather minor gain (of course, such a gain could be extremely valuable to a policy-maker who, in the absence of such a gain, would be constrained from undertaking some policy measure which has a large positive effect on his or her country's utility level). In a dynamic game setting, Sachs and McKibben (1985), using a simplified version of the model referred to above, demonstrated that the gains to the developed countries from coordinating their policies in the face of inflationary shocks were small; however, the gains to the developing countries were potentially large. Using different modelling frameworks, Canzoneri and Minford (1986) and Ishii et al. (1985) also confirm the rather limited gains from co-ordination. The reported gains in these studies are in the range 0.5–1.5 percent of GDP (Hughes Hallett (1986) provides a useful breakdown of the sources of the gains).

Hughes Hallett (1987) demonstrates that the USA would have obtained very large gains had it engaged in cooperative policies with the rest of the world since 1974, but other trading blocks would have gained very little. According to Currie et al. (1987) large gains are also to be made in circumstances where time inconsistency is ignored; however, when time-inconsistent policies are not ruled out there is little to be gained from coordination. McKibben and Sachs (1991), using the MSG model referred to earlier, demonstrate that when the coordination of both monetary and fiscal policies is considered the gains from coordination are potentially important, but that when only the coordination of monetary policies is considered the gains are relatively small. This would seem to be an important finding given that, at least in the short term, the adjustment of fiscal policy is often limited by institutional constraints.

The above researchers all assume that there is no uncertainty in the policy-makers' view of the "true model" or how the world economy operates. In a bid to introduce some model uncertainty, Frankel and Rockett (1988) use four different international models[24] to represent four different possible views of the world economy and they consider all possible combinations in which two countries can subscribe to any of the four models, whilst the true state of the world is given by any of the four models. Interestingly, they report that coordination is only welfare improving in a little over half the instances considered. Indeed in over a third of the combinations coordination made at least one of the countries worse off! However, Frankel (1989) demonstrates that this result is crucially dependent on governments not taking into account differences in their views of the world economy when formulating their policies. When they do, Frankel shows that the potential gains from coordination increase dramatically. Also, by using the same model as Frankel and Rockett, Holtham and Hughes Hallett (1987) demonstrate that a much higher proportion of gains can be achieved when cooperative gains in which one government expects the other government to be worse off are ruled out. It is, in fact, likely that governments would rule out such cooperation outcomes because they are the kinds of policies which are most likely to be reneged on. Ghosh and Masson (1988) turn the Frankel and Rockett conclusion on its head by showing that the existence of model uncertainty may in fact considerably increase the benefits of cooperation as long as the governments take the uncertainty into account in their design of coordinated policies.

The above evidence would seem to be rather mixed with respect to the benefits of policy coordination. A couple of papers, however, suggest that the reputational/credibility issues thrown up by the Rogoff point, discussed above, may have an important bearing on the potential benefits of coordination. For example, Currie et al. (1987) demonstrate using the OECD's Interlink model that the benefits of coordination with reputation are insignificant when economic shocks are small in magnitude, but rise substantially when the persistence of such shocks increases. For instance, a 1 percent permanent shock will in the long run yield a gain equivalent to 15 percent of GDP with coordinated policies. Using a selection of international macroeconomic models, Holtham and Hughes Hallett (1987) demonstrate that models which incorporate rational expectations yield the highest benefits with cooperation in the face of permanent shocks (around 4–6 percent of GDP). More specifically, in circumstances where the authorities operate closed loop policies (i.e. policies which are revised in the light of new information on past forecast errors) then coordinated policies are more robust than non-cooperative policies, and the associated gains increase with increasingly large shocks. Hence, as the degree of robustness increases the greater is the uncertainty.[25] This suggests that the potential benefits from policy cooperation with reputation may in fact be considerable.

Another source of uncertainty, which has not been widely addressed in this literature (see, though, Hughes Hallett, 1987) concerns the uncertainty that players have about other players' preferences.

 ## 6.5 Potential Impediments to Policy Coordination and the Appropriate Form of Such Coordination

Our discussion up to now has suggested that the case for international cooperation is, in principle, very strong, although the empirical evidence is somewhat more ambivalent. If there are gains to be had from cooperation, why then do we not observe greater cooperation in the recent floating rate period when the boom–bust cycle of the post-war period seems to have been most dramatic? Perhaps the simplest answer to this is to suggest that because the theory of coordination deals with fully optimal policies which are by their nature highly complex – and the potential gains to be had from such coordination are rather unclear – governments may believe the net benefits of such full-blown coordination to be extremely small. A more practical reason why we have not observed greater co-ordination since the inception of the floating exchange rate regime is simply the immense political difficulties facing governments in reaching agreement about the appropriate form of coordination. Such difficulties may, in turn, arise from differences in preferences, a poor distribution of the potential gains, disagreements over what is important, or simply a reluctance to surrender independence.

Instead of attempting full-blown coordination, governments have opted, as we indicated previously, for a more limited form of coordination through a shared target variable, namely the exchange rate. However, the evidence suggests that this form of coordination generates rather limited gains. For example, given that the gains from full-blown coordination are only of the order of 0.5–1.5 percent of GDP, the gains from a more limited form of coordination are likely to be much smaller (Hughes Hallett et al. (1989) estimate that the gains from coordination through exchange rate targeting are only 10–25 percent of the gains from full coordination). In fact it would probably be extremely difficult to find targeting schemes (even if the appropriate parities were actually known) which are Pareto superior to the best non-cooperative alternative, simply because the small potential gains mean that it would be extremely difficult to control their distribution in order to ensure incentive compatibility.

The fact that coordination has been conducted using exchange rate targets has itself perhaps been an impediment to a more complete form of coordination. This is because such targeting has not always been supported by the appropriate mix of monetary and fiscal polices, which are so central to the theoretical discussion of coordination, and the lack of success of these policies has, in turn, given coordination itself a bad name.

There is also the perennial problem for a macro-policy-maker with respect to what the appropriate policy mix should be to achieve any given objective – thus the well known adage that if a policymaker were to take counsel from a dozen economists each would come up with a different policy recommendation and each would give a different forecast of where the economy will actually be in the future! Such problems are likely to apply *a fortiori* in an international context. Thus, for example, it may be very difficult for governments to quantify the potential spillovers from their policies to the rest of the world and devise and agree on policies which attenuate the effects of such spillovers.

A further impediment to the coordination of policies relates to the freedom with which countries can manipulate their policies in order to make a credible threat to countries which adopt predator beggar-thy-neighbor type policies. This issue was mentioned briefly above when we discussed the sustainability of policies. A good example of this was the adoption of Reaganomics by the USA in the 1980s and the potential impotence of other trading blocs credibly to challenge this policy. Reaganomics entailed a combination of relatively tight monetary policy and lax fiscal policy which, from 1980 to 1985, resulted in a very sharp appreciation of the nominal and real values of the US dollar (the macro-policy mix adopted by Germany in the 1990s would seem to be a rerun, albeit perhaps for different reasons, of the Reagan experiment). The latter allowed the expansion of domestic output to proceed without a damaging explosion of inflation and also, because the USA has a relatively small traded goods sector, did not have a particularly deleterious effect on the output expansion (particularly since international trading companies switched towards supplying the domestic market). Such a policy could be regarded as optimal for the USA on a go-it-alone basis but also if some form of coordination was agreed it may be sensible for the USA to engage in a time-inconsistent manner and adopt such a policy anyway because of the lack of a credible threat from its trading partners (which as we have argued above may in fact be the case for Europe).

What form should coordination take? In practice two types of coordination have been adopted. Rules-based coordination (Currie, 1990) takes the form of regimes such as the gold standard, the Bretton Woods system, and the EMS. In these kinds of regimes rules have to be observed (say, with regard to the maintenance of an exchange rate parity under the Bretton Woods system) and the observation of such rules means that policy coordination is implicit. More explicit forms of coordination involve the kinds of *ad hoc* one-off agreements like the Plaza and Louvre Accords. Such agreements may be thought of as discretionary-based rules. Following Kydland and Prescott (1977), the closed economy rules versus discretion literature emphasized that rule-based policies, because of their reputational advantages, were more attractive than discretionary policies (although the more recent literature – see, for instance, Levine and Currie, 1987 – emphasizes that if discretionary policies are in fact time consistent they may also be expressed in the form of a rule and so the crucial distinction is between rules with and without reputation). Rules-based systems of coordination are also often viewed as offering the advantage of external discipline (this being especially useful perhaps for countries which have a succession of weak-willed governments or a country which has a strong unionized sector). Certainly this was one of the main advantages cited in favor of the ERM of the EMS, especially for countries like Italy and the UK.

Discretionary coordination, being a one-off bargain, however, may have advantages over rules-based systems in that it may be easier to incorporate important asymmetries into the coordination bargain (by their nature, rules-based bargains which may be very long-lived are much more likely to rely on symmetrical behaviour of the participants, although important asymmetries may develop in practice). Also, one-off discretionary deals may have the advantage that countries can bargain over a much wider range of issues than may be possible when setting up a permanent or quasi-permanent rules-based system (Currie (1990) cites the 1978 Bonn agreement as one in which the participants were able to strike a deal over a wide range of policy issues which could not have been struck under a rules-based system).

NOTES

We are very grateful to Andrew Hughes Hallett for his careful and extensive comments on an earlier draft of this chapter. Our stubbornness has perhaps prevented us from incorporating all of his comments into the current draft.

1 However, it is worth noting at this stage that this is simply an illustrative device. If the rest of the world (RoW) does not act as a single unit then we would have to consider the coalition properties of the RoW, introduce some form of Stackelberg leadership model or assume atomistic responses; each of these possibilities would vastly change the outcomes obtained and greatly complicate our discussion.

2 Frenkel and Razin (1988) examine the international transmission effects of fiscal policy in a model which features, *inter alia*, rational expectations and intertemporal budget constraints. A model – due to McKibben and Sachs (1991) – which also captures such features is discussed below; it is worth mentioning at this juncture that such a model comes to very similar conclusions to the basic MF model considered here.

3 As in many other discussions of these issues, we invoke this assumption for simplicity. However, it is important to note that considering symmetric countries may in fact

rule out the main potential gain from policy coordination, namely that countries are non-symmetric – see Hughes Hallett (1986).

4   These points draw on Currie (1990).

5   Such an objective may arise because the authorities may sense strong policy spillovers both from prolonged external disequilibria and from the policy interventions needed to straighten them out. Further, Sachs (1986) has argued that if countries attempt to coordinate policies by stabilizing their exchange rates (see the discussion below) this can result in the destabilization of current account balances; i.e. variability simply gets transferred from the exchange rate to the current account (and perhaps also to other asset prices such as interest rates).

6   Bruno and Sachs (1985) incorporate both demand and supply shocks into the MF model.

7   Two other multi-country descendants of the two-country MF model are the Liverpool model, which is New Classical (see, for example, Minford, 1989; Minford et al., 1986), and the Taylor model, which is New Keynesian (see, for example, J. B. Taylor, 1988). Such models, which incorporate *inter alia* rational expectations, tend to corroborate the results of the MF model although the spillovers are not as strong as suggested by that model.

8   That is, the approach which emphasizes the microeconomic underpinnings of macroeconomics – see Blanchard and Fischer (1989).

9   In particular, the model emphasizes the slow adjustment of wages and prices prevalent in certain countries, and also the European countries are assumed to suffer from hysteresis in unemployment.

10 This is a standard procedure in this class of computable general equilibrium models.

11 In the long run this generates an overall fiscal deficit. However, owing to an induced tax increase this does not violate the government's intertemporal budget constraint – the primary fiscal deficit (i.e. the deficit net of interest payments moves into surplus in the long run).

12 McKibben and Sachs also consider an anticipated fiscal expansion consisting of a gradual fiscal expansion engineered over a three-year period. It turns out that this produces a qualitatively similar picture to the once-for-all permanent expansion.

13 These results, for domestic and foreign output and the external balances, also occur when the expansion takes place in the foreign countries.

14 See Hughes Hallett (1989) for a useful discussion of this paper in the context of the policy coordination literature.

15 The example here is based on that in McKibben and Sachs (1991).

16 In the coordination context, the "cheating solutions" have been studied explicitly by Hughes Hallett (1986). The conclusion of this paper is that, although the possibility to cheat exists, the probability that any player would actually cheat is rather low. This is because the downside risks of retaliation are very high, while the upside gains of a successful cheat are actually rather small: the expected outcome is therefore a loss.

17 Stevenson et al. (1988) present an extensive range of applications of the Hamada diagram.

18 Numerous papers, using static game theory techniques, generally come to the conclusion that the non-cooperative outcome is suboptimal (see, *inter alia*, Hamada, 1979; Canzoneri and Gray, 1985; Corden, 1985; Eichengreen, 1985; Oudiz and Sachs, 1985).

19 The discussion here draws on Hughes Hallett (1989).

20 See MacDonald and Milbourne (1991) for a more extensive discussion.

21 This example draws on Currie (1990).

22 Although the example given in this paragraph is usually interpreted as one of time consistency (see, for example, Currie, 1990) it should perhaps, following the

discussion in the previous paragraph, be more correctly thought of as "player-domain" cheating.

23 A useful survey of this evidence is given by Currie et al. (1989).

24 Each of the models participated in the Brookings model comparison exercise reported in Bryant et al. (1988).

25 This is, in fact, a standard result in the control theory literature.

7

Purchasing Power Parity: Theory and Evidence

Since purchasing power parity (PPP) underlies much of the modern literature on the balance of payments and exchange rate determination (to be discussed in chapters 8–11) and also since it has been viewed as a theory of exchange rate determination in its own right, attention is turned in this chapter to an exposition of the concept and a review of the relevant empirical evidence.

The concept of PPP is generally attributable to Cassel, who formulated the approach in the 1920s. Cassel's theory essentially represents a synthesis of the work of the nineteenth-century economists Ricardo, Wheatley, and Thornton. Put in its most general terms, the PPP doctrine suggests that we should be able to buy the same bundle of goods in any country for the same amount of currency (or, put slightly differently, people value currencies for what they buy). The fundamental notion of the PPP theory is that the exchange rate depends upon price levels and not the other way around. This idea stemmed from the "bullionist controversy" where it was argued that an increase in English money supply had caused sterling's depreciation *vis-à-vis* Continental currencies during the wars against Napoleon. From the beginning, the PPP doctrine was related to a monetary interpretation of the exchange rate (on the genesis of PPP see Myhram, 1976; Frenkel, 1978; Officer, 1982).

The doctrine of PPP can be illustrated by making the distinction between its absolute and relative versions and this is done in the following section. Such versions rely for their derivation on items which appear in the current account of the balance of payments. A more recent version of PPP, labeled "the efficient markets view of PPP," relies on the capital account of the balance of payments, and this is considered in section 7.2. In section 7.3 it is demonstrated that PPP should be regarded as a long-run rather than a short-run concept. Criticisms of the PPP concept are considered in section 7.4 and, finally, in section 7.5 the empirical validity of PPP is examined.

7.1 The Absolute and Relative Purchasing Power Parity Concepts

7.1.1 Law of one price

Let us consider two countries, our own home country and a "foreign" country, where both countries produce only goods which are tradeable, the goods produced in each country are homogeneous (i.e. a washing machine produced in the home country is identical to a unit produced in the foreign country), there are no impediments to international trade, such as tariff barriers and transactions costs, there are no capital flows, the economies are operating at a full employment level and the price system "works." Given these, albeit heroic, assumptions, an important arbitrage condition, the law of one price, must hold:

$$P_t^i = S_t P_t^{i*} \tag{7.1}$$

where P_t^i is the price of good i, the asterisk denotes the foreign country and S_t is the exchange rate defined as the amount of home currency required to buy one unit of foreign currency. Thus, the price of good i in the home country must equal its price in the foreign country multiplied by the foreign exchange rate. Given these assumptions, if equation (7.1) does not hold then it would be profitable for arbitragers to trade.

For example, if P_t^i is for some reason greater than $S_t P_t^{i*}$ it would be profitable for economic agents in the foreign country to buy good i in that country, transport it to the home country and sell it at the higher price. Equally it would be profitable for arbitrageurs in the home country to convert funds into the foreign currency, buy good i in the foreign country and ship it home. This process of arbitrage will continue until it is no longer profitable; i.e. the equality (7.1) is again restored. Transaction costs would modify this result in the sense that they create a "neutral band" within which it is unprofitable to engage in arbitrage. Thus in the presence of transaction costs equation (7.1) would not necessarily hold exactly.

How does the adjustment in the above example take place? If the exchange rate is fixed or pegged, then the price of i will rise in the foreign country and fall at home as the commodity is arbitraged to the home country to restore equality (7.1). If the exchange rate is perfectly flexible then the pressure to convert the home currency into the foreign currency, in order for the home residents to obtain the cheaper foreign good, will cause the exchange rate to depreciate (S to rise). Thus, the price of good i will stay fixed in both countries and equation (7.1) will be restored by an exchange rate change rather than a price level adjustment. Hence under a system of fixed exchange rates PPP can be used to explain the change in reserves caused by changes in international exchange of commodities and under a system of flexible exchange rates it determines the exchange rate.

7.1.2 Absolute purchasing power parity

By rearranging equation (7.1) and summing all prices (using the same weights in constructing each country's price level) the absolute version of PPP is obtained:

$$S_t = \frac{\sum_{i=0}^{n} \alpha^i P_t^i}{\sum_{i=0}^{n} \alpha^i P_t^{i*}} \tag{7.2}$$

where the α terms denote the weights. Hence if the numerator is £50 and the denominator $100 then the pound–dollar exchange rate is £0.50 per dollar (which is the convention adopted here for expressing the exchange rate from the UK's point of view, i.e. with the UK as the "home" country), or $2 = £1, which is the conventional expression of the exchange rate if the USA happened to be the home country.

7.1.3 Relative purchasing power parity

The absolute version of PPP discussed above relates an exchange rate to the absolute price level of all $i = 1, \ldots, n$ traded goods in the two countries. In a period of relatively stable prices, exchange rates would not be expected to change very much. However, in a period of rapid inflation, such as the experience of the 1970s, it is likely that relative national price levels would be changing a lot, and therefore so would the exchange rate. The question is: by how much should an exchange rate change? In practice equation (7.2) is not a particularly useful construct because different countries use different price index weights to calculate price levels, an issue which is discussed in more detail later. Moreover, absolute PPP may not hold if there are restrictions on trade such as tariffs or quotas, if there are transport costs or if there is imperfect information about prices in the two countries. As a matter of practicality the relative PPP theory is used to overcome these problems. Thus, even if countries use different price weighting schemes or if these other factors come into play, as long as the weights and the other factors remain constant over time, changes in relative price levels will be reflected in the relative price indexes. Thus, if we write (7.1) in natural logarithms and drop the i superscript (the Ps now have the interpretation of overall price levels) we obtain

$$\ln S_t = \ln P_t - \ln P_t^* \qquad (7.3)$$

and taking first differences we get the proportionate change in the exchange rate, Δs_t, as a function of the difference in the proportionate changes in home and foreign prices. Thus

$$\Delta s_t = \Delta p_t - \Delta p_t^* \qquad (7.4)$$

where Δ is the first difference operator and $x_t = \ln X_t$.[1] The relative version of PPP simply states that, if relative prices double in the home country between a base period and some subsequent date, the exchange rate will change by an equal proportion, i.e. it will depreciate.[2]

■ 7.2 The Efficient Markets View of Purchasing Power Parity

Our derivation of PPP in section 7.1 relied on current account items, and this is how the approach has traditionally been motivated. Recently, however, a number of researchers have argued that PPP may be thought of in terms of certain parity conditions which relate to the capital account of the balance of payments. We label this approach to PPP the efficient markets view of PPP (EMPPP).[3] As we shall see this approach is at odds with the traditional view of PPP. The following derivation of EMPPP uses some of the parity conditions considered in chapter 3.

The two-country structure of the previous section is maintained. Additionally, it is assumed that each country issues a bond which is assumed to be a perfect substitute for the foreign-currency-denominated bond; uncovered interest parity (UIP) is therefore assummed to hold:

$$\Delta s_{t+1}^e = i_t - i_t^* \qquad (7.5)$$

The nominal interest rates in (7.5) may be decomposed into real and expected inflation components; using the Fisher decomposition:

$$i_t = r + \Delta p_{t+1}^e \qquad (7.6)$$

$$i_t^* = r^* + \Delta p_{t+1}^{e*} \qquad (7.6a)$$

where we assume that the real interest rate in the home and foreign country is constant (see chapter 3, p. 38, for a full description of these equations). On substituting (7.6) and (7.6a) in (7.5) we obtain:

$$\Delta s_{t+1}^e = (r - r^*) + (\Delta p^e - \Delta p^{e*})_{t+1} \qquad (7.7)$$

Now if it is further assumed that real interest rates are equalized across the two countries we may simplify (7.7) to

$$\Delta s^e_{t+1} = (\Delta p^e - \Delta p^{e*})_{t+1} \tag{7.8}$$

Note that equation (7.8) is effectively relative PPP, only the variables are expected, rather than actual, values. To arrive at the EMPPP view of the exchange rate, it is further assumed that expectations are formed rationally. That is, the change in the exchange rate and price levels is given by the following formulations:

$$\Delta s_{t+1} = \Delta s^e_{t+1} + \varepsilon_{t+1}, \tag{7.9}$$

$$\Delta p_{t+1} = \Delta p^e_{t+1} + v_{t+1}, \tag{7.10}$$

$$\Delta p^*_{t+1} = \Delta p^{e*}_{t+1} + v^*_{t+1}, \tag{7.11}$$

where the last term in each of these equations is an independently distributed random variable. On using equations (7.9)–(7.11) in (7.8) we obtain

$$\Delta s_{t+1} - \Delta p_{t+1} + \Delta p^*_{t+1} = \gamma_{t+1}, \quad \gamma_{t+1} = \varepsilon_{t+1} - v_{t+1} + v^*_{t+1}, \tag{7.12}$$

or

$$\Delta q_{t+1} = \gamma_{t+1}, \tag{7.12a}$$

or

$$q_{t+1} = q_t + \gamma_{t+1}, \tag{7.12b}$$

where q is the real exchange rate ($q \equiv S - P + P^*$). In words, (7.12) simply says that the real exchange rate follows a random walk. Thus the best prediction of the real exchange rate in any future period is simply today's real exchange rate. This has the very important implication that anything which pushes the nominal exchange rate away from its PPP rate (i.e. anything which causes a real exchange rate change) will be *permanent*: it will last into the indefinite future. This view of the determination of the real exchange rate is fundamentally at odds with the traditional view of PPP. Thus, and as we indicate in more detail in the following sections, a proponent of PPP (such as Cassel), whilst accepting that the nominal exchange rate may deviate from its PPP value in the short term, would argue that in the long run the nominal rate would return to its PPP value which, in turn, has the implication that real exchange rates will be mean reverting. The time-series properties of the real exchange rate are therefore crucially important in any attempt at discerning the validity of PPP. We shall discuss the empirical evidence on EMPPP in section 7.5.

Before considering such evidence, however, one criticism of EMPPP is worth elaborating; i.e. that it effectively ignores the distinction between the current and capital accounts of the balance of payments. So a real exchange rate appreciation that causes a current account deficit implies that it is financed by a capital account surplus (inflow). As such an inflow cannot carry on indefinitely – i.e. net foreign indebtedness cannot go to infinity – the real exchange rate must eventually revert to a level which balances the current account.

7.3 Further Interpretation of Purchasing Power Parity

The choice of appropriate price indexes to be used in the calculation of the PPP exchange rate amounts to much more than a ticklish technical detail. The matter has deep theoretical connotations. If the exchange rate is viewed as the relative price of traded commodities, as with the "law of one price" and in equations (7.1) and (7.2), the appropriate price indexes should include only traded goods. Proponents of this view include Angell (1926), Heckscher (1930), and Ohlin (1967). However, an alternative view, currently a focus of attention in exchange rate theory, is that the exchange rate, as an asset price, is the relative price of two monies (early proponents here include Hawtrey, 1919; Cassel 1928). In this case, since the value of money is the reciprocal of the general price level, the appropriate price index is the broadest one available – the gross national product (GNP) deflator if available, or, at least, the consumer price index.

If the exchange rate is viewed as an asset price and a broad price level index is adopted it will include both traded and non-traded goods and services and this will introduce some further complications. Perhaps the most important of these is that the traded goods PPP exchange rate (e.g. equation (7.1) or (7.2)) may no longer be the ruling exchange rate even if commodity arbitrage is perfect. In particular, at the very least this is a short-run problem (and it is a "problem" because of the effects on a country's trade flows and its economic activity in general). The essential reason why some goods or services are non-traded internationally is that they have to be consumed at the point of purchase and thus there are normally very high transaction costs facing a foreign resident wishing to purchase a service in the other country (e.g. consider the case of a US resident wishing to purchase a UK haircut). Moreover, the dividing line between traded and non-traded goods is fuzzy and continually changing.

However, the traded–non-traded goods issue is not necessarily seen as a problem for the computation of a PPP exchange rate because their prices may be linked by a variety of mechanisms (e.g. some traded goods serve as inputs into non-traded goods and vice versa; traded and non-traded goods may be produced by common factors of production; and traded and non-traded goods may be direct or indirect substitutes in consumption). The issue of traded and non-traded goods will be returned to below where it will be argued that it can create problems for the computation of PPP exchange rates – especially between countries at widely different levels of per capita income.

It may be questioned whether PPP should hold continuously. In fact few proponents of PPP would argue for a strict acceptance of PPP at all points of time.

Rather PPP is seen as determining the exchange rate in the long run and a variety of other factors may influence the exchange rate in conditions of short-run disequilibrium. Thus, assume that the "long-run," or equilibrium, exchange rate $\bar{S}$ between two currencies is determined by absolute PPP, namely

$$\bar{S}_t = \frac{P_t}{P_t^*} \tag{7.13}$$

but in the short run the actual exchange rate S may diverge from the long-run rate owing to the influence of other factors,

$$S_t = g(\bar{S}_t, X_t^i \dots X_t^n) \tag{7.14}$$

where $X_t^i \dots X_t^n$ represents the potential influences on the short-run exchange rate. What are these influences?

Basically the PPP doctrine captured in equation (7.2) or (7.3) asserts that currencies are demanded for transaction purposes, i.e. current account transactions. But capital account items are an important component of the balance of payments and often dominate current account transactions. Although capital accounts have been introduced in defining intertemporal PPP, notice that in equilibrium it is implicitly assumed that the reason agents hold bonds is to finance expected future transactions (i.e. they are a hedge against expected inflation).

Thus, for example, as will be shown in detail later, the current exchange rate may be influenced by expected future monetary developments in a country (see chapter 9 on the monetary approach to the exchange rate), so the exchange rate may move ahead of price developments – equation (7.1) or (7.2) will not then hold. Or, again, as in the Dornbusch (1976a) exchange rate "overshooting" model, exchange rates may jump about, overshooting their long-run values and only through a price level adjustment process extended over time eventually reaching their long-run levels. Indeed, De Grauwe (1989) identifies the overshooting phenomenon as the main reason why exchange rates may not be at equilibrium levels in the short run.

In addition to capital account transactions motivated by interest differentials, Cassel also recognized the importance of central bank intervention in keeping an exchange rate away from its PPP defined level (see, for example, Officer (1976) for a discussion of this point). However, a traditional proponent of PPP, such as Cassel, although recognizing the importance of short-run deviations from PPP, would nevertheless argue that in the "long-run" PPP will hold. A useful way of summarizing this traditional, or Casselian, view of PPP is to say that, in contrast to the prediction of the EMPPP, real exchange rates should be mean-reverting:

$$q_t = \alpha + \rho q_{t-1} + \omega_t, \qquad 0 < \rho < 1, \tag{7.12c}$$

where ρ is the parameter of mean reversion and ω_t is a random term. As long as ρ is some positive fraction, a shock or disturbance to the real exchange rate will eventually be offset (and the currency will return to a PPP-defined level).

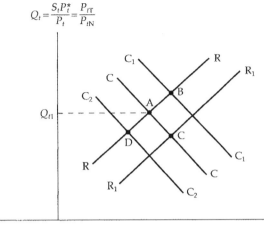

$$Q_t = \frac{S_t P_t^*}{P_t} = \frac{P_{tT}}{P_{tN}}$$

T/N
Ratio of traded to
non traded goods
in production (R) and
consumption (C)

Figure 7.1 Shocks to the equilibrium real exchange rate

To discuss **long-run factors affecting PPP** we will use the concept of the real exchange rate, Q, which was defined in section 4.2 as

$$Q_t = S_t P_t^*/P_t = P_{tT}/P_{tN} \tag{7.15}$$

where, it will be recalled, P_T and P_N are, respectively, the domestic prices of traded and nontraded goods, and we have added a time subscript, t. Thus, as $S_t = Q_t P_t / P_t^*$, S_t is determined alone by the ratio of domestic-to-foreign price levels only if Q_t is constant. However, as we are about to see, there are many factors which might impact a country's *equilibrium* real exchange rate – which we analyze using figure 7.1.

In figure 7.1 RR shows the ratio of traded to nontraded goods in domestic production as an increasing function of P_{tT}/P_{tN} (due to higher relative profitability in T goods); and CC shows the ratio of traded to non-traded goods in consumption as a decreasing function of the real exchange rate (due to the increasing relative price of T). The equilibrium real exchange rate is determined at Q_{t1} where excess demand for both goods is eliminated. Clearly, the equilibrium P_{tT}/P_{tN} and Q_t changes if the RR and CC functions shift relative to one another, and there are many factors which can cause this to happen. For example:

1   Tariffs, quotas and other restrictions on imports increase the relative profitability of traded goods so shifting RR to R_1R_1 and appreciating the equilibrium real exchange rate at point C.
2   A natural resource discovery such as North Sea oil and gas in the UK, Norway, and the Netherlands during the 1960s and '70s. Treating such natural

resources as a traded good, again the ratio of traded to non-traded goods in production increases and the real exchange rate appreciates at point C.

3   A faster rate of productivity growth in the traded goods sector relative to both domestic non-traded goods and foreign traded goods; for example, Japan, Korea, Germany for prolonged periods since end-WWII. Again RR shifts to the right and the equilibrium real exchange rate appreciates.

4   A change in domestic consumer preferences towards traded goods – so shifting CC to C_1C_1 and depreciating the equilibrium Q at point B.

5   Quite the opposite to the last point is that home demand growth may be biased towards non-traded goods. Genberg (1978) suggests that this might occur if the share of government spending in GDP increases – which of course it did in many countries during the 1960s, '70s and '80s – and government spending itself is more biased to non-traded goods than is private spending. In this case CC shifts to the left to C_2C_2, and the equilibrium real exchange rate appreciates.

6   The home country accumulates net foreign assets (a point considered in chapter 11) which allows it to enjoy interest income from the foreign country. The real exchange rate appreciates even though RR and CC remain in place. The resulting payments deficit is financed by the interest income. Contrawise, an increase in net foreign indebtedness requires a payments surplus on goods account in order to service the foreign debt. The real exchange rate must depreciate.

Biased productivity: the Balassa–Samuelson thesis

Furthermore, a problem arises when applying PPP to calculate an exchange rate between a developed country (DC) and a less developed country (LDC): a systematic divergence appears between the bilateral nominal and real exchange rates. This problem is known as the Balassa–Samuelson thesis. It depends on the supposition that traded goods prices determine the equilibrium exchange rate (i.e. $S_t = P_t^T/P_t^{T*}$ which represents a "balance of payments view" as the exchange rate is determined by the flow supply and demand for foreign currency); that both the DC and the LDC produce traded and non-traded goods; that wages are equalized between sectors because of the labour mobility (but not between countries); and, as Balassa (1964) observed, that productivity is higher in the traded goods sector of the DC compared with the LDC while productivity levels are similar in their respective non-traded goods sectors (the reason for this will be discussed in more detail below). An essential implication of the latter two assumptions is that, measured in a common currency, non-traded goods prices will be lower in the LDC than in the DC while traded goods prices will be equal to each other. As a result, a weighted averaged basket of traded and non-traded goods will be cheaper in the lower wage country – the LDC. Given that the nominal exchange rate is taken as being determined by the relative prices of traded goods, there will be a divergence between the nominal and real exchange rates. From the DC's point of view, the nominal exchange rate is weaker than the real exchange rate, i.e. the real exchange rate is appreciated relative to the nominal exchange rate. Its currency has greater purchasing power over a broad basket of the LDC's goods than over a basket containing only traded goods. Given the productivity differences, this result follows because of the generally lower level of wages in the LDC.

To demonstrate this argument suppose that

$$P_t^T = \frac{W_t^T}{X_t^T} \quad \text{and} \quad P_t^{T*} = \frac{W_t^{T*}}{X_t^{T*}} \tag{7.16}$$

$$P_t^{NT} = \frac{W_t^{NT}}{X_t^{NT}} \quad \text{and} \quad P_t^{NT*} = \frac{W_t^{NT*}}{X_t^{NT*}} \tag{7.17}$$

$$W_t^T = W_t^{NT} \quad \text{and} \quad W_t^{T*} = W_t^{NT*} \tag{7.18}$$

Equations (7.16) and (7.17) are a simple microeconomic definition of price as dependent upon production costs, constituted by wages W_t and the average productivity of labour X_t. Equation (7.18) says that wages are equalized in the respective sectors of each country as homogeneous labour is assumed to be perfectly mobile between the sectors within a country. The key assumption in this argument is that $X_t^{NT} = X_t^{NT*}$, which is made on the basis that many non-traded goods are services and international productivity differences here are generally not very great (e.g. a barber's productivity is likely to be fairly invariant between countries). However, $X_t^T > X_t^{T*}$ reflecting the idea that rich countries are so because of their higher labor productivity and that most of this advantage resides in traded goods sectors such as manufacturing. An implication of these features is that the ratio of prices of non-traded goods to traded goods is higher in a DC than in an LDC. The deduction is supported empirically by Kravis and Lipsey (1983).

To go further we need to convert all prices into a common currency, using the nominal exchange rate S_t to do so. Here it will be assumed that the "home" country is the DC, the "foreign" country the LDC and S_t, as usual, is expressed in terms of "home" currency per unit of foreign currency. The price indexes in the two countries are as follows:

DC's price index $\quad\quad P_t = aP_t^T + (1 - a)P_t^{NT}$ \hfill (7.19)

LDC's price index $\quad\quad P_t^* = aP_t^{T*} + (1 - a)P_t^{NT*}$ \hfill (7.20)

where a is the share of traded goods in the price index which, for convenience, is assumed to be common to both countries. Now, it will be recalled from equation (7.15) that the real exchange rate is $Q_t = S_t P_t^*/P_t$. Substituting (7.19) and (7.20) into this equation and distributing the S_t term we get

$$Q_t = \frac{aS_t P_t^{T*} + (1 - a)S_t P_t^{NT*}}{aP_t^T + (1 - a)P_t^{NT}} \tag{7.21}$$

But we know that $P_t^T = S_t P_t^{T*}$ by commodity arbitrage and that $P_t^{NT} > S_t P_t^{NT*}$ because of lower wages (but the same productivity) in the LDC compared with the DC. So in equation (7.21) it must be that Q_t is less than unity (as can be demonstrated by fitting some representative numbers in equation (7.21); e.g. let $P_t^T = S_t P_t^{T*} = 10$, $P_t^{NT} = 6$, $S_t P_t^{NT*} = 2$ and $a = 1/2$; then $Q_t = 3/4$).

What then is the relationship between the DC's bilateral nominal and real exchange rates *vis-à-vis* the LDC? The Balassa–Samuelson thesis assumes that the nominal exchange rate is determined by commodity arbitrage in the traded goods sector: namely $S_t^T = P_t^T / P_t^{T*}$ where Q_t is implicitly assumed equal to unity. But from equation (7.21) we have found that Q_t is less than unity if the real purchasing power of currencies over a broad basket of goods (i.e. including both traded and non-traded) is to be equalized. Hence, the nominal exchange rate, as determined by traded goods prices, exceeds the real exchange rate. The real exchange rate is lower than the nominal rate, i.e. has appreciated.

An implication of this divergence between nominal and real exchange rates is that a given sum of dollars (taking the USA as the DC) converted into an LDC local currency at the nominal exchange rate will buy a larger basket of commodities and services than can be bought at home. This is contrary to the PPP doctrine as this asserts that a dollar converted at the PPP nominal exchange rate should buy the same amount of real goods and services in the two countries.

A second implication is that the correct way to compare per capita incomes is not through exchange rate conversions, for the nominal exchange rate does not reflect the true real purchasing power of currencies. Rather, per capita incomes should be compared at the real exchange rate Q_t. Thus, the commodity and service items which appear in the US price index should be calculated at the LDC's domestic prices, as Kravis (1978) has done; or the items in the LDC's price index should be valued in US dollars. If the former, the price of American non-traded goods will be reduced to the LDC's level. And in the second case, the value of the LDC's non-traded goods will be raised to the American level. Either way, the LDC's per capita income will be raised relative to the USA's.

If a developing country grows more quickly than a developed country its real exchange rate appreciates relative to the developed country. Catching up most likely occurs because of increased labor productivity growth in the developing country's traded goods sector. This is shown in figure 7.2a by its production possibility frontier (PPF) shifting outward in a biased fashion – moving up the traded goods axis more than it does the non-traded axis. Thus, using the model of real exchange rate determination introduced in section 4.2, at an unchanged real exchange rate, Q_1, $T_2/N_2 > T_1/N_1$, the RR function in figure 7.2b shifts to the right, appreciating the real exchange rate.

As an income effect follows from the outward shift of the PPF, depending on the increase in real income and the size of the income elasticities for traded and non-traded goods, the CC function shifts and this too will affect Q. If the income elasticity of demand for N goods is greater than for T goods, CC shifts to the left and the appreciation of Q is magnified.

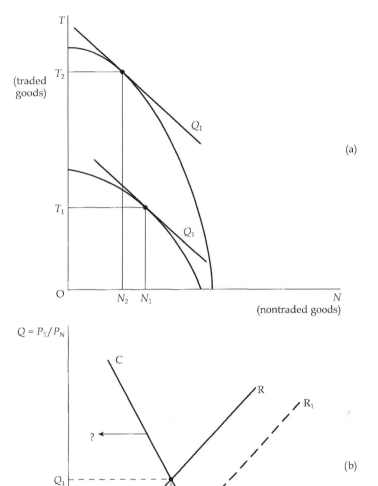

Figure 7.2 Narrowing productivity differentials and the Balassa–Samuelson theorem

7.4 The Empirical Validity of Purchasing Power Parity

This section considers some of the empirical evidence which tests the validity of PPP when exchange rates are flexible (the existence of PPP under fixed exchange rates is considered in chapter 8). The section is in two parts, corresponding to two levels of technical difficulty. The first part discusses some simple, non-regression-based, tests of PPP. The second part covers certain regression-based studies and studies which examine the time series properties of real exchange rates.

7.4.1 A comparison of real and nominal exchange rates and tests of the law of one price

In figures 7.3–7.5 the relationships between the nominal and real exchange rates for a selection of currencies (the real exchange rate is defined as $Q_t = S_t P_t^*/P_t$) are shown. On strict PPP grounds (i.e. the relationship considered in section 7.1) it is expected that the real exchange rate is independent of the nominal exchange rate. If, however, factors such as those described in section 7.3 have an independent effect on the exchange rate, it is expected that nominal exchange rate changes will result in real exchange rate changes. Which view does the evidence support? In figure 7.3 the logarithm of the UK pound–US dollar nominal

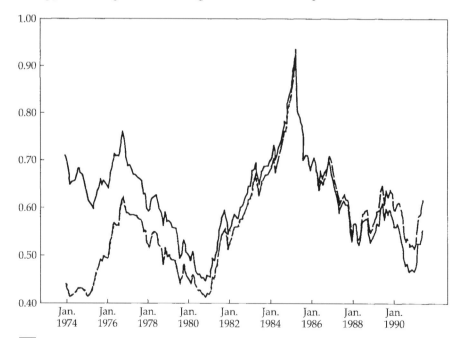

Figure 7.3 Sterling–dollar real and nominal exchange rates: —, real; ---, nominal

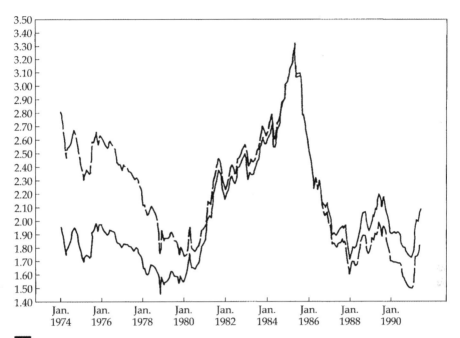

Figure 7.4 Deutschmark–dollar real nominal exchange rates: —, real; ---, nominal

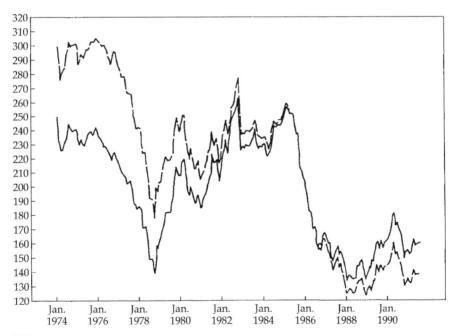

Figure 7.5 Japanese yen–dollar real and nominal exchange rates: —, real; ---, nominal

and real exchange rates is presented, where the latter has been calculated using consumer price indexes. It is clear that, for the period considered, nominal and real exchange rates move closely together. Thus, the nominal appreciation of the sterling rate from mid-1976 to 1980 is seen to be also a real appreciation and the nominal depreciation of the exchange rate thereafter is seen to be also a real depreciation. (This pattern also holds when wholesale price indexes are used, instead of consumer price indexes.) Notice that the close correlation between real and nominal exchange rates is borne out by the other dollar bilateral exchange rates considered – see figures 7.4 and 7.5. The broad conclusion from this evidence would be that attention needs to be focused on the factors which push the nominal exchange rate away from its PPP value (this is the topic of chapters 9 and 10).

One of the crucial assumptions underlying the derivation of the law of one price defined in section 7.1 was that traded goods are homogeneous. That is, a UK-produced unit of any good is identical to a US-produced unit. The empirical evidence strongly suggests, however, that, with the exception of agricultural and natural resource commodities, goods entering international trade are not close substitutes. For example, Isard (1977) takes the most disaggregated groupings of manufactured goods for which US, German, and Japanese prices are readily available (wholesale and export prices) and finds that for the period 1970–5 the law of one price fails to hold. Thus it is impossible to construct aggregate price indexes, such as in equation (7.2) above, which would be expected to obey the law of one price.

*7.4.2 Regression-based tests of purchasing power parity and the time-series properties of the real exchange rate

One extremely popular way of testing PPP has involved the use of regression analysis. For example, Frenkel (1978, 1981b) presents regression estimates of absolute and relative PPP based on a selection of aggregate price indexes for the interwar period and recent experience with floating exchange rates. The equations estimated are of the following form:

absolute PPP $\qquad \ln s_t = \alpha + \beta \ln p_t + \beta^* \ln p_t^* + u_t$ $\qquad$ (7.22)

relative PPP $\qquad \ln \Delta s_t = \beta \ln \Delta p_t + \beta^* \ln \Delta p_t^* + v_t$ $\qquad$ (7.23)

where u_t and v_t are disturbance terms. If PPP holds, it is expected that $\beta = 1$ and $\beta^* = -1$ and, in (7.23), the constant is equal to zero. Frenkel (1978) presents estimates of equations (7.22) and (7.23) for the dollar–pound, franc–dollar, and franc–pound exchange rates using the ratio of material prices indexes, the ratio of food price indexes and the ratio of wholesale price indexes for the period from February 1921 to May 1925. Frenkel's results are highly supportive of the PPP hypothesis in both the absolute and relative versions. Thus, in the majority of cases the hypothesis that $\beta = 1$ and $\beta^* = -1$ cannot be rejected at the usual significance levels. In the relative PPP case, the inclusion of a constant term is shown to be statistically insignificant.

However, when equations (7.22) and (7.23) are estimated by Frenkel (1981a) using data (wholesale and cost of living indexes) from the recent floating exchange rate experience for the dollar–pound, dollar–French franc and dollar–deutschmark exchange rates, it is shown that PPP in both its relative and absolute versions is not supported by the data. Results similar to Frenkel's are reported by Krugman (1978) for both the interwar and the recent floating experience. Krugman concludes: "There is some evidence then that there is more to exchange rates than PPP. This evidence is that the deviations of exchange rates from PPP are large, fairly persistent, and seem to be larger in countries with unstable monetary policy." (This point is picked up in chapters 9–12.) De Grauwe (1996) also points to the failure of PPP in the 1970s and 1980s and presents evidence showing the real exchange rate to "wander" with little or no tendency to move towards a long-run equilibrium level. His main explanation for this is the lack of a "nominal anchor" against which expectations can be measured, so giving a basis against which to measure long-run nominal and real exchange rates.

More recent tests of PPP have exploited important contemporary developments in the econometrics literature, particularly unit root testing and cointegration methods. Since these tests have generated a huge volume of new and important results, we attempt to provide a summary of the salient findings. There are basically two groups of tests in this recent literature. The first focuses on the time series properties of the real exchange rate, while the second uses cointegration methods to assess if there is an equilibrium relationship between *nominal* exchange rates and relative prices. Consider the real exchange rate tests first.

7.4.3 Real exchange rates and mean reversion

As we have seen the Casselian form of PPP predicts that real exchange rates should be mean-reverting, as in equation (7.12c). In the Casselian view the speed of mean reversion was seen as being relatively rapid, taking about two years in total. The degree of mean-reversion is usually summarized by the so-called half-life; that is, how long it takes for one-half of a disturbance to the real exchange rate to be extinguished. The formula for the half-life is:

$$\ln 0.5 / \ln (1 + \rho).$$

As we shall demonstrate, much of the recent literature on PPP reports half-lives which are regarded as being too slow to be consistent with traditional PPP. As we noted in section 7.2, a view diametrically opposite to traditional PPP is that of EMPPP, which suggests that shock to the real exchange rate should have a permanent effect – real exchange rates should follow a random walk as in expression (7.12b). The simplest way of trying to discriminate between these two hypotheses is to test if real exchange rates are non-stationary, against the alternative that it is mean-reverting.

7.4.4 Testing for unit roots in real exchange rates

In testing the null hypothesis of (7.12b) against (7.12c), the base-line test has involved a simple application of an augmented Dickey–Fuller statistic:

$$\Delta q_t = \gamma_0 + \gamma_1 t + \gamma_2 q_{t-1} + \sum_{j=1}^{n-1} \beta_j \Delta q_{t-j} + v_t. \qquad (7.24)$$

This kind of test has been implemented on a variety of real exchange rate data sets by numerous researchers (see *inter alia* Roll, 1979; Darby, 1980; MacDonald, 1985; Enders, 1988; and Mark 1990). The typical coefficient of mean reversion in these papers is often found to be around 0.97, which is statistically indistinguishable from unity. Such evidence would seem to be supportive of EMPPP and unsupportive of traditional PPP. However, as Campbell and Perron (1991), and others, have noted univariate unit root tests have relatively low power to reject the null when it is in fact false, especially when the autoregressive component is close to unity (which it often is with time-series data).

In an attempt to overturn the unit root result, alternative tests have therefore been adopted. The variance ratio test, popularized by Cochrane (1988), is potentially a more powerful way of assessing the unit root characteristics of series, since it can capture the long autocorrelations which are unlikely to be picked up in a standard ADF tests (and which will be important for driving mean reversion). If we take as the null hypothesis that the real exchange rate follows a random walk then the variance of the k'th difference should equal k times the first difference. That is,

$$Var(q_t - q_{t-k}) = kVar(q_t - q_{t-1}), \qquad (7.25)$$

or

$$V_k = (1/k).[(Var(q_t - q_{t-k})).(Var(q_t - q_{t-1}))^{-1}] = 1,$$

where V_k denotes the variance ratio, based on lag k. If the estimated value of V_k is unity then the real exchange rate follows a random walk. However, if the estimated value of V_k is less than one the real exchange rate is stationary or mean-reverting. An estimated value of V_k above one indicates that the series exhibits some kind of "super-persistence."

Huizinga (1987) calculates the variance ratio test for ten (industrial) currencies with k equal to a maximum of 120 months. He finds that the average estimated value of V_k is approximately 0.6, which is indicative of mean reversion; however, on the basis of standard errors, constructed using the standard $T^{1/2}$ formula, none of the estimated variance ratios are significantly below one. Glen (1992) and MacDonald (1995b and c) demonstrate that on using Lo and MacKinlay (1988) standard errors, which are robust to serially correlated and heterogeneous errors, significant rejections of a unitary variance ratio may be obtained, but the extent of any mean reversion is still painfully slow. For example, on the basis of WPI constructed real exchange rates MacDonald finds that the Swiss franc, pound sterling and Japanese yen all have variance ratios which are approximately 0.5 after 12 years (and these values are significantly less than unity). So on a single currency basis for the recent float the evidence noted here suggests that adjustment to PPP is painfully slow.

7.4.5 The power of unit root tests and the span of the data

On natural response to the finding of slow mean reversion observed in real exchange rate behavior, for the recent float, is to increase the power of the tests by increasing the span of the data. In so doing, it is not sufficient, as Shiller and Perron (1985) have indicated, merely to increase the observational frequency by say moving to a higher frequency data set (from quarterly to, say, monthly observations). Rather, it is important to increase the span of the data using low frequency observations, i.e. annual data, which will have a higher signal-to-nose ratio. In other words, the test should give the exchange rates a greater opportunity of returning to its mean value.

For example, assume that the estimated value of ρ is 0.85, and its estimated asymptotic standard error is $[(1 - \rho^2)/X]^{1/2}$, where X equals the total number of observations. Using 23 years of annual data the standard error would be approximately 0.11, with an implied t-ratio which is insufficient to reject the null of a unit root (i.e. the t-ratio for the hypothesis $\rho = 1$ is 1.34). However, with 100 annual observations the standard error falls to 0.05, implying a t-ratio for the hypothesis $\rho = 1$ of 6.8.[4] Defining $X = N.T$, where T denotes the and N denotes the number of cross-sectional units, then this example makes clear that by expanding the span in a time-series dimension increases the likelihood of rejecting the null of a unit root. The span may also be increased by holding T constant and increasing N. We now consider each of these alternatives.

In terms of the former method, a number of researchers have examined the mean-reverting properties of real exchange rates using approximately 100 years of annual data and find evidence of significant mean reversion with an average half-life across these studies being around four years (see Edison, 1987; Frankel, 1986, 1988; Abuaf and Jorion, 1990; Grilli and Kaminski, 1991; and Lothian and Taylor, 1995). Diebold, Husted, and Rush (1991) also use long time spans of annual data, ranging from 74 to 123 years, to analyze the real exchange rates of six countries. In contrast to other long time-span studies, the authors use long memory models to capture fractional integration processes. They find considerable evidence that PPP holds as a long-run concept and report a typical half-life of three years.

Although studies which extend the span by increasing T are interesting, they are not without their own specific problems in that the basket used to construct the price indices is likely to be very different at the beginning and end of the sample. This problem may be viewed as the temporal analogue to the spatial problem that arises in comparing price indices at a particular point in time. Also, such studies suffer from spanning both fixed and flexible rate regimes and are therefore not regime invariant. For these reasons, attention has turned from expanding T to extending N, the cross-sectional dimension.

In particular, researchers have turned to analyzing the behavior of real exchange rates in the recent floating period using panel data sets. A standard panel framework is:

$$s_{it} = \alpha_i + \beta'(p_{it} - p^*_{it}) + \{\Sigma_i \gamma_i D_i\} + \{\Sigma_t \delta_t D_t\} + u_{it}, \qquad (7.26)$$

where the i subscript indicates that the data has a cross sectional dimension (running from 1 to N), D_i and D_t denote, respectively, country-specific and time-specific fixed effect dummy variables (although not noted here it is straightforward to incorporate random effects into (7.26)). In a standard panel setting a number of modeling strategies are available for the disturbance term: it may be assumed to be random, heteroscedastic, autoregressive (with either common autoregressive terms across individual panel members or different autoregressive terms across members), it may be spatially correlated or some combination of these assumptions may be used. The earliest application of panel methods to testing PPP was Hakkio (1984) who used a monthly data set; the first paper to combine panel methods with annual data in a PPP test was MacDonald (1988b). These papers used conventional panel methods, such as the Kmenta estimator. The more recent panel exchange rate literature has involved testing for the stationarity of the residual series in (7.26) or reparameterizing the equation into an expression for the real exchange rate and testing the panel unit root properties of real exchange rates. In term of the latter, a rapidly growing literature has been inspired by the work of Levin and Lin (1992, 1994) who demonstrated that there are "dramatic improvements in statistical power" from implementing a unit root test in a panel context, rather than performing separate tests on the individual series.

The Levin and Lin approach involves testing the null hypothesis that each individual series is I(1) against the alternative that all of the series as a panel are stationary. Their approach allows for a range of individual-specific effects and also for cross-sectional dependence by the subtraction of cross-sectional time dummies. Frankel and Rose (1995), Wu (1996), Oh (1996) and MacDonald (1995b) have all implemented variants of the Levin and Lin panel unit root test on "overall" price measures (such as WPI and CPI) and find evidence of mean reversion which is very similar to that reported in long time spans of annual data, namely half-lives of four years. Another feature of these studies, which is quite similar to the long time-span studies, is the finding of price homogeneity when PPP is tested in a panel context using nominal exchange rates and relative prices. Oh (1996) and Wei and Parsley (1995) have examined the unit root properties of panel data for the Summers–Heston data set and tradable sectors, respectively, and report similar results to those based on aggregate data.[5]

Bayoumi and MacDonald (1998) examine the panel unit root properties of inter- and intra-national exchange rates. The former are defined for a panel of CPI and WPI based real exchange rates for 20 countries, over the period 1973 to 1993, while the intra-national data sets are constructed from Canadian regional and US federal data for the same period and the same number of real rates. The argument in the paper is that if indeed the predominant source of international real exchange rate movements is monetary in origin, observed mean reversion should be more rapid in international data than in intra-national data because monetary shocks are transitory relative to real shocks. This is in fact borne out by the panel data sets: for the international data set there is clear evidence of stationarity on the basis of the Levin and Lin test, while for the intra-national panel sets real rates are non-stationary and only very slowly mean-reverting.

One feature of recent PPP tests, involving either real or nominal exchange rates, is that they work better for DM-based bilaterals than US dollar bilaterals.[6] For example, this has been confirmed in a panel context by Jorion and Sweeney (1996) and Pappell (1997), who both report strong rejections of the unit root null (CPI) based real exchange rates when the DM is used as the numeraire currency, and also by Wei and Parsley (1995) and Canzoneri, Cumby and Diba (1996) using tradable prices. There are a number of factors to which the superior performance of PPP may be attributed when DM-based bilaterals are used. First, the existence of the ERM has attenuated the volatility of DM bilaterals relative to US dollar bilaterals, thereby producing a higher signal-to-noise ratio. Second, the geographical proximity of European countries facilitates greater goods arbitrage and therefore makes it more likely that PPP will occur. Third, the openness of European countries, in terms of their trade making up a greater proportion of their collective national output than in the US, means that PPP is more likely to hold when using measured price series. Lothian (1997) has given another reason why US dollar bilaterals are likely to work less well in a panel context than DM rates. He argues that the former are dominated by the dramatic appreciation and depreciation of the dollar in the 1980s (therefore the informational content of adding in extra currencies is less for a dollar-based system than a mark-based system).[7]

Pappell and Theodoridis (1997) attempt to discriminate amongst the potential reasons for the better performance of DM rates by taking measures of three of the potential candidates mentioned above: volatility, openness, and distance. Using a panel data base constructed for 21 industrialized countries, over the period 1973 to 1996, they find that it is both volatility and distance which are the significant determinants of this result; openness to trade proves to be insignificant. Pappell and Theodoris have also confirmed the Lothian prediction: evidence in favor of PPP for US dollar bilaterals strengthens the more post-1985 data included in the sample period.

Despite recent criticisms of panel unit root tests, we believe the evidence in this section indicates that when the span of the data sample is extended – either in a cross-sectional or time-series dimension – the power of unit root tests increases significantly (as does the size of the tests). *The stylized result is for half of a disturbance to PPP to be reversed after around four years.* Although such adjustment is reassuring for a believer in PPP, it is nevertheless probably still too long to be consistent with a traditional form of PPP. As we have noted, Cassel interpreted a half-life of about one year as consistent with a traditional form of PPP. Rogoff (1995) has referred to slow adjustment speeds in PPP calculations as the "PPP puzzle." How might this "puzzle" be explained? One obvious explanation is simply to say that there are real determinants of real exchange rates and they should be explicitly recognized in any modeling of the real exchange rate. Such an approach clearly represents an abandonment of PPP. An approach which is more in the spirit of Casselian PPP, however, is that which recognizes the important role that transactions costs, in the form of for example transportation costs, can play in explaining the PPP puzzle.

A number of researchers (see, *inter alia*, Heckscher, 1916; Beninga and Protopapadakis, 1988; Dumas, 1992; and Sercu, Uppal and Van Hulle, 1995) have argued that the existence of transaction costs, due largely to the costs of transportation, are a key explanation for the relatively slow adjustment speeds in PPP calculations. For example, in the presence of transaction costs, the price of good i in location j, p_j^i may not be equalized with its price in location k, p_k^i. If there are transportation costs, c^i, the relative price could fluctuate in a range:

$$1/c_i \le p_j^i/p_k^i \le c_i$$

Further, if the transportation costs depend positively on distance, the range of variation in the relative price will also depend on that distance. For example, Dumas (1992) has demonstrated that for markets which are spatially separated, and feature proportional transactions costs, deviations from PPP should follow a non-linear mean-reverting process, with the speed of mean reversion depending on the magnitude of the deviation from PPP. The upshot of this is that within the transaction band, as defined above, deviations are long-lived and take a considerable time to mean revert: the real exchange rate is observationally equivalent to a random walk. However, large deviations, those that occur outside the band, will be rapidly extinguished and for them the observed mean reversion should be very rapid. The existence of other factors, such as the uncertainty of the permanence of the shock and the so-called sunk costs of the activity of arbitrage, may widen the bands over-and-above that associated with simple trade restrictions (see Dixit, 1989; and Krugman, 1989).

Obstfeld and Taylor's (1997) attempt to capture the kind of non-linear behavior imparted by transaction costs involves using the so-called Band Threshold Autoregressive (B-TAR) model. If we reparametrize the AR1 model given by (7.12c) as:

$$\Delta q_t = \lambda q_{t-1} + \varepsilon_t$$

where the real rate is now assumed to be demeaned (and also detrended in the work of Obstfeld and Taylor, because the do not explicitly model the long-run systematic trend in real exchange rates), then the B-TAR is:

$$\Delta q_t = \begin{cases} \lambda^{out}(q_{t-1} - c) + \varepsilon_t^{out} & \text{if } q_{t-1} > c; \\ \lambda^{in} q_{t-1} + \varepsilon_t^{in} & \text{if } c \ge q_{t-1} \ge -c; \\ \lambda^{out}(q_{t-1} + c) + \varepsilon_t^{out} & \text{if } -c > q_{t-1}; \end{cases} \qquad (7.27)$$

where ε_t^{out} is $N(o, \sigma_t^{out})^2$, ε_t^{in} is $N(o, \sigma_t^{out})^2$, $\lambda^{in} = 0$, and λ^{out} is the convergence speed outside the transaction points. So with a B-TAR, the equilibrium value for a real exchange rate can be anywhere in the band $[-c, +c]$ and not necessarily to a zero point (the real rate is demeaned). The methods of Tsay (1989) are used to identify the best-fit TAR model and, in particular, one which properly partitions the data into observations inside and outside the thresholds. Using the data set of Engel and Rogers (1996), discussed above, Obstfeld and Taylor find that for inter-country CPI-based real exchange rates, the adjustment speed is between 20 and 40 months, when a simple AR1 model is used, but only 12 months for the TAR model. When dissagregate price series are used to test the law of one price the B-TAR model produces evidence of mean reversion which is well below 12 months, and indeed as low as two months in some cases. Obstfeld and Taylor also show that measures of economic distance – distance itself, exchange rate volatility, and trade restrictions – are all positively related to the threshold value and these variables also have a consistent inverse relationship with convergence speed.

Michael, Nobay, and Peel (1997) apply the exponentially autoregressive (EAR) model of Haggan and Ozaki (1981) (see also Granger and Terasvirta, 1993) to a monthly interwar database and a database consisting of two centuries of annual real exchange rate data. For each of the exchange rates considered, they are able to reject linearity in favor of an EAR process. An interesting further feature of the work of Michael et al. is that the estimated EAR parameters are consistent with Dumas's hypothesis; in particular, *real exchange rates behave like random walks for small deviations from PPP, but are strongly mean-reverting for large (positive or negative) deviations.*

In contrast to both Obstfeld and Taylor and Michael et al., O'Connell (1996) tests a TAR model for the post-Bretton Woods period and finds that there is no difference between large and small deviations from PPP – both are equally persistent. The difference between O'Connell's result and those reported above may relate to the fact he does not use a search algorithm to locate the thresholds (they are simply imposed) or to the fact that he uses aggregate price data (although this was also used in the above studies). In a bid to determine if these points are indeed responsible for the O'Connell's finding, O'Connell and Wei (1997) use a B-TAR model and disaggregate US price data set to test the law of one price. As in Obstfeld and Taylor, they confirm the point that large deviations from the law of one price are band reverting whilst small deviations are not. Bec, Ben-Salem, and MacDonald (1999) have highlighted an apparent flaw in some of the above tests, namely that the bands are defined using a non-stationary variable – the real exchange rate. Using a real exchange rate/real interest rate framework combined with a TAR model they define the bands using the real interest rate, which is a stationary variable. They report important non-linearities in seven real effective exchange rates, and half-lives which are always within one year; the slowest (for the United States) is nine months. Modelling PPP in a non-linear framework which explicitly recognizes the important role of transaction costs produces results which are consistent with traditional research. This would seem to be an important avenue for future research.

7.4.6 Testing PPP using cointegration methods

Most other recent tests of the PPP relationship have used cointegration methods to test if there is a cointegrating relationship between nominal exchange rates and relative prices. In particular, these tests focus on the application of cointegration methods to an equation such as (7.28):

$$s_t = \beta + \alpha_0 p_t + \alpha_1 p_t^* + \varphi_t. \tag{7.28}$$

If s_t, p_t, and p_t^* are integrated of order one – I(1) – then weak-form PPP (MacDonald 1993) exists if the residual term from an estimated version of (7.28) is stationary, or I(0). Strong-form PPP exists if in addition to weak-form holding homogeneity is also satisfied: $\alpha_0 = 1$ and $\alpha_1 = -1$. Symmetry implies $\alpha_0 = \alpha_1$. The distinction between weak- and strong-form PPP is important because the existence of transportation costs and different price weights across countries means that "there are no hypothesis regarding the specific values of α_0 and α_1 except that they are positive and negative" (Patel, 1990). This, in turn, has the implication that many of the unit root tests considered in the last section may be mis-specified to the extent that they impose a common factor restriction.

The basic message from cointegration-based tests of (7.28) is that the estimator used matters. For example, on the basis of the two-step Engle–Granger method, in which symmetry is generally imposed, Baillie and Selover (1987), Enders (1988), Mark (1990), and Patel (1990) find no evidence of cointegration in the sense that the residual series recovered from the estimated equation is non-stationary. However, and as is now well known, this procedure suffers from a number of deficiencies such as having poor small sample properties and, in the presence of endogeneity and serial correlation, the asymptotic distribution of the estimates will depend on nuisance parameters (Banerjee et al., 1986).

Since Johansen's (1988, 1990) full information maximum likelihood method produces asymptotically optimal estimates (because it has a parametric correction for serial correlation and endogeneity) a number of researchers have applied this method in testing (7.28). Thus, Cheung and Lai (1993), Kugler and Carlos (1993), MacDonald (1993) and MacDonald and Marsh (1994) all report strong evidence of cointegration, although symmetry and homogeneity are often strongly rejected for US dollar bilaterals, but not so for DM-based bilaterals. MacDonald and Moore (1996) use the methods of Phillips and Hansen (1990) and Hansen (1992) as an alternative (to Johansen) way of addressing issues of simultaneity and temporal dependence in the residual of (4). They also find strong evidence of weak-form PPP for dollar bilaterals, while strong-form PPP holds for most DM-based bilaterals. The average half-life in these kinds of studies turns out to be around three to four years.

Pedroni (1997) has proposed panel cointegration methods as an alternative to panel unit root tests. The construction of such a test is complicated because regressors are not normally required to be exogenous, and hence off-diagonal terms are introduced into the residual aysmptotic covariance matrix. Although these drop out of the asymptotic distributions in the single equation case, they are unlikely to do so in the context of a non-stationary panel because of idiosyncratic effects across individual members of the panel. A second difficulty is that generated residuals will depend on the distributional properties of the estimated coefficients and this is likely to be severe in the panel context because of the averaging that takes place. Pedroni proposes statistics which allow for heterogeneous fixed effects, deterministic trends, and both common and idiosyncratic disturbances to the underlying variables (and these, in turn, can have very general forms of temporal dependence). Applying his methods to a panel of nominal exchange rates and relative prices for the recent float, he finds evidence supportive of weak-form PPP.

Husted and MacDonald (1997) use panel cointegration methods to test PPP on a group of 20 countries against the US dollar and also DM for a sample period encompassing the recent float. Using the estimators of Hansen (1990) and Levin and Lin (1994) they find evidence in favor of cointegration. One particularly interesting feature of their work is that for DM-based bilaterals they find half-lifes of one year. In a further paper, Husted and MacDonald (1998) apply the Pedroni cointegration estimator to a monetary approach panel and confirm their earlier results.

7.4.7 Productivity differentials and the real exchange rate – empirical evidence on the Balassa–Samuelson hypothesis

As noted above, an alternative interpretation for the relatively slow mean reversion speeds is that there are important real determinants of real exchange rates. Perhaps the best known of these, discussed in section 7.3, is the Balassa–Samuelson productivity effect. A number of studies have examined the short-run interaction between real exchange rates and relative productivity using a variety of different measures to proxy productivity (see, for example, Hsieh, 1982; Marston, 1990; Micossi and Miles-Ferretti, 1994; DeGregario and Wolf, 1994). Although these models do tend to capture significant Balassa–Samuelson links, their specification is perhaps questionable. For example, they all rely on difference specifications (for bilateral and multilateral rates) and, as Chinn (1996) points out in his critical review of this literature, such tests are all likely to be misspecified (irrespective of whether the underlying time series process of the series are I(1) or trend stationary) because Balassa–Samuelson is about the relationship between the level of productivity and the level of the real exchange rate (i.e. if the series are I(1) then the theory implies that the series must be cointegrated and therefore a regression which relies solely on differences will be mis-specified from a statistical perspective).

Balassa–Samuelson studies which use cointegration methods to detect a relationship between the level of the real exchange rate and the level of productivity are Faruqee (1995), Strauss (1995), MacDonald (1995b), Strauss (1996), Chinn (1997), Chinn and Johnston (1996), Canzoneri et al. (1996), and Mark (1995).

Some of these studies, relying on a more general theoretical structure than Balassa
–Samuelson (such as the models of Mussa (1984) and Frenkel and Mussa (1985))
include other variables such as government fiscal balances. Faruqee (1995), for
example, uses the methods of Johansen to test for cointegration between the real
effective values of the dollar and yen (over the period 1950–90) and a Balassa–
Samuelson effect (measured as the ratio of CPI to WPI in the home relative to
foreign country), a net foreign asset position and terms of trade effect. Clear
evidence of cointegration is found for both currencies and for the dollar a set of
exclusion tests indicate that neither net foreign assets nor Balassa–Samuelson
alone can explain permanent movements in the exchange rate (although TOT can
be excluded); for the yen none of the variables can be excluded. Strauss (1996)
examines six bilateral DM rates (Belgian franc, Canadian dollar, Finnish Marka,
French franc, Pound sterling and the US dollar) for the period and, using sectoral
labor productivity as his measure of Balassa–Samuelson, finds strong evidence
of cointegration with the Johansen cointegration method. In a further paper,
Strauss (1995) uses total factor productivity for German mark bilaterals and finds
evidence of cointegration in eight countries out of 14.

Chinn (1997) uses a variety of cointegration estimators – Johansen, Phillips–
Loretan, and Pedroni – to assess the relationship between real exchange rates and
Balassa–Samuelson (as measured by total factor productivity), and a government
spending variable to proxy the demand side, although he also tests for the inclusion of a number of other variables such as a preference variable, the terms of
trade and the price of oil. Chinn uses an "effective" database (effective exchange
rates and effective explanatory variables, constructed using the weights implicit
in the effective rates), for 14 countries over the period 1970–91. Using single
equation time-series methods he finds the statistical links between real exchange
rates and the explanatory variables to be weak, although when panel estimation
methods are used a correctly signed and statistically significant productivity
effect is found (other variables are not significant). One interesting aspect of the
panel result is that the implied estimate of mean reversion is between 2.5 and
3 years, which is faster than that found in panel estimates of real exchange rate
when the only explanatory variable is the lagged real exchange rate. Chinn and
Johnston (1996) adopt a similar approach/data set to Chinn, the difference being
they focus on bilateral real (CPI) exchange rates. Their findings are also similar
to Chinn's, in that they find greater evidence of cointegration in a panel setting
than on a single equation basis; their estimate of mean reversion is, though,
slightly slower since the reported coefficient is around 4 to 5 years.

Canzoneri, Cumby, and Diba (1996) use panel cointegration methods to examine the Balassa–Samuelson effect. Using a panel consisting of 3 OECD countries,
over the period 1970 to 1991, and the US dollar as the numeraire they find strong
evidence of cointegration between the relative price of non-tradables (the second
component on the RHS of (10)) and the ratio of average products of labor (their
measure of productivity), thereby validating an important component of the
Balassa–Samuelson hypothesis. Indeed, they are unable to reject the hypothesis
that the slope coefficient in the cointegrating relationship is unity. However,
their panel tests of the proposition that exchange rates and the relative price of
traded goods prices are cointegrated finds some support in the data although

the slope of the coefficient in the cointegrating relationship appears not to be unity. However, in testing the stationarity of the difference between exchange rates and relative prices they are unable to reject the null of a unit root. Using the DM as the numeraire currency they confirm that the relative price of non-tradables and the ratio of average products of labor are cointegrated (with a unitary coefficient). In contrast to the US dollar results, nominal exchange rates and relative prices appear to be cointegrated with a cointegrating coefficient which is close to unity.

Using an annual database, spanning the period 1871–1994, Mark (1997) analyzes the importance of economic fundamentals in explaining systematic movements in the real value of the pound sterling–US dollar exchange rate. A variety of fundamentals are experimented with – relative real interest rates, relative money supplies, and relative productivity levels – but the only significant relationship occurs with the relative productivity measure (defined as per capita income). One interesting feature of this result is that it appears to be exchange rate regime specific (the significance and magnitude of this coefficient is most significant for the Bretton Woods period) which would seem to be evidence against the equilibrium approach of Stockman (1988).

The evidence in this section is supportive of the existence of a Balassa–Samuelson effect, although it would seem that it is not very strong. However, given that the studies overviewed here focus exclusively on the real exchange rates of industrialized countries, this is perhaps not surprising. Clearly the existence of a significant Balassa–Samuelson type effect strikes a blow against a traditional form of PPP. But are there other factors which introduce systematic variability into real exchange rates?

7.4.8 Modeling the real exchange rate

In moving from PPP-based relationships to explicit modeling of the real exchange rate, a number of researchers have used the real interest rate parity condition as their benchmark real exchange rate relationship. This may be derived from equation (7.7) by simply noting that we may define a period t real exchange rate from the period t nominal exchange rate and relative price terms in (7.7) and an expected $t + 1$ real exchange rate from the corresponding expected variables:

$$q_t = E_t(q_{t+k}) - (r_t - r_t^*), \qquad (7.29)$$

where we now use the rational expectations operator E_t and the forward date is now $t + k$ (rather than $t + 1$). Expression (7.29) describes the current equilibrium exchange rate as being determined by two components: the expectation of the real exchange rate in period $t + k$ and the negative of the real interest differential with maturity $t + k$. It is usually further assumed that the unobservable expectation of the exchange rate, $E_t(q_{t+k})$, is the "long-run" equilibrium exchange rate, which we define as $\bar{q}_t$:[8]

$$q_t = \bar{q}_t - (r_t - r_t^*), \qquad (7.30)$$

One strand of the literature based on (7.30) assumes the sticky price representation of the monetary model (see section 9.5). If one is prepared to make the further assumption that *ex ante* PPP holds then $\bar{q}_t$ may be interpreted as the flexible price real exchange rate (which, as was implied by our earlier discussion, must simply equal a constant, or zero in the absence of transaction/transportation costs) and so (7.30) defines the deviation of the exchange rate from its long-run equilibrium in terms of a real interest differential. Papers that follow this interpretation are Baxter (1994) and Clarida and Gali (1995).

Regression-based estimates of the relationship between the real exchange rate and the real interest differential may conveniently be split into two strands: those which assume that the equilibrium real rate is constant, and those which explicitly focus on trying to model the systematic determinants underlying determinants of $\bar{q}_t$.

Papers which assume the equilibrium real rate is constant focus on the following regression equation:

$$q_t = \beta_0 + \beta_1 r_t + \beta_2 r_t^* + \varphi_t, \qquad (7.31)$$

which may be derived from (7.30) by assuming $\bar{q}_t = \beta_0$. In an estimated version of (7.31) it is expected that $\beta_1 < 0$ and $\beta_2 > 0$. Some researchers put some structure on these coefficients. For example, when (7.31) is derived as a representation of the sticky price monetary model (see Edison and Melick, 1995), the assumption of regressive exchange rate expectations implies that the coefficients should be above plus 1 and minus 1, and inversely related to the underlying maturity. However, the relationship between real exchange rates and real interest rates can be derived without imposing regressive expectations and, since (7.31) is a reduced form, and given possibly substantial measurement error, the only requirement on the coefficients in (7.31) is that they be negative and positive, respectively.

A variety of researchers have used Engle–Granger cointegration methods (see, for example, Meese and Rogoff, 1988; Edison and Pauls, 1993; Throop, 1994; and Coughlin and Koedijk, 1990),[9] and have failed to uncover a statistically significant link between real exchange rates and real interest differentials.[10] However, paralleling the work with PPP and unit root testing in real exchange rates, these results seem to be estimation-specific. When the Johansen method is used to tie down the real exchange rate/real interest rate relationship, clear evidence of cointegration is found.

For example Edison and Melick (1995), MacDonald (1997), and MacDonald and Swagel (1998) used Johansen multivariate cointegration methods and found evidence of a unique cointegrating vector between a variety of real exchange rates and real interest rates; Edison and Melick find that this result only holds with long rates, while MacDonald and Swagel find it holds for both short and long rates. Relatedly, Johansen and Juselius (1992), Hunter (1992), and MacDonald and Marsh (1997) find that when PPP is tested jointly with UIP, again using Johansen methods, strong evidence of cointegration is found (up to two significant vectors) which is evidence supportive of a relationship between real exchange rates and real interest rates.

A number of researchers (Meese and Rogoff, 1988; Coughlin and Koedjik, 1990; Edison and Pauls, 1993; Stein and Allen, 1995; MacDonald, 1997; Clark and MacDonald, 1998; Stein, 1998)[11] do not assume ex ante PPP and propose that $\bar{q}_t$ may systematically change over time in response to *inter alia* productivity effects, fiscal imbalances, net foreign asset, accumulation, and terms of trade effects. The theoretical justification for the inclusion of these kinds of variables is given by the models of Mussa (1984) and Frenkel and Mussa (1986). However, despite allowing a broader range of variables to affect the real exchange rate, Meese and Rogoff (1988), Edison and Pauls (1993), and Coughlin and Koedjik (1990) fail to find any evidence of cointegration; all of these studies utilize the Engle–Granger two-step estimator. For example, one can sequentially regress the real exchange rate on the various candidates noted above and find no evidence of a cointegrating relationship for six bilateral real exchange rates. In contrast, using multivariate cointegration methods, Meese and Rogoff (1988) also find no evidence of cointegration and, additionally, confirm that their celebrated dictum that nominal exchange rate models cannot outperform a random walk, also holds for real rates.

In contrast to the above, Throop (1994), MacDonald (1997), and Clark and MacDonald (1998) find clear evidence of cointegration in these types of relationships. For example, Throop (1994) uses both a two-step estimator and a dynamic error correction model, over the period 1982, quarter 1 to 1990, quarter 3, to reveal significant evidence of cointegration in systems containing the effective US dollar, and the US bilaterals of the yen, the mark, and the pound sterling. Interestingly, the US effective is shown to dominate a random walk, in an out-of-sample forecasting contest, at horizons of 1 to 8 quarters; however, the evidence for bilaterals is more mixed – in one-half of the horizons it is able to beat a random walk. In MacDonald (1997) clear evidence of a significant cointegrating relationship is reported for the effective rates of the mark, yen, and dollar, and these are shown to produce dynamic real exchange rate models capable of outperforming a random walk at horizons as short as two quarters. Clark and MacDonald (1998) has as its goal the interpretation of multiple cointegrating vectors and the construction of a Behavioural Equilibrium Exchange Rate (or BEER) estimate of the equilibrium exchange rate (see below). They report two significant cointegrating vectors, for the effective systems of the US dollar, the German mark, and the Japanese yen. An example, for the effective US dollar over the period 1960 to 1996, here indicates the kind of relationships that may be recovered from this kind of system:

$$q_t = 0.084ltot + 2.701bs + 1.237nfa - 0.004\lambda + 4.595, \qquad (7.32)$$
$$\quad\;\;(0.04)\qquad\;(0.33)\qquad\;(0.10)\qquad\;(0.01)\qquad(0.014)$$

$$r_t - r_t^* = -0.014, \qquad (7.33)$$
$$\quad\;\;(0.003)$$

where *ltot* is the log of the terms of trade, *bs* is a Balassa–Samuelson effect (measured as the ratio of CPI to WPI in the home country relative to the foreign country), *nfa* is net foreign assets, λ is a risk premium and standard errors are in parenthesis. All of the coefficients are correctly signed[12] and all, apart from that on the relative debt term (the proxy for the risk premium), are statistically significant. The $\chi(4)$ test of whether the chosen restricted vectors span the cointegrating space has an estimated value of 5.49 and a marginal significance level of 0.24; the restrictions are easily satisfied at standard levels of significance.

Gagnon (1996) examines the $\bar{q}_t$ component using a panel equivalent to the Phillips–Loretan estimator (leads and lags in the regression). In particular, using an annual data set for 20 bilateral DM rates, over the period 1960 to 1995, he examines the effect of Balassa–Samuelson, *nfa*, and share of government consumption in total output. Two alternative measures of Balassa–Samuelson are used – real per capita income and the ratio of CPI to WPI in the home relative to the foreign country – and only the relative price measure proves to be statistically significant. The government consumption ratio also does not exhibit any explanatory power. The only variable found to have a robust and significant relationship with the exchange rate, in both the short- and long-run, is the NFA term; an increase in NFA equal to the sum of exports and imports produces a real exchange rate appreciation of 24 percent in the short run and approximately 10 percent in the long run. Adjustment speeds in his different specifications range from -0.23 to -0.5, with the average being -0.4.

Stein (1998), using the Johansen estimator, reports a significant cointegrating vector for the external value of the US dollar against the remaining G7 currencies (in effective terms). The sample period is 1973, quarter 1 through to 1993, quarter 3. The variables which appear statistically significant in the long-run relationship are home and foreign real interest rates and home and foreign income growth (the variables all appear in the form of moving averages). The dynamic error correction representation of the system is demonstrated to have high explanatory power (77 per cent) and is used to decompose the importance of long-term trends versus shorter-term high frequency components. In particular, the long-term trend accounts for 58 percent of the exchange rate variation, with business cycle factors generating the remaining 19 percent of variation. The unexplained element (23 percent) is attributed to purely speculative or transitory components.

Kawai and Ohara (1998) examine monthly bilateral real exchange rates (defined using both CPI and WPI measures) for the G7 countries, 1973–96. They also use the Johansen cointegration method to demonstrate considerable evidence of cointegration amongst real exchange rates and the kinds of explanatory variables discussed above. For example, relative labor productivity is statistically significant and correctly signed in over one half of the country pairs for which they define cointegration (productivity measure as industrial productivity per labor employed in the industrialized or manufacturing sector).

7.4.9 Behavioural Equilibrium Exchange Rates (BEERS) versus Fundamental Equilibrium Exchange Rates (FEERS)

Recently it has become fashionable to use (7.30) and its variants to address the issue of exchange rate assessment; that is, how far or how close an exchange

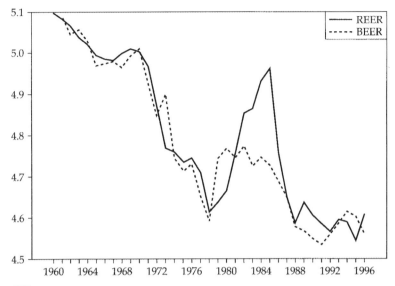

Figure 7.6 Real effective exchange rate and behavioral effective exchange rate for the United States

rate is from its equilibrium value. This approach, labeled a BEER by Clark and MacDonald (1998), is seen to have advantages over the FEER-based approach of Williamson (1985) and Driver and Wren-Lewis (1998) (see chapter 10 where this approach is discussed in some detail).[13] The Natural Real Exchange Rate (NATREX) model of Stein (1998) is a variant of the BEER. Amongst the disadvantages of the FEER approach are its relative intractability, its use of normative assumptions; and also it is unclear if the underlying exchange rate relationship is in any sense well-founded in a statistical sense.

The BEER approach may be used to construct data determined measures of equilibrium exchange rates such as that derived from equations (7.32) and (7.33). Clark and MacDonald refer to the gap between the actual and the data determined equilibrium as the current misalignment, a term which recognizes that in defining an equilibrium the underlying fundamentals may not be calibrated at their equilibrium values. However, it is not difficult to devise an alternative measure of equilibrium – where such fundamentals are calibrated at desired levels – and this is defined by Clark and MacDonald as the total misalignment. The BEER approach is seen to have advantages over the FEER in that it is highly tractable, can be assessed in terms of how good a representation of the data generating process it is, and is amenable to the construction of simple counterfactual experiments.

The BEER approach may be illustrated by referring to figure 7.6, where the BEER calculated from the sum of the two cointegrating vectors (7.32) and (7.33) is reported. The fitted values are interpreted as "equilibrium" values in the sense that they reflect the full adjustment of the real exchange rate to the set of identified

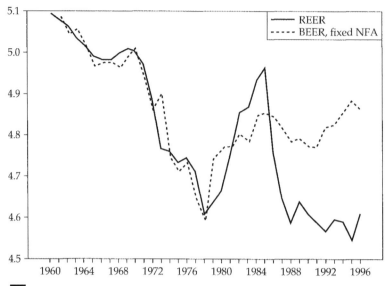

Figure 7.7 REER and alternative BEER for the United States, based on unchanged fiscal deficit and net foreign assets post-1980

fundamental economic variables, and the estimated level of the exchange rate is therefore consistent in a well-defined sense with economic fundamentals. Hence unexplained movements in the actual exchange rates are a measure of exchange rate misalignment because they reflect exchange rate behavior that cannot be accounted for by fundamentals, but rather by unobserved transitory and random factors. Perhaps the most striking feature of figure 7.6 is the extent to which the dollar was overvalued in the period 1980–6, a feature that Clark and MacDonald attribute to a speculative bubble or extrapolative expectations.

Of course, since the BEER is an explicitly behavioral concept, it does not necessarily follow that the fundamentals underpinning the BEER reported in figure 7.6 are themselves equilibrium values. In contrast, in the FEER approach economic fundamentals are calibrated at values which correspond to internal and external balance. However, the BEER approach can also be implemented in a similar manner by calibrating the variables in the cointegrating vectors at particular values. For example, in figure 7.7 a time path for the US BEER is derived by assuming that the large deterioration in the US fiscal deficit and net foreign asset position did not take place post-1980. It demonstrates that the post-1985 dollar depreciation would not have been as large as that which occurred. The gap between the actual real rate and the BEER in figure 7.7 reflects a *total* misalignment, where the difference between the actual and fitted values incorporates the effects of departures of the economic fundamentals from their long-run, sustainable, or desired levels. Reassuringly, the estimates of disequilibrium are very similar to those reported in Stein (1998) using the NATREX model (although the sample periods differ). The BEER approach to exchange rate assessment has recently become increasingly popular amongst practitioners.

◆ 7.5 Concluding Comments

This chapter has summarized the PPP hypothesis in both its absolute and relative versions. PPP is probably at its most useful as a description of the long-run exchange rate, when short-run relative price effects have worked themselves out or when inflationary forces dominate real changes (on the latter point, see Frenkel, 1976a). But does PPP in fact provide a theory of the exchange rate or is it rather a theory of the determination of prices? That is, which way does causation run? From prices to exchange rates as proponents of PPP would argue? From exchange rates to price changes? Or, as proponents of endogenous money would claim, are both prices and exchange rates simultaneously determined? These issues are still unclear and it is probably correct to say that both the exchange rate and prices are endogenous variables and are determined simultaneously (see, for example, Yeager, 1958).

The most glaring failure of PPP, which is obliquely referred to in figures 7.3–7.5, is that the theory as outlined fails to explain the large volatility of exchange rates that has been such a prominent feature of the recent floating experience. It is this phenomenon which we attempt to explain in the following chapters. However, more recent evidence, alluded to in the final section, suggests that some form of long-run PPP does have empirical support, although the adjustment speeds are probably too slow to be consistent with traditional, or Casselian, PPP. Perhaps the only resolution to this "PPP Puzzle" (Rogoff, 1995) is to adopt an explicitly real model of the exchange rate, such as that introduced in the preceeding section; an alternative resolution of the puzzle may lie in the use of the non-linear methods discussed in section 7.4.5.

NOTES

1 Recall that a change in a log value represents a proportionate change.
2 Strictly speaking absolute PPP is assumed to hold in the base period. In terms of (7.4), therefore, the assumption would be that absolute PPP held in the previous period.
3 So called because the various parity conditions rely on the efficient functioning of markets for their validity.
4 Increasing the span of the data is likely to affect the *size* of the test as well as its power. In the context of the example considered here the value of ρ is likely to fall as the span is increased.
5 Liu and Maddalla (1996) and Pappell (1997) both highlight the importance of residual correlation in panel unit root tests, a feature absent from the first set of critical values tabulated by Levin and Lin (1992) (used by Frankel and Rose (1995), Wu (1995), Oh (1995)) although not in the Levin and Lin (1994) paper (used by MacDonald (1995)). Pappell (1997) finds that for a number of different panels the null of a unit root cannot be rejected when monthly data is used, although it can be using quarterly data. O'Connell (1997) also takes the Levin and Lin test to task by noting that the power of the test relies on each new bilateral relationship being added to the panel adding new information. Although each relationship added may indeed contain some new information it is unlikely that this will be one-to-one given that the currencies are bilateral rates, are often defined with respect to the US dollar, and therefore will contain

a common element. Correcting for this common cross-correlation using a GLS estimator (although assuming that the errors are iid over time), O'Connell (1997) finds that the significant evidence of mean reversion reported in earlier studies disappears.

6   The superior performance of DM-based bilaterals was first noted by Frenkel (1981), in the context of a traditional regression based test of PPP.

7   See Jorion and Sweeney (1996) and Pappell (1997) for a further discussion.

8   This assumption has been invoked by, for example, Meese and Rogoff (1988).

9   Coughlin and Koedjik (1990) find some evidence for cointegration for one of the currencies in their data set, namely the German mark–US dollar.

10   Throop (1994), using an error correction relationship for the real exchange rate/real interest rate relationship, reports some evidence for cointegration on the basis of the estimated t-ratio on the error correction term; however, this is not significant on the basis of a small sample correction.

11   Equation 7.31 plays a pivotal role in the Natural Real Exchange Rate (NATREX) model of Stein and Allen (1995) and Stein (1998). Although the theoretical underpinnings of this model are rather different to the other papers discussed in this section, the kinds of variables cited as the fundamental determinants of real exchange rates are in fact very similar to those introduced here.

12   It is worth noting that the effective exchange rates discussed here are defined as the foreign currency price of domestic currency and therefore, can be thought of as the reciprocals of the real exchange rates discussed earlier. This of course means that although the coefficient signs in 7.32 and 7.33 are correct they are the opposite of what one would expect if the real rate was defined as in our earlier discussions.

13   See Faruqee, Isard and Masson (1998) for a novel implementation of the FEER approach.

8

The Monetary Approach to the Balance of Payments

The monetary approach to the balance of payments (MABP) argues, in contrast to Keynesian theory, that the balance of payments is a monetary phenomenon and not a real phenomenon, and should be analyzed using the familiar tools of monetary analysis, namely, the demand for and supply of money. Thus, it is argued that any disequilibrium in the balance of payments is a reflection of disequilibrium in money markets. In its most extreme version the MABP has a number of important conclusions.

1   In contrast to the models outlined in chapter 3, it implies that a devaluation can have only a transitory impact on the balance of payments.
2   A growing country will run a balance of payments surplus (this is in contrast to the Keynesian model where economic growth leads to a balance of payments deficit).
3   A country can only run a balance of payments deficit until it runs out of foreign exchange reserves.
4   Import quotas, tariffs, exchange restrictions and other interferences to international trade can have only, at best, a transitory effect on the balance of payments.
5   With pegged exchange rates a country cannot run an independent monetary policy.
6   A rise in the domestic rate of interest will result in a balance of payments deficit.

Why then does the MABP focus attention on the money market as the relevant market for the analysis of balance of payments issues, and how are the above important conclusions derived? It is the purpose of this chapter to explain why a view of the balance of payments different from those presented in chapter 3 is required, and the implications of this monetary view of the balance of payments for economic policy are spelled out. The outline of the remainder of this chapter is as follows.

In section 8.1 some familiar identities are presented to show that in an *ex post* accounting sense the MABP should give similar answers to balance of payments issues as the elasticities and absorption approaches. Since this is so, it is shown why proponents of the MABP say it is a preferable means of analyzing balance of payments issues. In section 8.2 a simple MABP model is outlined to illustrate the impact of devaluation and domestic credit expansion under fixed exchange rates. Some policy conclusions stemming from this model are then discussed. In the final two sections there is an assessment of the empirical evidence on two of the most crucial policy implications of the MABP: namely, the conclusion that under a system of pegged exchange rates a country cannot pursue an independent monetary policy and also the view that with fixed exchange rates inflation is an international monetary phenomenon.

8.1 What is so Different about the Monetary Approach?

In this section some simple and familiar identities are presented in order to illustrate the relationship between the elasticities, absorption and monetary approaches to the balance of payments. As will be seen, in an *ex post* general equilibrium sense these models are perfectly compatible and reconcilable and thus the question that naturally arises is why it is useful to analyze the balance of payments as a monetary phenomenon.[1]

Consider first the familiar balance sheet of the central bank:

Assets	Liabilities
D	H
F	

where H is high powered money, F is the foreign-backed component of H and D is the domestic asset component of H. The domestic money supply is then determined as some multiple of H:

$$M \equiv hH \equiv h(F + D) \qquad (8.1)$$

where h is the conventional money multiplier. For our discussion in this and the next section we shall assume that $h = 1$ (this is a simplifying assumption and does not materially affect any of the results discussed).

On taking first differences of (8.1) and rearranging:

$$\Delta F = \Delta M - \Delta D \tag{8.2}$$

where clearly ΔF is the change in reserves, ΔD is the change in the domestic component of the money supply or domestic credit expansion and ΔM is the change in the money stock which in the MABP literature is the flow demand for money, or hoarding (this concept will be discussed in some detail in section 8.2). Now it is known that with a fixed exchange rate system the change in reserves is equal to the sum of the current and capital accounts of the balance of payments, i.e.

$$\Delta F = B + K \tag{8.3}$$

where B represents the current account balance (a flow) and K is the capital account balance (also assumed to be a flow). Thus if both the current and capital accounts are in deficit the country must be losing reserves. Equation (8.2) explains why, for the country to be losing reserves, domestic credit expansion must exceed hoarding. Thus to control a balance of payments deficit domestic credit expansion has to be controlled relative to the flow demand for money. Alternatively, if ΔM is greater than ΔD then there is an excess flow demand for money which in an open economy can be satisfied by the public swopping bonds and goods for reserves, i.e. the country will run a balance of payments surplus.

The identities (8.1)–(8.3) are those relevant to MABP. It is now shown that the monetary approach identities, in an *ex post* accounting sense, should give the same result for the change in reserves as the elasticities and absorption approaches.

From national income accounting it is known that *ex post*

$$Y = A + B \tag{8.4}$$

where A represents aggregate absorption and B represents the trade balance (exports minus imports – other current account and capital account items are ignored for simplicity). The elasticities approach utilizes the relationship

$$B = X - M \tag{8.5}$$

and assuming that the Marshall–Lerner condition holds, as has been shown in chapter 3, a devaluation leads to an improvement in the balance of trade. The absorption approach, on the other hand, draws attention to the fact that the balance of trade can only be improved if income is increased relative to absorption (and, as we have seen, a country may require a combination of expenditure-switching (devaluation) and expenditure-reducing policies):

$$B = Y - A \tag{8.6}$$

Using (8.2), (8.3) (assuming for simplicity that $K = 0$), (8.4), (8.5) and (8.6), and taking all variables as *ex post* identities, then

$$\Delta F = B = X - M = Y - A = \Delta M - \Delta D \tag{8.7}$$

Thus, in an *ex post* sense the three approaches are equivalent. But as Whitman (1975) notes, perhaps identities are not very meaningful; one has to look behind the identities in order to see how variables are defined and what the implicit assumptions are underlying the approaches in order to give the above reconciliation. Nevertheless, the identity (8.7) does highlight the question that, if the three different approaches are potentially reconcilable, why do proponents of the MABP favor using equation (8.2) rather than (8.5) or (8.6). A quotation from Johnson (1977) should help to highlight the differences:

> the monetary approach should in principle give an answer [to balance of payments questions] no different from that provided by a correct analysis in terms of the other accounts. The main reason for preferring the monetary approach is that less direct alternative approaches have almost invariably attempted to explain the behaviour of the markets they concern themselves with, by analytical constructs in which the role of money in influencing behaviour, and the connection between these other markets and the money markets, are neglected as being 'of the second order of smalls', which may be a legitimate procedure for many economic problems, but cannot be so for an analysis which aims to explain and predict behaviour in the money market. (p. 253)

This quotation can be illustrated in the following way. Consider a closed economy in which there are goods, bonds and money. The overall aggregate budget constraint of such an economy must imply that the sum of the excess demands equals zero. Thus

$$ED_g + ED_b + ED_m = 0 \tag{8.8}$$

where ED represents an excess demand and the subscripts g, b and m represent goods, bonds and money respectively. In a fully employed economy closed to international trade in goods and assets, excess demand will be eliminated by changes in prices; but in an open economy such excess demands will be reflected in different net international flows in the balance of payments accounts. Clearly, if the country is small, in the sense of accepting world goods and bond prices as given, excess demands will be reflected solely in international flows. However, if, on the other hand, the country is not small but has some influence on world prices, it can be expected that excess demand will be eliminated by both price changes and international flows. The balance of payments flows will be constrained by

$$(X_g - M_g) + (X_b - M_b) + (X_m - M_m) = 0 \tag{8.9}$$

where X and M represent exports and imports, respectively. Thus the three accounts – the current, capital and money – must sum to zero.

The budget constraint implies that if two of the markets are in equilibrium so too must the third market be. Thus an analysis of the balance of payments could concentrate on the current and capital accounts and ignore the money account. With the elasticities approach, with no capital account, attention is concentrated on the current account and the money market is ignored. *But this will be valid only if the crucial nature of the money market is ignored.* Thus money is a *stock* concept and the demand for money is a demand for a *stock*, not for a continuing flow of money.

The money identity, equation (8.1), shows that in an open economy residents of that country can have an influence on the total quantity of money via their ability to convert domestic money into foreign goods and securities or conversely turn domestic hoods and securities into domestic money backed by foreign exchange reserves. The important point is that although stock disequilibrium in the money market will have as its counterpart a flow disequilibrium in, say, the goods market, such flows will only continue until stock equilibrium has been restored in the money market. But it is usual in non-monetary approaches to the balance of payments to have, say, goods flows depending only on prices and income, ignoring the underlying stock adjustment in money markets. We could of course "rectify" the traditional balance of payments model by incorporating a stock adjustment mechanism directly into the relevant functions. But proponents of the monetary approach would argue that it is more straightforward to concentrate directly on the underlying disequilibrium in the money market. A direct consequence of analyzing the balance of payments as a monetary phenomenon is that it is clearly seen to be a stock phenomenon and not a flow phenomenon.

Attention is now turned to an elaboration of some of the concepts discussed in this section in the context of a simple model of an open economy operating a fixed exchange rate.

8.2 The Global Monetarist Model

The essential feature of the MABP is that balance of payments disequilibrium should be viewed as reflecting disequilibrium in the money market. To illustrate the MABP consider, as a starting point, a version of the monetary approach which is to be found in the writings of a variety of its proponents, what Whitman (1975) has termed the "global monetary approach to the balance of payments" (GMABP). The global monetary model is attractive because of its inherent simplicity and also because it gives unambiguous analytical results and leads to strong policy conclusions. The "monetarist" element of the GMABP puts emphasis on the supply and demand for money as the relevant tools for analyzing balance of payments disequilibrium, and the global element of GMABP refers to assumptions pertaining to the integration of the world economy. An example of the integration of the world economy referred to may be given in terms of commodity markets. Global monetarism assumes that commodities produced in different countries are perfect substitutes and thus, in the absence of trade barriers, arbitrage will ensure that the law of one price holds (see chapter 7 on purchasing power parity, PPP).

Let us now turn to a simple model[2] which highlights the global monetarist view of the world and consider first the monetary assertions underlying the GMABP. For simplicity the capital account is ignored: concentration is only on current account transactions. The introduction of a capital account would only complicate the analysis without helping to elucidate the salient issues of the monetary approach.

The model consists of two countries, each producing a single commodity, and the commodities are assumed to be perfect substitutes. Each country has a "Cambridge" money demand function of the form

$$L = kP\bar{Y} \tag{8.10}$$

$$L^* = k^*P^*\bar{Y}^* \tag{8.10a}$$

where L is desired nominal money balances, k is the "Cambridge k" and represents the desired ratio of nominal money holdings to nominal income, P represents the money price of goods (or the price level) and $\bar{Y}$ represents the exogenously determined full employment level of real output. Henceforth terms with an asterisk denote foreign variables. The homogeneity of money in prices, as depicted in equation (8.10), reflects an absence of money illusion and the (long-run) neutrality of money; furthermore, wages and prices are assumed to be perfectly flexible. Although equation (8.10) gives the long-run stationary state effects of, say, an excess supply of money on the price level, in the short-run money market adjustment is assumed *not* to be instantaneous. Instead, as was discussed in the previous section, individuals in an open economy can alter the money stock via the balance of payments. The flow demand for money, which is normally classed as hoarding, is given by

$$H = \alpha(L - M) = H(P, M) \tag{8.11}$$

$$H^* = \alpha^*(L^* - M^*) = H^*(P^*, M^*) \tag{8.11a}$$

where H and H^* represent hoarding in the domestic and foreign countries, respectively, and α and α^* are the domestic and foreign rates of adjustment. Equations (8.11) and (8.11a) simply state that each individual believes that actual cash holdings at current prices can be adjusted by hoarding or dishoarding, i.e. by spending less or more than income respectively. Given the assumptions about the stock demand for money function – equation (8.10) or (8.10a) – it follows that a rise in the price level raises hoarding since it creates a stock excess demand for money, while an increase in the nominal quantity of money reduces hoarding since it creates a stock excess supply.

Next the money supply equation, noted in the previous section, is assumed to hold in each country:

$$M = F + \bar{D} \tag{8.1a}$$

$$M^* = F^* + \bar{D}^* \tag{8.1b}$$

where the domestic component of the money supply is assumed for the time being to be exogenous and is denoted as $\bar{D}$. Given the latter assumption the balance of payments feedback into the domestic money supply is defined by

$$H = \Delta M = \Delta F = B \qquad (8.12)$$

which states that for an exogenously determined domestic component of the money supply, $\bar{D}$, the money supply change is equal to the change in reserves which equals the trade balance surplus/deficit. Since a simple two-country model is being used here any hoarding/dishoarding in the home country will have its mirror image in dishoarding/hoarding in the foreign country and a corresponding change in F^* and M^*, i.e.

$$H = \Delta M = \Delta F = B = -SB^* = -SH^* = -S\Delta F^* = -S\Delta M^* \qquad (8.13)$$

where S, it will be recalled, is the exchange rate. Thus under fixed exchange rates the national money supply is *endogenous* rather than a policy instrument. This is in marked contrast to the assumptions, often implicit, underlying the Keynesian view of the balance of payments – namely that the monetary authorities sterilize the impact on the domestic money supply of international reserve flows ensuing from payments imbalance.

Desired nominal expenditure in each country, Z, Z^*, is assumed to be a function of nominal income and the flow demand for money or hoarding:

$$Z = P\tilde{Y} - H \qquad (8.14)$$

$$Z^* = P^*\tilde{Y}^* - H^* \qquad (8.14a)$$

Thus equation (8.14) is in contrast to simple Keynesian models of the balance of payments, which not only ignore modeling the money supply implications of balance of payments changes but also the effects of monetary repercussions on expenditure. But although the MABP resolves this problem of the Keynesian approach it does, as Whitman (1975) notes, retain and intensify another inconsistency, namely it combines long-run full equilibrium assumptions on the demand side with the essentially short-run assumption of the stationary state on the output side (i.e. income is exogenously given at the full employment level). Notice too that the expenditure functions in equation (8.14) imply a marginal propensity to spend out of income which is less than unity in the short run (because of the H term) but which is equal to unity in the long run when money market disequilibria have worked themselves out.

The global aspect of the GMABP is reflected by the equation

$$P = SP^* \qquad (8.15)$$

The law of one price holds in this one commodity world and this clearly *precludes* the terms of trade issues which are so crucial to the elasticities approach.

Thus there are three strands to the global monetarist view of the world. First, it is assumed that there is perfect commodity arbitrage and thus PPP holds continuously (equation (8.15) – this is the global element of the GMABP. The monetarist element of the GMABP is reflected in equation (8.10)): the effect of an

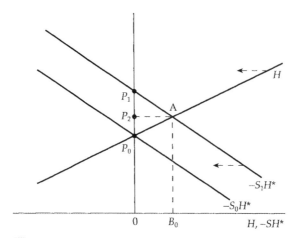

Figure 8.1 Devaluation and the price level in a two-country global monetary approach to the balance of payments model

increase of M on P is proportional. The third strand, which may be interpreted as the monetary approach to the balance of payments element, is that, with pegged exchanged rates, the domestic money supply becomes endogenous rather than exogenous (this is reflected in equations (8.1) and (8.13)), that the excess demand for money plays a key role in the functioning of all markets in the economy (equation (8.14)) and that such excess demand is a disequilibrium phenomenon (equations (8.10) and (8.11)).

The simple model described by equations (8.11)–(8.15) is illustrated in figure 8.1. The schedules H and $-S_0H^*$, drawn for given nominal M, M^* and S_0, represent the domestic and foreign rates of hoarding and dishoarding respectively as a function of the domestic price of goods, P. The domestic hoarding schedule will be upward sloping (i.e. $dH/dP > 0$) because an increase in the home price level, for a given nominal quantity of money M, will lead to a desire by the residents of the country to restore the real value of their cash balances, i.e. H increases in equation (8.11). This can only be achieved for a given M by a decline in expenditure/absorption relative to income (equation (8.14)) and an improvement in the balance of payments (i.e. a current account surplus), and thus the F component of the money supply will increase.

To understand why the foreign dishoarding function has a negative slope consider the effect of a rise in the home country's price from P_0. Given equation (8.15) it follows that $P^* = P/S$ and so P^* will rise as P rises; the rise in P^*, via equations (8.10a) and (8.11a), will encourage hoarding in the foreign country. This is shown in the *left*-hand quadrant of figure 8.1 where hoarding in the foreign country is *positive*.[3]

In figure 8.1, notice that at the equilibrium price P_0 there is neither hoarding nor dishoarding and this implies that the balance of payments must be in equilibrium, i.e. $B = 0$. This is therefore a position of long-run equilibrium and such an equilibrium requires that each country holds the desired quantity of real balances and that the arbitrage condition is satisfied.

8.2.1 Short-run dynamics

Devaluation

It is known that in the short-run, stock equilibrium need not obtain. Instead an alternative short-run definition of equilibrium is used, defined as a position where world income equals world expenditure, or equivalently, where the domestic rate of hoarding is equal to the foreign rate of dishoarding:

$$H = -S_0 H^*$$

The case of an exchange rate devaluation is illustrated in figure 8.1. The effect of a devaluation is to shift the foreign hoarding schedule upwards in exact proportion to the devaluation. For example, if the home currency is devalued by 10 percent and home prices also rise by 10 percent (in figure 8.1 P_1 is 10 percent higher then P_0), the price of goods in the foreign country, determined by $P^* = P/S$, will remain unchanged. Thus, foreign hoarding will remain at zero if the new $-S_1 H^*$ function passes through P_1. It will be useful to remember that, if home prices rise by less than the devaluation, home goods will become cheaper in the foreign country and the foreign price level P^* will tend to fall.[4] Furthermore, if the foreign price level does fall this will induce *dis*hoarding in the foreign country – which occurs in the right quadrant of figure 8.1.

The devaluation has no effect on the *position* of the home country's hoarding schedule but, as home prices rise, hoarding will increase along the H schedule.

Short-run equilibrium is depicted in figure 8.1 at A, where home hoarding is equal to foreign *dis*hoarding. At point A world aggregate demand still equals world aggregate output so world output will be unchanged (via equations (8.14) and (8.14a) desired nominal expenditure is $Z + Z^*$ with the positive H and negative H^* cancelling). But the home country will be running a balance of payments surplus equal to B_0 whilst the foreign country has a deficit equal to $-S_1 B_0$.

Notice that the home country's price level rises only to P_2, which is proportionately less than the devaluation $(= (P_1 - P_0)/P_0)$. This is made possible by a *reduction* in the foreign price P^* as money supply there is falling due to the payments deficit.

Point A is a position of short-run or instantaneous equilibrium because through equation (8.11) the money stock is rising in the home country to satisfy the higher level of money demand – which has increased in equation (8.10) due to the rise in P. The factor α, the domestic rate of adjustment, now comes into play and M rises relative to L, the flow demand for money falls and the domestic hoarding schedule shifts to the left.

Opposite factors are working in the foreign country: the foreign price level has fallen and via equation (8.10a) so has the demand for money. Dishoarding occurs

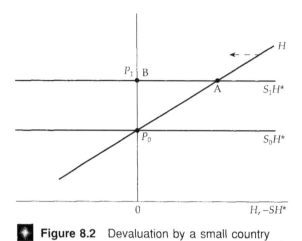

Figure 8.2 Devaluation by a small country

at the rate a, and, as the desire to dishoard decreases over time, the $-S_1H^*$ schedule also shifts to the left.

Ultimately the two hoarding schedules will intersect on the vertical axis, say at P_2, where the adjustment process is complete. As a result of devaluation by the home country, home prices, money demand and money stock have increased while, in the foreign country, prices, money demand, and money supply have decreased.

Small country assumption

What modification has to be made to the devaluation result if the home country is small, in the sense that it cannot affect foreign prices? The small country assumption may be captured by a modified version of (8.15):

$$P = S\bar{P}^* \tag{8.15a}$$

where the bar above P^* denotes that the foreign price level is parametrically, or exogenously, given to the domestic country.

In terms of figure 8.2 this means that domestic prices will rise proportionately with the devaluation since the foreign country's prices do not depend upon home country prices. In figure 8.2 devaluation raises the foreign hoarding schedule to S_1H^*, where P^* is constant. The home country has a temporary balance of payments surplus at A but, as was argued above, the H schedule will shift to the left at the rate governed by α until it intersects the vertical axis at B. It may be observed that the home country's money stock has increased as a result of the payments surplus and that in long-run equilibrium at point B the domestic money supply has increased in proportion to the rise in money demand, itself due to the rise in the domestic price level.

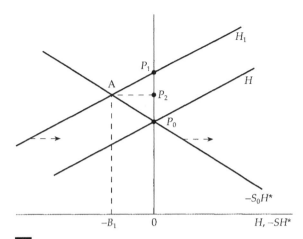

Figure 8.3 Domestic credit expansion in a two-country global monetary approach to the balance of payments model

Domestic credit expansion

Until now it has been assumed that the domestic component of the money supply, D, is fixed. This assumption is now relaxed and the effect is considered of a once-and-for-all increase in the domestic money supply brought about by an increase in D. For unchanged prices this implies, via equation (8.10), that individuals have excess money balances and this, through equation (8.11), will result in dishoarding in the home country and a balance of payments deficit as individuals attempt to offload the excess money balances by buying goods (and securities if the capital account is open). The initial effect of the expansion of D for the two-country case is illustrated in figure 8.3.

The increase in the domestic component of the money stock leads to a leftward shift in the hoarding schedule to H_1 where, at P_1, the proportionate rise in the price level is equal to that of the money stock. The domestic price level, however, rises only to P_2 as higher prices encourage (positive) hoarding in the foreign country. The effect of the latter, via equation (8.14a), is to release goods from foreign absorption and to direct them, through the country's balance of payments surplus, to the home country. The influx of goods restrains price rises in the home country to be proportionately less than the rise in the domestic money supply.

The home country's price level rises to P_2 but, with full employment, there is still an excess demand for goods, and thus at point A the home country is running a balance of payments deficit and losing reserves. The latter effect will push the hoarding schedule H_1 to the right over time.

The foreign country will be gaining reserves and experiencing an increased money supply. Thus, through equation (8.11a) it will be dishoarding which will also shift the $-S_0H^*$ schedule to the right.

Stock disequilibrium persists until the two schedules again intersect between P_1 and P_0, say at P_2. This is the only point consistent with full stock equilibrium.

8.2.2 Distribution of the world's money supply

The actual distribution of the increase in D on the home and foreign countries' money supplies and price levels can be seen to be a function of the *size* of the respective countries (see, for example, Swoboda, 1976). By arranging (8.10) and (8.10a) for the domestic and foreign price levels, respectively, and substituting the resulting expressions into equation (8.15), we obtain

$$d \ln M - d \ln k - d \ln Y - d \ln M^* + d \ln k^* + d \ln Y^* - dS = 0 \qquad (8.16)$$

where in equilibrium $M = L$, $M^* = L^*$ and d denotes the differential operator.

Since in the MABP model Y and k are assumed constant, and since the exchange rate is assumed fixed and therefore also constant, (8.16) may be simplified to

$$d \ln M = d \ln M^* \qquad (8.17)$$

Thus the increase in the world money supply is distributed in proportion to existing money stocks, the latter being related to the size of the countries (it will be exactly related if from equations (8.10) and (8.10a) $k = k^*$).

All of this is but old wine in new bottles! David Hume, the great Scottish philosoper had argued in the eighteenth century that there is a natural distribution of the world's money which is related to relative national incomes – as is the existing distribution of money stocks referred to in the last paragraph. Hume (1753!) wrote:

> Suppose that all the money in Great Britain were multiplied fivefold in a night ... must not all labour and commodities rise to such an exorbitant height that no neighbouring nations could afford to buy from us; while their commodities, on the other hand, became comparatively cheap, that, in spite of all the laws which could be formed, they would be run in upon us, and our money flow out; till we fall to a level with foreigners, and lose that great superiority of riches, which had laid us under such disadvantages? Now, it is evident, that the same causes, which could correct these exorbitant inequalities, were they to happen miraculously, must prevent their happening in the common course of nature, and must for ever, in all neighbouring nations, *preserve money nearly proportionable to the art and industry of each nation.* All water, wherever, it communicates, remains always at a level. Ask naturalists the reason; they tell you, that, were it to be raised in any one place, the superior gravity of that part not being balanced, must depress it, till it meets a counterpoise ... (p. 28)

And in a related footnote Hume hints at a monetary theory of the exchange rate!

8.2.3 The policy implications of the monetary approach to the balance of payments

At the outset of this chapter some of the implications of regarding the balance of payments as a monetary phenomenon were listed. These implications are now discussed in a little more detail in the light of the discussion in the previous sections.

Since balance of payments surpluses and deficits are reflections of monetary disequilibria, there is no need to have a government balance of payments policy since, as was shown, such payments imbalances are transitory and will automatically correct themselves. A deficit country may be able to sustain its deficit by sterilizing the effects of the deficit on the domestic money supply (i.e. increase D as F falls); however, since reserves are finite such a policy must eventually come to an end. Equally a surplus country may try to sterilize the effects of its surplus on the money supply but in the longer term it will eventually exhaust its stock of domestic credit assets.

Second, under a system of pegged exchange rates monetary policy has a very limited role to play. For the small country a change in the domestic component of the money supply leads to an offsetting movement in reserves: domestic credit policy can only alter the composition of the backing to the money stock. If, however, the global component of the GMABP is relaxed by allowing monetary variables to affect real variables in the short run and by assuming imperfect substitutability of goods and assets in different countries (see Dornbusch, 1973) it can be demonstrated that a change in the domestic-backed component of the money supply will have real effects in the short run even under fixed exchange rates. However, the requirement of long-run stock equilibrium and the impossibility of a country adopting a continuous sterilization policy (the "monetary" component of the GMABP) will ensure that for a small country an increase in D will lead to an exactly offsetting decrease in F: the *reserve offset coefficient* is equal to unity. When countries are not small the monetary component of the GMABP will ensure a proportional effect of money on prices in the long run.

A corollary of the last point is that, *under a system of fixed exchange rates, inflation is a world monetary phenomenon* and cannot be controlled by a national monetary policy. The only way a country can pursue an inflation rate different from the rest of the world is by relinquishing the commitment to intervene in the foreign exchange market at a fixed price; the exchange rate must be allowed to float freely. (As will be shown in the next chapter, it may well be impossible for countries even with floating exchange rates to pursue independent monetary policies.)

The third policy implication of the GMABP model is that devaluation has only a transitory effect on the balance of payments. Thus, and as was demonstrated in previous subsections, devaluation has an effect on the balance of payments only to the extent that it alters the demand for money relative to its supply. Nevertheless, the period of transition during which devaluation has an effect may be an important one for the policymakers, allowing them, say, to achieve an increase in the country's reserves or an increase in the domestic component of the money base (perhaps as a response to a budget deficit) without having a deterioration in the balance of payments. If, however, all markets adjust instantaneously following a shock then devaluation cannot have an impact, even in the short run.

Fourth, it has been demonstrated that if the global elements of the GMABP are relaxed, the monetary approach does still predict that monetary/exchange rate policy can have "real" effects in the short run although such effects will be vitiated in the long run. But some commentators (most notably Kaldor, 1970), by questioning the monetary component of the GMABP, have attacked the long-run ineffectiveness of the policy described above. For example, the crucial lynchpin relationship in the monetary approach is equation (8.10) which predicts that prices are homogeneous of degree one in money. This prediction, however, is based on the assumption that k, the inverse of the velocity of money, is constant and at least a stable function of a few key variables. Diehard Keynesians, taking their lead from, for example, the Radcliffe Report (1959), would presumably question this assertion by arguing that the velocity of money is highly unstable and thus the concentrating on the monetary consequences of the balance of payments is erroneous. Johnson (1977), however, has countered this by arguing that as long as k is not completely unstable we are justified in treating the balance of payments as a monetary phenomenon.

Rabin and Yeager (1982), although accepting that a well-defined and stable demand for money function may exist, argue that not all changes in the supply of money are desired or intended changes as suggested by the monetary approach. For example, the role of money as a medium of exchange necessitates it being used as a buffer stock and this may lead to unintended falls or rises in money balances.

> Money balances are pools into and out of which receipts and payments are made and so serve as buffers against short-term fluctuations in the timing and sizes of receipts and payments: since the fluctuations are unintended, the rise or fall in money balances can be unintended too.[5]

Although this point is clearly correct for an individual, it is unclear how relevant the concept would be in the aggregate.[6] For other criticisms of the monetary approach as outlined in this section, see Currie (1976), Coppock (1980) and Rabin and Yeager (1982).

*8.3 Sterilization and the Reserve Offset Coefficient

8.3.1 Empirical framework

Although the MABP has extremely strong policy implications it must be asked how well supported empirically the underlying theory is. In this section some answers to this question are given by considering a reduced-form MABP equation. The reduced form equation is derived from familiar equations introduced in this chapter. The differentiating feature of the present analysis is the introduction of a rate of interest into the demand for money. This effectively introduces a capital account into the balance of payments. The country is assumed to be small and the domestic good and non-money asset are assumed to be perfect substitutes for the corresponding foreign variables.

$$L = PkY^{\alpha_Y} i^{-\alpha_i} \tag{8.18}$$

$$M = h(F + D) \tag{8.19}$$

$$M = L \tag{8.20}$$

$$PkY^{\alpha_Y} i^{-\alpha_i} = F + D \tag{8.21}$$

where equation (8.18) is a Cagan-style money demand equation which posits that the demand for money balances depends upon real income and the interest rate and is homogeneous of degree one in prices; equation (8.19) is the money supply identity (note that in contrast to the previous two sections we have not constrained the money multiplier to be unity); and equations (8.20) and (8.21) represent conditions of equilibrium in money markets where demand is equal to supply.

Transforming (8.21) logarithmically, we obtain

$$\ln P + \ln k + \alpha_Y \ln Y - \alpha_i \ln i = \ln h + \ln(F + D) \tag{8.22}$$

On differentiating (8.22), rearranging and approximating the differential operator by the first difference operator, we get

$$\frac{F}{F + D}\Delta \ln F = \Delta \ln P + \alpha_Y \Delta \ln Y - \alpha_i \Delta \ln i - \Delta \ln h - \frac{D}{F + D}\Delta \ln D \tag{8.23}$$

which may be more compactly expressed as

$$r = \Delta \ln P + \alpha_Y \Delta \ln Y - \alpha_i \Delta \ln i - \Delta \ln h - d \tag{8.23a}$$

where

$$d = \frac{D}{F + D}\Delta \ln D$$

and

$$r = \frac{F}{F + D}\Delta \ln F$$

Notice that two interesting predictions of the monetary approach, not addressed hitherto, can be illustrated with equation (8.23a). It suggests that an increase in the home interest rate results in a balance of payments *deficit* (since it is a small country the interest rate increase will only be incipient). This is in contrast to a more traditional view of the effects of interest rates on the balance of payments (i.e. the Mundell–Fleming model described in chapter 5) where an increase in the domestic interest rate leads to a capital inflow and a surplus on the balance of payments. This apparent paradox may be explained in the following way. In the monetary approach, an increase in the domestic interest rate, caused perhaps by changed inflationary expectations, will lead to a reduced demand for money as people substitute from money to bonds and perhaps goods (if they do expect inflation). For a small open economy at full employment and facing given foreign prices and interest rates, this reduction in the demand for money will be reflected in an excess demand for foreign exchange reserves: a balance of payments deficit. The second point that emerges from (8.23a) is that if the economy is growing over time (i.e. $\Delta \ln Y > 0$) it will *ceteris paribus* run a balance of payments surplus. This is because income growth in this model increases the demand for money and, for a given rate of domestic credit expansion, can only be satisfied via the foreign exchange market.

Equation (8.23a) can be written in a form suitable for econometric investigation as

$$r = \beta_0 + \beta_1 \Delta \ln P + \beta_2 \Delta \ln Y + \beta_3 \Delta \ln i + \beta_5 d + \beta_6 \Delta \ln h + \mu_t \qquad (8.24)$$

where μ_t is an error term and it is expected that, if the MABP is correct, β_1 equals unity, β_2 and β_3 take values similar to those estimated in conventional money demand equations (say 1 and -0.01, respectively: see Laidler, 1992) and β_5 equals -1. (We shall discuss the term $\beta_6 \Delta \ln h$ below, in our discussion of the empirical evidence.) Perhaps the most crucial value, from the point of view of the verification of the MABP, is whether β_5, usually referred to as the offset coefficient, is exactly equal to -1 or not. For example, equation (8.24) could equally be derived from a Keynesian model, i.e. an observationally equivalent reduced form could be derived from a Keynesian structure. However, if (8.24) *was* generated from a Keynesian structure, the coefficient β_5 would lie in the interval -1 to 0, but would not be exactly equal to -1.[7]

In estimating equation (8.24), researchers have assumed that Y, P, i and d are all exogenous. The exogeneity of Y is justified on the MABP grounds of long-run full employment; i and P are assumed exogenous on the grounds that the country is small in world goods and financial markets; and if it is assumed that the authorities do not sterilize the effects of reserve changes on the money supply (i.e. if F increases D is not decreased) d may be assumed exogenous. The assumed exogeneity of the right-hand-side variables in equation (8.24) receives more attention below.

8.3.2 Empirical results

A variety of researchers have tested equation (8.24) for different countries and time periods. For example, a representative estimated equation by Bean (1976) for Japan over the period 1959–70 (quarterly data) is

Table 8.1 The offset coefficient and the monetary approach to the balance of payments

Author	Country	Data period	Estimation technique	β_5	R^2	DW
Bean (1976)	Japan	1959–70	OLS	−0.67 (8.32)	0.65	1.99
Connolly and Taylor (1976)	Various LDCs	1959–70	OLS	−0.82 (5.47)	0.65	NA
Genberg (1976)	Sweden	1951–70	TSLS	−1.11 (3.00)	NA	NA
Guittan (1976)	Spain	1955–71	OLS	−0.958 (9.65)	0.95	2.36
Kouri and Porter (1974)	Australia	1961–72	OLS	−0.47 (5.29)	0.82	1.87
Kouri and Porter (1974)	Germany	1960–70	OLS	−0.77 (18.40)	0.96	2.17
Kouri and Porter (1974)	Italy	1964–70	OLS	−0.43 (4.36)	0.66	2.55
Kouri and Porter (1974)	Netherlands	1960–70	OLS	−0.59 (7.58)	0.82	2.54
Zecher (1976)	Australia	1951–61	OLS	−0.82 (5.47)	0.65	NA

OLS, ordinary least squares; NA, not available; LDC, less developed country; TSLS, two-stage least squares; R^2, coefficient of determination; DW, Durbin–Watson statistic; t ratios are in parentheses under the β_5 coefficients.

$$r = 1.19\Delta \log P + 0.52\Delta \log Y - 0.11\Delta \log i - 0.67d \qquad (8.25)$$
$$(5.38)(6.36)(1.22)(8.32)$$

$$R^2 = 0.65 \qquad DW = 1.99 \qquad t \text{ statistics in parentheses}$$

Notice first that all coefficients are correctly signed in terms of the MABP and all, apart from the coefficient on the domestic interest rate, are statistically significant at the 95 percent level. The coefficients on P and i are close to the predicted values; however, both the income elasticity and the elasticity of the domestic component are less than predicted values of 1 and −1, respectively. (An explanation as to why β_5 may be less than −1 is given below.)

Since other researchers' specification of an MABP reduced-form equation differs slightly from equation (8.24), table 8.1 summarizes these other results for the crucial coefficient on d.

Examination of table 8.1 reveals that the MABP prediction that a change in the domestic component of the money base will be offset by an equiproportionate change in reserves finds mixed support from the empirical evidence. The studies by Connolly and Taylor, Genberg, Guittan and Zecher are all highly supportive of the proposition $\beta_5 = -1$ (in all these papers the coefficient differs insignificantly from -1); however, the results by Bean and by Kouri and Porter[8] tend to cast doubts on this proposition since the coefficient on β_5 is shown to differ significantly from -1 in these studies.

8.3.3 Problems with the empirical implementation of the monetary approach to the balance of payments reduced form equation

Some of the results reported in table 8.1 tend to question the robustness of one of the key propositions of the MABP, namely that a change in the domestic component of the money supply will result in an equiproportionate change in the foreign component. For example, Branson (1975a) has argued that the Kouri and Porter estimates β_5 are inconsistent with the MABP. But one reason why β_5 could be biased downwards may lie in the exclusion of certain key variables in the reduced form, i.e. there is a specification error. In particular, Magee (1976) argues that the exclusion of the exchange rate change will result in a specification error. Thus when the authorities increased d, the exchange rate under the Bretton Woods system was free to vary within a band and this movement may absorb some of the excess supply of money leading to a less than proportionate fall in r. Darby (1983) and Laskar (1983) have argued that a downward bias in β_5 may result from the exclusion of the expected change in the exchange rate from (8.23) (i.e. speculators may expect a change in reserves to lead to an exchange rate change).

Although four of the studies reported in table 8.1 give estimates of β_5 consistent with the MABP (i.e. estimates close to -1), critics of the approach have argued that this inverse relationship may reflect the intervention policies adopted by the central bank. Thus, an autonomous reserve inflow results in the central bank contracting the domestic component of the money base to stop the reserve flow affecting the money supply. Indeed, if the cause of the inflow is an excess demand for money the sterilization will lead to a magnification effect on reserves since the unsatisfied excess demand for money will continue to draw in reserves. Thus sterilization would be expected to lead to a magnification of the coefficient on d, so it would be expected to be greater than unity in absolute terms. If sterilization was an important feature of the countries' experience summarized in table 8.1, then the familiar problem of simultaneous equation bias would be imparted into ordinary least squares estimates of equation (8.24).[9] To account for any sterilization, a researcher would estimate equation (8.24) jointly with an equation specifying the authorities' reaction function for d. Of the studies reported in table 8.1, only Genberg (1976) utilized an estimator which accounted for simultaneous equation bias (i.e. two-stage least squares). The importance of failing to account for the bias imparted by sterilization in equations such as (8.24) is highlighted in a study by Obstfeld (1982) where it is shown that the coefficient β_5 falls from a significant -0.55 to a completely insignificant 0.003 once account is taken of the simultaneity bias (the country studied by Obstfeld is Germany over the period 1961–7).

The exclusion of exchange rate expectations from equation (8.23) may also lead to an over-estimate of the offset coefficient (for a discussion of the conflicting biases that exchange rate expectations may impart into equation (8.23), see Laskar (1983)). This is because a reserve outflow, say, may lead speculators to expect a devaluation of the exchange rate and this may lead to large capital outflows which in turn exacerbate the loss reserves. Taking account of simultaneous equation bias and the potential endogeneity of exchange rate expectations, Darby (1983) and Laskar (1983) show that non-reserve countries can exert a significant degree of control over domestic money supplies: β_5 differs significantly from unity.

However, simultaneous equation bias may still be present in estimates of equation (8.24) even after a researcher has accounted for the possibility of simultaneity from d to r. This is because in estimating equation (8.24) all the researchers mentioned in table 8.1 have assumed that P, Y and i are all exogenous and therefore are unaffected by the money supply. However, in the real world this is unlikely to be so. Indeed, an increase in d is likely to affect the other variables on the right-hand side of equation (8.24) and impart a further simultaneous equation bias. Hence, without proper specification and estimation it is not known whether the coefficients in equation (8.24) reflect a money demand equation or simply the effects of money supply on P, Y and i. As Magee (1976) points out, since such money supply phenomena work in the same direction as the demand-side influences researchers end up with ordinary least squares estimates which are biased in favour of the MABP.

*8.4 The International Transmission of Inflation: Some Evidence

In chapter 7 some empirical evidence on whether PPP holds during periods of floating exchange rates was considered. If exchange rates are fixed, then, as equation (8.15) makes clear, PPP becomes a relationship linking national price levels and inflation rates. The MABP outlined in this chapter provides a theory of the determination of such prices and *it is shown that inflation under a system of fixed exchange rates must be a worldwide phenomenon.*[10] In this section an attempt is made to shed some light on this proposition by examining some evidence on the behavior of national price levels/inflation rates during the Bretton Woods period, 1945–71.

Genberg (1978) usefully splits the statistical and econometric evidence relevant to the international transmission of inflation into two categories: those dealing with the dispersion and convergence of inter-country inflation rates and those testing the PPP relationship, using regression analysis, for the Bretton Woods period. In the former category of studies Pattison (1976), Genberg (1977) and Parkin et al. (1977) compute measures of the variance of inflation across OECD countries for the Bretton Woods period and find that there are relatively small differences across countries (although the differences tend to increase after 1967). Alternative tests of the international transmission of inflation have used regression analysis to estimate equation (8.15). For example, Genberg (1977) estimates the fixed exchange rate version of (8.15) for ten European countries, for the period 1955–70 (annual data), against the USA:

$$p_i = \alpha_0 + \alpha_1 p^* + \mu_i \tag{8.26}$$

$$\Delta p_i = b_0 + \alpha_1 \Delta p^* + \mu_i \tag{8.27}$$

where the *ps* are expressed in logarithms and the subscript *i* denotes country *i*. Under a regime of fixed exchange rates, if PPP holds, α_1 should be equal to unity and b_0 equal to zero. Genberg (1977) reports estimates of equations (8.26) and (8.27) which are consistent with such priors. However, in estimating equation (8.26) first-order autocorrelation was a problem in seven out of ten countries suggesting that there may be short-run deviations from PPP (the estimated mean lag for the re-establishment of PPP was about two years; this finding is confirmed in a further study by Genberg, 1978). Serial correlation was not a problem in the estimated version of equation (8.27) for eight out of ten countries, suggesting that although a country's price level may differ from its PPP level this divergence does not increase over time.

But as Genberg (1978) points out, the above tests say nothing about the reasons for divergences from PPP and what mechanisms lead to a restoration of PPP. A number of other researchers attempt to answer these issues by estimating alternative versions of equation (8.27):

$$\Delta p = \alpha_0 + \alpha_1 \Delta p^e + \alpha_2 x \tag{8.28}$$

where x is a measure of excess demand which may reflect monetary or fiscal impulses and Δp^e represents the expected inflation rate (i.e. inflationary expectations are one channel by which inflation may be transmitted internationally). Cross and Laidler (1976) and Laidler (1992) estimate versions of equation (8.28) for a variety of European countries where the lagged rate of change of foreign price enters the estimated equations as a proxy for inflationary expectations and excess demand is proxied by lagged income. Although the estimated results show that the rate of inflation for a country with fixed exchange rates will average over time to the rest of the world rate, the convergence rate is slow (between two and five years depending on the country); excess demand is also shown to be statistically significant. In a survey of other researchers' studies of equation (8.28), Genberg (1978) concludes that the estimates of α_1 (where Δp^* stands in for Δp^e) are "almost universally below unity ... [and] ... excess demand measures summarized by x are very often significant explanatory factors."

Interestingly, in some countries it is found that world excess monetary growth is a better proxy for excess demand than the domestic money stock.

NOTES

1 For a similar derivation see, for example, Mundell (1968) and Whitman (1975).

2 This model is adapted from Dornbusch (1973).

3 The slope of the two schedules may be seen in the following way. On substitution of (8.10) in (8.11) we obtain $H = \alpha(kPY - M)$ which clearly shows the positive relationship between H and P. For the foreign country a similar relationship holds, namely

$$H^* = \alpha^*(K^*P^*Y^* - M^*)$$

and from equation (8.15)

$$P^* = \frac{P}{S}$$

By substitution

$$H^* = \alpha^*\left(k^*\frac{P}{S}Y^* - M\right)^*$$

and $dH^*/dP > 0$. In figure 8.1 $dH^*/dP > 0$, as the positive quadrant for foreign hoarding is on the left-hand side.

4 Thus given that $P^* = P/S$ it follows that

$$\frac{dP^*}{P^*} = \frac{dP}{P} - \frac{dS}{S}$$

so if the proportionate devaluation is greater than the rise in home price, foreign prices will *fall*.

5 Rabin and Yeager (1982, p. 5).

6 Carr and Darby (1981) present empirical evidence for a number of countries which suggest that the aggregate buffer stock concept is important.

7 This point has been emphasized by Kreinin and Officer (1978).

8 Kouri and Porter (1974) estimate a reduced-form capital flow equation instead of equation (8.23).

9 Kouri and Porter (1974) demonstrate that if the authorities use a reaction function relating d to r, and other variables, the estimate of β_5 will be biased towards -1.

10 An alternative view of the international transmission of inflation appeals to "special factors," such as the monopoly power of trade unions and the business sector, commodity price rises and oil-price shocks. For discussions of the monetary approach/ special factors view see Laidler and Parkin (1975), Laidler and Nobay (1976), Johnson (1977) and Darby and Lothian (1983).

9

The Monetary View of Exchange Rate Determination

As was noted in chapter 2, the key issue in what we have termed the balance of payments view of the exchange rate was whether speculation would have a stabilizing impact on the exchange rate. Writing in the 1960s, advocates of flexible exchange rates strongly argued that speculation would be stabilizing and that this would tend to limit the extent of any exchange rate movements. However, one of the key features of the recent float has been the extreme volatility of exchange rates, as we pointed out in chapter 2 (see also the discussion in chapter 24).

How may the exchange rate volatility be explained? On the face of it, such volatility would seem to conflict with the views of Friedman (1953), and others, that a flexible rate regime would be one in which exchange rate movements were relatively stable. Such stability was ensured, or so it was argued, by the stabilizing behavior of speculators. One interpretation of the volatility then would be to argue that speculators have had a destabilizing effect on exchange rates. This was the position taken by McKinnon (1976), who argued that there was *insufficient* speculation because foreign exchange dealers in commercial banks were constrained from taking sufficient net open positions in foreign exchange because of institutional constraints (e.g. a foreign exchange dealer normally, at the end of a day's trading, has to balance his or her foreign exchange liabilities against his or her foreign exchange assets). Another interpretation of volatility would simply be to say that, regardless of the amount of speculative funds available, speculators have had a destabilizing effect because they have been ill-informed and acted in an irrational manner. This position has become extremely fashionable recently with the development of noise-trader models, and is discussed more fully in chapter 13. In this chapter and the next, however, we attempt to explain exchange rate volatility by appealing to the asset approach to the exchange rate.[1] As we shall see, this approach offers an explanation of exchange rate volatility which does not depend on the insufficiency of speculative funds or the irrational behavior of speculators. Indeed, *most asset market models assume that agents are rational maximizing individuals.*

In this chapter we show why it is useful to regard the exchange rate as an asset price and outline three versions of the asset approach which have attained a considerable degree of popularity:

1   the flex-price monetary approach to the exchange rate;
2   the sticky-price monetary approach to the exchange rate; and
3   the currency substitution model.

These three different asset views are particularly useful because they introduce a number of concepts prominent in the asset approach.[2] In discussing the flex-price monetary model we also introduce the concept of a rational speculative bubble which a number of researchers have proposed as a means of explaining excess exchange rate volatility.

9.1 The Asset Approach to the Exchange Rate

In order to explain the variability of exchange rates, international economists have moved away from the flow demand/supply analysis outlined in chapter 3 to the asset approach to the exchange rate (this switch in emphasis parallels the move from the elasticities and absorption approaches to the monetary approach to the balance of payments outlined in chapter 8).[3] It is argued that the exchange rate should be viewed as an asset price since it is by definition the price of one national money in terms of another (i.e. it is a relative asset price). Thus proponents of the asset approach (see, for example, Mussa, 1976, 1979a) argue that one should use tools normally used for the determination of other asset prices (such as bond and share prices) in analyzing the determinants of exchange rates, rather than analyzing the exchange rate in terms of flow demand and flow supplies. This argument would seem to have considerable force since, as we have seen, exchange rate volatility seems to be of a similar order of magnitude to the volatility of other asset prices.

For example, when considering an ordinary "normal" good it is customary to think of the flow demand and supply functions as depending on essentially different variables (e.g. demand is a function of tastes, incomes and relative product prices whereas supply is a function of technology and factor prices), the price being the outcome of the intersection of the demand and supply schedules. Price changes in this analysis are caused by shifts in the demand and supply schedules, the extent of the price change being contingent on relative elasticities. In contrast, the price of an asset changes because the market *as a whole* changes its view of what the asset is worth; buyers and sellers are therefore motivated by the *same* factors. Thus, the price of an asset, such as a share in BP or IBM, changes because the market as a whole changes its view of what the company, to which the asset is a title, is worth. The revision of a company's worth may be due to the arrival of new information about, say, the company's profitability. Crucially, the price may change (perhaps by a considerable amount) with little or no trade actually taking place: the price is simply marked up or down by dealers. It is very difficult to explain large price movements in the traditional flow model without substantial amounts of trade taking place. "The basic idea of the asset approach to the exchange rate is that essentially the same theory of the determination of prices of common shares is relevant to the determination of the exchange rate" (Mussa, 1979a).

A number of additional important implications, which we briefly note here and consider in more detail in future sections and chapters, follow from viewing the exchange rate as an asset price (or, more specifically, as the relative price of national monies). First, expectations will be important in the determination of the current exchange rate. Since monies are durable, in the sense that they can be held by investors for a number of periods, expectations about future exchange rates will affect the current exchange rate. Thus, if for some reason agents change their perception of the expected future exchange rate we would expect today's exchange rate to change by a similar amount; otherwise there would be a (possibly) large unexploited expected return available in the foreign exchange market. Since the exchange rate is the relative price of two monies one reason why agents may alter their beliefs about the expected exchange rate could be a change in the money supply (or the fiscal deficit, to the extent that it is financed by printing money) expected to prevail in the future. The importance of expectations in foreign exchange markets should result in a close correspondence between actual exchange rates and the markets' expected future exchange rate (this will be discussed further below and in chapters 11 and 12).

Two further implications of using a monetary framework to analyze the exchange rate have already been emphasized in the chapter on the monetary approach to the balance of payments. Thus, real factors can affect the exchange rate/balance of payments, but only to the extent that they first affect the demand for money. Also, since assets are stocks, equilibrium is defined as a situation where the stock demand for money is equal to the stock supply of money. Flows of assets across the foreign exchanges can occur, but such flows are a reflection of *disequilibrium* between money demand and money supply and must eventually cease.

A final implication of regarding the exchange rate as an asset price is that such prices are usually regarded as being determined in efficient markets. An efficient asset market, following Fama (1970), is one in which market participants exploit all profitable trading opportunities and force the current price to reflect all available information. Under certain circumstances this implies that exchange rates should behave randomly: they should follow a random walk.[4] A further implication of regarding the exchange market as an efficient market is that in such a market the forward exchange rate set today is usually taken to be the market's expectation of the spot rate in some future time period. The difference between the forward rate set at time t, with a maturity in $t + 1$, and the actual spot rate at $t + 1$ is the unexpected change in the exchange rate. In periods, in which there is a great deal of new information about, say, the future paths of money supplies, we should not be surprised if the unexpected change in the exchange rate is large and there are correspondingly large movements in spot exchange rates (the "news" approach to modeling the exchange rate is discussed in chapter 13).

In chapters 12 and 13 the efficient markets implications of viewing the exchange rate as an asset price will be discussed. In this chapter we concentrate on the other implications of regarding the exchange rate as an asset price: namely, the roles of money demand, money supply and expectations in the determination of the exchange rate. Consideration is initially given to the flex-price monetary approach to the exchange rate.

◆ 9.2 The Flex-price Monetary Approach to the Exchange Rate

The flex-price monetary model is in many ways an extension of the purchasing power parity (PPP) view of exchange rates outlined in chapter 7; essentially it appends a theory of the determination of the price level to a PPP equation in order to explain the exchange rate. The use of PPP in a theory of the determination of the exchange rate immediately introduces a problem for, as has been shown, PPP is not well supported empirically. Nevertheless, it is useful to examine the flex-price monetary approach (FLMA) as a first stepping stone in the study of more complex asset models and also because it offers an interesting explanation of recent exchange rate volatility.

The flex-price monetary model discussed here has the following characteristics which are common to the MABP models considered in chapter 8. We consider a two-country version of this model in which the domestic and foreign country each produce a good and these goods are assumed to be perfect substitutes. In the absence of restrictions to trade this means that PPP holds continuously:

$$s_t = p_t - p_t^* \tag{9.1}$$

where s_t, p_t and p_t^* are logarithmic values of the corresponding level terms. Additionally, each country issues money and a bond; the monies are assumed to be non-substitutable (i.e. the concept of currency substitution, discussed below, is ignored), whilst the bonds are assumed to be perfect substitutes. Since it is further assumed that asset-holders can adjust their portfolios instantly after a disturbance, and thus capital is perfectly mobile ($C_i = \infty$ as in equation (5.6)), uncovered interest rate parity must also hold:

$$\Delta s^e_{t+1} = (i - i^*)_t \tag{9.2}$$

where Δs^e_{t+1} denotes the (logarithmic) expected change in the exchange rate, one period ahead, and the i terms again denote interest rates. It is also worth explicitly writing down the (nominal) wealth constraint facing domestic residents (an equivalent relationship would also hold in the foreign country):

$$W = M + B + B^* \tag{9.3}$$

$$W = M + V \tag{9.3a}$$

where W denotes nominal wealth, M denotes domestic money, B denotes domestic bonds and $V = B + B^*$. Equation (9.3) simply says that agents can hold their wealth in the form of three different assets. However, since the bonds are perfect substitutes we may add them into one composite asset, V. Hence in thinking about asset markets it is legitimate to concentrate on either the money market or "the" (composite) bond market; if the money market is in equilibrium so too will the bond market be and, additionally, any disequilibrium in the money market will have as its equal and opposite disequilibrium in the bond market.[5] In the monetary approach (and this is common to all three versions of the monetary model considered in this chapter) attention is focused on the money market. The above point is worth noting because, as we shall see, it implies that bonds have no independent role to play in the determination of the exchange rate.

The money market consists of money demand and money supply relationships in the home and foreign countries. The money demand function is given by

$$m^D_t - p_t = \alpha_1 y_t - \alpha_2 i_t \qquad \alpha_1, \alpha_2 > 0 \tag{9.4}$$

$$m^{D*}_t - p^*_t = \alpha_1 y^*_t - \alpha_2 i^*_t \tag{9.4a}$$

where, of variables not previously defined, m^D is the natural logarithm of money demand and y is the natural logarithm of the level of real national income. Since the dependent variable and y in (9.4) are expressed as natural logarithms, α_1 has the interpretation of the income elasticity of the demand for money and, since i is expressed as a proportion (not a logarithm), α_2 has the interpretation of a semi-elasticity. Notice that we have assumed, for simplicity, that the income elasticity and interest rate semi-elasticity are equal across countries. Equations (9.4) and (9.4a) are typical Cagan demand for money functions, written in logarithmic form. The money supply is assumed to be exogenously determined by the monetary authorities and money markets are continuously equilibrated (i.e. money demand is always equal to money supply); thus

$$m^D_t = m^s_t = m_t \tag{9.5}$$

$$m^{D*}_t = m^{s*}_t = m^*_t \tag{9.5a}$$

Notice that the change in foreign exchange reserves must equal zero in this model because the exchange rate is assumed to be perfectly flexible: Δm_t must be equal to Δd_t – i.e. domestic credit expansion.

By substituting (9.5) into (9.4), subtracting the resulting foreign money market relationship from the domestic expression and solving for the relative price level we obtain

$$p_t - p_t^* = m_t - m_t^* - \alpha_1(y - y^*)_t + \alpha_2(i - i^*)_t \tag{9.6}$$

This expression may, in turn, be substituted into (9.1) in order to obtain a reduced-form equation which is our portrayal of the FLMA:

$$s = m_t - m_t^* - \alpha_1(y - y^*)_t + \alpha_2(i - i^*)_t \tag{9.7}$$

The predictions of the FLMA may be illustrated using the domestic country variables entering (9.7) (the effect of the foreign variables is equal and opposite to that discussed below). First, an x percent increase in the domestic money supply leads to an x percent increase in s (depreciation). This seems intuitive enough: countries which inflate their money supplies at a faster rate than their competitors, *ceteris paribus*, can expect to suffer a depreciation in the external value of their currency. Second, an increase in income leads to an exchange rate appreciation. This result is in sharp contrast to the result noted in chapter 3 where an increase in income led to an exchange rate depreciation. Third, an increase in the domestic interest rate leads to an exchange rate *depreciation* and again this is in marked contrast to the result obtained in chapter 3 where an increase in the home interest rate led to an appreciation of the exchange rate. How can these apparently conflicting results be reconciled?

The way to understand the "puzzling" effects of y and i is to recognize that these variables only affect the exchange rate via their effect on money demand. Thus an increase in income increases the transactions demand for money and, with a constant nominal money supply, money market equilibrium can only be maintained if the domestic price level falls; this in turn can only occur, given a strict PPP assumption, if the exchange rate changes. Thus the exchange rate appreciates in order to restore equality between real money demand and real money supply (i.e. the price level falls). Evidence in favour of this prediction may be found in the behavior of the Japanese yen and German mark exchange rates. On average, each of these currencies experienced appreciations in each of the years since the inception of the floating rate period and both Japan and Germany were countries which enjoyed high income growth rates relative to their trading partners.

The positive effect of the domestic rate of interest on the exchange rate again reflects the effect of interest rates on money demand. This follows from the assumed world in which we are operating. The easiest way to see what is happening is to recognize that a rise in the domestic interest rate reduces the demand for money, which needs a rise in the domestic price level to maintain equilibrium in the money market (a rise in real income would also do the trick, but we are assuming that real income is fixed at the full employment level). However, given that PPP holds, the domestic price level can only rise if the exchange rate depreciates.

Another way to look at the positive relationship between i and s is to recognize that nominal interest rates are assumed to obey the Fisher parity relationship outlined in chapter 3, i.e.

$$i_t = r_t + \Delta p^e_{t+1} \tag{9.8}$$

$$i^*_t = r^*_t + \Delta p^{e*}_{t+1} \tag{9.8a}$$

where r_t is the real interest rate and Δp^e_{t+1} is the expected inflation rate over the maturity horizon of the underlying bond. Assuming that real interest rates are equalized across countries, equation (9.7) may be rewritten as

$$s = m_t - m^*_t - \alpha_1(y - y^*)_t + \alpha_2(\Delta p^e - \Delta p^{e*})_{t+1} \tag{9.7a}$$

Thus an increase in the domestic interest rate reflects an increase in expected inflation and a reduced desire to hold real money balances. Given an exogenously fixed nominal money supply, the only way that real money balances can be altered is by an increase in the price level which is accommodated by an exchange rate depreciation.

 ## 9.3 Introducing Expectations

In the introductory remarks to this chapter it was argued that regarding the exchange rate as an asset price means that expectations about the future course of its determinants will be important for the current determination of the exchange rate. Equation (9.7) may be helpfully utilized to explain why it is possible for exchange rates to exhibit a great deal of variability relative to the *current* determinants of the exchange rate, such as current money supplies.

By substituting the uncovered interest rate parity term (equation (9.2)) in equation (9.7) and by defining $z_t = m_t - m^*_t - \alpha_1(y - y^*)_t$ we obtain

$$s_t = z_t + \alpha_2(s^e_{t+1} - s_t) \tag{9.7b}$$

where $\Delta s^e_{t+1} = s^e_{t+1} - s_t$. On gathering terms is s_t and rearranging, we obtain

$$s_t = \frac{1}{1 + \alpha_2} z_t + \frac{\alpha_2}{1 + \alpha_2} s^e_{t+1} \tag{9.9}$$

We now assume rational expectations, and therefore set subjective expectations, s^e_{t+1} equal to expectations conditional on the full information set (where this is deemed to include knowledge of the process of exchange rate determination and its underlying stochastic structure):

$$s_{t+1}^e = E(s_{t+1} \mid I_t) = E_t s_{t+1} \qquad (9.10)$$

where E is the rational expectations operator and I denotes the information set. Hence the imposition of rational expectations implies that we may rewrite (9.9) as

$$s_t = \frac{1}{1 + \alpha_2} z_t + \frac{\alpha_2}{1 + \alpha_2} E_t s_{t+1} \qquad (9.9a)$$

From the foregoing discussion it is clear that the factors determining the expected exchange rate in the monetary model are what agents expect the money supply and income to be in the future. Thus the expectation of the exchange rate in any future period will be given by

$$E_t s_{t+j} = \frac{1}{1 + \alpha_2} (E_t z_{t+j} + \alpha_2 E_t s_{t+j+1}) \qquad (9.11)$$

By repeatedly substituting for $E_t s_{t+1}$ in (9.9a) for n future time periods we obtain the rational expectations reduced-form exchange rate equation:

$$s_t = \frac{1}{1 + \alpha_2} \sum_{j=0}^{n} \left(\frac{\alpha_2}{1 + \alpha_2} \right)^j E_t z_{t+j} + \left(\frac{\alpha_2}{1 + \alpha_2} \right)^n E_t s_{t+n+1} \qquad (9.12)$$

The behavior of the last term in (9.12) is crucial in determining whether or not there exists a stable or explosive solution to the model. If the term in parentheses, $\alpha_2(1 + \alpha_2)^{-1}$, is less than unity the last term in (9.12) will go to zero as j goes to infinity. If, however, this term is greater than unity, (9.12) will have an infinity of explosive solutions, depending on the value taken by the expected exchange rate. *This explosive solution is usually referred to as the bubbles solution* and is discussed in more detail below. For the moment we impose the transversality, or terminal, condition that $\alpha_2(1 + \alpha_2)^{-1}$ is indeed less than unity (since α_2 has the interpretation of the interest rate semi-elasiticity of the demand for money, and will usually be expected to have a value of around 0.02,[6] this is not an implausible assumption) and we obtain the expectations-augmented FLMA

$$s_t = \frac{1}{1 + \alpha_2} \sum_{j=0}^{\infty} \left(\frac{\alpha_2}{1 + \alpha_2} \right)^j E_t z_{t+j} \qquad (9.13)$$

where we have set $n = \infty$. We may write in a more compact notation as

$$s_t = (1 - \beta) \sum_{j=0}^{\infty} \beta^j E_t z_{t+j} \qquad (9.13a)$$

where $\beta = \alpha_2(1 + \alpha_2)^{-1}$. Equation 9.13 shows, in the context of a simple monetary model with rational expectations, that the current exchange rate depends not just on current excess money supplies but also on expected future excess money supplies. The discounting factor α_2 discounts expected future money growth into the current spot rate in a manner analogous to that in which revisions in expected future earnings are discounted into equity prices.

The effect of current changes in the money supply on the exchange rate depends crucially on what people perceive as the stochastic structure underlying the authorities' money supply rule. For example, if the money supply increases by x percent in the current period and this change is believed to be temporary then via equations (9.12) and (9.13) the expected future exchange rate would be little affected and hence the current spot exchange rate would simply reflect the current money supply change. Exchange rate expectations are likely to be regressive under such a regime. By "regressive" we mean that, say, a current depreciation of the exchange rate generates an expectation that the exchange rate will eventually reappreciate. If, in contrast to the above example, the x percent increase in the money supply led to the expectation that domestic rates of monetary expansion would be x percent higher than foreign rates for the indefinite future, then the exchange rate would depreciate by far more than the current x percent change in the money supply.

For example, let us assume that the stochastic structure driving the fundamentals in (9.13) is given by the following first-order autoregressive process:

$$z_t = \theta z_{t-1} + \varepsilon_t \qquad \theta < 1 \tag{9.14}$$

where ε_t is a white noise disturbance. Because θ is assumed to be less than unity, (9.14) is a stable system in that a current disturbance to z_t will not be expected to last indefinitely into the future – such a process is stationary and its variance is bounded. Thus if ε in the current period were £100 million this would increase z_t by £100 million. In the next period, however, z would only be some fraction of the total and eventually the initial shock will be extinguished (of course other new shocks may affect z in the intervening period). If (9.14) describes the process driving fundamentals then it may be used to forecast the fundamentals in any future period. For example, for period $t + j$ (9.14) implies[7]

$$E_t z_{t+j} = \theta^j z_t \tag{9.14a}$$

On using (9.14a) in (9.13a) we obtain the following solution for the exchange rate:

$$s_t = (1 - \beta)(1 - \theta\beta)^{-1} z_t \tag{9.15}$$

Equation (9.15) is simply the solution to the infinite geometric progression in (9.13), given the model of fundamentals (9.14). It is clear from (9.15) that the effect a current change in z will have on the current exchange rate will depend critically on the magnitude of the parameters θ and β. For example, if, as we have suggested already, α_2 is around 0.02 then β will equal 0.019. If θ is, say, 0.9 then a 1 percent rise in z_t will result in an approximate 1 percent rise in the exchange rate – there is not an exchange rate magnification effect. This is simply because (9.14) implies that a current increase in z_t is expected to be reversed in the future;

it does not signal higher values for fundamentals in the future and a corresponding need to revise expectations upwards. However, if fundamentals are not driven by the stable system in (9.14) the story may be very different. For example, say θ in (9.14) equals 10 then in this case the exchange rate will increase by 1.21, which represents a fairly dramatic magnification effect. This is simply because a current increase in z_t is reinforced in the future by a continuing sequence of increases. Therefore, a current increase has a big influence on future expectations and, through the discounting process in (9.13), a big effect on the current exchange rate.

Equation (9.13) then gives an explanation for the volatility in exchange rates relative to current fundamentals, and is the correct light in which to view the issue of whether speculators have had a stabilizing or destabilizing influence on the exchange rate during the recent floating experience. Thus, it is often argued that it is regressive expectations that are stabilizing. But in the rational expectations monetary model expectations are regressive *because the underlying behavior of the money supply makes regressive expectations appropriate*. However, it is not only regressive expectations which are stabilizing; in the context of the above model what may be regarded as destabilizing expectations may be seen as stabilizing. Thus, large movements in the current exchange rate may reflect agents' beliefs that current changes in the money supply are suggestive of higher monetary growth in the future. On this basis there is little likelihood of the exchange rate depreciation being offset by a later appreciation. Such expectations, though, may be regarded as "stabilizing" because, as Mussa (1976) notes, they are the best possible prediction of future exchange rates, given the nature of monetary policy and the information available to asset-holders.

The above explanation of exchange rate volatility is in terms of the underlying instability of the variables driving the exchange rate. It is interesting to note at this juncture that although Friedman argued that speculation would have a stabilizing influence on the exchange rate (see chapter 3) this was contingent on the underlying economic structure being stable. Thus

> advocacy of flexible exchange rates is *not* equivalent to advocacy of unstable exchange rates. The ultimate objective is a world in which exchange rates, while *free* to vary, are in fact highly stable. *Instability of exchange rates is a symptom of instability in the underlying economic structure.* (Emphasis in last sentence added)

Thus, Friedman, writing in 1953, clearly anticipated the rational expectations exchange rate literature!

If the monetary model is the correct description of the exchange rate then its inherent simplicity clearly makes it an important tool for policy purposes. It implies, for example, that any change in the money supply has a proportionate effect on the exchange rate and hence on prices. Furthermore, the rational expectation version of equation (9.7) implies that monetary policy should be predictable and stable; instability in the money supply process implies unstable exchange rates. In the final section of this chapter we discuss the empirical evidence pertaining to the validity of the FLMA, in both is reduced-form (9.7) version and its expectations-augmented version.

■ 9.4 Rational Speculative Bubbles

This is a useful juncture at which to introduce the concept of a rational speculative bubble. The concept of a speculative bubble is often used to explain why asset prices like exchange rates take long swings away from their fundamental values, the dramatic appreciation of the US dollar in the early 1980s being a classic example – see Frankel (1985). Also the concept of a speculative bubble is often invoked, particularly in the popular press, as a way of explaining the exchange rate volatility that, as we have seen, has been such a prominent feature of the recent floating experience. Although the bubble concept has relevance to a broader range of models than the FLMA, the FLMA offers a particularly convenient framework for examining speculative bubbles because of its emphasis on the role of the expected exchange rate.

Consider equation (9.9a) again. As we have just seen, *one* rational expectations solution to that model is given by equation (9.13). Let us now label the exchange rate given by (9.13) as s_t^n, the "no-bubbles" solution. As we have seen, though, this solution only exists if a terminal, or transversality, condition is imposed, namely that the limit of the last term in (9.12) goes to zero. If it does not, then there are in principle an infinite number of rational expectations solutions for the spot rate, each of which can be written in the form

$$s_t = s_t^n + b_t \tag{9.16}$$

where b_t is the speculative bubble term which will be important if investors believe it to be so. For (9.16) to be a solution to (9.9a), an assumption has to be made concerning b_t and it is that

$$b_t = \beta E_t b_{t+1} \tag{9.17}$$

To see this, note that from (9.16) we may define the rationally expected exchange rate in the next period as

$$E_t s_{t+1} = E_t s_{t+1}^n + E_t b_{t+1} \tag{9.18}$$

Using the definition of $E_t s_{t+1}$ given by (9.18) and the definition of s_t given by (9.13) in (9.9a) we obtain

$$s_t^n + b_t = (1 - \beta)z_t + \beta E_t s_{t+1}^n + \beta E_t b_{t+1} \tag{9.19}$$

Given that s_t^n is defined by (9.13) this expression reduces to (9.17).[8] So as long as the restriction (9.17) is satisfied, the existence of a (rational) speculative bubble will be consistent with the satisfaction of (9.9a). Alternatively, it is clear that if we impose the restriction (9.17) on (9.19) we end up with a simple rearrangement of (9.9a); i.e. $(1 - \beta)z_t + \beta E_t s_{t+1}^n = (1 - \beta)\sum_{j=0}^{\infty} \beta^j E_t z_t$ and s_t^n is defined as simply equivalent to s_t.

A number of processes for the evolution of the bubble term have been proposed (see Blanchard and Watson (1982) and Blanchard and Fischer (1989) for an extended discussion), all of which satisfy the restriction (9.17). The simplest form of bubble process is to assume that the b_t is equal to a constant b (assumed to be greater than zero). From (9.16) and (9.17) this implies that the exchange rate will depreciate by an amount equal to βb *even when fundamentals are assumed to be constant*; this is a pure capital gain, unrelated to fundamentals, which investors receive from transferring their funds from the domestic currency to the foreign currency. A slightly more complicated process for the bubble would be to posit that it follows a deterministic trend, i.e.

$$b_t = b_0 \beta^{-\text{time}} \tag{9.20}$$

where time denotes a time trend. If (9.20) is the process driving the bubble, it indicates that the exchange rate will depreciate exponentially even if fundamentals are constant (assuming $b_0 > 0$). The process given by (9.20) illustrates well the notion that a current exchange rate depreciation becomes self-fulfilling as agents expect further depreciations in the future. However, these kinds of deterministic bubbles processes are not particularly realistic, since they effectively assume that the process continues *ad infinitum*. In practice, though, every bubble must eventually burst (i.e. the most widely-cited bouts of bubble mania – the South Sea bubble and the Tulipmania bubble in Holland – are not consistent with a deterministic process since they eventually burst). A more realistic class of bubbles, which allows bubbles to grow and burst, has been suggested by Blanchard and Watson (1982):

$$b_{t+1} = (\beta\pi)^{-1} + \varepsilon_{t+1} \quad \text{with probability } \pi$$

or

$$b_{t+1} = \varepsilon_{t+1} \qquad \text{with probability } 1 - \pi$$

where ε_{t+1} is a purely random term with an expected value of zero. This structure indicates that in any period the bubble has a probability π of continuing and a probability $1 - \pi$ of collapsing down to ε. Once collapsed, the ε term allows a new bubble to start. Note that this type of process also satisfies (9.17) and therefore may also be used to generate (9.9a).

There are a number of factors cited in the literature which limit the importance of speculative bubbles. For example, because the price of an asset can never be negative we can never have negative speculative bubbles. This is because with $b_t < 0$ it follows that the expectation of b in the distant future goes to minus infinity (see the discussion after equation (9.18)) and this in turn would imply a negative expected price, which we have just ruled out – no one would want to hold such an asset. Also, for assets which have some fixed terminal value, such as a redeemable bond, the price at redemption must be given by the redemption value and therefore there cannot be a speculative bubble at this date. It therefore follows, by backward recursion, that b must also equal zero in all past periods and so for this type of asset a bubble cannot get started. Of course exchange rates are asset prices which do not have a terminal value and therefore may be more inclined to reflect speculative elements. But the fact that the exchange rate is in a sense more like the price of a non-redeemable asset, such as a consol, also limits the possibility of the existence of positive speculative bubbles. Such assets effectively have an infinite life and Tirole (1982) has demonstrated, in the context of an infinite horizon model, that positive bubbles cannot arise. The idea is that an agent who sells a stock at a price higher than its fundamental value and leaves the market passes on a stock with a negative present value; this is clearly not an attractive investment for a rational maximizing agent (see Blanchard and Fischer (1989) for further problems with the rational speculative bubble concept).

◼ 9.5 The Sticky-price Monetary Approach

In this section a version of the monetary approach to the exchange rate due to Dornbusch (1976) is discussed. This model has the same properties as the FLMA in the *long run*; however, it differs fundamentally in its short-run properties because prices are assumed to be sticky. We label this model the sticky-price monetary approach (SPMA). As we shall see, such price stickiness gives another explanation for exchange rate volatility in terms of exchange rate overshooting. A useful way of characterizing this model is to say that equation (9.1) holds as a long-run phenomenon:

$$\bar{s}_t = \bar{p}_t - \bar{p}_t^* \tag{9.21}$$

where the bars denote variables at their long-run values. In the short run, though, (9.21) may be violated:

$$s_t \neq p_t - p_t^* \tag{9.22}$$

In this model the asset sector is assumed to be identical to the FLMA. For expository purposes we assume the foreign price level to be constant throughout our analysis and therefore we may legitimately ignore the foreign monetary sector: equations (9.4) and (9.5) are assumed to characterize domestic monetary conditions and the uncovered interest rate parity condition (equation (9.2)) is assumed to hold continuously. This means that asset markets continually clear. The stickiness of goods prices means that goods markets do not continuously clear (although they do clear in the long run). There is therefore an asymmetry of adjustment between goods and asset markets. The failure of PPP continually to hold results in two differences between this model and the FLMA.

First, in the FLMA the expected change in the exchange rate was demonstrated to be continuously equal to the expected inflation differential. The failure of PPP to hold in the short-run SPMA means that an alternative representation for the expected change in the exchange rate has to be used. In the short run it is assumed that the expected change in the exchange rate is equal to a constant proportion ϕ of the difference between the equilibrium value $\bar{s}_t$ and the current level s_t:

$$\Delta s^e_{t+1} = \phi(\bar{s} - s)_t \qquad 0 < \phi < 1 \qquad (9.23)$$

i.e. expectations are assumed to be governed by the same regressive expectations mechanism as that introduced in chapter 3.[9]

A second novel aspect of this model compared with the FLMA is that since PPP may be violated in the short run but not in the long run an equation describing the evolution of the price level from short to long-run equilibrium is required. It is therefore assumed that the price level adjusts in proportion to excess (over output) aggregate demand; i.e.

$$\Delta p_{t+1} = \Pi(d - y)_t \qquad \Pi > 0 \qquad (9.24)$$

where d_t denotes the logarithm of aggregate demand and Π is the speed of adjustment parameter. The demand function is assumed to have the form

$$d_t = \beta_0 + \beta_1(s - p)_t + \beta_2 y_t - \beta_3 i_t \qquad \beta_0, \beta_1, \beta_2, \beta_3 > 0 \qquad (9.25)$$

This demand function is closely related to the Mundell–Fleming demand function considered in chapter 5. Thus the $s - p$ term captures the effects of the real exchange rate on the trade balance and hence aggregate demand (i.e. if s rises relative to p demand will be switched towards home goods).[10] The y term reflects the effect of income on expenditure magnitudes such as consumption. The i term reflects the effect of the interest rate on domestic absorption and thus an increase in i results *ceteris paribus* in a fall in aggregate demand. The β_0 term is a shift parameter which, perhaps, reflects government spending. Assuming that output is fixed at the full employment level $\bar{y}$, then the change in the price level is given by

$$\Delta p_{t+1} = \Pi[\beta_0 + \beta_1(s - p)_t + (\beta_2 - 1)y_t - \beta_3 i_t] \qquad (9.26)$$

The workings of the above model structure may be illustrated in the following way using figure 9.1 which is from Dornbusch (1976a).

The 45° line shows the long-run factor of proportionality between the price level and the exchange rate, given that PPP holds in the long run and that p^* is fixed. Hence moving along the 45° line, PPP is assumed to hold. Below the 45° line the exchange rate has risen relative to the domestic price level, so there is excess demand for domestic goods; above the 45° line there is an excess supply of domestic goods.

The MM schedule captures money market equilibrium in an open economy in which uncovered interest rate parity holds at all times (i.e. capital is perfectly mobile). To see why MM has a negative slope recall that the demand for money is a positive function of the price level and a negative function of the rate of interest (it

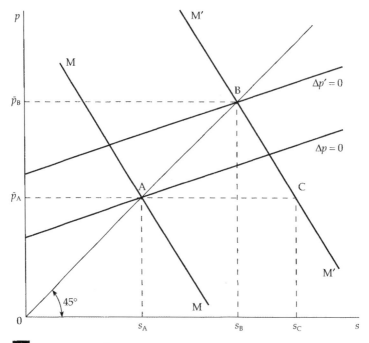

Figure 9.1 Overshooting and the sticky-price model

is also a positive function of real income, but real income is assumed fixed here). Thus, if the economy was initially in equilibrium at point A in figure 9.1 and for some reason the price level increased above $\bar{p}_A$, it would be necessary for the interest rate to increase to ensure that money market equilibrium is maintained. But a rise in i, with i^* fixed and uncovered interest rate parity holding at all times, is possible only if the exchange rate is expected to depreciate. Hence as p rises above $\bar{p}_A$, s, from (9.2), must fall below $\bar{s}_A$ – the long-run equilibrium exchange rate.[11]

Notice that the slope of MM depends on α_2 and ϕ, as can be seen by differentiating (9.45) in note 11; i.e. $dp/ds = -\alpha_2\phi$. So the smaller is the interest semi-elasticity of demand for money, or the slower is the speed of adjustment of s to $\bar{s}$, the flatter is MM.

The $\Delta p = 0$ schedule is drawn for short-run goods market equilibrium; i.e. excess demand for goods is zero. The positive slope of the $\Delta p = 0$ schedule is due to the assumption of continuous full employment and the fact that a rise in the price level – which would reduce aggregate demand – must be offset by a rise in the exchange rate.

The slope of the $\Delta p = 0$ schedule is less than the 45° ray, which indicates that the depreciation of the exchange rate is more than proportional to the rise in the price level. To see why this must be so, notice that a rise in the price level adversely affects international trade *and* reduces the real money supply. Thus, just to restore international competitiveness, the exchange rate would need to rise in proportion to the rise in the price level. However, the fall in the domestic real money supply means that the rate of interest has to rise to maintain money market equilibrium and this, in turn, will have a further deleterious effect on expenditure. Then in order to maintain full employment, the country must attract more foreign spending by a further depreciation of the exchange rate – so the proportional rise in s ends up being more than the proportional rise in p.[12]

Consider now an unexpected x percent increase in the domestic money supply from the initial equilibrium at A. It should be clear that since monetary homogeneity is a long-run property of this model (see equations (9.21) and (9.44) in note 11), the exchange rate and the price level must change in proportion to the increase in the money supply; we take the new long-run equilibrium to be at point B where the MM schedule has shifted rightwards and the Δp schedule has shifted upwards (i.e. the move to the new long-run equilibrium simply involves moving along the 45° ray). But in the short run prices are sticky and therefore goods market equilibrium is not immediately attained and the money market is not cleared via a price increase. Instead the money market is cleared in the short run by a fall in the domestic interest rate. Unlike the situation in the basic Mundell–Fleming model, this is possible because Δs^e is not equal to zero and therefore the current exchange rate can move to allow interest rates at home and in the foreign country to diverge. In terms of figure 9.1, the exchange rate jumps from A to C in the short run. Notice that the exchange rate *overshoots* the new long-run equilibrium exchange rate, i.e. $s_C > \bar{s}_B$. This follows from the uncovered interest parity equation which implies that the home interest rate can only be below the foreign rate if market participants expect the exchange rate to appreciate and the latter can only occur if the current spot rate moves by more than the long-run exchange rate.

The above overshooting of the exchange rate is captured concisely by equation (9.27), which may be thought of as an exchange rate multiplier (in response to the monetary change):[13]

$$\frac{ds}{dm} = 1 + \frac{1}{\alpha_2 \phi}$$

(9.27)

Thus the extent of any exchange rate overshooting is seen to depend upon the interest rate semi-elasticity of the demand for money and the degree of regressivity of exchange rate expectations. That this is so should be clear from our earlier discussion. For example, if we consider successively smaller values of the interest semi-elasticity of money, a given change in the money supply will require a much larger change in the interest rate to restore equilibrium the smaller is α_2, and, for a given ϕ, a relatively large change in the actual exchange rate is needed to generate a sufficient expected change in the exchange rate to offset it. An analogous reasoning explains why sucessively lower values of ϕ imply larger and larger exchange rate changes.

For B to be a position of long-run equilibrium, there clearly has to be zero excess demand in the goods market and thus the $\Delta p' = 0$ schedule must intersect the

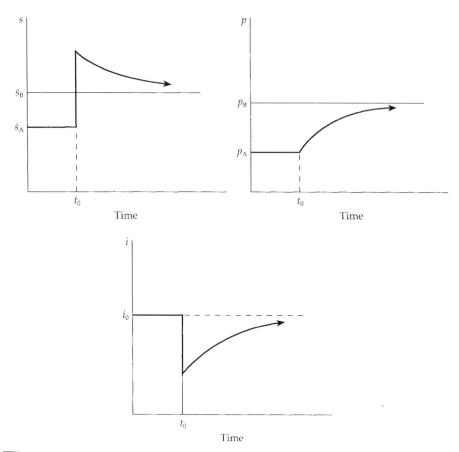

Figure 9.2 s, p, and i over time in the "overshooting" model

M'M' schedule at this point. But what is the adjustment process for prices from C to B? From our earlier discussion we know that at point C the exchange rate has depreciated (perhaps dramatically), thus changing the terms of trade, and the domestic interest rate has fallen. Both these factors, via equation (9.25), will boost aggregate demand. Thus over time, since output is fixed at the full employment level, prices must be rising (see equation (9.24)) and real money balances falling, pushing up interest rates in order to maintain money market equilibrium continuously. For the latter to be consistent with overall asset market equilibrium (i.e. equilibrium in both money and the international bond market) the exchange rate will be appreciating from the overshoot position C. Thus in this model rising interest rates are accompanied by an appreciating exchange rate.

The behavior of the exchange rate, the price level and the interest rate over time in the "overshooting" model is described in figure 9.2. It is important to stress that the exchange rate overshooting in the Dornbusch model is a result of the discrepancy of adjustment speeds in goods and asset markets; asset markets adjust instantly whereas goods markets adjust only slowly over time. This is in contrast to the FLMA where, as was shown, the exchange rate overshoots (or perhaps more correctly the exchange rate change is magnified) as a result of agent's expectations of the course of future exogenous variables.[14]

Many economists would argue that the SPMA offers a concise description of the real world behavior of exchange rates. For example, in the period 1979–81 the attempts by the Thatcher administration to reduce the UK money supply at times led to very high real interest rates in the UK relative to the USA and this in turn led to a sharp appreciation of the nominal sterling exchange rate (the reader is encouraged to work through the effects of a reduction of the money supply in the sticky-price model, using figure 9.1).[15] But since prices are also sticky downwards this, in turn, led to a *real* exchange rate appreciation, which affected the real sector of the economy; i.e. the high real exchange rate resulted in exporters becoming uncompetitive and going out of business, with the resultant loss of output and jobs. Thus, in his evidence to the Treasury and Civil Service Committee (1980a, p. 72), Dornbusch argued:

> If pursued over any period of time the high real exchange policy will lead to a disruption of industry; reduced investment, shutdowns, declining productivity, loss of established markets and a deterioration of the commercial position.

Thus he concluded that the high real exchange rate was a direct consequence of the high interest rate policy pursued by the UK authorities, and consequently a crucial issue for the policymaker in a world of high capital mobility, sticky prices and flexible exchange rates must be how to isolate the asset sector from the real sector. Dornbusch (1980a) recommended a tax on capital inflows: "It is quite apparent . . . that both from the point of view of public finance and from the perspective of macroeconomic policy, a real interest equalization tax is called for." Such a policy, for periods of tight money, has been supported by Liviatan (1980). Flood and Marion (1980) have argued that the effect of the capital account on the exchange rate may be divorced from the current account by introducing a dual exchange rate system. Such a system effectively means separating current and capital account items and having an exchange rate for each account.[16] More generally, the belief that exchange rates have tended to overshoot their equilibrium values during the recent float has led a number of researchers to advocate a complete overhaul of the international monetary system and, in particular, a move back to some form of exchange rate fixity. Such proposals are considered in some detail in chapter 24.

 ## 9.6 Currency Substitution

The specification of the monetary approach hitherto has relied on the implicit assumption that domestic residents do *not* hold foreign money; effectively we have assumed that the elasticity of substitution in demand between national money supplies is zero. However, in a regime of floating exchange rates, multinational corporations involved in trade and investment and speculators have an incentive to hold a *basket* of currencies in order to minimize the risk of revaluation effects of potential exchange rate changes on their wealth (in practice such operators will hold a portfolio of money and non-money assets; however, we shall leave inclusion of the latter in a theory of the exchange rate until the next chapter). Thus, much as in traditional portfolio theory, foreign exchange market participants have an incentive to hold a basket of currencies, the composition of the various currencies in the portfolio varying in accordance with their risk and expected rates of return characteristics (see chapter 19, note 12). The ability of foreign exchange market participants to substitute between different currencies has been made possible due to the lifting of exchange controls in the 1970s by most of the participating members of the floating regime. Girton and Roper (1981) were the first to use the term "currency substitution" to describe situations where agents hold more than one currency.

In this section we examine the implications of currency substitution for the behavior of exchange rates, the ability of central banks to adopt monetary targets and the implications it has for inflation.

9.6.1 Currency substitution and the monetary approach

In the flex- and fix-price monetary approaches monetary services are only provided by the domestic currency (i.e. equation (9.4)). However, as we have argued, this is probably an unrealistic assumption: various international companies have an incentive to hold a variety of currencies and therefore monetary services may be provided by other currencies. This may be illustrated by rewriting the demand for money function as:

$$m_t^D - p_t = \Omega + \alpha_1 y - \alpha_2 i \tag{9.28}$$

where Ω is a parameter which captures the degree of currency substitution towards the domestic currency.

Following King et al. (1977) we assume that Ω depends upon the expected change in the exchange rate: intuitively, an expected depreciation of the currency would result in agents holding a lesser proportion of domestic money balances (notice that this effect is separate from the traditional interest rate effect). The expected exchange rate change is, in turn, assumed to depend on expected monetary growth,[17] Δm^e, and the uncertainty with which such expectations are held, represented by the variance of monetary growth, $\text{var}(\Delta m^e)$. It is assumed that Ω has the following functional form:

$$\Omega = \beta_0 \Delta m_t^c + \beta_1 \text{var}(\Delta m_t^c) \qquad \beta_0 < 0, \beta_1 < 0 \tag{9.29}$$

On substituting this definition of Ω into (9.28) and on setting money demand equal to money supply (from (9.5)) we may solve the resulting expression for the price level and substitute into (9.1) to obtain

$$s_t = m_t - \beta_0 \Delta m_t^e - \beta_1 \text{var}(\Delta m_t^e) - \alpha_1 y_t + \alpha_2 i_t - p_t^* \qquad (9.30)$$

On using the uncovered interest rate parity condition, equation (9.2), to substitute for the domestic interest rate and by further assuming that $\Delta s_t^e = \Delta m_t^e$ (which is a kind of super-neutrality assumption) we obtain

$$s_t = m_t + (\alpha_2 - \beta_0)\Delta m_t^e - \beta_1 \text{var}(\Delta m_t^e) - \alpha_1 y_t + \alpha_2 i_t^* - p^* \qquad (9.30a)$$

where the term in square brackets denotes the influence of the foreign country, which we do not explicitly model here (we assume that the domestic country is "small"), and, since $\beta_0 < 0$, $\alpha_2 - \beta_0 > 0$. Thus in addition to the traditional monetary effects of m and y on the exchange rate, equation (9.30) also demonstrates the effect of currency substitution on the exchange rate. The coefficient on Δm^e is larger than it would be in the absence of currency substitution (i.e. $\alpha_2 - \beta_0 > \alpha_2$) because of the ability of agents to substitute between domestic and foreign money, exacerbating pressure for a currency depreciation or appreciation. This effect will be reinforced if the expected variability of monetary policy, var(m^e), changes in tandem with the expected change in m (i.e. note that β_1 is also assumed to be negative).

9.6.2 Currency substitution and monetary targeting

Until now we have discussed currency substitution in a rather abstract way, in the context of the FLMA. But does the concept have a "real world" applicability? A variety of central bankers would answer in the affirmative.

One notable feature of the 1970s and 1980s was the setting of monetary targets in an attempt to control inflation (the first country to adopt monetary targets was Germany in December 1974). However, the success of such a policy is contingent on the underlying stability of the money demand function. Although empirical studies of the money demand function suggested it was stable for the 1960s, evidence for a variety of countries for the 1970s implied that the relationship was unstable. One popular explanation for this instability has been argued to be currency substitution (see, for example, McKinnon, 1988).

For example, the Swiss and German monetary authorities set money supply targets of 5 and 8 percent, respectively, for the period 1977–9. The actual money supply outcome was an increase of 16.2 percent in Switzerland and 11.4 percent in Germany. These overshoots of the money supplies were blamed on a shift in foreign and domestic demand for financial assets based in deutschmarks and Swiss francs (in particular a shift away from the dollar which was argued to be overvalued). Since the Swiss and German authorities were unwilling to let the exchange rate take the adjustment (i.e. this would imply, on the assumption that prices are sticky, a *real* exchange rate change) by appreciating, they intervened in the foreign exchange markets to supply Swiss francs and German marks. Since the monetary consequences of this were not sterilized, increased money supplies inevitably resulted. These monetary overshoots led to the non-announcement of monetary targets by the Swiss authorities in 1979 and a more flexible target by the German authorities in 1979.

Several proposals have been made to overcome the effects of currency substitution on the ability of central banks to pursue monetary targets (see, for example, Vaubel, 1980). The first would be to define monetary targets net of international shifts in the demand for national money and to offset all such shifts via compensatory money supply adjustment. In principle this seems a perfect solution, but in practice the issue is complicated by the difficulties of central banks knowing when and by how much net *foreign* demand for its money has changed; i.e. the observable changes in money holdings are not a reliable indicator of the extent to which money demand has changed. Thus perhaps the central bank should try to trace the shifts in money demand back to their determinants, i.e. foreign income and foreign interest rates. But it has proved difficult to estimate such parameters and in any case they are likely to change as policy changes (i.e. the Lucas (1977) critique).

An alternative method for the curtailment of the deleterious effects of currency substitution would be to move full circle from monetary targets to (nominal) exchange rate targets.[18] It is argued that this would result in international shifts in money demand being reflected instantly by exchange market pressure, the monetary authorities then adjusting the money supply to keep the exchange rate constant. One problem, perhaps, with this idea would seem to be the difficulty for the authorities in discerning when exchange rate movements are due to currency substitution and when they are justified by, say, real factors (for other criticisms of exchange rate targets and for a discussion of other devices for countering currency substitution see Vaubel, 1980). The proposal of adopting exchange rate targets in order to deal with currency substitution has been made by McKinnon (1988) and is discussed in sections 17.3.2 and 24.5.1. The ideas for the reform of the IMS contained in McKinnon's 1988 article have their antecedents in some earlier work which we now discuss.

9.6.3 Currency substitution and inflation: the McKinnon hypothesis

Professor R. McKinnon has argued that currency substitution explains why countries' national monetary growth rates are not necessarily good predictors of national inflation rates. For example, in 1978 the US monetary growth was 8.2 percent and a monetarist would presumably argue that this should have a predictable effect on inflation after 18 months to two years. However, in 1979–80 the USA experienced inflation of 13 percent which implies an appreciably higher money growth two years earlier. The monetarist proposition holds only if one compares the "world" money supply with the "world" inflation rate. That the latter is the relevant money concept is due to currency substitution and an important asymmetry in the international monetary standard.

In 1977–8, owing to a belief that the dollar was going to depreciate, foreign exchange market participants were keen to reallocate their currency portfolios away from dollars toward European currencies. As we have seen, the Swiss and the German authorities were not prepared to let this substitution be fully reflected in the exchange rate and intervened in their foreign exchange markets, selling domestic currency for dollars. The effect of the latter was not sterilized and hence the domestic money supply rose. However, because European central banks hold their increased dollar reserves in dollar-denominated bonds their intervention has *no* effect on the US money supply (if, however, they hold their reserves as direct dollar deposit claims on the US central bank this will result in a reduction in the US base money). This asymmetrical operation of the international monetary system means that, in terms of the above example, currency substitution has led to an increase in the world money supply (effectively the weighted sum of US dollars and European monies). If we compare the world money supply figure in 1977–8 with the world inflation rate in 1979–80 we find a much more satisfactory correlation. For example, the world money supply increased by 10.27 percent and 10.98 percent in 1977 and 1978 respectively and world inflation increased by 11.1 percent and 13.5 percent in 1979 and 1980 respectively. Furthermore, McKinnon argues that the world money supply is a better predictor of US inflation than the US money supply is. For example, in 1978 US monetary growth was 8.2 percent and in 1979–80 US inflation averaged 13 percent. The latter figure, it is argued, is better explained by the effect on the international business cycle of the 11 percent world monetary growth in 1978.

McKinnon (1983, 1988) argues from the above evidence that certain money supply and intervention rules should be developed if price stability is to be achieved in the world economy (see also our discussion in section 17.3.2). First, each country should determine, in advance of any money demand shocks, a growth path for the money supply consistent with price stability. Second, countries then agree to cooperate by pursuing *symmetric unsterilized* intervention in the event of currency substitution moving exchange rates. Thus if the Swiss franc–US dollar appreciates because of currency substitution the Swiss monetary authorities should intervene by buying dollars for Swiss francs, not sterilizing the impact of this on the Swiss money supply, and depositing the dollars with the US central bank: the monetary base would then be increased in Switzerland as much as it is decreased in the USA. Assuming that money multipliers are the same in both the USA and Switzerland and that the velocity is the same in both countries then this type of intervention should lead to no change in the world money supply and have no inflationary impact.

Although the McKinnon hypothesis in its various strands seems appealing it is important to note that the methodology utilized by McKinnon (1983) has been the subject of a lively debate (the reader is directed to McKinnon and Tan, 1983; Ross, 1983; Goldstein and Haynes, 1984; McKinnon, 1984; Radcliffe et al., 1984). More generally, the concept of currency substitution itself has been empirically questioned by a number of researchers (see Spinelli (1983) for a useful summary of this evidence).[19]

*9.7 Empirical Evidence on the Monetary Model

We now consider how well supported empirically the monetary model is. In econometrically testing the monetary model researchers have concentrated largely on the FLMA and SPMA versions and we adopt this emphasis in this section.

Equation (9.7), rewritten here with a disturbance term, has been econometrically estimated for a number of currencies over the recent experience with floating exchange rates.

$$s_t = \beta_0(m_t - m_t^*) + \beta_1(y - y^*)_t + \beta_2(i - i^*)_t + u_t \qquad (9.7c)$$

where u_t is the disturbance term and the βs are the reduced-form coefficients. If the FLMA is correct, it is expected that $\beta_0 = 1$, $\beta_1 < 0$ and $\beta_2 > 0$. Additionally, β_1 and β_2 should take on values close, in absolute terms, to the estimated values of the income elasticity and interest semi-elasticity from money demand equations (see Laidler (1992) for a survey of such estimates). Because of the cleanness of the float of the deutschmark–US dollar exchange rate, in terms of the relatively low level of foreign exchange market intervention (and also, perhaps, because the mark is the only currency for which quotes actually reflect the price at which currency transactions take place), many researchers have concentrated on this exchange rate in their tests of equation (9.9). For example, Hodrick (1978) presents the following estimated version of equation (9.7) for the US dollar–deutschmark exchange rate over the period April 1973 to September 1975:

$$s_t = 1.52m_t - 1.39m_t^* - 2.23y_t + 0.073y_t^* + 2.53i_t + 1.93i_t^* \qquad (9.31)$$
$$(0.512) \quad (0.563) \quad (0.456) \quad (0.384) \quad (1.17) \quad (0.669)$$

$$R^2 = 0.66 \qquad DW = 1.61 \qquad SER = 0.37$$

standard errors in parentheses

where the coefficients are not constrained to be equal across countries. Notice that, apart from the coefficient on the German interest rate, i^*, all variables are correctly signed in terms of the FLMA and all, apart from y^*, are statistically significant at the 95 percent level. Indeed, Hodrick finds that the coefficients on the home and foreign money supply differ insignificantly from plus and minus unity as predicted by the approach. Other successful estimates of equation (9.7) have been presented by Bilson (1978) for the deutschmark–US dollar and by Putnam and Woodbury (1980) for the UK pound–US dollar using data from the early experience with floating (i.e. up to approximately the end of 1977).

Econometric estimates of the SPMA have been less commonplace in the literature (see, for example, Driskell, 1981; Smith and Wickens, 1990). However, one particularly useful way of discriminating between the FLMA and the SPMA is by estimating a reduced form first suggested by Frankel (1979a). Since this equation has been widely estimated in the exchange rate literature, it is worth deriving here. We refer to it as the *hybrid monetary model*. The model assumes that in the long run the nominal exchange rate is determined by the FLMA but that in the short run it deviates from this rate by an amount determined by the real interest differential between the home and foreign country. This is essentially the view taken by Dornbusch in the SPMA. The hybrid model, however, differs from the SPMA in that the expected inflation differential is also posited to be a determinant of the short-run exchange rate. The model is illustrated in the following way. The long-run exchange rate is given by

$$\bar{s} = \bar{m}_t - \bar{m}_t^* - \alpha_1(\bar{y} - \bar{y}^*)_t + \alpha_2(\Delta\bar{p}^e - \Delta\bar{p}^{e*})_{t+1} \tag{9.7d}$$

The short-run exchange rate may be derived from the mechanism describing the expected change in the exchange rate. As in the SPMA, the expected change in the exchange rate is governed by a regressive expectations component and, additionally, a term from the FLMA capturing the expected inflation differential:

$$\Delta s_{t+1}^e = \phi(\bar{s} - s)_t + (\Delta p^e - \Delta p^{e*})_{t+1} \tag{9.32}$$

Thus in long-run equilibrium when $s_t = \bar{s}_t$ the exchange rate is expected to change by an amount equal to the long-run inflation differential. An expression for the short-run exchange rate may be derived by substituting (9.32) into (9.2) to obtain:

$$s_t = \bar{s}_t - \frac{1}{\phi}[(i_t - \Delta p_{t+1}^e) - (i_t^* - \Delta p_{t+1}^{e*})] \tag{9.33}$$

Thus the current exchange rate may be above or below the equilibrium real exchange rate to the extent that there exists a real interest rate differential. For example, if the home country's real interest rate is below that of the foreign country, it follows that $s > \bar{s}$ and the exchange rate overshoots its long-run value.

Consider a once-for-all increase in the money supply in the context of (9.33). In terms of the Dornbusch model (i.e. if we only have nominal interest rates) the exchange rate must overshoot its long-run equilibrium in order to maintain interest rate parity. But if the money supply causes individuals to revise their inflationary expectations upwards, equation (9.33) says that the initial exchange rate depreciation will be greater in the hybrid model. This is because the fall in the real interest rate is greater in the hybrid model than in the Dornbusch model – i falls *and* Δp^e rises.

On using (9.7a) as our expression for the equilibrium exchange rate in (9.33) and, additionally, assuming that equilibrium values are given by their current actual values, we may derive the exchange rate equation

$$s_t = m_t - m_t^* - \alpha_1(y - y^*)_t + \alpha_2(\Delta p^e - \Delta p^{e*})_{t+1}$$
$$+ \frac{1}{\phi}[(i_t - \Delta p_{t+1}^e) - (i_t^* - \Delta p_{t+1}^{e*})] \tag{9.34}$$

Table 9.1 Predicted values for coefficients in three exchange rate models

	β_0	β_1	β_2	β_3
FLMA	1	–	+	0
SPMA	1	–	0	–
Hybrid	1	–	+	–

or as a reduced form

$$s_t = \beta_0(m_t - m_t^*) + \beta_1(y - y^*)_t + \beta_2(\Delta p^e - \Delta p^{e*})_{t+1}$$
$$+ \beta_3[(i_t - \Delta p_{t+1}^e) - (i_t^* - \Delta p_{t+1}^{e*})] + u_t \qquad (9.35)$$

where u_t is a disturbance term and the βs are reduced-form coefficients to be estimated by some appropriate estimator. In table 9.1 we indicate what proponents of the different versions of the monetary model would expect with respect to these coefficients.

Note that the different versions of the monetary model cannot be distinguished with respect to the coefficients on the relative money supply and income terms: the coefficient on the former variable is expected to be unity, whilst the coefficient on the latter should be negative and have a value close to the income elasticity recovered from an estimated monetary demand function (in the range 0.5 to 1, depending on the definition of the money supply chosen). The different versions of the model may, however, be distinguished with reference to β_2 and β_3. If the FLMA is correct β_2 is expected to be positive, but β_3 is zero since real interest rate differentials do not arise in this model. In contrast, in the SPMA emphasis is placed on the real consequences of monetary policy in the short run and therefore β_3 is expected to be negative and β_2 is expected to be zero. Frankel's eclectic hybrid view suggests that both effects will be present in an estimated exchange rate equation.

Frankel (1979a) presents econometric estimates of equation (9.35) for the deutschmark–US dollar exchange rate over the period from July 1974 to February 1978. His "best" equation is

$$s_t = 1.39 + 0.97(m - m^*)_t - 0.52(y - y^*)_t + 29.40(\Delta p^e - \Delta p^{e*})_{t+1}$$
$$\scriptstyle(0.12) \quad (0.21) \qquad\qquad (0.22) \qquad\qquad\qquad (3.33)$$
$$- 5.40[(i_t - \Delta p_{t+1}^e) - (i_t^* - \Delta p_{t+1}^{e*})]$$
$$\scriptstyle(2.04) \qquad\qquad\qquad\qquad\qquad\qquad (9.36)$$

$$R^2 = 0.91$$

where standard errors are reported in parentheses and R^2 denotes the coefficient of determination. In this equation notice that the coefficient for the relative money supply term is insignificantly different from unity, the coefficient on income is significantly negative and the expected inflation and real interest rate terms are both significant and have signs consistent with the hybrid view of the exchange rate;[20] thus both the sticky price and flex-price models would seem to have some validity. The high R^2 has also been interpreted as indicating that the estimated equation is remarkably successful in explaining the exchange rate in sample. However, since all the variables entering (9.36) are likely to be non-stationary the high R^2 reflects, in all probability, a common trend (i.e. the regression, in the sense of Granger and Newbold (1974) is "spurious").

The estimated values in equation (9.36) allow Frankel to estimate how much the mark–dollar exchange rate would have to depreciate for a once-and-for-all increase in the US money supply of 1 percent. The calculated fall in the real interest differential (i.e. the sticky-price model effect) gives a current exchange rate overshoot of 1.23 percent. However, if the monetary expansion signals to investors a new higher target for monetary growth the initial overshooting will be greater. Frankel estimates that, if agents' expected inflation rate is raised by 1 percent per annum, this will lead to a short-run exchange rate overshoot of 1.58 percent. Thus ignoring the expected inflation effect downwardly biases estimates of short-run exchange rate overshooting.

Although Frankel's reduced form exchange rate equation provides an interesting representation of the monetary approach, not least because it provides estimates of exchange rate overshooting, it is important to note that attempts to estimate equations (9.7) and (9.29) for the period beyond 1978 and for other currencies have not been particularly successful.

For example, Dornbusch (1980b), Haynes and Stone (1981) and Driskell and Sheffrin (1981) argue that once equations such as (9.7) and (9.29) are estimated for the mark–dollar exchange rate for the period extending beyond 1978 the relationship breaks down.[21] These researchers' results relate essentially to the "in-sample" fit of the equations in terms of their explanatory power (as indicated by the R^2 coefficient) and the fact that coefficient values differ dramatically, in terms of sign and magnitude, from their prior values. Perhaps, though, the most damning indictment of the monetary class of models is the finding of Meese and Rogoff (1983) that in an out-of-sample context the monetary class of models fails to outperform a simple random-walk model of the exchange rate. Without doubt the Meese and Rogoff result has had a pervasive influence on the profession. For example, Frankel and Rose (1995), summarizing the exchange rate literature that developed in the ten years after Meese and Rogoff, came to the following conclusion:

> the Meese and Rogoff analysis at short horizons has never been convincingly over-turned or explained. It continues to exert a pessimistic effect on the field of empirical exchange rate modelling in particular and international finance in general.

Frankel and Rose interpret a short horizon as anything less than 36 months. Following Mark (1995) and Chinn and Meese (1995), it is generally accepted that monetary models have predictability at "long" horizons; that is horizons greater than 36 months. Since the Meese and Rogoff results has had such a pervasive influence on the profession it is worth exploring here in more detail. Meese and Rogoff took the FLMA, the hybrid model and the Hooper–Morton model (which adds a wealth term and a risk premium to the hybrid model). These models were all estimated in static form: that is, the variables entered the equations in levels terms and only very limited dynamics were included, if at all. Additionally, Meese and Rogoff considered a wide array of univariate models and a vector autoregression (VAR) comprising exchange rates, relative short-term interest rates, relative inflation rates, and the current account. The currencies studied were the dollar–mark, dollar–pound, dollar–yen and the trade weighted dollar, and the sample period was March 1973 to November 1980, with the out-of-sample forecasts conducted over the sub-period December 1976 to November 1980. Out-of-sample forecasting accuracy was determined using the root mean square error (RMSE) criteria. The latter is defined as:

$$RMSE = \sqrt{\frac{\sum_t (F_t - A_t)^2}{n}}$$

where F represents the forecast (log) level of the exchange rate, A the actual outcome (log) exchange rate, and n is the number of forecasts made. A common way of representing the relative performance of a model is to give the ratio of the model's RMSE to that of the random walk. The simple random walk benchmark is:

$$s_t = s_{t-1} + \kappa + \varepsilon_t, \tag{9.37}$$

where κ is a constant (drift) term and ε_t is a random disturbance. This model provides a forecast of no change in the level of the exchange rate. Usually the model and random walk alternative are compared using the RMSE ratio:

$$Ratio = \frac{RMSE^m}{RMSE^{rw}} \tag{9.38}$$

where $RMSE^m$ is derived from the model and $RMSE^{rw}$ is derived from the random walk. A number below unity indicates relatively good performance by the model, while a number equal to one or greater indicates that the model is unable to beat a random walk.

In summary, Meese and Rogoff were only able to produce a value for *ratio* which was below one, for horizons of between one and 12 months ahead, in four instances out of a possible 224, which is a number less than that expected by chance for such a sample. The reason why the Meese and Rogoff finding has been interpreted as a particularly telling indictment against fundamentals-based models is that in their forecasting exercises they deliberately gave their models an unfair advantage by using actual (i.e. *ex post*) data outcomes of the fundamentals rather than forecasting them simultaneously with the exchange rate. Of course, a forecaster, using such models to generate "real time" forecasts, would have had to forecast the exchange rate *simultaneously* with all of the right-hand side variables.

One clue to the poor performance of the reduced forms used in the Meese and Rogoff study is the possibility of structural instability. Hence a more appropriate way of addressing the performance of structural models would be to allow the coefficients to evolve over time and this has been done in a number of studies (see Wolff, 1987; and Schinasi and Swamy, 1987). These studies report a consistent out-performance of a random walk at horizons as short as one or two months. Another clue to the poor out-of-sample forecasting performance reported by Meese and Rogoff relates to the dynamic properties of the data. As noted in chapter x, although deviations from PPP are mean-reverting there is nevertheless considerable persistence in the behavior of real exchange rates and this would need to be incorporated into any exchange rate modeling exercise. The same may be said for other "structural" relationships, such as money demand functions, which underpin the monetary model. Although in one of their models, Meese and Rogoff did allow for rich dynamic interactions using a VAR, it is now well known that such systems tend to be over-parameterized in terms of their use of information (indeed, Meese and Rogoff in a footnote cited this as a potential reason for the poor performance of the VAR model). Some results which address this issue are reported in the next section.

The forward looking monetary model, as given in equation (9.9b), has been estimated by Hoffman and Schlagenhauf (1983), Kearney and MacDonald (1988) and Ghosh (1991) for data samples involving the 1970s and 1980s. These papers all report results which are favorable to the forward-looking monetary model in the sense that the restrictions implied by the rational expectations hypothesis cannot be rejected. We tentatively conclude from this that the magnification story is supported by the empirical evidence.

*9.8 Recent Empirical Evidence on the Monetary Model

As in the PPP literature, more recent work on the monetary model has involved using cointegrating methods to analyze the "long-run" properties of the model. The first batch of cointegration-based studies used the Engle–Granger two-step method (see, for example, Baillie and Selover (1987) Boothe and Glassman (1987), Kearney and MacDonald (1986) and Meese (1986)) to test the stationarity of fundamentals:

$$z_t = s_t - m_t + m_t^* + \beta_0(y_t - y_t^*) \tag{9.39}$$

The general tenor of these results suggests that z_t is I(1) across currencies and time periods. This finding has been interpreted as *prima facie* evidence of a speculative bubble. However, as in the case of the empirical work on PPP these results seem to be estimation-specific.

For example, MacDonald and Taylor (1991a, 1993, and 1994) use the cointegration methods of Johansen to test the FLMA model for the US dollar bilateral exchange rates of the mark, sterling and yen. In contrast to the above studies, MacDonald and Taylor find strong evidence of cointegration for all of these

currencies, in the sense that they find statistically significant cointegrating relations. For the German mark, for example, they find that the first significant
vector may be restricted to:

$$s_t = (m_t - m_t^*) - (y_t - y_t^*) + 0.049i_t - 0.050i_t^* \tag{9.40}$$

which is clearly a very close approximation to a strict form version of the flex-
price monetary model. Perhaps the success in getting such a tightly defined relationship for the German mark reflects, at least in part, the relative success of the
Bundesbank in controlling the German money supply during the sample period
(1976 to 1990).[22] Having established a well-defined long-run relationship, this was
then used to produce a complicated dynamic error correction relationship of the
following form:

$$\Delta s_t = \underset{(0.073)}{0.244\Delta s_{t-2}} - \underset{(0.235)}{0.417\Delta_2\Delta m_t} - \underset{(0.343)}{0.796\Delta y_t} - \underset{(0.003)}{0.008\Delta^2 i_t^*} - \underset{(0.013)}{0.025z_{t-1}} + \underset{(0.003)}{0.005}$$

$$\tag{9.41}$$

where the z term denotes the error correction term derived from (9.40) and standard errors are in brackets. This model was shown to have an extremely good
in-sample performance in the sense that it passed a battery of statistical tests. Most
significantly, perhaps, it was able to outperform a random walk at horizons as
short as two months ahead.

The forecasting success of the monetary model is attributed by MacDonald
and Taylor to the use of econometric methods which capture both the short-
run dynamics and the longer run cointegrating relationships. The existence of
cointegration within the monetary class of models also has implications for
the estimation of the forward looking monetary model (9.9b). In particular, the
research reported above exploits a purely first difference specification of the
fundamental variables. However, as is well known if there exists cointegration
amongst a set of variables a formulation in differences will be mis-specified; the
appropriate specification is an error correction representation.

Although the findings of MacDonald and Taylor have been confirmed for other
currencies (see, for example, Kouretas (1997)) the approach has been criticized
by for example Cushman, Lee and Thorgeirsson (1996). They argue, for example,
that the significance levels used to determine the number of significant cointegrating vectors are only valid for much larger samples than those used by
MacDonald and Taylor. When a small sample correction is used the existence of
cointegration essentially disappears. However, given that cointegration tests,
such as the Johansen maximum likelihood test have relatively low power to reject
the null of no cointegration it may be preferable to use a lower significance level
than the standard 95 percent level.[23] Indeed, Juselius (1999) has argued that this
is especially relevant if the researcher can interpret the cointegration vector (s) in
an economically meaningful way (see La Cour and MacDonald, 1998).

In assessing the literature post-Meese and Rogoff, Frankel and Rose were cognizant of the findings of MacDonald and Taylor and Wolff and others. However, they preferred to downplay these results for two reasons. First, the above papers used actual data outcomes of the fundamentals, rather than forecasting the fundamental determinants of the exchange rates and, second, although these outperformed a random walk it was unclear if the difference was statistically significant. However, MacDonald and Marsh (1997) have addressed these issues and are still able to beat a random walk. Since their results would seem to completely alter the perspective on Meese and Rogoff, we consider them here in a little detail.

MacDonald and Marsh take a simple extension of PPP to tackle some of the criticisms made regarding other forecasting research. (Johansen and Juselius (1992) and Juselius (1995) adopt a similar modeling approach, although they use a different motivational framework). Although the approach is PPP-based we consider it here both because it has a direct bearing on the forecasting results considered above and also because the variants of the monetary model considered in this chapter are PPP-based. MacDonald and Marsh propose augmenting PPP with an interest differential. One simple way of motivating this augmentation is to consider the balance of payments equilibrium condition under which the current (*ca*) and capital (*ka*) accounts sum to zero. Assume that the long-run equilibrium current account is a function of competitiveness, while the capital account position depends on nominal interest differentials adjusted for expected exchange rate changes:

$$ca_t + ka_t = \alpha(s_t - p_t + p_t^*) + \mu(i_t - i_t^* - \Delta s_{t+k}^e) = 0 \qquad (9.42)$$

where variables have their usual interpretation, α is the elasticity of net exports with respect to competitiveness, and μ captures the mobility of international capital.

Assuming that capital is less than perfectly mobile ($\mu < \infty$) we can solve equation (9.42) for the exchange rate to give a long-run equilibrium relationship:

$$s_t = p_t - p_t^* - \frac{\mu}{\alpha}(i_t - i_t^* - \Delta s_{t+k}^e) + \varsigma_t \qquad (9.43)$$

where ς is an error term which should be $I(0)$. This relationship is labeled Casselian PPP by MacDonald and Marsh because Cassel, the modern proponent of PPP, recognized the role that interest rates could play in keeping an exchange rate away from its PPP determined value in both the short and medium run. Cassel appeared to neglect the role that persistent capital flows could generate systematic and long-lasting departures from PPP, although these of course did not dominate the foreign exchange market to quite the extent that they do now.

MacDonald and Marsh (1996, 1997) estimate exchange rate models for the mark, pound, and yen against the US dollar for the period January 1974 through to December 1992. The initial determination of the model only used data up to September 1989, i.e. 189 observations for model estimation, with the remainder saved for out-of-sample forecast tests. For each currency they were able to establish two significant cointegrating vectors, or long-run relationships. The first of

these was interpreted as a PPP relationship and the second an interest rate relationship. Using general-to-specific modeling methods, so-called simultaneous
econometric models (or SEMs) were constructed. These are models in which
all of the variables are potentially a function of contemporaneous values of the
other variables, lagged values of these variables and disequilibrium errors. The
key aspect of these models, which is appealing from a forecasting perspective, is
that they could actually have been used – real time – by someone wishing to forecast currencies. This is because all of the variables (not just the exchange rate) are
forecast simultaneously. As we have seen, previous forecasting exercises typically gave the modeled exchange rate the benefit of the doubt in the sense that
the actual outcomes of the regressors, rather than forecast outcomes, are used.

In addition to computing the ratio statistic, equation 9.38, for the three models
against a random walk, MacDonald and Marsh (1997) also compute this statistic
for their forecast against 150 professional forecasters supplied by Consensus Economics (these are the leading foreign exchange forecasters operating in the financial centers of the G7). Additionally, MacDonald and Marsh compute measures
of directional forecastability; that is, to what extent do forecasters get the direction of an exchange rate change correct.

The MacDonald–Marsh forecasting results may be summarized in the following way. For the one month horizon the random walk dominates across all three
currencies. For horizons greater than one month, however, the relative accuracy
of the models improves such that for each currency the ratio falls below unity. This
out-performance improves as the forecast horizon lengthens, suggesting that the
long-run equilibria are important.[24] Furthermore, many of the outperformances
turn out to be statisically significant. The forecasts of the professional forecasters
are only available at horizons three and twelve months ahead. In sum, MacDonald
and Marsh find that no forecaster ranks as consistently highly as the econometric
models, across currencies and/or horizons.

Finally, the proportions of correct directional forecasts are never below 0.5,
the expected number under pure chance. From performance over short horizons
which is not inconsistent with no directional forecast ability, the proportions rise
to between two-thirds correct and approximate perfection over those horizons
where the RMSE tests also indicate forecast ability.

The results of MacDonald and Marsh contrast with much of the literature on
forecasting the exchange rate. In particular, they suggest that forecastability of
exchange rates with respect to fundamentals starts at around two months rather
than the 36 months of Chinn and Meese (1995) and Mark (1995). The results of
MacDonald and Marsh (1997) have been confirmed in MacDonald and Marsh
(1999b), where a tri-polar modeling structure is used.

*9.9 Empirical Tests for the Existence of Speculative Bubbles

One of the simplest ways of testing for the existence of speculative bubbles is
along the lines of the variance ratio test, proposed initially for testing speculative

bubbles in bond and stock markets by Shiller (1981). In order to illustrate this kind of test let us assume that the FLMA is the "correct" model of the determination of the exchange rate. If s^* is defined as the present discounted value of actual future fundamentals – i.e. $s_t^* = (1 - \beta)\sum_{i=0}^{\infty}\beta^i z_{t+i}$ – then it may be interpreted, using the parlance of the stock market literature, as the "perfect foresight" or "*ex post* rational" exchange rate. It then follows from (9.13) that s_t^n is the optimal forecast of s^*, i.e. given our definition of s^* we may rewrite (9.13a) as

$$s^n = E_t s_t^*$$
(9.44)

Hence the perfect foresight price will differ from its expected value by a rational expectations forecast error:

$$s_t^* = s_t^n + u_t$$
(9.45)

It is a property of a rational forecast error that it must be orthogonal, or uncorrelated, with the rational forecast. Hence using (9.45) we may write the variance decomposition of s^* as

$$\mathrm{var}(s_t^*) = \mathrm{var}(s_t^n) + \mathrm{var}(u_t)$$
(9.46)

which, because variances cannot be negative, must imply the following variance inequality or ratio:

$$\mathrm{var}(s_t^*) \geq \mathrm{var}(s_t^n)$$
(9.47)

or

$$\frac{\mathrm{var}(s_t^*)}{\mathrm{var}(s_t^n)} \geq 1$$
(9.48)

Thus if the no-bubbles rational expectations solution to the FLMA is correct, the actual exchange rate (which should be equivalent to s_t^n) should be less volatile than the perfect foresight exchange rate. In the presence of a speculative bubble, however, this statement will not be valid. Instead the effect of a speculative bubble may be seen by substituting (9.16) into (9.45), which gives

$$s_t^* = s_t - b_t + u_t$$
(9.49)

and

$$\mathrm{var}(s_t^*) = \mathrm{var}(s_t) - \mathrm{var}(b_t) + \mathrm{var}(u_t) - 2\mathrm{cov}(s_t b_t)$$
(9.50)

Since there is no *a priori* reason to rule out the possibility that b_t and s_t might be positively correlated, it is impossible to write down an inequality like (9.48), the inequality could equally go in the opposite direction. Hence if in practice inequalities like (9.48) are violated by the data, this offers prima-facie evidence for the presence of speculative bubbles.

Using the FLMA as his model of fundamentals, Huang (1981) tested (9.48) for the US dollar–mark, US dollar–UK pound and UK pound–mark exchange rates for the period from March 1973 to March 1979. Generally speaking, the results are supportive of the existence of speculative bubbles in that Huang finds evidence of excess volatility of the current exchange rate relative to its perfect foresight value. Using a different model of fundamentals – namely the SPMA – Wadhwani (1984) also reports evidence of excess volatility for the dollar–sterling rate over the period 1973.I–1982.III. Although, as we have emphasized, the variance bounds test is predicated on a particular model of fundamentals, the fact that two researchers using different models of fundamentals find evidence of excess volatility perhaps points in the direction of support for the speculative bubbles concept.

Different types of bubbles tests have been conducted by Meese (1986), Evans (1986) and MacDonald and Taylor (1993). The former author uses two econometric estimators to estimate a version of equation (9.9). One of the estimators is demonstrated to be robust with respect to the presence of bubbles (an instrumental variables estimator) and one is not (ordinary least squares). A specification test (due to Hausman, 1978) is used to test whether the two sets of estimates are significantly different; if they are, this is taken to be *prima facie* evidence for the existence of a speculative bubble. For dollar–mark, dollar–yen and dollar–sterling exchange rates Meese finds evidence of speculative bubbles for the period from October 1973 to November 1982 (although, again, his results are contingent on a specific model of fundamentals, namely a version of the SPMA). Evans (1986) uses non-parametric methods to test for speculative bubbles present in the rational forward forecast error $s_{t+1} - f_t$ (see chapters 12 and 13 for an extensive discussion of this term) in the dollar–sterling exchange rate, 1981–4. Evans reports evidence which he interprets as being indicative of speculative bubbles (his tests, however, are contingent on the assumption of rational expectations and may instead reflect some form of irrationality or "peso effect" – see chapter 11). MacDonald and Taylor (1993) utilize the FLMA and the cointegration methodology (see chapter 7 for a further discussion) to test for speculative bubbles in the deutschmark–US dollar exchange market; the speculative bubbles hypothesis is strongly rejected.

■ 9.10 Concluding Comments

In this chapter we have outlined why it is useful to regard the exchange rate as an asset price determined in asset markets. By considering three versions of the monetary approach to the exchange rate we gave three stories to explain exchange rate volatility: agents' expectations of the future course of monetary policy; differential speeds of adjustment in goods and asset markets; and the desire by rational agents to hold a portfolio of currencies in a period of floating exchange rates. Although the early empirical evidence in favor of the monetary models has been heavily criticized, more recent modeling which appropriately captures the distinction between long-run equilibrium and short-run dynamics has offered some support to the monetary class of models (see MacDonald and Taylor, 1993). Furthermore, as MacDonald and Marsh (1997) demonstrate, the Meese and Rogoff result no longer rules the roost. We have also demonstrated in this chapter that variance bounds tests, which often rely on a version of the monetary model, are suggestive of the existence of speculative bubbles in foreign exchange markets; i.e. the evidence of excess volatility cited earlier may at least in part reflect such speculative elements.

One of the major problems with the versions of the asset approach discussed in this chapter is that they give no role to the current account in determining the exchange rate. However, this is hardly a good description of the real world since exchange rate changes *do* affect the current account and this, in turn, will affect the flow of savings and wealth. Furthermore, the range of assets considered in the monetary approach is severely limited since non-money assets are assumed to be perfect substitutes and drop out of the analysis: attention is focused on relative excess money supplies.

In the following chapter we consider a wider version of the asset approach which rectifies some of the above deficiencies of the simple monetary approach. In particular, we consider an asset model which incorporates wealth, relaxes the assumption of perfect substitutability between non-money assets and introduces an important role for the current account.

NOTES

1. An asset is a means of holding wealth. Ultimately it must take a real form, but paper claims improve the liquidity or convenience of holding real assets. Money is one such financial asset, as are bonds, equity etc.

2. The models introduced in this chapter do suffer from a number of deficiencies. For example, they give little or no account of the effects of exchange rate changes on the current balance and concomitant changes in wealth, and also concentrate on a very limited menu of assets: effectively, home and foreign money supplies. In chapter 11 we rectify these deficiencies by examining asset models which incorporate current account and wealth dynamics and asset models which consider a broader range of assets than relative money supplies. Although different asset market models utilize different assumptions about asset substitutability and the role of wealth, they all share a common theoretical assumption that asset markets clear instantly.

3. Mussa (1979a), for example, has shown that only when certain strong and unrealistic assumptions hold can the flow approach offer an explanation for exchange rate volatility.

4. See, for example, Levich (1979) for the circumstances required to hold for the exchange rate to follow a random walk. (This issue is discussed further in chapters 12 and 13).

5. This is a simple application of "Walras's law."

6. See, for example, Bilson (1978).

7. That is, on using current – period t – information to forecast fundamentals in $t + j$, (9.14) implies $E_t z_{t+j} = \theta^j E_t z_t + E_t \varepsilon_{t+j}$ and this expression simplifies to (9.14a) since $E_t z_t$ equals z_t and the expectation of ε_{t+j} is zero.

8   This follows because if (9.13) is used to substitute out for s_t^n and if (9.13) led one period is used to substitute out for s_{t+j}^n we are left with a term $(1 - \beta)z_t$ on the left-hand side and this will cancel the equivalent term on the right-hand side – all that remains are the two terms in b.

9   If agents have perfect foresight it can be demonstrated (see Dornbusch, 1976a; MacDonald, 1988b) that ϕ is a function of the model's structural parameters and variables.

10   Thus as we noted in chapter 7 the real exchange rate Q is defined as SP^*/P. In the current context the price levels refer to the prices of domestic output and therefore a rise in Q denotes an improvement in the domestic country's competitiveness. Given the assumption in the SPMA model that the domestic country is small we may set $P^* = 1$, and therefore the log of Q is simply $s - p$.

11   The downward sloping MM schedule may also be explained in the following way: substitute equations (9.5), (9.23) and (9.2) into (9.4) to obtain

$$p_t - m_t = -\alpha_1 y_t + \alpha_2 i_t^* + \alpha_2 \phi(\bar{s} - s)_t \tag{9.51}$$

In the long run with a stationary money supply, the current and expected exchange rate will be equal which implies, from equation (9.2), that interest rates will also be equivalent. Hence the long-run price level may be written as

$$\bar{p}_t = m_t + \alpha_2 i_t^* - \alpha_1 y_t \tag{9.52}$$

and by substituting equation (9.52) into (9.51) we obtain (i.e. solve for $\alpha_2 i_t^*$ in (9.52) and substitute for $\alpha_2 i_t^*$ in (9.51))

$$s_t = \bar{s}_t - \frac{1}{\alpha_2 \phi}(p - \bar{p})_t \tag{9.53}$$

This equation simply states that, given the condition of money market equilibrium and equalization of yields, if the current price level p_t rises above the equilibrium price level $\bar{p}_t$, monetary equilibrium requires a higher interest rate, and via equation (9.2) the expectation of a depreciation. The latter must imply that the current exchange rate s_t falls short of the equilibrium rate $\bar{s}_t$. The negative relationship between s and p is clear from (9.45).

12   The $\Delta p = 0$ schedule, which represents jointly goods and money market equilibrium, is derived in the following way. Goods market equilibrium is characterized by a situation where the excess demand for goods is equal to zero (i.e. $y = d$ and thus $\Delta p = 0$). Thus by setting $\Delta p = 0$ in (9.26) and on substituting the money market equilibrium condition ((9.4) substituted into (9.5)) for i we get

$$p_t = \frac{1}{\beta_1 + \beta_3/\alpha_2}\left[\beta_0 + \beta_1 s_t + \left(\beta_2 - \frac{\beta_3 \alpha_1}{\alpha_2} - 1\right)y_t - \frac{\beta_3}{\alpha_2}m_t\right] \tag{9.54}$$

which for given m and y demonstrates the positive slope of $\Delta p = 0$ in s–p space. Further, the slope $\Delta p = 0$ is less steep then the 45° ray for the following reason. From equilibrium, an increase in the price level results, via the $s - p$ term in equation (9.25), in a relative price change (domestic goods are more expensive vis-à-vis foreign goods) and decrease in the real money supply and as a consequence a rise in interest rates. Both these effects in the model result in an excess supply of goods. To offset the terms of trade effect the exchange rate would have to move by the same amount as p, but since interest rates have also risen s must rise more than proportionately to the relative price change.

13   Equation (9.27) is obtained by totally differentiating equation (9.51) to get

$$dp_t - dm_t = -\alpha_1 dy_t + \alpha_2 di_t^* + \alpha_2 \phi(d\bar{s} - ds)_t \qquad (9.55)$$

and by noting that homogeneity ensures that $d\bar{s}_t = dm_t$ and the assumption that y_t, i_t^* and p are constant or sticky ensures that their changes are equal to zero.

14   Frenkel and Rodriguez (1981) have argued that the exchange rate overshooting in the fix-price model is crucially dependent on the assumption of perfect capital mobility. If capital is less than perfectly mobile the exchange rate may undershoot its new long-run equilibrium value. A further example of exchange rate undershooting is given by Bhandhari et al. (1984). For a further discussion of the issues surrounding the over-shooting/undershooting question, see MacDonald (1988b).

15   It is worth noting that this monetary strategy entailed attempting to reduce the *rate of growth* of the money supply, rather than its level (as assumed in Dornbusch's version of the SPMA). A version of the SPMA which allows for changes in the rate of monetary growth is presented in Buiter and Miller (1981).

16   For a fuller discussion of dual exchange rate systems and their practicalities, see MacDonald (1988b).

17   Underlying the assumption that $\Delta m^e = \Delta s^e$ is a further assumption that expected income growth is equal to zero. This type of assumption has been termed "monetary super-neutrality" by Artis and Currie (1981).

18   For a discussion of the appropriate use of monetary and exchange rate targets see Artis and Currie (1981).

19   For example, Laney et al. (1984) argue that in 1981 US foreign currency holdings amounted to US$3 billion, whereas total narrowly defined money amounted to over US$400 billion.

20   Frankel uses long-term interest rates to proxy expected inflation differentials and short-run interest rates to measure real interest rates.

21   Similar poor results from estimating equations (9.7) and (9.36) have been reported by Hacche and Townend (1981) for sterling's effective exchange rate and by Backus (1984) for the Canadian dollar–US dollar exchange rate. See MacDonald (1991) and de Jong (1991) for a more comprehensive review of the expirical evidence on exchange rate models.

22   However, it is worth noting that for the other currencies studied by MacDonald and Taylor (1991b and 1994) estimated coefficients are often far from their expected values.

23   Additionally Cushman, Lee and Thorgeirsson (1996) find that a form of monetary model does hold when two other variables are included in the specification; see also Cushman (2000).

24   In support of this point, MacDonald and Marsh note that VARs with no *ecm* terms typically perform marginally worse than the random walk, and are uniformly less accurate than the models which include long-run equilibria over each forecast horizon. These results confirm that the error correction terms are important both in-sample (since they are significant in the SEMs) and out-of-sample (where they improve forecast performance).

10

The Monetary Model: Further Applications – Real Shocks and Exchange Regime Volatility

In the last chapter we analyzed various aspects of the monetary approach to the exchange rate. In this chapter we return to the monetary model to address a number of important issues. The first concerns the close correlation between real and nominal exchange rates we referred to in chapter 7. We noted there, that for most countries during the recent float the correlation between real and nominal rates has been approximately unity. How may this be explained? One natural explanation is in terms of the sticky price model discussed in the last chapter: with prices sticky in the short run, nominal exchange rate overshoots will inevitably mean that real and nominal rates move on a one-to-one basis. However, there is an alternative explanation for this correlation which also relies on a variant of the monetary model. This variant, due to Stockman (1980) and Lucas (1982), is labeled the General Equilibrium Model and is discussed in section 10.1. As we shall see, this model predicts that the close correlation between real and nominal exchange rates is in fact due to real rather than nominal shocks.

Another important issue, which has also been examined in the context of the monetary model, is that of regime volatility. This has been addressed by a number of researchers, and has been thoroughly analyzed by Flood and Rose (1995, 1999). They take a version of the monetary model and show that in the move from the Bretton Woods regime (of fixed but adjustable exchange rates) to the recent float the volatility of macroeconomic fundamentals remains unchanged, but the volatility of the exchange rate increases dramatically. It would seem then that by simply fixing the nominal exchange rate an important source of systemic volatility may be removed from the international monetary system. This clearly has important implications for the debate on the reform of the international monetary system and also for research on the economics of exchange rates. We consider regime volatility in section 10.2.

In section 10.3 we overview the empirical literature on the two competing hypotheses for explaining the volatility of real and nominal exchange rates. As we shall see, it seems natural to take this material after the discussion of regime volatility.

10.1 The General Equilibrium Monetary Model

The general equilibrium model is essentially a variant of the FLMA, but differs crucially from that model because it explicitly models cross-country real *shocks*. To impart a flavor of this model's predictions, we consider in this section what is perhaps the simplest variant of the model. The reader is directed to the excellent survey contained in Stockman (1987) for a fuller account of the model.

We return to the two-country, two-good world, with flexible prices used in the last chapter to motivate the FLMA. The key difference here is that, although agents are assumed to have identical homothetic preferences, they now make a distinction between home and foreign goods. The fact that agents have the same homothetic preferences essentially means that they can be lumped together into a representative agent, which is a common assumption in this literature. Additionally, it is assumed that all agents have the same resources.

In figure 10.1 we show the per capita supplies of the home and foreign good, assumed inelastic, and the indifference map which represents agents' preferences. In this world the equilibrium relative price of output is the slope of the representative agent's indifference curve at point A. This relative price is the real exchange rate, q. Note that in this setting tastes can affect relative prices but not quantities. So flatter (steeper) indifference curves would represent higher (lower) equilibrium values of the real exchange rate.

The nominal exchange rate, s, may be introduced by taking the money market equilibrium conditions from chapter 9, repeated here as equations (10.1) and (10.2):

$$m_t - p_t = \beta_0 y_t - \beta_1 i_t, \tag{10.1}$$

$$m_t^* - p_t^* = \beta_0 y_t^* - \beta_1 i_t^*. \tag{10.2}$$

For simplicity we assume $\beta_1 = 0$, and by rearranging for relative prices and substituting into the definition of the real exchange rate, $q(= s + p^* - p)$ we obtain:

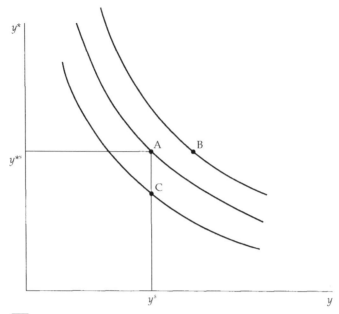

Figure 10.1 Preferences and supply in the General Equilibrium Model

$$s_t = m_t - m_t^* - \beta_0(y_t - y_t^*) + q_t. \tag{10.3}$$

As in the simple flex-price monetary, this model predicts that a k percent increase in m increases the relative price level by k percent and depreciates the nominal exchange rate by k percent. Again, as in the FLMA, an increase in y, by raising the demand for money and lowering domestic prices, appreciates the nominal exchange rate. However, in contrast to the simple FLMA, the real exchange rate, q, appears explicitly as a RHS variable and so an increase in q, which is here simply the relative price of imports, depreciates the nominal exchange rate in proportion. In terms of figure 10.1, this increase in q represents a flattening of the indifference mapping. There are essentially two ways this can occur.

First, a change in *tastes* which makes the indifference curve through A flatter will generate a rise in the real exchange rate. The second way it can occur is through a change in the supply of one or both goods. For example, hold the supply of the foreign good constant and consider an exogenous increase in the supply of the home good to a point such as B. At B we note that the intersection with the indifference mapping occurs where the indifference curves are flatter. It is important to note that in the case of the latter shock, there will be two influences on the nominal exchange rate. There will be the standard money demand effect of a rise in income (discussed above in the context of the standard FLMA) and also a relative price effect. The former effect, as we have noted, will appreciate the exchange rate while the latter produces a depreciation of the currency. Hence a supply-side shock has an ambiguous effect on the nominal exchange rate.

Obstfeld and Stockman (1985) have demonstrated that if the degree of substitutability between domestic and foreign goods is relatively small the relative price effect will dominate and so the combined effect will be to depreciate the exchange rate.

The punch-line from this model is that the kind of volatility we observe in real and nominal exchange rates is in fact being driven by volatility in the real exchange rate, rather than the other way around as in the sticky-price story of the last chapter. Essentially, causality runs from the real exchange rate to the nominal rate because of real shocks, rather than money market disturbances which in the presence of sticky prices produce nominal exchange rate overshoots which, in turn, produce real exchange rate volatility. So although the general equilibrium model is similar to the FLMA, it gives a very different story for volatility.

A linearized reduced form representation of this model is:

$$s_t = z_t + [\alpha_0 \tau_t + \alpha_1 \rho_t] \qquad (10.4)$$

where τ and ρ represent relative taste and technology shocks, respectively and z_t is the composite term containing the money market variables. We turn to a discussion of the empirical evidence relating to (10.4) after considering the Flood and Rose (1995) application of the monetary model.

10.2 The Monetary Model and Regime Volatility

Using US dollar bilateral exchange rates for the period 1957–84, Mussa (1986) demonstrated that the variance of real exchange rates in the floating rate regime was much greater than in the Bretton Woods fixed rate regime. Furthermore, Baxter and Stockman (1989) examine the variability of a number of macroeconomic variables – output, trade variables, and private and government consumption – and they are "unable to find evidence that the cyclic behavior of real macroeconomic aggregates depends systematically on the exchange rate regime. The only exception is the well known case of the real exchange rate." Flood and Rose confirmed this result using nominal effective exchange rates and a whole range of macroeconomic fundamentals. In sum, exchange rate volatility differs with the exchange rate regime whereas macroeconomic volatility does not. The idea that real exchange rate volatility is conditional on the exchange rate regime has been formalized by Flood and Rose (1995, 1999) using variants of the monetary model. We now consider their work.

Flood and Rose take as their starting point the basic FLMA, modified in two ways. First they add a well-behaved shock, ε_t, to the money market relationships in the home and foreign country. For example for the home country we now have:

$$m_t - p_t = \beta_0 y_t - \beta_1 i_t + \varepsilon_t \qquad (10.5)$$

Additionally, the absolute PPP condition is also assumed to hold up to an additive disturbance, v_t:

$$s_t = p_t - p_t^* + v_t. \tag{10.6}$$

Substituting (10.5) and the comparable foreign money market relationship into (10.6), we obtain a variant of the flexible price monetary model:

$$s_t = m_t - m_t^* - \beta_0(y_t - y_t^*) + \beta_1(i_t - i_t^*) - (\varepsilon_t - \varepsilon_t^*) - v_t \tag{10.7a}$$

which may be re-expressed as:

$$s_t - \beta_1(i_t - i_t^*) = m_t - m_t^* - \beta_0(y_t - y_t^*) - (\varepsilon_t - \varepsilon_t^*) - v_t. \tag{10.7b}$$

Flood and Rose then define three measures of fundamentals relating to the right and left-hand sides of (10.7b). Total Fundamentals (TF), which is taken to be the standard way of measuring fundamentals in the monetary model, is given by:

$$TF_t \equiv m_t - m_t^* - \beta_0(y_t - y_t^*)$$

while Augmented Fundamentals adds in the relative money demand disturbance from (10.7b) to give:

$$ATF_t \equiv m_t - m_t^* - \beta_0(y_t - y_t^*) - (\varepsilon_t - \varepsilon_t^*)$$

The latter measure of fundamentals is seen as more general since it does not require an explicit money demand model. Virtual Fundamentals (VF) are defined as the left-hand side of (10.7b):

$$VF_t \equiv s_t - \beta_1(i_t - i_t^*).$$

In contrast to traditional fundamentals, virtual fundamentals are always closely related to the exchange rate within the sample, given some assumed values for β_1. Flood and Rose are keen to stress that these three measures of fundamentals do not rely on a particular reduced form exchange rate relationship, and so their empirical work will not be affected by the kinds of instabilities (and other problems associated with reduced form estimates) noted in the last chapter.

The data period studied by Flood and Rose runs from 1960 to 1991 (monthly observations) and the countries studied are Canada, France, Germany, Holland, Italy, Japan, Sweden and the UK, with the United States taken as the foreign country. All three measures of fundamentals are first differenced to ensure stationarity and conditional volatility is used as their measure of volatility. Additionally, a variety of plausible values of β_0 and β_1 are used to construct the various measures of fundamentals and their results are shown to be insensitive to this choice.

In figures 10.2(a), (b) we report a representative set of results for VF and ATF, respectively. The striking feature of a comparison of these two figures is that the volatility of virtual fundamentals is much higher in regimes of floating exchange rates than during regimes of fixed rates, whereas there is no comparable large difference in the volatility of ATF (or indeed TF) across regimes. One immediate reaction to this result is that it is the failure to account for interest rate volatility in either of ATF or TF that explains the result. However, Flood and Rose also construct alternative measures of ATF and TF (from the sticky price monetary model) in which an interest rate differential enters. The results are effectively the same as those reported in figures 10.2(a), (b). Hence the excess volatility of the VF term must be driven by the exchange rate rather than the interest rate differential. Indeed, in a follow-up paper Flood and Rose (1999) demonstrate that the striking difference between the two sets of figures also holds if one simply compares the conditional volatility of the exchange rate with the conditional volatility of *all* of the right hand side variables in (10.7a).

How may this striking finding be explained or interpreted? The interpretation Flood and Rose draw is that this is another piece of evidence against traditional (macroeconomic) fundamentals-based models of the exchange rate. They argue that the key thing that changed as the international monetary system moved from fixed to floating exchange rates is not the underlying volatility of fundamentals but the regime itself, and correspondingly the structure of the market; the so-called market micro-structure has changed. In essence the change in the structure of the market attracts agents with a huge appetite for risk and their behavior imparts an excess volatility over-and-above the volatility inherant in macro fundamentals. We return to this point in the next chapter after introducing the portfolio balance model of the exchange rate.

 ## 10.3 Empirical Evidence on the General Equilibrium Approach

Proponents of the general equilibrium approach have appealed to certain stylized facts about the behavior of real exchange rates in support of their claim that their model explains the close correlation between real and nominal exchange rates. For example, Stockman (1987) noted that if real exchange rates are non-stationary then this implies that shocks to the real exchange rate are permanent, or real, shocks. However, as we saw in section 7.5 this point is contentious in the sense that there is now accumulating evidence to suggest that real exchange rates are mean-reverting and therefore real exchange rates contain important mean-reverting or stationary components. This evidence is more consistent with the sticky price story, especially for the adjustment speeds recovered from non-linear models of real exchange rate dynamics.[1]

However, perhaps the clearest piece of information against the general equilibrium model is that contained in the last section. If the general equilibrium story is correct then there should be no regime dependency in the behavior of the real exchange rate. However, the striking finding of Flood and Rose is that regime dependency is the key to understanding the behavior of exchange rates during the recent floating period. Of course the regime dependency point also undermines the credibility of alternative exchange rate models such as the sticky price model.

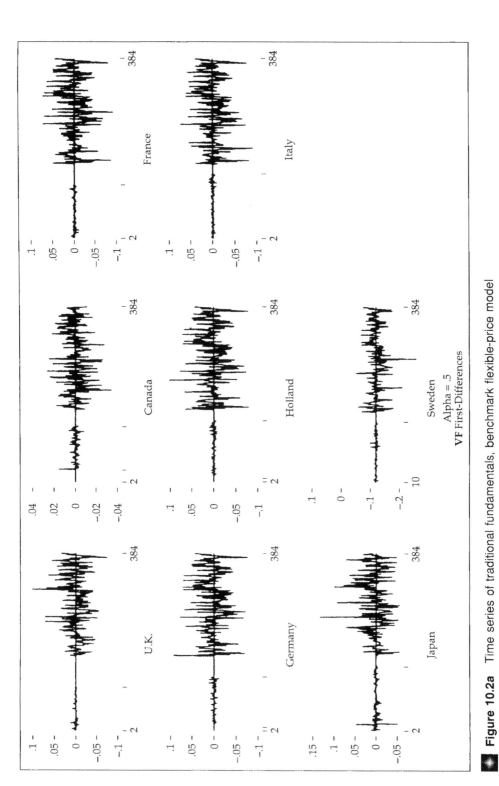

Figure 10.2a Time series of traditional fundamentals, benchmark flexible-price model
Horizontal axes are months, from 1960(I) to 1991 (end)

Source: Flood and Rose 1995

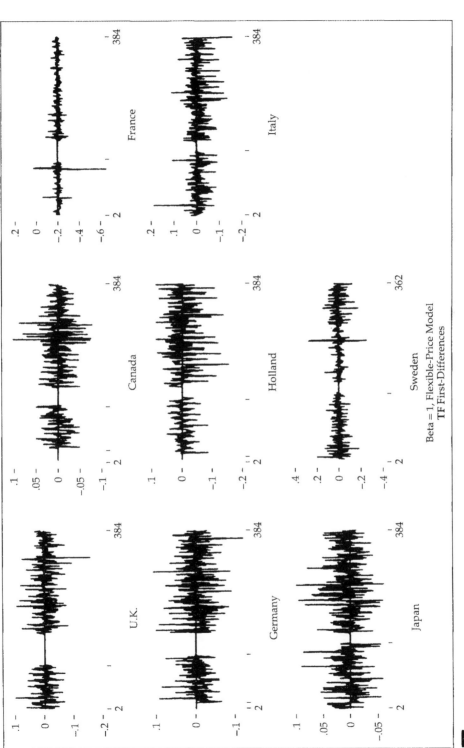

Figure 10.2b

Perhaps though the best way of assessing the relative merits of the different exchange rate models considered so far is to explicitly decompose the real exchange rate into components attributable to supply-side shocks and those attributable to demand-side shocks. In an influential paper Clarida and Gali (1995) have sought to do just that. In particular, they attempt to decompose the real exchange rates of the German mark, Japanese yen, UK pound and Canadian dollar into supply-side, demand side and nominal, or inflation, shocks. The sum of the demand and nominal shocks may be interpreted as those pertaining to the sticky price monetary model (or, as Clarida-Gali label it, the Mundell–Fleming–Dornbusch model), while the supply-side shocks are interpreted as relating to the Stockman model.

Clarida and Gali estimate trivariate vector autoregressive (VAR) models consisting of the change in relative output levels, the change in the real exchange rate, and a relative inflation rate. That is, denoting the 3×1 vector of variables as:

$$\Delta x_t \equiv [\Delta y_t, \Delta q_t, \pi_t]' \tag{10.8}$$

where y denotes relative output (home foreign), q denotes the real exchange rate, and π relative inflation (home against foreign). The VAR representation of Δx_t is then:

$$\Delta x_t = \sum_{i=1}^{p} \varphi_i \Delta x_{t-1} + \varepsilon_t, \tag{10.9}$$

where ε_t represents a vector of disturbances. The main novelty in the work of Clarida-Gali's work is to show how this vector may be interpreted as a set of supply, demand, and nominal disturbances. In particular, they show how using a set of identifying restrictions due to Blanchard and Quah (1989) the vector of disturbances may be defined as: $\varepsilon_t \equiv [z_t, \delta_t, v_t]'$, where z_t represents the supply shock, δ_t is the demand shock and v_t is the nominal shock. The economic intuition that allows the shocks to be interpreted in this way is: money shocks are not allowed to influence the real exchange rate or relative output in the long run; only supply shocks are expected to influence relative output levels in the long run; both supply and demand shocks are expected to influence the real exchange rate in the long-run. These restrictions are based on the long-run behavior of a modified version of the Mundell–Fleming–Dornbusch (MFD) model (modified to be stock-flow consistent and exhibit long-run neutrality of money).[2]

The expected sign patterns of the real shocks on output, the real exchange rate and the price level generated by the MFD model are as follows. A permanent demand shock should permanently appreciate the currency, increase the price level and output in the short run. A supply shock should produce a depreciation of the currency, a fall in prices and a rise in output. Finally, a nominal shock should also produce a nominal depreciation of the currency which, with sticky prices, will also generate a real depreciation; however, in contrast to the supply-side shock this will not be permanent. The nominal shock also produces a rise in the price level and a, perhaps, transitory effect on output.

Given this kind of framework, Clarida–Gali seek to answer two questions: what have been the sources of real exchange rate fluctuations since the inception of floating exchange rates and, second, how important are nominal shocks relative to real shocks? To answer these questions they use their estimated structural VAR models to estimate variance decompositions of the real exchange rate, impulse response functions of the set of VAR variables, to the underlying shocks and compute "real time" historical decompositions of the real exchange rate. Clarida–Gali estimate this model for the dollar bilaterals of the German mark, Japanese yen, UK pound, and Canadian dollar over the period 1974.I to 1992.I.

Clarida–Gali's impulse response analysis indicates that the responses of relative output, relative inflation and the real exchange rate to the underlying structural model are, in general, consistent with the underlying theoretical structure of the MFD model. For example, the US–German impulse response indicates that in response to a one-standard deviation nominal shock, the real exchange rate initially depreciates by 3.8 percent (the nominal overshoots by 4 percent), US output rises relative to German output by 0.5 percent and US inflation rises relative to German inflation by 0.3 percent. The output and real exchange rate effects of a nominal shock take between 16 to 20 quarters to die out. In response to a one-standard deviation relative demand shock, the dollar initially appreciates in real terms by 4 percent, relative output rises by 0.36 percent and there is a 0.44 percent rise in US inflation relative to foreign inflation. The effect on the exchange rate is permanent and after 20 quarters the real rate appreciates by 6 percent. A one-standard deviation relative supply shock produces a (wrongly signed) 1 percent dollar appreciation in quarter 2 and this quickly goes to zero (after 20 quarters the appreciation is only 0.2 percent). Other currency pairings produce similar results and, in particular, the perverse supply-side effect appears for the other currencies as well which would seem to indicate an unsatisfactory aspect of their modeling.

Following MacDonald and Swagel (1998), if we interpret the business cycle related component as the sum of the demand and money shock then CG's variance decompositions demonstrate that for all four real exchange rates the business cycle component constitutes approximately 90 percent of the variance of the exchange rates at quarter 40. Of this total, almost all is attributable to demand shocks in the case of the UK and Canada, while for Japan the split is 60 percent demand and 30 percent monetary with the split being approximately equal for the German mark. The proportion of the forecast error variance due to the supply shock is statistically insignificant at all forecast horizons. The very small supply-side specific component reported by Clarida–Gali has become something of stylized fact in the literature on the economics of real exchange rates.

Chadha and Prasad (1997) apply the Clarida–Gali approach to the Japanese yen–US dollar exchange rate over the period 1975 quarter 1 to 1996 quarter 1. Their impulse response analysis indicates a permanent real exchange rate depreciation in response to a supply shock (of around 8 percent), while a demand shock produces a permanent appreciation (of around 8 percent). The nominal shock produces an initial real depreciation which is eventually offset with the real rate settling down to zero by quarter 8. The fact that all shocks have a correctly signed effect on the Japanese yen exchange rate contrasts with the findings of Clarida–Gali and may be a reflection of the longer sample period used by Chadha and Prasad. Their variance decomposition analysis reveals a somewhat different split between the different shocks at quarter 40. In particular, the business cycle shocks total 78 percent (compared to 90 percent in Clarida-Gali), with the supply-side shock accounting for the remainder. Interestingly, supply and demand shocks each contribute about one-fourth of the forecast error variance after quarter 8, with nominal rates explaining the remainder. In contrast to Clarida–Gali, Chadha and Prasad find that the proportion of the forecast error variance due to the supply shock is statistically significant at all forecast horizons. Chadha and Prasad interpret their findings as suggesting that monetary and fiscal policy can have a substantial effect on the real exchange rate at business cycle frequencies, whereas the role of technology and productivity shocks is relatively small.

Clarida and Gali's results for the real US bilateral rates of the German mark, Japanese yen and UK pound are confirmed by MacDonald and Swagel (1998) for a longer sample period (1973 to 1997); the sum of demand and nominal shocks – the business cycle related components – dominate, as in CG, explaining approximately 90 percent of the variance of the mark and yen exchange rates after 40 quarters, with demand shocks being by far the most important component, especially for the UK. For the German mark, however, the business cycle component explains 70 percent of the forecast error variance with the supply-side shock explaining the remaining 30 percent. Interestingly, all of the forecast error variances are statistically significant at all forecast horizons and this is also the case for horizons of quarter 12 and above for the yen (all of the supply shock forecast error variances for UK pound are insignificant). Furthermore, MacDonald and Swagel also confirm the perverse sign of a supply-side shock on the real exchange rate and the statistically insignificant forecast error variances due to the supply-side shock. Interestingly, however, when considering real effective exchange rates (of the US dollar, UK pound, and Japanese yen) the supply-side shocks become correctly signed with respect to the exchange rate and although the aggregate effect of the business cycle component is similar to the bilaterals at quarter 40 (explaining 85 percent of the variance, rather than 90 percent) the composition of the business-cycle component is different. For example, for the UK bilateral 73 percent of the residual variance is due to the demand shock, 14 percent nominal, while for effectives the relative proportions are 59 percent and 25 percent. For the Japanese yen the difference is more marked, since the demand component moves from a 47 percent share in the bilateral to 25 percent in the effective, with the nominal share moving from 40 percent to 59 percent. The use of effective rates would therefore seem to be important in measuring the relative importance of demand shocks, but not the supply shocks which have a very similar influence to their role in the bilateral case.

Two further studies seek to address the issue of the relative dominance of demand shocks by specifying a richer menu of shocks, particularly on the supply-side. For example, Rogers (1995) expands the x vector in (10.8) to include the change in the ratio of government spending to output, and replaces inflation as the nominal variable with base money and the base money multiplier. The particular identification restrictions imposed allow him to construct fiscal and productivity shocks (both of which should produce a long-run appreciation on the real exchange rate), a demand shock (a long-run depreciation, due to having a model in which traded/non-traded distinction is made) and a monetary shock (no long-run effect). This particular specification is implemented on an annual data set for the UK pound–US dollar exchange rate over the period 1859–1992. The impulse response analysis reveals that 50 percent of the variance of the real exchange rate is due to monetary shocks (with a roughly equal split between money multiplier shocks and the monetary base shock), productivity (supply) shocks account for approximately 35 percent, with the remainder coming from the demand side. So supply shocks put in a more respectable performance in this paper. In a bid to discern if this is dependent on the sample period or the richer shock specification, Rogers implements his VAR specification for the same data sample as that used in Clarida–Gali, and the Clarida–Gali specification for his longer sample. In terms of the latter exercise, he finds that the longer sample does not increase the role of the supply-side shock, although it does increase the role of the monetary shock at the expense of the demand shock (interestingly, this is similar to the extended sample findings of MacDonald and Swagel). Implementing his model structure on the Clarida–Gali data set produces a similar result: the business cycle shocks dominate the total but the composition changes from the demand shocks being the dominant shocks to the nominal shocks contributing about one-half the total for all of the currencies considered by Clarida–Gali. So specification of shocks is important.

Weber (1997) also extends the Clarida–Gali model by specifying a richer menu of shocks. In particular, he splits supply shocks into labor supply and productivity components, and segments monetary shocks into both money demand and money supply; additionally, he also includes a relative aggregate demand shock. In terms of the real exchange rate, the long-run restrictions are that the real exchange rate depreciates in response to both a relative productivity and relative labor supply shocks and the real exchange rate appreciates in response to a relative demand disturbance. The long-run restrictions are imposed using the Blanchard–Quah decomposition. The data set consists of the three real bilaterals: US dollar–German mark, US dollar–Japanese yen, and German mark–Japanese yen. The period spanned is 1971 month VIII to 1994 month XII. Weber's results essentially confirm the findings of CG – demand shocks are the dominant force driving real exchange rates, although for the two cross rates involving the Japanese yen supply-side shocks (in the form of labor market shocks) do contribute a much larger fraction of the forecast error variance (around one-third) compared to the original CG study; and this result confirms the findings of Chadha and Prasad (1997). However, Weber notes that the demand shocks are highly correlated with the real exchange rate and, indeed, for the US dollar–German mark this is on a one-to-one basis; most intriguingly he demonstrates that the relative demand shock does not have a significant impact on output, which presumably it should have if it is to serve any purpose in representing a demand shock. Weber concludes by arguing that the aggregate demand (AD) shock is simply a "catch-all" term which reflects what is left of real exchange rate movements that cannot be forecast from the other variables in the system. It is therefore questionable to interpret such shocks as AD shocks when they contain such a large share of the residual variance.

The basic CG model suffers from other deficiencies in addition to those noted by Weber.[3] First, the basic identification procedure used forces all of the temporary shocks to have a monetary origin. Of course in practice, or in the data, this is unlikely to be the case. This means that a whole range of temporary supply shocks – oil price shocks, changes in fiscal policy – are subsumed as a monetary shock. The same kind of argument could be made for temporary demand shocks. Second, in setting up the identifying assumptions, it is assumed that the innovations to demand and supply are uncorrelated, which, for a variety of reasons, seems implausible (i.e. an increase in AD raises I, which raises the future capital stock and supply, as well as demand). Third, in the original CG study nominal shocks only have a miniscule effect on relative output and this raises the question of whether it is the way nominal shocks are specified, rather than the absence of important nominal effects that is to blame. Sarte (1994) has demonstrated that identification in structural VARs can be very sensitive to identifying restrictions particularly when residual series are used as instruments for the variables for which they are intended as instruments.[4]

The empirical work on structural VAR relationships may be summarized in the following way. The basic message from the original paper by Clarida and Gali is that supply-side shocks explain a miniscule and insignificant proportion of the variance of key real exchange rates. Extending the sample from that in CG seems to have the effect of increasing the importance of nominal shocks at the expense of demand shocks, while leaving the role of supply-side shocks unchanged, although supply-side shock does seem to be important for the Japanese yen. The measurement of shocks also seems to be important, especially on the demand side: defining the monetary variable to be monetary rather than price has an important bearing on the relative split between demand and nominal. The use of effective rates rather than bilateral measures seems to make a difference, particularly with respect to achieving correctly signed impulse response functions.

 ## 10.4 Concluding Comments

In this chapter we have taken the basic flexible price monetary model, first introduced in the last chapter, to address two key issues in the international finance literature. The first concerns the source of the close correlation between real and nominal exchange rates, which is a feature of the recent floating rate regime. The sticky price monetary model considered in the last chapter suggests that this correlation is due to the interaction of nominal exchange rate overshooting with sticky prices: causality runs from the nominal exchange rate to the real rate. However, and as we demonstrated in this chapter, the monetary model can also be used to introduce a role for supply-side shocks; that is, shocks to tastes and supply. In the general equilibrium model of Lucas and Stockman it is these real shocks which are the source of real exchange rate volatility and it is this which leads to nominal volatility. What does the empirical evidence indicate about the validity of these two interpretations? Perhaps the most complete empirical investigation of the source of the close correlation between real and nominal exchange rates is that of Clarida and Gali, who demonstrate that supply-side effects have a very small role to play in explaining real exchange rate behavior, the major source of real exchange rate volatility derives from shocks which are closely associated with the sticky price model (it is worth noting, however, that these results have not gone unchallenged). Perhaps the clearest piece of evidence against the general equilibrium model is the evidence of regime volatility which was the second key issue addressed in this chapter using the monetary model. The regime volatility point is that in moving from the Bretton Woods regime, of fixed but adjustable exchange rates, to the recent float, the only thing that changes, apart from the regime itself, is the volatility of the nominal exchange rate; there is no corresponding change in the volatility of the underlying fundamentals. Unfortunately, the regime volatility result has important implications for all fundamentals-based exchange rate models and not just for the general equilibrium model. We return to this point at the end of the next chapter.

NOTES

1 There is a small empirical literature which seeks to decompose real exchange rates into permanent and transitory components (see MacDonald, 1999, for an overview). In essence what this literature shows is that when univariate methods, such as the Beveridge–Nelson decomposition, are used the permanent component accounts for around 90 percent of the variance. However, when multivariate decompositions are used, and these are likely to be more appropriate, the proportion falls to about 50 percent.

2 The particular version is a stochastic version of Obstfeld's representation of the Mundell–Fleming–Dornbusch model.

3 Our discussion here is based on Stockman (1995).

4 As in Rogers (1995) and Weber (1997), MacDonald (1999b) advocates a wider range of shocks (both demand and supply shocks) and also a completely different way of estimating the effects of the shocks. In particular, MacDonald points out that in systems which are relatively rich in terms of the numbers of shocks the cointegratedness of the system must be recognized. The existence of significant cointegrating vectors is then used to impose a set of long-run restrictions. The impulse response functions and variance decompositions are then calculated using the generalized impulse response approach of Pesaran. This appears to give a more balanced approach.

11

The Portfolio Balance Approach to the Determination of the Exchange Rate

In chapter 5 one criticism of the Mundell–Fleming model was its neglect of the stock implications of flows. For example, a monetary expansion with perfect capital mobility results in an exchange rate depreciation, an expansion of output and a current account surplus in the new "equilibrium". The new "equilibrium" is not sustainable because of the stock–flow implications of the current account position. Similarly in the monetary class of models considered in the last chapter the flow implications of monetary policy are also ignored. Thus in the sticky-price monetary approach the stickiness of the price level means that any exchange rate overshoot has consequences for the real exchange rate and hence the current account; however, the wealth implications of any imbalance is ignored.[1]

In this chapter we attempt to remedy some of the stock–flow deficiencies inherent in other models by presenting a stock–flow consistent model. In particular, we present an asset model of the determination of the exchange rate in which the economy takes time to adjust to various shocks: there is therefore a split between the short- and long-run effects of such shocks. In the short run asset prices are determined by the stock requirements of asset markets, but the asset prices so determined may have consequences for real variables such as real wealth and the rate of savings over time. One important feature of the asset market model considered in this chapter is that, in contrast to the models considered hitherto, it assumes that bonds are imperfect substitutes and thus allows a role for portfolio diversification in terms of bonds between countries (the monetary class of models by assuming that bonds are perfect substitutes does not have a role for such diversification). Models which utilize imperfect substitutability and capture stock–flow interactions are termed portfolio balance models. The portfolio balance model has its origins and development in research conducted by McKinnon and Oates (1966), McKinnon (1969a) and Branson (1968, 1975a). It has been applied to the determination of the exchange rate by, *inter alia*, Branson (1977), Isard (1978), Genberg and Kierzkowski (1979), Allen and Kenen (1978) and Dornbusch and Fisher (1980). One particular feature of such portfolio balance models is that wealth is included as a scale variable in the asset demand equations. This is in marked contrast to the asset models considered in chapters 9 and 10.

In this chapter we present a model which captures the essential features of the portfolio balance model as it has been applied to the determination of the exchange rate. Before considering the model in any detail, however, some of the issues mentioned above are discussed in a little more detail. A related topic considered in this chapter is a review of the econometric evidence on the portfolio balance model.

Whither the current account?

The reader who has read the previous two chapters in the light of chapters 2, 3, and 4 may be forgiven for asking: what has happened to the current account? The emphasis in the monetary approach to the exchange rate is on asset markets and consequently the capital account: changes in monetary and real variables have their effects on exchange rates via asset markets. The current account may be thought of as being in the background in the different versions of the monetary approach. In the flex-price monetary approach there is nothing inconsistent with a country running a current account deficit or surplus and therefore accumulating or decumulating assets. Such imbalances, however, are due to the relevant propensities to save and invest in the respective countries (i.e. real magnitudes) and it is assumed that such factors are not influenced by exchange market developments.[2]

But how realistic is this? In the Dornbusch (1976a) model, for example, the short-run exchange rate overshoots to maintain money market equilibrium. This overshoot, as was shown in the previous chapter, implies a change in the real exchange rate (i.e. purchasing power parity (PPP) is violated in the short run) and thus in the terms of trade. This must, from a position of current account balance, lead to a current account imbalance and wealth must be changing. But in the Dornbusch model the change in the exchange rate has implications only for aggregate demand; the consequent wealth implications for current account imbalances have no effect on spending (via, say, a wealth effect on consumption) or on assets (i.e. if money demand is a function of wealth then a change in wealth will alter money demand). A realistic account of the dynamic adjustment from short-run asset market equilibrium to long-run equilibrium should highlight the role of the current account.

Casual empiricism also highlights a role for the current account and its effect on the exchange rate. For example, from June 8, 1977 until November 1, 1978 the dollar fell sharply against most currencies and, although the US economy was suffering relatively high inflation and nominal interest rates during this period, most commentators argued that the dollar's depreciation was much more than could be explained purely on the basis of these factors. Attention was also focused on the large and growing US current account deficit as an explanation of the large depreciation (nominal, real) of the exchange rate relative to inflation rates. The absence of current account effects from the models discussed in the previous chapter make them unsuited to explaining the dollar depreciation over 1977–8.[3]

Casual empiricism also suggests that the monetary approach ignores another important factor, namely, portfolio diversification. Thus, in chapter 9 it was assumed that non-monetary assets (bonds) were perfect substitutes and therefore had no role to play in the analysis of the determination of the exchange rate. However, a number of factors, such as differential tax risk, liquidity considerations, political risk, default risk and exchange risk, suggest that non-money assets issued in different countries are unlikely to be viewed as perfect substitutes. Thus, just as international transactors are likely to hold a portfolio of currencies to minimize exchange risk (i.e. currency substitution), risk-averse international investors will wish to hold a portfolio of non-money assets, the proportion of particular assets held depending on risk–return factors. In this chapter the imperfect subsitutability of home and foreign bonds is assumed to be driven by exchange rate risk. This, in turn, has the important implication that uncovered interest rate parity is not expected to hold. Indeed tests of the uncovered interest rate parity relationship do tend to question its validity and point towards the existence of a risk premium.[4] Thus equation (9.2) does not hold, but instead

$$i - i^* - \Delta s^e = \lambda \qquad (11.1)$$

where λ is a risk premium (in chapters 9 and 10 this term is assumed to equal zero). Thus if $\lambda < 0$ the return on the foreign country's assets (measured by $i^* + \Delta s^e$) is greater than that on the home country's assets (i.e. i) because foreign assets are viewed as more risky than home assets. If international investors decide that a currency has become riskier they are likely to reallocate their bond portfolios in favor of the less risky assets. This gives another explanation for the large depreciation of the dollar in 1977–8: the falling dollar meant that dollar assets were perceived to be riskier than, say, German and Japanese assets and portfolio managers were keen to switch from dollar bonds to mark- and yen-denominated bonds.

The above discussion has raised a number of points which are summarized as follows. First, if PPP does not hold in the short run, exchange rate changes caused by, say, a monetary shock will be real changes and, if the familiar Marshall–Lerner condition holds, these changes may be expected to influence the current account. A current account imbalance means that the country must be accumulating or decumulating assets and wealth must be changing. As Dornbusch

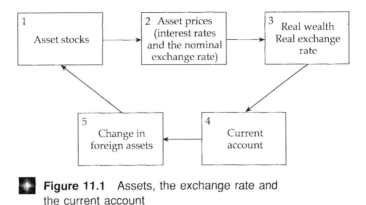

Figure 11.1 Assets, the exchange rate and the current account

(1980b) and Frankel (1983) have pointed out, changes in wealth could be expected to influence the exchange rate in a number of ways. If consumption is a function of wealth (as posited by the life-cycle hypothesis) then income will be changing and as a corollary so too will the demand for money and the exchange rate. If the demand for money is also a function of wealth, a change in wealth due to current account imbalance will lead to a changed demand for money and this can be expected to reinforce the exchange rate impact of the change in consumption. Wealth will also have an influence on asset market equilibrium if, as seems likely, international agents are risk averse and the riskiness of holding foreign assets implies that domestic bond-holders will hold a larger proportion of domestic bonds in their portfolios than foreign investors (for the same rate of return on home and foreign bonds). Thus with imperfect asset substitutability and risk aversion, greater proportions of an increase in wealth will be held in domestic bonds and this must have asset market consequences.

Imperfect substitutability of bonds has of course a separate influence on asset markets independently of wealth effects. Thus, as was argued above, if investors decide that a particular currency has become riskier they will diversify their portfolios away from bonds denominated in that currency.

The conclusion is reached on theoretical grounds and also from casual empiricism that the current account has an important role to play in a properly specified asset market model of the determination of the exchange rate. Hence although the exchange rate is at any point in time determined so as to clear asset markets (as in the monetary approach), the range of assets relevant to the determination of the exchange rate is likely to be wider than relative money supplies, and furthermore, because the current account is a flow concept, a current account imbalance will have an effect on the stock of assets over time and thus, for the reasons noted earlier, the exchange rate.

Later in this chapter a model of exchange rate determination is examined which incorporates the effects of both current account imbalances and portfolio diversification. Before discussing this model a simple example of the kind of dynamics underlying it is illustrated in figure 11.1.

The outstanding asset stocks determine a vector of asset prices (of which we have only considered the exchange rate in this section) and with an appropriate transmission mechanism they affect the real sector, e.g. real wealth and the real exchange rate. Changes in real variables such as these then affect the current account (4) and this will lead to a change in the stock of foreign assets (5), and the process 1–5 will be set in motion again until equilibrium is reached.

◆ 11.1 The Portfolio Balance Model

Our small country portfolio balance model is outlined in the following equations:

$$W = M + B + SF \tag{11.2}$$

$$\text{supply} = \text{demand}$$

$$M = m(i, i^* + \Delta s^e)W \qquad m_i < 0, \quad m_{i^*+\Delta s^e} < 0 \tag{11.3}$$

$$B = b(i, i^* + \Delta s^e)W \qquad b_i > 0, \quad b_{i^*+\Delta s^e} < 0 \tag{11.4}$$

$$SF = f(i, i^* + \Delta s^e)W \qquad f_i < 0, \quad f_{i^*+\Delta s^e} > 0 \tag{11.5}$$

$$Y^T = Y^T(q) \qquad Y^T_q > 0 \tag{11.6}$$

$$Y^N = Y^N(q) \qquad Y^N_q < 0 \tag{11.7}$$

$$C^T = C^T(q, w) \qquad C^T_q < 0, \quad C^T_w > 0 \tag{11.8}$$

$$C^N = C^N(q, w) \qquad C^N_q > 0, \quad C^N_w > 0 \tag{11.9}$$

$$Y^D = Y^T + Y^N + (i^* + \Delta s^e)SF \tag{11.10}$$

$$C = C^T + C^N \tag{11.11}$$

$$P = P_N^\alpha S^{1-\alpha} \tag{11.12}$$

where $\qquad q = \dfrac{S}{P^N} \qquad S = P^T \qquad w = \dfrac{W}{P} = \dfrac{M}{P} + \dfrac{B}{P} + \dfrac{SF}{P}$

Consider first the asset sector, given by equations (11.2)–(11.5). Domestic residents may hold their wealth in domestic money M, domestic bonds B and foreign bonds F (denominated in foreign currency). Since the bonds are assumed to be very-short-term assets, rather than consols, we do not need to consider capital gains or losses induced by interest rate changes. The asset demands depend upon the domestic and foreign rates of interest, which are assumed to be exogenously given, and are homogeneous of degree one in nominal wealth.[5] The partial derivatives indicate that for any asset an increase in the own-rate leads to an increase in demand and an increase in the cross-rate leads to a decrease in demand. It is also assumed that the bonds are gross substitutes (i.e. $b_i > f_i$ and $f_{i^*+\Delta s^e} > b_{i^*+\Delta s^e}$) and a greater proportion of any increase in domestic wealth is held in domestic bonds rather than foreign bonds. To simplify the analysis the asset demand equations are not dependent upon income. As Allen and Kenen (1978) point out, this introduces an important asymmetry into a portfolio balance model, namely that while conditions in goods markets do not have a direct effect on asset markets, asset market conditions directly affect goods markets since the exchange rate S features in both sectors. Although domestic residents can hold all three assets, foreign residents can only hold foreign bonds (and presumably also foreign money, which is non-traded). As in our currency substitution models the only way residents of the small country can accumulate F is by running a current account surplus (which, as we shall see below, equals positive savings). The supplies of both M and B are exogenously given by the authorities.

The real sector of the model is described by equations (11.6)–(11.9). Prices are assumed to be continuously flexible and the economy operates at full employment. Equation (11.10) represents domestic residents' disposable income which is assumed to be equal to income derived from traded and non-traded goods plus interest earnings on foreign bonds.[6] Equation (11.12) describes the small country's price level which is given by a simple Cobb–Douglas formulation.[7] The current account of the balance of payments is given as the difference between the consumption and production of traded goods (the trade balance) plus the interest earnings from the holdings of the foreign asset. The capital account of the balance of payments is simply the accumulation over the relevant period of the foreign asset F.

$$\Delta F = CA = Y^T(q) - C^T(q, w) + (i^* + \Delta s^e)SF \qquad (11.13)$$

Therefore the foreign asset can only be accumulated by the country running a current account surplus. Notice that the current account has two components: the trade account $Y^T - C^T$ and interest earnings. The equilibrium condition for the non-traded good is given as

$$Y^N(q) = C^N(q, w) \qquad (11.14)$$

Since, by definition, the non-traded good can only be consumed at home, relative price movements will ensure that (11.14) holds continuously.

The current account surplus or deficit can be shown to be linked to the economy's savings and dissavings in the following way. If agents have a *constant* desired target level of real wealth $\bar{w}$, then savings a may be represented as the excess of desired over actual real wealth, i.e.

$$a = \beta(\bar{w} - w) \qquad \beta > 0 \qquad (11.15)$$

Hence if actual wealth is below desired wealth agents will be saving, and conversely if w is greater than $\bar{w}$ agents will be dissaving. Since a is simply the difference between disposable income and consumption (i.e. $Y^D - C$) we have

$$a = (Y^T - C^T) + (i^* + \Delta s^e)SF \qquad (11.16)$$

where we have used condition (11.14) to justify the exclusion of $Y^N - C^N$. Equation (11.16) is simply an alternative representation of equation (11.13): the current account surplus/deficit is equal to savings/dissavings.

Before considering the workings of the model we must say a little about expectations. At all points of time, asset prices – the domestic interest rate, the exchange rate and the expected change in the exchange rate (given the small country assumption, the foreign interest rate is assumed to be exogenous) – are determined by the outstanding asset stocks. But the asset system (11.2)–(11.5), on its own, will be indeterminate, since we have three equations, only two of which are independent, and three unknowns. Thus we need to introduce a further relationship to capture expectations. Two assumptions are common in this vintage of model: either static expectations where $\Delta s^e = 0$ or rational expectations where we require the further equation

$$\Delta s^e = \Delta s + \varepsilon \qquad (11.17)$$

which says that the expected change in the exchange rate equals the actual change plus a white noise error. Given some expectational assumption, the asset sector determines the spot exchange rate S and the domestic interest rate i. In this chapter we shall assume that expectations are static. Although this may seem an unappealing assumption to make it does help to clarify the special features of the portfolio balance model without unnecessarily complicating the model dynamics.[8]

In illustrating the effects of various shocks in our asset market model, it will prove useful, for pedagogic purposes, to think of the model in terms of three separate periods: an impact period, a short-run adjustment period and long-run equilibrium. The impact period is concerned with the instantaneous adjustment of the asset markets following a shock. The short-run period is one in which the prices determined in the impact period have "real" effects and result in changes in flows over time. In particular, the asset prices determined in the impact period will have implications for the overall price level and this will result in a discrepancy between actual and desired wealth, which in turn has consequences for savings and the current account. Such flow magnitudes will eventually force the economy to a new long-run steady-state equilibrium with zero savings and a zero current balance.

The workings of the model can be illustrated diagrammatically in the following way. Consider first the asset sector. Figure 11.2 shows combinations of i and S which hold the demand for money equal to its supply (equation (11.3)) (MM), the demand and supply of domestic bonds in equality (equation (11.4)) (BB) and the demand and supply of foreign assets in equality (equation (11.5)) (FF). An

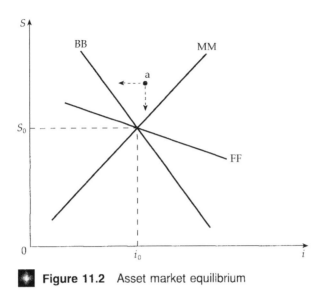

Figure 11.2 Asset market equilibrium

intuitive explanation of the relative slopes of the schedules in figure 11.2 is as follows. Taking money M and bonds B first, from a position of portfolio equilibrium an increase in the price of foreign currency will increase wealth by revaluing the foreign asset (i.e. making it larger in home currency terms) in equation (11.2) and thus will create an increased demand for both M and B to restore portfolio equilibrium. As the demand for money rises, for a given supply, i (the opportunity cost of holding money) must rise to maintain money market equilibrium – hence the positive MM curve in S–i space. The BB curve has a negative slope since the increased demand for bonds, for a given supply, raises their price and results in a lower rate of interest. The negative slope of the FF schedule may be explained by a fall in i which increases the attractiveness of foreign assets leading to a rise in S. Then BB is steeper than FF because domestic demand for domestic bonds is more responsive than domestic demand for foreign assets to changes in the domestic rate of interest (this follows from the assumed gross substitutability of assets).

The three schedules in figure 11.2 will shift in response to various asset disturbances. For example, an increase in the money supply will shift the MM schedule to the left since, for a given value of S, the interest rate must fall to restore portfolio balance. An increase in the supply of bonds shifts the BB schedule to the right since, for a given value of S, the interest rate on bonds must rise (price must fall) for the supply to be willingly held. An increase in the foreign asset F will result in the downward movement of FF since, for a given value of i, the maintenance of portfolio balance requires an exchange rate appreciation.

Because of the wealth constraint (11.2), we know that only two of the three asset equations are independent. Thus, if a given change restores equilibrium in two markets, the third market must also be in equilibrium. In order to analyze various shocks it is therefore legitimate to concentrate on only two schedules. In what

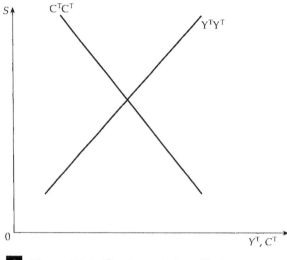

Figure 11.3   Goods market equilibrium

follows we concentrate either on the combination of BB and MM or on BB and FF. Using the combination BB and FF we may illustrate that the portfolio system is globally stable. Consider point a in figure 11.2, a point which is above the BB–FF intersection. For a given value of S the interest rate is too high for bond market equilibrium. This will generate an excess demand for such bonds, a rise in their price and a fall in their yield, namely i. Similarly, for a given i the exchange rate at a is too high for foreign asset market equilibrium: agents will attempt to sell foreign assets and convert the proceeds into domestic currency. This process will cause the exchange rate to appreciate (S falls). Hence at a the arrows of motion point towards the BB and FF schedules. Using similar reasoning, we may infer the arrows of motion for the other sectors in the diagram. So starting from a point such as a the system may be expected to follow the path indicated by the broken line.

In figure 11.2 we have looked at the short-run determination of the domestic interest rate and exchange rate from the point of view of asset market equilibrium. To illustrate goods market equilibrium, we introduce figure 11.3 which shows the domestic production and consumption of traded goods ($Y^T Y^T$ and $C^T C^T$) as positive and negative functions of the exchange rate. Thus for a given price of non-traded goods, an increase in the price of traded goods leads to a reduction in consumption as consumers switch from traded to non-traded goods (see equations (11.8) and (11.9)) and an increased relative production of traded goods (see equations (11.6) and (11.7)). An increase (decrease) in wealth shifts the $C^T C^T$ schedule to the right (left) and leaves $Y^T Y^T$ unaffected. An increase (decrease) in the price of non-traded goods shifts the $C^T C^T$ schedule to the right and the $Y^T Y^T$ schedule to the left. These latter shifts occur because, while we have S on the vertical axis in figure 11.3, a change in P^N for given S will also impact the real exchange rate as $q = S/P^N$. This in turn will affect the allocation of consumption and pro-

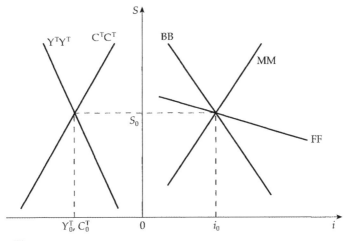

Figure 11.4 Asset and goods market equilibrium in the portfolio balance model

duction between traded and non-traded goods. As we shall see below, P^N will vary under pressure from excess demand for non-traded goods. In figure 11.4 we combine figures 11.2 and 11.3 to give a representation of joint asset and goods market equilibrium as i_0, S_0, Y_0^T, C_0^T. Consider now a number of shocks which upset the system's initial equilibrium. In particular, we consider an open market swap of money for bonds, an increase in the supply of bonds and an asset preference shift between home and foreign bonds.

11.2 Open Market Purchase of Bonds: Monetary Policy

11.2.1 Impact period

We consider the impact effect on asset markets of an open market purchase of bonds for money. An open market purchase of bonds for money by the central bank, in the impact period, will shift the BB and MM curves leftwards to BB', MM' in figure 11.5. At the initial equilibrium X, the open market purchase of bonds leaves asset-holders with an excess supply of money and excess demand for bonds. In their attempts to buy bonds, investors will push the domestic interest rate down and this, in turn, will lead to an increased demand for foreign bonds which will push the exchange rate upwards until the excess demand for foreign bonds is eliminated. If it is assumed that the domestic interest elasticity of demand for money is less than the domestic interest elasticity of the demand for foreign bonds, then the percentage change in the demand for foreign bonds will be greater than the percentage increase in the money stock. Given that there is a one-to-one relationship between S and F, this implies that the exchange rate change[9] will be larger than the money supply change: the exchange rate overshoots. The impact period equilibrium is given at point Y.

11.2.2 The short-run adjustment period and the move to the new long-run equilibrium

Although the valuation effect of the exchange rate on the foreign asset will on impact give a rise in nominal wealth, once we move to the short-run period this will be offset by the effect the exchange rate overshoot has on the price index and thus real wealth: actual real wealth in the short-run period will fall short of desired real wealth. This mismatch of desired and actual real wealth implies, via equation (11.15), that agents must be saving and thus running a current account surplus (see equation (11.13)) during the adjustment period. Thus the desire to restore the initial value of desired wealth can only be realized by the country running a current account surplus and accumulating the foreign asset. This is possible since in the impact period relative prices have moved in favor of the traded goods sector, inducing a switch in production from non-traded goods. The current account surplus over time forces the price of foreign currency downwards (i.e. F is rising and so S must be falling), leading to a diminution of the savings rate until equilibrium is restored.

The shifts in the C^TC^T and Y^TY^T functions are shown in figure 11.5:

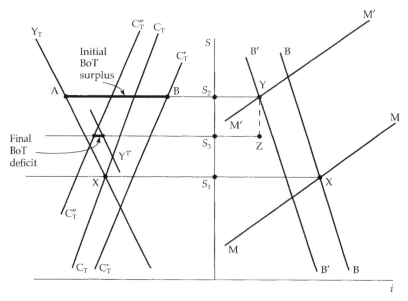

Figure 11.5 An open market purchase of bonds for money

Note: BoT: balance of trade.

1   C^TC^T initially shifts to the right to $C^{T'}C^{T'}$ (meaning less consumption of T goods) as residents increase their saving rate to restore their real wealth.

2   As real wealth increases back to its initial level, and the desire to save declines, C^TC^T gradually regains its initial position. However,

3   C^TC^T will shift further left beyond its initial position because the price of non-traded goods (P^N) has increased under the pressure of excess demand for non-traded goods (caused by the depreciation of S). Finally,

4   the increased P^N also causes the Y^TY^T function to shift to the right – meaning lower production of T goods.

Notice that at the new equilibrium the country is running a trade balance deficit. This may be explained in the following way. If in the initial equilibrium the price of traded goods equaled the price of non-traded goods, in the new equilibrium the relative price of traded goods will have fallen: the increase in the money supply has not led to a proportionate increase in the price level. This follows because in the adjustment period the home country has been accumulating foreign assets and in the new equilibrium interest receipts on the foreign assets must be greater than the initial equilibrium. Since the current account is the sum of the trade balance plus interest earnings and since a zero current balance is a condition of steady-state equilibrium, the positive interest earnings must be offset by a trade balance deficit. The latter is induced by a fall in the real exchange rate (i.e. P^N rises relative to P^T).[10] Isard (1977) has described this effect as the "knock-out punch" to PPP!

The adjustment of the asset equilibrium schedules in figure 11.5 from the impact equilibrium to the new long-run equilibrium is indicated by the arrow from Y to Z. Thus the accumulation of the foreign asset during the adjustment period will require an exchange rate appreciation for the maintenance of foreign asset equilibrium: the FF schedule shifts downwards. The accumulation of F over time also increases the size of the portfolio and thus the demand for bonds and money will rise. The increase in the demand for the former will lead to a leftward shift of the BB' curve (i.e. for a given exchange rate, the increased demand for bonds will force the price up and the interest rate down) and the increased demand for money will push MM' to the right over time.

In summary, the open market purchases set off portfolio and asset price adjustments. On *impact*, i falls and S depreciates, overshooting in fact, as the excess of money causes substitution into both domestic and foreign bonds. In the *short run*, as wealth on balance has fallen, residents increase their rate of saving via a current account surplus. As actual wealth now increases toward the desired level, the rate of saving falls and with it the size of the current account surplus – causing S to appreciate. In the *long run* asset markets adjust, with the accumulation of foreign bonds setting off a desire to hold more money and domestic bonds.

In figure 11.6 the profiles of the exchange rate, the trade balance and the capital account of the balance of payments are illustrated for the monetary shock. The monetary expansion takes place in period t_0 and the system has returned to long-run equilibrium in period t_n. In figure 11.6(c) the initial sharp depreciation of the exchange rate is denoted as the move from S_0 to S_1. As we have seen, the

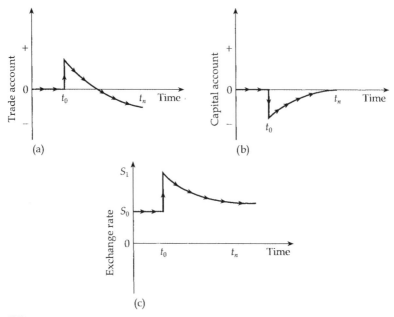

Figure 11.6 The adjustment profiles of (a) the trade account, (b) the capital account, and (c) the exchange rate

exchange rate appreciates during the adjustment period and because of the non-homogeneity of the system does not return to its initial equilibrium by t_n. The trade account initially moves into surplus at t_0, but over time the effect of the appreciating exchange rate means that the country will be running a trade account deficit. In the new long-run equilibrium t_n, the country runs a trade deficit which is "financed" by the interest earnings from the foreign asset. Since the condition of long-run equilibrium is that the current account equals zero, the capital account must also be balanced at t_n. Notice therefore that in contrast to the Mundell–Fleming model the expansionary monetary policy only has a transitory effect on the capital account: the stock–flow nature of the model ensures that this must be so.[11]

 ## 11.3 An Increase in the Supply of Domestic Bonds: Fiscal Policy

Consider now a once-and-for-all increase in the supply of bonds. (Although we have not explicitly modeled the public sector, this could follow from a bond-financed increase in government expenditure.)

An increase in the supply of bonds increases wealth[12] and, for a given domestic interest rate i, requires an increase in the exchange rate S to maintain the foreign exchange market in equilibrium; thus, the FF schedule in figures 11.7 and 11.8 shifts rightwards to FF'. For a given value of the exchange rate the increased supply of domestic bonds will require an increase in the domestic interest rate to maintain bond market equilibrium: the BB schedule shifts rightwards and the new equilibrium is at Y. The increased bond supply exceeds any wealth-induced increase in bond demand and the domestic interest rate is unambiguously raised.

The effect on the exchange rate of an increase in the stock of domestic bonds is in fact ambiguous. This is because the rise in the domestic interest rate will induce a reduced demand for foreign assets and this will tend to offset the increased demand for foreign fixed price bonds due to the wealth effect. The ultimate effect depends on whether F and B or B and M are the closer substitutes.

New bond issue and currency depreciation

Assuming that B and M are better substitutes than F and B, the issue of B causes currency depreciation at Y in figure 11.7 despite higher i attracting some capital inflow. This comes about because residents are, by assumption, not strongly attempting to swap foreign bonds, F, for B to obtain the higher rate of interest. The adjustment from Y to the new long-run equilibrium at, say, Z will be the same as for the open market operation – lower wealth reducing the demand for B and F.

On the production and consumption side too the outcome is the same as with the open market operation. Thus, at Y real wealth will have fallen, agents will be saving and real wealth will be reaccumulated over time, pushing C^TC^T first to the right and then back to the left as the level of actual wealth recovers. Moreover, as the price of non-traded goods will have risen owing to excess demand for them at the depreciated exchange rate S_2, the substitution effect out of non-traded into

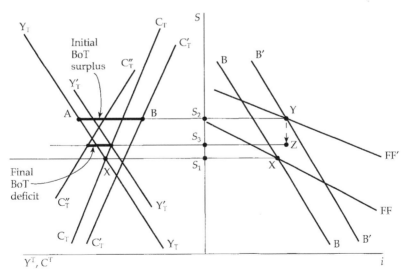

■ **Figure 11.7** An increase in the supply of bonds and currency depreciation

Note: BoT: balance of trade

traded goods will have the economy ending up with $C^{T''}C^{T''}$. On the production side, the rise in P^N works against traded goods production and Y^TY^T shifts to $Y^{T'}Y^{T'}$. Thus, the initial balance of trade surplus at S_2 turns into an ultimate trade deficit at S_3, which is financed by interest income on the foreign bonds accumulated through the earlier trade surplus.

New bond issue and currency appreciation

If F and B are regarded as better substitutes for each other then the exchange rate will be appreciated (lower) at Y in figure 11.8 because the shift in demand from F to B as a result of the rise in i will be greater the closer are F and B regarded as substitutes (relative to B and M).

This coupling of appreciation and bond financing actually occurred in the USA during the period 1981–5. Let's see how this plays out in figure 11.8.

With the issue of new bonds raising wealth, FF and BB shift so that S appreciates to S_2, the price level falls, and actual wealth increases relative to desired wealth. These events set off the following adjustments:

1   C^TC^T shifts left to $C^{T'}C^{T'}$ owing to the wish to reduce actual real wealth to the desired level – which is achieved through a trade and current account deficit and capital inflow at S_2.

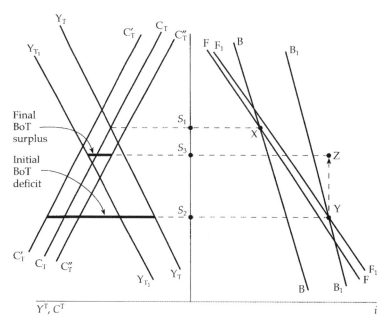

Figure 11.8 An increase in the supply of bonds which causes currency appreciation

Note: BoT: balance of trade

2   As actual real wealth gradually falls back to its desired level, $C^{T'}C^{T'}$ steadily shifts back to C^TC^T. However,
3   the consumption of traded goods will fall even more than this to $C^{T''}C^{T''}$ because the relative price of non-traded goods has fallen. Finally,
4   Y^TY^T shifts left to $Y^{T'}Y^{T'}$ due to the lower price of non-traded goods which encourages greater traded goods production.

Thus, the initial position at S_1 is one of trade balance (assuming no accumulation of foreign assets). Following the issue of bonds the currency appreciates to S_2 when there is a payments deficit financed by capital inflow. This is a version of the famous "twin deficits." But S_2 cannot be sustained as interest payments must be made on the accumulated foreign debt. The exchange rate depreciates from its overshot position at S_2 to S_3 so creating a balance of trade surplus exactly equal to the interest payments. At which point the current account is balanced so that actual wealth remains at its desired level.

In the long run, a higher exchange rate than S_2 is needed due to the increase in wealth raising the demand for F and B – so BB and FF again shift to pass through Z.

11.4 Asset Preference Shift

If, due to a perceived increased riskiness, domestic bonds become more attractive than foreign bonds, what effect will this have in the impact period and in the short-run adjustment to a new equilibrium? Such a shock is illustrated in figure 11.9.

At the initial equilibrium the increased demand for domestic bonds can only be satisfied by a reduction in the rate of interest, giving the leftward shift from

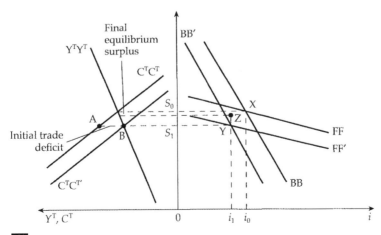

Figure 11.9   A shift in asset preferences

BB to BB'. Equally the attempt to move out of foreign bonds can, in the impact period, only be satisfied by a leftward shift of the FF schedule. Thus the impact effect of a change in asset preferences from foreign to domestic bonds results in a reduction in the interest rate and the exchange rate: from i_0 to i_1 and from S_0 to S_1.

Moving from the impact period to the short-run adjustment period, we find that private sector wealth has increased due to the fall in the price of the traded good and thus w must be greater than $\bar{w}$ and agents dissaving. This is illustrated in the left-hand side of figure 10.8 where the initial current account deficit is equal to AB. Over time this deficit will result in a loss of the foreign asset and a reduction in wealth which pushes $C^T C^T$ to the right and the exchange rate upwards. If the domestic economy lost foreign assets during the adjustment period it would end up with a final equilibrium at a point such as Z.

 ## *11.5 Econometric Evidence on the Portfolio Balance Approach

Given the nature of the asset sector in the portfolio balance model it seems intuitively plausible that the impact or very-short-run exchange rate equation derived from this model will have the following form (i.e. in the impact period the exchange rate is determined by disturbances to the asset equilibrium conditions):[13]

$$S_t = f(B_t, M_t, F_t) \tag{11.18}$$

To be consistent with the empirical results presented in the last chapter, we explicitly date variables in this section. Equation (11.18) has been empirically implemented by Branson et al. (1977) and Branson and Haltunen (1979) for the recent floating exchange rate experience. In empirically implementing the portfolio model, Branson et al. replace the small country assumption with a two country model and thus include the foreign country's demand for the home country's domestic bond, its own "foreign" bond and foreign money but not the home country's money as monies are assumed not to be substitutes in asset portfolios. Accordingly equation (11.18) is replaced by

$$S_t = f(M_t, M_t^*, B_t, B_t^*, F_t, F_t^*) \tag{11.19}$$

In a two-country setting asset accumulation emanating from the current account will have the same effect on the exchange rate as in the small country case as long as domestic residents' preference for the domestic bond is greater than their preference for the foreign bond.

Branson et al. (1977), by arbitrarily dropping the B and B^* terms from equation (11.19), econometrically estimated the equations

$$S_t = f(M_t, M_t^*, F_t, F_t^*) \tag{11.20a}$$

$$S_t = q_0 + q_1 \overset{+}{M}_t + q_2 \overset{-}{M}_t^* + q_3 \overset{-}{F}_t + q_4 \overset{+}{F}_t^* + \varepsilon_t \tag{11.20b}$$

for the deutschmark–US dollar exchange rate over the period August 1971 to December 1976 (the sign of the effects of asset changes on the exchange rate are represented by a plus or minus sign above the assets and are interpretable in terms of our discussion in the theoretical section). The money supply terms are defined as Ml and the foreign assets are proxied by cumulated current account balances. Although all of the estimated coefficients had the hypothesized signs, after correction for autocorrelation only one coefficient was statistically significant. To allow for any potential simultaneity bias induced by foreign exchange market intervention by the German authorities (i.e. $M_t = F_t + D_t$ and thus, if F_t is changed to modify S_t, M_t will be correlated with the error term, introducing simultaneous equation bias), Branson et al. (1977) estimated equation (11.20) using two stage least squares, but this did not lead to a substantial improvement of the results. In Branson and Haltunen (1979), equation (11.20) is estimated for the mark–dollar rate for the larger sample period from August 1971 to December 1978, but the results are very similar to those in the earlier paper. In a further paper, Branson and Haltunen (1979) estimate equation (11.20) for the Japanese yen, French franc, Italian lira, Swiss franc, and the pound sterling (all relative to the US dollar) for the period from July 1971 to June 1976. Their ordinary least squares results show most equations with statistically significant coefficients and signs which are consistent with the priors noted in equation (11.20). However, little reliance can be placed on their results since they suffer from acute autocorrelation. The latter could reflect a dynamic misspecification of the model or the exclusion of variables relevant to the portfolio approach. Indeed, Bisignano and Hoover (1983), in their study of the Canadian dollar, include domestic non-monetary asset stocks and report moderately successful econometric results. A further problem with the Branson implementation of the portfolio model is that the use of bilateral exchange rates and cumulated current accounts implies that third country assets and liabilities are perfect substitutes. Bisignano and Hoover (1983) use strictly bilateral asset stocks in their study and this could be a further reason for their successful results (the use of cumulated current accounts by researchers is usually out of necessity and not choice: few countries publish the details of the ownership of assets).

Alternative tests of the portfolio balance approach have exploited the insight of Dooley and Isard (1982) that the portfolio model can be solved for a risk premium. It is argued that the risk premium term λ_t is a function of the factors that determine the supply of outside assets, i.e. government bonds. Thus, λ_t may be written as a function of the relative supplies of bonds:

$$\lambda_t = \frac{1}{\beta} \frac{B_t}{F_t S_t} \tag{11.21}$$

The idea being that an increase in the relative supply of domestic bonds requires an increased risk premium for these assets to be willingly held in international portfolios. On substituting (11.21) into equation (11.1) the following equation is obtained:

$$\frac{B_t}{F_t S_t} = \beta(i_t - i_t^* - \Delta s_{t+k}^e) \tag{11.22}$$

or, re-expressing the left-hand side in logs,

$$b_t - s_t - f_t = \beta(i_t - i_t^* - \Delta s_{t+k}^e) \tag{11.23}$$

Thus, in order to diversify the resultant risk of exchange rate variability, investors balance their portfolios between domestic and foreign bonds in proportions that depend on the expected relative rate of return (or risk premium). Following Frankel (1983) equation (11.23) can be used to derive a generalized asset market representation of the exchange rate which is econometrically testable.

By rearranging equation (9.32) as

$$\phi(s - \bar{s})_t = \Delta p_{t+k}^e - \Delta p_{t+k}^{e*} - \Delta s_{t+k}^e \tag{11.24}$$

and by simultaneously adding the interest differential to $-\Delta s_{t+k}^e$, subtracting Δp_{t+k}^e $- \Delta p_{t+k}^{e*}$ from the differential and solving for s_t the following equation is obtained:

$$s_t = \bar{s}_t - \frac{1}{\phi}[(i_t - \Delta p_{t+k}^e) - (i_t^* - \Delta p_{t+k}^{e*})] + \frac{1}{\phi}(i_t - i_t^* - \Delta s_{t+k}^e) \tag{11.25}$$

which states that the exchange rate deviates from its long-run value by an amount proportional to the real interest differential and the risk premium. Furthermore, substituting from equation (9.7) for the long-run equilibrium exchange rate (and again assuming that long-run values are given by their current actual values), the following equation can be derived:

$$s_t = m_t - m_t^* - \alpha_1(y_t - y_t^*) + \alpha_2(\Delta p_t^c - \Delta p_{t+k}^{e*})$$
$$- \frac{1}{\phi}[(i_t - \Delta p_{t+k}^e) - (i_t^* - \Delta p_{t+k}^{e*})] + \frac{1}{\phi}(i_t - i_t^* - \Delta s_{t+k}^e) \tag{11.26}$$

Relative bond supplies enter equation (11.26) via the last term. Thus, by substituting (11.23) into the last term in (11.26) and solving for s_t the following reduced-form relationship may be obtained:

$$s_t = \gamma_0(m - m^*)_t - \gamma_1(y - y^*)_t + \gamma_2(\Delta p^c - \Delta p^{c*})_{t+k}$$
$$- \gamma_3(i - i^*)_t + \gamma_4(b - f)_t \tag{11.27}$$

where the γs are the reduced-form parameters, which are related in an obvious way to the underlying structural parameters. Note that this relationship is simply a version of the real interest differential model, discussed in the previous chapter, extended to include the relative bond supply term. Therefore the signs of γ_0 to γ_3 have the same interpretation as in the last chapter and the positive sign on γ_4 implies that an increase in the supply of domestic bonds relative to foreign bonds should result in an exchange rate depreciation because domestic bonds have become relatively risky.

Frankel (1983) tests equation (11.27) for the dollar–mark exchange rate in the period from January 1974 to October 1978 and a representative equation is reported here:

$$s_t = 0.50(m - m^*)_t - 0.056(y - y^*)_t - 0.358(i - i^*)_t$$
$$(0.31)(0.21)(0.47)$$

$$+ 1.851(\Delta p^e - \Delta p^{e*})_{t+k} + 0.313(b^* - f)_t \qquad (11.28)$$
$$(0.69)\phantom{1.851(\Delta p^e - \Delta p^{e*})_{t+k} + }(0.05)$$

$$R^2 = 0.95$$

standard errors in parentheses

In this equation it is assumed that the USA is the home country and Germany is the foreign country; however, b_t^* and f_t are, respectively, German holdings of the domestic (i.e. German) and home (US) bond (this is why the labeling is perhaps a little confusing) and therefore the coefficient on $(b^* - f)_t$ should have a negative sign if the above modeling strategy is appropriate. Equation (11.28) is referred to as the "small country portfolio model." Referring back to equation (11.27) notice that the signs on money, income, interest rates, and the inflation rate are all correct, although only the last-mentioned term is statistically significant. The risk premium term, $(b^* - f)_t$, although statistically significant is wrongly signed: an increase in the foreign asset relative to the home bond leads to an exchange rate depreciation, in contrast to the prior expectation. Thus, Frankel's estimates, at best, give somewhat mixed support to the portfolio balance approach.

A version of equation (11.27) has also been estimated by Hooper and Morton (1983) for the dollar effective exchange rate over the period 1973.II–1978.IV and they found that the risk premium term was neither significant nor correctly signed.

The above noted tests of the portfolio model all use "in-sample" criteria to assess the model's performance. In addition to testing the out-of-sample performance of the monetary models considered in chapter 9, Meese and Rogoff (1983) also assessed the out-of-sample forecasting performance of the portfolio model represented by equation (11.27) (see our discussion in section 9.1 for details of the Meese and Rogoff methodology). In common with their findings for the simple monetary models, Meese and Rogoff demonstrated that the portfolio balance equation was unable to beat the simple random walk. However, it is important to re-emphasize the point made in chapter 9 that when proper account is taken of the data dynamics such a model may well outperform a random walk.[14]

A somewhat different approach to assessing the validity of the portfolio model than using in-sample or out-of-sample criteria is that proposed by Obstfeld (1982). He proposes estimating a four equation structural version of the portfolio model for the deutschmark–US dollar exchange rate over the period 1975–81 (the four equations are for money demand, money supply and home and foreign bond market equilibrium). The idea is to simulate the model over the sample period, under conditions of perfect foresight, and assess whether sterilized intervention (which amounts to a swap of domestic bonds for foreign bonds, with no implication for the money supplies in the home or foreign countries) would have been successful. If the portfolio balance model is appropriate such intervention should be effective in changing the exchange rate since bonds are assumed to be imperfect substitutes. In fact Obstfeld finds that sterilized intervention only has a miniscule effect on the exchange rate compared with non-sterilized intervention, which has a big effect. However, Kearney and MacDonald (1986) implement a similar methodology for the sterling–dollar exchange rate over the period 1973–83 and find that sterilized intervention does seem to have a relatively big effect on the exchange rate. The effectiveness of sterilized intervention in the UK relative to Germany is attributed by Kearney and MacDonald to the UK's investment currency scheme whereby foreign exchange reserves were rationed throughout the period up to 1979.

In sum, the above selection of empirical studies on the portfolio balance approach are not particularly supportive of the model. But perhaps this should not be surprising: the paucity of good data on non-monetary aggregates (in particular their distribution between different countries), and, as noted above, the relatively primitive specifications of the reduced forms tested, perhaps do not give the portfolio balance approach a fair "crack of the whip". We return to some empirical evidence on the validity of the portfolio balance model in chapter 12 where we examine the literature which seeks to model the risk premium.

 ## 11.6 Summary and Concluding Comments

We now briefly summarize some of the salient results of this chapter. First, it has been demonstrated that in the context of a model in which non-money assets are imperfect substitutes asset shocks can result in exchange rate overshooting (and this is distinct from the overshooting, discussed in chapter 9, in the sticky-price monetary model). This overshoot, however, is reversed over time as the country accumulates or decumulates foreign assets via the current account. Second, asset shocks can affect the long-run terms of trade, or real exchange rate, in our model because of the existence of at least one outside asset: for example, a 10 percent increase in M does not result in a 10 percent increase in the price level because of the interest payments accruing from the outside asset. Third, a current account surplus in the model is associated with an appreciating exchange rate.

How useful is the portfolio balance model in explaining the determination of the exchange rate? Although the extant econometric evidence is perhaps not encouraging (although, as we have suggested, there may be good reasons for this), casual empiricism suggests that the approach may, at least at certain times, be a useful framework for analysing the determination of the exchange rate. For example, consider the behavior of the deutschmark–US dollar exchange rate in the period 1978–9. During this period German money supply growth oustripped German income growth and far exceeded US monetary growth; however, the mark–dollar exchange rate sharply appreciated. This phenomenon has been termed "the mystery of the multiplying marks" by Frankel (1982b) – the price of the currency rises as its relative supply increases. The monetary approach to the exchange rate would seem to be ill-suited to explaining this phenomenon. However, the key to understanding the appreciation of the mark–dollar in this period lies in the large current account deficit that the USA was running and the current account surplus in Germany. The analysis of this chapter suggests that the consequent increasing (decreasing) German (US) wealth should result in an appreciation of the mark–dollar exchange rate.

NOTES

1 In the flex-price monetary approach wealth effects are ignored because the flexibility of the price level ensures that the economy moves timelessly from one stock equilibrium to the next.

2 Notice, however, that the flex-price monetary model is one in which short- and long-run equilibria coincide and thus we are always in steady-state equilibrium. A common feature of steady-state equilibrium in balance of payments and exchange rate models is that the current account should equal zero (more is said about "steady" states in the rest of this chapter).

3 The monetary model outlined in the previous chapter would seem to have worked well for the dollar appreciation in 1976 and 1977. Thus although the USA had a current account deficit in the period it experienced rapid income growth and, via increased money demand, it would be expected that on the basis of equation (11.10) the exchange rate would appreciate.

4 As we noted in chapter 3, the problem with such tests is that they are testing a joint hypothesis of perfect asset substitutability and rational expectations and thus in rejecting the joint hypothesis it is impossible to discern if this is due to imperfect asset substitutability or the irrationality of expectations or both! (More is said about this issue in the next chapter.)

5 Strictly speaking the asset demand equations (11.3)–(11.5) should be real demands and equation (11.2) should be real wealth, but the assumed homogeneity of asset demands to wealth ensures that the price deflator drops out.

6 For simplicity we assume that the government taxes all domestic residents' interest earnings on domestic bonds.

7 Notice that the inclusion of S in this definition of the price level is similar to that used in the extended Mundell–Fleming model discussed in chapter 5. This inclusion has important implications for the results in this chapter.

8 Examples of portfolio balance models in which expectations are assumed rational are Dornbusch and Fischer (1980), Branson (1983) and Branson and Buiter (1983). See also MacDonald and Taylor (1989e) for a discussion.

9 The interest rate change will also be larger than the money supply change.

10 This result is familiar from closed economy theory. For example, Patinkin (1965) shows that the existence of an outside asset, which is regarded as wealth by the private sector, will give non-homogeneity results between money and prices, even in the "long run."

11 The stability of the model in terms of the movement from the initial to the new equilibrium depends on the Marshall–Lerner condition holding (e.g. the initial exchange rate depreciation leads to a current account surplus: an accumulation of F) and requires that the trade effect of increasing F outweighs the investment income effect. See Branson (1977) for a further discussion.

12 This is not uncontroversial. For example, the Ricardian equivalence theorem, as expounded by Barro (1974), argues that bonds are not net wealth since agents realize they have to finance the increased bond supply by future tax payments. However, as Tobin and Buiter (1976) point out, as long as agents ignore the future tax burden to *some* extent, bonds will be net wealth. This is the approach adopted here.

13 See Branson et al. (1977) for a further discussion.

14 We noted in chapter 9 that researchers who have correctly identified the dynamic processes in simple monetary equations have been successful in beating the random-walk model – see MacDonald and Taylor (1993). That such dynamic modeling has not been applied to portfolio balance models probably reflects the problems facing a researcher in assembling in high-quality data base for non-money assets.

12

Spot and Forward Exchange Rates and the Efficient Markets Hypothesis

On a number of occasions throughout the book we have referred to the relationship between the forward exchange rate, the expected spot exchange rate and the actual spot exchange rate. For example, in chapter 3 we noted that if speculators are risk neutral the forward exchange rate will equal the expected spot rate or, if speculators are risk averse, the forward rate will equal the expected spot rate plus a term which may be interpreted as a risk premium. The view that the forward rate wholly, or in part, mirrors agents' expectations of the exchange rate is usually referred to as the economists' view or, more correctly perhaps, the *academic* economists' view. It contrasts starkly with an institutional-based view of the determination of the forward rate, particularly as reflected in the dealing rooms of commercial banks, where the forward rate is thought of as the residual set to ensure that covered interest rate parity is always maintained.[1] A statement which typifies this view would run along the following lines: "forward rates have got everything to do with interest rates and nothing to do with expectations of the future spot rate." This view is usually labelled the Cambist view.[2] Our discussion of the relationship between forward and spot rates in this chapter is motivated by the economists' view of the determination of the forward rate. However, it is worth noting, as Llewellyn (1980) suggests, that the analytical conclusions stemming from these two separate approaches are in fact very similar.[3]

If forward rates do indeed incorporate a risk premium, one may be tempted to conclude that the existence of risk should have a negligible effect on international trade flows. That is, the existence of forward contracts should allow agents involved in international trade completely to hedge any risk. However, there are two points worth noting here. First, if the risk premium is very large, the cost of forward cover is likely to be correspondingly large as well and this may act as a disincentive for producers to engage in international trade. Second, forward contracts are generally only available (certainly on a widely quoted basis) for relatively short time horizons (up to a year). But a company thinking about investing in the traded goods sector may be interested in hedging the exchange risk for the life of the capital investment. Since this is not possible such companies may well be discouraged from, say, expanding into the traded goods sector. Both of these arguments imply that the existence of exchange risk premia may have a deleterious effect on international trade and, ultimately, employment, output, and economic growth. It is the argument that a flexible exchange rate system substantially increases the riskiness of international trade that has led many to advocate reform of the international monetary system and, in particular, a move to a system characterized by greater exchange rate fixity. Such reforms are considered in chapter 24. In this chapter we are more concerned with the narrower question of the existence, or otherwise, of a risk premium.

The outline of the remainder of this chapter is as follows. In section 12.1 we present a graphical description of the relationship between spot and forward exchange rates and also discuss a well-known survey conducted by the publication *Euromoney* on how good the forward rate is as a forecasting mechanism relative to professional (American) foreign exchange forecasters. In section 12.2 we look in more detail at the optimality of the forward rate as a predictor of the future spot rate. Section 12.3 summarizes a series of econometric tests which seek to test the optimality of the forward rate as an exchange rate forecasting device. As we shall see, such tests indicate that the forward rate is not an optimal predictor and we seek to explain this in section 12.4 in terms of a risk premium. In the next chapter we attempt to rationalize the apparent sub-optimality of the forward rate in terms of so-called expectational failures.

■ 12.1 Spot and Forward Exchange Rates

In figures 12.1–12.4 we present some evidence appropriate to the issue of how good a predictor the forward rate is of the spot rate for the bilateral US dollar rates of the German mark and the pound sterling. The sample period chosen is January 1974 to October 1990 and the data frequency is quarterly. In figures 12.1 and 12.2 spot rates are plotted against appropriately aligned forward rates (i.e. with quarterly data and a three-month forward exchange rate we have to lag the forward rate a single period in order to discern its predictive properties).[4] It is fairly clear from these diagrams that although both rates exhibit similar trending

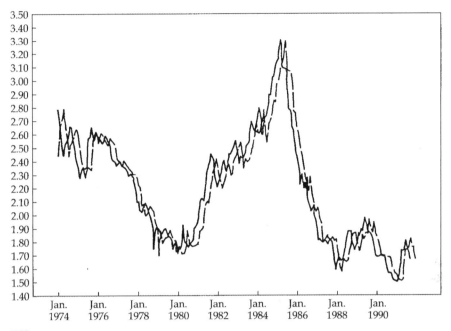

Figure 12.1 Deutschmark–US dollar spot and (lagged) forward rates:
—, spot; ---, forward

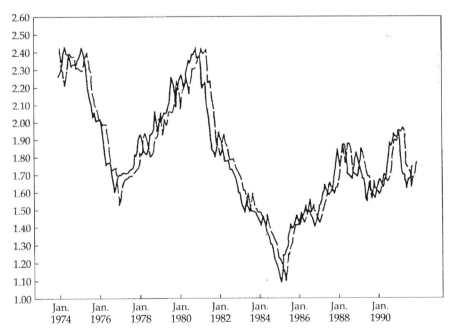

Figure 12.2 Pound sterling–US dollar spot and (lagged) forward rates:
—, spot; ---, forward

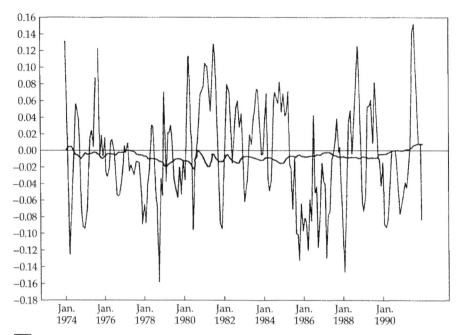

Figure 12.3 Deutschmark–US dollar actual changes and forward premia: —, actual change; —, forward premium

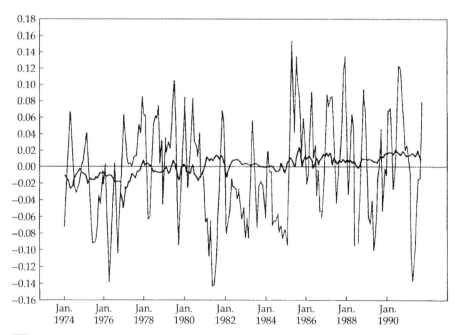

Figure 12.4 Pound sterling–US dollar actual changes and forward premia: —, actual change; —, forward premium

properties the predictive powers of the forward rate are very poor. This poor predictive performance is confirmed in figures 12.3 and 12.4 where the forward premium is plotted against the actual change in the exchange rate. Since these diagrams involve the same basic variables as in figures 12.1 and 12.2, transformed by subtracting the spot rate from each variable, it is perhaps unsurprising that they produce further evidence against the poor predictive powers of the forward rate. Indeed, they tend to dramatize the difference between the two rates: the forward premium is relatively constant around zero whilst the exchange rate change is highly variable around this base line.

It is important to note at this stage that although figures 12.1–12.4 suggest that the forward rate is not a good predictor of the future spot rate it may still be an optimal predictor in the sense that it reflects all available information efficiently. As we shall see below, in an efficient market the large discrepancy between the forward premium and the exchange rate change, portrayed in figures 12.3 and 12.4, may reflect the arrival of new information to the market, which by its nature is unpredictable.

The forward rate is often interpreted as the market's consensus, or mean, measure of the expected spot rate. However, it has recently become fashionable for various economic information institutions (most notably the company Money Market Services) to provide alternative measures of the consensus constructed by directly surveying foreign exchange market participants' views of what they expect the exchange rate to be at a variety of horizons (such data are discussed in some detail in the final section of this chapter). Does a survey-based measure of the consensus do any better than the forward rate? In figures 12.5 and 12.6 we have plotted the actual (quarterly) exchange rate changes for the two currencies referred to above, and the quarterly change predicted by exchange rate forecasters as reflected in their mean response to a survey questionnaire (these data are discussed again in more detail in chapter 13).[5] As is clear from these figures the survey data seem to offer little improvement in terms of forecasting performance over the forward rate. Is this finding borne out by a more formal analysis of the data? This is something we discuss briefly now and in more detail in chapter 13.

In 1981 Richard Levich, on behalf of the publication *Euromoney*, attempted to gauge the accuracy of leading American foreign exchange forecasters. Levich compared the forecasting performance of 13 American forecasting agencies, for the period 1977–80, by calculating each company's percentage forecast error and comparing it with the corresponding forecast error for the forward exchange rate. Taken overall his results suggest that the companies, which represent some of the leading US forecasters, do not do as well as the forward rate on the basis of this criterion; they are not, in the sense defined, accurate.[6] However, a company or individual considering the appropriate moment at which to make an investment in a foreign currency may be more concerned about whether a forecaster gets the *direction* of the exchange rate movement correct, rather than whether the forecaster always beats the forward rate in terms of having a lower forecast error. This will be particularly so for the hedger who is considering a strategy of placing all or none of his or her funds in a foreign currency – the so-called

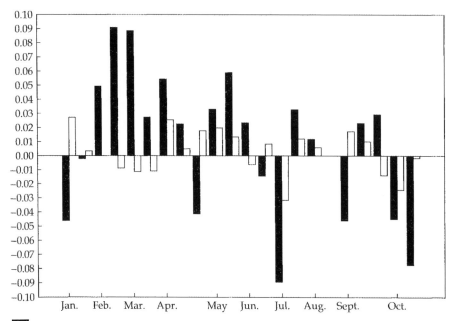

Figure 12.5 Deutschmark–US dollar actual (■) and expected (□) changes

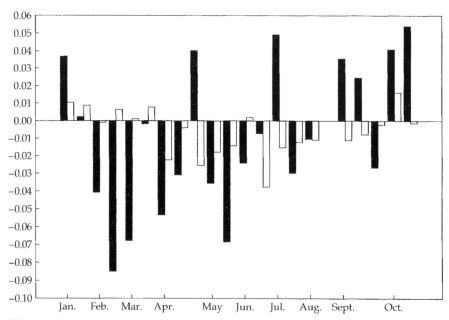

Figure 12.6 Pound sterling–US dollar actual (■) and expected (□) changes

all-or-nothing strategy. Using the correctness criterion, Levich finds that the forecasters do substantially better. In particular, a small group of forecasters are consistently able to get the direction of an exchange rate correct by an amount not explicable by chance. In a follow-up study, Levich (1982) repeated the exercise for the same companies with a year's extra data. The companies in this updated study seemed to do substantially worse than in the previous year and this was attributed to the dramatic sustained US dollar appreciation which was unforeseen.

The results of the Levich exercise have been confirmed using a UK data set by Brasse (1983).[7] She analyzed the exchange rate forecasts of six leading exchange rate forecasters using a monthly data base over the period 1977–82 and came to very similar conclusions to Levich: the forecasters appear to be less accurate than the forward rate, whilst there is some evidence to suggest that some of the forecasters get the direction of the exchange rate movement correct by an amount not explained by chance. The US evidence of Levich would therefore not appear to be country specific.

Brasse (1983) also emphasizes a point from the forecasting literature, that even if individual forecasters produce biased forecasts their forecasts nevertheless may reflect information which is not available to other forecasters (this is because information is costly to gather and therefore forecasting units end up specializing in particular pieces of information to the exclusion of others). Hence some combination of such forecasts (and this combination need not be the simple mean forecast) may actually produce an unbiased forecast, or more generally a good forecast, because it combines all the "good" bits of information which are used in isolation by forecasters. Although we return to this topic briefly in chapter 13 it is perhaps worth questioning at this juncture the realism of this kind of argument. After all, the foreign exchange market is a market in which one would expect all agents to have access to the same information set. Perhaps, therefore, the different performance of forecasters picked up in the above studies simply reflects the skills of the forecaster in interpreting the information rather than differing information sets.

 ## 12.2 The Efficient Markets Hypothesis and the Forward Market for Foreign Exchange

In this section we formalize the relationship between the forward rate and the expected spot rate into an operational form which is testable using standard econometric methods. The formulation relies on exploiting the so-called efficient markets hypothesis (EMH). This hypothesis, which is at the heart of any testing strategy in the financial economics literature, relies on the efficient exploitation of information by economic actors and is often, therefore, referred to as "informational efficiency". In a general sense an asset market is usually described as informationally efficient if the asset price in question always "fully reflects"

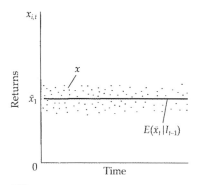

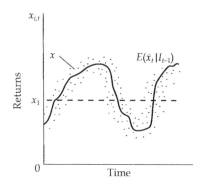

Figure 12.7 Market efficiency with constant equilibrium return

Figure 12.8 Market efficiency with nonconstant equilibrium return

available information (Fama, 1970). If this is a characteristic of an asset market then it should not be possible for a market operator to earn abnormal profits. As Levich (1979) has emphasized, in order to implement the hypothesis empirically, and to make sense of the term "fully reflect", some view of equilibrium expected returns or equilibrium prices is required. Using equilibrium expected returns, for example, the excess market return on asset i may be thought of as

$$Z_{i,t} = x_{i,t} - E(\bar{x}_{i,t} | I_{t-1})$$

where $x_{i,t}$ is the one-period percentage return, I_{t-1} is the information set, a bar denotes an equilibrium value and Z represents the excess market return. If the market for asset i is efficient then the sequence $Z_{i,t}$ should be orthogonal to the information set (i.e. $E(Z_{i,t} | I_{t-1}) = 0$) and serially uncorrelated. This example makes clear that the EMH is a *joint hypothesis* because it assumes that agents in forming their expectations in period $t - 1$ are rational, in the sense that they do not make systematic forecasting errors, and they know expected market equilibrium prices or expected equilibrium returns. This clearly raises an important issue for the testing of the EMH. Thus a researcher in rejecting the EMH for some asset cannot discern whether the rejection is due to the irrationality of market participants or to his misspecification of the equilibrium expected returns. Levich (1979) has usefully demonstrated this issue with two examples which counter the oft-cited view that market efficiency necessarily implies that asset prices should follow a random walk.

In figure 12.7 actual market returns $x_{i,t}$ are assumed to vibrate randomly around the constant equilibrium expected return $\bar{x}_1$. In figure 12.8 actual returns again fluctuate randomly around the expected equilibrium return, but in this case the expected equilibrium return is assumed to be non-constant. In figure 12.7 prices follow a random walk with drift (equal to $\bar{x}$). In figure 12.8 returns and the underlying prices do not follow a random walk since prices and returns are serially correlated around their mean values. Thus even if asset prices do not follow a random walk, the market may still be efficient (i.e. $Z_{i,t}$ will be serially uncorrelated):

randomness in price movements is neither a necessary nor a sufficient condition for market efficiency. This is a point which a number of researchers of the efficiency of foreign exchange markets have failed to appreciate.

Grossman and Stiglitz (1980) have pointed to a conundrum underlying our definition of efficiency. For example, if asset prices *do* fully and instantly reflect all available information then presumably there will be no incentive for individuals to collect and process information since this will already have been reflected in market prices. How can market prices simultaneously reflect all relevant information *and* give agents potential profits to induce arbitrage? This paradox is in fact more apparent than real, since data are collected at discrete periods and all that is necessary for market efficiency is that arbitrage has occurred within the period. This assumption allows us to analyze the effects of information on asset prices without modeling the actual arbitrage process (see Begg, 1982).

Efficiency can be more precisely defined with reference to the information set available to market operators (i.e. I_{t-1} in our examples above). For example, and following Fama (1970), a market is described as *weakly efficient* when it is not possible for a trader to make abnormal returns using only the past history of prices/returns. If by increasing the information set to include publicly available information (i.e. information on money supplies, interest rates, and income) it is not possible for a market participant to make abnormal profits, then the market is said to be *semi-strong* form efficient. *Strong-form* efficiency holds when it is impossible for a trader to make abnormal profits using a trading rule based on either public or private information.

12.2.1 Some basic relationships

As we have mentioned, the EMH may be thought of as a joint hypothesis consisting of some statement about how equilibrium returns are determined combined with the view that agents rapidly arbitrage away any profitable opportunities that may arise, using the available information at their disposal. The latter leg of the joint hypothesis may be thought of as equivalent to the rational expectations hypothesis, although it need not be exactly equivalent.[8] In what follows we think of the EMH as a joint hypothesis consisting of a statement about what determines the forward exchange rate combined with the assumption that agents are endowed with rational expectations.

As applied to the foreign exchange market, the EMH may be described in the following way. The first component of the joint hypothesis refers to the assumed equilibrium condition which may be interpreted as referring to the relationship between the forward rate and the expected spot rate. This relationship may be stated in the following way:

$$f_t^{t+k} = s_{t+k}^e + \lambda_t \tag{12.1}$$

where f_t^{t+k} denotes the forward rate contract defined in period t, maturing in $t + k$ (in future we simply write this as f_t, where it is understood that the maturity horizon corresponds to the lead operator used for the spot exchange rate), s_{t+k}^e denotes the expected spot rate for period $t + k$ and λ_t has the interpretation of a (time-varying) risk premium (required to compensate agents from exposure to open positions in the currency in question at time t) and may be more precisely defined as having two components:

$$\lambda_t = \mu + \gamma_t \qquad (12.2)$$

where μ denotes a constant risk premium term and γ_t denotes the time-varying component of the risk premium. As in previous discussions, lower-case letters here signify that the natural logarithm operator has been applied to the underlying level of the variable (and all exchange rates are defined as the home currency price of one unit of foreign exchange). Instead of presenting the model in logarithmic levels it will prove advantageous (particularly, as we shall see, in terms of the econometric results presented in the following section) alternatively to present the model in terms of changes or, more correctly, quasi-changes, as

$$fp_t = \Delta s_{t+k}^e + \lambda_t \qquad (12.1a)$$

where the variables are again in logs and fp_t has the interpretation of the forward premium equal to $f_t^{t+k} - s_t$ and $\Delta s_{t+k}^e = s_{t+k}^e - s_t$. This first component of the joint hypothesis is usually discussed in the context of either risk neutrality or risk aversion. On the basis of the first view of risk we have the proposition that agents will act to ensure that the forward premium (discount) equals the expected foreign currency appreciation (depreciation), whilst on the latter view agents act to ensure that the premium equals the expected currency appreciation adjusted for the potentially time-varying risk premium. Agents are assumed to force these equalities on the basis of the exploitation of available information. The rational expectations leg of the joint hypothesis may be summarized by the equation

$$\Delta s_{t+k} = \Delta s_{t+k}^e + \eta_{t+k} \qquad \Delta s_{t+k}^e = E(\Delta s_{t+k} \,|\, I_t) \qquad (12.3)$$

where $\Delta s_{t+k} = s_{t+k} - s_t$ is the actual change in the exchange rate, E is the mathematical expectations operator, I_t is the information set on which agents base their expectations and, if agents are rational, η_{t+k} should be a random forecast error, orthogonal, or uncorrelated, to the information set.

On using (12.1a) and (12.3) we obtain a statement of the joint hypothesis under risk aversion as follows:

$$fp_t = \Delta s_{t+k} + \varepsilon_{t+k} + \lambda_t \qquad (12.4)$$

where $\varepsilon_{t+k} = -\eta_{t+k}$ of equation (12.3). In words, equation (12.4) simply states that the forward premium should equal the sum of the exchange rate change, a random forecasting error and a risk premium.

Equation (12.4) makes clear why figures 12.3 and 12.4 do not necessarily indicate a violation of the EMH. Thus the forward premium set in period t will not be a good predictor of the future exchange rate change if there is a lot of new information hitting the forward exchange market (the arrival of such information will result in potentially large forecast errors) and/or if there are important time-varying risk premiums. Hence figures like 12.3 and 12.4 are of limited usefulness in describing how good a predictor the forward rate is of the exchange rate change.

Seigel paradox

The variables entering the efficiency relationships above are all assumed to be logarithmic transformations of the underlying actual values (i.e. $f_t = \log(F_t)$). There is in fact a very important practical reason for using the log transformation. Thus, if we were to examine whether the actual forward rate F_t was an unbiased predictor of S_t we would get two different answers depending on whether we defined the exchange rates as the home currency price of a unit of foreign exchange or the foreign currency price of a unit of home currency. This follows because the expectation of a variable (i.e. $E_t S_t$) and its inverse (i.e. $E_t(1/S_t)$) are not equivalent when the variable is in levels. This is referred to as the Seigel (1972) paradox, which, in turn, is simply an application of a well-known statistical theorem called Jensen's inequality. Since, however, $E_t(-s_t) = -E_t(s_t)$ the problem does not arise when the variables are defined in logarithms.[9]

*12.3 Econometric Estimation of the Efficient Markets Hypothesis

The optimality of the forward rate is usually assessed by implementing a two-step testing strategy. The first stage involves testing whether the forward exchange premium is an unbiased predictor of the corresponding exchange rate change. This, in turn, involves specifying a regression equation of the following kind and estimating it appropriately (by, say, ordinary least squares):

$$\Delta s_{t+k} = \alpha_0 + \beta_0 fp_t + u_{t+k} \tag{12.5}$$

If agents are *risk neutral* (which enable us to set λ_t in (12.4) to zero) and rational, it follows that for (12.4) to be satisfied we would expect $\alpha_0 = 0$ and $\beta_0 = 1$. The vast majority of researchers who test (12.5) take this to be the null hypothesis. If agents are *risk averse*, however, then a significant constant term in (12.5) could reflect a constant risk premium, and *a significant deviation of β_0 from 1 could reflect a time-varying risk premium*, irrationality or both (this will be explained in more detail below). It is often argued that if agents are rational the error term in (12.5) is expected to be independent and identically distributed (iid); a finding of non-iid errors in (12.5) is therefore indicative of irrationality. However, it is wrong to make any prior predictions about the nature of the error term in (12.5). This is because in the presence of heteroscedasticity – a common feature of financial markets – the error terms may have a changing variance from period to period and therefore we would not expect the error term to be identically distributed. The existence of heteroscedasticity does not conflict with the rational processing of information. Further, in circumstances where the forecast horizon is longer than the observational frequency, the EMH does not even require that the error term be serially uncorrelated. This may be illustrated by means of the following example.

Overlapping contracts

If the forward premium in (12.5) has a three-month (quarterly) maturity and we have monthly observations on this premium we will for each month of the quarter have a forecast error and these errors will be expected to be related over time. More specifically, consider two forward rates, one negotiated in period t and the other in $t - 1$, where t denotes a month. Although the forward rates are quoted monthly they mature in three months' time. Hence the former rate matures in $t + 3$ and the latter in $t + 2$. We may think of the forecast error in the period when the period-t contract matures, u_{t+3}, as containing a sequence of forecast revisions, arising from new information, which occur in each period from t through to $t + 3$. That is, there will be a revision in $t + 1$, u_{t+1}, and in $t + 2$, u_{t+2}, and any revision that occurs in $t + 3$. Similarly, the forecast error for the forward rate maturing in $t + 2$, u_{t+2}, can be thought of as containing the news occurring in $t + 2$ plus the news from $t + 1$, u_{t+1}, and period-t news, u_t (since this contract would have been negotiated in $t - 1$). Hence it is clear that the two forward contracts, one written in t and the other in $t - 1$, will contain common forecast errors: in terms of our example, $t + 1$ and $t + 2$. Therefore, in cases where we have such overlapping contracts it is expected *a priori* that the error term in an equation like (12.5) will be serially correlated. In general terms any $k - 1$ successive forecast errors will share at least one news item and hence may be correlated. This is consistent with assuming that the forecasting errors follow a moving-average error process of $k - 1$ (in terms of the above example the error term is expected to follow a second order moving-average process). As we shall see below, the existence of such moving-average errors creates problems for the estimation of an equation like (12.5).

Orthogonality

The second stage in an EMH testing strategy normally involves testing whether the forward rate forecast error is orthogonal, or uncorrelated, to information available to agents at the time they form their expectations. Such an orthogonality test is usually conducted by estimating a regression equation of the form

$$f_t^{t+k} - s_t = \Gamma X_t + \omega_{t+k} \tag{12.6}$$

where X_t is a $1 \times k$ row vector, which is the econometricians' observed portion of the "true" information set I_t available to agents, Γ is a $k \times 1$ vector of parameters and ω_{t+k} is an error term. Equation (12.6) may be derived from (12.5) by simply subtracting fp_t from both sides of (12.5) and introducing a vector of information variables into the resulting expression. The null hypothesis is that Γ should equal zero. If this condition is violated then information available to agents at time t

has remained unexploited. Again, with overlapping contracts, the error term in (12.5) will follow a moving-average error process.

Choice of estimator

The existence of a moving-average error in equations like (12.5) and (12.6) introduces a complication into their estimation. Normally the presence of autocorrelation requires the use of a generalized least squares (GLS) estimator instead of ordinary least squares (OLS). However, because the error term in (12.5) and (12.6) has the interpretation of a rational forecast error the use of GLS to estimate such equations will violate certain orthogonality conditions (see Flood and Garber, 1980; Hansen and Hodrick, 1980). In dealing with this problem most researchers follow Hansen (1982) and estimate the point estimates in (12.5) and (12.6) by OLS (since they will be unbiased and consistent)[10] and then construct the variance–covariance matrix of these estimates using the generalized method of moments (GMM). Hansen has demonstrated that the application of GMM will produce a consistent estimator of the covariance matrix.

12.3.1 *Tests of the forward premium as an optimal predictor of the exchange rate change

A large number of researchers have implemented (12.5), using a variety of currencies and time periods, for the recent floating experience, and report results which are *unfavorable* to the unbiasedness hypothesis; i.e. they are unfavorable to the null hypothesis that $\alpha_0 = 0$ and $\beta_0 = 1$. For example, Bilson (1981), Longworth (1981), Fama (1984), Gregory and McCurdy (1984), all report a result which seems to suggest a resounding rejection of the unbiasedness hypothesis, namely, a significantly negative point estimate of β_0. This result seems particularly robust given the variety of estimation techniques used by researchers and the mix of overlapping and non-overlapping data sets. Indeed, the finding that β_0 is closer to -1 than $+1$ has become something of an industry paradigm (see MacDonald and Taylor, 1992). To the extent that the forward premium only reflects the expected change in the exchange rate, this result would seem to suggest that agents get the direction of the exchange rate change completely wrong! However, and as we shall see below, this is not an uncontroversial conclusion. Often the constant term – the α_0 term in (12.5) – has a statistically significant effect, perhaps reflecting the importance of a (constant) risk premium term. A good example of the kind of result obtained by researchers is given below (the result is from Fama, 1984), where standard errors are in parentheses.

$$\Delta s_{t+k} = 0.81 - 1.15(f - s)_t \tag{12.7}$$
$$\quad\;\;(0.42)\quad(0.50)$$

Currency: Swiss franc-US dollar

Fama did not have an overlapping data set and therefore both the coefficient estimates and their associated standard errors in (12.7) could have been estimated by OLS. However, since (12.5) was also estimated for a number of other US dollar bilateral rates, Fama exploited the fact that the error terms were likely to be correlated across the different equations (i.e. a shock that affects the US dollar will *ceteris paribus* affect all US dollar bilateral rates) by using the seemingly unrelated regression estimator (SURE), which should give more efficient estimates. Before trying to interpret (12.7), and particularly the estimate of β_0, we discuss briefly the extant evidence on (12.6).

Tests of equation (12.6) may be split into those which include only lagged forecast errors in the conditioning information set, which we categorize as type A tests (in terms of Fama's (1976) nomenclature such tests are weak-form tests), and those which include information additional to lagged forecast errors in the information set, which we label type B tests (or, following Fama (1976), semi-strong-form tests).

Type A tests have been conducted by, *inter alia*, Gweke and Feige (1979), Frankel (1979b), MacDonald (1983b), Cumby and Obstfeld (1984), Gregory and McCurdy (1984) and MacDonald and Taylor (1991a). These authors use a variety of different sample periods (i.e. recent float and interwar float), estimation techniques and currencies (usually bilateral dollar rates). Their basic finding is that the EMH is rejected for a number of currencies for the recent and interwar floating experiences. For example, Hansen and Hodrick (1980) estimate equation (12.6) using a weekly data base over the period 1973–9 and find that the orthogonality property is violated for three currencies (the Swiss franc, the Italian lira and the German mark). Hansen and Hodrick estimate their version of equation (12.6) using OLS (since it is consistent), but correct the standard errors for the implied moving-average error structure using Hansen's GMM. MacDonald and Taylor (1991a) also use Hansen's GMM to conduct type A tests for the interwar period, but in contrast to Hansen and Hodrick, MacDonald and Taylor use the GMM procedure to correct for both the implied moving average error *and* conditional heteroscedasticity (Hansen and Hodrick assume conditional homoscedasticity); they find very strong rejection of the EMH for dollar – sterling, franc–sterling and franc–dollar rates (this result contrasts with other tests of the EMH for the interwar period).

Given the rejections of the null hypothesis reported when researchers conduct type A tests, it is hardly surprising to find that type B test results are even more strongly rejected. Thus, Gweke and Fiege (1979), Hansen and Hodrick (1980), Hsieh (1984) and MacDonald and Taylor (1991a) all report regressions of the current period forecast error on own lagged forecast errors and lagged forecast errors from other foreign exchange markets, and find that the joint null $\Gamma = 0$ is resoundingly rejected.

An alternative way of testing error orthogonality conditions is to use the vector autoregressive (VAR) methodology, originally proposed by Sargent (1979) in the context of testing the rational expectations model of the term structure of interest rates. A VAR model is a time-series model which, in the current context, may be thought of as consisting of two regression equations. The equations feature the forward rate and the spot rate as the dependent variables of these two equations, with the regressors in the equations being a number of lagged values of the spot and forward rates (the lags are usually chosen using a lag length criterion and the same number of lags of each of the variables appears in each of the equations). This methodology has been applied to testing the efficiency of the forward foreign exchange market by Hakkio (1981), Baillie et al. (1983) and MacDonald and Taylor (1989d). The approach, although it can be viewed as an alternative representation of (12.6), has a number of important advantages over the simpler regression-based tests discussed above.[11] First, no special problems arise from overlapping data and serially correlated disturbances. Second, the information set upon which the tests are conditioned is made explicit. Third, since this approach exploits the time-series properties of the data, the tests should be more efficient – they should have greater power to reject a false null hypothesis in any particular application. The main disadvantage of the approach, in contrast to the regression based tests, is that it fails to accommodate conditional heteroscedasticity which is widely recognized to be a feature of (particularly high-frequency) exchange rate data.[12] *All of the papers noted above which use this methodology provide a resounding rejection of the EMH.*

More recent tests of the unbiasedness of the forward exchange rate have used cointegration and unit root testing methods. In particular, if the unbiasedness proposition is valid then as Liu and Maddala (1992) have pointed out the forward premium should be a stationary, or I(0), variable. A number of researchers have tested this proposition (see, for example, Hakkio and Rush (1989), Mark, Wu and Hai (1993), Crowder (1994), MacDonald and Marsh (1997) and MacDonald and Moore (2000)) and the results are rather inconclusive since a finding in favor of stationarity seems to be estimation-specific (see Engel (1995) for an excellent overview of this recent literature).

Conclusion

Thus researchers using a variety of estimation techniques (those robust to conditional heteroscedasticity (GMM) and those not (the vector autoregressive and maximum likelihood methodologies)) report evidence which is unfavorable to the joint null hypothesis. How then may such rejection be rationalized? There are essentially two ways in which researchers have sought to explain such rejection. The first, and most popular, is to argue that agents are risk averse and therefore λ_t is non-zero in (12.4). Alternatively, researchers have sought to explain rejection in terms of a failure, in some sense, of the expectations component of the joint hypothesis. In the remainder of this chapter we consider the former interpretation. Expectational interpretations of the failure of the null hypothesis are left to the next chapter.

*12.4 A Risk Premium Story to explain why β may not be unity

A large amount of research effort has been expended in trying to rationalize the findings noted above. Perhaps the most popular explanation lies in the existence of a non-zero time-varying risk premium which drives a wedge between the forward and future spot rates.

A useful starting point in any discussion of time-varying risk premiums is Fama's novel way of analyzing the degree of variability of the components of the forward premium. In addition to equation (12.5) Fama considers the "companion" regression equation

$$f_t - s_{t+k} = \alpha_1 + \beta_1(f_t - s_t) + \varepsilon_{2,t+k} \tag{12.8}$$

Since the regressor in (12.5) and (12.8) is the same variable and the sum of the regressands equals the regressor, the equations are entirely complementary (i.e. $\alpha_0 = -\alpha_1$ and $\beta_0 = 1 - \beta_1$). The usefulness in estimating both equations lies in their ability to interpret the data. By using the standard formulae for β_0 and β_1, the definition of the risk premium implied by (12.1) and the rationality equation (12.3), it is straightforward to demonstrate that the probability limits of the βs may be written as (see Fama (1984) and MacDonald and Taylor (1989e) for further details)

$$\beta_0 = \frac{\text{var}(s_{t+k}^e - s_t) + \text{cov}(\lambda_t, s_{t+k}^e - s_t)}{\text{var}(\lambda_t) + \text{var}(s_{t+k}^e - s_t) + 2\text{cov}(\lambda_t, s_{t+k}^e - s_t)} \tag{12.9}$$

$$\beta_1 = \frac{\text{var}(\lambda_t) + \text{cov}(\lambda_t, s_{t+k}^e - s_t)}{\text{var}(\lambda_t) + \text{var}(s_{t+k}^e - s_t) + 2\text{cov}(\lambda_t, s_{t+k}^e - s_t)} \tag{12.10}$$

In the rather extreme case where λ_t and $s_{t+k}^e - s_t$ are uncorrelated, β_1 would capture that component of the variance of the forward premium due to the variance of the risk premium and β_0 would reflect that part of the variance of the premium due to variability of the expected change of the exchange rate. In practice the interpretation of the βs is unlikely to be so clear cut, since the covariance terms are unlikely to be zero. However, even in the presence of non-zero covariance terms, (12.9) and (12.10) offer a neat interpretation of the empirical finding of a negative β_1. Thus since the denominator and the variance term in the numerator of (12.9) must be positive, it follows that $\text{cov}(\lambda_t, s_{t+k}^e - s_t)$ must be negative and greater than $\text{var}(s_{t+k}^e - s_t)$ in absolute magnitude. This in turn implies that $\text{var}(\lambda_t)$ must be greater than $\text{var}(s_{t+k}^e - s_t)$. In order to get a feel for the magnitude of the difference we may subtract (12.9) from (12.10) to obtain

$$\beta_0 - \beta_1 = \frac{\text{var}(\lambda_t) - \text{var}(s_{t+k}^e - s_t)}{\text{var}(f_t - s_t)} \tag{12.11}$$

Thus, the difference between the βs in (12.9) and (12.10) is determined by the relative variances of the risk premium and the expected rate of change of the exchange rate. Fama (1984) calculates this difference for nine major dollar rates and finds a range for (12.11) from 1.58 (Japanese yen) to 4.16 (Belgian franc). Moreover, in six out of the nine cases the estimate of (12.11) is more than two standard errors away from zero, and in all cases it is more than one and a half estimated standard errors away from zero. Fama thus confidently concludes that the variance in the risk premium is reliably greater than the variance in the expected change in the exchange rate.

The negative covariation between the risk premium and the expected depreciation implied by most reported point estimates of β_0 proved puzzling to Fama (1984), who argued that "A good story for negative covariation . . . is difficult to tell." Intuitively, a negative β_0 means that the greater the expected depreciation of the dollar, the greater the expected return that one should require bidding for a dollar-denominated security (all exchange rates are defined as dollars per unit of currency). Hodrick and Srivastava (1986) provide a solution to this apparent paradox. They point out that the risk premium in this empirical work is the expected profit from an open forward *purchase* of dollars, and so this is in fact denominated in foreign currency (the maturing long dollar position is eventually sold in the spot market). The expected (dollar-denominated) profit from an open forward *sale* of dollars is $-\lambda_t$ and the widely reported negative estimate of β_0 suggests that this will be positively correlated with the expected rate of dollar depreciation.

Notice that the Fama story, since it assumes that agents are rational, is only an *interpretation* of why efficiency is rejected. We shall consider other interpretations in the next chapter. Before we do so, however, how might the risk premium be modeled from a theoretical perspective?

12.4.1 A model of the risk premium

We have referred to the risk premium frequently in this chapter and in previous chapters. However, we have said nothing about the theoretical determinants of the premium. In this section we seek to remedy this imbalance by presenting a model of the risk premium which is widely used in the financial economics literature to model the "closed economy" risk premium (i.e. the premium contained in a risky asset, such as a share, over the return on a riskless asset) and in the international finance literature to model the open economy risk premium. The model was first developed, in the closed economy context, by Lucas (1978) and has been applied to the open economy context by, *inter alia*, Grauer et al. (1976), Kouri (1977), Stockman (1978), Fama and Farber (1979) and Lucas (1982). Since most derivations of the model are highly technical we attempt to give an intuitive feel for the model whilst, hopefully, not completely abandoning rigor.[13]

We start first with a closed economy. In such a setting a representative agent (or investor) is assumed to be maximizing the present discounted value of utility, subject to a set of sequential budget constraints (see section 4.6 for a two period discussion of this model). The agent's utility function is given by

$$U_t = E_t \left[\sum_{i=0}^{\infty} \beta^i u(c_{t+i}) \right] \qquad (12.12)$$

where E_t denotes the conditional expectations operator $E_t = E(.\,|\,I_t)$; I_t denotes the full information set; u denotes utility; c denotes the consumption good available to the agent in each period; β is the subjective discount factor, and is assumed to lie in the interval between 0 and 1; and U_t represents the present discounted value of utility. The utility function is assumed to have all the standard properties, such as time separability and strict concavity (implying risk aversion), and is continuously differentiable. Equation (12.12) simply states that the individual is interested in the utility obtained from the present discounted value of current and all future levels of expected utility. The individual is assumed to maximize this function subject to a sequence of budget constraints. These constraints are of the form (for period t to $t + 1$)

$$a_{t+1} = r_t(a_t + y_t - c_t) \tag{12.13}$$

where a_t denotes real wealth, y_t denotes labor income, $y_t - c_t$ therefore denotes saving from labor income and r_t denotes one plus the real interest rate. Hence the increase in the agent's real wealth from period to period depends upon his or her rate of saving and the rate of interest.

If (12.12) is maximized subject to a set of (sequential) budget constraints like (12.13) the following first-order (or Euler) condition is obtained:

$$u'(c_t) = \beta E_t[u'(c_{t+1})r_t] \tag{12.14}$$

where $u'(.)$ denotes marginal utility. Equation (12.14) is a condition of welfare maximization and states that in equilibrium the marginal utility from the chosen consumption in period t should equal the marginal utility of the chosen consumption in period $t + 1$ scaled by the real rate of return on the representative asset and the subjective rate of time preference. By noting that c_t is available in period t, we may rearrange (12.14) as

$$1 = \beta E_t\left[\frac{u'(c_{t+1})r_t}{u'(c_t)}\right] \tag{12.14a}$$

One implication of the kind of model portrayed in (12.12)–(12.14) is that if the real rate of return is constant ($r_t = \alpha$) the representative agent will attempt to smooth consumption over time, in order that the respective marginal utilities are equalized. If, as in (12.14a), the real rate of return is stochastic, then it will do the work to ensure (12.14) is satisfied. Thus, if for some reason consumption is low in the present, relative to levels expected to prevail in the future, the asset price has to adjust to ensure that a high yield is obtained when consumption is relatively high. More generally, conditional on consumption choices this equation offers a theory of asset prices or, alternatively, conditional on asset prices it offers a theory of consumption (Deaton, 1992).

In an open economy context, and conditional on consumption choices, the maximizing behavior of consumers generates a risk premium (i.e. in the open economy context this is equivalent to the determination of the return term r_t). This may be seen in the following way. Assume that r_t in (12.14) is the return from taking an uncovered position in a foreign-currency-denominated bond. Using the kind of logarithmic expressions referred to previously this may be written as $r_t = i_t^* - (p_{t+1} - p_t) + (s_{t+1} - s_t)$, where all variables are expressed as natural logarithms, i.e. the nominal foreign interest rate adjusted for the holding period inflation rate (where p is the price of the consumption good) and the exchange rate depreciation over the holding period.[14] On using this definition of the real return in (12.14) and noting that the model discussed here is defined with respect to the levels of the variables we obtain

$$1 = \beta E_t \left[\frac{u'(c_{t+1})(1 + i_t^*)}{u'(c_t)} \frac{P_t}{P_{t+1}} \frac{S_{t+1}}{S_t} \right] \tag{12.15}$$

Consider, additionally, the alternative investment strategy where the individual takes a *covered* position in the foreign bond. In this case, instead of (12.15) we have

$$1 = \beta E_t \left[\frac{u'(c_{t+1})(1 + i_t^*)}{u'(c_t)} \frac{P_t}{P_{t+1}} \frac{F_t}{S_t} \right] \tag{12.16}$$

where the forward rate has been substituted for S_{t+1}. The covered interest rate parity condition implies that the return entering (12.16) will be identical to the return on an identical domestic bond. On taking the difference between (12.15) and (12.16) and dividing the resulting expression by β and $(1 + i_t^*)$ we obtain

$$E_t \left(Q_t \frac{S_{t+1} - F_t}{S_t} \right) = 0 \tag{12.17}$$

where $Q_t = [u'(c_{t+1})/P_{t+1}]/[u'(c_t)/P_t]$, which has the interpretation of the intertemporal marginal rate of substitution of money,[15] and the term $(S_{t+1} - F_t)S_t^{-1}$ is what we have referred to previously as the forward forecast error and may be interpreted here as the profit from forward market speculation. We have almost reached our desired point of defining the risk premium. Before doing so, however, it is important to note that (12.17) offers a way of testing the model. Thus the product of Q and $(S_{t+1} - F_t)S_t^{-1}$ should be orthogonal, or uncorrelated, with period-t information (i.e. remember that E_t is the expectations operator conditional on period-t information). Therefore, as long as one can somehow define the elements in Q this hypothesis can be tested.

The risk premium may be defined by first noting that the definition of the conditional covariance (that is conditional on the information set $cov[.;. | I_t]$) of two random variables is

$$cov(z_t; x_t) = E_t(z_t x_t) - E_t(z_t)E_t(x_t) \tag{12.18}$$

where z_t and x_t are random variables. Using (12.18) we may rewrite (12.17) in terms of the expected profit from a forward speculation, which in this context is the risk premium, as

$$E_t\left(\frac{S_{t+1} - F_t}{S_t}\right) = \mathrm{cov}\left(Q_t;\ \frac{S_{t+1} - F_t}{S_t}\middle|\ I_t\right)[-E_t(Q_t)]^{-1} \tag{12.19}$$

Since the intertemporal marginal rate of substitution of money is always expected to be positive, we may say that the risk premium is proportional to the intertemporal marginal rate of substitution of money and the profit from foreign exchange speculation. Further, since the period-t spot and forward rates are contained in the period-t information set, we may rewrite (12.19) in what is perhaps a slightly more familiar way as

$$\frac{F_t}{S_t} = E_t\left(\frac{S_{t+1}}{S_t}\right) - \mathrm{cov}\left(Q_t;\ \frac{S_{t+1} - F_t}{S_t}\middle|\ I_t\right)[-E_t(Q_t)]^{-1} \tag{12.20}$$

which is simply an alternative (non-logarithmic) version of (12.1); i.e. we have defined the risk premium term λ_t (the second term on the right-hand side of (12.20)) in terms of the parameters of the representative agent model. Equation (12.20) makes the point that the forward rate need not be an unbiased predictor of the future spot rate if the second term on the right-hand side of (12.20) is non-zero. It is important to note that this can occur *even when agents are risk neutral* (a situation that will be characterized by the linearity of the utility function underlying (12.12)). With risk neutrality, the Q term in (12.20) will be defined exclusive of consumption (see Stockman, 1978; Frenkel and Razin, 1980).

 ## *12.5 Empirically Implementing Equation (12.20)

In trying to implement empirically the implications of the representative agent model as given by (12.20), a researcher is immediately faced with the problem of how to model the unobservable entry Q. A variety of approaches have been adopted in the literature and we now briefly discuss the three main ones.

12.5.1 The capital asset pricing model/latent variable approach

A number of studies have exploited the capital asset pricing model (CAPM) so widely used in pricing the riskiness of domestic shares. This well known model[16] relates the expected risk premium on a stock to the expected risk premium on the market scaled by a conditional risk premium term which captures the share's inherent riskiness, described as the share's β:

$$r_i - r_f = \beta(r_m - r_f) \tag{12.21}$$

where r_i is the return on stock i, r_f is the risk-free return, r_m is the market return and $\beta = \mathrm{cov}(r_i - r_f;\ r_m - r_f)/\mathrm{var}(r_m - r_f)$.

Hansen and Richard have exploited this kind of model in order to derive a tractable version of (12.19). In particular Hansen and Richard (1984) posit that the expected normalized profit on a long position (i.e. the expected risk premium) may be written as

$$\frac{E_t(S_{t+k} - F_{t,k})}{S_t} = \beta_t^c E_t(R_{t+k,k}^b - R_{t,k}) \tag{12.22}$$

where $\beta_t^c = \text{cov}_t[(S_{t+1} - F_{t,k})/S_t; R_{t+k,k}^b]/\text{var}_t(R_{t+k,k}^b)$, $R_{t,k}$ denotes the known dollar return of investing one dollar at t in a risk-free rate maturing in $t + k$ and $R_{t+k,k}^b$ is the k-period return on an appropriate bench-mark portfolio (essentially the R terms in this equation are a measure of the Q terms in the theoretical model – see Hansen and Richard (1984) and Hodrick (1984) for a detailed description of how (12.22) may be derived from (12.19)). Notice that the β term in (12.22) is time dependent.

Hansen and Hodrick (1983) test a "latent variable" version (a latent variable approach is adopted because of the unobservable nature of the bench-mark portfolio) of (12.22) using semi-weekly data for five bilateral US dollar rates over the period from February 5, 1976 to December 29, 1980. The use of a latent variable model forces restrictions on the coefficients in the estimated equation and if the model is valid the data should not result in the rejection of these restrictions. In fact, Hansen and Hodrick find evidence against the model's restrictions. Interestingly, using the estimated βs as a measure of risk, it was demonstrated that the Swiss franc and Japanese yen are the most risky currencies whilst the French franc and UK pound are the least risky – a somewhat counterintuitive result.

Hodrick and Srivastava (1986) re-estimate (12.22) for the same currencies as in Hansen and Hodrick's study but for an extended non-overlapping sample (February 1976 to September 1982) and use a different information set (in particular, they define the set to consist of forward premiums rather than the forward forecast error as used by Hansen and Hodrick). Interestingly, this simple change results in the model's restrictions being easily rejected (this result parallels the results of Levine (1987) who utilizes a somewhat different model of the risk premium – see the last section of this chapter). Both Hansen and Hodrick and Hodrick and Srivistava assume that the β in (12.22) is constant. In an attempt to discern if their reported rejection is due to the non-constancy of the βs (i.e. there is nothing inherent in the model to suggest that β should be constant), Hodrick and Srivastava test the model over a number of sub-samples, corresponding to periods of uncertainty in foreign exchange markets, and find some evidence against the hypothesis of no structural change. The time-varying nature of the βs is attributed to non-linearities between the forecast errors and the forward premiums (when the forecast errors are projected onto squared forward premiums, in addition to forward premiums, the squared variables prove highly significant and the hypothesis that the coefficients are time invariant cannot be rejected). Giovannini and Jorion (1987) also find support for the existence of time variation of the βs in their study of the latent variable model (their specification allows the βs to be a function of the nominal interest rates of the USA and the "foreign" country). Campbell and Clarida (1987) extend the latent variable model by incorporating other returns. More specifically, they consider the co-movement of risk premiums in the term structure of interest rates and the forward market and are unable to reject the single latent variable model.

12.5.2 Testing the orthogonality condition directly

An alternative way of testing for the risk premium implied by the representative agent model has been discussed by Mark (1985). In particular Mark uses the methodology of Hansen and Singleton (1982) which directly exploits the orthogonality condition (12.17). Put simply this method involves regressing the variable in parentheses onto a set of variables assumed to be in the agent's information set. If the model is valid these variables should be jointly statistically insignificant. Therefore, in contrast to the applications of this model outlined in the previous section, Mark effectively works directly with the model's first-order conditions. In order to do this some assumption has to be made about the particular form of the utility function (in order to calculate the appropriate marginal utilities). Mark assumes that the particular form of the utility function is in the constant relative risk aversion class[17] and only one consumption good enters the function. Using monthly data on exchange rates,[18] real consumer expenditure and the consumer expenditure deflator over the period from March 1973 to July 1983, Mark finds that this class of model does have some power in capturing time-varying risk premiums. However, as is common in these kind of estimates the estimated value of the risk aversion parameter tends to be large and not precisely estimated, in a statistical sense.

12.5.3 Autoregressive conditional heteroscedasticity models of the risk premium

Perhaps one of the most popular methods of implementing (12.20) is the autoregressive conditional heteroscedasticity (ARCH) framework originally proposed by Engle (1982). Domowitz and Hakkio (1985) were the first to apply this class of model to the forward foreign exchange market. By imposing some structure on the representative agent model outlined above,[19] Domowitz and Hakkio derive the following logarithmic representation of the risk premium:

$$E(s_{t+1}) - f_t = 0.5(h_{t+1} - h^*_{t+1}) \qquad (12.23)$$

where h_{t+1} and h^*_{t+1} denote, respectively, the conditional variance of the home and foreign money supplies. An increase in h_{t+1}, by increasing the variance of the purchasing power of domestic money, will induce a fall in domestic interest rates, which through the interest rate parity condition will induce a fall in f_t (the spot rate, and therefore its expectation, are unchanged): the risk premium falls. In the empirical implementation of the risk premium, the representative agent model is effectively abandoned and an *ad hoc* representation of (12.20) is implemented. More specifically, Domowitz and Hakkio estimate the following model:

$$s_{t+1} - s_t = \lambda_t + \beta(f_t - s_t) + \varepsilon_{t+1} \tag{12.24}$$

$$\lambda_t = \beta_0 + \theta h_{t+1} \tag{12.25}$$

$$\varepsilon_{t+1} \mid I_t \sim N(0, h_{t+1}^2) \tag{12.26}$$

$$h_{t+1}^2 = \alpha_0^2 + \sum_{j=1}^{n} \alpha_j^2 \varepsilon_{t+1-j}^2 \tag{12.27}$$

where λ_t is the risk premium ($= 0.5(h_{t+1} - h_{t+1}^*)$) which is assumed to be a function of the conditional variance of the forecast error ε_{t+1}, and I_t is the time t information set. Equation (12.24) simply states that the conditional variance of the rate of depreciation depends upon the past n realizations of the squared forecast errors. Note that (12.25) has a number of implications for the behavior of the risk premium. First, the time-series properties of the risk premium are determined solely by the movement of the conditional variance. Second, (12.25) implies that the risk premium can be positive or negative and change sign, depending on the values of β_0 and θ.

By assuming that the order of the ARCH process equals 4, Domowitz and Hakkio estimate (12.24) using five currencies for part of the recent floating experience and report rather mixed results: thus although there is fairly strong evidence of ARCH effects (i.e. non-zero as) the null hypothesis of no risk premium ($\beta_0 = \theta = 0$) cannot be rejected for any of the currencies (some evidence of rejection is reported when equation (12.24) is specified in levels; however, any inferences drawn from such a non-stationary system must be rather limited). One interpretation offered by Domowitz and Hakkio for their poor results is that the type of bilateral model estimated ignores any cross correlation between exchange markets (such correlation is shown to have an important impact on efficiency tests by *inter alia* Gweke and Fiege (1979), Edwards (1983), and MacDonald (1983a)). Kaminsky and Peruga (1988) attempt to capture such effects by re-estimating the Domowitz and Hakkio model in a multivariate context (the currencies studied are the bilateral dollar rates of the British pound, German mark and Swiss franc) and find that the hypothesis that $\theta^b = \theta^g = \theta^s = 0$ (where the superscripts have an obvious interpretation) is easily rejected at all conventional significance levels; Domowitz and Hakkio's rather negative findings, therefore, are perhaps a reflection of their failure to account properly for foreign exchange market interdependences (a multivariate ARCH framework has also been used by Nerlove et al. (1988) to model exchange rate changes).[20]

Although the ARCH model would seem to have some strong intuitive appeal, it suffers from a number of problems. First, the approach is inherently *ad hoc* in that the conditional variance depends solely upon past squared innovations, and second the method does not specify the *source* of changes in the conditional variance. As Hodrick (1987) has emphasized, the fact that the ARCH model **forces** the conditional variance to take its largest value after the largest residual error of the sample is not particularly insightful, since in some particular instances such large errors may result from the resolution of some market uncertainty and in fact lead to a small conditional variance (Hodrick gives the example of a change in the monetary/fiscal regime which was preceded by a period of debate about the direction of policy – the resolution of the policy uncertainty results in a reduction of conditional variance on the part of rational agents). Often the ARCH model will be effective because it picks up some underlying misspecification such as a regime change. If this is the case a better approach to modeling risk may lie in the use of a time-varying parameter model.

12.5.4 The portfolio balance–mean variance approach to risk

As we noted in chapters 9 and 11, one of the key distinguishing features of the monetary and portfolio classes of exchange rate models is that in the former group non-money assets are assumed to be perfect substitutes, whilst in the latter group such assets are assumed to be imperfect substitutes. Such imperfect subsitutability was argued to be a direct result of the existence of an exchange risk premium. A number of researchers (most notably Frankel, 1982c, 1983) have exploited this difference between the models in order to test for the existence of a risk premium. The essential idea underpinning such tests may be illustrated in the following way. The essence of the portfolio balance approach may be captured by

$$B_t(S_tF_t)^{-1} = \gamma(i_t - i_t^* - \Delta s_{t+k}^e) \tag{12.28}$$

where B_t denotes the domestic non-money asset, F_t denotes the comparable foreign non-money asset, γ is a measure of relative risk aversion and the term in parentheses is the expected excess return of the domestic asset over the foreign asset – equal to the risk premium λ_t. Using a two-period mean–variance maximization problem it can be shown – see Frankel (1982a) – that $\gamma = (\vartheta\theta)^{-1}$, where ϑ is the Arrow–Pratt measure of relative risk aversion and θ is the conditional variance of exchange rate depreciation. If ϑ goes to zero (i.e. agents are effectively risk neutral) γ becomes infinitely large and (12.28) simply reduces to uncovered interest rate parity; i.e. the home and foreign non-money assets become perfect substitutes.

Equation (12.28) may be put into a form amenable to econometric estimation by inverting it and by assuming that the expected change in the exchange rate is formed rationally (i.e. $\Delta s_{t+k} = \Delta s_{t+k}^e + \varepsilon_{t+k}$):

$$i_t - i_t^* - \Delta s_{t+k} = \gamma^{-1}(B_t(S_tF_t)^{-1}) + \varphi_{t+k} \tag{12.29}$$

where $\varphi_{t+k} = -\varepsilon_{t+k}$. Frankel (1982c) uses monthly data over the period from July 1973 to August 1980 to estimate (12.29) by maximum likelihood. The null hypothesis is that agents are risk neutral, and therefore ϑ should equal zero. In fact

Frankel reports that the estimated likelihood function is very flat, with the maximum occurring where $\vartheta = 0$. This would seem to suggest that agents are risk neutral and that the inefficiency finding is due to some form of expectational errors. Simpler regression-based tests of (12.29) also lead to the conclusion that $\vartheta = 0$. Rogoff (1984) replicates Frankel's study using weekly data for the Canadian dollar–US dollar exchange rate, and he also reports statistically insignificant estimates of γ.

However, as Frankel (1983) emphasizes, failure to reject a null using an equation like (12.29) is not the same as acceptance. Indeed any test of (12.29) is likely to have very low power because of the variability of the error term which by definition reflects unexpected exchange rate changes of "news." As we argued earlier (and again in the next chapter), news is likely to be an important feature in foreign exchange markets (and indeed has been an empirical regularity of the recent floating experience – see Mussa, 1979a) and thus perhaps the risk premium and news should be modeled jointly (we examine the news approach to exchange rate modeling in the next chapter). Although the error term in (12.29) was shown to reflect expectational errors, the actual regression errors may consist of expectational errors *plus* measurement error if there has been error in the measurement of the right hand side variables or if the asset demand equations have not been correctly specified. Further, the error term may be correlated with the right-hand-side variables if simultaneity is an issue. To the extent that there are simultaneity and errors-in-variables problems, estimates of the coefficient in (12.29) are likely to be biased and inconsistent.

A number of researchers have tried to improve the performance of (12.29) by recognizing that measurement error is likely to be especially important for this class of model, since the types of assets used are collected from a variety of governmental agencies in different countries. Danker et al. (1985) and Rogoff (1984) all estimate versions of (12.29) and show that, although the unbiasedness hypothesis can be rejected, portfolio balance variables do not explain such rejection.

12.5.5 Miscellaneous risk models

Some other models which do not fall neatly into any of the above categories are considered in this section. In contrast to the above models, Korajczyk (1985) attempts to *measure* the risk premium. His approach may be illustrated by considering again the logarithmic definition of the real exchange rate for period $t + 1$:

$$q_{t+1} = s_{t+1} - p_{t+1} + p_{t+1}^* \tag{12.30}$$

which on first differencing becomes

$$s_{t+1} - s_t = q_{t+1} - q_t + \Delta p_{t+1} - \Delta p_{t+1}^* \tag{12.31}$$

On using the standard covered interest rate parity relationship ($s_t - f_t = i_t^* - i_t$) to substitute for s_t in (12.31), assuming nominal interest rates are governed by the standard Fisher relationship (i.e. $i_t = r_t + E_t \Delta p_{t+1}$, where r_t is the real interest rate) and taking conditional expectations, we obtain

$$E_t s_t - f_t = E_t \Delta q_{t+1} + E_t(r_t^* - r_t) \qquad (12.32)$$

which indicates that if the real exchange rate evolves as a pure random walk (i.e. $E_t q_{t+1} = q_t$)[21] the risk premium, regardless of how it is determined, should equal the real interest differential. Korajczyk tests this hypothesis by estimating equation (12.32) with monthly data (April 1974 to December 1980) for seven exchange rates against the dollar using a McCallum-type instrumental variables procedure:

$$s_{t+1} - f_t = \theta_0 + \theta_1 E_t(r_t^* - r_t) + \theta_2 Z_t + u_{t+1} \qquad (12.33)$$

where Z_t is a vector of variables known at time t and the null hypothesis is that $\theta_0 = \theta_2 = 0$, $\theta_1 = 1$. In general, Korajczyk is unable to reject these restrictions and argues that his results are supportive of the existence of time-varying risk premiums (conditional on the assumption of rational expectations). However, if covered interest rate parity is treated as an identity then the assumption of a random-walk exchange rate is the only behavioral assumption in the analysis and Korajczyk's methodology amounts merely to a rather convoluted way of testing the martingale property of real exchange rates. Furthermore, Levine (1987) has demonstrated, using a similar data base to that used by Korajczyk's, that when the forward premium is included in the Z vector in (12.33) it consistently proves to be statistically significant: real interest differentials are not the only systematic component of forward forecasting errors (which they should be if the model is correctly specified).

Wolff (1987) uses Kalman filtering techniques to model the risk premium as a latent variable. Wolff uses this methodology to identify and estimate premiums as autoregressive processes, whilst Taylor models the premium as a latent variable depending upon domestic and foreign yield volatility.

12.6 Concluding Comments

In this chapter we have discussed the so-called "economists' view" of the determination of the forward exchange rate (the view that the forward rate may be decomposed into the expectation of the spot rate and a risk premium) using the EMH. In particular, we examined the joint null hypothesis of rational expectations and risk neutrality which has the implication that the forward premium on foreign exchange should be an unbiased predictor of the future exchange rate change. The overwhelming message from the empirical literature is that it is not. One reason for this may be attributable to the assumption of risk neutrality which researchers utilize in their econometric testing. We spent some time exploring this interpretation of the rejection of unbiasedness. In particular, we discussed how one may interpret a coefficient on the forward premium which differs significantly from unity when agents are risk averse, using a framework developed by

Fama (1984). A theoretical model of the forward rate risk premium was then presented and we discussed the empirical tests for the existence of a risk premium. A fair assesment of such empirical evidence would be to stay that it is not supportive of the existence of a time-varying risk premium (although there is some evidence suggestive of a constant risk premium). This evidence, combined with a widely expressed view that a time-varying risk premium is a rather vacuous device which "has no function but tautologically to save the theory" (Mankiw and Summers, 1984),[22] suggests that perhaps the rejection of the unbiasedness may be attributable to some form of expectational failure. This is the topic we turn to in the next chapter.

NOTES

1 An interesting and lucid discussion of the Cambist view is presented in Llewellyn (1980).

2 In terms of the model of spot and forward rates discussed in chapter 3, the Cambist approach is only concerned with the activities of the interest arbitrageurs who may be taken to be the commercial banks. The efforts of this group to take advantage of interest differentials results in the forward exchange rate being set as a residual (i.e. at point B on figure 3.4), as indeed the empirical evidence would seem to suggest. There is no speculative role in the Cambist view of the world (and therefore no influence for s^e and/or λ).

3 The "economists' model," which predicts that the forward rate is an unbiased predictor of the spot rate, and the Cambist view, which predicts that the forward rate is determined by relative (Euro) interest rate differentials, give the same result under two alternative scenarios: in a world of uncertainty both relationships will give the same result if speculators are risk neutral; in a world of certainty the same result will pertain if purchasing power parity holds and interest rates reflect expected inflation.

4 Thus in any period t we have an observation of the spot rate S_t and an observation of the forward rate F_t. The forward rate, with quarterly data and a three-month contract, is the market's expectation of the spot rate in the next period, $t + 1$. Hence in order to examine the predictive properties of the forward rate we must align the two rates by either leading the spot rate by one period (so that we have S_{t+1} and F_t) or, alternatively, lagging the forward rate one period (so that we have S_t and F_{t-1}).

5 The survey data were provided by Consensus Economics of London.

6 A statistically insignificant minority of companies were able, at some forecast horizons, to produce more accurate forecasts than the forward rate. Levich does not attribute this finding necessarily to a market inefficiency; rather it may be a reflection of the fair return available to agents in the presence of a risk premium (in the forward rate).

7 See also Blake et al. (1986) for a further analysis of this data set.

8 It need not be because it is normal when imposing rational expectations to say that agents have access to the *full* information set. However, when a researcher tests the EMH he or she may only use a subset of the full information set, such as the past history of the variable being studied. Such a test, following the taxonomy described in Fama (1976), is usually referred to as a weak-form test of the EMH.

9 In any case, McCulloch (1975) has argued that the operational implications of using the levels of the variables are likely to be slight.

10 The OLS point estimates may only be consistent for (12.6), depending on the information set used.

11 See MacDonald and Taylor (1989e) for a detailed discussion of this technique.

12 See, for example, Boothe and Glassman (1987) and Hsieh (1984).

13 See Hodrick (1987) for an excellent – and rigorous – presentation of the model.

14 This relationship is made operational by assuming perfect foreseight; i.e. the actual price/exchange rate changes are equal to their expected values.

15 This follows because $1/P$ is the purchasing power of a unit of home currency and therefore $u'(c)/P$ is the utility-denominated value of a unit of home currency.

16 See the many texts on corporate finance such as Copeland and Weston (1988).

17 That is $u(c_t) = \delta c_t^{1-\gamma}(1 - \gamma)^{-1}$ where γ is the coefficient of relative risk aversion ($\gamma < 1$) and δ is some arbitrary constant.

18 The exchange rates studied are the Canadian dollar, the Dutch guilder, the German mark, and the UK pound, all against the US dollar.

19 In particular, the consumption good and money (which appears in the form of the marginal utility of money in (12.20)) are assumed to follow first-order autoregressive processes and preferences are assumed to be given by a Cobb–Douglas functional form.

20 Using weekly data and forward rates of one-month maturity, MacDonald and Taylor (1991a) implement the GARCH-in-mean model for the 1920s experience with floating exchange rates. The implications of their exercise are that ARCH effects do appear to be important for this time period (this finding would seem to cast some doubt on previous work for this period which assumed homoscedasticity) and that the GARCH-in-mean premium model is supported by the behavior of the franc–sterling and franc–dollar exchange rates.

21 See *inter alia* Roll (1979), Adler and Lehmann (1983), and MacDonald (1985a, b) for evidence supportive of this hypothesis.

22 See also Goodhart (1988) for a discussion.

13

Expectational Explanations for the Rejection of the Efficient Markets Hypothesis and the "News"

In terms of the issues addressed, this chapter follows on directly from chapter 12. In the previous chapter we considered the implications of the efficient markets hypothesis (EMH) for the foreign exchange market. We noted there that the joint hypothesis of rationality and risk neutrality is resoundingly rejected by the extant evidence and one interpretation (it is only an interpretation because of the jointness of the hypothesis being tested) that may be placed on this finding is that it is due to a risk premium. However, the empirical evidence summarized in the last chapter suggests that this is not a particularly good interpretation. An alternative interpretation may lie in a failure, in some sense, of the expectations leg of the joint EMH. The most obvious such failure would simply be to posit that agents are sub-optimal processors of information; i.e. they are irrational. However, such an interpretation, because it conflicts with such a central tenet of mainstream economics, is anathema to many international economists. Nevertheless, such an interpretation has recently become increasingly fashionable as a result of the popularity of the noise-trader model introduced into the stock market literature by De Long et al. (1990). A less obvious expectational failure relates to certain distributional problems which stem from potential regime changes – the so-called "peso effect" (Krasker, 1980). In this chapter we examine these expectational explanations for the failure of the EMH in some detail.

To the extent that the failure of the EMH *is* due to expectational errors of some kind then this may have important implications for economic policy. For example, in our introduction to the last chapter we mentioned that if flexible exchange rates are responsible for the existence of risk premiums, and if such premiums have important deleterious effects on international trade, one may want to consider an international monetary regime characterized by an alternative exchange rate regime. Similarly, here, if flexible exchange rates are driven in large measure by ill-informed speculation, then policymakers may again want to consider moving away from an international monetary system based on flexible exchange rates, although the form this takes may differ from that implied by the existence of a risk premium.

The outline of the remainder of this chapter is as follows. The implications that "peso effects" and rational speculative bubbles can have for the testing of market efficiency is discussed in section 13.1. As we shall see, the existence of these kinds of effects means that the inefficiency findings reported in the last chapter are perfectly consistent with the rational processing of information. In section 13.2 we then go on to examine one of the main sources of non-rational information processing in the guise of chartism and some of the empirical evidence pertaining to this concept. The literature which uses survey data to discriminate between the risk and expectations stories for the rejection of the EMH is considered in section 13.3. In section 13.4 the concept of economic news in explaining why the forward rate may be a poor predictor of the future exchange rate is examined (as we shall see, the news approach is not an explanation for the rejection of market efficiency). In the final section of the chapter we introduce the noise trading model which many opponents of the EMH argue should become the new paradigm for thinking about the determination of asset prices. It is perhaps worth emphasizing that some of the topics introduced in this chapter, in a sense, are stand-alone topics in that they are relatively self-contained and can be read on their own (the technical analysis–chartist section being a case in point).

13.1 Peso Effects, Rational Speculative Bubbles, and Econometric Inference

One of the most popular expectations rationalizations for the rejection of the EMH is the so-called peso problem (see Krasker, 1980). The peso effect gets its name from the behavior of the Mexican peso in the early 1970s. In 1976 the peso was sharply devalued. However, in the period leading up to the devaluation the forward rate on the peso was at a discount relative to the spot rate. That is, agents were expecting the peso to be devalued for a number of periods before the devaluation actually occurred. Clearly, if a researcher were to use data from the period before the devaluation he or she would inevitably find that the forward rate was a biased predictor of the future spot rate. But how should one interpret such bias? Krasker argues that such biasedness does not reflect an inefficiency; rather it reflects deviations of the sampling distributions from the normal. This may be seen by referring to the following simple example.

Consider again the rational expectations solution to the flex-price monetary approach (FLMA) (equation (9.13a)), reproduced here as

$$s_t = (1 - \beta) \sum_{j=0}^{\infty} \beta^j E_t z_{t+j} \tag{13.1}$$

and the following simple representation of the fundamentals z_t:

$$z_t = \bar{z}_t + u_t \tag{13.2}$$

$$\bar{z}_t = \bar{z}_{t-1} + g\omega_t \tag{13.3}$$

$$\omega_t = \begin{cases} \omega_{t-1} & \text{with probability } \pi \\ 0 & \text{with probability } 1 - \pi \end{cases} \tag{13.4}$$

where u_t is a white noise disturbance and the fundamentals are assumed to have a systematic part $\bar{z}_t$ and a non-systematic part u_t. Equation (13.3), and the assumed nature of probability given in (13.4), imply that there is a probability $1 - \pi$ of a discrete reduction of g in the rate of change of the systematic fundamentals. It is fairly easy to demonstrate (see MacDonald and Taylor (1989e) for an extended discussion) that as long as π differs from 0.5 the rational expectations forecast error $s_{t+k} - E_t S_{t+k}$ will be non-symmetrically distributed (i.e. skewed) and therefore any inferences made about the regression parameters in (12.5) will be invalid; i.e. tests of whether β_0 is significantly different from unity will not be valid. Regime changes have been fairly commonplace during the recent floating experience as governments moved from interest rate targeting to monetary targeting and back again to interest rate targets. To the extent that such regime changes are important to agents, this perhaps gives a rationalization for the rejection of the EMH which does not rely on risk premiums. More technically, in using time-series data, such as those on spot and forward rates, a researcher assumes (usually implicitly) that the data are ergodic. Put simply this means that the data used have sample moments (mean, variance and covariance) which approach the true population moments and so the data may be used to make inferences about the probability distribution. So potential changes in government policy which do not occur in-sample, or expected devaluations which also do not occur in-sample, mean that the data are not ergodic and inferences may not be drawn about the probability distribution.

A similar kind of story to the peso effect may be told if agents are rational and, additionally, if rational speculative bubbles are important. For example, consider again (13.1) and assume, as we did in chapter 9, that if the actual exchange rate is equal to the fundamental value plus a speculative bubble term then the rational expectations forecast error may be written as

$$s_{t+k} - E_t s_{t+k} = \varepsilon_{t+k} + b_{t+k} - \beta^{-1} b_t \tag{13.5}$$

Therefore,

$$\Pr[(s_{t+k} - E_t s_{t+k}) \geq 0] = 0.5\{\Pr(\varepsilon_{t+k} \geq 0) + \Pr[(b_{t+k} - \beta^{-1} b_t) \geq 0]\}$$
$$= 0.5(0.5 + \pi)$$

and this implies that although the rational forecast error will have a zero conditional mean it will have a non-zero median (i.e. it will be distributed asymmetrically). Again, as in the peso problem, this may invalidate standard econometric inference procedures (see MacDonald and Taylor (1989e) for a further discussion).

The above examples are both consistent with the view that, although the forward exchange rate is a biased predictor of the actual exchange rate change, it may still be consistent with the rational processing of information. We now consider some evidence, and a popular method of forecasting exchange rates used by market operators, which suggests that the sub-optimality of the forward rate may simply be due to irrationality.

 ## 13.2 Technical Analysis and Chartism

Perhaps one of the earliest pieces of evidence to suggest that the market inefficiency finding is due to sub-optimal information processing came from the literature on filter, or trading, rules. Such rules, developed originally in the context of the stock market by Alexander (1961), suggest that certain market operators, known as technical analysts or chartists, can consistently make profits in excess of a simple buy-and-hold strategy. Such analysts believe that exchange rates exhibit certain trends and that past changes in exchange rates can be used to forecast future movements. In their concentration on exchange rate trends, technical analysts pay little or no attention to the fundamental determinants of exchange rates. Rather, the market price contains all relevant information, whether this be rational or irrational, and therefore the investor does not need to go behind the price (i.e. to fundamentals) to forecast its future path. The description of technical analysts as chartists arises because such investors often rely on producing a chart of either the actual price over time or some transformation such as a moving average, and look for particular patterns in the charts (technical analysis is in fact a broader concept than chartism, in that a technical analyst may use a variety of statistical and mathematical techniques to analyse the price, in addition to a reliance on charts – see Feeny (1989) for an elaboration of this distinction).

Three basic kinds of charts are used by the chartist. The *line chart* involves plotting the closing price of an asset against time. Such a chart, by definition, excludes all intra-day price information and the rationale given for this is that it is the closing price which is most important because it reflects the market's final assessment of the day's trading (also, of course, it is easy to produce and convenient to interpret). The *bar chart*, in addition to providing the closing price (in the form of a tick to the right of the bar), also describes the day's price range in terms of a vertical bar, where the end points indicate the high and low (often these charts also include information on the volume of trade). Such daily charts usually contain around nine months of information.[1] A variant on the bar chart is the Japanese inspired *candle chart*, which superimposes the day's price range onto the day's opening and closing prices. Such charts tend to be very colorful and elegant, with the open–close range drawn with a thick line (the color red is used if the close was higher than the open, whilst black is used when the close is lower than the open). The charts get their candle-like appearance from the superimposition of the price range onto the open–close price range as a thin black line (the candle's wick).[2]

The third type of chart which is commonly use by chartists is the *point-and-figure chart*. The key feature of this type of chart is that it records price changes of a certain magnitude irrespective of how long it takes the price to change (i.e. is the time dimension is ignored). Each entry on the chart represents a price movement of a prespecified amount, referred to as the box size. Up movements are recorded with a cross, whilst down movements are marked with an open circle. Each time the price changes direction, usually by an amount greater than the box size (the "reversal size") a new column is started. So the horizontal axis of a point-and-figure chart is dependent on how sensitive the price is to a change in direction, whilst the vertical scale is determined by the box size (i.e. the number of price units that go to make up a box). The reason for plotting price change in this way (without any time dependence) is that each trader has a view of the price at which he or she will enter the market and will do so once that price is reached, irrespective of how long it takes. An example of a point-and-figure chart for the US dollar–pound sterling exchange rate is given in figure 13.1.

Chartists are primarily interested in tracking the trend in an exchange rate, or indeed other asset prices and, in particular, using charts to determine when the trend is going to be continued or when it is going to be reversed. In fact a number of chart-based indicators have been developed to aid the trader in deciding continuations and reversals of trends. Before we examine such indicators we first say a few words about the concept of a trend. A trend is defined as capturing the overall direction of the market. An uptrend line is defined as joining a series of successively higher lows, while a downtrend line joins three or more lower highs. Often such trends are portrayed as straight lines although they need not be in practice. The penetration of a trend line (or a "trend channel," a pair of parallel lines surrounding the trend line) is often taken to be an indication of a significant change in price direction. Although, as we have argued previously, foreign exchange dealers are generally required to balance their books at the end of a day's trade, they may nevertheless on a succession of days go long, say, in

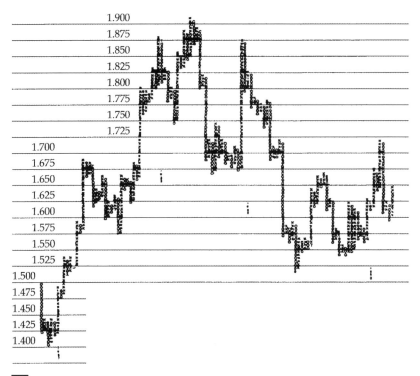

Figure 13.1 A point-and-figure chart: US dollars per pound sterling
Source: Allen, 1990

a particular currency and this can push the price up to levels where it is over-extended and therefore vulnerable to a move in the opposite direction; the currency is "overbought" (similarly a sequence of net short positions could result in a currency being "oversold"). Thus, an individual trading on the basis of, say, an uptrend may want to take into account whether the currency is in fact over-bought or oversold (see, for example, Feeny (1989) for a discussion of a range of such indicators).

In connection with the trend, perhaps the most important chartist concepts are those of *support* and *resistance*. A support price is a level at which the market does not believe the exchange rate can fall through. Therefore once a price which has been following a downward trend reaches this level there will be increased buying of the currency. Similarly, when an exchange rate has been following a rising trend a resistance level is reached when excess selling occurs, forcing the rate back down. If, however, the exchange rate does not obey these laws of motion this may be interpreted by the market as a significant signal. For example, if a previously defined resistance level is penetrated the market may take this as a strong buy signal and indeed once this occurs the role of the resistance level may be reversed (that is, it becomes a support level). The following quote from H. Allen (1990) emphasizes the importance of support and resistance levels:

Considerable "psychological" importance may be attached in the market to support and resistance levels. Looking at the daily financial press will confirm this – currencies are often seen to hover around what the market regards as significant bilateral rates. To quote from the *Financial Times*:

> "Earlier in the day, the dollar had already stalled, having failed to break resistance at DM1.8300" (F.T. 28.6.88);
> "Elsewhere the D-Mark held above a support level of Y71.43 against the yen . . ." (28.6.88);
> "the US currency today broke through what traders regard as the psychologically important levels of DM1.80 and Y130 . . ." (25.6.88).

As illustrated by the last quotation, certain numbers may become focal points for market psychology – with round numbers being particularly renowned for offering support and resistance. Traders cautious of this possibility may tend to avoid placing trading orders right on these round numbers, lest their role as support and resistance levels means that the market price will never quite get there.   (p. 45)

On point-and-figure graphs support and resistance levels stand out as thick black areas of thick boxes.

Having defined a trend, chartists, as we have suggested, are particularly interested in determining price reversals and continuation patterns with respect to the trend. Perhaps the best known reversal pattern, and one regarded as having good predictive powers, is the head-and-shoulders pattern, which is in fact prevalent in all speculative markets. A typical head-and-shoulders pattern is illustrated in figure 13.2, which reveals its classic three-part formation: a large middle peak (the head) with two smaller peaks on either side (the shoulders). This pattern is not regarded as having been formed until the price has closed through the "neckline." There are a number of variations on the head-and-shoulders pattern: the inverse head-and-shoulders is, as the title suggests, an inverted image of the basic head-and-shoulders pattern, which occurs at the bottom of a market; complex (or, perhaps, in a coloquial vein, drunken) head-and-shoulders patterns have two heads or double shoulders. Edwards and Magee (1966) give the classic interpretation of the evolution of the basic head-and-shoulders pattern in terms of a stock that was initially underpriced in the market. In figure 13.2(a) the outline of the classic head-and-shoulders pattern is given and in figure 13.2(b) some data for the deutschmark–dollar exchange rate is plotted, which supposedly indicates a head-and-shoulders pattern.

There are a huge number of other specific patterns which may be detected with either bar chart analysis or point-and-finger graphs. For example, "tops and bottoms," "saucers," "triangles," "price gaps and reversals," and "flags and pennants." For a detailed discussion of these patterns see Edwards and Magee (1966) and for an application to the foreign exchange market see H. Allen (1990).

As most proponents of technical analysis recognize, and indeed as our discussion above illustrates, chartism is basically an art form rather than a scientific method. Some scientific rigour, however, may be injected into technical analysis by the use of mechanical trading rules which can be used to generate precise price signals. Perhaps the most popular of these is the construction of a simple

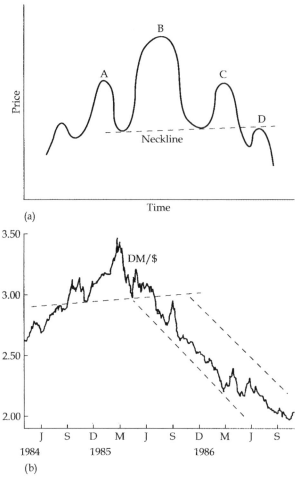

Figure 13.2 The head-and-shoulders reversal pattern: (a) a classic head-and-shoulders pattern; (b) a supposed head and shoulders in the deutschmark–dollar rate (daily data)
Source: Allen, 1990

moving average of the price to capture the underlying trend. Such moving averages are constructed by taking the average of the previous N periods' prices and this can then be plotted on a bar chart, with buy and sell signals being generated when the average crosses the price line. For example, a closing price which turns out to be above the moving-average line would generate a buy signal whilst, conversely, a price below the moving average would generate a sell signal. More complex trading decisions may be taken on the basis of two moving-average plots. Thus a common trading strategy involves buying when the shorter average cuts the longer one from below. Many variants on this kind of cross-over pattern are listed in the literature. Other types of mechanical rules are the overbought/oversold indicators mentioned earlier and the use of filter rules, which are discussed below.

What then of the empirical evidence on the use and success of chartist techniques? In order to assess the extent of use made of chartist techniques in practice, Allen and Taylor (1990) conducted a survey of chief foreign exchange dealers in the London foreign exchange market; they found that a high proportion of dealers used some form of chart analysis in forming their trading decisions. More specifically, Allen and Taylor found that at short horizons (i.e. periods of up to one week) over 90 percent of dealers used some form of chart analysis, and about 60 percent judged charts to be at least as important as fundamentals. Interestingly, as the time horizon was expanded the weight given to fundamentals by the dealers expanded dramatically. Perhaps one of the most interesting aspects of their study is the finding that one or two traders can, solely on the basis of using past price behavior, beat the simple random-walk model in an out-of-sample forecasting context.

Filter rules as tests of chartism

The notion that exchange rate changes signal information about future changes has been confirmed by a variety of filter rule tests. We now consider some of these tests. A particular form of a filter rule test has been usefully summarized by Poole (1967), who defines the exchange rate as the foreign currency price of a unit of domestic currency (and therefore a rise denotes an appreciation of the domestic currency):

> The test is performed by seeing whether a hypothetical speculator could profit from the following scheme: when the rate has risen by x percent from a trough, a speculator buys, when the rate has fallen by x percent from a peak the speculator sells out his long position and sells short as well. The x percent filters out the random fluctuations and allows the hypothetical speculator to identify the trend. If there are genuine trends in the series, the filter analysis will show positive returns for the hypothetical speculators. If trends do not exist, the gross return should be zero. (p. 37)

Using a number of different values for x, Poole constructed a variety of trading rules for the Canadian dollar (1950–62) and for nine currencies from the interwar experience with floating exchange rates (all data are daily), and unearthed high gross returns. Although Poole concluded that this amounted to rejection of the EMH, such a conclusion is erroneous since he did not adjust his filters for interest rates or transactions costs. Logue and Sweeney (1977) compare the Poole strategy with a buy-and-hold strategy for the French franc–US dollar exchange rate in the period from January 1970 to March 1974 (daily data). Of the 14 rules they tried and reported, only one failed to outperform the buy-and-hold strategy (and by a very narrow margin). Logue and Sweeney did account for transactions costs in their study and also argued that taking interest earnings into account would not have changed their conclusions.

A further trading rule study has been conducted by Dooley and Shafer (1976) who test a variety of filters for five currencies (all adjusted for interest rates and transaction costs) for the period March 1973 to September 1975. They find that 1, 3 and 5 percent filters are very profitable for the period; for example, a 1 percent filter rule for the French franc would have yielded an annual return of 16 percent for the sample period 1976–81. Thus if market participants had calculated Dooley–Shafer rules for the early floating experience, the inference is that they could have been applied to the post-1976 period to make substantial profits. One problem with this conclusion is that no statistical measure of the significance of such profits is provided and also no adjustment for the potential riskiness of the investments is made.[3]

Although the above filter results are suggestive of market inefficiency they do not conclusively indicate it. This is because the profits reported in the above studies have not been adjusted for the inherent riskiness of the positions taken. It is therefore unclear if the reported profitability of the studies simply reflects the reward for taking a risky position. A number of researchers, however, have attempted to incorporate riskiness into their computations of trading rule models.

In calculating his filter rules Sweeney (1986) uses a capital asset pricing model to adjust for the inherent riskiness of the investments and finds that statistically significant profits still exist. Bilson (1981) uses equation (12.5) to define a simple forecasting rule which he uses to generate a series for expected profits (he is careful to use information which would have been actually available to agents). It is demonstrated that predictable profits could have been made for the period from February 1980 to January 1981[4] and, on the basis of a mean–variance framework, that the profit–risk ratio is too large to be accounted for by either risk aversion or transaction costs. Hodrick and Srivastava (1986) repeat Bilson's analysis for a longer time span, and although they also report favorable risk–return trade-offs (somewhat less favorable than Bilson's) they argue that such trade-offs appear to be quite volatile and sensitive to the model used to form expected profits and their variances. Using a variety of forecasting equations, Longworth et al. (1983) produce profits which are supportive of Bilson's initial conclusion.

One of the first studies to propose an empirical test of chartist behaviour formally was that of MacDonald and Young (1986), who derive a time-series representation of the exchange rate based on three trading principles generally used by technical analysts. These are the "overbought"/"oversold" principle, which relates to the level of the exchange rate (a currency is often regarded as overbought when its price is high relative to a moving-average trend); the evolution of an exchange rate in accordance with bull and bear trends (a currency on a bull trend signals to agents that they should buy the currency); and overreaction and correction, whereby traders overreact to news and then "correct" by moving in the opposite direction by a smaller amount. One interesting feature of this study is the finding that the trading rules model outperforms, on an in-sample basis, the forward exchange rate as a forecasting device. To the extent, therefore, that exchange rates are being driven by some form of trading rule strategy and forward rates are simply a reflection of interest rates, it is perhaps not surprising that the forward premium is such a poor predictor of the exchange rate change (we shall return to this issue below).

A very interesting and novel model of the exchange rate which incorporates chartism behavior is that of Frankel and Froot (1990). Their model was motivated by the dramatic appreciation of the US dollar from 1981 to 1985. Although this could be reasonably well explained by fundamentals in the early part of the appreciation, such fundamentals could not explain the last part of the appreciation (in particular the final 20 percent of the total appreciation). They propose that the dollar's behavior in this period, and indeed more generally the behavior of any currency, may be explained by a combination of chartist and fundamentalist behavior. In a stylized way, they argue that the exchange rate may be thought of as being determined by portfolio managers, who are viewed as the agents who take positions in the market. Portfolio managers, in turn, form their expectations as a weighted average of two "in-house" groups who form their expectations on the basis of chartist techniques or in terms of fundamentals:

$$\Delta s^m_{t+1} = \omega_t \Delta s^f_{t+1} + (1 - \omega_t)\Delta s^c_{t+1} \tag{13.6}$$

where Δs^m_{t+1} denotes the expected rate of change of the spot rate expected by porfolio managers, Δs^f_{t+1} and Δs^c_{t+1} are similarly defined variables for fundamentalists and chartists, respectively, and ω_t denotes the weight given to fundamentalist views (notice that this weight is time dependent). Using survey-based expectations Frankel and Froot demonstrate that throughout the period of the dollar's appreciation less and less weight was put on the views of fundamentalists (i.e. ω became smaller and smaller) and more and more emphasis was placed on chartists' expectations.

The evidence from the trading rules literature discussed in this section suggests that the reason why the forward exchange rate appears to be a sub-optimal predictor of the future spot rate is ineffective information processing by agents. Indeed the consistency with which researchers uncover potentially exploitable profits is in marked contrast to the difficulty which researchers have had in estimating the risk premium (see chapter 12). In order to shed further light on which of these two competing views is correct we turn to the literature which uses survey data to capture agents' expectations.

13.2.1 Deterministic chaos

The predictability of exchange rate changes that filter rule tests pick up has been reinforced by work on the time-series properties of exchange rates which suggests that there is substantial non-linear dependence in high frequency exchange rate movements (see Hseih, 1989). These kinds of results are not inconsistent with the common assertion that exchange rates follow random-walk processes (Mussa, 1979a), because the latter usually rely on data of a different observational frequency (usually monthly) and use testing methods which are not well-suited to unearthing time dependence in exchange rate movements (particularly non-linear time dependence). Indeed a visual inspection of the logarithmic change of an economic time series, such as an exchange rate, may indicate that the series is random, even though the application of sophisticated statistical techniques reveals substantial persistence. The observed time dependence in exchange rate changes is, in fact, consistent with time dependence in the movements of other asset prices. For example, Poterba and Summers (1988) and Fama and French (1988) have noted that stock returns (effectively the logarithmic difference of stock prices) exhibit considerable persistence (for a detailed analysis of the persistence of a number of asset prices, including the exchange rate, see Cutler et al. 1990).

Such persistence in asset price movements may be interpreted in a number of ways, such as those considered in this and the last chapter. However, a recent strand in the financial economics literature, which has its origins in the natural sciences, interprets the (non-linear) dependence as evidence of *chaotic processes*. So-called *deterministic chaos* is when a non-linear dynamic system, which is deterministic, produces a variable such as the exchange rate which visually appears to be random but is in fact completely deterministic (i.e. the visual dependence will not reveal any non-linear dependence in the data). A better flavor for chaos may be derived from some of the standard definitions in the literature. For example, Devaney (1989) defines a chaotic system as (a) being unpredictable, (b) being indecomposable and (c) having an element of regularity. Baumol and Benhabib (1989) define chaos as a condition "in which a dynamic mechanism that is very simple and deterministic yields a time path so complicated that it will pass *most* standard tests of randomness" (emphasis added). Baumol and Quandt (1985) define chaos as "a fully deterministic behavior pattern which is, *in at least some respects*, indistinguishable from a random process" (emphasis added). A number of methods to test for the existence of chaos have been proposed in the literature (a useful summary is given by Hsieh) and these are generally of the form of tests for non-linear dependence in the price of the asset.

De Grauwe and Dewachter (1990) demonstrate that the fundamentalist–chartist model, summarized in (13.6) below, implemented with the sticky-price monetary model of the exchange rate, can produce very complex exchange rate behavior which appears to be random but nevertheless is generated from a deterministic process. The application of chaotic techniques to modeling exchange rate movements appears promising, although the methodology as applied to asset prices is still at a relatively early stage.

*13.3 Survey Data, Expectations, and Risk

We have now examined a number of explanations for the failure of the efficiency hypothesis in the forward foreign exchange market, and such explanations fall into one of two groupings: those concerned with risk and those concerned with a failure, in some sense, of the expectations component of the joint hypothesis. But the problem with each of these explanations is that, in order to invoke one, the researcher must (normally) *assume* that the other component of the joint hypothesis is valid. For example, Fama's interpretation of a negative β_1 coefficient reflecting time-varying risk premiums, discussed in section 12.4, relies on the assumption that rationality is maintained. Clearly one would like to be able to conduct *single* hypothesis tests of the joint hypothesis in order to discern which component of the joint is at fault. A number of researchers (see Dominguez, 1986; MacDonald, 1990a; MacDonald and Torrance, 1988a, 1990; Frankel and Froot, 1989) have argued that this is possible if an independent measure of expectations is available to the researcher. Thus in moving from (12.1) to (12.4) the researcher has to assume rationality of expectations. If a separate measure of expectations exists then the rationality of such expectations is testable and also the construction of the risk premium is facilitated since, by definition, it is the difference between the forward rate and the expected spot rate.

In section 12.1 we mentioned the survey that *Euromoney* has conducted since the mid-1970s; such surveys are conducted annually. However, since the inception of the *Euromoney* studies a number of other bodies have started to produce high-quality surveys of market participant's expectations of a variety of asset prices, such as the exchange rate. Indeed, there now exists a variety of highquality exchange rate survey data bases. As should be clear from our earlier discussions these data bases are potentially very attractive to researchers because they offer an independent measure of expectations, and a number of important studies have resulted from their wide availability. We now briefly discuss some of these studies and indicate what they imply for the apparent finding of foreign exchange market inefficiency.[5]

One way of motivating survey-based tests of the EMH is to consider again the coefficient β_0 from equation (12.5). By noting that $\Delta s_{t+k} = \Delta s_{t+k}^e + u_{t+k}$, this coefficient may be written as

$$\beta_0 = \frac{\text{cov}[u_{t+k}, (f-s)_t] + \text{cov}[\Delta s_{t+k}^e, (f-s)_t]}{\text{var}[(f-s)_t]} \tag{13.7}$$

On manipulating (13.7) β_0 may be written as equal to unity minus a term, β_0^{re}, arising from any failure of rational expectations and minus a further term, β_0^λ, arising from the presence of a risk premium (see Frankel and Froot (1986) for further details):

$$\beta_0 = 1 - \beta_0^{re} - \beta_0^\lambda \tag{13.8}$$

where

$$\beta_0^{re} = \frac{\text{cov}[u_{t+k}, (f-s)_t]}{\text{var}[(f-s)_t]}$$

and

$$\beta_0^\lambda = \frac{\text{var}(\lambda_t) + \text{cov}[\Delta s_{t+k}^e, \lambda_t]}{\text{var}[(f-s)_t]}$$

The availability of survey data means that both β_0^{re} and β_0^λ can be distinguished, and therefore in principle it should be possible to discern whether rejection of the null is due to risk or irrationality. Thus β_0^{re} may be estimated from a regression of the form

$$s_{t+k}^e - s_{t+k} = \alpha + \beta_0^{re}(f - s)_t + v_t \qquad (13.9)$$

the intuition being that if agents are rational there should be no relationship between the forecast error and information available in period t, such as the forward premium, and β_0^{re} should equal zero. The parameter β_0^λ may be estimated from a regression of the form

$$s_{t+k}^e - s_t = \gamma_0 + \gamma_1^\lambda(f - s)_t + u_t \qquad (13.10)$$

as $1 - \hat{\gamma}_1^\lambda$. Again the intuition here is that if the forward premium consists only of the expected exchange rate change, $\hat{\gamma}_1^\lambda$ should be insignificantly different from unity (conversely, if only a small component of the forward premium reflects expectations – the largest component reflecting a risk premium $-\hat{\gamma}_1^\lambda$ will be close to zero).

Recently a number of researchers in the USA and the UK have used survey data to obtain estimates of β_0^{re} and β_0^λ. Do their findings shed any light on the rejection of the joint null, noted earlier? Frankel and Froot (1989) estimate (13.9) and (13.10) using a variety of survey data sets (AMEX, *The Economist* and Money Market Services (MMS), (US)) for a period covering the early 1980s (the data sets are pooled across a number of currencies). The main conclusion to emerge from this work is that the unbiasedness proposition fails both because of deviations of β_0^{re} from unity and also because of the existence of a *constant* risk premium (i.e. a significant estimate of γ_0 in (13.10)); the hypothesis that γ_1^λ equals unity cannot be rejected (and therefore they conclude that the risk premium is not of the time-varying variety). In contrast to Frankel and Froot, MacDonald and Torrance (1988a, 1989) find, using survey data generated by Money Market Services (UK) Ltd, that the unbiasedness proposition fails both because of deviations of β_0^{re} from unity and because of the existence of a time-varying risk premium (i.e. estimates of γ_1^λ which differ significantly from unity). Indeed the estimates of the risk premium γ_1^λ reported by MacDonald and Torrance are much larger than estimates obtained from standard mean-variance models (see, for example, Frankel, 1982c).

Dominguez (1986) tests the efficiency of MMS (US) one-week, two-week, one-month, and three-month forecast data for the US dollar against the UK pound, the German mark, the Swiss franc, and the Japanese yen for the period 1983–5. Dominguez reports significant evidence of biasedness and violation of the error orthogonality condition. MacDonald (1990a) uses MMS (UK) survey data to estimate a number of error orthogonality conditions and finds that variables (particularly forward premiums) in the period-t information set remained unexploited.[6]

Canova and Ito (1988) use a weekly vector autoregressive (VAR) model (sample period: 1979, week 1 to 1985, week 52) to generate a series for the expected Japanese yen–US dollar exchange rate. The main purpose is to use this series as an alternative and independent means of generating the risk premium term. Of course, the procedure relies crucially on the variables entering the conditioning information set. Canova and Ito use Japanese and US stock prices and short-term interest rates and the yen–dollar spot rate in their VAR model.[7] Amongst their results, Canova and Ito show that their generated expectational series is much more accurate than the equivalent survey series described in Frankel and Froot (1989), they confirm the findings of Fama (1984) and Hodrick and Srivastava (1986) regarding the negative correlation between the risk premium and the expected appreciation of the yen,[8] and they also demonstrate that the time series of the risk premium is time varying and non-stationary. From the perspective of the survey data literature the import of the Canova and Ito study would seem to be that using simple mechanical forecasting formulae would have enabled them to improve their exchange rate forecasts.

The above survey-based studies all utilize consensus survey measures, such as the mean or median responses. This is fine if agents' forecasts are homogeneous, as they should be if the rational expectations hypothesis is correct. However, if forecasters form heterogeneous expectations then concentration on a consensus measure of the survey may miss important insights into how agents process information. Since the existence of heterogeneous expectations is central to the market microstructure hypothesis we introduce that topic here as a way of motivating survey-based studies which exploit disaggregate data.

13.4 Market Microstructure

As we saw in chapter 9 there is considerable scepticism in some quarters regarding the usefulness of macroeconomic fundamentals in explaining exchange rate movements. This has led a number of researchers to advocate moving away from a macro-based analysis of the foreign exchange market to one which is based on the market microstructure (see, for example, Frankel and Rose (1995) and Flood and Rose (1999)). By this is meant focusing on an array of institutional aspects of the foreign exchange market – price formation, the matching of buyers and sellers (i.e. market makers and brokers), and optimal dealer pricing policies. An alternative way of motivating this literature is to say that on a day-to-day basis we observe approximately $1 trillion volume of gross trading in foreign exchange markets, 80 percent of which is between market makers alone. *Annual* world trade flow is $4 trillion. It would seem difficult to explain this huge volume of trade in foreign exchange in terms of the standard list of fundamentals.

In standard macro-based exchange rate models, such as the flex-price monetary model considered in chapter 9, the assumption of homogeneous expectations is central – as we have seen this is usually expressed as $E(.\,|\,I_t)$. At the heart of the market microstructure literature is the idea that the huge volumes of trade that we observe can only be explained by the interaction of *heterogeneous* agents. Such heterogeneity may arise from a number of sources, such as differences in information, beliefs, preferences, and wealth. But who are these heterogeneous agents? A description of a particular market is the crucial first step in understanding the efficiency of pricing and allocation in that market, and is a key element in the market microstructure literature (see, for example, Flood (1991) for an excellent survey).

The foreign exchange market is dominated by *market-makers* who trade directly with each other (60 to 80 percent) and indirectly through *brokers* (15 to 35 percent). The market makers are essentially the commercial banks (i.e. they represent the inter-bank market). *Customers*, who make up 5 percent of the market, usually go through banks since their credit-worthiness cannot be detected by brokers. Therefore the foreign exchange market combines two disparite auction structures for the same commodity: the inter-bank direct market and the brokered market. The former market may be thought of as a decentralized, continuous, open bid, double auction market (some participants provide prices on both sides of the market as reflected in the bid–ask spread). Brokers represent a quasi-centralized, continuous, limit-book, single auction market. As Flood (1991) points out there is some evidence to suggest that the degree of centralization of a market can have an important bearing on market performance. For example, a centralized brokerage type market is thought to benefit dealers because it ensures orders are executed according to price priority. Indeed the efficiency gains of a centralized market, and the associated economies of scale, would lead one to expect a natural monopoly arising for brokerage services. That this has not occurred in the foreign exchange market is something of a puzzle.

The other efficiency aspect of the market relates to the concept of "temporal consolidation," which concerns how rapidly trade actually takes place. As we have noted, the foreign exchange market is a continuous market, and in such a market trading occurs at its own pace as and when it is required. In contrast, in a call market trading occurs at pre-appointed times (the calls) with orders arriving retained until the next call. Compared to the standard textbook Walrasian tâtonnement model – the classic call equilibrium model – a continuous trading system is thought to alter allocations, the process of price discovery, and the ultimate equilibrium price relative. This is essentially because with continuous trading, transactions which occur at the start of the trading process (i.e. the trading day, say) will satisfy some consumers and producers, thereby causing shifts in supply and demand which can affect later consumers. In contrast, though, the periodic batching associated with a call market can also have a deleterious effect on investors' decision making and associated allocations. Hence in such a market investors are prepared to pay a *liquidity premium* to trade immediately. Similarly, the existence of periodic calls can delay price information, thereby imparting price uncertainty into the decision-making process. In sum, the two extremes of a continuous market and call market represent a trade-off between informational and allocative efficiency, respectively.

Another important aspect of the market microstructure concerns how agents communicate prices. In an "open bid" market, offers to buy or sell at prespecified price are announced to all in the market at the same time. At the opposite extreme there is "sealed bid" market in which orders are known only to those placing the order. Although the foreign exchange market more closely resembles an open bid market its form of price communication is in fact somewhere between the two extremes. For example, although direct trading in the foreign exchange market allows any individual to contact a market maker for a price quote, the bilateral nature of trade means that there cannot be a simultaneous provision of all market makers' quotes. This raises the possibility of arbitrage opportunities since it may be possible to find two market makers' bid–ask quotes which do not overlap. Further, in the indirect segment of the market brokers hold "limit books" which contain a record of quoted bid–ask spreads, these are not open for public inspection and only the best bids are revealed. Clearly knowledge of the concealed limit orders could be of potential speculative value to market makers: for example, an unbalanced book may suggest a price movement in a particular direction. Clearly the costs involved in finding the best quote are probably suboptimal from an efficiency perspective and market participants are viewed as willing to pay a liquidity premium to reduce search costs; this premium is usually reflected in the market-maker's spread.

The market microstructure literature is not, however, limited to simply describing a structure of the market, such as the foreign exchange market. Rather it goes beyond this to examine issues such as the determination of both market makers' and brokers' bid–ask spreads, where variables such as inventory and the quantity transacted (i.e. volume) are seen as crucially important. An overview of these topics is beyond the purview of this chapter (see Flood (1991) for a further discussion).[9] Instead, for the remainder of this section, we focus on an assumption which is central to the market microstructure literature, namely the existence of heterogeneous expectations. We utilize the extant survey-based literature to get a feel for this issue.

Disaggregate survey data has been used in essentially one of two ways to gain a perspective on market microstructure issues. The first group of tests try to determine if there are indeed different patterns of expectations formation among different classes or groups of agents, while the second seeks to relate a measure of heterogeneity, such as the dispersion of expectations, to a variety of "indicators" of market microstructure, such as volume, volatility, and the bid–ask spread.

The first set of tests usually focus on a variant of the test first proposed by Ito (1990). According to this test, individual-specific effects emanate from a constant bias and not from the use of different modeling techniques. For example, suppose individual j forms a forecast at time t and this consists of two parts: X_t, based on publicly available information, I_t, and an individual effect, g_j. For a given forecast horizon the expected exchange rate for the individual will be the sum of these two parts plus an individual random disturbances term u_{jt}:

$$s_{j,t}^e = X_t + g_j + u_{j,t}. \tag{13.11}$$

The average forecast at time t is then:

$$s_{A,t}^e = X_t + g_A + u_{A,t}. \tag{13.12}$$

Normalizing such that g_A equals zero and subtracting (13.12) from (13.11) we get:

$$s_{j,t}^e - s_{A,t}^e = g_j + [u_{j,t} - u_{A,t}]. \tag{13.13}$$

The *individual effect* in (13.13) may be estimated simply by regressing the difference between an individual and average forecast on to a constant term: a non-zero g_j indicates that an individual's forecasts are biased compared to those of the average forecaster. From an empirical perspective the attractive feature of (13.13) is that it is unnecessary for the econometrician to know the exact structure of the conditional information set used by agents, X_t. However, a so-called *idiosyncratic effect* may be obtained by incorporating a piece of relevant publicly available information, such as the forward premium (fp_t), into the regression:

$$s_{jt}^e - s_{At}^e = g_t + [\beta_j - \beta_A]fp_t + [u_{jt} - u_{At}]. \tag{13.14}$$

An idiosyncratic effect (that is, an individual specific weight placed on a publicly available piece of information) would be picked up if $\beta_j - \beta_A \neq 0$.

Ito (1990), MacDonald and Marsh (1996) and Chionis and MacDonald (1997) use the framework given in (13.13) and (13.14) to examine the importance of heterogeneity in the foreign exchange market. For illustrative purposes we take the results of MacDonald and Marsh. They used a dissaggregate panel data set consisting of the expectations of 150 professional forecasters located in the financial centers of the G7. The survey data was provided by Consensus Economics of London and related to two forecast horizons, 3 and 12 months ahead, for the US dollar bilateral exchange rates of the mark, yen, and pound sterling. In sum, MacDonald and Marsh show that there is considerable evidence of both individual and idiosyncratic effects at both horizons. Across the two currency horizons and three exchange rates, the percentage of the total number of forecasters who exhibit a significant individual effect ranges from 32 to 47 percent. The other studies which focus on variants of (13.13) and (13.14) come to similar conclusions.[10]

The existence of heterogeneous expectations formation amongst foreign exchange forecasters has also been confirmed in studies which examine the unbiasedness of expectations (see MacDonald (1992b)) and the expectations formation processes of individuals (see Benassy-Quere, Larribeau, and MacDonald (1999)). Having established that the expectations of agents are indeed heterogeneous, the next question to address is: does such heterogeneity drive indicators of market microstructure such as volume and volatility? A number of survey-based papers, relying on some form of Granger causality testing, have answered this question in the affirmative (see Frankel and Froot (1990), MacDonald and Marsh (1996) and Chionis and MacDonald (1997)).

 ## *13.5 The News Approach to Exchange Rate Modeling

In this section we shift the emphasis of our discussion somewhat by introducing the "news" approach to modeling the exchange rate. Our main reason for addressing this topic here is that it may be viewed as an extension of the efficient markets model considered in this and the previous section and because it emphasizes the importance of expectational revisions in explaining why the forward exchange rate may be a poor predictor of the future exchange rate (but it does *not* purport to explain why the forward rate is a *biased* predictor of the future spot rate).

The new information or "news" approach may be illustrated in the following way. If the vector z_t contains all variables – suitably transformed to induce stationarity[11] – relevant for the process of exchange rate determination (thus we are completely agnostic about the appropriate menu of fundamentals) then our equation for the evolution of the exchange rate change is

$$\Delta s_{t+1} = \gamma z_{t+1} + \varphi_{t+1} \tag{13.15}$$

where φ_t is a serially uncorrelated error (and reflects the usual kinds of error imparted in any modeling strategy). In forming their (rational) expectations agents will use this model and hence their expected change in the exchange rate from t to $t+1$ will be

$$\Delta s_{t+1}^e = \gamma z_{t+1}^e \tag{13.16}$$

On subtracting (12.16) from (12.15) we obtain

$$\Delta s_{t+1} - \Delta s_{t+1}^e = \gamma(z_{t+1} - z_{t+1}^e) + \varphi_{t+1} \tag{13.17}$$

which says that the error in forecasting the exchange rate change is driven by new information about the fundamental determinants of the exchange rate and a random error term (which if the fundamentals model is the true model may be interpreted as measurement error and is likely to be small). On using the definition of the forward premium from (12.1a) we may rewrite (13.17) as

$$\Delta s_{t+1} = fp_t + \gamma(z_{t+1} - z_{t+1}^e) - \lambda_t + \varphi_{t+1} \tag{13.18}$$

which simply reinforces the point made above that in periods when there is a lot of new information about fundamentals (i.e. the term in parentheses is large) there will not be a close correspondence between Δs_{t+1} and fp_t. At least two problems confront a researcher interested in implementing the news approach. First, he or she has to take a position on the variables entering the fundamentals vector. As we shall see, most researchers in defining the fundamentals set use some version of the asset approach to the exchange rate, such as the monetary approach to the exchange rate. Second, some method has to be utilized in order to generate the news. How then do researchers deal with these specific issues and, more generally, how well supported is the news approach by the empirical evidence?

 ## *13.6 Empirical Studies of the News Approach

The first news study was by Frenkel (1981a) and he used time-series methods to generate the news. Frenkel estimated a news equation of the form

$$s_t = a_0 + b_1 f_{t-1} + b_2(z_1 - z_1^e) + w_t \qquad (13.19)$$

where the fundamentals vector z_t was defined to include only relative interest rates (i.e. $z_t = (i - i^*)_t$) and w_t is assumed to be a white noise process.[12] Equation (13.19) was estimated for the US dollar–UK pound, US dollar–French franc and US dollar–German mark exchange rates, over the period from June 1973 to June 1979, using an autoregression to generate the expected interest rate series. In all of Frenkel's estimated equations b_2 is positive, but only in the case of one equation (for the US dollar–UK pound), given below, is b_2 statistically significant (at the 5 percent level):

$$s_t = \underset{(0.02)}{0.031} + \underset{(0.02)}{0.959 f_{t-1}} + \underset{(0.18)}{0.432[(i - i^*)_t - (i - i^*)_i^e]} \qquad (13.20)$$

$$R^2 = 0.96 \qquad DW = 1.78$$

(estimation technique, instrumental variables; standard errors in parentheses)

The positive association between the exchange rate and interest rate news is asserted to be supportive of the FLMA. An autoregressive approach to generating the news is also favored by Edwards (1982), who estimates a news representation of the FLMA (i.e. the unanticipated exchange rate is related to unanticipated money supplies, income and interest rates) for the same currencies as Frenkel (and also the Italian lira–US dollar) over the period from June 1973 to September 1979. Edwards reports results which are reasonably supportive of the FLMA news reduced forms in that the coefficients on some variables are statistically significant and correctly signed. Copeland (1984) also estimates a news representation of the FLMA for the pound sterling–US dollar rate (using autoregressive models to generate news) and reports results which, after accounting for potential simultaneity bias, are reasonably supportive of the approach. MacDonald (1985b) uses autoregressive models to generate news for an FLMA reduced form from the 1920s experience with floating exchange rates; results which are generally supportive of the news approach in that the equations exhibit a reasonable explanatory power and the coefficients on the news variables are well determined are reported.

Bomhoff and Korteweg (1983) also use a time-series methodology to generate the news, but their approach is more sophisticated than those discussed hitherto in that they allow the parameters in the estimated news equation to be time dependent. Using a multistate Kalman filter, news about relative money supplies, income and the price of oil is generated for six currencies over the period 1973–9 (quarterly data). Bomhoff and Korteweg summarize their evidence in the following way:

> Between 16 and 60 percent of the variation of the unexpected rate of change of the various spot rates can be explained by the current and lagged effects of randomly arriving new information. . . . Furthermore, most "news" terms appear to be correctly signed and significant at the 90 percent level or better. Interestingly, "news" affects the current exchange rate with long lags; in some instances there are lags of over

one year before the domestic or foreign monetary impulses have their effect on spot rates. (p. 174)

Given that Mussa (1979a) has suggested that a successful model of the exchange rate should be able to explain at least 10 percent of the quarter to quarter exchange rate change, Bomhoff and Korteweg (1983) regard their results as offering considerable support to the news approach.

A number of researchers have implemented the news approach using more information than simply the past history of the variable being forecast. In particular, Branson (1983), Edwards (1983) and MacDonald (1983a, b) use either vector autoregressions or a version of Barro's (1978) methodology to generate the news.

A version of equation (13.19) has been estimated by MacDonald (1983a) for a selection of six currencies against the US dollar (the Canadian dollar, the Austrian schilling, the UK pound, the French franc, the German mark, and the Swiss franc) over the period 1972.I–1979.IV using the ZSURE estimator. The variables entering the z vector are the growth of home and foreign money supplies and news about these variables is generated by regressing them on variables such as the inflation rate, income, interest rates, the current account surplus and the budget deficit (along the lines suggested by Barro (1978)) and retrieving the residuals. The reduced form exchange rate equation tested is

$$s_{t+1} - f_t = a + b_1 \sum_{i=1}^{3} u_{t+1-i} + b_2 \sum_{i=1}^{3} u^*_{t+1-i} + \varphi_{t+1} \tag{13.21}$$

where u denotes the money growth residual (i.e. the news). Equation (13.21) may be obtained from (13.18) by subtracting fp_t from both the right- and left-hand sides and by assuming that the risk premium term is zero. Following the FLMA, it is expected that domestic monetary news is positive and statistically significant and the foreign news term is significantly negative; it is further expected that the lagged news terms should not have a significant role to play in determining the current forecasting error. MacDonald (1983b) implements the approach for three currencies from the interwar floating period (monthly data, February 1921 to May 1925). A selection of the results from the two periods is reported in table 13.1.

Although a number of coefficients are significantly different from zero in this table, notice that many are wrongly signed, suggesting that an unanticipated increase in home money results in an exchange rate appreciation. Another interesting feature of the studies by MacDonald was the finding that lagged news terms were statistically significant (in some cases lag $t - 4$ was significant). Although publication lags could explain some of the significant lagged news terms (perhaps at lag 1) the rest of the significant lagged news terms are perhaps harder to rationalize (see MacDonald (1988b) for a discussion). They may for example reflect some kind of expectational error, as discussed previously, or they may be picking up a time-varying risk premium. Interestingly, when MacDonald (1983b) used interest rate news in the interwar news equations, more promising results, broadly supportive of the monetary approach, were reported.

Table 13.1 Monetary news and the exchange rate in two periods of floating exchange rates: $s_{t+1} - f_t = b_0 + b_1 u_{t+1} + b_2 u^*_{t+1}$

Exchange rate	Time period	b_0	b_1	b_2	Estimation technique
Pound–dollar[a]	1972.1–1979	0.047	−0.156	0.172	ZSURE
		(0.60)	(1.06)	(0.14)	
Franc–dollar[a]	1972.1–1979	−0.003	−0.291	−1.155	ZSURE
		(0.38)	(0.46)	(1.02)	
Mark–dollar[a]	1972.1–1979	−0.015	−2.017	3.173	ZSURE
		(1.85)	(3.27)	(2.68)	
Dollar–pound	February 1921–May 1925	−0.364	0.071	0.003	OLS
		(2.57)	(2.45)	(1.11)	
Franc–dollar	February 1921–May 1925	0.059	0.497	−3.854	OLS
		(1.15)	(1.06)	(0.49)	
Franc–pound	February 1921–May 1925	0.013	1.623	0.070	OLS
		(1.17)	(1.60)	(0.90)	

[a] The original reported results included lagged news items; t ratios are in parentheses.
Source: MacDonald, 1983a, b

In an attempt to implement the portfolio balance approach in a news context, Branson (1983) models news about money supplies, the current account and price levels as residuals from vector autoregressions (the unanticipated measure of the exchange rate is generated in a similar way). Branson's news approach is implemented by cross-correlating the exchange rate residual separately with each of the relevant news variables. For the exchange rates studied, the results are found to be supportive of the porfolio balance view since the current account and relative price terms generally have the correct sign; the money news signs are somewhat more ambiguous because of the simultaneity of money that existed during the estimation period.

In a somewhat separate news literature from that outlined above, a number of researchers regress the *actual* exchange rate change on news about whether monetary authorities in the USA and UK have maintained their monetary targets (where the news is generated using survey data). This is illustrated by the following equation:

$$s^a_t - \hat{s}_t = a_0 + a_1(\dot{m}^a_t - \dot{m}^e_t) + w_t \tag{13.22}$$

where $\dot{m}^a_t$ denotes the announcement of how much monetary growth has overshot its target, m^e denotes the expected monetary overshoot recorded immediately before the announcement, s^a_t denotes the log of the spot rate at the time of the announcement and $\hat{s}_t$ denotes the log of the spot rate immediately before the announcement. The $\dot{m}^e_t$ term is taken to be the median value of a survey of money market operators conducted in both the USA and the UK by MMS. Although, for obvious reasons, this literature cannot be thought of as a test of the EMH (the use of the actual exchange rate change precludes this) it is nevertheless believed to be useful in discriminating between market participants' beliefs about the future course of monetary policy (see Cornell (1983) for a further discussion).

For example, if market participants expect a monetary overshoot – i.e. $\dot{m}^a - \dot{m}^e > 0$ – to be reversed in the future they will expect a tightening of monetary policy, an increase in the expected real interest rate and an appreciation of the currency on the announcement day: the estimate of a_1 should be negative (much as in the sticky-price monetary approach). This is referred to as the policy anticipation effect in the literature – see Urich and Wachtel (1981). If, however, agents expect the overshoot to be an indicator of future monetary laxity they will revise upwards their expectations of future inflation and, much as in the FLMA model, the exchange rate should depreciate: the estimate of a_1 should be positive. This effect is referred to as the expected inflation effect. For the USA and the UK, the evidence (see, *inter alia*, Cornell, 1983; Engel and Frankel, 1984; MacDonald and Torrance, 1989) strongly supports the view that an overshoot of the monetary target is expected to be reversed by a future tightening of monetary policy.

The above results suggest that the news approach to the determination of the exchange rate is reasonably well supported by the data, and future research on this topic should usefully extend the range of news terms considered and the methods of generating the news. Nevertheless, a difficulty remains: as Davidson (1985) points out, the volatility of exchange rates appears to be greater than the volatility of the conventional news items. This finding is supported by the literature on variance bounds tests (see chapter 9) which demonstrates that the volatility of the kinds of variables used in empirical news studies is much less than the volatility of exchange rates (this finding corresponds to that in the stock market literature which indicates that stock prices are more volatile than dividends). How can this be explained? It may be possible to supplement the news approach in a number of ways.

First of all it is quite possible that non-quantifiable news elements, such as political announcements and rumours, dominate the quantifiable elements which researchers use in their news models. By their very nature these elements cannot be captured in the kinds of models discussed in this section.

Second, as discussed in detail in chapter 9, high relative volatility of exchange rates may be due to the presence of rational speculative bubbles.

A third rationalization for the greater volatility of exchange rates relative to the news is that market participants may be using a different economic model from that prescribed by international economists. It is relatively easy to demonstrate that the use of the wrong economic model can introduce greater exchange rate variability than the use of the "correct" economic model (see Dornbusch (1980b) for a further discussion). Even if agents possess the "correct" economic model, they may be swayed by fashions as to which variables are "newsworthy". For example, in one period current account news may be fashionable, in the next it may be fiscal or monetary discipline. This brings us neatly to the noise-trader view of the determination of asset prices.

13.7 The Noise-trader Paradigm

In the light of a variety of empirical studies mentioned in this and the last chapter it could be argued that the EMH has been seriously undermined as a way of thinking about the determination of asset prices like exchange rates, and an alternative paradigm which presents a more realistic portrayal of the behavior of investors is required. In fact the widely-noted rejection of the EMH for foreign exchange markets is paralleled by a similar rejection in the stock market literature and this has led a number of prominent financial economists to advocate replacement of the EMH with the so-called noise-trader or "fads" model. This seems an appropriate juncture at which to introduce this model.

In the stock market literature, a large number of researchers have demonstrated that actual stock prices are too volatile relative to their fundamentals to be consistent with the efficient processing of information (see the summary in MacDonald and Taylor (1991d)). Casual empiricism and, in particular, the dramatic worldwide bull market in stocks in the 1980s and Black Monday in October 1987 have led a number of commentators to conclude that stock prices are not the outcome of rational maximizing behavior but rather the expression of market psychology, unrelated to fundamentals (both types of empirical evidence – the formal and the casual – are presented in Shiller's (1990) excellent book). This view, which goes back at least to Keynes, has recently been formally articulated into a model which many researchers now regard as the alternative paradigm which replaces the EMH. This new paradigm is labelled the noise-trader model. The model is in fact an attempt to combine the technical analysis behavior that we discussed in a previous section, and which is known to characterize the trading behavior of agents, with a more traditional view of economic behavior based on rational maximizing behavior. Since this model has general applicability to the determination of all asset prices, we discuss it here in fairly general terms.

The noise-trader model relies on two groups of agents. The "smart money" agents are assumed to be maximizing rational individuals who base their trade largely, although not exclusively, on fundamentals. The other group, the "noise-traders," are assumed to display irrational behavior. Their trades are based on noisy information which is generally unrelated to economic fundamentals. The interaction of these two groups can create asset prices which are far away from their fundamental values. To see this let us look at the two groups in a little more detail.

The essence of this model is that the actions of noise-traders push asset prices, like exchange rates, far away from their fundamental values. If, as we have mentioned, smart money agents operate in a rational maximizing way on the basis of fundamentals, one would suppose that their actions would prevent the exchange rate from ever moving away from its fundamental value. However, the noise-trader model is one in which risk plays a crucial role, especially with respect to the behavior of smart money. In particular, such individuals are constrained from pushing, or arbitraging, an exchange rate back to its fundamental value once it has moved away owing, specifically, to two types of risk.

Fundamental risk arises when an exchange rate is overpriced in relation to fundamentals. In this instance smart money should short the currency in the expectation that the price will fall back to fundamentals. However, uncertainty is introduced into the decision-making process because some favorable piece of news may come along which suggests that the price should go on rising. Fear of such a loss will limit the arbitrageur's original position and keeps the activity of short selling from driving the price all the way down to the fundamental value. *Unpredictability of the future asset price* is another source of risk that limits short selling in much the same way as in the previous example. Therefore if stock market prices are currently rising and indeed overpriced the investor may decide to sell the stock, but if the market becomes even more overpriced he or she will lose out even more in the future if he or she has made the (wrong) decision to sell today. Of course, if the arbitrageur does not know the true value of the security and is not able to detect price changes that reflect deviations from fundamentals, this presumably makes arbitrage even riskier. Clearly, trying empirically to verify whether there are arbitrage limitations is difficult because often it is impossible to discern if a price movement is a result of fundamentals or insufficient arbitrage.

The other type of operators are noise-traders. What type of view of the world do they have? What we are referring to with noise traders is the concept that agents' demand for an asset changes, not in response to fundamental factors but rather to noise, i.e. random price movements. Clearly in a world in which all traders trade randomly such demand shifts would cancel out and there would be no aggregate shifts in demand. It is much more likely, however, that the judgment biases affecting investors tend to be the same across investors. Indeed a considerable amount of empirical evidence from the psychology literature indicates that subjects tend to make the same mistake or judgment biases; they do not make random mistakes. For example, Alpert and Raiffa (1982) have indicated that experimental subjects tend to be overconfident, which makes them take on more risk. Andreassen and Kraus (1988) indicate that experimental subjects also tend to extrapolate past time series which can lead them to chase trends. This kind of work tends to be backed up by survey data collected by economists. For example, during the week of the stock market crash of October 19, 1987, Robert Shiller sent out 1000 questionnaires to institutional investors and 2000 questionnaires to private investors and found that the vast majority of investors took the signal of the initial price fall on the morning of the 19th as an indication of further price falls. Indeed this was seen as the most popular piece of "news" on that day. Interestingly, when asked about why the market fell on the 19th the vast majority of respondents said the market was overpriced and that it was a theory of investor psychology, rather than fundamental factors such as profits or interest rates, which was responsible for the overpricing.

The source of the noise used by the noise-traders could literally be taken to be anything that they *believe* to be useful in predicting exchange rate behavior. It could be a sunspot theory or the pronouncements of some financial guru who perhaps uses astrological methods to predict asset prices! Usually, though, noise-traders are taken to use the kind of chartist techniques introduced earlier as their means of forecasting asset price movements.

The interaction of the noise-trader group with the smart money arbitrageurs results in the determination of the *risk-adjusted* equilibrium asset price. The key implication of this model is that the risk incorporated in the asset price is generated by the behavior of noise-traders and is not captured in standard models. This suggests that the inability of researchers, reported in the last section, to discover a significant risk premium may be a reflection of an inappropriate modeling strategy. Many prominent economists believe that the noise trading model replaces the efficient markets model which we have discussed in this and the previous chapter. It remains to be seen, however, whether the model will be as widely embraced as the EMH has been over the last four decades.

NOTES

1   Both line and bar charts can be plotted for a much longer basis than the daily basis referred to in the text. For example, weekly bar charts covering a period of around five years and monthly charts covering a period of 20 years are commonplace. The use of these longer-term charts help to put any short-term fluctuations reflected in the daily bar charts into perspective.

2   For a list of the typical candle chart patterns, and their interpretation, see Feeny (1989).

3   Hodrick (1987) has attempted to compute a rough measure of the significance of Dooley and Shafer's reported profits and finds that they are not significantly different from zero.

4   Bilson uses a pooled time-series cross-sectional analysis to generate his profit series (i.e. he effectively collapses the equations for a number of currencies into a single equation).

5   See MacDonald (2000) for a comprehensive overview of this literature.

6   Froot and Ito (1988) test the "consistency" of MMS (UK and US) expectational data. Such tests amount to testing whether the long-term forecast *implied* by a short-term forecast is consistent with the survey-based long-term forecast. Such a test is effectively an application of the cross-equation restrictions tested in the context of a BVAR model of the forward and spot rates (see the discussion above). Froot and Ito demonstrate that the different forecast horizons are inconsistent.

7   Canova and Ito us a Kalman filter technology to ensure that their k-step-ahead forecasts are only based on information available at period t.

8   It is further demonstrated that the variance of the estimated risk premium term is larger than the variance of the expected change in the exchange rate and the covariance between the risk premium and the expected change in the exchange rate is larger than the covariance of the forward premium with the realized change in the spot rate.

9   See Lyons (1996, 1997) for useful models.

10 While these papers focus on the role of idiosyncratic interpretations of publicly available information, Lyons (1991) and Ito, Lyons, and Melvin (1998) focus on the existence of private information in the foreign exchange market. For example, Ito et al. examine the volatility in the Tokyo foreign exchange market over the lunch hour under trade and no-trade scenarios. They find that private information is the most likely explanation for the observed patterns.

11 That is, to have a constant (or non-time-dependent) mean.

12 Frenkel's study was conducted prior to the explosion of interest in the stationarity of economic time series, and he therefore uses s_t and f_{t-1} instead of Δs_t and fp_t respectively.

14

Currency Crises and Speculative Attacks

This chapter discusses currency crisis and speculative attacks. Section 14.1 points to the commonality of experiences in three recent "famous" international financial crises, emphasizing that each occurred in a domestic environment of weak financial institutions. Sections 14.2 and 14.3 discuss, respectively, the first- and second-generation models of speculative attack. Section 14.4 reviews some econometric evidence on these models. Section 14.5 turns from macro- to micro-economic indicators of potential speculative attack. Section 14.6 then discusses the possibility of contagion between one country's financial crisis and that of another. The penultimate section examines interest rate, foreign exchange and credit risk, and the final section considers various matters of economic policy to prevent or to combat currency crisis context.

14.1 Recent International Financial Crises

In the last two decades huge losses have been incurred in emerging market financial crises. Thus, according to Calomiris (1998), of 90 emerging market crises since 1982 about 20 had bank losses of 10 percent or more of GDP. This is large even in comparison with the losses sustained in the US banking crises of the early 1930s and the late 1980s when on each occasion about 4 percent of GDP was lost.

It is worth emphasizing that recent international financial crises were preceded by relaxation of regulatory controls on emerging market financial systems – a process known as *financial liberalization*. Financial liberalization is based on the belief that financial intermediaries and markets will efficiently allocate financial resources if only they are allowed to. Such a conviction rests on the assumption that financial intermediaries and financial markets in emerging markets are up to the task of coping with informational problems about as well as is the case in mature financial markets such as those of North America and the European Union.[1]

Moreover, as even mature financial systems remain under regulatory control, a further implicit assumption of the "liberalization now" school is that a nation's regulators are up to the job. This job itself needs to overcome asymmetric information between the regulators and the regulated in order to avoid undesirable behavior on the part of the latter. In the absence of proper regulation, banks and other financial intermediaries might be operated with nasty external diseconomies. For example, (i) if "crony capitalism" is taken to include the practice of banks channeling funds to associates with unprofitable projects, the externality is a lower rate of return on a nation's savings; (ii) if the stability of a banking system increases with the amount of equity capital in it, a generally accepted proposition, bank capital has an external economy. But bank owners have an incentive to minimize their equity/assets ratio – thereby increasing gearing – as this raises the rate of return on it.

Unfortunately, as Espinosa and Hunter (1994) observe, financial liberalizations in emerging markets have often been into environments of severe asymmetric information between borrowers and financial intermediaries, and between the latter and the regulators. Moreover, neither the financial intermediaries nor the regulators in these countries have much experience of coping with it. Thus, as too much financial liberalization can be dangerous, there must be some optimal degree of financial repression which would be a good idea to approximate.[2]

Each of the three most stunning recent financial crises – Latin America 1982/3, Mexico 1994/5, and East Asia 1997 – display an interaction between domestic financial weakness and international financial crisis. The main similarities between them are that they were each preceded by:

1   financial liberalization;
2   large-scale capital inflow which was consequent upon it – as domestic banks were allowed, especially in the later two crises, to diversify their sources of funds into the international interbank market (in the Latin American crisis of 1982/3 there was proportionately more government guaranteed foreign borrowing by non-banks); and
3   a large-scale build-up of international indebtedness. Furthermore,
4   these financial crises occurred suddenly and deepened rapidly;
5   foreign lenders made large-scale withdrawals of funds;
6   domestic asset prices fell sharply; and
7   the crises spread to other emerging markets in a similar external positions.

But there were also differences: (i) in 1982, as many capital account controls were still in place, pressure on exchange rates was to a relatively large extent through the current account so that the Latin American crises of the early 1980s were to some extent "slow motion" events following years of current account deficits and almost a decade of so called "petrodollar" recycling. In contrast, the two later crises were "fast motion" – largely because capital accounts were wide open and a country's foreign exchange reserves could be depleted very quickly; (ii) the global macroeconomic situation was much better in the 1990s than it had been the early 1980s; (iii) the affected countries were exchange rate peggers in the 1990s while they had mainly been floaters in the early 1980s; and (iv) in the 1990s it was private rather than public sector international indebtedness that was the focus of concern.

As our main interest is in the international aspects of financial crises we turn to a discussion of speculative currency attacks.

14.2 First-Generation Speculative Attack Models

The first-generation speculative attack model, as developed by Krugman (1979), Flood and Garber (1984) and Blanco and Garber (1986), combines elements of the monetary approach to the balance of payments (see chapter 8) and the flexible price monetary approach to the exchange rate (see sections 9.2 and 9.3). The former theory is used to make the simple point that a rate of domestic credit expansion faster than the rate of growth of demand for domestic money causes a fall in foreign exchange reserves – which ultimately destroys the peg. The monetary approach to the exchange rate is used to (a) calculate (from the current and expected fundamentals) the shadow floating exchange rate (i.e. as in equation (9.13)). This is the rate used by agents to gauge whether a currency is overvalued or not. Therefore, the shadow rate is the exchange rate to which the actual exchange rate will gravitate if it is above (more depreciated) than the officially pegged rate. And, (b) to support the observation that a speculative attack on a currency will occur *before* foreign exchange reserves are exhausted. This is because in the monetary approach to the exchange rate, the current exchange rate, s_t, is determined not only by current fundamentals but also by the discounted value of *expected* excess money supplies (equation (9.13) again). Thus, if investors actually ignored expected excess money supplies, the pegged and shadow exchange rates would coincide just as foreign exchange reserves ran out – because the shadow rate would be determined by purchasing power parity and, given an assumption of perfect commodity arbitrage, the domestic price level has not yet changed. However, given forward-looking agents and expected excess money supplies, the shadow exchange rate must depreciate relative to the pegged rate sooner than this, and investors will rush to reduce their holdings of domestic money – so provoking the speculative attack. Another point worth noting is that the exchange rate will not jump to a new market rate as such a transition would imply that some profitable opportunities for currency speculation had been ignored. Rather the transition will be smooth – to a floating rate that approximates the old pegged rate, thereafter depreciation sets in.

We will now discuss the first-generation speculative attack model in a little more detail, relying on a version of it by Agenor, Bhandari, and Flood (1992). This assumes perfect foresight, a small country, and fixed output at $\bar{y}$; purchasing power parity and uncovered interest rate parity both hold.

With all variables other than interest rates stated in natural logs, begin with a standard money demand equation

$$m_t - p_t = \phi \bar{y} - \alpha i_t \qquad \phi, \alpha > 0 \qquad (14.1)$$

While money supply is

$$m_t = \gamma D_t + (1 - \gamma) R_t \qquad 0 < \gamma < 1 \qquad (14.2)$$

where m_t is the nominal money supply, p_t the domestic price level, D_t is domestic credit created by the central bank, R_t the domestic currency value of foreign exchange reserves (the money multiplier assumed equal to unity). The term γ is the initial share of domestic credit in the money supply.

The rate of domestic credit expansion, $\dot{D}_t$, is constant at

$$\dot{D}_t = \mu \qquad \mu > 0 \qquad (14.3)$$

Furthermore, fixing and standardizing the foreign price level to unity ($= 0$ in logs), gives purchasing power parity as

$$p_t = s_t \qquad (14.4)$$

And uncovered interest parity is as usual

$$i_t = i^* + E_t \dot{s}_t \qquad (14.5)$$

where the i's are, respectively, the home and foreign interest rates (the latter is fixed), E_t the expectations operator, and $\dot{s}_t$ the expected change in the exchange rate.

Under perfect foresight $E_t \dot{s}_t = \dot{s}_t$. Holding domestic output at the standardized value of unity ($= 0$ in logs) and substituting equations (14.4) and (14.5) into (14.1) yields money demand as

$$m_t = s_t - \alpha \dot{s}_t \qquad (14.6)$$

Notice that with a pegged exchange rate money demand in (14.6) fixed as the last term on the right $= 0$.

The equation for foreign exchange reserves assuming a fixed exchange rate, $\bar{s}^-$, is found by substituting (14.6) into (14.2)

$$R_t = (\bar{s} - \gamma D_t)/(1 - \gamma) \qquad (14.7)$$

Then substituting (14.3) into (14.7) tells us the rate at which foreign exchange reserves are run down

$$\dot{R}_t = -\mu/\Theta \qquad (14.8)$$

where $\Theta = (1 - \gamma)/\gamma$.

Thus, if foreign exchange reserves are constantly depleting, because $\mu > 0$, agents will expect that the authorities will eventually abandon the peg. Exactly when, it turns out, depends on the type of regime that is expected to follow the peg. Here we assume that the new regime will be a clean float.

The shadow floating exchange rate, it can be shown, is given by

$$\hat{s}_t = \gamma(D_0 + \alpha\mu) + \gamma\mu t \qquad (14.9)$$

where D_0 is domestic credit at time 0, t the number of time period since time 0, and the other variables are the same as before. Thus, the shadow floating exchange rate depreciates at the rate $\gamma\mu t$.

As the pegged rate regime collapses when the shadow floating rate infinitesimally rises above the pegged rate, the exact time of collapse is

$$t_c = (\Theta R_0/\mu) - \alpha \qquad (14.10)$$

where t_c is the time of collapse, R_0 initial reserves, and the other terms are as before.[3] Collapse occurs all the sooner the larger is the initial proportion of domestic credit in the money stock (the smaller is Θ), the lower is the initial stock of reserves, the higher is the rate of credit expansion, and the higher the semi-interest elasticity of demand for money (why? -- because with currency depreciation, inflation is expected and the associated increase in the nominal rate of interest will reduce money demand).

This model is summarized in figure 14.1. Until the time of speculative attack and the collapse of the peg at t_c, the money stock is constant but it is composed of a growing amount of domestic credit and falling amount of foreign exchange reserves. Until this time the exchange rate peg holds at $\bar{s}$. But with expectations of excess money supplies, at time t_c the shadow floating rate depreciates relative to the pegged rate, so provoking speculative attack. This reduction in the demand for domestic money immediately empties foreign exchange reserves and reduces the money stock. After t_c the currency is floating and depreciates as shown in the lower part of figure 14.1.

14.2.1 Extensions of the first-generation model

Further insight into the first-generation model may be gleaned from figure 14.2 where we plot equation (14.9) and the pre-attack fixed exchange rate, $\bar{s}$. The two lines intersect at point A, where $D = D^A$. If a speculative attack were to occur at a point where D was smaller than D^A, speculators would suffer a capital loss on

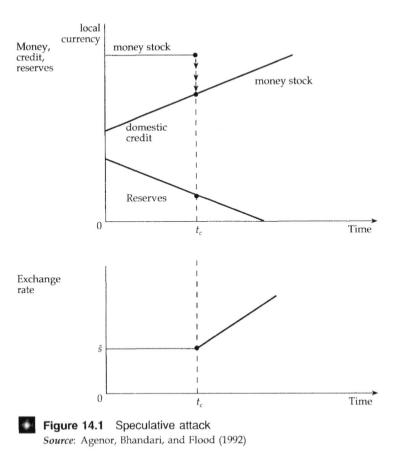

Figure 14.1   Speculative attack
Source: Agenor, Bhandari, and Flood (1992)

reserves purchased from the central bank; there will be no speculative attack, therefore, when $D = D^A$. Alternatively, however, when $D > D^A$ there is a capital gain to be had from speculating against the currency and buying reserves from the central bank. Speculators will forsee this capital gain and compete against each other for the potential profit. It is this competition which ensures that the attack is driven back to the point where $D = D^A$. It therefore follows that exchange rate jumps will be ruled out by speculative competition and a forseen attack will occur when $\bar{s} = \hat{s}$.

It is widely accepted that in the speculative crises of the 1990s the money-supply effects of reserve losses were sterilized. Sterilization may be introduced into the above model by holding the money supply fixed throughout the attack at $\bar{m}$. With the exchange rate fixed at $\bar{s}$ the money market equilibrium (14.6) becomes:

$$\bar{m}_t - \bar{s}_t = -\alpha \dot{s}_t \tag{14.11}$$

Immediately after the attack the domestic money market condition will be given by:

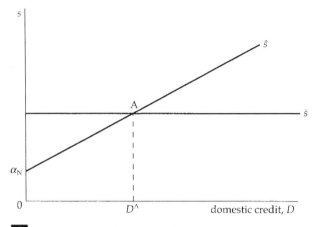

Figure 14.2 Attack time in first generation model

$$m_t - \hat{s}_t = -\alpha(i_t^* + \mu) \qquad (14.12)$$

where $\hat{s}_t$ is the flexible exchange rate which grows at the rate μ if the domestic money supply is assumed to grow at that rate. By subtracting equation (14.12) from (14.11) we see that $\hat{s}_t$ is greater than $\bar{s}$ no matter how high $\bar{s}$ is set by the authorities. So this simple model predicts that no fixed exchange rate regime can survive, even momentarily, if the monetary authorities plan to sterilize an attack and agents understand these plans.

The above models are useful in revealing some important aspects of a speculative attack. However, their main deficiency lies in the fact that they assume perfect foresight. In reality agents are unsure about when the attack will actually take place and they are also uncertain about how much the exchange rate will change if there is an attack. In Flood and Marion (1997) a stochastic version of the speculative attack model is developed. Essentially their modification results in using a version of the risk-adjusted interest rate parity condition which, as we saw in chapter 11, is one way of representing the portfolio balance model of the exchange rate. Their condition is:

$$i_t - i_t^* = E_t \Delta \hat{s}_{t+1} + \beta_t(b_t - b_t^* - \hat{s}_t), \qquad (14.13)$$

where the second term on the right-hand-side is a time-varying stochastic risk premium and has two elements. First, the term in brackets is the relative quantity of domestic government bonds to foreign bonds held by the private sector (see chapter 11) and the coefficient on this term, β_t, is assumed time-varying. Flood and Marion demonstrate that if agents maximize expected utility that is increasing in expected wealth and decreasing in the variance of wealth then:

$$\beta_t = zVar_t(\hat{s}_{t+1}),$$

where z is a taste-determined constant and $Var_t(\hat{s}_{t+1})$ is the conditional variance of the period-ahead shadow rate. The assumed form for β_t introduces a non-linearity into the model and this in turn can generate multiple solutions. The important implication of this stochastic model is that although currency crises can still arise as before, due to inconsistent policies, they can also arise from self-fulfilling prophecies about exchange market risk. For example, if for some reason agents expect more currency variability in the future $-Var_t(\hat{s}_{t+1})$ becomes larger – this will affect the domestic interest rate, through (14.13) and this in turn will affect the demand for money and make the exchange rate more variable if the fixed rate is abandoned. So such a shift in expectations can alter the relevant shadow rate for determining if an attack is profitable and changes the attack time. The existence of such non-linearities means that an economy can jump suddenly from a no-attack equilibrium to an attack equilibrium.

Equation (14.13) also sheds further light on our discussion of exchange rate volatility in chapter 10. There we noted the Flood and Rose (1995) finding that the volatility we observe in exchange rates when they are flexible appears to be unrelated to fundamentals. Flood and Marion (1997) demonstrate that when an exchange rate is flexible, equation (14.3) can produce several perfectly viable equilibria. Such equilibria may correspond to exchange rate regimes with differing volatility. Equally, however, movements across these equilibria could produce exchange rate volatility without corresponding changes in fundamentals.

14.3 Second-Generation Models

Our discussion of the first-generation models finished by introducing a non-linearity into private sector behavior. The second-generation models also emphasize non-linearities, particularly those relating to government behavior. Flood and Marion (1997) succinctly summarize the difference between the first- and second-generation models. In the first generation models inconsistent policies prior to the attack can *push* the economy into a crises while in the second-generation models, even with consistent polices, attack-conditional policy changes can *pull* the economy into an attack. The following simple example (taken from Flood and Marion (1997)) illustrates this push–pull distinction.

In the simple first-generation model considered above, domestic credit was assumed to grow at a constant rate which we label here μ_0. The policy non-linearity says that if there is no attack on the fixed exchange rate domestic credit continues to grow at the rate μ_0 but if there is an attack it grows at the faster rate, μ_1. Figure 14.3 is a modified version of figure 14.2 to allow for two shadow exchange rate lines, one corresponding to a rate of credit expansion μ_0 (which intersects the $\bar{s}$ line at point A) and the other related to the higher credit expansion, μ_1 (which intersects the $\bar{s}$ line at point B). Assume $\mu_0 = 0$, so that the policy setting the fixed rate would survive indefinitely for some amounts of domestic credit.

Suppose D lies somewhere to the left of D^B. If no attack occurs the shadow rate will be on the $S\mu_0$ line. If there is an attack the shadow rate will jump to $S\mu_1$ which, because it is still below the fixed rate line, would imply a capital loss for

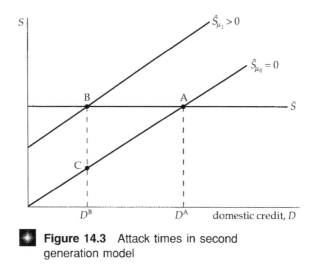

Figure 14.3 Attack times in second generation model

speculators. Hence for $D < D^B$ no attack will occur. If the level of domestic credit is at D^B then with $\mu = \mu_0$ the shadow rate is at point C. However, if the currency is attacked the shadow rate jumps from C to B. The attack will be successful but there would be no profit for speculators. So in this scenario the economy could sit indefinitely at C or it can move to point B. There are multiple equilibria, but no profit incentives to drive the economy from C to B. When domestic credit lies in the range D^A to D^B there clearly would be profit incentives to mounting a specu-lative attack and so multiple equilibria may arise. For example, if agents believe that there is no possibility that the market will mount an attack, the economy could stay indefinitely on $S\mu_0$. However, if speculators believe that the market is going to force a speculative attack then no speculator will want to hold the domestic currency and all agents will participate in the attack, pushing the currency off the fixed rate. If the foreign exchange market is dominated by a large Soros-type player, with the power to singlehandedly move the market, then the economy will only face the attack equilibrium (i.e. there will be a unique equilibrium), as occurred to sterling in 1992. If on the other hand the market is dominated by many small credit-constrained traders then as suggested by Obstfled (1986) there will be multiple equilibria. The second-generation models are silent on the coordina-tion necessary for a group of such traders to mount a speculative attack.

14.4 Econometric Estimates of Speculative Attack Models

For pre-1990 crises, a number of econometric studies have suggested that the stand-ard first-generation models do have predictive properties. Blanco and Garber (1986), for example, use a version of the Krugman–Flood–Garber model for the Mexican Peso to predict the timing of the probability that the shadow rate would exceed the fixed rate one quarter ahead was between 2 and 5 percent in tranquil periods, but rose above 20 percent before the 1976 and 1982 devaluations. Interest-ingly, both domestic credit growth and standard money demand variables were significant determinants of these probabilities.[4] A similar approach was used by Cumby and van Wijnbergen (1989) to analyze the attack on the Argentinian crawling peg of the early 1980s. They found that the growth of domestic credit was a significant determinant of the attack. A number of other researchers have used panel data sets to analyze if the above single-country studies generalize to groups of currencies. For example, Klein and Marion (1994) used a panel frame-work to examine 80 devaluation episodes in Latin American countries over the period 1957–91. Their main finding was that the monthly probability of abandoning a fixed exchange rate increased when a currency was overvalued in real terms and decreased with the level of foreign exchange reserves (they also found that so-called structural factors – such as, the openness of the economy and political factors – influenced the monthly probability).

As we have noted, casual empiricism has suggested that the currency crises of the 1990s – for example, the speculative attack against EMS currencies in 1992 – were not motivated by indisciplined monetary and fiscal policies. To get a feel for the sources of the '90s crises a number of researchers have used empirical models which incorporate a wide array of potential explanatory variables to distinguish between the run up to a currency crises and tranquil periods. For example, Eichengreen, Rose, and Wyplosz (1995) examine a panel of 20 industrial countries for a sample period 1959–93. They take their measure of a speculative attack as a variant of the Girton–Roper (1977) exchange market pressure variable (see chapter 15). In particular, they define speculative pressure, K_t as a weighted average of exchange rate changes, interest rate changes, and the negative of reserve changes. The idea is that at the time of the attack reserves will fall sharply, interest rates will rise (reflecting the expected depreciation) and the exchange rate will be unchanged – K_t will increase if the crises is predictable. Of course if the crises was largely unanticipated, K_t may move little – if at all. In practice, Eichengreen, Rose, and Wyplosz define extreme values of K_t to be those which are at least two standard deviations above the mean. By this measure Eichengreen, Rose, and Wyplosz find that crises "tend to occur when unemployment is high and when political circumstances are unpropitious." Flood and Marion (1997) interpret these findings to mean that data-defined crises are hard to predict using panel methods. One reason for this has already been given. The other reason why panel methods may perform poorly is that by looking for common patterns in the data they may miss heterogeneous sources of currency crises across countries and across time. Kaminsky, Lizando, and Reinhart (1998) and Sachs, Tornell, and Velasco (1996) have had greater success in applying similar methods to that of Eichengreen, Rose, and Wyplosz for developing countries. The greater success rate for these countries may reflect the greater variation in the data.

 ## 14.5 Microeconomic Indicators

As domestic and international financial crises are bound together, investigation of potential problems in domestic banking and financial system could be inform-ative. Such microeconomic indicators include: falling bank risk-adjusted capital ratios, rising proportions of non-performing loans, growing proportions of loans to known risky sectors (such as commercial real estate), widening spreads between deposit and lending rates (in particular, the latter increasing as banks raise lending rates – which can be afforded only by borrowers with the most risky projects), and growing dependence on short-term liabilities, especially when denominated in foreign currency.

A problem with all banking systems is the moral hazard caused by the existence of asymmetric information between a bank and the regulatory agencies. Hence, an individual bank might see deterioration in these indicators but act in a way that is not beneficial to the system as a whole. For example, in hope of turning things around it might raise loan rates – which can be afforded only by those with the most risky projects, financed by short-term foreign loans. Given asymmetric information, a problem which is worse the poorer are a country's accountancy standards and data collection systems, the regulatory agencies may not be able to respond until the whole banking system is under threat of collapse. Also, even if it is known that a banking system is getting into trouble, "regulatory forbearance" may occur – i.e., the regulators do *not* implement various preventative actions, such as closing down failing banks. This could be because of "cronyism" amongst the bank owners and the regulators, or, because the scale of the problem, once it has become known, is too big for the regulators to handle given the resources at their command. But regulatory forbearance creates, what have been called in the US context, "zombie banks", the living dead, whose continuing competitive presence squeezes the life (i.e. profit margins) out of the remaining healthy banks.

Demirguc-Kunt and Detragiache (1998), in a fascinating paper, test for the causes of banking crises from a microeconomic point of view. They use the theory that banks operate with asymmetric information with respect to borrowers and that they, the banks, face credit, interest rate, and foreign exchange risks. They estimate the probability of banking crises in a panel data set of 65 countries over the 1980–94 period using a reduced form multivariate logit model. Proxies are chosen to reflect the realization of these risks. For example, deterioration in the macroeconomic environment (lower growth) increases borrower defaults – realizing credit risk; a rise in interest rates may realize interest rate risk (because banks borrow short term, having to pay the higher rate for funds, and lend long term at fixed rates); and currency depreciation realizes foreign exchange risk (when domestic banks have net foreign currency liabilities). Note that higher interest rates and currency depreciation are likely to increase borrower default (credit risk) – as when domestic corporations have to roll over domestic currency debt and service foreign currency debt. Furthermore, a proxy for financial liberalization is used (the ratio of credit-to-the-private-sector to GDP – which will increase as banks are freed on their use of funds from mainly buying government securities), as was a proxy for moral hazard (i.e. banks not operating in the interests of depositors). The proxy for moral hazard is whether a government explicitly guarantee bank deposits.

Demirguc-Kunt and Detragiache's econometric tests find good support for the above microeconomic theory of causality of banking crises. They conclude:

banking crises tend to emerge when the macroeconomic environment is weak . . . High real interest rates tend to increase the likelihood of a banking crisis . . . We have found some (not very strong evidence) that a proxy for the degree of financial liberalization significantly increases the likelihood of banking crises . . . [And] that the presence of an explicit deposit insurance scheme tends to increase the probability of systemic banking problems. (Demirguc-Kunt and Detragiache, 1998, pp. 103–4)

Also, while currency depreciation was not found to cause banking crises in a statistical sense, all eight of their reported regressions had the expected sign.

Can a *domestic* banking crisis somehow be fitted into the speculative attack models – which are macroeconomic rather than microeconomic in nature? Garber (1998) argues that this is a simple matter if a government is expected to monetize its way out of a banking crisis. Monetization itself would be necessary if (implicit) guarantees to depositors have been given and no other means of raising the necessary public finance is available. Thus, the banking crisis feeds an expectation of an increase in the rate of domestic credit expansion. Hence, μ in equation (14.3) increases and this brings forward the time of the collapse of the pegged exchange rate regime as in equation (14.10).

14.6 Contagion

Contagion may occur in a situation where investors, foreign and domestic, have less than complete information on the true economic and financial condition of a country. Then an event that reveals information about one country may be taken as revealing new information about similar countries. As an example, in East Asia during the 1990s until the summer of that year much capital inflow was through the inter-bank market. This involved two levels of asymmetric information: between a domestic non-bank as borrower and a domestic bank, and between the domestic bank and foreign banks. Beginning with Thailand, when foreign lenders eventually realized that Thai banks were financing highly risky projects – especially in Thailand's non-traded goods sector (e.g. real estate), and had much higher than previously known proportions of non-performing loans, they withdrew from lending to Thailand. At the same time they also withdrew from lending to the rest of East Asia because deterioration in financial conditions in Thailand were taken as a signal of problems elsewhere. Another example is the "Tequila effect" from Mexico's December 1994 currency collapse on much of the rest of Latin America, especially Argentina. In order to maintain the credibility of its currency board peg to the dollar Argentine interest rates were sharply increased, with the result that Argentina suffered a severe economic recession during 1995.

Other things apart, the contagion is "justified" if the inference about the third country is correct. Notice that this way of looking at the problem of contagion does not agree with the sometimes stated view that "contagions don't happen because a country with sound fundamentals has never been forced to devalue by one." But statements such as this do not allow for asymmetric information on the true state of fundamentals. In the presence of asymmetric information any country's foreign exchange market might be roiled by disturbances in another country's financial markets. Even so, it is worth noting that in the study by Kaminsky and Reinhart (1998) no country experienced a currency crisis that had less than 20 percent of its indicators indicating one.

A series of contagious devaluations may occur even without informational problems – as when countries are in international competition with one another. An element of this might have been present in the depreciation of the Japanese yen during 1997, which reduced the export competitiveness of other East Asian countries. Similarly, countries leaving the gold standard along with the UK in September 1931 might have done so in order to defend their competitive positions.

■ 14.7 Interest Rate, Foreign Exchange, and Credit Risk

Some idea in a simple model of how financial crises hurt emerging market economies is shown in figure 14.4.[5] Here the exchange rate is determined assuming uncovered interest parity (UIP), i.e. an emerging country's spot exchange rate, S_t, which solves $i = i^* + (S_{t+1}^e - S_t)/S_t$ for given i, i^* and S_{t+1}^e which are, respectively, the domestic and foreign bank deposit interest rates, and the emerging country's expected exchange rate (price of foreign exchange, say, the US dollar). In figure 14.4 the vertical line is the emerging country's interest rate on bank

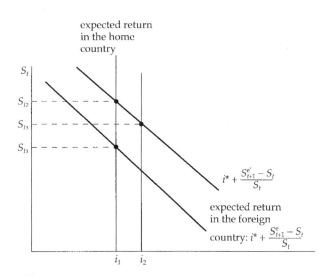

Figure 14.4 The effect of asset preference shift against an emerging economy and a possible domestic interest rate adjustment

deposits, i_1, and the negatively sloped line the expected return in the foreign country, the USA, adjusted for the expected exchange rate change, i.e., $i^* + (S_{t+1}^e - S_t)/S_t$. The negative slope occurs because an increase in S_t reduces the expected rate of return on the US asset as the price of buying dollars rises. In figure 14.4 UIP is satisfied at the current exchange rate S_{t1}.

Problems for an emerging market economy may arise if there is a shift of sentiment against its currency – i.e. as reflected in a rise in the expected exchange rate (a depreciation) from S_{t+1}^e to S_{t+1}^{e1}. Such a shift in sentiment may be caused by any of the macroeconomic or microeconomic fundamentals mentioned above. For whatever reason, if the expected exchange rate depreciation increases, the expected rate of return in the foreign country increases and the negatively sloped function in figure 14.4 shifts to the right. Thus, the *equilibrium* spot exchange rate immediately depreciates from S_{t1} to S_{t2}.

The emerging market government now faces a number of hard choices:

1 It could change the course of economic policy – as the IMF would be suggesting if conditional loans were being sought. To turn sentiment around to favor the domestic currency, economic policy at both the micro- and macroeconomic levels will probably need to be changed.

2 Let the exchange rate depreciate to its new equilibrium level, S_{t2}. But if domestic banks and non-bank corporations have borrowed heavily from abroad, *foreign exchange risk* will be realized and profits squeezed. Foreign exchange rate risk depends mainly on the ratio of a bank's or nonbank's foreign currency denominated liabilities to its assets. In emerging markets, having experienced heavy capital inflows, this ratio is probably greater than unity for many non-banks and especially banks, so that depreciation of the home currency reduces profitability. Firms in the non-traded goods sector who have borrowed heavily abroad will be especially hard hit as their foreign debt denominated in domestic currency will have increased just as their profits are squeezed by a fall in the price of non-traded goods relative to traded goods.

3 Defend the exchange rate by raising the domestic interest rate, say, to i_2. This would be easy to accomplish through unsterilized intervention in the foreign exchange market – supporting the currency while letting the domestic money supply fall. But, while a large currency depreciation is avoided (the exchange rate depreciating only to S_{t3}), or at least put off, now *interest rate risk* is realized, especially by domestic banks. Interest rate risk, depends mainly on the ratio of interest rate sensitive liabilities to interest sensitive assets. For banks, as this ratio is usually greater than unity, a rise in interest rates reduces bank profitability. If the banks' capital ratios (capital to assets) fall the stability of the banking system may be threatened and their ability to finance business reduced.

While both interest rate and exchange rate risk can be hedged if suitable financial derivatives are available (frequently in emerging markets they are not) neither emerging market banks nor nonbanks used them much because of their expense.[6]

A third line of attack on bank profitability is via *credit risk*. This is realized when many of the domestic customers of emerging market banks themselves stop servicing their bank loans. Something like this must have happened throughout East Asia after the currency crises of 1997 as exchange rates were depreciated and domestic interest rates increased – resulting in a spate of non-bank and bank bankruptcies.

4   Introduce foreign exchange controls. In the short term the advantage of effective foreign exchange controls is that neither interest rates nor the exchange rate need be increased. But there are several disadvantages including: first, to the extent, which might be large, that banks have lent to many non-viable enterprises, both the banks and their borrowers are effectively protected and the economy may stagnate, perhaps for years – somewhat as in the days of import-substituting industrialization. Secondly, if foreign investors are prevented for a time from transmitting their capital out of the emerging market in question, international borrowing in the future may become much more expensive as risk premiums are raised. Thirdly, the resulting excess demand for foreign exchange at the un-devalued exchange rate will have to be coped with somehow – probably through a combination of an (inefficient) official allocation scheme and an illegal blackmarket.

14.8 Possible policy responses

It is well known that the policy choice of pegged exchange rate, independent monetary policy and open international capital market is infeasible as only two of them at a time can be adopted and the third must be given up. But in East Asia during the 1990s, as earlier in other places, there was a reluctance to do so. In particular, while retaining pegged exchange rates and open capital markets, in East Asia in 1997 the urgency to use an independent monetary policy to support domestic financial systems increased. Thus, in 1997, a policy of quickly raising interest rates to support the exchange rate was not adopted because this would have damaged their financial systems and real economies.

Many policy reforms have been suggested in response to the emerging market debt crisis of 1997. Some of these revolve around the policy dilemma just referred to. Thus,

1   *Exchange rate pegging* could be dropped in favor of a float. As no country practices clean floating some form of managed float would be chosen (i.e. floating with *ad hoc* intervention). Suggestions include wide-band target zones (real or nominal) and crawling pegs. However, if exchange rate pegging is deemed to be an optimal policy – perhaps because floating rates are thought to be too volatile, or, because a peg is seen as being a good way of imposing monetary discipline (e.g. Argentina's currency board, established in 1991) – the cost of dropping the peg has to be balanced by the expected advantages derived from running open capital markets and an independent monetary policy. Somewhat more subtly, Jeffery Sachs argues that, while exchange rate pegging can be used to reduce inflation expectations early in an economic and currency reform, a managed float should be adopted as soon as inflation expectations have been brought

down. But, again, this leaves the question of subsequent exchange rate volatility unanswered.

2 *Open capital markets.* The freedom of capital movements, especially short-term movements, could be reduced – the choice made by Malaysia in 1997. Reducing capital movements by taxing short-term capital inflows has been tried but abandoned by Chile.[7] The cost of restricting capital movements is that it reduces a country's ability to borrow abroad, so that domestic saving and investment must be more closely matched. The benefit is in allowing more scope for monetary policy in a pegged exchange rate environment.

3 *Monetary policy independence* could be reduced. Increased IMF *surveillance* (e.g. by the IMF adopting and policing a "code of good practices") and *pre-qualification* for IMF financial aid in an international monetary crisis is directly aimed at increasing monetary and other macroeconomic policy discipline in emerging markets.

At first sight some other suggested policies may not appear to have an important monetary policy component, but they in fact do so. Thus,

1 The frequently stated call for stronger *fiscal discipline* may be interpreted in the financial arena as reducing the probability of a need for monetization of a budget deficit.

2 Policies that directly relate to *reform of domestic banking and financial systems* also have monetary implications. (The Basle Committee on Banking Supervision has already established the "Core Principles on Effective Banking Supervision" with some emerging market central banks.) If failing financial systems have to be supported by increased liquidity and lower interest rates a central bank in effect monetizes the financial crisis. It may do so in the traditional way of buying government securities, or by directly injecting reserves into the banking system by buying their dud assets.

3 *New mechanisms* for, and increased levels of, international financial support e.g. the IMF acting as a lender of last resort. These may be analyzed in the following way. Suppose that exchange rate expectations are driven by fundamentals then the ability to draw on a pool of international funds has the effect of allowing economic fundamentals to get even more out of line before pressures in exchange markets become unbearable. In this respect an increase in the size and availability of a pool of borrowable funds acts similarly to an exogenous increase in foreign exchange reserves. The argument that improving access to international funds will cause moral hazard is very much related to this argument. The moral hazard argument is that a country knowing that it will be bailed out by the international community will allow its economic fundamentals to deteriorate more than otherwise, as well as putting off meaningful reform of its financial sector. The notion of increased IMF surveillance can be understood as an attempt to reduce the scope for this moral hazard; and pre-qualification into a lender-of-last-resort scheme as a means of reducing adverse selection.

Other suggestions for economic and financial reform do not so obviously relate to the policy dilemma that we have been discussing. For example, *improved information systems*, in particular on the accuracy, scope, and timeliness of economic and financial data. This may be viewed in different ways as: (i) as a means of reducing asymmetric information between emerging markets as borrows and the lenders. Better information on fundamentals should reduce moral hazard both for public sector (governments and the IMF) and private sector (international banks and capital markets) lenders. (ii) as a means of better informing market-participant's exchange rate expectations. Discontinuity in the flow of information (e.g. the sudden revelation that emerging market banks have much higher than previously known non-performing loans) can give rise to sudden changes in exchange rate expectations and plunge a country into an immediate foreign exchange crisis without any chance for a government to make gradual adjustments to economic fundamentals. According to some sources, this might have been the case with Thailand in mid-1997. The hope is that a steadier flow of reliable economic and financial information may render changes in exchange rate expectations and, therefore, in exchange rates, smoother. And that more gradual exchange markets developments – e.g. a currency bumping gently against its lower intervention band – will exert market-discipline emerging market decision-makers.

Sachs and Radelet (1998) argue that an institution such as the IMF should act as an *international bankruptcy court* to fulfill functions rather like bankruptcy courts at the national level. In essence this proposal is aimed at reducing volatility in international capital markets. The argument is that bankruptcy courts exist because of asymmetric information concerning the true credit worthiness of a company. With incomplete information on an otherwise solvent company, and without the formal closure procedures offered by bankruptcy law, an otherwise solvent company could be subjected to a "grab race" by its creditors – so causing it to fail. This would be against the best interests of both the company and the creditors. In other words, an important effect of bankruptcy law is that it is stabilizing to domestic financial systems. The idea behind the Sachs and Radelet (1998) proposal is that international creditors also suffer asymmetric information and on mere rumor could start a grab race for a country's assets – so setting off destabilizing capital outflows. An international bankruptcy court could guard against this by giving creditors confidence that they could get most of their investments out at some future date. Something akin to what an international bankruptcy court would do has already been tried on an *ad hoc* basis – the Brady bailout plan (1989) for Mexico where about 500 international banks agreed to choose between either lowering the interest rate on, or the outstanding value of, their loans to Mexico.

Unfortunately, many of these suggested policy responses to international financial crisis are politically unrealistic. They are so because they require too much national sovereignty to be handed over to an international institution or to international law. However, what is realistic in the view of Eichengreen (1999) is first improving formation in international financial markets through better accountancy standards – to be achieved via the International Accounting Standards Committee; secondly, as riskiness in the *sources*, as well as the *uses* of commercial bank funds, is a factor in the strength of banking systems, the former should also be taken into account in the calculation of risk adjusted capital ratios under the Basle Accord;[8] thirdly, short-term bank borrowing abroad could be restricted by taxing it in some way; finally, exchange rate flexibility could be increased.

NOTES

1 For example, well functioning financial intermediaries must be efficient information gatherers (to avoid moral hazard by and adverse selection of borrowers), they must be able to promote incentive alignment, and they must be efficient monitors.
2 A state of financial repression is what financial liberalization is aimed at reducing.
3 Equation (14.10) is found, first, by noting that with pegging $s_t = \bar{s}$; and secondly, by substituting 14.2 into 14.9 which is allowed because under the assumptions $s_t = p_t$ (i.e. PPP) $= m_t$ (neutrality of money).
4 See also Goldberg (1993).
5 For asset preference shift against a currency in the more sophisticated portfolio balance model see section 11.4.
6 The Indonesian company Bakrie and Brothers (with main interests in rubber plantations, telecommunications and oil industry infrastructure) provides an example of realized interest and exchange rate risk. In 1996 its net profit margin was over 10 percent, but following the collapse of the Indonesian currency and sharp increase in local interest rates in 1997, net profit margin fell to minus 15 percent (*The Economist*, January 30, 1999, pp. 58–97).
7 Chile's scheme, introduced in 1991, required Chilean banks borrowing abroad to deposit 30 percent of the proceeds with the Chilean central bank, with no interest being paid on the deposit. In 1998, however, this deposit scheme was given up.
8 On the Basle Accord see section 19.3.

15

Exchange Rate Target Zones and "Dirty Floating"

Section 15.1 discusses the theory of exchange rate target zones – how a pegged exchange rate may behave within its fluctuation band. Section 15.2 explains various applications of this theory to the estimation of exchange rate realignment expectations and section 15.3 shows how to calculate devaluation probabilities. Section 15.4 offers a model of "dirty floating."

The term "dirty floating" refers to the fact that an exchange rate is ostensibly floating yet, at irregular intervals, it is subjected to intervention by the exchange authorities. Virtually all exchange rates that "float" do so in this manner. While the theories of target zones and dirty float appear to be concerned with quite different subjects, this is in fact not the case. The theories of target zones and dirty floating combine elements of exchange market intervention and a floating exchange rate. Thus, within the intervention points of a target zone the exchange rate may be left free to float. Under dirty floating, exchange market intervention by the authorities is more discursive as there are no formal intervention points, nevertheless floating and intervention are combined.

15.1 Target Zones

15.1.1 Target zones – theory

There are many examples today and in history of pegged exchange rate regimes. In these systems a central rate, or, "par value," and a fluctuation band, or, "zone," for an exchange rate is declared and the monetary authorities commit to manage monetary conditions so as to make the commitment stick. This was the case under the Bretton Woods system 1959–71, the EMS 1979–99, and the many arrangements today where less developed countries peg to a foreign currency or currency basket. The classical gold standard, circa 1875–1914 and the interwar gold standard 1925–31, for adherents was an implicit pegged exchange rate system as currency prices of gold defined central rates and the gold points set the width of fluctuation bands.

Somewhat strangely it was not until Krugman (1988) that serious consideration was given to theoretical aspects of how exchange rate target zones actually work. This chapter discusses the main theoretical aspects of the target zone literature as well as considering various empirical evaluations of it.

The following discussion assumes that "the market" believes that the authorities are willing to defend the zone – requiring that they use monetary policy to defend it. That is, we assume that the chosen exchange rate policy is perfectly credible. As a simplification, it is further assumed that the zone is defended only when the exchange rate reaches either the upper or lower edges of the zone (so called "marginal intervention"). The exchange rate is determined as

$$s_t = m_t + v_t + \alpha_2 E_t[ds_t]/dt \qquad (15.1)$$

where, in natural logarithms, s is the domestic currency price of foreign exchange, m the money supply (which is an exogenous policy variable), α_2 is the semielasticity of demand for money, v is a "general purpose" term that includes anything else that impacts the demand or supply for money (e.g. changes in real income) and t is a time subscript. Most simply v is taken to be the cumulative value of velocity (Miller and Weller, 1991). Shocks to velocity are random with mean = 0, and normally distributed such that the cumulative value of v follows a continuous-time random walk. The sum of m_t and v_t is usually referred to as the composite fundamental term, f_t. The final term, $E_t[ds_t]/dt$, is the *instantaneous* rationally expected rate of change of the exchange rate. Purchasing power parity ($s = p - p^*$) and uncovered interest parity ($i = i^* + E[ds]/dt$) are assumed to hold continuously. Moreover, as the country is small, p^* and i^* are parameters (therefore equation 15.1 bears an obvious relationship to the models considered in chapter 9).

Figure 15.1a shows how the exchange rate behaves in response to shocks to v. If the exchange rate was permitted to float freely, according to equation (15.1), it would move along the dashed 45° line as s is homogeneous of degree one in m and v. However, there is a target zone with s_U as the maximum depreciation and s_L the maximum appreciation permitted. According to the theory of target zones the "S" shaped curve defines the movement of the exchange rate in the presence of shocks.

To see how the exchange rate behaves inside the band suppose that the random shocks to v are positive, then $m + v$ increases and to balance the domestic money market i falls. But given that uncovered interest parity holds, a fall in i is possible only if $E[ds]/dt$ is negative – the exchange rates is expected to appreciate – we explain why in a moment. If so, in equation (15.1), s increases by

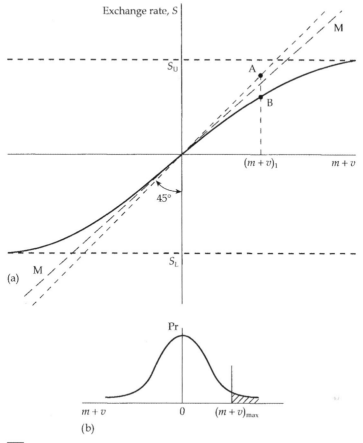

Figure 15.1 (a) Target zone honeymoon effect and smooth pasting; (b) probability distribution of $m + v$

less than if the latter term had not become negative. Exchange rate variability is thereby reduced. This is called the *honeymoon effect*, and represents a free benefit from the announcement of a (credible) target zone.

But why is the exchange rate expected to appreciate following a positive shock to v? Suppose that the exchange rate has already reached its upper limit – a further random increase in v will be offset by a policy-induced reduction in m. Thus, s cannot rise because $m + v$ has an upper limit; but it might fall because the next random shock to v may be negative – in which case $m + v$ and s fall. Thus, on balance, s must be expected to fall. It is this expected appreciation, given that uncovered interest parity holds at all times, that allows i to fall below i^*. Moreover, this argument holds for any value of s between its upper limit and central rate. To see this consider figure 15.1b, which shows the probability distribution of $m + v$ (for convenience it is assumed that $m = 0$, i.e. $M = 1$).

If no intervention by the central bank was ever expected, the expected change in the value of $m + v = 0$. But intervention is expected to occur should the exchange rate hit the upper edge of the zone. This implies that $(m + v)_{max}$ exists. Now, because the right tail of the probability distribution in figure 15.1 is truncated, the expected value of $(m + v) < 0$. It therefore follows, since $E(m + v)$ is an argument in the next period's exchange rate, that $E[ds]/dt < 0$. That is, the exchange rate is expected to appreciate because of the expected fall in $m + v$.[1]

Moreover, the phenomenon of *smooth pasting* – i.e. the tangency of the "S" curve in figure 15.1a with the upper and lower bands – can be explained as follows. In figure 15.1a, as $m + v$ gradually increases above zero, within the target zone s gradually falls more and more below its free market value (on the 45° line). For example, at $(m + v)_1$ the difference is AB. Also, to clear the domestic money market, i is gradually falling further below i^* – which is possible, given uncovered interest parity, only if s is expected to appreciate by successively larger amounts. The latter phenomenon can be understood by referring again to figure 15.1b. As the exchange rate moves closer and closer to its upper bound, the center of the probability distribution of $m + v$ moves closer and closer to $(m + v)_{max}$ so the shaded area increases. This means that as s rises towards is upper bound, the expected value of $(m + v)$ declines continuously and, given the proportionality between $m + v$ and s in equation 15.1, s itself is expected to take gradually lower (i.e. appreciated) values.

A further comment on this new "target zone literature" is in order. As Miller and Weller have done, the theory can be extended to real target zones (as with Williamson's (1983) target zone proposals), with similar conclusions on the notion that target zones not only reduced exchange rate variability outside the zone but also squash variability within the zone.

15.1.2 Target zones – evidence

The empirical tests of the target zone model may be catalogued into two categories: those which seek to test the predictions of the model and those which test the key underlying assumptions invoked. As we have seen, one key prediction of the model is that at the upper band a currency is expected to appreciate, whilst at the lower edge of the band the currency must be expected to depreciate. This implies that the expected change in the exchange rate should be negatively correlated with the exchange rate; that is, at the upper band we have a depreciated value of the currency but the expectation of an appreciation – a negative Δs^e_{t+k}. In testing this relationship a researcher needs a measure of the expected change in the exchange rate. This may be obtained from the uncovered interest parity condition. Thus, if the band is indeed credible (as the model assumes) then one would not expect there to be any risk of a currency depreciation/appreciation *outwith* the band. So within the band uncovered interest parity is expected to hold exactly and therefore the interest differential may be used to capture the expected change in the exchange rate: there should be a negative correlation between the interest differential and the exchange rate. Svensson (1991) and Flood, and Rose and Mathieson (1991), comprehensively examine this relationship and find more evidence of a positive relationship rather than a negative one.

A further prediction of the model is that the exchange rate should behave in a non-linear way within the band compared with the supposed linear relationship of a pure floating rate (i.e. the 45° line). This is clear from figure 15.1a. Given that a number of prominent currencies have been tied to the exchange rate mechanism of the European monetary system for much of the recent floating experience this has led a number of researchers to question whether the generally poor empirical performance of linear exchange rate models (discussed in chapters 9 to 13) may be due to the choice of an inappropriate functional form. Using a generalized version of the monetary model of the exchange rate as the fundamental model, Meese and Rose (1990) and Flood, Rose, and Mathieson (1991) implement this idea using a number of non-linear transformations for a number of different currencies: however, little improvement in the performance of the non-linear model is shown to occur over the results derived from the linear model. A simpler way of testing whether exchange rates are non-linear within bands is to plot actual exchange rates against some composite measure of fundamentals. If the model is valid, the classic S-shaped (smooth pasting) pattern should emerge. However, plots produced by Flood, Rose, and Mathieson (1991) do not suggest a clear-cut relationship.

In addition to testing the predictions of the target zone model a number of researchers have sought to test two of the key model assumptions, namely whether the zone is indeed credible and also whether foreign exchange market intervention only occurs at the margins of the band. Svensson (1991) suggests testing the former proposition by examining whether the forward exchange rated at various maturities lies inside or outside the target zone band. If it lies outwith the band this suggests that investors expect the currency to either depreciate or appreciate, depending on which edge it is at, and there must therefore be profitable arbitrage opportunities and a lack of credibility in the band. Svensson (1992) summarizes such tests by arguing that they clearly indicate that perfect credibility is rejected for most exchange rate target zones and sample periods. One problem with such tests, however, is that in using forward rates they may not be solely picking up expectations of a currency change, but rather a combination of the expected change and a time-varying risk premium (which in itself would indicate a violation of the credibility hypothesis). In order to get a direct measure of expectations some researchers have utilized the expected exchange rate produced from surveys of exchange rate dealers (see the discussion in chapter 12). This line of research also suggests that the target bands have not been credible.

The other key assumption of the model, that foreign exchange market intervention should only occur at the margins, seems also to be rejected by the data. For example, Dominguez and Kenen (1991) demonstrate that most of the intervention actually occurs within the band, rather than at the edges (see also Giavazzi and Giovannini, 1989; and Edison and Kaminsky, 1991).

15.1.3 Target zones – a modification and some further evidence

It is clear from the evidence presented above that the basic target zone model proposed by Krugman is not well supported by the extant empirical evidence. A number of researchers have therefore attempted to save the model by making one or two key modifications which seem to be warranted by the way in which actual target zone systems like the EMS have behaved in practice. Such modifications seem to result in the model being better supported by empirical tests.

One key feature of the EMS target zone system which the basic target zone model ignores is the possibility of realignments, or shifts, of the central parity. For example, between September 1979 and January 1987, inclusive, the French franc–German mark exchange rate was devalued on six occasions. If market participants at least in part anticipate such realignments, the target zone cannot be perfectly credible as is assumed in the basic target zone model. Indeed the tests of credibility referred to above suggest that the EMS target zone has not been perfectly credible. Bertola and Caballero (1992) propose a variant of the Krugman model in which the movement of the exchange rate is in natural logs equal to the sum of the exchange rate within the band, x_t, and the central parity rate, c_t:

$$s_t = x_t + c_t \tag{15.2}$$

Using this expression the expected change in the exchange rate may, in turn, be defined as

$$E_t \frac{ds_t}{dt} \equiv E_t \frac{dx_t}{dt} + E_t \frac{dc_t}{dt} \tag{15.3}$$

Where $E_t(dx_t/dt)$ is the expected rate of currency depreciation within the band and $E_t(dc_t/dt)$ is the expected rate of realignment. On using this definition of $E_t(ds_t/dt)$ in (15.1) and subtracting c_t from the resulting expression we obtain an equation describing the exchange rate within the band as

$$x_t = h_t + \alpha_2 E_t \frac{dx_t}{dt} \tag{15.4}$$

where h_t is the new composite fundamental and is equal to $f_t - c_t + \alpha_2 E_t(dc_t/dt)$. Equation (15.4) has two immediate implications for empirical tests. First, even if uncovered interest rate parity holds continuously, this extended target zone model suggests that one cannot say *a priori* what the relationship between the exchange rate and the interest rate differential will be like (remember that in the basic Krugman model it is supposed to be negative). This is because uncovered interest rate parity holds for the total expected change in the exchange rate which from (15.3) is equal to two elements. As in our discussion of the Krugman model one would expect there to be a negative association between the expected rate of currency depreciation within the band and the exchange rate, but one cannot say anything about the relationship between the expected rate of alignment and the exchange rate. Since the latter component of (15.3) is time varying it could easily swamp the former, resulting in a positive or negative relationship between the exchange rate and the interest differential (hence the positive association referred to above may be explained in this way). A second implication of (15.4) for an empirical test is that one should include the expected rate of realignment in one's measure of the composite fundamentals term. Rose and Svensson (1991) plot the composite fundamentals term h_t against the exchange rate and find that it conforms more closely to the pattern predicted in figure 15.1(a) in that it has a slope of less than unity (which is supportive of the so-called honeymoon effect); however, it does not have the flat slope at the edge of the zone, usually associated with the smooth pasting phenomenon.

In order to explain the latter contradiction attention has focused on the kind of intervention most often practised by central banks. In the Krugman model (marginal) intervention need only take place at the edge of the band – hence the smooth pasting effect. In practice central bank intervention will often take place well within the band (i.e. it is intra-marginal, or leaning-against-the-wind, intervention). To take account of this in terms of the imperfect credibility version of the model noted above, Lindberg and Soderlind (1992) suggest that the intra-marginal interventions result in the expected change of the composite fundamentals term (i.e. h_t) towards the central parity – proportional to the distance to central parity. This is demonstrated to imply that the relationship between the exchange rate and the fundamentals is much closer to a simple linear relationship than that implied in the original Krugman model. Indeed, the relationship is shown to be similar to that pertaining in an ordinary managed float (i.e. without any intervention bands). The schedule MM in figure 15.1(a) illustrates this. This relationship seems more like the empirical relationship of Rose and Svensson (1991) referred to above. The extended target zone model therefore seems well suited to explaining how exchange rates are determined within target bands. For an application of the target zone theory to the gold standard periods see Hallwood, MacDonald and Marsh (1996).

As we have seen a key feature of the target zone model is that exchange rates should be mean reverting within the band, and this is stressed by Svensson (1991). Anthony and MacDonald (1998, 1999) test this key property of the target zone model and for the ERM experience they find some evidence in favour of mean reversion (particularly towards the end of the ERM experiment) and also that the size of the band is not curial in determining this finding.

15.2 Target Zone Credibility

A target zone is credible – in the sense that the market believes that the exchange rate will be contained within it – if it is believed that the monetary authorities are committed to managing fundamentals to that end. Thus, to maintain credibility, an exogenous shock to fundamentals, say a fall in real economic activity, that would otherwise push the exchange rate outside of the target zone, must be offset by a monetary contraction – for instance, by open market sales of domestic securities. Thus, as we said before, at the edges of the target zone monetary policy must be geared exclusively to the exchange rate and not, say, toward influencing business conditions. But when the exchange rate is in the interior of the zone the monetary authorities do have some freedom of action.

How can we tell whether monetary authorities under various pegged exchange rate regimes – from the gold standard to the European Monetary System – have behaved in such a way as for financial markets to regard a commitment to a peg (and its fluctuation band) to be credible?[2] To answer this question some measure of *realignment expectations* is needed.

This measure has been developed in Svensson (1991), Svensson (1993), and Bertola and Svensson (1993). A finding of statistically significant realignment expectations suggests that the authority's commitment to a given exchange rate peg is not credible. The market may be interpreted as expecting a devaluation (if monetary policy is deemed to be too loose), or, upvaluation (if too tight).

15.2.1 Calculating realignment expectations: the simplest test

This method of calculating realignment expectations utilizes the concept of uncovered interest parity which says that the interest differential between two countries is equal to the expected rate of change of the exchange rate.

In order to bring the following argument together we repeat equation (15.2): in natural logarithms the exchange rate at time t, s_t, is

$$s_t = x_t + c_t \tag{15.5}$$

where, again, c_t is the central parity and x_t is the proportionate deviation from parity. Taking time derivatives

$$E_t[ds_t]/dt = E_t[dx_t]/dt + E_t[dc_t]/dt \tag{15.6}$$

which, again, says that the rationally expected rate of change of the exchange rate can be divided into the expected movement "within the band," $(E_t[dx_t]/dt)$, plus the expected rate of depreciation of the central parity, $(E_t[dc_t]/dt)$.

Furthermore, for any given x_t, the movement within the band is bounded by the lower (strong) and upper (weak) intervention points

$$(x_t^l - x_t)/dt \le E_t[dx_t]/dt \le (x_t^u - x_t)/dt \tag{15.7}$$

where x^l is the lower bound of s_t, and x^u, the upper bound.

On using equations (15.6) and (15.7) we discover the confidence interval for realignment expectations

$$(i_t - i_t^*) - (x_t^u - x_t)/dt \le E_t[dc]/dt \le (i - i^*) - (x_t^l - x_t)/dt \tag{15.8}$$

where i_t is the home country's interest rate and i_t^* is a comparable interest rate in the foreign country. The term $(i_t - i_t^*)$ – the interest differential – has been substituted for $E_t[ds_t]/dt$ because we are assuming that uncovered interest parity holds.[3] (The forward premium could have been used instead.)

Equation (15.8) defines the minimum and maximum bounds of the market's rationally expected central parity realignment. Svennson called this the "*simplest test*" for realignment expectations.

A numerical illustration may be helpful. Suppose that a pegged exchange rate regime had a plus/minus 0.5 percent fluctuation band around its central parity, that the exchange rate happened to be at the center of the zone (i.e. $x_t = 0$ and, therefore, $x_t^u - x_t = 0.5\%$), but that the expected change in the exchange rate as measured by the interest differential was 5 percent. It follows that $4.5\% \le E_t[dc]/dt \le 5.5\%$ and we are confident that depreciation of the central parity is expected. Suppose again that the exchange rate is in the centre of its zone but that the expected depreciation is only 0.25 percent. Thus, $-0.25\% \le E_t[dc]/dt \le 0.75\%$. In this case the range of expectations spans both a possible appreciation of the central parity and a depreciation. As this range spans zero, the null hypothesis of no realignment cannot be rejected.

15.2.2 Calculating realignment expectations: the drift adjustment method

Svensson complements the simplest test for realignment expectations with that of the "*drift adjustment method*" which uses an econometric estimate of expected reversion of the exchange rate to parity within the target zone (Svensson, 1993, p. 768).

Rearranging equation (15.6) obtains a statement of the rationally expected realignment expectation as

$$E_t[dc]/dt = E_t[ds]/dt - E_t[dx]/dt \qquad (15.9)$$

This realignment expectation can be calculated if the two terms on the RHS are known. The expected change in the exchange rate, $E_t[ds]/dt$, is known from the interest differential, and Svensson (1993) gives a simplified method for calculating the expected movement of the exchange rate within the band. He takes this to be a linear function of the current deviation, x_t, of the exchange rate from the central parity.[4] The expected movement of the exchange rate within the band, therefore is

$$x_{t+m} - x_t = a_0 + a_1 x_t + u_t \qquad (15.10)$$

i.e. the expected movement in the band depends on the current deviation from the center of the band. And if a_1 is significantly less than zero we have mean reversion.[5]

The final step in implementing equation (15.9) is to take the 95 percent confidence intervals for mean reversion – calculated using equation (15.10) – and to combine them with the interest rate differential (or forward premium) data, which proxy for $E_t[ds]/dt$, to calculate the "95 percent" confidence intervals for realignment expectations.

You could turn now to section 16.1.3 for an econometric application of the drift adjustment.[6]

◆ 15.3 Calculating the Devaluation Probability

Another development of the target zone model is to break realignment expectations into their individual components. Thus, the expected rate of realignment, measured as the interest rate differential, can be interpreted as the expected devaluation size multiplied by the frequency of realignment.

To illustrate, suppose that, conditional on there being a devaluation, the devaluation will be 5 percent. An expected rate of realignment of 2.5 percent implies that the expected frequency of realignment is 0.5 per annum. That is, the market expects a 5 percent devaluation within the year to happen with a 50 percent probability. Equivalently, the expected time to a 5 percent devaluation of a currency is two years. Thus, though the average expected rate of realignment may appear to be small it can be consistent with quite substantial devaluation expectations.

Following Mizrach (1995) the expected exchange rate change is determined as follows:

$$intsp_t^k = [(1 - p_t^k)E_t[\Delta s_{t+k} \mid nodeval] + p_t^k E_t[\Delta s_{t+k} \mid deval]]/k \qquad (15.11)$$

where $intsp_t^k$ denotes the interest rate differential (home minus foreign country's) on bills of maturity k years, p_t^k denotes the time t probability of a devaluation (home currency) during the subsequent k years, and s_t denotes the spot exchange rate. What this equation says is that the interest differential equals the probability weighted change in the spot exchange rate under the alternative scenarios of a devaluation and no devaluation.

There are four independent terms in equation (15.11) – the interest differential, the expected change in the exchange rate conditional on no devaluation, the expected change in the exchange rate conditional on a devaluation, and the probability of devaluation. The one that we are after is the probability of devaluation, $p_{t,}^k$ which can be isolated if the other three independent terms are known or can be proxied.

The easiest one to calculate is obviously the interest rate differential, but care must be taken to use comparable interest rates. The term $E_t[\Delta s_{t+k} \mid nodeval]$ is simply the movement of the exchange rate within the band which can be modeled as in equation (15.10). This leaves $E_t[\Delta s_{t+k} \mid deval]$ which Mizrach (1995) models as a linear function of the size of the last devaluation. Other methods can also be used to estimate the size of the latter term, for example making it proportional to the deviation of an exchange rate from purchasing power parity.

Having recovered the time series of probabilities of devaluation from equation (15.11) it is then possible to regress $p_{t,}^k$ on its determinants. The set of

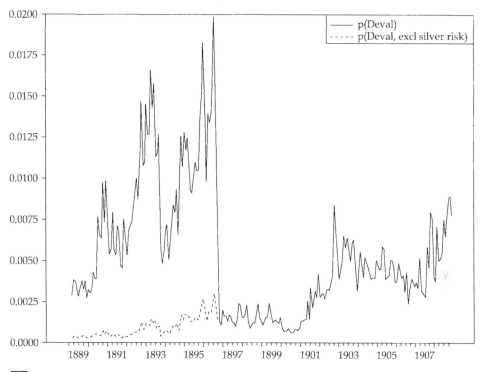

Figure 15.2 An example of probability of devaluation

determinants of the probability of devaluation includes things such as macro-economic fundamentals, interest rate term structures and, perhaps, dummy variables to capture political or other non-economic events.

As an example of the application of this model, Hallwood, MacDonald, and Marsh (1998) apply it to the USA during the period 1890–1908 when, for part of this period, American continued adherence to the gold standard was in doubt. We use two dummies to capture the effects on the probability of realignment of, first, the Silver Purchase Act, 1890–3 (which partly untied the US money base from gold) and, secondly, political pressure for a return to a bimetallic silver–gold stand-ard which lasted from at least 1890 until the defeat of the silver candidate in the presidential election of November 1896. We also use three fundamentals: the relative (US minus UK) year-on-year growth rates of money (measured as notes and coin in circulation), relative year-on-year income growth rates, and the real exchange rate. All fundamentals being lagged one period. The first dummy takes a value of one if the Silver Puchase Act is on the US statutes (1890/7 to 1893/10) and a zero otherwise. The second dummy takes a value of one if the bimetallism debate is still active in the US, defined as the period from the start of our sample, 1890/1 to 1896/11.

Our results are illustrated in figure 15.2 where it is shown that the probability of dollar devaluation peaks at about the time the 1890 Act was repealed, and again at the time of the 1896 presidential election – which turned out to be closely run.

That the dollar was under pressure on the exchanges mainly because of political factors is evident from the dashed line which nets out silver risk – in other words US macro-fundamentals were not out of line with the commitment to the gold peg.

The probability of dollar devaluation falling sharply after 1896 can be interpreted as a long-lasting shift in sentiment in favor of the dollar. It has been a puzzle for a hundred years as to why the Fisher equation (see section 3.5) for real interest parity apparently did not hold after 1896 and into the early years of the twentieth century. With real interest parity the Fisher equation predicts that a rise in a country's inflation differential will cause its interest rate differential likewise to increase – so keeping real interest rates between a pair of countries unchanged. Yet during this period US inflation increased relative to that in the UK but the US interest differential over UK rates did not. This fall in US real interest rates relative to UK rates is entirely consistent with a shift in sentiment in favor of the dollar – speculators trying to demand a lower real return on short-term dollar denominated assets.

15.4 Dirty Floating

The term "dirty floating" was used soon after the general move to floating exchange rates in the early 1970s. What it means is that a monetary authority states an official policy of letting the exchange rate float, yet frequently intervenes in the foreign exchange market to manage the exchange rate.

Perhaps dirty floating is best analyzed using the exchange market pressure model of Girton and Roper (1977). In this model demand and supply for base money are always equal. Thus,

$$H = F + D = PY^{\beta}exp^{-\alpha i} \qquad \beta, \alpha > 0 \qquad (15.12)$$

where H is the money base, F is foreign exchange reserves, D domestic securities held by the central bank, and $PY^{\beta}exp^{-\alpha i}$ a Cagan-style money demand function.

Writing the last equation in logs, taking time derivatives and noting that F and D are both expressed as proportions of H, gives

$$\dot{f} + \dot{d} = \pi + \beta\dot{y} - \alpha i' \qquad (15.13)$$

where all variables are expressed as rates of change in, respectively, reserves, domestic securities (known as domestic credit expansion, or, DCE), the price level, real income, and the rate of interest.

To find the international consequence of DCE, inflation etc. subtract the foreign country variables from these home country variables, giving

$$\dot{f} - \dot{f}^* = -\dot{d} + \dot{d}^* + \beta\dot{y} - \beta^*\dot{y}^* + \pi - \pi^* - \alpha(i' - i^*') \qquad (15.14)$$

Now add e – the rate of appreciation of the exchange rate (stated as the amount of foreign currency per unit of home currency, so an increase is an appreciation – e is the reciprocal of s) to both sides of the last equation to give

$$\dot{f} - \dot{f}^* + \dot{e} = -\dot{d} + \dot{d}^* + \beta\dot{y} - \beta^*\dot{y}^* + \dot{q} - \alpha(i' - i^{*\prime}) \qquad (15.15)$$

where $\dot{f} - \dot{f}^* + \dot{e}$ is dubbed "exchange market pressure" (EMP), a *decrease* in EMP signifying an increase in "pressure" against a monetary authority (as the rate of increase in foreign exchange reserves and/or appreciation of the currency has fallen); and $\dot{q}$ ($= \pi - \pi^* + \dot{e}$) is the rate of appreciation of the real exchange rate. Thus, EMP increases with an increase in the home country's rate of DCE or rate of interest (both of which inducing dishoarding); and it decreases with an increase in the rate of growth of real income and the real exchange rate (both of which inducing hoarding).

Notice that with a floating exchange rate the monetary authority can choose how to absorb shocks to the RHS variables: it can let either $\dot{f}$ or $\dot{e}$ or both change. If the authority does not want the exchange rate to move too much (because, for example, it does not want a lot of volatility), it can use its foreign exchange reserves. Alternatively, if it is targeting reserves, it can let $\dot{e}$ "take the strain."

Notice also that if $\dot{f} = 0$, there is no foreign exchange intervention, equation (15.15) reduces to the monetary approach to the exchange rate; while, if instead $\dot{e} = 0$ we have the monetary approach to the balance of payments.

Also, the EMP model is relevant when a country contains its exchange rate within an official fluctuation band or "target zone." The authorities can allow the exchange rate to float freely within the upper- and lower-edges of the zone; only necessarily having to intervene with foreign exchange reserves when the exchange rate threatens to penetrate either edge.

Girton and Roper (1977) test the EMP for the Canadian–US dollar. They treat Canada as a small country and estimate the equation

$$\dot{f}_c + \dot{e}_c = \beta_0 + \beta_{1c}\dot{d}_c + \beta_{2us}\dot{h}_{us} + \beta_{3c}\dot{y}_c + \beta_{4us}\dot{y}_{us} + v \qquad (15.16)$$

where, respectively, "c" and "us" stand for Canada and the USA; and the expected signs are $\beta_{1c} < 0$, $\beta_{2us} > 0$, $\beta_{3c} > 0$, and $\beta_{4us} < 0$. In their linear regression of this equation the expected signs are found at high levels of significance.

Finally, Hallwood, MacDonald, and Marsh (1996) test equation (15.16) using monthly data for the interwar gold standard period. The gold standard, while often viewed as a fixed rate system, in fact featured a fluctuation band (defined by the gold points). The results are reported in table 15.1. The dependent variable is exchange market pressure and the exchange rate is the pound/dollar rate.

The results are hardly econometrically startling but in the first column we find four correct signs out of five, two of them being statistically significant. In the second column terms have been added for the expected movement of the exchange rate "within the band," $E[dx]/dt$, and the expected "movement of the band" (at the time meaning an expectation of sterling devaluation), $E[dc]/dt$. This is allowed because in equation (15.8), using uncovered interest parity, the interest differential is equal to the expected movement of the exchange rate, which is itself composed of $E[dx]/dt + E[dc]/dt$. (Any risk premium is subsumed into the latter term.) Both of these factors are expected to affect exchange market pressure on the pound. The negative and significant sign for $E[dc]/dt$ is

Table 15.1 Exchange market pressure model of interwar gold standard

	UK/US	
d	−0.853	−0.836
	(2.70)	(2.56)
d*	0.007	−0.014
	(0.02)	(0.04)
π − π*	−0.533	−0.696
	(1.36)	(1.56)
y* − y	−0.058	−0.060
	(1.70)	(1.62)
i*′ − i′	−11.015	
	(2.44)	
E[dx]/dt		−2.200
		(1.68)
E[dc]/dt		−3.665
		(2.58)
Std. Error	0.0156	0.0170
No. Obs	72	72

d denotes the growth in domestic credit (domestic credit defined as money base less reserves), π denotes the growth in the inflation rate, y denotes the growth in income, and i′ denotes the growth in the interest rate. An asterisk denotes foreign (US) variables. Seasonal dummies are included in the estimated equation. All equations are estimated using McCallum–Wickens instrumental variables. The instrument set is the dependent and each explanatory variable lagged by two and three periods, together with a constant, time trend and seasonal dummies (unlagged). The figures in parentheses under the coefficient estimates are t-statistics computed with GMM standard errors.

expected as expectations of a devaluation increase exchange market pressure – for example, by encouraging capital outflows. For more on the gold standard see the next chapter.

NOTES

1 This argument is symmetrical for the part of the zone between the central rate and the lower limit of s. Thus, if the exchange rate reached the lower intervention point, a fall in v is expected by the market to be offset by a rise in m. Hence, on average s is expected to rise.
2 Under the gold standard there was no international commitment to a predefined target zone. Rather, target zones existed as biproducts of mint par parity and gold-movement transaction costs, the latter of which defined gold export and import points which acted as a fluctuation band.
3 As Svensson (1993, p. 766) points out, if agents arbitraging between national money markets demand a risk premium, the interest differential measures the expected change in the exchange rate plus the risk premium.

4 It is possible to make this assertion because according to Krugman (1988, 1991) in a credible target zone the exchange rate should be mean reverting.
5 Notice that equation (15.10) is in the form of a test for a unit root where $a_1 = p - 1$.
6 It turns out in our calculations that realignment expectations during various phases of the gold standard were almost identical whether using the simplest test or the drift adjustment method. Notice the great advantage of the drift adjustment method for the gold standard is that the gold points were not known for sure – those of *The Economist* were only estimates.

16

The International Gold Standard: Theory and Experience

The history of the international monetary system is like a person's biography. The interesting questions are: how did she get to be what she is? What skeletons are in the cupboard? What can we learn? These questions are relevant today given the widespread dissatisfaction with floating rates, discussions of blueprints for international monetary reform, and monetary union in Europe. In this and the next chapter we investigate, respectively, the gold standard ("classical" period, circa 1875–1914, and interwar, circa 1925–31), and, in chapter 17, the Bretton Woods–IMF system and the current decaying dollar standard. Section 10.3 discusses exchange rate volatility under different exchange rate regimes, chapter 18 discusses monetary union, and chapter 24 international monetary reform. In this chapter, section 16.1 discusses the classical gold standard and section 16.2 the gold standard during the interwar period.

16.1 Credibility and Exchange Rate Regimes

Time-inconsistency problems arise when policymakers have incentives to deviate from announced policy once private decision-makers have adjusted to it (Kydland and Prescott, 1977). A central bank, having announced a policy of low-inflation, may subsequently engineer an inflation-surprise in order to reduce unemployment. If private decision-makers anticipate this, the low-inflation policy is not credible, inflation-expectations will not fall, and the inflation–unemployment trade-off will remain unfavorable. History appears to show that to avoid time-inconsistency a central bank should adopt a commitment-mechanism which credibly makes monetary policy non-discretionary – and the gold standard appears to be one such.

Another modern view is that an exchange rate regime can be interpreted in the context of policy rules versus discretion. Giovannini (1993) sees pegged exchange rates as "natural" – because they provide a credible policy *rule* that stabilizes inflation expectations more effectively than does, say, monetary targeting. The advantage of pegging is that the policy is overt and everybody knows when the rule has been broken; but monetary targeting is opaque: which monetary aggregate is in play, can it be controlled, when has the target been missed? Pegged international systems have been abandoned in the face of serious shocks – such as the Napoleonic Wars, the First World War, the Great Depression, and the Vietnam War – which have excessively increased the cost of adherence to the regime. On this view floating exchange rates are "interlude regimes" – a mere "escape clause" utilized when the going get too tough. But Wyplosz (1993) mentions that it is not clear that pegged exchange rates constitute a "rule" while floating is "discretion." After all, floating is sensibly accompanied with rules – e.g. on fiscal deficits and monetary targets. Besides, pegging allows for some policy discretion.

During the gold standard era a monetary authority would buy or sell gold at a fixed price.[1] But, given transaction costs, the gold export and import points defined, respectively, upper and lower bounds of an exchange rate fluctuation band.[2] Similarly, in pegged systems, such as the EMS and the Bretton Woods system, currencies were restricted to a narrow band. As is shown in section 16.1.1, fluctuation bands allow for some degree of discretionary monetary policy: some monetary expansion is possible if an exchange rate is allowed to depreciate within the band. Indeed, research (e.g. by Eichengreen, Watson, and Grossman, 1985; and Goodhart, 1972) establishes that the Bank of England did practise discretionary monetary policy during the successive episodes of commitments to pegged exchange rates. It is a mistake to call the international gold standard "automatic," believing that changes in a country's interest rates and money-base were entirely governed by its balance of international payments.

If a pegged exchange rate regime can be classified as a "policy rule with limited discretion," credibility of commitment is in focus. Monetary policy may not be consistent with the commitment to the exchange rate peg. If a monetary authority uses its scope "within the exchange rate band" to accommodate deflationary real shocks it may overdo it and cause a devaluation. When discretion is practised the very commitment to an exchange rate peg may not be deemed to be time-consistent. This may have been the case with some Latin American countries that have tried on and off during the last three of decades to use exchange rate pegs to anchor inflationary expectations *before* reducing their fiscal deficits.

In this and the next chapter a recurring theme is the credibility of national commitments to pegged exchange rates from circa 1875. Bordo and Kydland (1992) examine time-consistency features of the classical gold standard period, finding that adherence by the monetary authorities to the "rules of the game" constituted a credible commitment not to inflate. They contrast the experience of strong adherents to the classical gold standard with the weakly committed Italy finding that interest rates on Italian government bonds included a large and variable risk premium – a fact which they explain in terms of inflation expectations not having benefited from a credible monetary policy. A similar argument about the USA in the 1890s is made by Friedman and Schwartz (1963), Schwartz (1987), and Hallwood, MacDonald, and Marsh (1999).

16.1.1 The classical gold standard: circa 1875–1914

From the voluminous literature on this subject we will discuss three of the most important topics:

1 the UK's position at the heart of the system;
2 short-term capital flows and the credibility of commitments to pegged exchange rates (via fixed gold prices); and
3 the "transfer problem" and long-term capital flows.

But before doing so we will discuss some important time-series properties of pegged exchange rates versus floating rates. These have been investigated by Alogoskoufis and Smith (1991) for the UK and US from the classical gold standard until 1987. They find that inflation rates are a first-order autoregression and they compare ρ values for various historical sub-periods.

In a first-order autoregression

$$x_t = \rho x_{t-1} + v_t \tag{16.1}$$

where ρ lies between plus/minus unity. The closer is ρ to positive unity the greater is the effect of x_{t-1} on x_t. That is, the more "persistent" is the time series as a shock to x_{t-1} more strongly influences $x_t \ldots x_{t+n}$. Values of ρ close to zero cause the effect of shocks quickly to die out.

Their findings on inflation persistence are shown in the first column of table 16.1. In both the UK and the US inflation persistence (high ρ values) is greater during periods of floating exchange rates. For example, taking 1967 (when the pound was devalued) as the post-Second World War divide between fixed and floating rates, ρ jumps from 0.27 during the 1948–1967 period to 0.74 during 1968–87. For the US, the respective ρ values are 0.25 and 0.70.

Alogoskoufis and Smith (1991) also estimate expectations augmented Phillips curves for the different time periods as

$$\Delta w_t = \alpha_0 + \alpha_1 \rho \Delta p_{t-1} - \alpha_2 \Delta u_t - \alpha_3 u_{t-1} + \xi_t \tag{16.2}$$

where in logs w_t is the nominal wage, ρ the first-order autoregression coefficient, p the consumer price index, u_t the unemployment rate and ξ_t a white noise error term. It is an increase in $\alpha_1 \rho$ that measures an upward shift in the Phillips curve due to increased inflation expectations. Calculated values of $\alpha_1 \rho$ are shown in the second column of table 16.1.

These findings relate to the loss of credibility of commitment and the time-consistency of monetary policy under floating exchange rates. The evidence is that in table 16.1, $\alpha_1 \rho$ jumps dramatically in 1914 and again in the late 1960s. In other

Table 16.1 How current inflation depends on past inflation p, and the expectations augmented Phillips curve $\alpha_1 p$

	p	$\alpha_1 p$	Exchange Rate regime
UK			
1. 1857–1987	.76	0.95	
2. 1857–1913	.26	0.30	fixed – gold standard
3. 1914–1987	.74	0.91	fixed *and* floating
Post-World War II			
4. 1948–1987	.80	0.78	
5. 1948–1967	.27	0.28	fixed – Bretton Woods
6. 1968–1987	.74	0.46	mainly floating
USA			
7. 1892–1987	.64	0.64	
8. 1892–1913	.20	–0.17	fixed – gold standard
9. 1914–1987	.63	0.63	fixed *and* floating
Post-World War II			
10. 1948–1987	.62	0.53	
11. 1948–1967	.25	0.23	fixed – Bretton Woods
12. 1968–1987	.70	0.81	mainly floating

All p and $\alpha_1 p$ values are statistically significant except for p numbers 5, 8 and 11, and $\alpha_1 p$ numbers 5 and 8. Wald tests for the significance of shifts between the crucial periods 2 *versus* 3, 5 v. 6, 8 v. 9, and 11 v. 12 are statistically significant.
Source: Alogoskoufis and Smith (1991)

words, wage setters began to give a greater weight to past inflation – as a predictor of expected inflation (presumably because they expected the effect of past inflation on the real money supply to be accommodated) – just at the time when pegged exchange rates were abandoned and the prospect for monetary accommodation increased.

16.1.2 The UK's position in the classical gold standard

What are the main reasons for the success of the classical system? According to Gallarotti (1995) one reason is the dominant political philosophy of the day, laissez faire – which allowed markets to "work," discouraged fiscal deficits, and favored monetary discipline. Also the UK, as the world's dominant economic and financial power, acted beneficially for the international monetary system. She was the main source of long-term capital loans – lending long and borrowing short as long-term capital outflows exceeded her current account surpluses (Lindert, 1969). The UK also practised free trade, so allowing other countries to repay international debts in commodities rather than gold. Thus, the UK did not drain gold from debtor nations, rather, she promoted the reflow of international finance (Morgan-Webb, 1934). This contrasts with the experience of the interwar gold standard when both the US and France drained gold from other members of the system.

According to Cassel the classical gold standard was successful because it was a sterling standard: "the pre-[first world] war gold standard may not inadequately be described as a sterling bloc held together by London's position as the world's financial centre and by the pound sterling as a generally recognized means for international payments."[4] Sterling balances held in London economized on gold and were used to settle international balances. World trade was largely financed in sterling bills of exchange drawn on British banks. Lindert (1969) points out that by 1913, foreign exchange (including some French francs and German marks) made up about 19 percent of the world's "gold and foreign exchange" reserves, rising from about 10 percent in 1880. Thus, classical gold standard was really a gold-exchange standard, with sterling as the key currency.

However, London was *not* the "conductor of the international orchestra" with the Bank of England setting interest rates for the system as a whole. Rather, as Eichengreen and Flandreau (1996) point out, it was a multi-polar system with London, Paris, and Berlin having their own spheres of influence. Furthermore, tracing Granger "causality" between changes in central bank discount rates Tullio and Wolters (1996) show that the Bank of England often followed discount rate changes in Germany and, sometimes, in Paris. Besides, as an open pegged system the monetary approach to the balance of payments applied and money in the UK was endogenous (McCloskey and Zecher, 1976). Although not widely recognized, the same also applied to the USA in the period 1929–33 – and the Great Depression there had international causes (see section 16.2.5).

The key factor in the success of the classical gold standard was that it was a credible system.[4] Financial markets seem to have been convinced that the pound, franc, and mark would not be devalued, and this set up a virtuous interaction: exchange rate credibility promoted stabilizing short-term capital flows which helped to stabilize exchange rates. It was not the size of the UK's gold reserve that bred confidence in the key currency, rather it was the Bank of England's dexterity in managing its bank rate to this end that was the crucial factor. Bloomfield (1959) and Goodhart (1972) show that bank rate was managed procyclically – in order to reduce long-term capital outflow when the current account weakened with economic expansion.

16.1.3 Credibility and short-term capital flows

Figure 16.1 shows the dollar–sterling fluctuation-band, or, "target zone" for *The Economist's* contemporaneous estimate and one by Clark (1984). The fact that the dollar–pound exchange rate sometimes penetrated these estimated gold points does not necessarily mean that they did not set credible bounds to the exchange rate. This is because the gold points almost certainly varied over time – for instance, as interest rates changed (Office, 1996).

To discuss the matter of credibility in more detail we use Hallwood, MacDonald, and Marsh (1996). In the target zone theory of Krugman (1991) (see section 14.1.1)

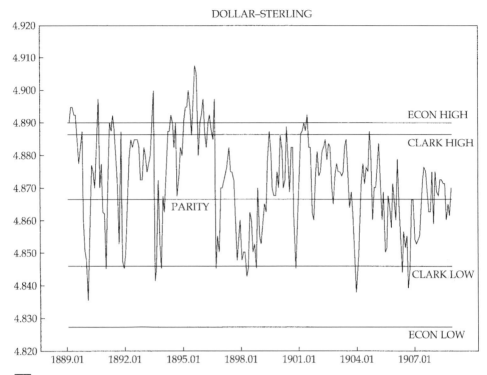

DOLLAR–STERLING

Figure 16.1 Spot rate and gold points

exchange rates between the gold points should be mean reverting – movement of an exchange rate near one of the gold points should be back towards the centre of the zone. That is, in an AR(1) process, ρ should be significantly less than unity. The time-series of exchange rates should be a stationary process. For this to be so, it must be the case that the fundamental determinants of an exchange rate should not leave a currency permanently weak at the gold export point (or strong at the gold import point). Variance ratio and unit root tests of the US dollar–pound and French franc–pound exchange rates, 1889–1908, indicate strong evidence of mean reversion.

Another test for the credibility of commitment is to use uncovered interest parity to test the prediction that the difference between a pair of comparable short-term interest rates in two countries, should not deviate by more than the maximum allowable movement of the exchange rate "within the band." If the deviation in these interest rates is any greater than this, then "the market" is deemed to expect an exchange rate realignment.

Realignment expectations for the franc–pound and dollar–pound exchange rates are reproduced, respectively, as figures 16.2 and 16.3. The two lines in each figure are 95 percent confidence intervals. Only when both are of the same sign (e.g. above the zero line) are realignment expectations taken to be statistically significant.

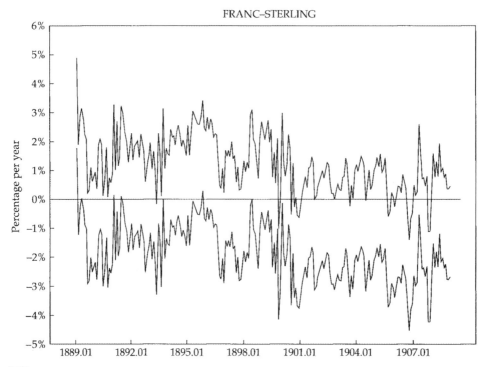

FRANC–STERLING

Figure 16.2 Realignment expectations for the franc–pound exchange rate

Note: When both confidence intervals are positive, franc devaluation is expected; vice versa for the pound. If they are of opposite sign accept statistically that no realignment is expected.

The striking fact about the franc–pound exchange rate is that markets rarely questioned the gold commitment in either France or the UK. The case of the US dollar is somewhat different as until 1896 the dollar was often expected to devalue (a significant positive realignment expectation). The USA's political commitment to the gold standard was threatened by the "free silver movement," which advocated the remonetization of silver. The defeat of the Democratic "free silver" candidate in the election of 1896 marks the end of significant dollar realignment expectations in figure 16.3. See also Section 15.3.

16.1.4 Long-term capital flows under the classical gold standard

During this period long-term capital flowed from the Old World (especially the UK, France, and Germany) to the New World (in particular the USA, Canada, and Argentina), and real resources were transferred via trade account surpluses in the former and deficits in the latter. Several mechanisms have been emphasized as affecting real transfers: the monetary, the real exchange rate, the relative price between traded and non-traded goods (Taussig, 1927), and the terms of trade. The latter three mechanisms can be grouped together because they are strongly

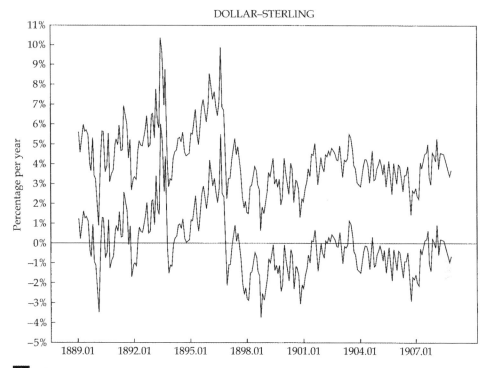

DOLLAR–STERLING

Figure 16.3 Realignment expectations for the dollar–pound exchange rate

interrelated. It can be shown that the real exchange rate is equal to the ratio of traded to non-traded goods prices, and that on certain assumptions it is equal to the reciprocal of the terms of trade.

Monetary analysis

In the monetary analysis of the gold standard by McCloskey and Zecher (1976) relative prices do not enter into balance of payments adjustment. This could be true if countries are "small," the exchange rate is fixed, *and* all goods are traded goods. In this case all prices are given parametrically and are unaffected by changes in the desire to hoard. In this model a rise in the rate of saving in the capital exporting country releases resources for transfer to the capital importing country – see section 4.6 for an intertemporal utility maximizing model of the current account. The former's trade account goes into surplus and its capital account into deficit. Incipient changes in interest rates give rise to appropriate changes in the long term capital accounts.

Relative price adjustments

More realistically, as the main capital exporting countries were "large" and had substantial non-traded goods sectors, relative price adjustments played a major role in the transfer process.

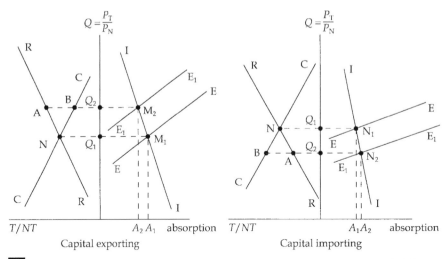

Figure 16.4 Relative price adjustment and sustained long-term capital flows

Figure 16.4 shows internal and external balance in a pair of capital exporting and importing countries. It is based on the model set out in section 4.2. RR is the ratio of traded to non-traded goods in a country's domestic production. A real depreciation increases profitability in traded goods production – so raising the ratio T/NT in production. CC is T/NT in domestic consumption, and it is a negative function of Q as appreciation raises the relative price of traded goods. Where RR and CC intersect, the trade account = 0. II, internal balance, is a negative function of Q as real appreciation reduces foreign demand which is balanced by greater domestic absorption. EE is external balance – greater absorption increases imports and Q needs to depreciate to balance the external account. EE is drawn for some given level of "sustainable" capital flow which, we assume, starts out at zero. Initially both economies are in equilibrium at M_1 and N_1.

To affect a real transfer of resources, the capital exporting country needs to develop a trade surplus and this requires its real exchange rate to depreciate – say, to Q_2 – which will cause resources to move into its traded goods sector and domestic consumption to move toward its non-traded goods. The trade surplus is measured relative to A–B. As this trade surplus is financing a "sustainable" capital outflow, the EE function shifts to E_1E_1 as absorption at any real exchange rate must be reduced.

Notice that in the capital exporting country the rate of saving has increased because its absorption has fallen from A_1 to A_2.

In the capital importing country, capital inflow enables absorption to increase at any exchange rate and EE shifts to the right. At the new equilibrium, N_2, the equilibrium real exchange rate has appreciated, absorption increased and a trade deficit appeared.

Thus, the transfer "problem" story can be told as running from an exogenous increase in the propensity to save in the capital exporting country – the desired lower level of absorption allowing larger "sustainable" long-term capital outflow (EE shifts left). With greater savings there is an incipient fall in the domestic long-term interest rate relative to those in a capital importing countries. The depreciation of the real exchange rate plays the crucial role of inducing resources to be reallocated out of the capital exporting country's non-traded goods sector and into its traded goods sector. Or, the story could be told the other way round. A rise in the demand for capital in a capital *importing* country causes its real interest rate to rise relative to that in the capital exporting country. "Sustainable" capital inflow increases, shifting EE to the right in the capital importing country and to the left in the capital exporting country. The equilibrium real exchange rate appreciates in the former country and depreciates in the latter country.

The cushioning effect of international capital flows Economic historians have argued that international capital flows under the gold standard had beneficial effects additional to those already discussed. With *monetary shocks*, changes in the balance of payments (B) and money supply (M) are inversely related. Thus, an autonomous increase in M is worked off through dishoarding via both the current account and the capital account – the latter as domestic interest rates fall. With *non-monetary shocks* B and M are directly related. Consider two examples: (i) there is a sudden switch in home demand to foreign goods causing both B and M to fall. But the fall in M will cause the domestic rate of interest to rise as residents sell bonds in an effort to replenish M in their asset portfolios. The higher *i* attracts capital inflow which does indeed cushion the effect of the real shock on the country's balance of payments (the sum of the negative current account and positive capital account) and domestic money supply. Effectively the country is borrowing in order to enjoy increased consumption of foreign goods. (ii) There is a fall in national production due to, say, a harvest failure which causes either imports of food to rise or exports to fall. Again B and M both fall and *i* rises. The induced capital inflow represents borrowing from abroad to soften the effect of the harvest failure on real consumption.

16.2 The Gold Standard During the Interwar Period

Dozens of countries, following the British lead in April 1925, rejoined the international gold standard only to abandon gold six years later. The USA hung on until March 1933, and France and a few other "gold block" countries until September 1936.

We will discuss four main questions concerning the interwar gold standard:

1 Were exchange rate commitments under it credible?
2 Did countries play by the "rules of the game"?
3 Was the gold standard culpable in causing the Depression on a global scale?
4 Did its adherence to the gold standard contribute to bringing the Depression to the USA?

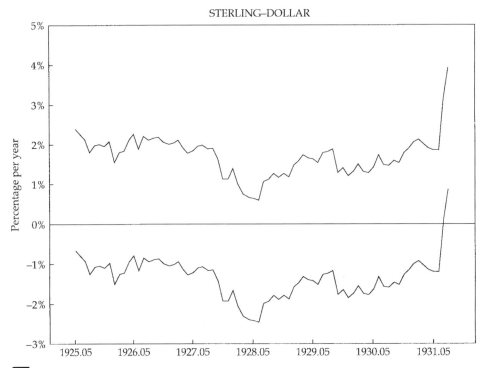

Figure 16.5 Interwar realignment expectations: pound–dollar exchange rate
Note: When both confidence intervals are positive pound devaluation is expected.

16.2.1 Credibility and realignment expectations

While the interwar "experiment" with gold is often disparaged, it is a remarkable fact that exchange rates of some important European currencies fared as
well as or better than they did under the European Monetary System. Officer
(1993) has calculated gold points for the pound against the dollar and found that
they were never challenged. Hallwood, MacDonald, and Marsh (1996) calculate
realignment expectations for the pound–dollar rate using the methodology described in section 15.2.2. These expectations are reproduced in figure 16.5, which
shows that realignment expectations only turned to favor a devaluation of the
pound against the dollar (both confidence intervals positive) in the summer of
1931 – just before gold was in fact abandoned in September. Thus, financial markets, it seems, deemed the UK's adherence to the gold standard as a credible commitment, and short-term capital flows, at least until almost the very end, must
not have been particularly destabilizing of the pound–dollar exchange rate. The
fact that the time series for the pound–dollar exchange rate was mean reverting
– in accordance with target zone theory – supports this conclusion.

The USA suspended gold convertibility eighteen months after Britain in March
1933. Figure 16.6 measures realignment expectations for the franc–dollar exchange
rate. As the franc remained on gold, the series here also measures the credibility

Figure 16.6   Franc–dollar realignment expectations
Note: If both confidence intervals are positive the dollar is expected to devalue.

of the American commitment to gold. In this case, when both confidence intervals are *below* the zero line markets are deemed to have expected a devaluation of the dollar.[5] Comparing figures 16.5 and 16.6 it can be seen that the struggle to "save the dollar" was a much more drawn-out affair than that to "save the pound."

16.2.2 Playing by the "rules of the game"

Did central banks play by "the rules of the game" in letting the foreign account to a large extent determine changes in base money, or did they set other objectives such as targeting domestic monetary conditions? Eichengreen, Watson, and Grossman (1985) find that the Bank of England did *not* play by the rules, as bank rate was keyed onto domestic business conditions. Hallwood, MacDonald, and Marsh (1996) regress their time series of pound–dollar realignment expectations on key macroeconomic variables – see table 16.2 – and find that they were sensitive to monetary policy. Yet it remains true that realignment expectations did not (in a statistical sense) favor a devaluation of the pound until just before the end.

Table 16.2 Fundamental determinants of realignment expectations – interwar

	UK/US	FR/US
$r-r^*(-1)$	–0.012861	0.000568
	(2.42)	(0.15)
$\pi-\pi^*(-1)$	–0.678636	–0.175159
	(2.24)	(3.01)
$m-m^*(-1)$	0.073279	–0.002736
	(3.46)	(0.22)
bop-bop*(–1)	0.007605	–0.005111
	(2.95)	(1.78)
$y-y^*(-1)$	–0.006547	0.010847
	(3.02)	(1.78)
real(–1)	0.536438	0.710324
	(2.02)	(1.94)
$E[dc]/dt(-1)$	0.726229	0.713541
	(10.97)	(10.00)
R^2	0.849	0.882
Std. error	0.0033	0.0034
χ^2-test	25.071 (0.00)	76.899 (0.00)
No. observations	74	53

Figures in parentheses under the coefficient estimates are t-statistics computed with GMM standard errors. r denotes reserves, π denotes inflation, m denotes money supply, bop denotes the balance of payments (exports/imports), y denotes income, and real denotes the real exchange rate. All independent variables are lagged by one period, and a * denotes a foreign (US) variable. χ^2-tests are tests that the fundamental determinants excluding the lagged dependent variable are insignificant. The figures in parentheses after the test statistics are the marginal significance level.

There is no paradox here. Since an exchange rate is free to vary within the fluctuation band, the exchange rate commitment does not mean that a central bank cannot practise limited monetary management. Indeed, it is recognized that the wider exchange rate bands of the Bretton Woods system would allow precisely this. Thus, since markets deemed the pound–dollar rate credible, the conclusion should be that for all but about the last two months of the 1925–31 period that the UK was on gold, the Bank of England did play by the "rules of the game."

16.2.3 The gold standard and the world depression of the 1930s

What evidence is there that the operation of gold standard was instrumental in causing and prolonging the Great Depression in the capitalist world? Specifically, was there a shortage of monetary gold compared to the demand for it? Sumner (1991), establishes that it was not monetary contraction in an absolute sense, rather it was a contraction in the sense that the world's demand for monetary gold increased by much more than the world stock of monetary gold and, as a result, the world price level was forced sharply downward.

Sumner argues that the world price level will *fall* if the demand for monetary gold exceeds the supply of monetary gold. By definition it is true that

$$PD = gG \tag{16.3}$$

where P is the world price level, D is the real demand for monetary gold, g is the price of gold and G is the quantity of gold. (Thus, gG is the nominal value of the stock of monetary gold.) Hence, rearranging 16.3 and writing in natural logarithms

$$\ln P = \ln (gG) - \ln D \tag{16.4}$$

establishes the assertion that, *ceteris paribus*, the world price level will fall if the real demand for gold increases relative to supply. Furthermore, the real demand for monetary gold, D, has two components, r_w, the world's gold-reserve ratio (i.e. the ratio of gold to currency stocks), which is controlled by the monetary authorities; and c, the real demand for currency, which indirectly generates a demand for gold. A rise in r_w or c raises the demand for gold and lowers the world price level.

Sumner (1991) finds that during the year following the stock market Crash, October 1929–October 1930, the world's real demand for monetary gold increased by 14.6 percent while its supply increased by only 5.3 percent. This resulted in a 9.3 percent fall in the world price level. Furthermore, looking at the reasons for the increase in the real demand for monetary gold, most of it was due to a rise in the gold-reserve ratio, r_w (which increased by 9.6 percent), while the real demand for currency, c, increased by 5.0 percent. This may be interpreted as tight money, executed by a rise in the gold-reserve ratio (the only variable controlled by the central banks), having the major deflationary impact. During 1931 and 1932 the real demand for currency increased sharply but central banks did not offset the deflationary impact of this sufficiently by *reducing* the gold-reserve ratio (indeed, it increased again in 1932). Under the circumstance of rising real demand for currency on the part of the public, monetary policy remained far too tight.

Sumner (1991) also assesses the contribution of individual countries to the rising demand for monetary gold. The US, the UK, France, and the rest of the gold block are all guilty of raising their gold reserve ratios in the year immediately after the Crash. Thereafter both the US and UK relaxed monetary policy but, in America's case, by no means enough to offset the rise in demand for currency. However, France, in particular, and the rest of the gold block, continued to pursue tight money policies (by raising their gold reserve ratios) in the teeth of the Depression. Thus, over the period December 1926 to December 1932 the world price level fell by 37 percent and France alone was responsible for almost one-half of this fall.

However, while the rigors of the gold standard are strongly implicated in causing the global depression, some authorities, notably Friedman and Schwartz (1963), argue that the USA, through its Federal Reserve, brought the depression on itself and that its adherence to the gold standard was not important.

16.2.4 The gold standard and the Depression in the USA

Did monetary contraction and depression in the USA result from unconstrained Federal Reserve policy, or was the Fed and the US a victim of the commitment to gold? Friedman and Schwartz (1963) argue that the gold standard commitment was not a factor in the American monetary contraction because the Fed had plenty of gold.[6] Brown (1940), Eichengreen (1992), Kindleberger (1986), and Temin (1989) argue the opposite case but their evidence is rather inconclusive. An attempt to settle this matter is that of Hallwood, MacDonald, and Marsh (1997).

There are three key magnitudes: realignment expectations on the value of the dollar, gold flows between the US and the rest of the world, and American bank failures. Hallwood, MacDonald, and Marsh (1997) use Granger "causality" tests and vector autoregressions to determine the direction of causality between them. Their evidence on US monetary policy and international interactions supports the argument that the Federal Reserve's monetary policy was indeed constrained by international considerations. Specifically, the fact that bank failures caused with a lag (on both the Granger causality and VAR tests) dollar devaluation expectations suggests a domestic cause of the weakening of the USA's adherence to the gold standard. In other words, even more stringent monetary contraction (the very thing that the Fed has been blamed for by Friedman and Schwartz), and resulting bank failures, would have caused even greater fragility of the dollar on the foreign exchanges. Even more significantly for the "international cause" argument is that there is a positive feedback from gold outflows to bank failures (a lagged effect on the Granger causality tests and a contemporaneous effect from the VAR). That is, an international interaction was adversely affecting the US banking system. Furthermore, gold outflows were having a lagged effect on dollar devaluation expectations (this time from both of our tests), which must also have been a worry for the Fed. These findings would seem to support the positions of Eichengreen, Kindleberger, and Temin rather than that of Friedman and Schwartz. The Federal Reserve was indeed being hemmed in by the USA's commitment to the gold standard. The Federal Reserve found itself in a dilemma: if it increased the money base to "save the banks," which it did try to do with open market purchases in the spring and early summer of 1932, it was not playing by the "rules of the game" given the preponderance of gold outflows between September 1931 – when sterling left gold – and June 1932. However, if it did nothing, which turned out to be the preferred policy, this risked the bank failures that, as we have shown, also put pressure on the dollar. Under these circumstances the USA's adherence to the gold standard had become untenable. Remarkably these results are fully consistent with the hypothesis of Brown (1940) that devaluation expectations caused a withdrawal of gold which in turn precipitated waves of bank failures.

16.2.5 The demise of the gold bloc, 1933–6

The gold bloc grew out of the failure of the World Economic Conference in June 1933 to reconstitute an international gold standard following the USA's suspension of it in March – but Roosevelt would have nothing to do with it. Thus it was that Belgium, France, the Netherlands, and Switzerland (and, initially a few peripheral players) formed the "gold bloc."

An interesting question about the gold bloc concerns what ultimately brought it down. Is its failure just one more piece of evidence against pegged exchange rates and independent national monetary policies, or, were other factors at work? Eichengreen (1992) and Hogg (1987) give similar purely politico-economic explanations centering on their currency over-valuation *vis-à-vis* the dollar and pound, and resulting balance of payments deficits and gold loss. Thus, to protect their gold reserves, the gold bloc countries were forced to deflate their price levels with resulting very high rates of unemployment. This explanation for abandonment of the gold standard closely resembles that which seems to explain the UK's abandonment of gold five years earlier. Moreover, the fact that Belgium was embroiled in a major banking crises as well as straitened economic circumstances when it devalued against gold in March 1935 has a resemblance to the circumstances under which the USA had suspended gold.

However, the European political landscape had changed mightily in the few years to 1937, in particular with the rise of the Third Reich. It is worth noting that the classical gold standard operated in Europe at a time when a balance of power held and that it was promptly abandoned in 1914 when that balance cracked. Throughout the interwar period the European balance of power was far from being stable, the French having been left by the Americans and the British to face Germany virtually alone – French alliances with various East European nations being of little military value.

Important political-military events occurred in March 1935 when Germany announced the reintroduction of conscription – which was against both the Versailles Treaty and the Locarno Pact; October 1935 when Italy invaded Abyssinia (which for complicated reasons destroyed any protection that France might have enjoyed under the League of Nations and the principle of "collective security" – see Kissinger (1994)); and March 1936 when Germany reoccupied the Rhineland, so eliminating France's surrogate buffer state and access to its eastern European allies. At the time of the latter event, the French Foreign Minister Flandin commented that "once Germany had fortified the Rhineland, Czechoslovakia would be lost and that, soon after, general war would become unavoidable" (quoted by Kissinger, 1994, p. 305). It can hardly be argued, therefore, that the Second World War broke on France as a complete surprise; indeed, it was signalled well ahead of the outbreak.

Concurrent financial events in France can be linked to these political–military developments: the financially conservative Laval government fell over the Abyssinian débâcle; in March 1936 there was a run on the banks in north and north eastern France (Einzig, 1937); French investors moved gold to London bank vaults, presumably for safe keeping; and an increase in French defence spending equal to about a third of French gold reserves was announced just two weeks before gold was abandoned.

As France was the key player, both Netherlands and Switzerland abandoning gold a few hours after France, we have econometrically investigated the circumstances under which France was forced off the gold standard in 1936 (Hallwood,

MacDonald, and Marsh, 1999). First, exchange rate expectations, using money market interest rates, were calculated for the French franc (Ff) and Dutch guilder against the Swiss franc (Sf) – the latter being chosen as Switzerland was unlikely to be a belligerent in any ensuing war. Strikingly, the Ff was strong against the Sf until early 1935 whereafter it become weak; similarly for the guilder. Secondly, we regressed these realignment expectations on a set of explanatory economic variables and political–military war dummies for March 1935, October 1935, and March 1936. Our economic model fits the data quite well. Our main finding is that the March 1935 dummy is significant – indicating a shift in the relationship between realignment expectations and explanatory economic fundamentals. The Ff suddenly weakened, as measured by an increase in the probability of Ff devaluation – much more than can be explained by economic fundamentals alone; similarly, but to a lesser extent, with the Dutch guilder.[7]

NOTES

1 For example, Britain had fixed the price of gold since 1717 at £3 17s 10 1/2d per ounce of gold 11/12ths fine, and the USA from 1873 at $18.8047 per ounce of gold 9/10ths fine. At these prices the mint par parity dollar–pound exchange rate was 4.8665.

2 Given transaction costs (e.g. lost interest during the time it took to ship gold across the Atlantic, mint and abrasion expenses, normal profit, and any risk premia), the gold import and export points formed a currency fluctuation band for the dollar/pound rate of about plus/minus 0.5 percent around mint par parity.

3 Quoted by Bordo (1984), pp. 75–6.

4 Bordo and MacDonald (1997) examine the degree of monetary independence confined on a credible country which participated in the classical gold standard, and show that it was about 1 year. Such independence was only feasible with fixed rates because the system was so credible.

5 As the exchange rate here is the franc–dollar rate, if "the market" expects a devaluation of the dollar, there will be *fewer* francs per dollar.

6 Friedman and Schwartz (1963) wrote "that a shortage of free gold did not in fact seriously limit the alternatives to the [Federal Reserve] System. The amount was at all times ample to support large open market purchases . . . The problem of free gold was largely an ex post justification for policies followed, not an ex ante reason for them" (p. 406).

7 March 1935 was the date of both the German announcement of a conscription army and that of the Belgian devaluation. The latter too could have shaken confidence in the Ff and the guilder. But perhaps not, as Belgium was beset with a banking crisis which neither France nor Netherlands were to experience, while it was the Swiss banking system which was not above suspicion.

17

The Dollar Standard Today and During the Bretton Woods Era

Many economists were of the opinion that the gold standard imposed a too harsh financial discipline on domestic economies and that output and employment were sacrificed for external equilibrium. This view, along with the unhappy experience with floating exchange rates during the 1920s, provided the motivation after the Second World War to devise a new managed international monetary system, but one which was still linked to gold to secure price-stability and which retained pegged parities for currencies. The managed elements of the system came in the provisions for adjusting the parities of currencies and for supplementing international reserves through borrowing from a new international organization, the International Monetary Fund (IMF). This new system, the Bretton Woods system – called after the place where the arrangements were finalized – represented a partial move away from gold.

The system, however, evolved in a manner unforeseen by its designers. Little use was made of the provisions which permitted discretionary management. Parities for currencies were changed infrequently and the demand for additional international reserves was met not by extra borrowing facilities at the IMF, or, even by new gold, but by vastly increased dollar holdings. The flood of dollars which engulfed the world economy in the early 1970s – which could not be exchanged for gold from the US reserves because of the latter's inadequacy – led to mistrust in the dollar and to a series of crises which wrecked the system. From the turmoil there emerged the flexible exchange rate system, sometimes described as "dirty" floating, and, perhaps somewhat surprisingly, not a lesser role for the dollar but rather the demonetization of gold. The latter event, reduced monetary discipline (see, for example, Alogoskoufis, 1992; and Alogoskoufis and Smith, 1991), and is almost certainly associated with the unprecedented world inflation of the 1970s and '80s. Nor has the experience with floating exchange rates been edifying. Nominal exchange rates move around so much that they distort real exchange rates and real economic activity; future exchange rates are largely unpredictable; the insulation property of floating rates has turned out to be chimerical; and the lack of discipline in international monetary affairs was a major contributor to the international debt crisis. Despite this, today, no plan for international monetary reform has a realistic chance of adoption and more, rather than fewer, countries are adopting floating exchange rates (but see chapter 18 on the EU).

The main elements of how the international monetary system came to this impasse are described in this chapter. Section 17.1 outlines the origins, objectives, and evolution of the Bretton Woods system. Section 17.2 examines the dollar standard as it developed in the 1960s and early 1970s; and section 17.3 discusses how it has worked, with increasing instability, during the last three decades (on this also see section 9.6). Section 17.4 discusses how the East Asian dollar standard operates.

 ## 17.1 The Bretton Woods System to 1971

As early as 1941 plans were being prepared in the UK and the USA for the postwar economy. These were heavily influenced by the experience of the 1930s which had witnessed the collapse of the gold standard, the Great Depression (in which the gold standard was culpable – see sections 16.2.3 and 16.2.4), volatile exchange rates, trade-protection, and competitive devaluations.

The main monetary institution created at Bretton Woods in 1944 was the International Monetary Fund. The first of its Articles of Agreement set out the objectives of a new international monetary system:

- to promote exchange rate stability;
- to give confidence to member countries by making available the IMF's resources with adequate safeguards;
- to promote international monetary cooperation by consultation and collaboration on international monetary problems;
- to facilitate the balanced growth of international trade and high levels of employment and real income;
- to establish a multilateral system of payments for current account transactions;
- to shorten the duration and lessen the degree of disequilibrium in the balance of payments.

Action was most clearly visible on the first two objectives. Member countries were required to state par values for their currencies in terms of gold and then to intervene in the foreign exchange market to keep the market exchange rate within one percent of the par value. In practice, members expressed par values against the US dollar and the US stood ready to convert dollars into gold at the price of

$35 per ounce – the so-called *asset convertibility* of the dollar. The system had the characteristic of a gold-exchange standard, with the dollar (in the early years at least) for many countries preferable to gold, as dollar reserves could be deposited in America to earn interest.

IMF resources mainly come from member subscriptions (i.e. quotas), the size of which depend on a country's economic importance. The quotas initially were paid one-quarter in gold and three-quarters in the member's currency. Quotas determine a country's voting weight on the Executive Board and its borrowing capacity. Quotas are reviewed at intervals of five years and a four-fifths majority is required in favor of any change – the one provision in the Articles of Agreement for a general increase in international liquidity. Two other sources of money for the IMF are the General Agreements to Borrow (1962) with the G10 countries plus two others: up to $24 billion can be borrowed through the GAB; and the New Arrangement to Borrow, set up in 1997, with 25 countries, for the IMF to borrow up to $47 billion.[1]

17.1.1 Role of the IMF in the early days

In 1952 the IMF introduced a general policy for the use of its resources as well as commencing surveillance of members' macroeconomic policies. The latter now involve annual consultations between the IMF and each of the members on balance of payments and domestic macroeconomic policies and it has become a main means of attaining the third objective of Article 1. With regard to resource use, the IMF announced "tranche" arrangements under which countries could borrow. The right to the first, or gold tranche (now called the reserve tranche), was automatic. A country can also request access to four further tranches, each being of 25 percent of quota, so that total borrowing can amount to 125 percent of a country's quota. Borrowing on these four credit tranches was conditional upon the country pursuing certain economic policies stipulated by the IMF and on repayment within three to five years.

As a result of several new lending facilities introduced since the 1970s it is possible for a country to borrow conditionally up to four and a half times its quota. Also introduced at this time was the so-called stand-by arrangement, which is a line of credit, only drawn upon if required. The main advantage of the stand-by credit is that the fact of its existence may help to restore confidence in a country's currency, while only a small commitment charge is involved if foreign currency is not in fact drawn. Total lending by the IMF under its various facilities is shown in table 17.1. The EFF, CCFF, SAF, and ESAF arrangements were introduced mainly to help low-income members facing cyclically low commodity prices, necessary structural adjustments, and needing longer-term loans.

As lending by the IMF is constrained by its resources its liquidity ratio (unlent funds/total funds) falls sharply during times of heavy borrowing by members. This was especially true in 1997 and 1998 at the time of the East Asian economic and financial crisis – see figure 17.1. The danger in this is that the IMF may find itself with insufficient resources should other members require large-scale loans.

Table 17.1 Use of IMF credit, 1998

	$ million
General resource account	20,586
stand-by arrangements	12,098
supplemental reserve facility	8,726
EFF arrangements	6,331
supplemental reserve facility	675
CCFF	2,156
SAF and ESAF arrangements	895
TOTAL	21,482

EFF: extended fund facility; CCFF: compensatory and contingency fund facility;
SAF: structural adjustment facility; ESAF: enhanced structural adjustment facility.
Source: IMF *Survey*, March 8, 1999

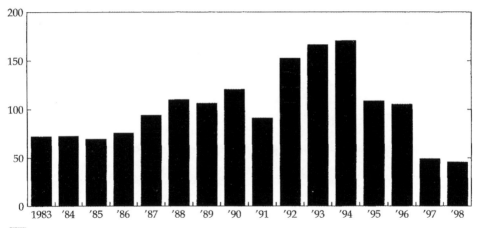

Figure 17.1 IMF liquidity ratio
Note: Figure for 1998 is as of April 30, otherwise all figures are for end of period, in
percentages.
Source: IMF, *Survey Supplement*, Sept. 1998

17.1.2 Heyday of the Bretton Woods system

The main conditions necessary for the operation of the Bretton Woods System
lasted only from about 1959 to 1971. Current account convertibility was widely
achieved only in 1959, the convertibility of the dollar into gold ceased in 1971
and, by 1973, most major countries had renounced par values for their currencies.
Moreover, as discussed in sections 17.2, 17.3 and 17.4 below, the US dollar came
to play such a predominant role as a reserve asset – a role that was not widely
envisaged in 1944 – that some authorities have described the international monetary system at this time as being a *dollar standard*.[2]

The 1960s had witnessed a period of rapid growth in world production and international trade. The decade, however, was not without its problems. There was concern about the disruptive effects of short-term capital movements, especially on the key currencies – the dollar and sterling. Doubts about the foreign payments positions of the reserve currency countries led to speculative short-term capital flows which disrupted the system. In an effort to cope with this, in 1961 the IMF extended the use of its resources to help members in difficulties caused by short-term capital outflows.

Robert Triffin (1960) was concerned about the *adequacy of international liquidity*: the ratio of international reserves to the value of world imports declined from 73 percent in 1954 to 51 percent in 1961 and 35 percent in 1968 (IMF, 1970a). To deal with this problem the IMF concluded the General Arrangements to Borrow (GAB) with the ten major industrial countries – allowing the IMF to borrow from members with payments surpluses in order to assist members with deficits. The GAB had the undesigned effect of negating the scarce currency clause: the IMF could now obtain a scarce currency, effectively eliminating the need for up-valuation of the scarce currency.

The GAB contributed to the *adjustment problem*. Exchange rates of countries with chronic balance of payments disequilibria were adjusted too infrequently. This aggravated the *confidence problem* – the confidence of markets in the ability of central banks to defend par values declined during the course of the 1960s. The confidence problem largely accounts for disruptive short-term capital flows.

The GAB was significant in two further respects. The borrowings represented the first occasion on which the IMF borrowed to supplement its resources and as such they have been the forerunner of other borrowing arrangements such as the oil facilities (1974–6) and the supplementary financing facility (1979). Secondly, they had an important political dimension, by promoting consultation among G10 members they soon came to influence Fund policy on many matters. Indeed, the GAB can "be viewed as an additional defence of an essentially conservative, strong-country oriented economic order which weakened possible pressures for reform which might otherwise have been taken more seriously" (Brett, 1983).

17.1.3 Failure of the "grand design" (1972–4)

While international monetary turmoil was occurring during 1971–3, discussions were taking place in the IMF to design a new monetary constitution for the world. One suggestion was an SDR standard – the SDR (Special Drawing Rights) would become the numeraire and main reserve asset of the international monetary system. The perceived advantage was that growth in the demand for international liquidity could be accommodated by the managed creation of SDRs. But the SDR has never been able to displace the dollar as the major international reserve asset.

In 1972 the IMF set up the Committee of Twenty (C20) to consider reform of the international monetary system. However, political differences between its members prevented it agreeing on a new system (Williamson, 1977). The main points of contention were as follows. The major American preoccupation was to

achieve symmetry of adjustment obligations between surplus and deficit countries by introducing "trigger adjustment criteria." (The US wished to promote more
frequent exchange rate adjustments by surplus countries than had been the case
up to 1971.) But, secondly, the Europeans and Japanese wished to remove some
of the USA's advantages as a key currency – the seigniorage[3] and the supposed
ability to avoid adjusting its payments deficits. While, thirdly, the developing countries on the C20 wanted a greater transfer of real resources to promote development via the so-called "link" (i.e. the distribution of new SDRs to be determined
as a matter of foreign aid). In the absence of any agreement on these matters, the
oil shock of 1973 and the accompanying international monetary turmoil gave an
excuse for the emissaries to adjourn the C20.

So nothing came of the "grand design." What did happen, in 1976, was that
the Articles of Agreement of the IMF were belatedly altered to allow members
to float their exchange rates; but this was a *fait accompli*. At the same time the
official price of gold was abolished. Member-country central banks were allowed
to buy gold at any price they wished. The status of gold is now ambiguous. Though
demoted at the IMF, it can be included in a country's foreign exchange reserves
valued at market prices and used in settlement between countries. However, given
the great variability of the free market price, countries are rather unwilling to
use it in official settlements. Members of the IMF retain an obligation to promote
stable exchange rates by fostering orderly underlying economic, financial, and
monetary conditions and the IMF has a surveillance function over these policies.
International cooperation does remain as an obligation but this discipline has proved
to be too weak, and it has not prevented the wildly fluctuating exchange rates
nor the world inflation which accelerated after the link to gold was abandoned.
(See chapter 6 on international cooperation.)

17.2 The Dollar Standard

The word "standard" refers to the dollar as the *ultimate* standard of value – the
dollar as a "world money." This had not been the intention at Bretton Woods when
the world powers devised an international monetary system for the postwar
world – gold had been chosen as the ultimate base money.

However, the dollar was so sought after by America's trading partners that
it became preeminent. One view is that "for twelve years after World War II,
the world was unambiguously on a dollar standard; the gold convertibility of the
dollar was incidental and *irrelevant*" (Ruff, 1967, italics added). If this was true
then it is hard to see that the Bretton Woods system ever did operate as originally envisaged. However, as Triffin and others were to argue, toward the end of
the 1950s the question of the convertibility of the dollar into gold was a major
issue. Indeed, in 1967 several major central banks agreed with the US *not* to exchange
their unwanted dollar holdings for American gold in order to relieve pressure on
US gold reserves. What is important here is that the agreements *not* to exchange
dollars for US gold caused a *de facto* demonetization of gold. Accordingly, it is
justifiable to date the rise of the dollar standard from the mid 1960s.[4]

17.2.1 Early views on the dollar standard

In 1966 Despres, Kindleberger, and Salant (DKS) and Kindleberger (1965) pointed out that the international reserve-creation process had in fact developed outside of the plans laid down at Bretton Woods. Triffin's view that a shortage of international liquidity was bound to occur was quite simply wrong. DKS argued that the creation of dollar reserve assets was demand determined and the USA played the role of an *international financial intermediary*.[5]

The main question concerned whether short-term capital flows to the USA were placed voluntarily or involuntarily by European investors and central banks? DKS said that they were voluntary, arguing that Europe had high liquidity preference – a feature which led to a spectrum of low short-term and high long-term interest rates in European capital markets. America had low liquidity preference which resulted in the interest rate structure being twisted in the direction of relatively (to Europe's) high short-term and low long-term interest rates. Accordingly, beneficial flows of short- and long-term capital between Europe and America were bound to arise – long-term interests rates in Europe fell while its high liquidity preference was satisfied by holding liquid US assets. Thus, "the US is no more in deficit when it lends long and borrows short than is a bank when it makes a loan and enters a deposit on its books" (DKS, 1966, p. 526). America was a financial intermediary performing inter-temporal asset conversion for the Europeans.

However, Halm (1968) and Aubrey (1969) argued that the international monetary system remained unstable because America was vulnerable to "a run on the bank" – its gold reserves were small in relation to its external liquid liabilities. Yet, according to Lindert (1969), the USA's reserve position was not very different to that of the UK on the eve of the Second World War – and there was little doubt that the latter country was secure on the gold standard. Secondly, the structure of international interest rates was not guaranteed always to induce short-term capital flows to the USA; and, thirdly, there seemed to be no reason why European banks could not provide the liquid assets apparently desired by European investors. Rather than the financial intermediary view, the stock of dollars held as a reserve asset can be argued to depend upon more general factors.

The demand for dollars

The demand for dollars was (and is) boosted by its role as a *vehicle currency*. In effect, the transaction cost of exchanging, say, rupees for dinars is lower when using the dollar as a vehicle than directly exchanging the two currencies (Magee and Rao, 1980; Chrystal, 1984; Black 1989). As Chrystal (1987) points out, the use of the dollar in international exchange reduces dealers' costs, e.g. banks have only to have correspondent relationships with US banks and do not have to hold a large portfolio of other currencies. The dollar also has an advantage over other currencies as a *numeraire* because many commodity prices are quoted on international markets in dollar terms. Finally, so long as the US price level remained relatively stable, as it did in the 1950s and for much of the 1960s, the dollar performed well as *a store of value*.

The supply of dollars

Under the Bretton Woods system the supply of dollars was largely demand determined – a view implicit in the DKS argument. This is a major claim in favor of the dollar standard (there could never be a liquidity shortage) provided, that is, that the US pursued a policy of monetary and price level stability.

The supply of dollar foreign exchange reserves is demand determined because any country could, within limits, choose the extent of its own balance of payments surplus with the USA. For example, if a country wished to reduce the rate of growth of reserves it could cut interest rates and adopt other means of inflating the domestic economy, which would normally reduce the size of its balance of payments surplus and rate of accumulation of dollar reserves. Conversely, reserves could be increased by adjusting the domestic economy so as to run a balance of payment surplus. Or, domestic interest rates could be raised to encourage borrowing from the USA. In principle, all dollar accumulation could be viewed as *voluntary*. The USA's role in this system was to practice *benign neglect*, allowing other countries to determine the US balance of payments.

Given its existence how did (and does) the dollar standard operate? We answer that question with reference to work by Genberg and Swoboda (1993) and McKinnon (1982, 1988).

17.2.2 Genberg–Swoboda on a pure dollar standard

Genberg and Swoboda (1993) use the global monetary approach to the balance of payments model discussed in chapter 8. In this model excess money supply is worked off via dishoarding through an official settlements deficit; and excess money demand is met via a payments surplus. Although the G–S (1993) analysis refers to the pegged exchange rates of the 1960s, in the following discussion we will use the present tense as under dirty floating some of what they say is still relevant – dirty floating against the dollar implies that something like a weak peg against the dollar is retained.

An important institutional feature of the dollar standard is the ability of the USA to create foreign exchange reserves. As a stylized fact, the USA holds only gold as a reserve asset, the rest of the world (ROW) holding both gold and dollars. Crucially, these dollars are held mainly as US Treasury securities, which means that any reduction in the US money supply through a US payments deficit is replaced by foreign official purchases of these securities. As a result, the USA has the power to increase the world's foreign exchange reserves, while the ROW does not. For example, an increase in the US money supply leads to an American official settlements deficit and to a corresponding increase in the foreign exchange reserves of the ROW, but to no reduction in the US money supply (i.e. the US reserve offset coefficient = 0 – see section 8.3 on the offset coefficient). But when any other central bank (pegging its currency against the dollar) increases its money supply this, *ceteris paribus*, leads to an official settlements deficit *and*, as its currency is not held as a foreign exchange reserve, to a reduction in its reserve

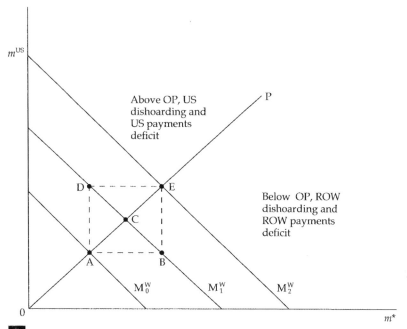

Figure 17.2 Symmetric and asymmetric reserve creation
Note: Slope of OP depends upon relative demands for national monies, given by y/y^*, which determines "the natural distribution of the world stock of money."

position (i.e. for the other members of the system the reserve offset coefficient $= -1$).

A model of this asymmetric reserve creation process, due to G–S (1993), is presented in figure 17.2. M^{US}, M^* and M^W, are the money supplies of, respectively, the USA, the ROW, and the world as a whole (where $M^{US} + M^* = M^W$). The lines denoted $M^W_0 \ldots M^W_2$ represent combinations of M^{US} and M^* for increasing levels of world money supply. If the weighted exchange rate between the US dollar and the ROW is unity, the slope of each M^W line $= -1$. The line OP is the ratio of equilibrium money supplies in the US and the ROW that give official settlements balance in both the USA and the ROW.

Defining two types of foreign exchange reserves as "outside assets" (e.g. gold or SDR) and "inside assets" (e.g. the liabilities of the Federal Reserve) imagine the case where all foreign exchange reserves are outside assets. In this case there is a symmetry in the effect of money creation in the US and in the ROW. Thus, if the ROW increases its money supply the initial move in figure 17.2 is from A to B. But the ROW now has a payments deficit which leads to an increase in US gold (or SDR) reserves and money supply. The system moves up M^W_2 from B to C, with full equilibrium at point C. Similarly, if the US increases its money supply from A to D, its payments deficit leads to an increase in money in the ROW and long-run equilibrium is also at C. Thus, each "country" has an equal influence over the world's money stock.

Now consider the dollar standard where all foreign exchange reserves are dollars held in US Treasury securities. If the ROW increases its money supply there is a temporary movement from A to B. But the resulting payments deficit causes a fall in foreign exchange reserves and money supply of the ROW, and the system moves back from B to A – the reserve offset coefficient is -1. Contrast this with the power of the USA over world liquidity. If it increases its money supply so that the system moves A to D, its payments deficit does not lead to contraction in the US money supply, rather, it causes the reserve-base of the ROW to increase. There is a further money multiplier effect on the quantity of money in the ROW, and the system moves on from D to E. Clearly the dollar standard is highly asymmetric in the way it operates. It is also clear that the USA bears a great responsibility as Federal Reserve policy, in effect, sets the money supply of the world system as a whole.

Using this framework Genberg and Swoboda (1993) argue as follows:

1 In accordance with DKS (1966), world foreign exchange reserves increase via a US official settlements balance of payments deficit. The size of this is *endogenously* and simultaneously determined by the net balance of the desire to dishoard in the US and hoard in the ROW. G–S (1993) dub the ratio of "other Group of 10" to US real GDPs (y^*/y) *demand pressure for the dollar* and a rise in this ratio signifies an increased desire to hold dollars as foreign exchange reserves by the "other G10" countries. Reserve increases caused by an increase in y^*/y are voluntary. *Supply pressure* is measured by the ratio of US money to "other G10" money (M/M^*). An increase in this ratio signifies an excess supply of dollars – the US settlement deficit and reserves elsewhere increasing.

From 1960 to end 1967, G–S show that neither strong demand nor supply pressure was exerted on the dollar and that world foreign exchange reserves increased at a moderate rate. The next two years were a transitory period, but in the years 1969 to 1971 both demand and supply pressure on the dollar became very strong. That is, y^*/y and M/M^* both increased sharply and the US official settlements deficit increased enormously. As only that part due to demand pressure was voluntarily held by the "other G10," the supply pressure probably contributed to the increase in the stock of dollars being involuntarily held by the "other G10" – just as in Halm (1968) and Aubrey (1969) – and was instrumental in bringing the system down.[6]

2 As for the powerlessness of the "other G10" to manage their own money supplies, G–S calculate a reserve offset coefficient for these countries over the period 1960–71 of 0.67 in the year following a monetary expansion. Clearly, these countries had little independent control over their own money supplies, most certainly in the long run.

3 G–S show that their GMABP model – featuring endogenous reserve creation under a pure dollar standard – can explain the acceleration of world inflation from the early-1960s. This result complements that of earlier writers such as Heller (1976) which treated growth in foreign exchange reserves as exogenous and, therefore, unexplained. We extend this discussion on world inflation in the next section.

17.3 Reserve Creation and the US and World Price Levels

According to Ronald McKinnon (1969) the world price level is closely connected to the US price level. This was especially true when most exchange rates were pegged against the dollar. To some extent the connection is still there today as many exchange rates are not allowed to float completely free of the dollar. The US was, and is, the dominant supplier or buyer in many international markets and, through commodity arbitrage, US prices influenced price levels in competitor and supplier countries. Also, the US price level influenced the supply of international liquidity, and it still does. Thus, with a stable US price level and pegged exchange rates, inflation in Europe made Europe less competitive. Europe would eventually experience balance of payments deficits and its foreign exchange reserves would fall. Sooner or later this was taken as a signal to European governments to adopt anti-inflationary economic policies. Hence, European price levels could not rise much above that of the USA. Conversely, if Europe's price level was rising less quickly than that of the USA, increasing competitiveness relative to the USA would lead to balance of payments surpluses and to accumulation of dollars in foreign exchange reserves. Rising foreign exchange reserves would cause an increase in European money supplies, lower interest rates, raise expenditure, increase the rate of economic expansion and raise prices. Thus the European price level could not fall much below the stable US price level.

It should be clear, therefore, that stability of the world price level, under the pegged exchange rate dollar standard extant until spring 1973, required stability of the internal value of the dollar. A stable US price level would provide the link between the monetary and real spheres, much as gold was supposed to have done under the gold standard. But with the dollar standard, and given a stable US price level, it was the stable price of *all* US goods and services which governed the world price level. Thus, with accelerating monetary growth in the USA and a rising American price level from 1969, "supply pressure" on the "other G10" foreign exchange reserves increased. They thus had to choose between more inflation at home or lowering the price of the dollar in terms of domestic currency.

But it would not be strictly correct to say that the "other G10" independently chose appreciation against the dollar – which was in fact arranged in the Smithsonian agreement of December 1971 – as these countries had something more than just a helping hand from the USA. The USA was concerned about the real over-valuation of the dollar which was depressing private sector economic activity there. But how could the dollar be devalued within the rules of the Bretton Woods system? Either, the USA's trade partners could lower their domestic currency prices of gold while the US retained the $35 per ounce price; or, the US could raise the dollar price of gold. The first approach could not be coordinated, essentially because of a "free rider" problem – not up-valuing against the dollar meant that competitive advantages were retained. And the second approach was not followed because the US worried that other countries would simply also raise their own gold prices, so leaving the US real exchange rate unchanged. What did happen on August 15, 1971 was a piece of pure real politick on the part of the USA. It closed the gold window, forcing the dollar to float against gold.

17.3.1 The dollar standard "on the booze"

In 1972 Haberler wrote that the "greatest, nay indispensable, American contribution to the working of the international monetary system is to curb inflation" (p. 4). But the USA was already failing in this duty. The nub of the problem was that it was becoming increasingly expensive for the USA to curb inflation. At first the cost of failure to stabilize the US price level could be measured by the loss of gold reserves through its balance of payments deficits. As $35 per ounce, fixed in 1934, the official price of gold was becoming increasingly undervalued compared with the general price level. Moreover, the cost of keeping American inflation down could be seen in terms of rising unemployment – a cost which successive administrations were increasingly reluctant to bear. In failing to stabilize the price of US goods, the USA effectively gave up the role of providing the anchor for the world price level.

Commenting in 1983 on the huge US payments deficits, *The Times* of London wrote:

> It is a common place that a country with a large current account deficit should have a weak currency. There is no doubt that this simple principle applies very effectively to France, Italy and dozens of smaller deficit nations around the world. But it does not seem to work with the United States. The American deficit next year will be at least five times the size of the French, but the dollar is at the top of the foreign exchanges' popularity list while the franc is near the bottom . . . Fifty years ago, when President Roosevelt and his Treasury Secretary, Morgenthau, were manipulating the gold price from day to day, Keynes described American policy as "a gold standard on the booze". Today we have a grossly overvalued dollar, record real interest rates, the largest budget deficit ever known and the prospect of a current account shortfall which is a multiple of the worst previously registered by any nation. The combination may fairly be described as *the dollar standard on the booze*.

Indeed, the difficulties of the dollar standard are deepening. As we explain in the next section, expectations of changes in the value of the dollar lead to surges of international capital into or out of the dollar and this magnifies the adverse monetary consequences of linking currencies (even weakly through "dirty" floating) with the dollar.

17.3.2 The dollar standard in an era of volatile exchange rate expectations

McKinnon (1982, 1988) has extended his ideas on the behavior of the dollar standard to cover the present system of floating exchange rates. (See also section 9.6.)

The heyday of the dollar standard was during the 1950s and 1960s when it was approximately true that:

1   The dollar was the only reserve currency and the rest of the world (ROW), not the USA, intervened in foreign exchange markets to stabilize exchange rates.
2   The rest of the world held its foreign exchange reserves as US Treasury securities rather than as Federal Reserve liabilities. (As we have seen this is true today of the dollar component of foreign exchange reserves.) This gave (and gives) rise to *passive sterilization* of US balance of payments deficits on the US money base – base money "lost" through a US payments deficit was (and still is) replaced by foreign central banks when they buy Treasury securities. And
3   The ROW was (and remains to some degree) unable effectively to sterilize the effect of capital inflows/outflows on its own money base.

Thus, *currency substitution* out of the dollar raises base money in the ROW without reducing it in the US – the world's money base is thereby increased. The world's money base is reduced when currency substitution is *into* the dollar. The ROW's foreign exchange reserves and money supply decline while the currency inflow into the US is passively sterilized in the USA. In effect, the ROW's central banks and private sector swap ownership of US securities – which has no effect on the US money base – while the reduction in the ROW central bank's assets reduces the money base of the ROW.

McKinnon supposes, and there is some evidence for this, that at the aggregate level, the world's demand for money is a stable function of a few variables. The share of the dollar in this stable demand, however, is a negative function of the expected rate of depreciation of the dollar.

Assumptions (2) and (3) imply that control of world base money is entirely at the discretion of the Federal Reserve. Respectively, passive sterilization stabilizes America's money; and assumption (3) amounts to the claim that the ROW has no control over its own base money. For example, if the ROW attempted to lower its money base by raising interest rates, capital inflow from the US would thwart the attempt.

Since only the USA's money base is independently controlled, McKinnon draws the startling conclusion that:

$$M^W = A / \beta(\Delta s^e) \tag{17.1}$$

where M^W is the world money base; A is the domestic assets of the Federal Reserve: β is the dollar's share of world base money, and β depends inversely on the expected rate of depreciation of the dollar, Δs^e.

In the 1960s, β was close to unity, i.e., the dollar was virtually the only reserve currency (the sterling area was then on the way out), and Δs^e changed little under the pegged exchanged rate regime. Thus, not only was β close to unity, it was also stable around that value. America set the world's money base and changes in Federal Reserve assets had a predictable effect on it.

However, in the last three decades β has fallen sharply as the share of dollars in foreign exchange reserves has been reduced to about 55 percent in the early 1990s. That is, the world money base multiplier, $1/\beta$ is larger today than in the 1960s. Moreover, expectations of dollar depreciation, Δs^e, have become highly volatile, which implies that not only is the base multiplier larger, it is also much more unstable.

Policy implications

McKinnon (1982b) recommends that the US should abandon "passive steriliza-tion" – it should allow its money supply to *fall* along with dollar outflow. If so, the world would have a system of "*symmetrical non-sterilization*" with neither the ROW nor the US sterilizing the effect of capital flows.

Moreover, long-run world base money control could be secured by coordi-nated domestic base money expansion by each central bank raising its assets at a rate that just satisfies the rate of growth in world money demand. Such a policy would need a considerable amount of agreement between the world's financial powers. Success in this would be most likely if the number of coordinating nations was kept small. McKinnon argues that it would be sufficient if such coordination was between just the US, Germany, and Japan.[7]

17.3.3 The adjustment problem

It is clear that under the dollar standard there is no shortage of international liquidity. Why then did the adjustable peg Bretton Woods system breakdown? The answer lies with the system's adjustment problem. Existing parities needed to be adjusted from time-to-time due to differential rates of inflation and product-ivity growth. But countries with persistent payments surplus to a large extent sterilized reserve inflows – so as to preserve competitiveness. Deficit countries, especially the USA and, to a lesser extent the UK, had their payments deficits financed for them as their currencies were held as reserve assets. This might have been alright so long as incremental reserves were voluntarily held. But even so, the process was not painless because as the dollar and pound became overvalued both countries turned to ever greater governmental expenditures to maintain employment levels.

Sooner or later adjustment had to come. Either the surplus countries would come to the realization that a large part of their reserve accumulation was *invol*unt-ary (the surge in "supply pressure" of international liquidity during 1969–71 bears this out); or, the US would come strongly to desire to correct the real over-valuation of the dollar. The year 1971 saw the confluence of these two factors. The US closed the gold window in August so indicating that it would no longer support the dollar. First thoughts were that fixed exchange rates need not be abandoned, and under the Smithsonian Agreement of December 1971 a new set of currency pegs with a devalued dollar and increased price of gold were agreed. But these did not stick and about eighteen months later they were abandoned by the major G10 countries.

That the adjustment problem was binding during the 1960s is born out by Giovannini (1993, figure 2.8). He calculates realignment expectation for the pound–dollar and mark–dollar exchange rates using the same target zone methodology as we described in section 15.2. He finds statistically significant devaluation expectations for the pound especially in 1957, 1965, and, even 1967 through end-1969 (i.e. after the November 1967 devaluation). And the vulnerability of the dollar is indicated by significant expectations of *up*-valuation of the mark–dollar rate in 1961, and then more-or-less persistently from mid-1967 until end-1969.

These repeated expectations of currency realignments during the Bretton Woods period compare *unfavorably* with those that we have calculated for the two gold standard episodes (see chapter 16). And this is despite wider fluctuation bands compared with the gold points, and restrictions on short-term capital flows. On the other hand, the Bretton Woods experience compares *favorably* with that of the EMS in the 1980s – which is one of repeated currency realignments.

Overview

Thus, a sifting of the contemporaneous financial evidence of exchange rate realignment expectations leads to the conclusion that the credibility of currency pegs has *declined* from one pegged regime to the next: in the historical order of classical gold standard, interwar gold standard, Bretton Woods system, European Monetary system. Some possible reasons for this are:

1   Declining resolve – as viewed by actors in financial markets – of governments to defend declared exchange rate pegs; that is the ability of governments to make a credible commitment has declined and the time inconsistency problem has increased. Financial actors realize this and make "one-way" speculative bets on exchange rate movements.
2   Fiscal deficits have become larger and more persistent, so exerting greater pressures in foreign exchange markets.
3   Monetary policies have become more active.
4   Increasing inflation persistence has increased (see section 16.1.2).
5   Decreasing wage-price flexibility as reflected in the steepening of Phillips curves (see section 16.1.2).
6   Increasing volumes of short-term capital flows which make exchange rate pegs more difficult to defend.
7   Increased differential shocks between countries which are better coped with by floating exchange rates (see chapter 18 on monetary union) – though Bayoumi and Eichengreen (1994) do not find much evidence for this.

■ 17.4 The East Asian Dollar Standard

By the 1990s, as inflation in the USA had settled down to low and stable levels, the dollar again offered itself as a useful nominal anchor against which to peg exchange rates. Argentina and some other countries latched onto this by establishing currency boards with the dollar as the peg – see section 18.2.3. Here we discuss the East Asian dollar pegs.[8]

An East Asian monetary standard (Thailand, Korea, Indonesia, Philippines, Malaysia, Hong Kong, Taiwan, Singapore) existed before 1997 with these countries in effect pegging in narrow ranges against the US dollar. Why did they peg to the dollar? It was not necessarily because of their trade patterns: while it is true that the USA was (and is) their largest single export market, the largest single source of imports was (and remains) Japan. However, much of intra-East Asian trade, and especially that of Japan, is invoiced in US dollars, and as these dollar prices tended to be invariant to the yen/dollar exchange rate (i.e. there is "pricing to market"), it made sense for East Asian countries to peg to the dollar rather than the yen.

The advantages for East Asian countries of pegging to the dollar can be listed as: (i) simplification of monetary policy – which was set to target the exchange rate. (ii) domestic price level stability was encouraged at what by the 1990s had become a stable US price level – the dollar serving as a good nominal anchor, something that a yen peg could not have been since the Japanese wholesale price level has been falling for over a decade. (iii) competitive devaluations between the East Asian countries were avoided; (iv) the dollar peg helped to maintain stable real exchange rates with the USA and each other.

However, the East Asian dollar standard collapsed in the financial crises of summer 1997, and many of the East Asian countries listed above shifted to floating exchange rates. Three main factors undermined the East Asian dollar standard:

1 The yen/dollar rate still floated with adverse effects for the East Asian dollar standard. It destabilized the competitive positions of the dollar bloc countries, imparting to them a business cycle inversely related to the yen/dollar rate. This cyclical factor was intensified by fluctuations in Japanese direct foreign investment in East Asia which was also inversely related to the yen/dollar rate. Thus, a yen/dollar depreciation reduced an important source of balance of payments financing just at the time that it was needed.

2 The dollar peg, together with a virtual absence of foreign exchange controls and moral hazard on the part of badly-run East Asian banks, led to heavy short-term international borrowing – as borrowing in foreign currencies, especially the Japanese yen, was at lower interest rates than at home. Typically, East Asian banks did not cover themselves against exchange rate risk because the cost of forward cover would have eliminated the cost advantage of borrowing abroad. And as the borrowing was short term, banks simply took the chance that the exchange rate would not devalue in the meantime. Certainly this was a risky venture, but some East Asian banks were anyway facing bankruptcy – having been poorly run and regulated – and the competitive advantage gained from using cheap foreign funds just might have returned them to solvency. Unfortunately, competitive forces caused such a doubtful practice to spread throughout East Asian banking systems – as banks with the lowest cost of funds could win the most business.

There is a precedent for this sort of systemic breakdown – bad banks driving out good banks. In the domestic American context Edward Kane pointed to doubtful practices in the late 1980s of insolvent (but supported by government handouts) or near-insolvent financial institutions. Many failing S&Ls (akin to building societies), in hopes of regaining profitability, made dubious commercial real estate loans and investments in junk bonds financed with deposits raised at above market rates of interest. Kane dubbed these near-insolvent banks "zombies" – the living dead – and argued that their unsound practices spread to otherwise solvent institutions (so that they too could compete). Thus, it was that large sections of the US banking industry had to be bailed out at an undiscounted cost of over $500 billion. As the East Asian dollar standard was brought down in 1997 by similar systemic failures but in an international context, we could say that it was destroyed by "internationalized zombies"!

3 With interest rates in the East Asian dollar zone being set in the USA, the exchange rate pegs to the dollar prevented central banks from injecting liquidity – so lowering interest rates and the cost of funds – in order to "save" their banking systems. Rather, interest rates were kept high for so long that many East Asian banking systems were convulsed and, ultimately, the resulting banking difficulties undermined confidence in their currencies. This was far from being the first time in history when faults in domestic financial systems destroyed international monetary arrangements. Both the USA's and Belgium's ejection from the gold standard in, respectively, 1933 and 1935, were intimately related to domestic banking difficulties.

As a *postscript* to the East Asian dollar standard McKinnon (1999) argues against permanently floating exchange rates in East Asia because the benefits of pegging to the dollar would be lost. Furthermore, in his view, floating would not necessarily reduce risk premia on East Asian interest rates because floating is likely to destabilize domestic prices and, therefore, interest rates. However, domestic financial reforms are needed, such as recapitalization of the banks, better bank regulators, and rules preventing banks borrowing foreign currencies unhedged.

NOTES

1 For more details see IMF, *Survey*, February 10, 1997.
2 In view of the fact that in some quarters it is believed that the Bretton Woods conference "chose the American dollar as the backbone of international exchange," it is worth emphasizing that this was not in fact the case. But the Articles of Agreement did allow for the possibility, later taken up by the USA, for a member to maintain its commitment to a parity exchange rate by pegging against gold; other member's then fulfilled their commitments by pegging against the dollar.
3 Seigniorage accrues to the issuer of a currency. In the case of the dollar as a reserve asset, seigniorage is collected by the USA if the rate of interest paid on foreign central bank deposits is less than the return on the corresponding assets acquired by the USA.
4 While Tew (1977) dates the rise of the dollar standard from 1971, the *de jure* demonetization of gold, this now seems to be a minority view. Several authorities in Bordo and Eichengreen (1993) date the rise of the pure dollar standard from at least the middle of the 1960s.
5 If the gold backing for the dollar was as important as Triffin said, why did the UK on the eve of the First World War maintain an unquestioned position on the gold standard with, according to Lindert (1969), a similar ratio of gold to external liquid

liabilities? At this time the UK was lending long and borrowing short, just as the US did during the 1960s. Was the UK then the early twentieth century precursor of the US? While Lindert (1969) doubts that she was (arguing that sterling liquid liabilities were being accumulated simply because British exports were too small), he does explain why other countries voluntarily held increasing amounts of foreign exchange reserves rather than gold: for the interest income, as countervailing power against the creditor nation, the benefit of lower transaction costs, and as a shock-absorber to stabilize gold reserves. But these motives for holding a foreign currency instead of gold might well have been as strong in the 1960s, which implies that Triffin's concern was overdone.

6   Genberg and Swoboda (1993) comment that the system could have been saved if only the "other G10" had followed that logic of the system and increased their money supplies more quickly – so moderating the increase in M/M^*, accepting a higher rate of inflation. But another solution was also at hand – countries such as Germany and Japan could have stemmed their involuntary accumulation of dollars by increasing the value of the mark and the yen against the dollar – as was allowed for under IMF rules. Thus, as, *inter alia*, Williamson (1993) and Corden (1993) comment, the Bretton Woods system was brought down not so much by its "liquidity problem" as by its "adjustment problem."

7   McKinnon rejects the notion that the world's money supply problems are due to payments deficits caused by disequilibrium exchange rates under the "system" of dirty floating. Rather, exchange rate targeting is necessary owing to exchange rate overshooting.

8   Much of the discussion in this section is based on McKinnon (1999).

18

Monetary Unions

To examine theoretical and empirical matters relating to monetary unions this chapter is divided into seven main parts. Section 18.1 outlines three seminal contributions on the theory of monetary union – those of Mundell, McKinnon, and Kenen. Section 18.2 outlines the optimum currency area model of Melitz (1995), which is based on the idea of selecting monetary union partners with whom the covariances of equilibrium real exchange rates is low. This model is easily extended to compare choices between regimes of pegged rates, currency boards and dollarization. Section 18.3 discusses the general equilibrium model of Bayoumi (1994), which also rests on the idea that suitable partners for monetary union are subjected to similar shocks – and, therefore, share low correlations in equilibrium real exchange rates. Section 18.4 lists *ad hoc* benefits and costs of monetary union. Section 18.5 discusses empirical evidence on the nature of shocks and, therefore, the strength of the economic case for monetary union between various groups of countries. Finally, sections 18.6 and 18.7 discuss problems that arise with fiscal policy in a monetary union.

18.1 Benefits and Costs of a Monetary Area: Seminal Ideas

Should a country join a monetary union – so adopting a common currency with its partners? Before looking at the seminal contributions let's get the answer into broad perspective. The answer turns on the benefits and costs of doing so. A monetary union offers benefits by enhancing the functions of money as a numeraire (prices become less opaque as the prices of more goods are stated in a common currency), medium of exchange (lowering the costs of changing one money for another), and store of value (a more stable price level). Another benefit that might be reaped is from economies of scale if the creation of a monetary union leads to concentration in production. The costs of monetary union occur when shocks change a country's equilibrium real exchange rate *and* there is some nominal wage-price stickiness. If wages and prices could in fact change quickly, so that the new equilibrium real exchange rate is quickly gained, "giving up" the nominal exchange rate would not matter as the equilibrium real exchange rate would be achieved via a change in the price level. But with nominal wage and price rigidity and a single currency, a shock causing a country's equilibrium real exchange rate to depreciate will cause a rise in the rate of unemployment and lost output. Notice that such a shock could occur either in the home country (e.g. a switch of demand away from its goods), or, in another member of the monetary union (e.g. a rise in productivity in a key sector).

Mundell (1961). The key factor in Mundell's argument is the degree of factor mobility between regions within a nation or between nations. If mobility is low, monetary union is undesirable. This could even mean breaking up an existing monetary union. To illustrate, suppose that in a large country demand switches from goods produced in area A to those produced in area B. Excess supply appears in area A and excess demand in area B. If labor is highly mobile it migrates from area A to area B: unemployment is not a problem. But if factors are geographically immobile a change in the real exchange rate between the two areas is called for.

Area A's real exchange rate is:

$$K_A = S.(P^B/P^A) \tag{18.1}$$

where S is the exchange rate between areas A and B $(= 1)$ and the Ps are regional price levels. To eliminate excess supply a depreciation of K_A is needed. If prices are flexible this is accomplished by a fall in area A's price level and a rise in area B's. But if prices are inflexible (perhaps due to national wage bargaining, long-term contracts, or intractable inflation expectations) disequilibrium will persist. Rather than wait for a drawn-out recession to reduce region A's price level, the alternative is to break up the monetary union allowing the nominal exchange rate, S, between the two areas to depreciate.

This analysis has the merit of pointing to potential problems for nations that are considering joining a monetary union. The combination of internationally immobile labor, sticky wages-prices, and the abandonment of the exchange rate instrument could condemn a nation finding itself in the position of area A to a period of prolonged unemployment.

McKinnon (1963). Whether a change in the nominal exchange rate will be sufficient to change the real exchange rate and so eliminate excess supply or demand, according to McKinnon, depends on an economy's degree of openness – measured by the ratio of traded to non-traded goods in national production or consumption.

Suppose that a country has a current account deficit. We know that to correct it the price of traded goods, P_T, must increase relative to the price of non-traded goods, P_{NT} – then production shifts into, and home consumption out of, traded goods. It is the change in the exchange rate which is supposed to cause this alteration in relative prices.

McKinnon (1963) argued that, typically, in an *open* economy changes in the exchange rate would not alter the ratio of prices between traded and non-traded goods, i.e. $d(P_T/P_{NT})/dS = 0$, as rising traded good prices quickly and obviously feed into the consumer price index and cannot help but be noticed by labor, which bargains for real wages. Thus, P_{NT} rises along with P_T. Therefore, in an open economy, the exchange rate may as well be fixed – the country becoming a member of a currency area or monetary union. In a relatively *closed* economy $d(P_T/P_{NT})/dS > 0$ on the, perhaps, somewhat artificial assumption that labor does not immediately notice the inflationary effect of devaluation. There are two possible reasons for this: (i) in a closed economy the traded goods sector contributes minimally to the consumer price index, so devaluation may have a less-than-obvious effect on the rate of inflation; and (ii) the large nontraded goods sector may be able to absorb the switch in demand towards it without a noticeable rise in prices.

The logic of the McKinnon argument is that only relatively closed economies can effectively use the exchange rate instrument. Herein lies an argument for monetary union in the EU. All member countries are open economies as measured by the share of imports in GDP. For example, in 1987, Belgium's ratio was 76 percent and even the large EU economies were each over 25 percent. By contrast, the ratio for the USA, Japan, and the EU (external trade) was in the neighborhood of 12 percent.

Kenen (1969) argued that countries with diversified industrial and export structures (such as those in the EU) should try to reap the benefits of a fixed exchange rate, because demand fluctuations and supply shocks at the microeconomic level will tend to cancel each other out. Thus, variation in real exchange rates (via adjustment of nominal exchange rates) is rarely required. As we shall see in the next section, in more recent work on optimum currency areas the relevance of economic structures and asymmetric shocks is emphasized.

The Mundell, McKinnon, and Kenen models of the optimum currency area have been described as "single criterion cases" (Ishiyama, 1975) and as such may be regarded as overly-restrictive in scope. Furthermore, as Tavlas (1994) points out the criteria may be conflicting. For example, a country may be open – suggesting joining a monetary union, but it may not have internationally mobile labor – suggesting the opposite.

A preferable approach would be to lay down explicit lists of the benefits and costs likely to be associated with the creation of a currency area. This has recently been accomplished in formal models by Melitz (1995) and Bayoumi (1994).

■ 18.2 Melitz and the Covariance of Equilibrium Real Exchange Rates Approach

Melitz (1995) offers a theory of the optimum currency area based on maximizing the net benefits of a monetary union. His main insight is that *the cost to a country of giving up the nominal exchange rate in the face of wage-price stickiness depends on its trade weighted covariance of equilibrium real exchange rates with its trade partners.* If this covariance is high, a given change in the home country's nominal exchange rate will appropriately move its real exchange rate with each trade partner. The cost of giving up the nominal exchange rate instrument will therefore be high. But if the covariance of equilibrium real exchange rates is low, a given devaluation may be appropriate for some but not all trade partners. It would not then be so costly to give up the nominal exchange instrument.

For example, if phylloxera once in a while severely damaged only the French wine industry (God forbid), its equilibrium real exchange rate would depreciate against all of its trade partners – hence the covariance of French equilibrium rates with its trade partners would be high and nominal devaluation would be appropriate against all of them. However, if the disease, at the time as it struck France, also struck other important wine-producing countries – say, Italy and Spain – France's equilibrium real exchange rate might not depreciate against them though it still would against say, the UK and Sweden. In this case, the nominal exchange rate instrument is less useful as franc nominal devaluation would only be appropriate for the non-wine growing countries.

Thus, Melitz models the cost of monetary union to a given country (call it "home") to depend upon both its extent, u, and degree, x, of openness. Here u is the share of a country's trade absorbed in a monetary union and so ranges from 0 to 1 (e.g. if 35 percent of a country's trade is with members of the monetary union $u = 0.35$); and x is the ratio exports/GDP. Begin by assuming that all trade partners of home are taken into a monetary union, $u = 1$, the cost, $C(u, x)$, is:

$$C(1, x) = f(\text{cov}(1), x) \tag{18.2}$$

$$\text{cov}(1) > 0 \qquad f'(\text{cov}(1)) > 0 \qquad 0 < x < 1 \qquad f'(x) < 0$$

Here $f(\ )$ depends on wage–price stickiness and the production function which together determine the amount of lost output when the real exchange rate remains over-valued. Cov(1) is the weighted average expected covariance of home's equilibrium relative prices with all foreign countries – which depends, as explained above, on the expected shocks hitting home and its various trade partners – the more asymmetric the shocks the higher the covariance.

Of course, a country will not be joining a universal monetary union so $u < 1$. In considering which countries the home country should first form a monetary union it is reasonable to assume that it will pick them so as to minimize the cost of giving up the nominal exchange rate instrument. Therefore, for any $u < 1$, the other members will be chosen so as to minimize covariance with them. This is because if covariance is low the nominal exchange rate instrument is not of much use and is not therefore costly to give up.

The cost of monetary union for "home" with this group of *lowest covariance members* is:

$$C(u, x) = [cov(u)/cov(1)].f(cov(1), x) \tag{18.3}$$

$$f'[(cov(u)/cov(1)] > 0 \qquad f''[cov(u)/cov(1)] > 0$$

where $cov(u)/cov(1)$ is simply the proportion of home's *lowest* total covariance absorbed within the monetary union for any $u < 1$. By "lowest" we mean that for any proportion, u, of home's trade absorbed into a monetary union, that the countries included have the lowest covariances with home, while those with higher covariances are not included. The signs of the first and second derivatives are reasonable because, the lowest cost countries will join first, and successively higher cost countries later.

Benefits. The benefits of monetary union for home are as with other writers the benefit of improving money as a numeraire, medium of exchange, and store of value. Thus,

$$R(u, x) = g(u, x) \tag{18.4}$$

$$g'(u) \text{ and } g'(x) > 0$$

where R is home's gross benefit which depends positively on the extent of the union (u) and degree of openness (x).

18.2.1 The optimum currency area

Figure 18.1 shows the size of the optimum currency area, as measured by u (the share of home's foreign trade included within it), being determined by the marginal cost and marginal benefit of enlargement. Thus, as the optimum u increases, the country "home" wants to join in monetary union with successively more countries. Likewise, as these other countries' optimal u's increase the prospective partners will want to join with "home" – provided that their cost functions (equation 18.2) include "home" among their cost-minimizing set of countries. In other words, we take it that there is a direct relationship between the size of the optimal u's and the number of countries wishing to join a given monetary union.

Figure 18.2 shows that the size of home's optimum currency area increases directly with the a rises in the degree of openness, x. This increase in optimum size occurs as: (i) $g'(x) > 0$, because the more open is an economy prior to joining a currency union the less well does its own money function as a unit of account, medium of exchange and store of value. And (ii) $f'(x) < 0$, because it is less painful to give up the nominal exchange rate instrument because it works less well the more open is an economy.

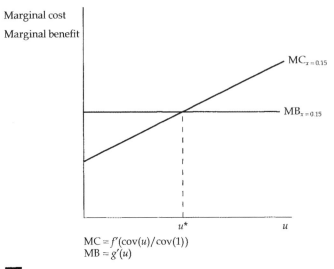

$$MC = f'(\text{cov}(u)/\text{cov}(1))$$
$$MB = g'(u)$$

Figure 18.1 The optimum currency area

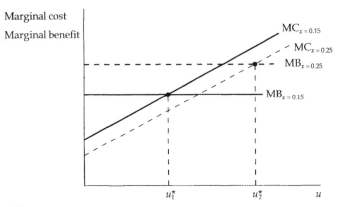

Figure 18.2 The size of the optimum currency area increases with openness

18.2.2 The size of the optimum monetary union versus the size of the optimum pegged exchange rate zone

A zone of pegged exchange rates is different to a monetary union because under the former "giving up the nominal exchange rate instrument" is not complete. Room is left for the exchange rate to fluctuate within a band and for *ad hoc* exchange

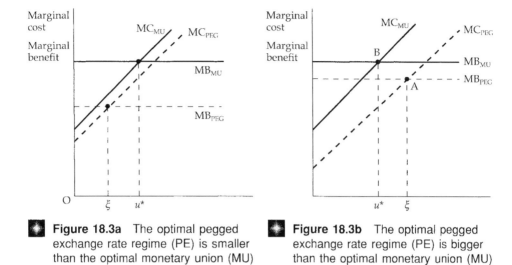

Figure 18.3a The optimal pegged exchange rate regime (PE) is smaller than the optimal monetary union (MU)

Figure 18.3b The optimal pegged exchange rate regime (PE) is bigger than the optimal monetary union (MU)

rate realignment. Thus, writing ξ for the proportion of trade coming under a pegged exchange rate regime (instead of u) we get:

$$C(\xi, x) = cC(u, x) \qquad 0 < c < 1 \qquad (18.5)$$

for $\xi = u$. That is, costs are less by the fraction c in a pegged system than in a monetary union of the same size because the exchange rate instrument is not entirely given up.

But benefits are less too:

$$R(\xi, x) = rR(u, x) \qquad 0 < r < 1 \qquad (18.6)$$

for $\xi = u$. That is, benefits are less by the fraction r in a pegged system because a separate currency is retained.

With both marginal costs and benefits being lower in a pegged system, depending upon which falls more, the optimal pegged regime may have either a smaller or a larger share of home's foreign trade (ξ) coming under it compared with the optimal u for monetary union. These two cases are shown in figures 18.3a and 18.3b.

Thus, in figure 18.3a benefits have fallen by more than costs and the optimal pegged regime has a smaller proportion of home's trade under it compared with monetary union. But in figure 18.3b the reverse is true. With respect to figure 18.3b Melitz makes the most interesting observation that while it might have been optimal for the UK to be a member of the EMS (a pegged regime), it may not be optimal for it to be a member of the monetary union, because in moving from A to B the rise in costs is more than the rise in benefit.

18.2.3 The choice between pegging, currency boards, and dollarization

In a currency board arrangement a country fixes its exchange rate *without* any fluctuation band. Currency boards are currently operated by Argentina, Bulgaria, and Estonia. A currency board is more like a monetary union than is a pegged exchange arrangement because of both the absence of a fluctuation band and the presence of a strict monetary policy rule linking changes in the money base to the balance of payments. However, a currency board is not monetary union because a separate currency is retained and the monetary policy rule can be changed without consultation with another country.

Thus, again we expect both the costs and benefits of a currency board to be less than in a monetary union. Writing κ for the proportion of trade coming under a currency board's fixed exchange rate – i.e. if tied to the US dollar, its trade with the USA and other countries pegged to the dollar – costs and benefits become:

$$C(\kappa, x) = qC(u, x) \qquad 0 < q < 1 \tag{18.7}$$

$$R(\kappa, x) = vR(u, x) \qquad 0 < v < 1 \tag{18.8}$$

for $\kappa = u$. Thus, costs and benefits are lower with a currency board than with monetary union.

We can imagine a hierarchy of non-floating exchange rate regimes through which a country might pass as perceived costs and benefits change over time. Thus, initially there might be a pegged exchange rate (which could include some sort of managed float or crawling peg). Dissatisfaction with this – perhaps due to the persistence of inflation (i.e. benefits are perceived as being low in relation to the cost of operating the system) – could lead to a currency board. This would be true if the increase in benefits expected from adopting a strict monetary policy rule outweigh the expected increase in costs. If so, in figure 18.4, $\kappa > \xi$, and the country adopts a currency board moving from point A to point B.

However, as Argentina's experience in 1995 showed, the costs of operating a currency board can be very high. At end-1994 the value of the Mexican peso collapsed and caused a run on most Latin American currencies – the so-called "tequila effect." We can think of the Mexican devaluation setting off a contagion across Latin America that these countries too would change their monetary policy rules. Argentina's currency board held out as interest rates there were very sharply increased. But the economic cost was enormous as Argentina was plunged into a severe economic recession.

Hence, in recent years, following Argentina's 1999 discussions with the USA on the official *dollarization* of Argentina, there have been predictions by senior economists that in the near future most of Latin America will have been dollarized.[1] Dollarization, the US dollar replacing the domestic currency, amounts to a monetary union with the USA. A move from either a pegged exchange rate or a currency board to dollarization is shown at point C in figure 18.4 by marginal

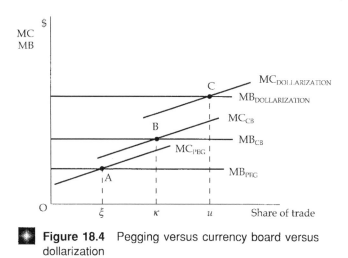

Figure 18.4 Pegging versus currency board versus dollarization

benefit increasing by more than marginal cost. The latter increases as an independent monetary policy is given up altogether, and the expected marginal benefit of dollarization is assumed to be high relative to other regimes because of the perceived failures of pegged and currency board arrangements.

18.3 Bayoumi's General Equilibrium Model of the Optimum Currency Area

Bayoumi (1994) incorporates the three criteria of Mundell, McKinnon, and Kenen in a general equilibrium model of the optimum currency area. The key assumptions are that each of two countries, j and k, are fully specialized in production of a single differentiated good which they trade with each other; the production functions are $\ln y = \alpha \ln x + \varepsilon$ ($\ln x$ is labor input, $\alpha < 1$, and ε is a random productivity shock with expected value $= 0$); labor supply is fixed and labor markets are competitive (hence, $W \times E = MRPL$ where W is the local currency nominal wage, E the amount of foreign currency per unit of domestic currency, and MRPL is the marginal revenue product of labor); W is sticky downwards, and a third country, m, with a fixed price level serves as the numeraire for exchange rates.

Suppose that j and k are subjected to asymmetric shocks, $\varepsilon_j > 0$, $\varepsilon_k < 0$. As $MRPL_k$ has decreased so must $W_k \times E_k$ which, if exchange rates are floating, is easily achieved via currency depreciation – E_k falling. Also, as $MRPL_j$ has increased so must $W_j \times E_j$ – which can be achieved via currency appreciation, E_j rising. Thus, k's necessary real exchange rate depreciation *vis-à-vis* j is achieved without disruption via an increase in the ratio E_j/E_k.

The story is quite different if j and k form a currency union, so fixing the nominal exchange rate between themselves. While they continue to float against m their common floating rate cannot move to satisfy both countries at once. Bayoumi assumes that it stays somewhere in the middle, satisfying neither country completely. Given the same shocks as before, the same change in the real exchange rate between j and k is required but now the excess demand for labor in j causes W_j and the price level in j to rise. In k wages need to fall to maintain labor market equilibrium but W_j is sticky downwards, so unemployment results.

Clearly, the more asymmetric are the shocks, the bigger are the welfare-reducing disequilibria in j and k's economies. Bayoumi gives the costs of these disequilibria for country j as:

$$B_{jk}(\varepsilon_j - \varepsilon_k)H \tag{18.9}$$

and for country k as:

$$B_{kk}(\varepsilon_j - \varepsilon_k)H \tag{18.10}$$

where B_{jk} is the share of good k in country j's consumption, B_{kk} the share of good k in country k's consumption, $(\varepsilon_j - \varepsilon_k)$ measures the size of the asymmetric shocks, and $H = \alpha/2(1 - \alpha)$. Thus, the cost of a currency union between j and k increases as the following variables increase: the size of the asymmetric shock, the share of good k in country j's consumption (B_{jk}), the share of good k in country k's consumption ε_{kk}, and α.

The benefit of currency union between j and k in Bayoumi (1994) depends directly on the proportion of trade between them, B_{jk} and B_{kj}, and the level of transaction costs on this trade. It is assumed that transaction costs are eliminated with currency union. (Other benefits could also be taken into account such as the achievement of economies of scale.) Whether currency union is welfare-increasing depends on the balance of the costs and benefits.

Thus, for country k the net benefit of joining a currency union in the face of a negative shock is greater the larger the cost of transacting across currencies, the greater the share of good j in country k's consumption, the lower the share of good k in country k's consumption and the smaller the shocks. So we note that openness (defined as a high level of cross or, "diversified" consumption) favors a currency union. This is McKinnon's criterion but reached from a different argument. Also a diversified industrial structure – which would tend to reduce the size of aggregate shocks – supporting Kenen's use of this criterion. Furthermore, if labor is mobile between regions, a portion of country k's unemployed will move to country j where there is excess demand for labor. So while country k's output is still lower, country j's output rises – thus cutting the cost of forming a currency union. This is Mundell's argument – labor mobility between regions is desirable.[2]

 ## 18.4 *Ad hoc* Benefits of a Pegged Exchange Rate or Common Currency

1   Increased allocative efficiency may occur as elimination of exchange-risk, at the margin, will promote integration of production and international exchange: both trade and investment flows between the EU members may be stimulated

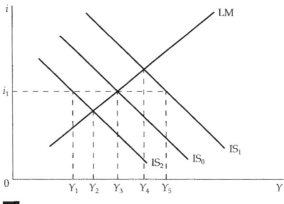

Figure 18.5 Real shocks and income instability

(on this argument see IMF, 1984). To put it another way, elimination of exchange rate risk within a monetary union removes exchange rate hedging as an argument in a firm's location decisions.

Against this, pegging exchange rates, as opposed to monetary union, may only shift risk to some other quarter – possibly the bond market if interest rates become more variable due to the gearing of domestic monetary conditions to the fixed exchange rate. In general, fixing the exchange rate increases the volatility of real economic activity if shocks originate in the domestic real sector, but lowers it if the shock originates in the domestic monetary sector (De Grauwe, 1992 based on Poole, 1970).

To see this, recall that with a fixed exchange rate the domestic interest rate is fixed for a given foreign interest rate and exchange rate expectations (i.e., $\Delta s^e = 0$). We stick with the simplest of cases. In figure 18.5 the IS curve is stochastic and the LM curve is deterministic – reflecting the notion that shocks originate in the real sector. The fixed exchange rate imposes interest rate targeting and at i_1, given the existence of real shocks, income varies between Y_1 and Y_5. Had the exchange rate been allowed to float, so that the interest rate was free to vary, income would fluctuate only between Y_3 and Y_4. On the other hand, when LM is unstable (due to, for example, unstable money demand) and IS is deterministic, a fixed exchange rate – with consequent interest rate targeting – leaves income stable at Y_2 in figure 18.6. However, with a floating exchange rate and monetary targeting, LM shifts about and income is destabilized, varying between Y_1 and Y_3.

2   If risk-adjusted interest rates fall as exchange-risk is reduced or eliminated, dynamic welfare gains may result from an enhanced rate of capital formation. This could happen in high inflation/interest rate countries if bond and money markets expect that inflation will be permanently reduced.

3   We know that floating exchange rates since 1973 have been associated with overshooting and wide divergences of real exchange rates from purchasing power parity which, in turn, have had deleterious real economic effects (see sections 2.5,

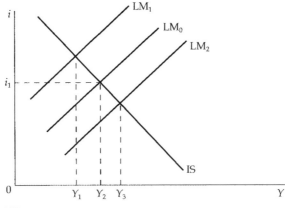

Figure 18.6 Monetary shocks and income instability

6.4, 24.4 and chapter 11). Elimination of exchange rate overshooting and the smoothing of real exchange rates should promote economic stability. This argument is especially strong given that intra-EC trade in 1990 amounted to nearly 60 percent of the EC's total trade. That is, an overshooting exchange rate between a pair of countries doing little trade with each other may not matter much, but it matters a lot when they trade a great deal.

4   In the old European monetary system an economy arose through the financing of intra-area current account deficits in local currencies rather than in US dollars as these currencies do not have to be earned through payments surpluses with the USA. A related economy in the holding of international reserves may arise if random trade imbalances with the rest of the world are smaller than the aggregate of the members' individual temporary imbalances.

5   Transaction costs incurred in changing one currency for another will be eliminated if a common currency is adopted. In the case of the EU this saving is estimated to be about one-half of one percent of EC GNP (*European Economy*, 1990).

6   Some members of an EC monetary union may gain monetary credibility as a result of giving up their own monetary independence and having their monetary conditions governed by an independent European Central bank: a reduction in their rate of inflation would occur – sooner or later – as inflation expectations adjusted downward.[3] This argument may have some appeal for inflation prone countries but it also has a dubious aspect: would not greater independence for a nation's existing central bank achieve the same end? And is it necessarily true that low inflation countries will continue being so once their monetary policy is handed over to a Eurofed? Perhaps yes, if the Eurofed operates like the Bundesbank.

7   Following Edwards and Hallwood (1980) there is a welfare gain if variability in *relative* prices is reduced. But will fixing the exchange rate reduce relative price instability? It may well do so if some prices are more sensitive to movements in the exchange rate (e.g. those of traded goods) than are others.

18.4.1 *Ad hoc* costs of a common currency

1 If inflation remains stubbornly high in a member country, or, a country enters into monetary union at an overvalued exchange rate, it may have to pass through a period of deflation with high real interest rates, reduced economic growth and higher unemployment, i.e. a country's short-run Phillips curve may not be vertical and the short run may not be all that short.

2 Low-income countries may attract mainly low value added (low wage) direct foreign investment (*broadening*) while high income countries *deepen* their advantage in high value added activities such as R&D, management, product development, and ownership. Buckley and Artisien (1987), and Cantwell (1987) provide evidence that, in several industries, the broadening–deepening process is happening. Greece, Portugal, Spain, and Ireland may be candidates for peripheral status. In the absence of exchange rate and tariff instruments to keep or attract high value added activities, use of inter-regional transfers provides some compensation. Portugal, Greece, and Ireland already receive regional aid amounting to about 3 percent of GDP.

Notice that this argument suggests that the members of a monetary union may be left more open to asymmetric shocks, so raising the costs of membership.

3 Monetary policy may be set in a way that does not suit all members – a factor that led to the disruption of the EMS in September 1992. In the EMS, because of its dominant position in monetary affairs, Germany effectively set monetary policy for the EC as a whole. The Bundesbank set high interest rates in an effort to stem the inflation deriving from the high cost of unifying Germany. However, several European economies, especially Britain's, were in recession and wanted low interest rates. Short of devaluing the pound, British interest rates were governed by those in Germany. The European central bank will probably find that it is not able to accommodate the desires of all members on interest rate and, hence, exchange rate policy. A feature of the Bayoumi (1994) model – see section 18.3 – is that a monetary union's (external) exchange rate is an average of what would have been the equilibrium exchange rates of the members had they not been in a monetary union. Thus, if some members experience asymmetric shocks the external exchange rate cannot move to satisfy each of them.

4 As we discuss at greater length in sections 18.6 and 18.7, a member of a currency area is likely to find increased constraints on its fiscal policy. In the EU this is now a matter of international agreement between the members. Coordination of fiscal policy between the members is needed to internalize fiscal externalities and to avoid free-rider problems.

18.5 Estimating Shocks

As empirical inquiries into the EU as an optimal currency area often make comparison with the USA, it is as well at the outset to enquire into how real exchange rate adjustment between US regions takes place. Tootell (1992) found that in the USA marked changes in relative inter-regional prices and prosperity is the mechanism through which regions adjust to differential economic shocks. Specifically, in the USA purchasing power parity tends to hold between regions in traded goods but *not* in non-traded goods – implying that the non-traded goods sector absorbs shocks specific to a regional economy. In otherwords, real exchange rates between regions are adjusted by changes in regional price levels caused by changes in the prices of non-traded goods.

Tavlas (1994) points out that studies of the suitability of the EU for monetary union reach mixed results. In an early study Bayoumi and Eichengreen (1992) compared the degree of correlation of shocks in the EC12 with that between major regions in the USA, finding that both demand and supply shocks were more closely correlated in the 1962–88 period in the USA than in the EC12. This suggested that the USA is more like an optimal currency area than is the EC12. However, noting that supply shocks are the important ones as (macroeconomic) demand shocks can, presumably, be largely rubbed out in a monetary union, they also found that supply shocks in a small group of EC countries (Germany, France, Benelux, and Denmark) were highly correlated – suggesting that they may form an optimal currency area. Using a different statistical technique, Caporale (1993) also found high correlation between shocks across the EC12.

A more recent study by Bayoumi and Prasad (1997) is supportive of the view that shocks hitting the EU countries are no more asymmetric than those hitting the US regions. But they qualify this with the finding that labor is less mobile in the EU than in the US – so that the same type of shocks could cause a greater loss of output in the EU than in the US.

Furthermore, among the EU countries there is one country that experienced a markedly different pattern of shocks compared with the EU average. This is the UK. The Bayoumi and Prasad (1997) model is set up to explain short-term variation in industry growth rates in various EU countries. For this group as a whole and for the UK taken separately about one-half of the variation is explained by the model. The sources of variation are broken down into "aggregate shocks" which affect the whole area, "industry shocks" experienced by the same industry across countries, and "country shocks" unique to a given country. While in the EU as a whole the explained variation is divided evenly between the three causes this was not the case in the UK. For the UK, 41 percentage points of the 48 percentage points of explained variation was due to country specific shocks. If this finding is confirmed and the pattern persists it indicates that the UK experiences with asymmetric supply shocks questions the desireablity of monetary union. And it might also help to explain why a pegged exchange rate for the pound in the EMS was a less questionable choice than monetary union – see section 18.2.2.

Bayoumi and Eichengreen (1994) investigate the pattern of shocks in 15 European countries, 13 countries from the Americas and 11 countries from East Asia. Their findings for Europe are similar to those outlined above – only a small group of EU countries in northern Europe experience highly correlated supply shocks – so suggesting a case for a "two speed" Europe.

Significant supply shock correlations in East Asia were sparse – suggesting that a yen block is likely to be torn apart – but that both Taiwan and Korea did have a significantly correlated supply shocks.

In Latin America there were even fewer significant correlations of supply shocks. Given that Latin American countries have long been searching for viable exchange rate regimes, this finding, if confirmed in other studies, is of great relevance. It suggests that monetary unions, currency boards based on the US dollar, or, even, pegged rate regimes are not necessary suited to the Latin American case. But, as small open economies, neither are they suited to floating rates.

18.6 Fiscal Federalism

Fiscal policy in a monetary union is discussed under the heading, of what is called in public finance, "fiscal federalism." Fiscal policy has three broad functions: those of allocation, distribution, and stabilization. With regards to the *allocation* function, should social goods (i.e. non-rival or non-excludable in consumption) be provided on a centralized or decentralized basis? The accepted principle is that social goods should be supplied at the level of government that most closely matches the spatial distribution of benefits with costs. When benefits are spatially limited the voting area should be similarly limited since it is through the ballot box that preferences are revealed. This makes an economic case for subsidiarity in the EU.

The *distribution* function, however, may be required to be moved up to the federal level if population mobility is quite high over a period of years. Otherwise those favoring tax regimes that promote income equality (most often those with low incomes) will move to the jurisdictions that offer this, while those that do not (those with high incomes) move to areas that offer less progressive tax regimes. As a result little income redistribution will occur.

There is a good case for centralizing the *stabilization* function at the federal level, or, at least, coordinating it from there. A change in a country's fiscal stance may create externalities for other members of a monetary union. For example, depending upon circumstances, an expansionary fiscal policy by nation A may yield an external benefit (stimulating growth and employment) or an external diseconomy (increased inflationary pressures) in the union as a whole. In either case, the externality is not internalized by nation A so it is not driven to adopt the socially optimal fiscal stance from the union's point of view. As this is true for the other members of the union there is no guarantee that the aggregated balance of national fiscal policies will be that which is most desirable. Moreover, in the case where economically and politically costly disinflationary fiscal policy is called for in the union a free-rider problem arises. As a result, either the sum of disinflationary policies is insufficient, or the burden of adjustment falls heavily on a few countries, e.g. those in the weakest financial position.

In the EU fiscal federalism is qualitatively different from that in the USA. In the USA the federal budget is large relative to individual state budgets so centralized budgetary policy can be set without need to coordinate the independent states. This is especially so as the states are committed to balanced budgets. However, in the EU the federal budget is small and would be ineffective as a stabilization device. Moreover, in the USA the large federal budget acts both as an effective automatic stabilizer for the macroeconomy and as an automatic devise for the geographic redistribution of income to disadvantaged areas.

Statistical estimates by Bayoumi and Masson (1995) and Sala-i-Martin and Sachs (1992) indicate that in the USA interregional Federal government automatic adjustments in regional Federal taxes and transfers have a 30 percent cushioning effect. In other words, a region experiencing a negative shock has a real GDP which is that much higher than it otherwise would have been. Estimates for another federal country, Canada, are for a 17 percent cushioning effect.

The stabilization effect of the "federal" EU budget is much less powerful because the EU as such has a tiny budget in relation to EU GDP. However, national budgets are large in the EU and Bayoumi and Masson (1995) estimate from a sample of five members a cushioning effect of similar magnitude as that of the federal budget in the USA.

Herein lies the danger of EU imposed ceilings on national budget deficits. Bayoumi and Eichengreen (1995) simulate the effect of legislative restraints on budget balances in reducing the effectiveness of automatic stabilizers on the volatility of real GDP. They find that a balanced budget amendment in the USA would worsen the size of the negative output gap between actual and potential real GDP in the first year following a fall in consumption. They observe that ceilings for national budget deficits in the EU could have the same sort of effect there, especially as budget deficits at lower levels of government (county, city and town) in the EU were found to behave less anti-cyclically than was the case in the USA.

Under the circumstances discussed above fiscal design in the EU should try to recognize: (i) the primacy of national fiscal policies; (ii) the need to coordinate these policies; and (iii) leave sufficient scope for national fiscal deficits to allow for effective stabilization.

 ## 18.7 More on Fiscal Policy in a Monetary Union

We discussed fiscal policy spillover effects between countries with fixed exchange rates in section 6.1, and this is clearly relevant in the monetary union context. We showed that the result of a larger budget deficit in one of the two countries locked together with fixed exchange rates was higher aggregate demand and interest rates in both countries, and an appreciated floating exchange rate against the rest of the world. We also commented that such spillovers could be inflationary for the partner country and, therefore, would be unwelcome. In general, spillovers are more unwelcome the more out of phase are national business cycles, or, what amounts to much the same thing, the less symmetric are shocks.

An international welfare gain could, therefore, result from international policy coordination – as in figure 6.5. The objective of policy cooperation would be to move from a non-cooperative Nash or Stackelberg equilibrium to a Pareto optimal position on the contract curve. However, the Mastricht Treaty does not in fact try to promote a cooperative search for fiscal policy Pareto equilibria. Rather, it only sets limits on the scope for increasing fiscal imbalances at the national level.

Whether this moves the member countries closer to or further away from Pareto optimality is incidental to the Mastricht Treaty. Thus, in figure 6.5, if the policy instrument is constrained so that the Nash or Stackelberg equilibria are ruled out, a move from the right toward the contract curve from these equilibria might be forced. However, the fiscal constraint could be so tight as to reduce *welfare* below the level of the Nash or Stackelberg equilibria *and* prevent the contract curve being approached from the left.

NOTES

1 For example, Rudiger Dornbusch, BBC World Service, February 21, 1999.
2 Interestingly, a third country, outside of the currency union, suffers a welfare loss from the currency union between j and k as it does not share in lower transaction costs but it suffers the lower availability of good k. But if other benefits materialize – such as economies of scale in the currency union – this result might not follow.
3 There is some evidence showing that inflationary expectations in Ireland fell after joining the EMS. Prior to 1979 Ireland's exchange rate was tied to the pound sterling and Britain's exchange rate policy was accommodated to British inflation. But once in the EMS the Irish government accepted a much stronger exchange rate discipline and inflationary expectations moderated (Kremers, 1989). The Irish experience also shows that it does matter which monetary union you join: tying to inflationary Britain left Irish inflation expectations high, while effectively tying to the DM had a purging effect. Moreover, Britain's relatively brief participation in the exchange rate mechanism led to a drastic fall in the UK's inflation rate as the Bank of England's monetary policy was tied to that of the Bundesbank.

19

International Capital Flows

19.1 International money and capital flows
19.2 Eurobanking
19.3 Regulation: the Basle capital accord
19.4 Measuring international capital mobility
19.5 International bond markets

Through which intermediaries and markets does short-term and long-term capital move? How big are the flows? Why have they grown so quickly in recent years? How mobile is long-term capital?

We saw in earlier chapters that short-term capital is mobile in the sense that returns on similar short-term assets are equalized between countries under uncovered interest parity. But how internationally mobile is long-term capital? Are returns on physical assets, or, rather, the claims on them, equalized between countries so that the world's capital stock is optimally allocated between countries?

We proceed to deal with this and related questions in the following way. In section 19.1 we describe the vast size of international short-term and long-term capital flows. The next two sections discuss short-term capital movements: section 19.2 covers the eurodollar market and eurobanking; and section 19.3 the issue of regulating international money markets and financial intermediaries. We then turn to discuss long-term capital movements. Section 19.4 introduces the accepted paradigm that long-term capital is rather *immobile* between countries and section 19.5 discusses issues related to international bond markets.

19.1 International Money and Capital Flows

Measures of the flow of international short- and long-term capital are shown in table 19.1. International financing is broken down into gross and net *international bank lending*, net issues of *international money market instruments*, net issues of *international bonds and notes* and annual *portfolio investment*. Annual flows of *direct foreign investment* and *foreign exchange reserves* and daily flows of foreign exchange turnover are also recorded.

Table 19.1 International capital flows (US dollars billion) (annual increases, except stocks end 1997)

	annual average increase 1992–4	1995	1996	1997	stocks end 1997
International bank lending					
gross	245	644	604	1222	10,383
interbank redepositing	60	314	184	722	5,098
net	185	330	420	500	5,285
International debt securities issues					
net money market instruments	3	17	41	20	184
net bonds and notes	195	251	502	576	3,358
total net issues	198	268	543	596	3,542
Direct foreign investment		369	358	448	3,000[a]
Portfolio investment		764	1,163	1,040	
Foreign exchange reserves[b]	87	215	164	52	1,732
	1986	1989	1992	1995	1998
Foreign exchange trading per day	188	590	820	1,190	1,600
daily global FX turnover As percentage of:					
global FX reserves	37	76	86	84	92
annual world exports	7	16	17	19	22

[a] estimated from BIS (1997), p. 33.
[b] including gold valued at $35 per ounce.
Sources: BIS (1997, 1998); IMF (*International Financial Statistics*) and IMF (*International Capital Markets*) 1998

The outstanding stock of international bank lending at $10,383 billion is enormous, being six-times the stock of world foreign exchange reserves. Almost one-half of this sum is in the form of inter-bank redepositing. Net international bank lending measures lending to "ultimate" users. As the outstanding net stock of securities issues amounted to $3,542 billion, the total outstanding net stock of international capital intermediated to end-users via either international banks or money/capital markets was $8,827 billion. Of this total 60 percent was via bank lending – a proportion that has been gently falling during the 1990s from 67 percent at end-1991. The bulk of international bonds are issued by corporations, state enterprises, governments and international organizations such as the World Bank and its subsidiaries.

Direct foreign investment takes the form of equity investment in a foreign country which gives the investor some degree of control over the entities purchased. Since the mid-1980s this category of international capital flow was, until the mid-1990s, about equivalent in size to international bond financing, thereafter the latter accelerated ahead.

International portfolio capital flow, involving the purchase on secondary markets of foreign equities and bonds, at over one trillion dollars per year is very large. Pension funds, insurance companies, and investment companies (i.e. open-end funds investing in transferable securities and money market instruments) are the main institutions active in moving international portfolio capital. This activity ballooned in the 1980s as restrictions on foreign equity investment were either reduced or removed so allowing portfolio diversification. At end-1996 US portfolio capital held outside of the US by the three identified institutions amounted to $985 billion, that for the UK $422 billion, Netherlands $158 billion, and Canada $150 billion.[1]

Notice how large is the level of daily foreign exchange trading which dwarfs world foreign exchange reserves and annual world trade.

19.2 Eurobanking

A Eurobank is an intermediary in non-domestic financial markets which are commonly described as "external" or "offshore." Eurocurrency markets are made by banks that accept time and other interest-earning deposits and make loans in currencies other than the country in which they are located, i.e. in a foreign currency. Hence, eurodollars are dollar deposits in commercial banks situated outside the USA, and euroeuros are euro deposits in banks located outside the Euro area. The eurodollar is easily the largest eurocurrency.

Ultimately, a eurodollar is a liability of a domestic American commercial bank, similarly with the other eurocurrencies and their domestic commercial banks. Circulation of eurocurrencies from one owner to another takes the form of liability transfers on the books of commercial banks in the home currency country (Bell, 1973). Thus, suppose that a non-bank makes a dollar deposit with a eurobank by writing a cheque against its account with a domestic US commercial bank. The eurobank now has a liability to the new depositor and, after the cheque clears, an asset – a deposit – with the commercial bank. If the first eurobank lends the dollars on the inter-bank market to a second eurobank, the first eurobank exchanges the asset with the domestic US commercial bank for an IOU from the second eurobank. Now the deposit at the US commercial bank is an asset of the second eurobank. And so on until a loan is made to an ultimate user who then gains ownership of the same dollar deposit. The deposit leaves the eurodollar system if, after it is spent by the ultimate borrower, it is not redeposited with another eurobank.

The prefix "euro" was given because the eurodollar system originated in Europe, in London in fact. Today the prefix is not strictly accurate as eurodollars and other eurocurrencies are also the assets or liabilities of banks located outside of Europe, but the prefix has stuck. Indeed, European eurocurrency banking centers

– notably London, Luxembourg, Paris, and Frankfurt – account for a little over one-half the eurocurrency market. Japan has a small share. Offshore banking centers – in Bahamas, Singapore, Bahrain, Hong Kong, Cayman Islands, Panama, and the Netherlands, Antilles – account for much of the rest. Eurocurrency activity on US soil hardly existed before 1981 because Federal regulations prohibited US resident banks from accepting non-dollar deposits. However, in 1981, in an effort to win back business lost to foreign financial centers, the Federal Reserve created an "international banking facility" which allows banks operating under it to operate as eurobanks.

19.2.1 Origin of the eurodollar market

A number of factors were responsible for the development of the eurocurrency markets – the eurodollar was the first on the scene. First, in 1957, the Bank of England introduced tight controls on non-resident use of sterling, which caused UK banks to search for a new currency through which to finance world trade – they chose the US dollar as the preeminent convertible currency. Secondly, some holders of dollars, notably the Russians, preferred to hold dollar deposits in banks outside of the USA where they were thought to be safe from US control. Thirdly, in 1958, several major European currencies were made convertible – so allowing residents to hold dollars rather than having to turn them in to their central banks. In 1958 the eurodollar market amounted to less than $1 billion. It has grown an annual average compound rate for much of the period since then of about 20 percent.

The main factor that is responsible for the rapid growth of the eurocurrency markets is their efficiency in intermediating funds between ultimate lenders and borrowers – multinational corporations and other private sector entities, governments and governmental agencies such as UK local authorities and nationalized industries in many countries, and some central banks. As figure 19.1 shows eurobanks work with narrower interest rate spreads than do national-based commercial banks. That is, the former offer higher rates of interest on deposits and lower rates on loans than do the latter banks. How are they able to do this? In the early days an important factor was America's Regulation Q which put a ceiling on the deposit rate of interest that domestic American banks could offer clients. Outside of the USA, free of this regulation, eurobanks could attract dollar deposits by offering higher interest rates. Two other US government regulations helped, in effect, to raise loan rates of interest. The 1963 Interest Equalization Tax, introduced to protect the US balance of payments from capital outflows, added a tax on to loans made by American banks to foreign clients. Then, the 1965 Voluntary Foreign Credit Restraint Guidelines (made compulsory in 1968) was aimed at limiting the amount of lending to foreigners by US banks.

While important in the early days for the development and growth of the euro-dollar market these US government regulations do not explain its continued

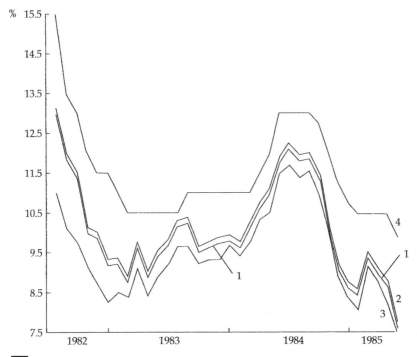

Figure 19.1 Dollar and Eurodollar interest rates: (1) Eurodollar deposit rate; (2) Eurodollar loan rate; (3) commercial bank deposit rate; (4) loan rate

success once they were swept away. For this we must look to the fact that euro-banks have lower costs than do domestic commercial banks. This is because the latter are burdened by bank regulations concerning reserve requirements while eurobanks are not. The need to carry minimum liquid reserves burdens domestic banks with low-yielding assets, which eurobanks are able to avoid. Eurobanks may also gain economies of scale given that their loans are usually much larger than those made by domestic-bound banks.

The inter-bank market. Eurobanks operate a large inter-bank market in eurocur-rencies. Inter-bank liabilities amount to well over one-half of the eurobanks' gross liabilities. In the inter-bank market funds flow from one bank to another, indeed, some of the smaller eurobanks in London rely on it entirely as a source of funds (Ellis, 1981). There are a number of reasons for the existence of the inter-bank market: first, commercial banks will sometimes borrow in the eurocurrency mar-ket to satisfy local national bank regulations on cash or liquidity ratios – this is known as "window dressing." Secondly, funds flow from eurobanks with surplus deposits to those which have identified end-users. Thirdly, eurobanks arbitrage short-term capital between convertible currency countries. In fact, most arbitrage capital moves through the eurocurrency markets and most of the deposit funds are short-term.

19.2.2 The eurodollar credit multiplier

Eurobanks are a variety of *non-bank financial intermediary* because they hold their reserves with commercial banks. Commercial banks, of course, hold their reserves as cash and deposits directly with a central bank. Proponents of the non-bank financial intermediary view include Dufey and Giddy (1978), Llewellyn (1980), Niehans (1984) (and less explicitly Klopstock, 1968).[2]

To derive the eurodollar credit multiplier define the supply of US dollars as:

$$M = M_p + M_E \tag{19.1}$$

where M is the money supply measured in dollars; M_p is the amount of dollars held by the private sector *excluding* eurobanks; and M_E is the dollars held by eurobanks with domestic US banks as reserves, that is as demand deposits – which are, of course, a component of the US money supply.

Define the stock of dollar liquid assets held anywhere in the world by the non-bank public, L, as:

$$L = M_p + E \tag{19.2}$$

where M_p is again the amount of dollars held by the private sector (excluding eurobanks); and E is the public's holding of eurodollars.

Divide equation (19.2) by equation (19.1) and then divide each term on the right-hand side by E. This yields:

$$L = M.\{[(M_p/E) + 1]/[(M_p/E) + (M_E/E)]\} \tag{19.3}$$

Equation (19.3) says that the amount of dollar liquid assets, L, held by the public will be greater than the dollar money supply, M, if the "eurodollar multiplier," the term in { }, is greater than unity. The eurodollar multiplier depends upon two factors: M_p/E which, if constant, is the *reciprocal* of the redeposit ratio (i.e. the proportion of each dollar lent by a eurobank that gets redeposited back into the eurodollar banking system – as opposed to the US domestic banking system); and M_E/E, the eurobanks' reserve ratio.

Eurobanks maintain low ratios of deposits at US banks to their liabilities – this holds out the prospect of a very high eurodollar multiplier. However, the redeposit ratio is also small (its reciprocal is large) and this reduces the size of the multiplier probably to about unity.

But this type of multiplier analysis is incomplete because it ignores the role of interest rates in determining bank assets and liabilities (à la Tobin, 1967). As non-bank financial intermediaries, eurobanks must attract both depositors and borrowers by offering competitive interest rates, something that we know that they do from figure 19.1. Thus, as Llewellyn (1980) amongst others observes, the size of the eurodollar market depends upon the relative share that it can attract of total US dollar deposits. This observation, of course, would apply to any non-bank financial intermediary, e.g. building societies (S&Ls). So, if the share is constant, growth of the eurodollar market depends upon the growth of the credit in the USA. Similarly with other eurocurrencies and the growth of home-country credit.

A related point is that the eurobanks can have only a minimal impact on over-all liquidity. In the first place, eurobanks offer only an alternative method of holding liquid assets (as in equation (19.2)); and, secondly, since eurobanks offer more attractive interest rates than do US banks, there may be some inducement – at the margin – to wealth-holders to diversify into liquid assets.

19.2.3 Eurobanks as a debt management system

Hogan and Pierce (1980, 1982) provide a systematic explanation of the eurocurrency system as international system for managing debt that is consistent with the non-bank financial intermediary view of eurobanks. The Hogan and Pierce argument highlights the role of eurobanks in the ballooning of international debt and gives further insight into the economic characteristics of the eurobanking system. The essence of their argument is that the spectacular growth of international debt through the eurobanking system is due to the persistence of the *same* group of countries being in balance of payments deficit while another group is in persistence surplus. Their schema is laid out in table 19.2 – other aspects of international debt are discussed in chapters 14 and 23.

The world is divided into just three countries which for convenience we shall call the USA, Latin America, and Europe. The USA is always in balance of payments equilibrium (this is only a schema!), Latin America is in persistent payments deficit, while Europe has a persistent payments surplus. Eurobanks are in existence and they are assumed to hold assets and liabilities after a transfer to them of $100 by an American non-bank. In year 1, Latin America has a balance of payments deficit of $100 which, given the assumptions, must be matched by a $100 European payments surplus. If Latin America financed its payments deficit from foreign exchange reserves and the next year corrected the deficit, the eurobanks would not be called upon. They would have no function to fulfill. However, it is assumed that Latin America borrows $100 from the eurobanks, so financing its payments deficit, and does nothing to correct that payment's deficit. Europe too allows its payments surplus to persist from one year to the next, and deposits the $100 payments surplus with the eurobanks because they offer the most advantageous terms. The circuit is thus primed to run on year after year: table 19.2 shows just three years of payments disequilibrium.

Eight important points concerning the operation of the eurodollar market can be made:

1   Eurobank assets take the form of loans to Latin America ($300) and deposits with a US bank ($100), and after three years total $400.
2   The *size* of the eurodollar market is growing by $100 per annum and after three years totals $400 whether measured in terms of the eurobank's assets

Table 19.2 Balance of payments disequilibria and the growth of Eurocurrency debt

Eurobanks have $100 million to lend[a]
    BOP deficit country 'Latin
    America'   *BOP surplus country 'Europe'*

Year 1 $100 million deficit $100 million surplus
         ⌈borrow $100 million from⌉ Eurobanks   ⌈deposit $100 million with⌉
         ⌊Eurobanks   ⌋ ←intermediate   ⌊Eurobanks   ⌋

Year 2 $100 million deficit $100 million surplus
         ⌈borrow $100 million from⌉ Eurobanks   ⌈deposit $100 million with⌉
         ⌊Eurobanks   ⌋ ←intermediate   ⌊Eurobanks   ⌋

Year 3 $100 million deficit $100 million surplus
         ⌈borrow $100 million from⌉ Eurobanks   ⌈deposit $100 million with⌉
         ⌊Eurobanks   ⌋ ←intermediate   ⌊Eurobanks   ⌋

Eurobanks after three years
Assets   *Liabilities*
$300 million   ('Latin American' loans) $300 million   (European deposits)
$100 million   (deposits with US banks) $100 million   (US non-bank's deposits)

$400 million $400 million

[a] A US non-bank is assumed to transfer funds from a chequing account with a US commercial bank to a Eurobank. The Eurobank's assets at this stage read: assets $100 million (deposit with a US commercial bank); liabilities $100 million (deposit of the US non-bank).
Source: Following Hogan and Pierce, 1982

(as in the first point) or liabilities, $300 to European depositors and $100 to the original American non-bank depositor.

3 It is made clear that annual growth in the size of the eurodollar market is governed by the size of world balance of payments deficits.

4 Eurodollar debts will continue to grow so long as balance of payments deficits persist.

5 The growth of eurodollar debt is non-inflationary: for each amount borrowed there is an equal amount saved: Latin America's excess of spending over income is matched by Europe's excess of income over spending. The recycling of payments surpluses does not lead to an increase in world aggregate demand. Hogan and Pearce have qualified this point, pointing out that "the growth of international debt can continue without new money creation anywhere. On the other hand, if governments do create new money it is as likely as not that some of this will find its way into the hands of the eurobanks where it may serve to generate even greater deficits and, *ipso facto* an even faster growing total of international debt" (1982, pp. 83–4). But the eurobanks play an intermediary role; money creation is initiated elsewhere.

6 Eurodollar debt is the debt of Latin America. However, if Latin America defaulted on its debt, then, as intermediaries, the eurobanks would still be liable to their depositors.

7 Notice that growth of the eurodollar market does not need either the creation of new dollars by the USA or even a US balance of payments deficit.

8 As Hogan and Pearce observed, "there can be no increase in debt without a flow of money" (1982, p. 80); the flow of money in question is the $100 million asset that the eurobanks hold on the books of a US commercial bank. This money is constantly flowing through the eurobanks to Latin America and is redeposited with them by Europe. Latin America's creditors though, are the eurobanks only in the sense that the eurobanks play an intermediary function – the ultimate creditor, which has reduced spending below income, is Europe.

◈ 19.3 Regulation: The Basle Capital Accord

Failure of a foreign subsidiary of an international bank – due perhaps to bad loans or to illegal activities – could threaten the solvency of the "mother" international bank and could have serious implications for a national banking system (try to imagine what consequences might follow if one of Britain's major banks failed). Moreover, a contagion could spread to otherwise solvent banks in the same country and, perhaps, internationally. The failures of the Herstatt Bank and the Franklin National Bank in 1974 fortunately were not serious enough to bring down a banking system but the international debt crisis following Mexico's 1982 threatened moratorium on servicing its debt was. Indeed, the whole debt crisis episode of the 1980s – when hundreds of international banks wrote off billions of dollars as loan-losses – shows that international banks have been failures at properly identifying loan-risks. These and other examples from recent decades, including the notorious Bank of Credit and Commerce International case revealed in 1991, and the East Asian financial crises of summer 1997, make a case for the supervision of international banks.

Why have international banks made so many bad loans and, for that matter, why are domestic banking systems among the most heavily regulated of sectors in any country? There are several problems: (i) depositors in a bank have much less information about the bank than do its managers (i.e. asymmetric information exists – caused by the high cost of gathering information on the true riskiness of a bank's assets). A bank therefore has scope to make more-risky loans (aiming for higher expected returns) than depositors would prefer. Moreover, (ii) moral hazard problems arise from deposit insurance and the lender of last resort function of central banks: commercial banks make more-risky loans because in case of failure they expect to be "bailed out." (iii) Banks making loans to some developing countries fell into a "lenders trap" in which it was rational to make successively more-risky loans to a debtor country in order to "protect" the value of loans made earlier (Cline, 1984).

And (iv) competition between banks can lead to a "race to the bottom" in the holding of bank capital – which leaves them with only a thin cushion against loan-losses. Thus, for an individual bank after taxes are taken out:

$$\text{profit/equity capital} = \text{profit/assets} \times \text{assets/equity capital} \qquad (19.4)$$

where the ratios are, respectively, the return on equity, the return on assets and the equity multiplier (which is the reciprocal of the capital ratio). Thus, for a given return on assets, the return on equity can be progressively increased by raising the equity multiplier. Unfortunately, if some banks pursue profit in this way, or, countries differ in their regulated minimum capital standards, there is an external diseconomy for the international banking system as a whole. Aggressive lending by some banks squeezes the return on assets for the others so reducing their return on equity. These banks then face the uncomfortable choice of watching their business being taken by the aggressive banks or raising their own equity multipliers. Here we see that the case for international bank supervision rests on the market failure that the return to bank capital is not fully internalized as an individual bank may have an interest in reducing its level below what is good for the system as a whole. In other words, bank capital is a public good because more of it not only reduces the risk that an individual bank will fail, it also increases the soundness of the whole international banking system. Some sort of government intervention is justified. In the context of international banks – which operate simultaneously in the jurisdictions of several monetary authorities – it is international regulation that is needed.[3]

International regulation of banks' capital standards is a recent phenomenon, having been agreed in the *Basle Capital Accord* of 1988 (but not becoming legally effective until 1992). The Accord is an international agreement on capital adequacy measurement and standards. It addresses explicitly only credit risk. Defines: (a) eligible capital elements; (b) variable risk weights applicable to several main categories of on and off-balance sheet exposure; and (c) overall minimum capital ratio of 8 percent of risk-weighted assets, with core (Tier I) capital – the fully harmonized definition in terms of components – being "not less than 4 percent" (BIS, 1998, p. 148). The 8 and 4 percent rules represented a substantial increase for some international banks. The Basle Accord was strengthened in 1996 by setting minimum capital standards for market risk – i.e. those risks faced with banks associated with changes in interest rates, exchange rates, commodity prices and equity prices (collectively "market risk").

The Basle Accords grew out of the Basle Committee (of Group of Ten central banks) which was initially set up to deal with the lack of bank supervision that was perceived following the major failures of international banks during the course of 1974. By 1983 it had established the principle of "parent country" regulation, but little else of a practical value was achieved mainly because each central bank preferred to defend its own regulatory practices. However, parent-country control alone was not a solution as it ran into the difficulty of collecting and interpreting non-standardized information on the activity of a parent-bank's foreign subsidiaries – a loophole that BCCI was able to exploit for years. According to Kapstein (1991), the catalyst of an international agreement on bank regulation was the 1987 bilateral agreement to regulate international banks in their jurisdictions between the Federal Reserve and the Bank of England. Faced with a "zone of exclusion" (Kapstein, p. 2) for their own banks from the territories of the two largest eurocurrency centers, other Group of Ten countries the next year agreed to the

Basle Capital Accord. The European Community virtually included it into its Single Market banking directives and several other leading offshore banking centers have indicated that they too will voluntarily adopt the regulations.

Notice that the Basle Capital Accord sets capital standards only against risks incurred in the "use of funds" by banks. Following the 1997 East Asian financial and banking crisis it became clear that banks also face risks on the other side of their balance sheets – the "sources of funds". Heavy borrowing by some East Asian banks in the international interbank market left them vulnerable when this source of funds all but dried up. It is possible that the Basle Capital Accord will one day be extended to include capital standards related risks on the source of funds.

Basle Concordat

Another area of international agreement on bank supervision is the Basle Concordat. This was agreed in 1975 as a set of rules for apportioning responsibilities for the supervision of banks' foreign affiliates between home and host country supervisors. Because of various loopholes it was revised in 1983, introducing the principle of "consolidated supervision" with its scope being widened to include supervision of some previously unsupervised financial centers. A further amendment in 1992 was aimed at strengthening it so as to set minimum standards for banking establishments still not subject to consolidated supervision.

19.4 Measuring International Capital Mobility

How internationally mobile is capital? If it is highly mobile, expected returns on similar financial assets and the real assets that back them between a pair of countries will be equalized. If not, rates of return will differ. But "financial assets" fall into two categories: "short-term," held in the form of deposits with financial intermediaries and money market instruments such as treasury bills, commercial paper, and negotiable CDs; and "long-term" held in the form of capital market instruments, such as bonds, mortgages, stocks, and other direct equity stakes – as with direct foreign investment by multinational corporations.

Short-term capital mobility

How can the degree of short-term capital mobility be measured? A frequently used measure is the condition of covered interest parity (CIP) – discussed in section 3.2 and 3.3. It implies that there will be no net capital flows between financial centers when interest rates adjusted for the cost of forward cover are equalized. However, since as we argued at the beginning of chapter 12 that in the Cambist view (see Llewellyn, 1980), CIP is likely to be an identity in practice (because banks set forward rates in such a manner that CIP always holds) it is not a particularly good measure of capital mobility. The uncovered interest parity (UIP) alternative to CIP is used in many theoretical models (for example the sticky price model of section 9.5) as the measure of short-term capital mobility. But as we saw in section 3.4, getting an empirical fix on UIP is not straightforward because of the difficulty in measuring exchange rate expectations. To the extent that expectations are rational (and this, as we have seen in chapter 13, is a debatable issue for financial markets) then both direct (see section 3.4) and indirect tests (see section 12.3)[4] of UIP suggest that time-varying risk premia are likely to be an important reason for the failure of short-term interest rates to be equalized across financial centers.

An alternative, and simpler, measure of short-term capital mobility, and in particular how it has evolved over time, may be obtained by comparing the differential between the yield on onshore and offshore assets (see Frankel, 1993). If capital is perfectly mobile there should be no difference between these yields. But a plot of the yield on a 3-month UK Treasury bill and a 3-month UK Euro bill for part of the recent experience with floating exchange rates shows a gap between these two rates of return for the sample period. But the important point to note is that this gap is diminishing over time. This seems intuitive enough. In the early part of the floating rate period there were controls on the short-term movement of capital which prevented arbitrage equalizing net yields. The removal or reduction of these controls, combined with the financial deregulation process in the 1980s, explains why the gap has been decreasing over time.

Long-term capital mobility

The seminal paper on long-term capital mobility is that of Feldstein and Horioka (1980) (FH). They argue that the implication of highly mobile long-term capital, and the consequent equalization of returns, is either a zero or a low correlation between rates of national saving ($NS = S + (T - G)$) and investment in a given country. For example, if national saving increases in a "small" country (defined as not being able to affect the world rate of return), the increment will flow to all countries in the system as national savers seek the best rates of return, and the correlation between rates of national saving and investment is zero. Similarly, if the country is large (defined as being able to affect the world rate of return), the extra saving will force both the domestic and world real rates of return downward but, unless the country is very large, the correlation between rates of domestic saving and investment will be low.

For a small country the FH effect may be illustrated using figure 19.2, where the terms have an obvious interpretation. Assume the initial equilibrium is at point A. Say the government embarks on a fiscal expansion financed by issuing government debt (so either G increases, T decreases or some combination of the two). If the economy in question is closed to capital account transactions the new equilibrium will be at a point such as B, where both national savings and investment are lower. If, however, capital is perfectly mobile, the real interest rate stays at r_0 and the reduction in national savings is offset by savings supplied from the international pool of savings (equal to the horizontal distance CA).

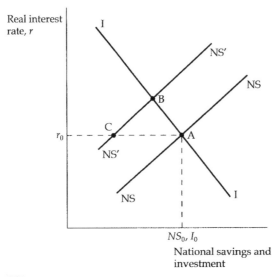

Figure 19.2   Long-term capital flow

The hypothesis of perfect long-term capital mobility can be tested using:

$$(I/Y)_{i,t} = \alpha + \beta(S/Y)_{i,t} + u_{i,t} \qquad (19.5)$$

where $(I/Y)_i$ is the rate of domestic investment in country i, and $(S/Y)_i$ the rate of national saving. The assumption here is that the saving rate is exogenous – which to a large extent it is in the long run; i.e. netting out the effect of the business cycle. Average saving rates between countries in fact show large persistent differences with, for example, Japan at the high end at about 37 percent and the UK at the low end at about 18 percent. If long-term capital is highly mobile β is expected to be zero (small country) or a value substantially less than unity (large country). In these cases, since the extra saving must end up somewhere, an increase in domestic saving causes capital outflow as residents buy foreign financial assets. Thus, fluctuations in the rate of domestic saving causes fluctuations in a country's net investment abroad.

This latter assertion is shown by subtracting $(S/Y)_i$ from both sides of equation (19.5) and rearranging:

$$[(I - S)/Y]_{i,t} = \alpha + (\beta - 1)(S/Y)_{i,t} + u_{i,t} \qquad (19.6)$$

where $(I - S)/Y$ is net foreign investment. Thus, if $\beta = 0$, implying that real rates of return are equalized internationally, a country's rate of net foreign investment depends on its saving rate.[5]

A statistical finding that $\beta = 1$ suggests that long-term capital is highly immobile. Thus, in equation (19.5), the rate of domestic investment varies exactly with the rate of domestic saving; and in equation (19.6), the rate of net foreign investment is not associated with the rate of domestic saving. In either case, if the rate of domestic saving increases, residents buy more domestic (rather than foreign) financial assets which reduces the rate of return on them relative to that in the rest of the world. The international capital market is fractured.

Feldstein and Horioka (1980) estimate equation (19.5) using annual cross-section data for 16 OECD countries over the 1960–74 period. Using OLS they obtain:

$$(I/Y) = 0.035 + 0.89(S/Y) \qquad\qquad (19.7)$$
$$\underset{(0.018)}{} \quad \underset{(0.074)}{} \qquad\qquad R^2 = 0.91$$

with standard errors in parentheses. Thus, $\beta = 1$ cannot be rejected at the 95 percent level.

This finding of long-term capital *immobility* has stood up to intense econometric and theoretical scrutiny. At the econometric level it is robust to cross-sectional versus time-series data, data period, country sets, variable definitions (net rather than gross values), functional forms, reduced form specifications, model structures, and estimation techniques.

At the theoretical level one argument is that the world rate of return, r^*, is endogenous because, at least with some developed countries, each contributes significantly to the world pool of saving. (Thus, an increase in saving in country X would force the world rate of return downward and encourage a larger share of saving to be invested at home.) But, it is difficult to imagine that any country, save perhaps the USA, could have such a major effect on r^*. Besides which, as Dooley, Frankel, and Mathieson (1987) point out, in cross-section data r^* is exogenous to all countries.

19.4.1 Why is long-term capital internationally immobile?

A number of reasons may account for the immobility of long-term capital.

1 The *currency risk premium* argument is that the portfolio preferences of large long-term investors, such as pension funds, mutual funds and insurance companies, are governed by currency risk and risk aversion, especially because liabilities are usually stated in domestic currency and long-term hedging instruments are not readily available.[6] Thus, arbitrage in a long-term security establishes

$$i_{t+k,t} = i^*_{t+k,t} + \Delta S_{t+k,t} + \lambda_{t+k,t} \qquad\qquad (19.8)$$

where $i_{t+k,t}$ is the rate of return at time t on a security $t + k$ years from maturity in the home country, $i^*_{t+k,t}$ in the foreign country, $\Delta S_{t+k,t}$ is the expected average annual rate of currency depreciation over $t + k$ years, and $\lambda_{t+k,t}$ is the currency risk premium. As in equation 10.1 for short-term securities, if $\lambda_{t+k,t} < 0$ investors prefer to invest domestically and the domestic rate of return on assets of maturity

$t + k$ at time t will be lower than the expected rate of return on the equivalent foreign asset.

A relevant issue here is the term structure of returns – meaning the return on long-term assets relative to that on short-term assets. If, domestically, arbitrage between them is perfect, perfectly elastic short-term capital outflow from a high saving country would equalize long-term returns between countries – a point made by FH (1980) and Dooley, Frankel, and Mathieson (1987). This is because short-term capital outflow would move downward the whole term structure of returns. However, even domestic arbitrage along the yield curve is far from perfect – as is recognized in the liquidity and preferred habitat theories of the term structure.

The currency risk premium argument is supported empirically by Yamori (1995) who finds no correlation between saving and investment in Japanese regional data – where currency risk is not a factor.

2   Government restraints on capital flows. This is much less of a problem today following widespread financial liberalization. For example, the FH sample is one in which there were fairly severe restrictions on capital flows, so perhaps it is not surprising that capital is found to be imperfectly mobile for a period in which it was heavily controlled. Frankel (1994) makes this point nicely in his survey of measures of capital mobility. In fact he re-estimates the Feldstein Horioka equation into the 1980s and shows that it begins to "work" as capital restrictions are reduced and financial deregulation kicks in.

3   Institutional rigidities such as US laws requiring commercial banks to invest some of their funds in the local economy.

19.4.2 Consumption-based test of international capital mobility

The problems associated with the Feldstein–Horioka tests of international capital mobility has led researchers to seek alternative ways of assessing long-term international capital mobility. The most popular of these is based on the intertemporal maximizing model introduced in section 4.6, and we label this approach the *consumption-based test of international capital mobility*.[7] Essentially this approach represents an extension of the famous Hall (1978) random-walk model of consumption to the open economy.

Consider again the so-called first order, or Euler, condition derived from the representative agent model of section 12.4 (in particular, equation 12.14a; see also equation 4.25), where we have assumed that the marginal utilities of consumption are given by actual consumption and used a log transformation:

$$\Delta c_{t+1} = \beta + (1 + r_t) \tag{19.9}$$

Now recall that this kind of expression is derived for a representative agent in the domestic economy. If it is assumed that a representative agent follows the same maximizing procedure in the foreign country, we have

$$\Delta c^*_{t+1} = \beta^* + (1 + r^*_t) \tag{19.10}$$

where, as before, an asterisk denotes a foreign magnitude. Now if capital is perfectly mobile across countries, the real interest rates in (19.9) and (19.10) should be equalized – the null hypothesis of perfect capital mobility. Under the null, we obtain that there should be perfect correlation between the change in consumption in the domestic relative to the foreign country:

$$\Delta c_{t+1} = \alpha + \Delta c^*_{t+1} \tag{19.11}$$

where $\alpha = \beta - \beta^*$. The intuition for this result is as follows. In the home country the representative agent has the objective of smoothing her consumption over time. It is access to financial markets which facilitates this process. If the representative agent did not have the ability to borrow and lend freely at the going real interest rate, then as output-income fell consumption would have to correspondingly fall. The consumption-based test of international capital mobility simply takes this prediction one step further. If the interest rate at which agents borrow and lend is indeed locked to the foreign rate, then the consumption smoothing we observe in the home country should be the same as that observed in the foreign country even if income growth in the two countries is quite different. Other things equal (a strong statement, perhaps, in terms of the current application), the home country resident should be able to enjoy the same level of welfare as the foreign resident.

Bayoumi and MacDonald (1995) use a regression-based approach to test the implications of the consumption-based model. In particular, they estimate equation (19.12) as

$$\Delta c_t = \alpha + \beta \Delta c^*_t + u_t \tag{19.12}$$

where, an * here denotes the rest of the world excluding the home country, and if capital is perfectly mobile β should be insignificantly different from unity. Equation (19.12) may be thought of as the consumption-based analogue to the Feldstein–Horioka equation. However, Bayoumi, and MacDonald (1995) argue that (19.12) represents a very stringent test of international capital mobility because it may be that investors within a country do not have perfect access to domestic capital markets, far less international markets – they may be liquidity constrained.[8] They therefore propose distinguishing between *intra-* and *inter*national capital mobility. In terms of a regression-based test, what this amounts to is including the current change in domestic and foreign income into an equation like (19.12) (and using an appropriate estimator which accounts for potential simultaneity).

Using an annual data set for the period 1971 to 1992, Bayoumi and MacDonald (1995) estimate the income modified version of the consumption-based model for a group of 15 OECD countries. It turns out that Japan is the only country in their sample which appears to be fully integrated with the rest of the world. The remaining countries fail the capital mobility test and the reasons for this may be attributed to two sources. For all countries apart from Austria and Japan, consumption appears excessively sensitive to current income, which is indicative of internal capital market failures. For seven countries, all of them continental European countries, there is a failure for interest rates to be equalized with their partner countries and there would therefore seem to be welfare gains from the further integration of such countries' capital markets (as has in fact been happening over the last five years or so).

Obstfeld (1995) has implemented the consumption-based test for the G7 over the period 1951–88 (annual data). The tests are implemented on two sub-samples of the complete sample (they correspond to the Bretton Woods and recent floating periods), namely 1951–72 and 1973–88. Obstfeld finds considerable evidence that the coefficient on the rest-of-the-world consumption are close to unity and, furthermore, are rising over time. However, many of the coefficients are also imprecise in the sense that they are insignificantly different from zero.

19.5 International Bond Markets

We saw in table 19.1 that while the single largest conduit for international capital flow was through the intermediary of international banks, flows through the direct channel[9] of international bonds were also large – the net stock of outstanding international bonds at end-1997 amounting to $3,358 billion with annual net flows of about $500–$600 billion.

The term "international bond" includes "foreign bonds" and "eurobonds." A *foreign bond* is a bond issued by a foreign corporation or government in the domestic capital market of another country. They are normally sold through a host-country investment bank (the underwriter or, in Britain, a merchant bank) and are traded on the host's financial market. A foreign bond is subject to the security laws of the host country. A *eurobond* is issued in countries that do not use the currency of its denomination as domestic currency. Usually a eurobond is issued by a syndicate of underwriters and is often simultaneously launched in several countries. The secondary market in eurobonds is made by market-makers who trade over-the-counter, the main location being London – with Frankfurt, Amsterdam, and Zurich also being significant centers. Annual new net eurobond issues run about twice the rate of foreign bond issues.

The modern theory of finance argues that direct finance (defined in note 9) through a bond or equity market is marked by asymmetric information. This may give rise to adverse selection and moral hazard problems.[10] That is, there is a good chance that a borrower that issues bonds is a bad credit risk. Lenders are more likely to purchase bonds issued by, say, a foreign corporation: the lower the cost of collecting information about that corporation, the greater its net worth (high net worth makes lenders feel more comfortable as it acts as a sort of collateral), and the lower the cost of monitoring the borrower. Corporations (and other borrowers) with these desirable characteristics are most likely to be found in developed countries – because of the existence there of bond-rating agencies such as Standard and Poor and because information is generally more widely available than it is in developing countries.

It is because of the problem of asymmetric information that *international agencies* intermediate between the international bond markets – where the World Bank for example sells its bonds – and developing country borrowers. Buyers of World Bank bonds, presumably, are confident that the World Bank will collect sufficient information on the entities to which it lends, that it efficiently monitors loans and is vigilant in enforcing the restrictive covenants (i.e. terms and conditions) attached to the loan. It will probably have occurred to you that the international banks play virtually the same role *vis-à-vis* developing country borrowers. That is, they specialize in reducing the asymmetric information – except that their main source of funds for international loans to developing countries is not bonds, rather it is customers' deposits.

19.5.1 Growth of international bond markets

Several factors have encouraged the growth of international bond markets. First, it is advantageous to borrow in a currency other than the domestic currency if the expected borrowing cost inclusive of the risk premium is thereby reduced. That is, if in equation (19.8) $i_{t+k,t}$ is greater than the value on the right hand side.

Secondly, advantages may rise from reducing risk by diversifying portfolios into international bonds. Following the work of Tobin (1958) and Markowitz (1959) a portfolio-holder's utility depends upon combinations of expected return and risk – the so-called, mean–variance model. For any given expected rate of return, a wealth-holder will always prefer the portfolio with less risk. Portfolio theory establishes that diversification reduces risk for the same rate of return whenever changes in rates of return on the different assets (or liabilities) in a portfolio are not perfectly positively correlated. Moreover, the more independent are the movements in returns the greater is the advantage of diversification. The advantage of international diversification derives from the fact that the correlation of returns on bonds is lower between countries than it is within a given country (owing, *inter alia*, to less than perfect correlation of international business cycles). The objective of international diversification is to exploit this advantage. The argument holds both for bonds, notes, equity currencies, and other financial assets.[11]

The advantages of diversification into international bonds can be shown using the efficiency locus (or investment opportunity set) familiar from the theory of finance.[12] Jorion (1989) calculated the efficient investment frontier for combinations of US bonds and stocks using data from the period 1978–88, and compared this with the frontier that included foreign stocks. As figure 19.3 shows, at any given level of risk, say volatility = 14 percent, the expected return on the internationally diversified portfolio is a lot greater than the US-only portfolio. The advantage of international diversification has also been shown by Grubel (1968), Jacquillat and Solnik (1978), and Solnik (1974). Solnik found that a well diversified international portfolio of stocks could reduce risk by over one-half.

Thirdly, a corporation may issue an international bond in order to hedge risk. Suppose that a corporation has a subsidiary in another country that is expected to earn a stream of profits denominated in a foreign currency. The position can

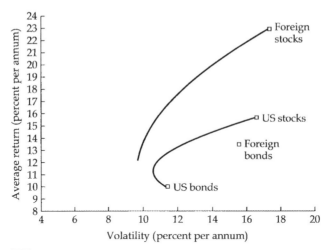

Figure 19.3 Efficiency loci for US-only and unhedged internationally diversified portfolios, 1978–88
Source: Jorion, 1989

be hedged by issuing an international bond in the same foreign currency. Then there can be some (no doubt inexact) matching of assets (the profits stream) and liabilities (service cost of the bond) denominated in the foreign country. On this argument, the growth in postwar years of the international bond markets matches the growth and spread of multinational corporations.

Fourth, an entity such as a nationalized industry may be encouraged by the government to borrow in international capital markets so as to raise money to finance a balance of payments deficit. This strategy was adopted by the British Labour government in the 1973–5 period. It has also been widely used by Latin American governments.

Fifth, borrowing in international bond markets may be because of the non-existence or thinness of national bond markets, especially in relation to inter-national bond markets. This is typically the case in Latin America. Corporations wishing to raise capital by selling bonds have to turn to the international bond market. As mentioned earlier, borrowing by developing countries in the inter-national bond market is small – owing to the perceived high risk of bonds issued by Latin American governments and corporations. For example, in 1990 develop-ing countries accounted for only $2.7 billion of completed new issues out of a global total of $132 billion. In the same year the outstanding stock of develop-ing country international bond debt amounted to only $33 billion – out of global bond issues of $1.47 trillion (BIS, 1991). Outstanding developing country debt in the same year was over $1.2 trillion – i.e. most developing country foreign debt is owed to banks rather than bond holders.

Sixth, not withstanding the previous point, financial liberalization in emerg-ing markets and transition economies from the late 1980s onward has allowed domestic borrowers to turn to lower cost international sources of bond financing.

Finally, taxation of foreigners using a domestic bond market played a role in forcing some bond markets "offshore" to avoid the tax – so creating the eurobond market. In effect, taxation breaks the equality (19.10) and provides a motive for borrowers and lenders to avoid the tax. The American Interest Equalization Tax of 1963–74 was designed to help improve the USA's balance of payments by reducing capital outflow. The tax raised the cost to foreigners of issuing foreign bonds in the USA. Similarly, in 1964 Germany imposed a tax on interest paid on DM bonds to foreigners. The aim in this case was to reduce capital inflow. Both cases represent an interference in the market: in the case of the dollar creating a desire to supply dollar-denominated bonds (to benefit from low American interest rates); and, in the case of the DM, an unsatisfied demand for DM denominated bonds – to benefit from expected currency appreciation.

NOTES

1   The data for these countries are the only ones that can be extracted from BIS (1998), tables V.4 to V.7.
2   In fact, it took economists quite a long time before realizing that eurobanks are really non-bank financial intermediaries. The first approach was to model them as a system of fractional reserve banks (Klopstock, 1968; Machlup, 1971; Carli, 1971; Makin, 1972; Lee, 1973). As reserves in relation to deposits were low – and despite high rates of cash drain out of the system – estimates of the eurocurrency credit multiplier were often high: anything up to 18! The perceived existence of high credit multipliers was a cause for alarm in some quarters because it was thought that there was a powerful mechanism of credit creation lying outside the control of any central bank. In the inflationary 1970s the idea was plausible. However, even in the early days there were dissenters from the "fractional reserve" view. Friedman (1969) saw eurobanks as just a part of the US banking system which operated on lower reserve requirements – but he still came up with a large credit multiplier. Other economists doubted the analogy to fractional reserve banking. Lutz (1974) pointed out that eurodollar deposits were *not* a means of payment so eurobanks were quite different from domestic commercial banks. Einzig (1970), in similar vein, pointed out that eurobank transactions are loan transactions – a concept supported and thoroughly developed by Hogan and Pierce (1982) – see the section 19.1.4 "eurobanks as a debt management system." Others pointed out that as eurobanks did little maturity transformation, the degree of liquidity creation must have been small (Hewson and Sakakibara, 1975b; Hewson, 1976).
3   An example of the confusion that can exist over the lender of last resort in the international context is given by Kapstein (1991). When the Banco Ambrosiano failed in 1982 the Bank of Italy gave full backing to depositors in the parent bank in Italy but refused the same for the depositors in the Bank's subsidiary in Luxembourg where its Eurocurrency activities were handled.
4   The indirect tests, which involve regressing the actual change in the exchange rate onto the forward premium, are predicated on the assumption that covered interest parity holds.
5   An alternative way of stating equation 19.6 is: $KA = k(r - r^*)$, where KA is the capital account, r and r^*, the real rate of return on long-term capital in, respectively, the home and foreign countries (or the rest of the world), and k measures the degree of long-term capital mobility. If capital is perfectly mobile k is infinity.

6   With mutual funds, the risk aversion is more likely to be with investors who probably expect eventually to spend most of their mutual fund investments in their domestic economy.

7   This approach is dealt with in some detail in Obstfeld and Rogoff (1998).

8   For example, Campbell and Mankiw (1989) note this as a potential explanation for the failure of the random-walk consumption model to work in a closed economy.

9   With direct finance the ultimate borrower and ultimate lender stand face-to-face (through an underwriter). In the case of indirect finance, a financial intermediary – such as a commercial bank – separates lenders and borrowers. Lenders usually have little idea about the identity of borrowers.

10 Asymmetric information in this case is a situation where the borrower has good (even complete) information on how a loan will be used while the lender is at least partly in the dark. The borrower may use the borrowed funds wastefully – there is a moral hazard. This possibility raises the riskiness of a loan because it may not be repaid. Adverse selection is the case where the potential borrowers that come forward are the most likely to use borrowed funds improvidently. After all why do they need to borrow in the first place? Will not the most successful, low credit risk corporations, be able to finance investment out of profits, so leaving mainly high risk corporations seeking loans.

11 The subject of currency substitution is discussed in chapter 9.

12 The construction of the efficiency locus can be illustrated for the case of combinations of a single stock mutual fund (i.e. unit trust) with a single bond fund. The return to the portfolio, R_p, is:

$$R_p = w_s.E(r_s) + w_b.E(r_b)$$

where $E(r_s)$ is the expected return on the stock fund and $E(r_b)$ that on the bond fund, w_s is the share of the portfolio invested in stocks and w_b the share invested in bonds ($w_b = 1 - w_s$). By the rules of combinations of random variables:

$$\sigma_p^2 = (w_s\sigma_s)^2 + (w_b\sigma_b)^2 + (w_s\sigma_s)\,(w_b\sigma_b)p_{sb}$$

where each σ^2 is the variance of a variable and p_{sb} is the correlation coefficient between the return on stocks and bonds. Notice that the lower the degree of correlation, the lower the variance – or riskiness – of the entire portfolio. The investment opportunity locus is calculated simply by varying the weight, w_s, from 0 to 1. It is true that stocks are more risky than bonds but also, historically, have higher returns, so when $w_s = 1$ the variance of the portfolio is σ_s^2 – the extreme right-side ends of the investment opportunity loci in figure 19.3. When $w_s = 0$ the variance of the portfolio is σ_b^2 – the left end of the loci. The advantage of internationally diversifying a portfolio stems from the fact, e.g. in the case of the USA, correlation between domestic stocks is about 0.9 while between US stocks and the stocks of other countries only about 0.43.

20

Developing Countries, Balance of Payments Adjustment, and the International Monetary Fund

Developing country members of the International Monetary Fund (IMF) are easily the most frequent users of IMF conditional loans. However, the terms and conditions attached to these loans are sometimes regarded by them as being too harsh and imposing unacceptable economic and political costs. Sometimes potential borrowers will not accept the IMF's conditions and will turn a loan down. Some borrowers fail to abide by the loan conditions and have the credit-lines cut off. However, many other developing countries accept and abide by the IMF's conditionality clauses and adjust their balance of payments to sustainable levels.

This chapter discusses the economic reasoning behind and criticisms of the IMF's approach to balance of payments adjustments, and considers the effects of the IMF's "medicine" on the members' balance of payments and general economic performance. The chapter opens in section 20.1 with a discussion of developing country exchange rate arrangements. This subject is interesting because payments deficits could not arise if exchange rates were allowed to float freely. Why do developing countries operate pegged or managed exchange regimes? Section 20.2

then considers factors affecting developing country real exchange rates. Section 20.3 examines the IMF's role in balance of payments adjustment and states the IMF's objectives and the policy means chosen to attain those objectives. As the IMF's view of balance of payments adjustment is rooted in the monetary approach to the balance of payments, the main outline of that theory as it is applied by the IMF is set out in section 20.4. Following this there is a brief account in section 20.5 of the new structuralist school's criticism of IMF policies, and the debate between the two sides is considered in a schematic economic model. The final sub-sections of the chapter explain why the IMF is so often concerned with including clauses in its conditional loans which aim at reducing price distortions. It is shown empirically that price distortions hinder economic performance – with the implication that the IMF is generally correct to pursue policies which reduce their incidence.

20.1 Developing country exchange rate arrangements: to peg or not to peg?

Whether a country should peg or manage-float its exchange rate is a matter of whether it should join a monetary union (see chapter 18 on monetary unions). Five factors are likely to be relevant here: the country's size, its degree of openness, its degree of international financial integration, its inflation rate relative to the world average, and its trade pattern. Small countries are most likely to be price-takers in world markets and so cannot expect to induce balance of payments adjustment through terms of trade effects induced by changing the exchange rate. Similarly, an economy's degree of openness is important because the more open it is, the less effective will be a change in the exchange rate in altering the price ratio between traded and non-traded goods. In both of these cases, depreciation is not effective because it is likely to translate into generalized domestic inflation. A high degree of integration with international financial markets may favor floating because there should be plenty of international capital available to stabilize the exchange rate even if the current account fluctuates unexpectedly. A large inflation differential with the rest of the world also favors floating as a pegged exchange rate would be untenable. Dependence upon a few commodities in the export structure is ambiguous – shocks are more likely to be asymmetric favors floating (as a change in the nominal exchange rate against all trade partners is appropriate). However, a floating rate in these circumstances might be unstable (no opposite offsetting shocks), so pegging is favored. Finally, geographic trade concentration favors pegging against the dominant trade partner (s).

Heller (1978), Savvides (1990), and Weil (1987) find that country characteristics and regime choice line up well. However, Honkapohja and Pikkarainen (1992) do not find such convincing empirical support. They argue that it is a misspecification to include the inflation differential among the explanatory variables (as this may be an effect of regime choice rather than a cause); and they use per capita income as a proxy for Mundell's criterion of "economic flexibility" (if low flexibility, float). Their probit and logit analysis indicates that small countries tend to peg, as do those with low commodity diversification, but "other country characteristics, like the level of economic development, openness of the real or financial sector, geographical diversification of trade, and fluctuations in the terms of trade have in practice hardly any power in explaining the choice of a country's exchange rate system" (Honkapohja and Pikkarainen, 1992, p. 19).

20.1.1 What to peg against?

Having chosen to peg the exchange rate, a developing country faces the question of which other exchange rate to peg against? If it were to choose the US dollar it would also be electing to float against all currencies not also pegged to the dollar. Relevant questions are: how will the choice affect the country's terms of trade, or its internal distribution of income, or its resource allocation? These questions have been considered by Lipschitz (1979). To simplify, assume that the country is a price taker in foreign trade, and that it sends all of its exports to the USA while obtaining all of its imports from Japan.

It turns out that the choice of an exchange rate against which to peg makes no difference to the developing country's terms of trade T. This ought to be intuitively obvious because we have already said that the country is a price-taker. More formally,

$$T = \frac{P_x^{US} S^{US}}{P_m^J (S^{US}/S_{Y/\$})} = \frac{P_x^{US}}{P_m^J} S_{Y/\$} \tag{20.1}$$

where S^{US} is the developing country's domestic currency price of the dollar, $S_{Y/\$}$ is the yen price of the dollar, P_x^{US} is the price of exports in dollars and P_m^J is the price of imports in yen. The middle expression in equation (20.1) is the ratio of export prices to import prices measured in domestic currency. After cancelling terms the developing country's terms of trade is seen not to depend upon the foreign currency peg. It depends only upon the commodity prices set in the two big trade partners *and upon the exchange rate between those two countries.* Moreover, if the yen–dollar exchange rate never diverged from purchasing power parity (PPP), exchange rate fluctuations cannot affect the developing country's terms of trade.[1] But when this exchange rate does diverge from PPP there is a shock to T, and it does then matter whether the developing country is pegging to the yen, the dollar or against a currency basket. Shocks to the terms of trade will affect the internal distribution of income, the allocation of resources between the traded and non-traded goods sectors and the level of real income.

Consider first the impact on the internal distribution of income. If the exchange rate is pegged to the US dollar, the price of exports is fixed.[2] Thus, a shock to the terms of trade must show up in import prices. If the yen appreciates against the dollar (i.e. $S_{Y/\$}$ declines), from equation (20.1) the developing country's terms of trade deteriorate as import prices rise, and real income falls (from equation (3.2)). In this case, supposing that there are two classes in society, workers (paid wages) and capitalists (collectors of residual income), workers suffer a greater fall in their real incomes than do capitalists. This is because the fall in the capitalists' income is partly cushioned by rising profitability in the import-competing sector, so workers bear a disproportionately large share of the burden of falling real national income.

However, continuing with the assumption that T has fallen because the real exchange rate of the yen has risen against the dollar, this last result is reversed if the developing country is pegging against the yen. Now import prices are fixed, so the deterioration in the terms of trade shows up as falling export prices. If exportables are included in the consumer price index, the fall in export prices *raises* real wages! Correspondingly, as the developing country's real income has indeed fallen, capitalists will have to experience a particularly sharp fall in their real incomes.

Suppose that the developing country has chosen to peg against a currency basket made up of the yen and the dollar. The interesting case is when the basket is made up of the average of the import and export weights (if the basket is weighted more to the dollar or to the yen the previous results stand). In this case Lipschitz shows that the income distributional effects depend upon the share of importables and exports in GNP. If the shares are equal, changes in the terms of trade have no effect on income distribution; but if the share of exports is greater than the share of importables, which is likely, the shock of deterioration in the terms of trade will be mainly felt by a reduction in capitalists' real incomes. This result is reversed in the case of improving terms of trade: most of the gains go to the capitalists.

Consider how the choice of exchange rate peg may affect the allocation of resources between the traded and non-traded sectors as the terms of trade fluctuate. If the domestic currency is pegged to the US dollar – so fixing export prices – deterioration in the terms of trade (as the yen appreciates against the dollar) again causes the price of imports to rise. If both export and non-traded goods prices are fixed, resources will move into the importables sector (i.e. the non-traded goods sector shrinks). However, if the peg is against the yen, import prices are fixed and worsening of the terms of trade is through a fall in export prices. This relative price movement will release resources from the exportables sector and into the importables and non-traded goods sector (i.e. the non-traded goods sector expands).

Are there any criteria which should guide a developing country in choosing an exchange rate peg? According to Branson and Katseli-Papaefstratiou (1981), a country's choice of currency peg should be determined by the geographic structure of its foreign trade. In particular, if its foreign trade is mainly with a single partner, it should peg to that country's exchange rate – this will help to stabilize relative prices by constraining exchange rate fluctuations. (The dilemma set for the developing country in the discussion above was partly caused by the fact that there was no overlap in the geographic structure of its export and import trade.) They find support for their assertion: choice of exchange rate peg by developing countries does seem to be governed by geographic trade structures, with countries whose foreign trade is mainly with, for example, the USA or France pegging their exchange rates against, respectively, the dollar and the French franc. Moreover, the study by Flood et al. (1989) supports the view that the evolution of exchange rate regimes is governed by change in objective determinants. In particular, the gradual shift by some developing countries away from fixed exchange rates to more flexible rates over the 1969–87 period was found to be related to changes in the underlying stochastic structure of their economies (e.g. of variability in money growth and inflation rates).[3]

If in a developing country prices are sticky and/or internal resources are immobile between sectors, changes in relative prices caused by exchange rate fluctuations between third countries may translate into unemployment (with a deterioration in the terms of trade) or inflation (with an improvement). Thus, even if developing countries were always to follow a disciplined monetary policy, which, of course, many do not, balance of payments deficits could still occur, being caused by fluctuations in their terms of trade, T, over which they have little control. When a developing country does get into payments difficulties it must use its foreign exchange reserves and if these become inadequate it may approach the IMF for loans.

20.2 Liberalization, the Equilibrium Real Exchange Rate, and Economic Policy

Economic liberalization philosophy began sweeping developing countries in the late 1970s. It is necessary to understand the effects of the various liberalization-shocks on a country's equilibrium real exchange rate as these relate to subsequent economic policy. Thus, the level of the real exchange rate ($Q = SP^*/P = P^T/P^N$) affects a country's current account, resource allocation and internal balance. To understand these matters we use the micro–macroeconomic internal–external balance model introduced in section 4.2. We first consider some static shocks and then discuss some issues related to dynamics.

Considering substitution effects, a *cut in import tariffs* depreciates the equilibrium real exchange rate because it creates an excess demand for traded goods, T, and an excess supply of non-traded goods, N, at Q_1 in figure 20.1. CC (the ratio of T to N in consumption) shifts rightward as the consumption of traded goods rises; while RR (the ratio of T to N in production) moves leftward as the T good sector experiences greater competition.[4] That trade liberalization causes real depreciation is supported in the empirical work of Edwards (1989), Le Fort (1988), and Tokarick (1995).

Reduced government spending as a share of GDP is another feature of liberalization philosophy. If, as is likely, this mainly reduces the demand for N goods, CC moves rightward in figure 20.2 as the share of N in consumption falls. The equilibrium real exchange rate depreciates, reflecting the fall in the relative price of N goods.

A *positive terms of trade shock* (i.e. increased export prices in relation to import prices) appreciates the real exchange rate as the positive income effect increases the demand for N goods, raising their relative price.

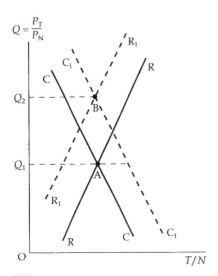

Figure 20.1 The real exchange rate and a tariff reduction

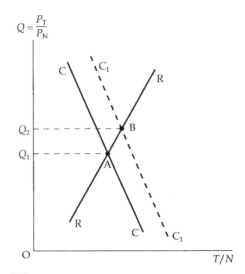

Figure 20.2 The real exchange rate and reduced government spending

Dynamic effects

Edwards (1989) notes that in a dynamic framework matters are more complicated. For example, suppose that a shock depreciates the *equilibrium* real exchange rate, the *actual* real exchange rate may fail to depreciate sufficiently quickly (perhaps because the nominal rate is pegged and prices adjust slowly), and this will give rise to a trade deficit. This may be financed by borrowing from abroad. As international indebtedness increases an obligation is incurred to repay that foreign debt through a trade surplus at a future date. Thus, the rate of depreciation of the real exchange rate is slowed down by the foreign borrowing, but it ends up having to depreciate even more than if there had not been any foreign borrowing because of the need to generate a trade surplus.

Compare the cases where a country chooses to repay outstanding foreign debts with that where it settles just to pay the interest on that debt. The real depreciation must be greater when it chooses to pay off foreign indebtedness as it must generate a larger trade surplus. This is the case analyzed in the two-period model of Edwards (1989). In the other case, the real exchange rate only has to depreciate enough to create a trade surplus large enough to pay the interest on the outstanding debt. This is as in the portfolio balance real exchange rate model of Allen and Stein (1989, 1991).

Thus, shocks cause a country's real exchange rate to take on some trajectory over time. But it will be very difficult for a government to know exactly what this is as it depends on the nature of the shock, the amount and terms of foreign borrowing, substitutability in production (the slope of RR) and consumption (CC slope), the relative strength of income effects, the rate of time prefence, and whether shocks are expected to be temporary or permanent (which may govern the terms of access to foreign finance). In fact, Edwards (1989) notes that

> it is not possible to know how the effect of import tariffs and terms of trade shocks on the equilibrium exchange rate will be distributed through time. (p. 51)

This is a point of great practical importance for a developing country's government concerned with exchange rate policy. It means that it is difficult to know whether a real exchange rate is adjusting close to its equilibrium path – no policy action needs to be taken; or whether policy action is required because it is well off its equilibrium path and is causing resource misallocation and macroeconomic disequilibrium.

Monetary control and inflation

Suppose that a government attempts to maintain international competitiveness by following a policy of nominal exchange rate depreciation at the same rate as the domestic inflation differential over the world average rate of inflation. This amounts to a policy of targeting the real exchange rate.

A potential problem with this arises if the real exchange rate is shocked, for example, by a sharp improvement in a country's international terms of trade (examined in Montiel and Ostry, 1991, 1992). In this case the real exchange rate would need to appreciate to reflect the increased demand for N goods. If there is no nominal exchange rate variability (at least from a steady inflation path in their model), all shocks to the real exchange rate show up as a variation in the rate of inflation – hence Montiel and Ostry's conclusion that neither nominal exchange rate targeting nor monetary targeting can act as nominal anchors for the domestic price level.

What are the reasons for this somewhat uncomfortable conclusion? Failure of the real exchange rate to appreciate will lead to a trade surplus as the terms of trade improvement leads to an increase in export earnings. The trade surplus will lead to an inflationary increase in the money supply. Notice that if the government were to succeed in sterilizing the monetary effect of a payments surplus, real interest rates will rise – due to an increased demand for money as income increases along with the improvement in the terms of trade. Now, if the capital account is open and international capital is highly mobile, the domestic real interest rate will not be able to increase relative to the world rate, and money will have become entirely endogenous. Thus, lacking exogenous control over the domestic money stock, monetary policy cannot be used to target the price level.

20.3 The IMF: its Role

As the role of the IMF in the international financial and economic system was touched on in chapter 17 we need to add only a few more details here. The IMF's main objectives – when confronted with a member country seeking funds to finance a balance of payments deficit – is to restore payments equilibrium as quickly as possible. One Fund staff member has written *"the unique function of the Fund is to promote the adjustment process"* (Dale, 1983, emphasis added); and another embroiders the point: "The ultimate aim of Fund financial assistance is to restore viability to the balance of payments in the context of price stability and sustained economic growth, without resort to measures that impair the freedom of trade and payments" (Guitian, 1981). However, Polak (1991b) points out that these objectives are not necessarily consistent with each other. Over the last decade the IMF has begun to place greater emphasis on the objectives of structural adjustment and economic growth. This is shown by the introduction for the use of low income countries of the Structural Adjustment Facility (in 1986) and the Enhanced Structural Adjustment Facility (1988); see table 17.1. Moreover, the IMF has shifted its interpretation of the "Guidelines on Conditionality" from emphasis on the aggregate budget deficit and its rapid reduction to greater consideration for the specific content of government expenditure and tax programs (Tanzi, 1987); e.g. the IMF now recognizes that targets for the fiscal deficit should include measures to reduce price distortions, to promote economic growth in the medium and long term and to reduce poverty.

The IMF has an array of policies from which it can select. The main ones are as follows:

1 monetary policy, usually the setting of ceilings on the rate of domestic credit expansion;
2 devaluation;
3 reduced price distortions, e.g.
   (a) by increasing energy prices and reducing food subsidies;
   (b) by interest rate reform – through raising or eliminating ceilings on interest rates;
   (c) by trade liberalization;
4 wage freezes;
5 targets for the growth of net foreign indebtedness.

Very important are demand management policies. The IMF's view is that domestic demand (or "absorption") must be constrained to a level consistent with the level of domestic production plus any sustainable net capital inflows, otherwise a balance of payments deficit is unsustainable. Important among demand management policies is the control, or restriction, of domestic bank credit expansion. Selection of this policy instrument, and the setting of targets for domestic credit expansion (DCE), follows from the IMF's analysis of the causes of payments deficits, an analysis which is rooted in the monetary approach to the balance of payments (see chapter 8). Use of monetary policy instruments is often accompanied by targets for public sector borrowing, i.e. fiscal targets which are usually set in terms of target levels of aggregate government spending and income and sometimes with reference to spending levels on various public sector programmes and tax-revenue schemes.

However, for balance of payments adjustment to be anything other than temporary, the IMF often seeks the attainment of certain other objectives.

1 The view on improved resource allocation is that this will lessen the constraint on the level of domestic demand imposed by a *given* availability of resources. The policies used here usually involve exchange rate adjustment, interest rate adjustment and other price adjustment policies, especially public sector pricing and subsidies.
2 From the late 1970s the IMF has paid attention to "supply-side" measures – so as to reduce the balance of payments constraint on demand from the side of increased domestic production from *enhanced* domestic resources. This is especially important where the root-causes of developing country payments deficits lie in external events (such as higher energy prices), which are structural in character rather than cyclically reversible. Such structural deficits can be reduced by increasing domestic supply (e.g. of energy resources) rather than by simply cutting domestic demand.

The distinction between supply-side and demand-side measures is somewhat overdrawn, however, as measures taken by governments in conjunction with IMF conditional loans will often simultaneously affect both sides. For example, the IMF will often combine targets for reduced fiscal deficits with measures to reduce fiscal distortions by, for example, rationalizing personal and company income taxes so as to reduce their distortionary effects; similarly with the structure of import duties; and user fees charged for publicly provided goods are encouraged to move into closer association with the cost of provision (Gray and Linn, 1988). Indeed, in 1990 Managing Director Camdessus stated that "growth" was the Fund's main objective. He argued that balance of payments equilibrium was consistent with "high quality growth", while disequilibria were associated only with unsustainable "flash-in-the-pan growth", financed by running down international reserves (quoted by Polak, 1991b).

IMF policy measures are not universally accepted as ideal; dissenters include some recipients of IMF conditional loans and a group of economic theorists known as the *new structuralist school*. Section 20.5 assesses the economic merits of the IMF's policies and the relevance of the arguments put by the new structuralist school against them.[5] The weight of this evidence is shown to lend more support to the IMF's position – but the case is not entirely clear cut. For now we turn attention to the monetary model which for over four decades has strongly influenced the IMF's view of balance of payments adjustment.

20.3.1 The IMF and domestic financial distress

Since a spate of international financial crises in the 1990s, sparked by *domestic* financial difficulties (related to poorly regulated, under-capitalized domestic bank borrowing in foreign currency unhedged on the short-term international inter-bank market) there have been calls for the IMF to expand the scope of its policy advice and conditionality clauses to include improved conditions in domestic financial systems. As we have indicated in (chapters 14 and 19) (see also Crockett, 1997), a country's international financial difficulties often cannot be separated from problems in its domestic financial system. As Eichengreen (1999) points out, the intertwining of domestic and international financial systems in developing countries stems from relaxation of controls on international capital movements during the 1980s. Thus, a balance of payments crisis can now easily be sparked in the capital account even by a *suspected* domestic banking crisis which induces investors to take their money out of a given country. Hence, the need for a sound domestic financial system to support a country's position in the international financial system. Indeed, given that contagion may spread a financial crisis from one country to another, as is thought to have happened in the East Asian financial crisis of 1997 and the American crisis of 1998 (the Failure of Long Term Capital Management causing interest rates to rise and stock markets to fall around the world), an improvement in one country's financial system creates an externality for the stability of the entire international financial system.

We can think of any element which improves the soundness of a domestic financial system as being an international public good but, being so, will be underinvested in. One such is bank capital, discussed in section 19.3. Eichengreen (1999) lists other factors to include anything that reduces asymmetric information in financial markets – so that markets can better discipline borrowers; and modification of creditor rights in international bond issues so as to reduce the chances of "grab races" which could destroy an otherwise solvent borrower (see section 14.8). Furthermore, as volatile short-term capital flow may have negative externalities for the international financial system, the flow should be reduced toward the socially optimal level by taxes on them.

Amongst these perhaps the most pressing need is to reduce asymmetric information in international financial markets. As in domestic financial markets, this is achieved through the adoption of common reporting standards. Thus, Eichengreen (1999) argues for the development and adoption of common international standards in accountancy and auditing, the establishment of investor rights over monitoring, and laws preventing insider trading. To the extent that information remains asymmetric, so weakening market discipline, complements to better information are also required. These include better standards of regulation by domestic bank and securities regulators, and better incentive alignment been domestic banks and their creditors. The latter being created by requiring banks to operate with larger cushions of capital – so that bank owners have more to lose if badly run.

While some experts have suggested that standards such as mentioned above should be set by to-be-created supranational institutions (such as an international bankruptcy court – see section 14.8), or, even by the IMF itself, Eichengreen (1999) sees this as politically impractical and favors working for the achievement of common international standards through existing international *private sector* bodies. These include the International Accounting Standards Committee, the International Organization of Supreme Audit Institutions, Committee J of the International Bar Association (on reforming bankruptcy laws), and the International Corporate Governance Network.

Nevertheless, the IMF has a crucial role to play in recognizing international standards and in encouraging compliance with them by making the standards "official" and *conditioning its lending on compliance.*

While some commentators may argue that such "micro-managed" conditionality clauses unduly impinge on national sovereignty, the counter argument is that the right of a nation to integrate into the international financial system should also bring with it the obligation to contribute to the stability of that system, or, at least, not to detract from it. And the way to do the latter is not to create external diseconomies through a poorly functioning domestic financial system.

Some other commentators have suggested that the IMF should be abolished because its lending causes moral hazard on the part of borrowers. The strong counter argument to this is that IMF membership is the only practical means of encouraging countries to invest in international public goods; and membership is desirable only if some benefit (loans) may be garnered. Besides, IMF conditional lending, phased release of funds, and surveillance of performance are designed to reduce moral hazard.

◆ 20.4 The IMF's Monetary Approach to the Balance of Payments

In the early days the IMF sought a robust theory of the balance of payments upon which a consistent set of adjustment policies could be based – it was provided by a paper published in 1957 (Polak, 1957). The underlying assumption of this model, largely taken over and applied by the IMF with some modifications, is that balance of payments deficits have common causes and that payments adjustment can be most efficiently achieved by applying the limited set of adjustment policies mentioned in section 20.3. In the early days empirical evidence showed that the demand for money was a stable function of a few economic variables. The velocity of circulation of money was stable, at least in the long run. Thus, changes in money supply should have predictable effects on nominal national income.

As a matter of fact, in many developing countries monetary policy is subservient to fiscal policy (Johnston and Brekk, 1989). High rates of DCE are used to finance large fiscal deficits. As a result, in many cases exchange rates are depreciating and the current account is in chronic deficit despite the use of import controls and official currency inconvertibility.

Why do these undesirable features occur together? The monetary effect of high DCE, according to the monetary approach to the balance of payments, is to encourage *dis*hoarding by domestic wealth-holders as they seek to rid themselves of excess money balances. If the exchange rate is fixed or somehow managed, foreign exchange reserves will be depleting and net international indebtedness rising as the government directly or indirectly – through public corporations – borrows foreign exchange to intervene on the foreign exchange market. Almost certainly, measures will have been introduced to protect foreign exchange reserves: e.g. domestic currency will have been made inconvertible for capital account transactions and tariff and non-tariff barriers will have been raised against imports (having the unfortunate effect of heightening price distortions in the domestic economy).

Letting the exchange rate depreciate, by devaluation of a pegged rate or in a dirty float, somewhat relieves pressure on foreign exchange reserves. The following shows how. Even though DCE may still be high, the depreciation will induce an increase in hoarding – or a decrease in the rate of dishoarding – as the higher exchange rate raises the general price level. The higher price level in turn raises the demand for money. The combination of high rates of DCE and an ever higher exchange rate could offset each other exactly. Indeed, in a clean float, they would have to as the nation as a whole cannot dishoard domestic currency through a balance of payments deficit. A higher price level is therefore needed to make wealth-holders willingly hold the growing money stock. With currency depreciation caught up in a inflationary spiral (but not as the cause which is the budget deficit financed by DCE), the government may choose to halt the incipient capital outflow by imposing (or strengthening) foreign exchange controls. If this is successful the rate of depreciation of the exchange rate will be reduced. But this will have the unfortunate effect of causing the real exchange rate to appreciate, with consequent contractionary effects on the domestic traded goods sector. These effects are also likely to be present if the exchange rate is pegged or if there is "dirty" floating.

As the budget deficit and capital outflow persist, foreign exchange reserves will be falling. Under these conditions pressure for trade-protectionism measures are likely to be rising, with tariff and non-tariff barriers being increased. The effect of these will be to cause a one-off increase in the domestic price level – so increasing the desire to hoard. But the respite to the balance of payments deficit will be temporary. The persistence of DCE ahead of the long-term trend growth rate of desired hoarding still leaves wealth-holders wishing to dishoard. Moreover, once-in-a-while devaluations act similarly as they cause one-time increases in the price level – again with only temporary relief to the balance of payments deficit.

Eventually the IMF will be called in, usually before hyperinflation has caught hold but probably not before net foreign indebtedness has become unmanageable and the domestic economy is badly distorted by the price effects of tariffs and controls over foreign trade. Capital markets and interest rates too will have become badly distorted if financial repression (see the next chapter) has been adopted as an ancillary means of financing the budget deficit.

As pointed out earlier, the IMF wants the adjustment of the fundamental factors causing payments deficits and economic distortions. Just financing the payments deficits under these circumstances is bound to fail, giving only temporary respite. Adjustment requires a fundamental change in a country's economic and financial conditions. The budget deficit needs to be reduced and all of the factors to which it gave rise reversed: rapid DCE halted, price distortions removed, financial repression ended, capital account currency convertibility made legal. To achieve these ends the IMF will make its loans conditional on factors such as these.

In terms of the monetary approach to the balance of payments the IMF's objective is to cut the rate of *dis*hoarding. As high rates of DCE are due to the budget deficit an essential step is to reduce that deficit. If these objectives are met, tariffs and exchange controls become redundant, at least from the macroeconomic point of view. Moreover, removal of these is expected to improve resource allocation and to raise the rate of economic growth.

There is a more extensive discussion of economic and financial reform in both the developing countries and the formerly centrally planned economies in the next two chapters where the subject of the order of economic and financial liberalization is discussed: experience shows that rapid and indiscriminate liberalization of an economy is not necessarily desirable. This lesson has been learned by the IMF which now accepts that gradualism rather than a "big bang" approach to economic and financial adjustment is preferable.

 ## 20.5 The New Structuralist Debate

The new structuralists' case against the routine application of "standard" (monetary-based) IMF adjustment packages in developing countries is that their economic structures are quite different from those of developed countries and that, as a group, they are themselves structurally diverse. Adjustment packages that might work well when applied to developed countries, or even some developing countries, may be ineffective, or worse, when applied to other developing countries.

Taylor (1983), noting that developing countries are structurally diverse, points out that "no single set of institutions or equations can capture all of this variety" (p. 191). He develops several macroeconomic models which incorporate many different structural characteristics. Manipulation of these models yields a wide variety of results with virtually no outcome being determinate on the basis of *a priori* economic reasoning. Different assumptions about key parameter values can yield policy outcomes quite counter to those that are sometimes asserted by the IMF. By way of example consider the following.

1   A *reduction* in the real money supply (due to lower nominal money) could be inflationary if "interest rate cost push" is strong (i.e. the aggregate supply curve in price-level-income space shifts upwards). This might arise if firms have to hold large stocks of circulating capital financed by borrowed money: Buffie (1984), Lim (1987), and Van Wijnbergen (1982) provide theoretical and empirical support for this proposition.
2   An upward-shifting aggregate supply curve could also be caused by devaluation as the cost of imported inputs rises or, if wages are indexed to prices.
3   Devaluation can worsen the current account deficit (an example of "elasticity pessimism") and cause a reduction in the rate of economic growth. The latter effect could stem from the effect of reduced real wages on the level of aggregate demand. Reduced spending by workers may not be made up by higher spending by others so that aggregate demand and economic growth rates fall. The theoretical possibility that devaluation may cause excess supply and

deflation, via income redistribution and differences in the spending propensities of workers and capitalists, was first set out by Diaz-Alejandro (1963).

4 If food subsidies are reduced as part of a programme of reduced government expenditure, the demand for non-food goods would be reduced if the demand for food is inelastic. Growth incentives would also be reduced and the rate of economic growth would suffer.

5 Devaluation may have a contractionary effect on spending as it reduces residents' net real wealth (i) via inflation and the real balance effect and (ii) by raising the domestic currency value of foreign debt.

6 Devaluation raises import prices in terms of domestic currency and, if *ad valorem* tariffs are being levied, the amount of tariff revenue collected by the government will rise. The resulting smaller budget deficit is contractionary (Krugman and Taylor, 1978).

Furthermore, Spraos (1986) argues that as the demand for money function is not necessarily stable and payments deficits may have non-monetary causes – such as a recession in export markets – monetary targeting by the IMF as part of conditional loan packages may not be appropriate. This argument echoes that of Rabin and Yeager (1982) who also question the general validity of the monetary approach to the balance of payments – see p. 168 for a fuller discussion. Some country studies support the new structuralists' case that the IMF should tailor its adjustment polices to suit specific circumstances. Green (1983) argued that an IMF credit-adjustment package for an extended fund facility loan in 1981 was refused by the Tanzanian authorities because the IMF did not take account of microeconomic and structural issues particular to the Tanzanian economy. The argument was that the devaluation demanded by the IMF was inappropriate as a means of improving the current account deficit. Export bottlenecks existed and required imports to alleviate them, while any temporary gains from devaluation would be quickly wiped out by the inflation brought on by the devaluation. In the case of Jamaica it has been argued that the conditions for IMF loans negotiated during the 1970s showed pro-market bias and operated under the assumption that markets worked efficiently (Sharpley, 1983). Indeed, a joint IMF–World Bank report in 1986 conceded the point, concluding that Jamaica's economic difficulties were deep-seated, requiring structural adjustment supported by World Bank structural adjustment loans – of which five were granted during 1982–7 (Robinson and Schmitz, 1989).

It has been admitted by IMF sources that fiscal adjustments required by the IMF may not always have been entirely appropriate (Tait, 1989). However, it is claimed that the IMF itself has no political agenda of its own and that it is entirely motivated by the best academic thinking. A major consideration that motivates the IMF is the need to reduce fiscal deficits so as to reduce crowding out of private sector investment and to improve the macroeconomic environment so as to encourage capital repatriation – especially important in Latin American countries – yielding a source of funds for the financing of both balance of payments deficits and private domestic investment (Tanzi, 1989). Moreover, many developing countries voluntarily invite IMF tax missions to advise on tax reforms – the advice is informed by both theoretical considerations and practicalities as faced by a particular developing country (Tanzi, 1990).

20.5.1 New structuralists versus the International Monetary Fund: devaluation

The IMF's case for and the new structuralist's case against devaluation as a means of adjusting balance of payments deficits can be contrasted in a simple model. The model is based upon the following three assumptions:

1 the economy is divided into two sectors:
   (a) *non-traded goods*, such as housing and other items of social infrastructure, many services and, very often, commodities which are produced and consumed only in the domestic economy;
   (b) *traded goods*, a major export industry based upon a raw material produced in a mineral or agricultural sector, together with a sector of limited scale producing import-competing goods.
2 There is perfect mobility and constant productivity of factor inputs when they move between industries *within a sector*. This is the basis of the division of the economy into two sectors.
3 There is diminishing marginal productivity of factor inputs when they move between sectors, so that the transformation curve between traded and non-traded goods is concave to the origin.

Given the underlying production and utility functions, the levels of production and consumption will depend on the relative price of traded and non-traded goods (measured in local currency).

Figure 20.3 shows the full employment, flexible price, production possibility frontier for a small open economy that is running a balance of current account deficit. As has been amply demonstrated by Corden (1977), both expenditure reduction and expenditure switching are involved in the adjustment process. Relative prices between traded and non-traded goods are shown by the slope of RR_1. The domestic price of traded goods equals SP^*, where S is the exchange rate and P^* is the fixed exogenous foreign price of traded goods. The latter follows because we have made the "small country" assumption. The domestic price of non-traded goods is set in the long run to clear the market for non-traded goods, but in the short run we take the price of non-traded goods to be inflexible downwards. Initially consumption is at C, on indifference curve IC_1, and production is at P. Absorption exceeds income by RU as measured in terms of traded goods, and this is also the size of the balance of payments deficit. At unchanged relative prices consumption slides up or down the income–consumption curve OZ, but production remains at point P.

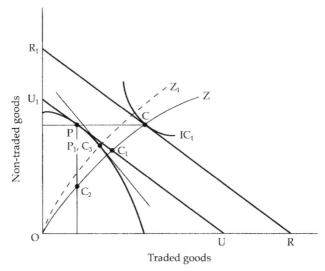

Figure 20.3 Balance of payments adjustment with resource mobility

Beginning at the consumption point C, consumption will sooner or later begin to fall along OZ. This will be so owing to either a negative wealth effect – induced by the payments deficit (as foreign indebtedness increases and permanent income falls) – or the implementation of expenditure reduction policies by the government – such as lower government spending and higher taxes. In the absence of a change in relative prices, consumption would need to fall to C_2 for the domestic demand and domestically produced supply of traded goods to come into balance and therefore for the payments deficit to be eliminated. If so, there will be an excess supply of non-traded goods, equal to PC_2, and unemployment will result, at least in the short run.

However, when wealth effects, or the application of expenditure reduction policies, have reduced consumption along OZ (at the initial relative price ratio) to C_1, absorption equals income – but there is still an excess demand for traded goods and an excess supply of non-traded goods. At this point, the government, instead of allowing unemployment to worsen, could choose to devalue the exchange rate, so raising the domestic nominal price of traded goods as well as their price relative to non-traded goods. The production point is then induced to move from P to P_1 and consumption from C_1 to C_3 where the payments deficit is removed.

A general point that is often raised with regard to currency depreciation is that it can be quickly offset by inflation. Empirical evidence, however, shows that nominal exchange rate depreciation does generally cause the real exchange rate to depreciate, even after three years, so that devaluation can alter the relative prices of traded and non-traded goods (Donovan, 1981; Kamin, 1988; Edwards, 1989).

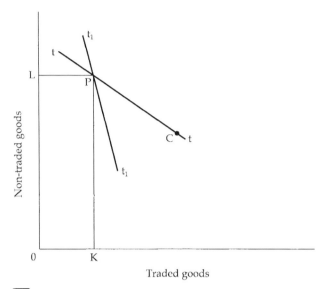

Figure 20.4 Balance of payments adjustment with resource immobility

New structuralist arguments against currency depreciation usually revolve around factors such as *import dependence* and *resource immobility*, particularly between the traded and non-traded sectors. These can be treated as arguing that the production possibility curve is degenerate: in the extreme case of zero resource mobility it becomes a rectangular box with one corner at the point where domestic production happens to lie. Resources cannot be reallocated from the non-traded goods sector to the traded goods sector (an important adjustment mechanism in the case made above for the effectiveness of devaluation).

In figure 20.4, where the rectangular production possibility curve reflects the assumption of perfect resource immobility, production and consumption are initially at P and C respectively with a payments deficit. An appropriately chosen devaluation could reduce consumption of traded goods and, at P, the payments deficit would be removed. However, the whole burden of this adjustment is on the consumption of traded goods. This is unwelcome, new structuralists argue, in circumstances such as the following.

1 *Food import dependence*: reduced availability and a higher price of food has *inegalitarian* income distributional consequences as the poor spend a larger proportion of their income on food than do the rich.
2 *Input-import dependence* (where imported capital goods etc. are vital to the domestic economy): reduced availability of traded goods
   (a) if vital to the production of non-traded goods, would move production to a point somewhere down the line PK – there would be unemployment in the non-traded goods sector;

(b) if vital to the production of traded goods, would move production to a point somewhere to the left on the line LP with unemployment in the traded goods sector;

(c) if vital to production in both sectors, would cause production to lie somewhere within the degenerate production possibility curve with unemployment in both sectors.

New structuralist arguments are taken up again in section 21.1.

20.5.2 Empirical evidence

Empirical evidence tends *not* to support the new structuralist's case against devaluation. Even so, the evidence is somewhat mixed. A study of 12 *least* less developed countries showed that a 10 percent devaluation on average improved the current account by 1.5 percent of GNP (Gylfason and Radetzki, 1991). An earlier study of 12 developing countries agreeing to implement IMF devaluation inclusive adjustment packages (during 1970–6) showed that real export growth improved both in the short run (one-year comparison) and long run (three-year comparison) (Donovan, 1981). However, as in the case of other economic magnitudes, the improvements were not achieved in all 12 countries. For the group as a whole, real import growth actually increased following devaluation, a feature which reflects both the removal of certain import barriers and the improved (in the short run only) rate of real GDP growth. Real trade balances tended to improve sharply particularly in the short run. However, rates of inflation fell only marginally. A study of 64 devaluation episodes in developing countries by Kamin (1988) found that devaluation improved trade balances and that this was due to a rise in exports rather than a fall in imports.

As far as African countries are concerned empirical evidence covering countries that adopted Fund-supported adjustment programmes in the 1973–86 period showed that inflation rates were reduced, though other statistically significant effects were hard to find (Greene, 1989a). However, there was some (weak) evidence that the current account balance and economic growth improved.

The removal of tariff and non-tariff barriers against imports acts similarly to exchange rate devaluation as it raises the domestic price of exports relative to imports and depreciates the real exchange rate. This should encourage growth of the export sector, and this is especially so when imported goods are used as inputs into the export sector. Empirical investigation of 23 sub-Saharan African countries supports this hypothesis (DeRosa, 1990). Using simulation techniques it was shown that the effect of reducing average tariff rates from 30 percent to 10 percent would be to raise the value of exports by between 15 and 33 percent. Moreover, as it is likely that both exports and imports will be rising following the tariff reductions it is not possible on *a priori* grounds to predict the effect of trade liberalization on the balance of trade – a view supported by the theoretical model of Ostry (1991).

Some other evidence – from the World Bank (1991) – is more supportive of the IMF's approach, interpreted as combining macroeconomic discipline with microeconomic adjustment. In particular the latter requires that price distortions are reduced; specifically that domestic prices move closer to world prices so that they are more reflective of true opportunity costs. The expectation is that as price distortions are reduced resource allocation will improve and that this will engender a positive effect on the rate of economic growth. The World Bank study calculated rates of return on 1200 projects that it had financed in the 1969–89 period and, as table 20.1 shows, these rates of return were highest where policy distortions (measured by the degree of trade restrictiveness, foreign exchange premiums, real interest rate and size of fiscal deficit) were lowest. The data in table 20.1 are clearly supportive of the hypothesis that price distortions harm economic performance.

20.5.3 Adjustment and income distribution

Devaluation

The effect of devaluation on income distribution is not at all clear despite new structuralist claims that it will have inegalitarian effects. *A priori* it is quite impossible to tell which classes – rich or poor – will benefit or suffer from the devaluation. (See also our discussion above of the terms of trade and income distribution.) The outcome depends upon too many factors. For example, if agricultural crops are sold only or mainly on local markets, as in Indonesia and Bolivia, the relatively higher price of traded goods will tend to squeeze real incomes in the farming sector; but if a large proportion of crops are exported, as in Ghana, farming sector real incomes will tend to rise following a devaluation (Johnson and Salop, 1980; Heller et al., 1988). However, in the 12 *least* less developed countries in their empirical simulations Gylfason and Radetzki (1991) found that, if the nominal wage is rigid, a 10 percent devaluation causes real wages to fall by 2.9 percent on average and real GNP by 0.5 percent. Krugman and Taylor (1978) had argued that devaluation could be deflationary and so the latter finding is supportive. However, Donovan (1981) found mixed evidence on this matter; and Kamin (1988) found no evidence that devaluation had a contractionary effect.

Such is the complexity of the income distributional effects of devaluation in developing countries, together with the array of fiscal measures which governments can, and do, employ along with a devaluation, that the outcome for income distribution is likely to be more a matter of political choice than the working of crude economic forces. Devaluations in Latin America might have produced inegalitarian outcomes because the military dictatorships in power favored the rich, while the more egalitarian results of devaluations observed in Malaysia may be explained by the observation that the poorer income groups there are better represented in government (Cline, 1983). Moreover, since the late 1980s, the IMF cooperates with bilateral and multilateral aid agencies to direct foreign aid to the poor in cases where the application of IMF adjustment policies suggest that there is a need – Ghana in 1988 is one such case (see Polak, 1991b).

Table 20.1 Economic policies and average economic rates of return for projects financed by the World Bank and IFC, 1969–89

Policy-distortion index	All projects (%)	All public projects (%)	Public agricultural projects (%)	Public industrial projects (%)	Public projects in non-tradeable sectors (%)	All private projects (%)
Trade restrictiveness						
High	13.2	13.6	12.1	—[a]	14.6	9.5
Moderate	15.0	15.4	15.4	—[a]	16.0	10.7
Low	19.0	19.3	14.3	—[a]	24.3	17.1
Foreign-exchange premium						
High (200% or more)	8.2	7.2	3.2	—[a]	11.5	—[a]
Moderate (20%–200%)	14.4	14.9	11.9	13.7	17.2	10.3
Low (less than 20%)	17.7	18.0	16.6	16.6	19.3	15.2
Real interest rate						
Negative	15.0	15.4	12.7	17.9	17.9	11.0
Positive	17.3	17.5	17.0	17.8	17.9	15.6
Fiscal deficit (% of GDP)						
High (8 or more)	13.4	13.7	11.7	10.3	16.6	10.7
Moderate (4–8)	14.8	15.1	12.2	21.0	16.8	12.2
Low (less than 4)	17.8	18.1	18.6	14.1	18.2	14.3

[a] Insufficient number of observations.
Source: World Bank, 1991

Credit and fiscal policies

The array of fiscal policies that can be deployed to reduce government expenditure and/or raise public sector income is broad, and the choice will sometimes have clear income distributional consequences. Reduced price subsidies, particularly on food, tend to reduce the real income of the poor more than that of the rich – similarly with reduced public expenditure on health and education. But other considerations are also important, as Johnson and Salop (1980) and Heller et al. (1988) point out. If egalitarian objectives are important, deep cuts may be made in the income of relatively highly paid civil servants. Broadening the tax base and reducing tax evasion tend to be egalitarian measures. With credit policies the government's choice of policy composition is important. Policies taken to reduce the extent of "financial dualism" (Myint, 1971), where cheap credit is channeled to large firms and higher income groups in the urban sector at the expense of higher interest rates charged to rural, poorer, borrowers, have the effect of moving income distribution in an egalitarian direction. Recent research on World Bank lending for structural reform could find no systematic relationship between adjustment and income distribution (Ribe and Carvalho, 1990). And Heller et al. (1988) observe that it is largely a matter of choice whether an adjustment package has favorable or unfavorable effects on income distribution. Moreover, the poor are more likely to benefit from a planned adjustment than from automatic adjustment through increased rates of inflation.

NOTES

1 Writing equation (20.1) in natural logs

$$\Delta T = \Delta p_x^{us} - \Delta p_m^{J} - \Delta s_{y/\$}$$

and noting that if PPP holds

$$\Delta s_{Y/\$} = \Delta p^{J} - \Delta p^{us}$$

It follows that, substituting the second of these equations into the first, $\Delta t = 0$. Thus, only if PPP between the USA and Japan does not hold will the LDC's terms of trade T be affected by exchange rate developments.

2 Evidence from Latin American experience supports the proposition that pegging against the US dollar does indeed (approximately) fix domestic prices, including export prices, to levels determined in the USA (Connolly, 1983).

3 One problem with this study though is that it may confuse cause with effect: i.e. the economies may have become more unstable because they had abandoned their nominal exchange rate anchors rather than abandoned their anchor because they had become more unstable.

4 The income effect of the tariff reduction on the CC function is to shift it as the deadweight cost of tariffs is reduced and real income increases. Which way it shifts depends on the relative strengths of the income elasticities of demand for traded and non-traded goods.

5 The structuralist school's views are also discussed in section 21.1.

21

The Order of Liberalization in Developing Countries

This chapter discusses the issue of economic and financial reform in developing countries and the next chapter discusses the same issue in the formerly centrally planned or, transition economies (TEs) of Europe. Discussion of this matter is appropriate in a book on international money and finance as both groups of countries are increasingly integrated into the world financial system. The character of this integration conditions how quickly and in what order financial and economic reforms should be executed. The experience of several developing countries in recent decades demonstrates that hurried reforms, which have paid no attention to proper sequencing, end in financial chaos and with the reimposition of government controls over the financial sector, i.e. financial repression. Moreover, economic and financial developments in developing countries can affect the international financial system, e.g. the international debt crisis of the 1980s.

Section 21.1 discusses the case for financial liberalization in developing countries. This case rests on the argument that price and other financial and economic distortions retard economic growth and therefore should be removed. The seminal works on financial liberalization in developing countries, by McKinnon (1973) and Shaw (1973), were part of a wider historical sweep in which many economists came to the realization that the market system should be freed to play a major role in promoting economic growth and development.

Perhaps to the surprise of the early proponents of financial reform, the first experience with financial liberalization in developing countries was not a happy one. The reasons for this are discussed in section 21.2. Chastened by these experiences, by the early 1980s many economists were arguing that, ideally, financial reform should be *sequenced*. This is the subject of section 21.3. It is argued that, as no reform programme could possibly immediately create a complete set of markets (there would be no missing markets), "second best" problems are bound to arise.[1] Thus, the removal of any given price distortion may reduce rather than raise welfare. For example, a strong conclusion in the literature on financial liberalization in developing countries is that the early removal of foreign exchange controls will probably affect capital flows and exchange rates in a way that damages the liberalizing country's economy.

As was shown in chapter 20, International Monetary Fund (IMF) (and, more recently, World Bank) thinking on the selection of adjustment policies is guided by macroeconomic, balance of payments and microeconomic considerations. The main microeconomic consideration is that price distortions, especially negative real interest rates, overvalued real exchange rates and, in the TEs, administered price structures are detrimental to efficient resource allocation and economic growth. However, as we have indicated, price reform necessarily takes place in a world of second best, so the removal of one price distortion while other considerations remain may not raise welfare. It is because of the second best problem, and concerns over equity issues, that debate has arisen over the ideal way in which to liberalize the economies of developing countries and the TEs.

 ## 21.1 Distortions and Economic Performance

Many developing countries, typically those in Latin America and also some in Africa and Asia, display features that have been associated with financial repression (which is a condition that gives rise to "disequilibrium credit rationing"[2]), macroeconomic mismanagement and import-substituting industrialization. The stylized facts are that

1   fiscal deficits are large, as much as 20 percent of gross domestic product (GDP);
2   financing of government budget deficits is predominantly through the banking system (in developing countries 47 percent from the central bank and 7 percent from deposit banks during 1975–85, compared with 12 percent and 23 percent respectively in developed countries (World Bank, 1989a));
3   rates of monetary expansion and inflation are high;
4   real deposit rates of interest are usually negative, while free market real loan rates of interest are relatively high;
5   the export sector suffers from an overvalued real exchange rate;
6   domestic money and capital markets are cut off from the world financial system by exchange controls; and
7   tariffs, quotas, and other non-tariff barriers are high.

Financial depth, as measured by, for example, the ratio M2/GDP, is an indicator of how well developed a country's financial system is. When the ratio is relatively low, the flow of loanable funds from lenders to borrowers is restricted. Examination of table 21.1 reveals that high economic growth in developing countries is associated with greater financial depth, high savings rates, and lower incremental capital–output ratios (ICORs) than is the case with countries that

Table 21.1 Financial depth, saving and growth in developing countries, 1965–87

Country group by GDP growth rate[a]	M2/GDP	Gross national savings/GDP	ICOR
High[b]	43[e]	28	3.80
Medium[c]	31	18.5	4.24
Low[d]	24	19	9.9

[a] High, medium, low ranked respectively as over 7 percent, 3–7 percent and less than 3 percent per annum.
[b] Seven countries.
[c] 51 countries.
[d] 72 countries.
[e] 1977–87.
Data are weighted averages multiplied by 100 and are based on a sample of 80 developing countries. M2 is currency in circulation plus demand, time and saving deposits at banks. Investment is gross domestic investment.
Source: World Bank, 1989a

have performed less well. Encouragement of greater financial depth has become a policy objective of the IMF and World Bank.

Financial depth itself depends, to some extent, on the willingness of wealth-holders to place savings with financial intermediaries (e.g. deposit banks, mutual funds, pension funds, life insurance companies) or to hold bonds or equity. Crucial here is the real rate of interest on, say, deposits. When this is *positive*, financial deepening is encouraged; but if it is negative, wealth-holders will seek other, less liquid, means in which to hold their wealth. Empirical evidence gathered by the World Bank (1989a, table 2.3) supports these assertions: grouping 80 developing countries according to the average level of real interest rates in 1974–85 showed that those developing countries with positive real interest rates had more financial depth, a higher rate of investment and faster economic growth than did countries with moderately negative real interest rates; and these in turn had superior performance compared with a third group of developing countries which had strongly negative real interest rates.

Negative real interest rates are associated with financial repression. Nominal interest rates in many developing countries are regulated by usury laws or are administered by the government; one result is that in many cases *real* deposit rates of interest are negative. Interest rate ceilings distort the economy as low deposit rates of interest discourage saving and divert saving into unproductive inflation hedges (e.g. real estate, foreign exchange). Moreover, a reduced level of saving in domestic currency deposits reduces the capacity of the financial system to make loans, so real loan rates of interest are often high. High loan rates not only compress the amount of investment but may also reduce its quality as only borrowers with high risk–return projects may be willing to pay the high loan rates.[3]

Financial intermediation is hindered by two other factors: segmented capital markets and extraordinarily high reserve ratios imposed on banks. The segmentation of capital markets is partly due to governmental efforts to cope with the high loan rates charged by banks. This is done by the government establishing public sector development banks designed to give low cost loans to favored enterprises. But loans are often not allocated efficiently. Moreover, as loan rates charged by development banks are below market rates, the subsidization of capital costs may lead to unduly high capital–labour ratios.

High reserve ratios – of the order of 50 percent or more – imposed on the banks also reduce the efficiency of financial intermediation. Reserve ratios act as a tax on the banks, diverting funds from commercial loans to the central bank and to the financing of the government's budget deficit. Financing the budget deficit is the main reason for imposing the high reserve ratios in the first place. In these circumstances, a strong positive relationship exists between the bank's *real* lending rate of interest and the rate of inflation, as well as a negative relationship between inflation and the *real* deposit rate of interest (McKinnon, 1981a). When inflation is high the government effectively imposes an inflation tax on the banks' reserve holding as well as all holders of local money. If the banks are to make even modest profits, they must recoup the "tax" from their clients – the depositors and the borrowers – which is done through the wide interest rate spread. But the wide spread reduces the efficiency of banks as financial intermediaries and drives some lenders and borrowers into the informal, unregulated, credit market.

The case for financial liberalization is that it will improve both the level of saving and the efficiency of the banking system in allocating investment funds: interest rate ceilings should be removed, reserve requirements reduced, and segmentation of financial markets diminished. The World Bank (1989a, ch. 4) judges that many developing countries in the 1980s made some, but not sufficient, progress towards financial liberalization. And a survey of monetary control techniques in nine developing countries by Johnston and Brekk (1989) was encouraging as it revealed that they were moving towards market-based instruments of monetary control (such as open market sales of treasury bills and central bank paper) rather than relying on interest rate and quantitative credit controls. The advantage of these reforms is that the market is allowed to allocate credit for investment purposes and the distortionary effects of direct controls are reduced.

The need for market-based reforms has not gone unchallenged. In the *new structuralist* view (e.g. Taylor, 1983; Van Wijnbergen 1983a, b; Kohsaka, 1984; Buffie, 1984), financial liberalization is not necessarily desirable. (See also our discussion of the new structuralists versus the IMF, p. 421–9.) According to the new structuralist scenario, the McKinnon–Shaw view on the benefits of financial liberalization is flawed because they failed to model financial institutions in developing countries correctly. In particular, McKinnon and Shaw failed to take into account the important role of the unregulated, "curb" market which also directs funds to borrowers. The essence of the new structuralist's criticism is that deregulation of the "official" market will lead to higher deposit rates of interest and this will divert deposits from the unofficial market (as well as from inflation hedges): financial deepening will indeed occur. But the rate of capital formation will not necessarily rise. Indeed, it may very well fall. The reasoning on this point is that, as the banks have to hold reserves against deposits, while no reserves are held by the unofficial money lenders, the diversion of savings to the banks will reduce the amount of funds available for lending. Indeed, there is empirical evidence which challenges that given earlier on the efficacy of financial deepening. Gonzales Arrieta's (1988) review of the empirical evidence on the relationship between national saving rates and real interest rates, and between real interest rates and GDP growth rates, did not find overwhelming support for the view that financial liberalization is necessarily desirable. Moreover, a number of country studies – e.g. by Van Wijnbergen (1982), Buffie (1984), Lim (1987), Karapatakis (1992) – have found that rising real interest rates have effects which, at least in the short run, are stagflationary – an effect which depends on the practice of full cost pricing, a rise in the cost of capital being passed on as higher prices. In Karapatakis's model,[4] increased lending by the banks finances the purchase of both working capital (e.g. raw materials) and fixed capital – but there is a one-period gestation lag between the increase in fixed capital and the increase in final output. Thus, increased bank lending shifts the aggregate demand function to the right before the aggregate supply curve shifts, so causing inflation.

However, there are many reasons that suggest that the unregulated sector is itself an inefficient intermediary. In particular, it is far from being a national market – which suggests that informational inefficiencies are higher than in a national banking system, many loans are for consumption purposes, it operates with high transaction costs (relative to large-scale banking which typically enjoys economies of scale) and funds are effectively siphoned off through monopolistic spreads between loan and deposit rates of interest. In effect, leakages from the unofficial market are at least as great as those from the banks (Owen and Fallas, 1989). Besides, thorough financial reform should lead to a substantial reduction in leakages from the banking system as reserve requirements are brought down.

Moreover, the relative efficacy as a financial intermediary of the banking system versus the unregulated market can be deduced from modern finance theory. Financial intermediaries such as banks exist partly because of the relative *in*efficacy of direct finance (e.g. through equity or bond markets). Both direct and indirect finance suffer from the problems of adverse selection and moral hazard (Jensen and Meckling, 1976; Fama and Jensen, 1983).[5] But because banks are specialists in selecting between potential borrowers, they have devised standard legal contracts to lessen moral hazard problems and have standardized monitoring routines, and they should be more efficient than (direct) financial markets at moving funds from borrowers to lenders. At least this is what modern principal–agent theory concludes.

To take an example of *dis*-disintermediation (i.e. diversion of funds back to the banks away from the fringe markets) consider the case of Uruguay. Severe regulation of the banking system beginning in the mid-1960s led to a fall in bank deposits by 65 percent by 1974 with a concurrent fall in bank lending for investment purposes. A lot of savings were diverted to the unregulated direct finance *parabancario* market (Perez-Campanero and Leone, 1991). There is no suggestion that growth of this market was due to anything other than regulation-induced disintermediation from the banks and would be accompanied by worse adverse selection and moral hazard problems (especially as norms devised to make borrowers reveal information about themselves were weak). It is therefore little wonder that reversion of most lending to the banking system (*dis*-disintermediation) was predicted by Perez-Campanero and Leone to raise rates of return on loans in that country.

As table 21.1 shows, there is also empirical evidence supporting the view that financial liberalization is beneficial to the rate of capital formation and rate of economic growth. Relaxing interest rate ceilings, so allowing positive real rates of interest, increases financial depth, raises the rate of saving and improves the quality of investment – as the ICOR falls. The last follows because, as the banks do not have to charge such high real loan rates, the adverse selection problem diminishes. Also, the reflow of funds out of the curb market back to the commercial banks should reduce informational problems in financial intermediation, so raising the quality of investment.

The last was indeed true in Uruguay following financial liberalization in the mid-1970s: the ICOR fell by 40 percent (to 4.0) between 1967–74 and 1975–81 (Hanson and de Melo, 1983). Positive associations between the real deposit rate of interest and the rate of economic growth have also been found by Fry (1978, 1988) and Gelb (1989). Other evidence on the positive effect of financial liberalization relates to the relationship between financial deepening and economic performance. The IMF (1983c), using cross-sectional data, found positive correlations between the growth rate of real financial assets and real GDP, and the World Bank (1989a) also linked the rate of economic growth to positive real interest rates and financial deepening.

To sum up on the new-structuralist view that financial liberalization would have a negative impact, three general points can be made which largely invalidate it.

1   Since it is admitted that the unofficial money market largely owes its existence to interest rate controls on the banking system, it is implicitly admitted that the unofficial money market is the relatively inefficient credit conduit.
2   If the first point is accepted, it is to be expected that regeneration of the banking system will increase the rates of capital accumulation and economic growth. Thus, even if the effect of financial liberalization in the short run is stagflationary, in the longer term the net present value of the policy is likely to be positive.
3   Thus, if the policy is judged to be beneficial in the longer term, even the short-term stagflation may be avoided by foreign borrowing (a payments deficit shifts the aggregate demand curve to the left), repaying the accumulated foreign debt out of higher GDP.

■ 21.2 Unhappy Experience with Financial Liberalization

Despite the arguments in favor, financial liberalizations in Latin America (Argentina, Chile and Uruguay) in the 1970s and early 1980s ended as disastrous failures: widespread bankruptcies, high inflation, rising unemployment, and the reimposition of financial repression. This occurred because no attention was paid to the correct *order of liberalization*. The nature of the integration of the liberalizing countries with the world economy was an important factor here (McKinnon, 1982a, 1989; Diaz Alejandro, 1985; Edwards and Edwards, 1987; World Bank, 1989b). Prior to the adoption of broad-based liberalization measures (of the banking system and foreign exchange and trade regimes), it is necessary to improve the macroeconomic background: particularly to reduce or to eliminate the government budget deficit and to reduce inflationary expectations.

To understand what went wrong it should be remembered that financial repression had been introduced in the first place in order to extract funds – to finance the fiscal deficit – directly from the commercial banks (through the high reserve ratios) and indirectly from both the banks and the non-bank public through the inflation "tax." Faced with the inflation "tax" the natural response of the non-bank public was to find inflation hedges and to practise currency substitution.

With respect to the inflation tax, faster expected monetary growth is reflected in a widening of the difference between the official and black (or parallel) market exchange rates and this is taken by the private sector as a signal that the inflation tax is increasing (Agenor, 1990a, b). Increased currency outflows through the unofficial market are induced and the inflation tax base is narrowed. Financing fiscal deficits by monetary expansion is self-defeating because the inflation tax base will be shrinking and ever higher rates of monetary expansion are required. Foreign exchange is increasingly diverted from the official market through, for example, under-invoicing of exports and over-invoicing of imports. To support the official exchange rate foreign exchange reserves (owned and borrowed) are used to absorb excess demand for foreign exchange on the official market and the domestic money supply contracts unless sterilized.[6]

The basic problem is that the financial liberalizations did not provide for financing of the budget deficit, even though they did relieve the domestic private sector from financing that deficit (e.g. when it chose currency substitution). With the fiscal deficit still in existence recourse was then made to foreign saving. This is why financial liberalization was so quickly followed by large current account deficits. In many cases the mechanism that brought the latter into existence was a sharp appreciation of the real exchange rate – caused by high real interest rates (needed to balance the market for loanable funds) – and induced capital inflows.

A simple stock adjustment model that helps to explain capital inflow following financial liberalization (in particular the removal of exchange controls) is provided by Edwards (1984). Capital inflow ΔK_t is determined by the model

$$\Delta K_t = \min[\theta(D_t^* - D_{t-1}), \overline{\Delta K}_t] \tag{21.1}$$

where D_t^* is the desired level of foreign debt (which for simplicity is assumed to bear a positive and stable relationship with a growing level of real GDP) and D_{t-1} is the actual stock of foreign debt.[7] The θ term is a one-period partial adjustment factor. The symbol $\overline{\Delta K}_t$ is the increase in foreign debt allowed by government regulations. Capital inflow will be the lower (minimum) of $\theta(D_t^* - D_{t-1})$ and $\Delta \bar{K}_t$. Assuming that capital-import controls have been binding for some time, a gap will have developed between the desired and actual levels of foreign debt as in each previous period $\theta(D_t^* - D_{t-1}) > \Delta \bar{K}_t$. When the capital account is liberalized, foreign capital borrowing will surge by the amount $\theta(D_t^* - D_{t-1})$, causing the exchange rate to appreciate. Indeed, the exchange rate will overshoot as capital inflow will tail off over time as the actual stock of foreign debt approaches the desired stock, and capital inflow diminishes.

Macroeconomic *in*stability results from this adjustment process. Profitability in the non-traded goods sector increases sharply causing an investment boom which, due to bottlenecks (e.g. in real estate), causes inflation. As the real exchange rate appreciates the traded goods sector contracts. Foreign debt climbs rapidly – partly to finance the resulting current account deficit and partly to finance capital flight. Capital flight occurs because the overvalued exchange rate is viewed as unsustainable. Then, when the exchange rate is sharply devalued, profitability in the non-traded goods sector falls, so inducing another round of economic adjustment.[8] Net foreign debt rose sharply and governmental indebtedness even faster (partly because the government had to take over the foreign debts of failing private companies and partly because of capital flight).

To stabilize international indebtedness the current account deficits have to be reduced, but how then could the budget deficits be financed if not by foreign borrowing? The governments are again forced to turn to the domestic private sector as the main source of saving and this requires the reimposition of financial repression.[9]

Thus, if financial liberalization is desirable, how is it best achieved? The answer to this question requires a discussion of the topic of "the order of liberalization."

21.3 The Order of Liberalization

While we have argued that low price-distortion economies have performed better than high price-distortion economies it does not necessarily follow that the *immediate* removal of all price distortions is desirable. Rather, economic reforms need to be sequentially ordered (McKinnon, 1982a; Edwards, 1984; Corbo and de Melo, 1987; Edwards and Edwards, 1987; Kahkonen, 1987; Fry, 1988; World Bank, 1989b; Collier and Gunning, 1992; Falvey and Kim, 1992). The economic collapse of the Southern Cone countries of Latin America in the early 1980s, described above, following incorrectly ordered and perhaps hasty financial and economic liberalizations, demonstrates the necessity of finding the correct order of liberalization. As indicated earlier, a relevant consideration is the theory of second best. Unambiguous results in a second best world are not always clearly defined. This leaves room to argue over just about anybody's preferred order of liberalization as results vary with the assumptions made.

Not only is the *order* of liberalization a matter of discussion but so too is its *pace*. In the light of the poor results that followed the Latin American financial and economic liberalizations in the 1970s and early 1980s, many economists now recognize that financial liberalization in developing countries is most successful when it is gradual (Kahkonen, 1987; McKinnon, 1989; Villanueva and Mirakhor, 1990). For example, Villanueva and Mirakhor examined the financial liberalization programmes[10] of two groups of countries: the "rapid liberalizes" (Argentina, Chile, Malaysia, Philippines, Turkey, and Uruguay) and the "gradual liberalizes" (Indonesia, South Korea, Singapore, Sri Lanka, and Taiwan). One reason for the relative success of the second group was found to be that they first provided a relatively stable macroeconomic environment – i.e. manageable budget deficits and slower rates of money growth – before reducing the degree of interest rate management and credit rationing. With interest rates stabilized, widespread bankruptcies were avoided and the rate of investment was maintained. However, a major problem for the rapid liberalizes was that they virtually abandoned management of interest rates and allocation of credit before the fiscal position was made sustainable. When they were free to do so the banks sharply raised interest rates and this led to widespread bankruptcies and the distortion of investment into more risky ventures.[11]

There are five broad areas where economic reforms and liberalization measures need to be taken:

1 reduction of the fiscal deficit;
2 liberalization of the domestic financial system;
3 liberalization of foreign trade;
4 liberalization of foreign exchange controls; and
5 exchange rate management.

An order of liberalization that is now accepted by at least some economists is the following sequence:

$$\text{reduce fiscal deficit} \rightarrow \text{financial liberalization trade reform} \rightarrow \text{reform exchange rate} \rightarrow \text{reform capital account}$$

Reducing the government's fiscal deficit as a necessary first step is pretty much universally accepted in the literature. Without reducing that deficit, financial liberalization would be seen by the private sector as being unsustainable and reversible (as was true in the cases of Argentina and Uruguay, discussed earlier). This intertemporal distortion would then be very likely to affect adversely the amount of intermediation that domestic banks would perform. This is because the rise in the real deposit rate of interest would be viewed as temporary, so it might not tempt wealth-holders to diversify into bank deposits, preferring instead to invest in inflation hedges or foreign currencies.[12]

There is support in the literature for the second policy in the liberalization sequence being financial liberalization combined with trade reform. Financial liberalization may be welfare raising for the reasons discussed in section 21.1:

allowing banks to pay higher real deposit rates of interest enables them to expand their role in the economy as efficient financial intermediaries. However, the increased flow of finance needs to be conditioned by correct price signals, otherwise investment may be taking place in the "wrong" sectors – i.e. not according to a country's comparative advantage and not where social rates of return are highest. It appears to be the case, therefore, that the more distorted are relative prices to begin with, the greater is the need to combine trade reform (tariff reduction and removal of quotas and other non-tariff barriers) with financial liberalization.

Financial liberalization also makes trade reform desirable. The infant industry argument for protection is partly based on the assumption that domestic capital markets are insufficiently forward looking (a fact which is reflected in the very high loan rates of interest typical in many developing countries). Reform of the financial system, therefore, weakens or removes the infant industry argument for protection. The order of trade reform is also a consideration according to Michaely et al. (1989) and the World Bank (1989b). Based on a study of 19 developing countries Michaely et al. (1989) found that a trade "liberalization introduced with a strong measure, rather than by minor and marginal policy steps, is likely to survive in the long run. A weak, hesitant, and very gradual attempt is much more likely to be reversed" (p. 4). Moreover, they found that the more entrenched are protectionist policies the greater is the benefit of a sharp change in policy, as this marks a clear break with the past. (It was also found, not surprisingly, that an inflationary fiscal background led to the reversal of a trade reform policy.)

More detailed analysis may be applied to determine the appropriate mix of trade reform and devaluation. Collier and Gunning (1992) apply a flexible price monetary approach to the balance of payments to a general equilibrium model of a small open economy. There is a small budget deficit, the Marshall–Lerner condition holds, labor, but not capital, is perfectly mobile between the importables, exportables and non-traded goods sectors and the capital account is closed.[13] Trade liberalization and an appropriate devaluation in the impact period leave the balance of payments and price level unchanged (liberalization lowers import prices and devaluation raises them). Then, the devaluation gradually stimulates exports as capital is slowly reallocated into this sector. The effect of the latter is to raise real income and the demand for money. The excess demand for money is satisfied by exchange rate appreciation. Hence, the authorities must be prepared to depreciate the exchange rate in the impact period more than is necessary for long run equilibrium – i.e. a managed "overshoot." This liberalization overshoot policy is *coherent* in the sense that price signals always point one way – to the reallocation of resources out of importables and into exportables. Coherence should contribute to the credibility of the reform package. Noncredible policies are likely to fail: e.g. if it is viewed that trade liberalization will be reversed, an import surge is likely to occur which will undermine the reforms.

An *incoherent* reform package gives conflicting resource allocation signals. One such case offered by Collier and Gunning (1992) is the aid-for-trade-liberalization packages sometimes offered to some African countries by the World Bank, which have been adopted by several African franc-zone countries. Thus, a small open economy reduces import restrictions and is given aid to support the balance of payments. To simplify matters the exchange rate is assumed to be unchanged. Liberalization of the trade account lowers import prices, raises real income and causes a consumer boom which "benefits" the non-traded goods sector (and foreign suppliers). The corresponding excess demand for foreign currency (the balance of payments deficit) is mopped up with the foreign aid and, as the domestic money supply falls, the domestic price level falls over time. The resulting depreciation of the real exchange rate stimulates exports. This policy package is incoherent because it signals an allocation of resources first into the non-traded goods sector and then out of that sector and into the exportables sector. Investment in the non-traded goods sector first rises and then falls. Similarly, labor moves into and then out of this sector. The price of assets such as land may also pass through a damaging boom-and-bust.

Even modifying the aid-for-trade-reform package to include devaluation does not entirely undo the incoherence, so, surprisingly, aid is not necessarily beneficial in the context of economic reform. The problem is similar to the Dutch "disease": a natural resource gift – natural gas in the Dutch case – appreciates the exchange rate and causes de-industrialization. But would the recipients of such a gift really be better off without it? Hallwood, Kemp and Wood (1983) argue that this is not so if the natural resource asset is transformed into capital goods rather than consumer goods. This would also seem to be the case with foreign aid. Incentives should be put into place to discourage a consumer boom and encourage an investment boom – especially in the export sector.

Several authors argue that trade reform should come before removal of exchange controls and the opening of the capital account.[14] One argument here is that freeing of the capital account may well cause a sharp exchange rate appreciation (as happened in Chile and Uruguay) and this would send price signals which conflict with those generated by the trade reform; e.g. an exchange rate appreciation offers protection to the importables sector just at the time when the trade reform is designed to remove it. A related argument is that the increased intermediation of funds by the banks ought to be conditioned by a non-distorted price structure. In fact, there is a good deal of agreement in the literature that opening of the capital account should be the last step in the liberalization process.

Finally, there is the matter of choice of exchange rate regime. Dual exchange rates (i.e. different rates for different classes of international transactions) and segmented foreign exchange markets (i.e. official and black market rates) should be removed early in the reform process. Dual exchange rates give distortionary price signals, while wide differences between the official and black market exchange rates encourage capital outflows. Apart from these stipulations, exchange rate policy is a tool as well as an objective of the liberalization process.

When the liberalization process is begun in a developing country inflation is usually well in excess of the average for the world as a whole and inflationary expectations have become deeply embedded. A forward-looking downward exchange rate crawl (i.e. based on a published table of future nominal rates), but at a slower pace than is suggested by current inflationary expectations, should help – if the government's resolve is credible – to cause inflationary expectations to be revised downward (Edwards and Edwards, 1987; McKinnon, 1989). Neither fixed nor floating rates may be credible brakes on inflationary expectations. The former may be expected to collapse (Chile's experiment with fixed rates during the period 1979–82 had to be abandoned when the real exchange rate became too highly appreciated), while the latter may be expected to be no more than accommodating inflation. But, if it is believed that fixed exchange rates are beneficial, and there is empirical evidence showing that those Latin American countries that have pegged their exchange rates to the US dollar have much lower and less variable rates of inflation than those countries that have not (Connolly, 1983), the rate should be fixed when it becomes possible to do so. But this will probably be near the end of the reform process when domestic monetary policy and international commodity arbitrage have imposed internal price stability.

In the next chapter we turn our attention to the financial and economic liberalization process in the formerly centrally planned economies. There distortions and second best problems are even more deeply embedded than in the worst of the developing countries.

NOTES

1 The general theory of second best was developed by Meade (1956) and Lipsey and Lancaster (1956–7).
2 The term "disequilibrium credit rationing" seems to be due to Goodhart (1991).
3 However, willingness on the part of borrowers to pay higher interest rates does not necessarily signal a better investment for the bank or society. This is the adverse to be willing to pay the highest interest rates. Goodhart (1991) points out that the adverse selection problem can be used to support arguments for interest rate ceilings. Moreover, since interest rate ceilings require banks to practise credit rationing, there is even a case for government direction of loans through directed credit programmes. Those interested in pursuing these arguments further should also see Stiglitz and Weiss (1981).
4 In fact, Karapatakis turns out to be critical of the neo-structuralist school.
5 See note 8 in chapter 19 for a definition of these terms.
6 The theory of the determination of the parallel market exchange rate has developed a large literature (e.g. Agenor, 1992; Dornbusch et al., 1983; Phylaktis, 1991). In this literature the exchange rate is treated as an asset price with foreign currency held as part of a diversified portfolio. Currency substitution into "black" dollars increases if the expected net return on them increases – being determined by the expected rate of depreciation of the official exchange rate and the cost of illegal activity (which includes the expected cost of getting caught). The parallel exchange rate is instantaneously determined at the level where residents are just willing to hold the existing stock of black dollars. The parallel market premium (i.e. the difference between the parallel and official exchange rates) also affects the size of the stock of black dollars, an increase in the premium increasing the supply: exporters the official market) and importers reduce purchases of black dollars because of their increase relative cost. In long-run equilibrium, the premium finds the level where asset-holders are just willing to hold the increment to the stock of black dollars. It may be noted that a

devaluation of the official exchange rate is unlikely to reduce the premium permanently unless the authorities adopt a credible policy of monetary restraint. The reason is straightforward: continued excess money growth in the long run leaves the desire to dishoard unchanged. Only in the short run may the devaluation of the official rate reduce the premium – because the devaluation increases the domestic price level, raising the desire to hoard, i.e. hold more domestic currency for transaction purposes rather than black dollars.

7 It has been shown that in the case of Uruguay domestic firms took advantage of the opening of the capital account to borrow in foreign currencies so as to finance real investment programmes (Perez-Campanero and Leone, 1991). At the time foreign exchange risk did not seem to be so great as investment projects seemed to be profitable, foreign exchange reserves were relatively large and the overhang of foreign debt was relatively small.

8 It is argued by Edwards and Montiel (1989) that delayed adjustment of fiscal deficits to long-run equilibrium values destabilize the economy both by moving macroeconomic variables (such as the nominal and real exchange rates, foreign exchange reserves, the price level and unemployment) away from equilibrium in the first place and, when the adjustment does finally take place, causing these variables to *overshoot* their long-run equilibrium values. So, for example, a large fiscal deficit financed by monetary expansion first causes the real exchange rate to appreciate, squeezing profitability and wages in the traded goods sector, and worsens the current account deficit. After adjustment takes place, the real exchange rate overshoots to the extent of its depreciation owing to the induced competitive weakness of the traded goods sector.

9 The discussion in the text assumes that the budget deficit remains large – as in Argentina and Uruguay. But Chile eliminated the budget deficit and still experienced chaos following liberalization. The reason there was that inflationary expectations remained high. With backward-looking wage indexation, inflation was slow to fall; and with the nominal exchange rate fixed from 1979 to 1982 the real exchange rate appreciated enormously.

10 Financial liberalization included interest rate and credit rationing policies, supervision of the banking system and banking regulations.

11 It is interesting to note that the case for gradualism in economic and financial reform in developing countries has not been expressed anything like as often in reference to the reform of the formerly centrally planned economies. Indeed, the opposite is the case: a "big bang" approach seems to be preferred by many, but not all, writers. See chapter 22.

12 Unless the fiscal deficit is removed (or at least reduced) the government will be expected again to resort to financial repression as the only means of financing the budget deficit.

13 The nearest real world example is said to be the post-1986 Nigerian trade reform.

14 For a contrary view that it does not matter whether the trade account is opened before or after the capital account see Kahkonen (1987), but his results are admitted to be rather "model specific."

22

Exchange Rates and Transition Economies

Transition economies (TE), or formally central planned economies are introducing rational price-structures to replace the distorted price-systems of central planning, and as part of the process they are integrating themselves into the international economy. An important relative price is the real exchange rate, because it acts as a bridge between efficient resource allocation in traded and non-traded goods on the one hand and macroeconomic internal–external balance on the other.

This chapter discusses the linkages that exist between economic transition and real and nominal exchange rates. Section 22.1 discusses some stylized facts, especially emphasizing the structural gradualness of the transitions that are occurring. Section 22.2 argues that successful economic transition can be seen as a fanning out of the internal and external balance functions introduced in section 4.2. Section 22.3 examines various shocks to a TE's equilibrium real exchange rate; and section 22.4 examines exchange rate overshooting early in the transition process. The final two sections discuss aspects of exchange rate policy in TEs.

22.1 Economic Reforms

While economic reform in some east European TEs began prior to the fall of Communism, strongly pro-market reforms date from 1989 at the earliest. There was a presumption even among solid pro-market advocates that wide-ranging reforms should be delivered into an appropriate "technical" universe of market-orientated institutions and legal frameworks. As these could not simply be wished into existence, "big bang" never occurred. Indeed, such was the scope of second-best problems that no economically sensible ordered sequence of reforms has been designed, and the actual sequencing of reforms in TEs has not followed any strict blueprint.

As a stylized fact traded goods sectors were liberalized before non-traded goods sectors, the soft budget constraint for non-traded goods being retained to ensure the provision of social goods and infrastructure via subsidized losses. This is not to deny that some reforms have occurred in non-traded goods, only that they have gone much further in the traded goods sector. The early opening of the traded goods sector was a relatively easy method for introducing rational commodity prices into a transforming economy. Retention of the non-traded goods sector in public ownership on the other hand was thought to be desirable because it could be used as a social cushion against the harshness of market reforms.

Thus, during the course of the transition during the 1990s, market-failures have remained. There was (and is) the continuing existence of a large number of monopolized industries, rigid labor markets, underdeveloped banking systems and capital markets, the pre-existence of inefficient and subsidized industries, and inadequate legal systems. An important element is that non-traded goods production largely remained subsidized through the soft budget constraint within the state sector so as to soak up the labor which is almost certainly being released by the liberalized traded goods sector.

The economic implication of the above is that the application of price equilibriating processes has developed only slowly. A good statement of this is:

> maintaining price controls in some sectors may diminish the advantages of price liberalization in others. *Liberalization must be fairly comprehensive to bring its full efficiency benefits.* (Sundakov, Ossowski, and Lane, 1994, p. 431, italics added)

Also:

> competition can function in an effective and desirable way only when enterprises have the means and incentives to pursue their individual interests, and when the institutions of financial discipline are in place, such as the absence of systematic subsidies and capricious taxation, the separation of lenders from borrowers, a mechanism to remove unsatisfactory management, and the ultimate threat of bankruptcy. (Hardy, 1992, pp. 310–11)

Thus, during the transitional process relative prices have become effective signals for resource allocation only gradually, and in the meantime large but shrinking sectors of TEs have remained rather unresponsive to relative price signals.

22.2 Microeconomic–Macroeconomic Equilibrium

Figure 22.1 (which repeats figure 4.1) shows internal and external balance in macroeconomic and microeconomic equilibrium.

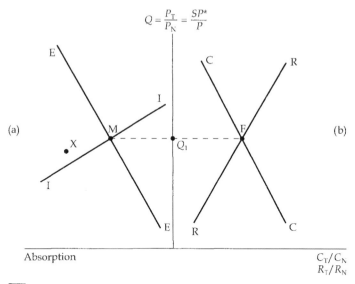

Figure 22.1 Microeconomic–macroeconomic internal–external balance

As the real exchange rate, $Q = SP^*/P = P_T/P_N$, is the relative price of traded-to-nontraded goods

$$C_T/C_N = f(Q) \qquad f' < 0 \tag{22.1}$$

$$R_T/R_N = g(Q) \qquad g' > 0 \tag{22.2}$$

where C_T/C_N is the ratio of traded (T) to non-traded (N) goods in consumption and R_T/R_N their ratio in domestic production (with $C_T + C_N$ = absorption, and $R_T + R_N$ = real GDP). $f' < 0$ as absorption increasingly favors traded goods as Q appreciates (falls) and reduces their relative price;[1] and $g' > 0$ as real depreciation raises the competitiveness of traded goods production. In figure 22.1b, f is represented by CC and g by RR.

The trade balance, TB, can be written as

$$TB = H[g(Q) - f(Q)] \qquad H_Q > 0 \tag{22.3}$$

As excess supply of T goods is a positive function of Q, the trade surplus is greater the larger are f' and g' in absolute value, i.e. the flatter are CC and RR.

The slopes of the microeconomic functions in figure 22.1b govern those of the macroeconomic functions in figure 22.1a. Thus, the more responsive are the shares of traded goods in production and consumption to a change in Q the flatter will be the external balance function, EE, as any given increase in Q will cause a larger trade surplus (in figure 22.1b and equation 22.3) which, to maintain external balance, will need to be offset by a larger *increase* in absorption in figure 22.1a.

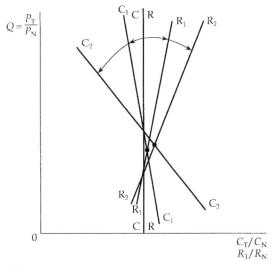

Figure 22.2 The opening of an RR/CC fan

Similarly with internal balance on II: the more sensitive are CC and RR to a change in Q, the flatter is II – as a given increase in Q causes a larger trade surplus, which needs to be offset by a larger *reduction* in absorption to maintain internal balance.

As the transition proceeds the absolute values of f' and g' will begin to increase from previously low values under central planning – see figure 22.2. "Complete" central planning could be defined as $f' = g' = 0$ where the central planner is entirely responsible for production and consumption allocation, hence the vertical superimposed CC/RR functions. However, the introduction of market allocation processes into such a system allows consumption and production decisions to become price-sensitive and the signs of the respective derivatives will appear.[2] But the transition in RR is gradual as it has not been possible to create a market economy in resource allocation all at once. Similarly, CC will over time become more responsive to the real exchange rate as domestic consumers and, especially, producers gradually become more price-sensitive.[3]

If a transition is going well, we liken the gradual increasing slopes of the RR and CC functions to a slow opening of a fan. But if a transition is not going well the fan will not be opening very much at all.

The flatter the RR/CC and II/EE functions become, the stronger will be the balance of payments adjustment mechanisms. Thus, if RR and CC have become quite flat a deviation of the *actual* Q from its *equilibrium* will cause strong balance of trade disequilibrium which might quickly set off automatic adjustment – perhaps through changes in the money stock, along the lines of the monetary approach to the balance of payments; or, if an economy is off of its internal balance function – which is quite likely, via wage and price adjustments in labor and commodity markets. Hence with relatively flat schedules, reflecting the fact that transitional reforms have begun to bite, balance of payments disequilibria tend to set off strong macroeconomic and microeconomic resource reallocation processes.

In contrast, in a situation where the schedules are still steep as they were under central planning – because the transition has hardly started or has been blocked in some way, the automatic adjustment forces will remain weak. In this case, when the actual real exchange rate is away from the equilibrium rate, there is not much to induce Q to trend to its equilibrium value, or, if there is a tendency to return it will be a slow drawn-out process. For example, the gap between a pair of near vertical RR and CC functions – even well away from equilibrium – will yield only a small payments deficit, so the adjustment in the money stock is rather minor. Similarly, with the gap between a pair of near vertical EE and II schedules: macroeconomic disequilibrium need not be all that great, even though at the microeconomic level the economy is not in a healthy condition.

22.3 Shocks to the Equilibrium Real Exchange Rate

In this section we consider three shocks to a TE's equilibrium real exchange rate. If as seems likely the adoption of transitional polices cause the share of traded goods in production to increase, i.e. R_T/R_N increases, the RR function shifts to the right in figure 22.3b to R_1R_1. The trade balance improves at Q_1 as the equilibrium real exchange rate appreciates to Q_2. This appreciation comes about either through a rise in the domestic price level – caused perhaps by excess demand

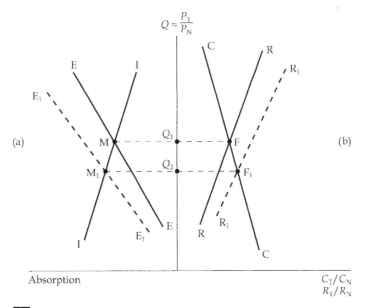

Figure 22.3 A positive shock to the share of traded goods in production (R_T/R_N increases)

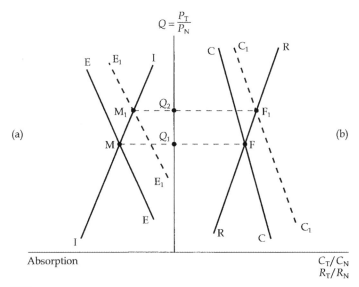

Figure 22.4 A positive shock to the share of traded goods in consumption (C_T/C_N increases)

for non-traded goods, or through nominal exchange rate appreciation due to a strengthening external account. There is likely to be a positive income effect – at least in the long run as reform policies take hold – and this will shift the CC function, depending upon the relative strengths of the income elasticities of demand for traded and non-traded goods. If the former is greater than the latter, the CC function will shift to the right and this will moderate the real appreciation.

The external balance function in figure 22.3a shifts from EE to E_1E_1 as the strengthened external account allows absorption to increase at any Q. Internal–external balance moves from M to M_1 as absorption must increase down the internal balance function to offset the effect of the switch of demand away from domestic goods as a result of the real exchange rate appreciation.

If transitional policies raise C_T/C_N, perhaps due to the opening of foreign trade and increased availability of foreign goods, the CC function shifts to the right in figure 22.4b to C_1C_1 and the equilibrium real exchange rate depreciates to Q_2. External balance in figure 22.4a moves from EE to E_1E_1 and the new internal–external balance from M to M_1. Absorption decreases up II to maintain internal balance which has been disturbed by the depreciation of the real exchange rate which has switched foreign demand towards the TE's goods.

Given the revealed sequencing of reforms in TEs, subsidies to the traded goods sector have already been removed when they are finally withdrawn from the nontraded goods sector. How does the latter policy affect the equilibrium real exchange rate?

In figure 22.5b, RR shifts to the right as production of non-traded goods falls and resources are reallocated to the traded goods sector. EE shifts to E_1E_1 as a

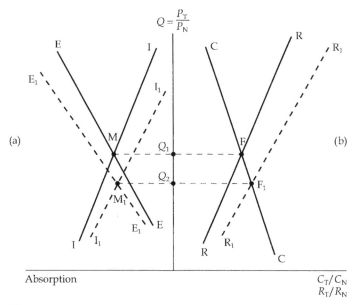

Figure 22.5 Removal of subsidies to non-traded goods

greater level of absorption can be supported at any Q. If, as a result of the removal of subsidies, structural unemployment increases, the internal balance function in figure 22.5a shifts to the right as absorption at any Q must be reduced. Hence, the real exchange rate appreciates – the relative price of non-traded goods has increased. Income effects on CC could stem from the increased equilibrium rate of unemployment, but we ignore these here.

■ 22.4 The Real Exchange Rate in Asset Market Equilibrium

Assuming excess demand for goods under central planning, the freeing of foreign trade provided an opportunity to turn excess money balances – known as a *monetary overhang*[4] – either directly into imported goods for immediate consumption or into superior stores of value, such as imported cigarettes (as in Calvo and Frenkel, 1991). Accordingly, the share of traded goods in consumption increased on the freeing of the foreign account and the CC function shifts to the right as in figure 22.4b. However, this real depreciation is temporary because when the monetary overhang is worked off, the rightward shift of CC undoes itself.

Alternatively, the monetary overhang may be worked off when prices are liberalized and wealth-holders divest excess money balances into domestic goods. In this case, excess demand for goods leads to a rapid inflation which, to maintain the equilibrium real exchange rate, requires a corresponding proportionate depreciation in the nominal exchange rate. In this case the behavior of the real exchange rate depends on the relative rates of domestic price inflation and nominal exchange rate depreciation. If domestic prices are sticky relative to the exchange rate a real exchange rate overshoot may occur.

22.4.1 Asset market equilibrium: real exchange rate overshooting

Excessive depreciation of real exchange rates at the beginning of the process of economic reform was a common phenomena. Calvo and Frenkel (1991) and Richards and Terseman (1995) link this to asset market considerations. A well-known paradigm is that asset markets clear more quickly than do goods markets, and this can give rise to nominal exchange rate overshooting. Calvo and Frenkel (1991) predicted this for the early stages of transition. Below we set out how real exchange rate overshooting may occur in a model with a distinct transitional economy flavor.

In equilibrium, asset portfolio shifting by residents will tend to equalize the return on domestic and foreign liquid assets. The foreign asset may be a storable commodity, such as cigarettes, or it could be foreign currency which pays no interest. The domestic asset is taken to be money balances which also pay no interest. This was the main form of holding liquid assets in many TEs. Given expectations of inflation (which is likely given the existence of monetary overhangs, and the likelihood of monetization of budget deficits), the return on the domestic asset is expected to be negative. For returns to be equalized in equilibrium the foreign asset must be bought at a price which is expected to *fall* relative to the price of domestic goods. This implies that in figure 22.4b, CC will shift even further to the right in instantaneous asset market equilibrium than is in fact shown. The depreciation of Q being caused by a sharp rise in the nominal exchange rate, S. Beyond the impact period Q (= SP^*/P) will begin to appreciate, so yielding the negative return on the foreign asset. Notice that if Q did not on impact depreciate enough, the return on the foreign asset would be greater than on the domestic asset and that there would still be an incentive to accumulate the foreign asset – so further depreciating S and Q.

The appreciation of Q from its overshot position will be brought about by a combination of nominal exchange rate appreciation and domestic inflation. To see this define the domestic price level as:

$$P = aP_T + (1 - a)P_N \qquad (22.4)$$

where a is the share of traded goods in domestic consumption, $a > 0$. Also let

$$P_T = P_T^* S = S, \text{ by defining } P_T^* = 1, \qquad (22.5)$$

and assume no foreign inflation. Therefore, the rate of domestic inflation is given by:

$$\dot{P} = a\dot{S} + (1 - a)\dot{P}_{\dot{N}} \tag{22.6}$$

and

$$\dot{S} = (1/a)\dot{P} - [(1 - a)/a]\dot{P}_{\dot{N}} \tag{22.7}$$

If the nominal exchange rate is appreciating from its overshot position, $\dot{S} < 0$, it follows that the price of non-traded goods is inflating faster than the general price level, P. Or, to put it the other way around, the price of traded goods is inflating less quickly than the general price level. Hence, the real value in terms of domestic currency of the foreign storable traded good is declining in terms of command over domestic goods.

22.4.2 Empirical evidence on TE exchange rate overshooting and equilibrium real rates

Hallwood and MacDonald (1997a, b) confirm that real exchange rates in the early 1990s were mean reverting from overshot levels to equilibrium levels in several TEs. As we have just seen a number of factors may be cited as explaining this under-valuation: a large pent-up demand for foreign assets, which are in limited supply; substitution from the domestic currency as the monetary overhang from the planning period generates a rapid burst of inflation; in the absence of knowledge of where the equilibrium rate is, convertibility forces the monetary authorities to allow the currency to become undervalued. The real rate then appreciates from its original overshoot, due both to the self-correction to the initial under-valuation and also because the transformation process itself imparts an appreciation. A number of factors can be cited in support of the latter phenomenon. First, productivity effects are seen as crucially important, both because of a Balassa–Samuelson effect and also due to a demand-side effect – the rising income in the transitional process increases the demand for non-traded goods which generates a real appreciation. Second, non-traded prices are set too low prior to the transition. When they are freed they rise to match production costs, thereby appreciating the real exchange rate. Third, on the tradable side, goods were, in general, of poor quality and badly marketed prior to the transition; after the transition these factors improve and this is reflected in an improvement in the terms of trade. Finally, since potential returns on capital are high in these countries, this leads to a net long-term capital inflow which also appreciates the real rate.

Rather than present a formal model, Halpern and Wyplosz (1997) use three different measures of the real exchange rate to bring out the driving forces of real exchange rates in transitional economies. The three *equilibrium* real rates are the CPI-based real rate, q, the US dollar wage real exchange rate, ω and the relative price of non-traded to traded goods prices. In practice they focus on q and ω. Halpern and Wyplosz posit the following model for q:

$$q = k + \gamma_1(a^T - a^N) + \gamma_2(\rho^T - \rho^N) + \gamma_3\theta. \tag{22.8}$$

where q is defined as the foreign currency price of domestic currency, k denotes the terms of trade (or more directly a quality of traded goods measure), the second term is a Balassa–Samuelson effect. The ρ^T term represents the excess of (sectoral) real wages over (sectoral) productivity which is initially assumed positive in the traded sector and negative in the non-traded sector. The correction of this imbalance over time imparts an appreciation into the real exchange rate. The final term, θ, represents the relative wage between the non-traded and traded sectors. Initially, the wages in the non-traded sector are assumed to be below those in the traded sector but over time the gap should close, thereby imparting an appreciation into the real exchange rate. The reduced form for the US dollar wage is:

$$\omega = (\rho - \rho^*) + (a - a^*) + q \tag{22.9}$$

where a represents aggregate marginal productivity of labor, ρ is the aggregate excess of wages over labor productivity, and an asterisk denotes a foreign magnitude. The key element in this relationship is seen to be the influence of aggregate productivity, instead of sectoral productivity, on the real exchange rate.

The empirical model is estimated for ω rather than q, but both (22.8) and (22.9) are used to motivate the kind of explanatory variables entering the dollar wage equation. In particular, they focus on: a number of indicators of economic effectiveness (the k term), such as human capital (proxied by education), the size of government, and the size of the agricultural sector; average productivity (a) is measured by GDP per worker; data on differences in productivity and effectiveness across sectors ($a^T - a^N$ and $\rho^T - \rho^N$) are not available for most countries and are therefore not modeled.

The empirical tests were undertaken on a large panel data set for the following country groupings: OECD, Africa, Southeast Asia, Latin America, and transition economies (in total they have 80 countries in their panel). Halpern and Wyplosz are able to distinguish between these different groupings using fixed and random effects estimators. Their measure of aggregate average productivity (GDP per worker) produces a large and significant coefficient which is shown to be sensitive to the inclusion of regional and country dummies – it declines quite dramatically as such dummies are added in. Conversely the coefficient on investment in human capital (proxied using secondary school enrolment) rises as the regional and country dummies are introduced. They also find that a 10 percent decline in the size of agriculture relative to industry increases the dollar wage by between 1 and 2 percent. A 10 percent increase in the size of the government raises wages by 3 to 6 percent. This effect is interpreted as measuring the effect of public services and infrastructure on aggregate productivity.

These panel estimates are then used to back out measures of the equilibrium exchange rate for the transitional economies. The estimates are derived with and without a planned economy dummy. The measure of equilibrium without the dummy is seen as an upper bound, to be reached once the market economy institutions are in place and functioning smoothly. The rate with the dummy gives the lower bound and hence the "true" measure of equilibrium lies somewhere in between. With the exceptions of Slovenia and Hungary, all countries started the transition process with significantly undervalued exchange rates. At the time of writing, countries which aggressively pursued market reform policies (namely, the Czech Republic and Poland) have real rates which are not very far from equilibrium (the lower bound); the same appears to be true of Croatia, Slovenia, and possibly Hungary. The remaining transitional countries studied (Bulgaria, Romania, and the Slovak Republic) all have real rates which are undervalued.

Perhaps not surprisingly, the basic upshot of the work of Halpern and Wyplosz is that PPP is not a suitable vehicle for analyzing transitional real rates. Also the need for real appreciation during the transition period has important implications for the choice of exchange rate policies and regime. For example, if a transitional economy decides to peg its exchange rate to a western country then during the transitional period the real exchange rate appreciation will require a higher inflation rate at home relative to overseas (if the authorities have a low inflation target then the nominal exchange rate should be allowed to float freely). Finally, given the need for a real exchange rate appreciation during the transition period, trying to resist it would only produce destablizing capital inflows.

■ 22.5 On Knowing the Correct Real Exchange Rate

If the economy is to the left of the II and EE functions, e.g. at point X in figure 22.1a, there is excess demand for goods and for foreign exchange. Automatic adjustment through rising prices in the goods and foreign exchange markets should eventually clear both markets by adjusting spending and Q to their appropriate levels. A classic prescription is that it is futile for the government to interfere with this process – e.g. by maintaining the level of the real money supply. However, it may hurry the process along by the (also classic) adoption of policies of expenditure reduction (to lower absorption) and expenditure switching (to be rid of excess demand for foreign exchange) – see section 4.5.

Notice that in figure 22.2 the intersections of the fanning CC and RR functions define a set of equilibrium real exchange rates. Not withstanding Halpern and Wyplosz (1997), in practice it is very difficult to calculate the equilibrium real exchange rate as small wobbles in either of two steep functions can make a large difference. One of the lessons of our discussion is, then, that it is probably impossible to define a trajectory over time for a transforming economy's equilibrium real exchange rate. This concurs with Edwards' (1989) conclusion made with respect to developing countries. The starting point – that passed on from central planning – is arbitrary, and the slopes and positions of both CC and RR will be changing. This makes exchange rate policy in the TEs particularly difficult to resolve. McKinnon (1991) has argued that the policy toward the nominal exchange rate should be passive, adjusting with the price level. The discussion here supports this view because, with steep CC and RR functions, approximate macroeconomic balance can occur with a quite wide range of real exchange rates. In other words, a government should not overly worry about finding the correct real exchange rate.

22.5.1 Policy-targeting of *Q*?!

It has been shown above that the equilibrium real exchange rate is determined by the relative abundance of traded and non-traded goods in macroeconomic equilibrium. As such, targeting its level is tantamount to government price-fixing and it is almost bound to set off undesirable side effects. Attempting to fix *Q* above the equilibrium level by allowing *S* to depreciate at a faster rate than the rate of inflation, perhaps in an attempt to stimulate exports, will lead to accelerating inflation. While attempting to fix the real exchange rate below the equilibrium level by allowing the rate of currency depreciation to be less than the rate of inflation, perhaps in an attempt to reduce the rate of inflation, is likely to run into a foreign exchange crisis as reserves are depleted. In support of these points Richards and Terseman (1995) argue that as the equilibrium real exchange rate is changing, it is not possible to target both the nominal exchange rate and the price level. With a pegged exchange rate, endogenous changes in the money stock caused by balance of payments disequilibria will ultimately determine the price level, and/or a given pegged rate will not be defensible.

Implicit real exchange rate targeting may come about in another way. Suppose that the government, having added various transitional reforms, finds that the real exchange rate has appreciated due to the combination of a pegged exchange rate and inflation, and that the equilibrium rate of unemployment has also increased – perhaps due to the withdrawal of subsidies to the non-traded goods sector ahead of the ability of the traded goods sector to absorb the excess labor. Thus, there is a rightward shift of the II function in figure 22.1a. If the government sees the cause of rising unemployment as being due to the appreciation of *Q* – rather than to a higher equilibrium rate of unemployment – it may attempt to engineer a real exchange rate depreciation through an increase in the nominal exchange rate. But such a real depreciation will take the economy to the left of the appropriate II function as demand switches toward domestic goods. This is both inflationary and futile because the real exchange rate depreciation will eventually have to reverse itself once the government tires of the accelerating rate of inflation that it is causing.

22.6 Choice of an Exchange Rate Regime by a TE

We have argued that in a transitional economy resource allocation in response to changes in the real exchange rate are very likely to be price-inelastic. That is, the RR and CC functions are likely to begin rather steep relative to what they will eventually become and in comparison with those of fully-fledged market economies. Does this observation have any relevance to the choice of an exchange rate regime by a TE?

We think that this price-inelasticity in TEs extends Williamson's (1983, 1994) proposal for the management of nominal exchange rates within a wide target zone of, say, plus/minus 15 percent. In a transitional economy, even with low inflation, because of the low price-responsiveness of resource allocation, variations in the nominal exchange rate of this magnitude will probably not make that much difference to either macroeconomic stability or to resource allocation between traded and non-traded goods. But foreign exchange markets do need some sort of lead by the authorities. The problem is, that with resource allocation being unresponsive to the real exchange rate, the real exchange rate does not have a strong center of gravity on which to anchor itself. (It would have such an anchor if resource allocation and, therefore, the trade balance were more responsive to the real exchange rate – as with elastic RR and CC functions.) The level of the real exchange rate, and more especially the nominal exchange rate for a given price level, is left open to, perhaps, volatile speculative pressures. This argument is even more true when considering the very short run – the sort of time period in which speculators operate. In this time-frame resource allocation at the macroeconomic level is highly inelastic with respect to the real exchange rate, and the real and nominal exchange rates have no macroeconomic anchor – they are entirely left to asset market equilibrium considerations which may operate with discount rates that effectively discount out of view longer-term expectations for macroeconomic variables. All this amounts to a transitional government aiming for macroeconomic balance, especially containing the rate of inflation, while adopting a policy toward the nominal exchange rate that allows it to float within quite wide limits. Some constraint of wild fluctuations in the nominal exchange rate is desirable, but there is no particular advantage to managing the nominal exchange rate within the constraint band.[5]

NOTES

1 We assume throughout that substitution effects dominate.
2 Under "complete" central planning the production possibility frontier between T and N goods is rectangular with its interior corner located at the point chosen by the central planners. Changes in relative prices will not alter this allocation. As market processes are introduced, the production possibility frontier gains some curvature – showing that a change in relative prices can affect the allocation of production. Similarly, with "complete" central planning the community indifference curves are rectangular, with the corner point chosen by the central planner. The introduction of market processes again introduces curvature and price responsiveness.
3 It is likely that the rate of change of CC will be faster than RR because it is probably easier to reallocate consumption than restructure production.
4 Monetary overhangs are thought to have existed in Bulgaria, Romania, and the Soviet Union. Cottarelli and Blejer (1992) estimated that by end-1990 the overhang in the Soviet Union was about 20 percent of GDP and would have required an increase in the price level of about 50 percent.
5 Begg, Halpern and Wyplosz (1999) and McKinnon (1993) also support the idea of a wide-band target zone. They also argue that the choice of exchange rate regime is of secondary importance compared with the priorities of fiscal reform and achieving monetary discipline.

23

International Debt

Now passed the crisis stage, international indebtedness still remains a major problem for many developing countries. In the first three sections of this chapter we describe the debt problem, the growth of international indebtedness and the burden of debt on economic growth. Section 23.4 describes an economic model that explains capital flight from debtor countries in terms of differential perceptions of risk between investors in debtor and creditor countries. Capital flight is shown (in section 23.5) to worsen the problem of governmental foreign indebtedness. Section 23.6 explains why international banks continued to increase lending even as default risk increased. In the last two sections various debt reform proposals are discussed.

It is recommended to read this chapter in conjunction with chapter 14 on currency crises and speculative attack.

 ## 23.1 The Debt Problem

The international debt crisis dates from 1982 when Mexico, followed by a host of other developing countries, could not service its debts and had to have them rescheduled. Between 1980 and 1990 there were about 300 multilateral debt relief agreements. Foreign debt has been a problem for debtor countries since at least the 1960s when the Pearson Commission emphasized the need for increased foreign aid and debt relief. In 1982 international debt became a "crisis" for the creditor banks as they faced writing-off loans. While the banks coped, many

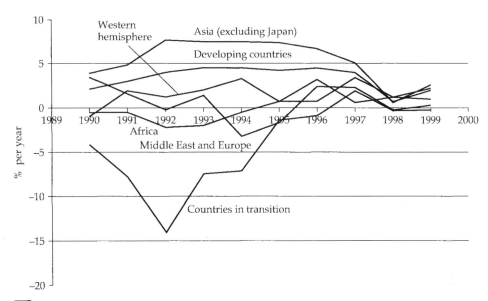

Figure 23.1 Real per capita annual GDP growth, developing countries and transition economies, 1990–9

Source: IMF, *World Economic Outlook*, October 1998, table 5, page 177

developing countries were burdened by high levels of foreign indebtedness. The 1980s have been termed a "wasted decade" for many developing countries as their per capita income grew at an annual average of only 1.9 percent, and it was negative or zero in three regions, only being positive in Asia. In the decade of the 1990s, however, annual average per capita income growth picked up to 3.3 percent and it became positive in all developing country regions – see figure 23.1. It was sharply negative in countries in transition (i.e. the formerly centrally planned economies) until mid-decade.

In 1993 the foreign indebtedness of developing countries was almost $1.5 trillion – most of it owed to private creditors, rising to about $1.9 trillion at the turn of the century. The World Bank identifies 25 *low-income* countries, almost all in Africa, as being "*severely* indebted". A further 20 *middle-income* countries, 12 of them in Latin America, are also classified as "severely indebted". The debt crisis was until the late-1990s – when it burst upon East Asia (see chapter 13) – largely confined to Africa and Latin America, although by 1993 in Latin America rates of economic growth were beginning to recover and this continent was able to re-enter international capital markets. African countries are primarily indebted to official donors (bilateral and multilateral), while Latin American and Asian countries are most heavily indebted to international banks.

As shown in figure 23.2 external debt as a percentage of exports of goods and services fell during the course of the 1990s. Similar easing was experienced by developing countries in "the" debt service ratio – i.e. debt service payments (interest plus amortization) as a percentage of export earnings – figure 23.3.

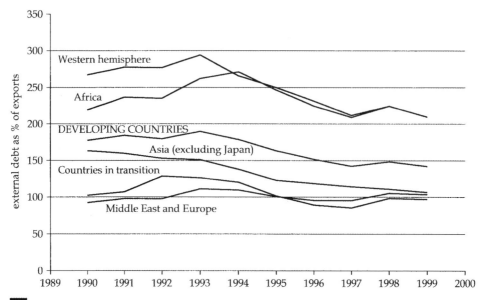

Figure 23.2 External debt as percentage of exports of goods and services: developing countries and transition economies, 1990–9

Source: IMF, *World Economic Outlook*, October 1999, table 38, page 230

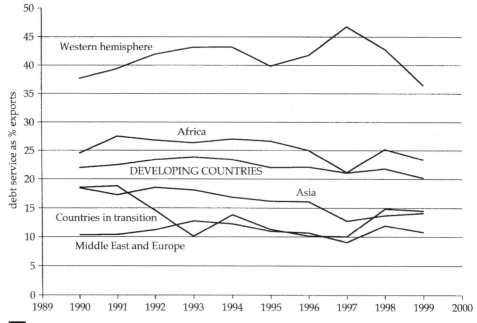

Figure 23.3 Debt service payments as percentage of exports of goods and services, developing countries and transition economies, 1990–9

Source: IMF, *World Economic Outlook*, table 33, page 219

23.2 Growth of International Debt

The increase in a country's net foreign indebtedness is equal to the current account deficit which has to be financed by borrowing from abroad. Using the national income accounting identities,[1] the proximate causes of a current account deficit are

$$(X - M) - R_F = (S - I) + (T - G) \tag{23.1}$$

where the current account (the trade account $X - M$ plus net interest paid abroad, R_F) is equal to the sum of net private and public sector saving.[2] It follows that if net foreign indebtedness is not to increase, the trade surplus must be large enough to finance interest payments abroad – which requires positive net domestic saving (i.e. public plus private).

Anything that causes I to rise relative to S, G relative to T, M relative to X or R_F to increase can cause net foreign indebtedness to increase. As a broad generalization, in the ten years up to the debt crisis of 1982 each one of these factors was unfavorable for the developing countries as a group, certainly those dependent upon oil imports. Both external and internal factors were responsible. The internal factors were either self-inflicted – especially the failure to raise domestic savings rates and to constrain budget deficits – or resulted from failure to adjust to external shocks. In fact, in the analytical model of Edwards and Montiel (1989) it is shown that the existence of "devaluation crises" provoked by payments deficits is not so much due to the occurrence of "shocks" (internal or external) as to failure to adjust to them quickly.

The oil-price shocks of 1973–4 and 1979–80 played havoc with non-oil developing country trade balances. Hallwood (1980) and Hallwood and Sinclair (1981) show that about three-quarters of the growth in developing country trade deficits was due to higher oil prices. The counterpart – on the right-hand side of equation (23.1) – was that, as domestic expenditure on oil increased, savings fell relative to investment and fiscal balances deteriorated as some governments subsidized petroleum prices.

The effect of the second oil shock was compounded by a sharp rise in real interest rates, worsening terms of trade, and export-volume loss due to the world recession of 1981–2 (table 23.1). In 1982, and for several years thereafter, threatened sovereign default was largely handled by capitalizing interest arrears and rescheduling debt repayments. By the late 1980s it was more widely recognized that many debtors were *insolvent* and that debt forgiveness was necessary – as acknowledged at the Group of Seven's Toronto Summit in 1988. At about the same time the International Monetary Fund (IMF) began to pay greater attention to the idea of an international debt facility through which debt may be forgiven; and the Brady plan (1989) incorporated an element of debt forgiveness.

The main aspects of the East Asian international financial crisis of 1997 are discussed in chapter 14. We suggested there that speculative attack against East Asian currencies was probably justified on the basis of either or both macroeconomic or microeconomic (financial system) fundamentals.

Table 23.1 The effect of exogenous shocks on the external debt of non-oil developing countries

Effect	Amount (billion dollars)
Oil-price increase in excess of US inflation, 1974–82 cumulative	260
Real interest rate in excess of 1961–80 average, 1981 and 1982	41
Terms of trade loss 1981–2	79
Export volume loss caused by world recession, 1981–2	21
Total	401
Memorandum items	
Total debt 1973	130
1982	612
Increase 1973–82	482

Source: Cline, 1984

23.2.1 The debt-service ratio

Although no measure of a country's debt burden can show the optimal level of external debt, the debt-service ratio (DSR) – the ratio of debt service to export earnings – is useful. When it is high (say, over 25 percent) it indicates that a country is vulnerable to adverse changes in its foreign trade or the level of international interest rates. Because a country's primary obligation is to service foreign loans, domestic interest rates may have to be raised and vital imports may have to be cut with economic performance suffering.

The DSR can be written as DSR = DS/X where DS is debt service and X is export earnings – both expressed in a foreign currency, say, the US dollar. It follows that

$$\frac{\mathrm{dDSR}}{\mathrm{DSR}} = \frac{\mathrm{dDS}}{\mathrm{DS}} - \frac{\mathrm{d}X}{X} \tag{23.2}$$

The DSR increases if debt service grows at a faster rate than export revenues.

The annual absolute increase in debt service (dDS) depends upon four factors: this year's trade deficit (with a positive sign), the interest rate paid on this increment to foreign debt outstanding, the change in the rate of interest (if any) paid on debt outstanding at the beginning of the year, and the change in repayments of principal (known as "amortization"). The annual absolute dollar increase in debt-service obligations is given by

$$\mathrm{dDS} = i\mathrm{TD} + \mathrm{d}iD + \mathrm{d}A \tag{23.3}$$

where iTD is the interest paid on the current year's trade deficit (i is the interest rate and TD the trade deficit); diD is the change in the amount of interest paid on debt outstanding at the beginning of the year (di is the change in the rate of interest) and dA is the change in annual repayment (or amortization) of principal.

Dividing equation (23.3) through by DS and substituting into equation (23.2) yields

$$\frac{d\text{DSR}}{\text{DSR}} = \frac{i\text{TD}}{\text{DS}} + \frac{di\text{D}}{\text{DS}} + \frac{dA}{\text{DS}} - \frac{dX}{X}$$

(23.4)

Thus, the DSR rises if the trade deficit, the interest rate or annual amortization rises, or if the export growth rate falls. Annual amortization changes with the time profile of the repayment schedule: if the average maturity of debt lengthens, *ceteris paribus*, annual amortization falls. Most debt rescheduling agreements push current amortization off into the future thereby reducing the present level of A (dA/dDS is negative). But the success of this tactic depends rather on the ability to reduce the trade deficit or to raise the rate of export growth. Recurrent failure here means that sooner or later a second and a third rescheduling is needed. As many countries have repeatedly had their debt rescheduled it is clear that rescheduling is often only a palliative.

23.3 Debt and Economic Growth

After the debt crisis broke in 1982, the hope was that developing countries could "grow their way out of debt" (see Cline, 1984). Faster economic growth would raise debt-service capacity and reduce the ratio of debt to income. In fact, even if a country is able to achieve a balanced trade account, the rate of growth of nominal income must be at least as great as the nominal interest rate paid on debt outstanding if the debt to national income ratio, D/NI, is not to rise. That is,

$$\frac{D}{\text{NI}} = \frac{D}{Y/S}$$

(23.5)

where D is debt outstanding (measured in foreign currency) and Y is nominal income which is converted at the exchange rate S into foreign currency. Noting that the proportionate growth of debt is equal to $(\text{TD} + R_\text{F})/D$, taking logarithms and differentiating equation (23.5) with respect to time yields

$$\left(\frac{\dot{D}}{\text{NI}}\right) = \frac{\text{TD}}{D} + \frac{R_\text{F}}{D} - \dot{Y} + \dot{S}$$

(23.6)

where R_F/D is the average interest rate paid on debt outstanding which can be simply stated as i. If the debt–income ratio is to remain constant at some desired level (perhaps the maximum level considered by international banks to be consistent with solvency)[3] and the trade account is brought into balance we can write

$$\dot{Y} - \dot{S} = i \tag{23.7}$$

which says that the rate of growth of nominal income measured in foreign currency (the left-hand side) must grow at a rate equal to the interest rate paid on foreign loans. Notice that inflation in a *debtor country* is no way out from under a debt burden because S will rise, in some exchange rate models, at the same rate as the rate of inflation, leaving the left-hand side in equation (23.7) unchanged. Thus, it is the rate of *real* economic growth which must equal the foreign *real* rate of interest.[4]

One possible way from under the debt burden is for creditor countries to lower real interest rates. Then, if purchasing power parity holds approximately, in equation (23.7) S will fall (appreciate) so raising the growth rate of real income measured in foreign currency. A good bout of (unanticipated) inflation is usually good for debtors – "General" inflation to the rescue, but only so long as it is occurring in the creditor countries.

23.3.1 Debt overhang

While sustaining the rate of real economic growth is a clear objective for debtor countries, the debt "overhang" is a constraining factor. The reasons are that (i) debt service absorbs profits that otherwise could have been reinvested in capital accumulation (in 1984 in Latin America, interest payments on international debt amounted to 5.5 percent of gross national product (GNP) (BIS, 1990, p. 40); and (ii) when the overhang becomes big enough, the source of foreign savings dries up and, if it is not replaced by increased domestic savings, domestic real loan rates of interest rise (Borensztein, 1989). In Latin America the current account deficit (representing use of foreign savings) fell from 4.4 to 1.3 percent of GNP between 1980 and 1989, while the domestic savings rate also fell (from 20 to 19.3 percent), with the result that the rate of investment fell by 3.8 percent of GNP to 19.6 percent in 1989 (BIS, 1990, table 39). Other empirical evidence for the hypothesized negative relationship between debt and growth is found in Borensztein (1990). For example, in the Philippines a $1.3 billion reduction in international bank debt was calculated to increase the demand for funds for productive investment by 2 percent of GNP. In Argentina, Brazil, and Mexico debt service has crowded out investment rather than consumption with private investment being sharply reduced – in 1985 to only $2\frac{1}{2}$ percent of gross domestic product (GDP) in Argentina, and 10 percent in Mexico (country studies by Dornbusch and de Pablo, 1989; Cardoso and Fishlow, 1989; Buffie and Krause, 1989).

A related view of the causes of the slowdown in economic growth in Latin American countries since the early 1980s is the *confidence gap theory* (Blejer and Ize, 1989). In this theory sources of foreign saving, domestic saving *and* the domestic demand for investment funds collapse together. The main reason is that poor macroeconomic management and the impact of adverse external events lead to greater uncertainty throughout a debtor's economy. This is particularly true of the belief in the viability of the domestic financial system. Blejer and Ize argue that in many Latin American countries during the 1980s there developed a general lack of confidence in the economic system as a whole. The virtual suspension of foreign leading, following the debt crisis of 1982, further weakened remaining confidence in the economy when it was realized that very severe adjustment policies would have to be put into effect – with the political system itself in jeopardy.

 ## 23.4 Capital Flight

Rates of economic growth in debtor countries have suffered because of large-scale capital flight – domestic savings being placed abroad.

Capital flight is defined as "capital outflow motivated by the desire of residents to obtain financial assets and earnings outside of the control of the domestic authorities," i.e. not subject to taxation – especially the inflation "tax" (Dooley, 1988a, p. 428). Dooley estimated that by 1984 seven major debtor countries together had a total stock of external claims of $183 billion, of which two-thirds ($121 billion) was flight capital. Flight capital represented 36 percent of their external indebtedness. In a later estimate, by the beginning of 1988 flight capital amounted to one-half of 15 big debtors' external debts and as much as 80 percent in the case of Mexico and 75 percent in the case of Argentina.[5]

Flight capital can escape a country by various means. For example, in black leather satchels, in intra-family transfers, through under-invoicing of exports and over-invoicing of imports, via unofficial currency markets or through banks that retain secrecy of account information.

Why does capital flight occur? A persuasive hypothesis is that flight capital is one leg of a round-tripping of capital between debtor and creditor countries (Khan and Haque, 1985; Eaton, 1987; Dooley, 1988a). This round-tripping is caused by differences between residents and non-residents in their perceptions of the riskiness of returns on financial claims against entities (corporations, banks, government) in a given developing country.

Residents of a typical Latin American country of the 1970s, 1980s and into the 1990s experienced high rates of inflation tax. However, foreign lenders, because their assets are denominated in foreign currency, do not face the risk of the inflation tax.[6] They do, however, face default risk. But, for a long time after private bank lending to developing countries took off in the early 1970s, default risk was seen by the lenders as being of low probability – the maxim then was that "countries cannot go bust." Thus, initially default risk was perceived as low. Foreign creditors invested in the debtor country while developing country residents invested abroad. In terms of the balance of payments accounting identities, capital inflow financed the capital outflow.

Round-tripping is an international portfolio adjustment process. As such it would come to an end once portfolios reattained equilibrium. What brought about this end for many Latin American countries was the run up in default risk as perceived by foreign banks and the choking of capital inflow.[7] Flight capital remained abroad so long as the inflation tax remained high. But in many Latin American countries (excluding Brazil) around 1990 or 1991, inflation rates were falling and real exchange rate overvaluation was corrected. As predicted by Dornbusch (1985) and Edwards (1984), capital flight reversed. The resulting improvement in the balance of payments then helped to reduce the problem of governmental foreign indebtedness. For some countries perhaps the debt crisis was over, until reappearing in the mid-1990s.

Dooley (1988a) finds empirical evidence supporting the "differential perceived risk" hypothesis. Capital flight is positively associated with a debtor nation's rate of inflation (the proxy for the inflation "tax") and negatively associated with the risk premium on foreign loans (the proxy for default risk). The latter implies that as the capital inflow dries up so will capital flight. Cuddington (1986) also finds that capital flight is positively related to currency overvaluation (a proxy for the perceived exchange rate "tax") as well as the rate of inflation.

A different model of capital flight is developed by Razin and Sadka (1989). Capital flight is a response to international differences in *net* rates of return on financial investments. Assuming that foreign exchange controls are ineffective and that a developing country government cannot tax income on residents' foreign assets, capital flight continues until the after-tax rate of return on domestic investment is equal to the world rate of return. Thus, in the presence of taxation, the gross rate of return on domestic investment in the developing country must exceed the world rate of return. This represents a misallocation of investment funds and a reduction in the rate of investment in the developing country. In the presence of such a distortion, Razin and Sadka suggest that quotas on capital exports be made effective.

In yet another model of capital flight Edwards (1984) applies a foreign indebtedness stock-adjustment model – as discussed in section 21.2 – to Southern Cone countries. During the long periods of controls on foreign loans a large stock of desired foreign borrowing built up. When the controls were lifted in the late 1970s there was a surge of foreign borrowing which caused exchange rates to appreciate. But some residents recognized that the appreciation was temporary and would be reversed, so they placed funds abroad.

Capital flight has not featured prominently in East Asia presumably because inflation has generally remained quite low, economic growth rates high, and risk premia on international loans low until 1997. Indeed, it is arguable that these risk premia remained too low for too long. The BIS (1998, p. 127) records that the major sovereign rating agencies, Moody's and S&P, lowered their credit ratings of several East Asian countries *after* the currency crises of 1997 had hit. Had risk premia been increased gradually as fundamentals worsened, international capital inflow may have been reduced gradually, rather than all but collapsing in the third quarter of 1997.

23.5 Governmental and National Foreign Indebtedness

In the 1970s and 1980s it was often the practice for debtor country governments to guarantee foreign loans as well as borrowing on their own behalf – practices which in the 1990s became less prevalent.

In view of massive capital flight from many developing countries during the 1980, it is desirable to show the proximate causes of increased *governmental* foreign indebtedness (i.e. public and publicly guaranteed debt), as a country's debt problem was more that of governmental debt than of national indebtedness. The proximate causes of increased governmental indebtedness are derived in the following way:

$$\Delta F = \text{BOP} = \text{current account surplus} + \text{capital account surplus} \qquad (23.8)$$

where ΔF is the increase in foreign exchange reserves and BOP is the official settlements balance. The capital account surplus is made up of three elements which are substituted into equation (23.8) yielding

$$\Delta F = \begin{array}{l} \text{current} \\ \text{account} + \\ \text{surplus} \end{array} \begin{array}{l} \text{net long-term} \\ \text{private capital} + \\ \text{inflow} \end{array} \begin{array}{l} \text{government} \\ \text{foreign} \\ \text{borrowing} \end{array} \begin{array}{l} \text{gross private} \\ - \text{ short-term} \\ \text{capital outflow} \end{array} \qquad (23.9)$$

Rearranging equation (23.9) gives

$$\begin{array}{l} \text{government} \\ \text{foreign} \\ \text{borrowing} \end{array} = \begin{array}{l} \text{current} \\ \text{account} + \Delta F + \\ \text{deficit} \end{array} \begin{array}{l} \text{gross private} \\ \text{short-term} \\ \text{capital outflow} \end{array} \begin{array}{l} \text{net long-term} \\ - \text{ private capital} \\ \text{inflow} \end{array} \qquad (23.10)$$

Hence, a government's foreign borrowing will be greater, *ceteris paribus*, the larger is the current account deficit or the increase in foreign exchange reserves or gross private capital outflow, and the smaller is the level of net long-term private capital inflow. However, the increase in a country's *net* foreign indebtedness is determined only by the size of the current account deficit: net long-term capital inflow in excess of the current account deficit will go into foreign exchange reserves or gross private capital outflow. In practice it can matter a lot which of the last two items predominates as far as a government's debt-service problem is concerned. If gross private capital outflow is large, a government may still face debt servicing difficulties even though net indebtedness has not increased by very much. This is simply because the government is unable to use the interest income earned by residents on their foreign private investments to service public and publicly guaranteed foreign debts.

23.6 The Lenders' Trap

If in the early 1980s so many Latin American and other developing countries had built up debt-service obligations to levels which obviously threatened their creditworthiness, why did the international banks continue to make loans to them on such a large scale? One answer is that they did their best to get out. The share of bank debt in total developing country foreign debt in fact fell quite sharply after 1982. Even so, new loans were made. Why? Once having made loans to a client state, banks can become locked in even if there is a threat that the client cannot service the debt. For the banks the choice is stark: either lend more money so that the service payments on the old loans can be made (in effect capitalizing the interest payments), or declare the borrower to be insolvent and prepare to write off the loan.

New lending will be the chosen alternative so long as the expected benefit of new lending exceeds the expected cost. Following Cline (1984) the expected benefit of new lending is

$$E(B) = (P_0 - P_1)D \qquad (23.11)$$

where P_0 and P_1 are respectively the probabilities of default before and after the new loan is made and D is the outstanding debt prior to the new loan. The expected cost of new lending is

$$E(C) = P_1 L \qquad (23.12)$$

where L is the dollar value of the new loan. Net benefit of the new loan expressed as a percentage of outstanding debt is

$$N(B) = E(B) - E(C) = P_0 - P_1 (1 + L/D) \times 100 \qquad (23.13)$$

Hence, whether to make new loans depends upon the "before" and "after" probability of default and the size of the new loan relative to debt outstanding. A bank will make a new loan in circumstances where P_0 is high and L/D is small but the new loan is expected to bring about a marked reduction in the probability of default. For example, in Mexico in 1982, the banking community rushed in with new loans. This was not surprising. Cline assesses that P_0 was "substantial" while P_1 was low and the required new loans amounted to only 7 percent of outstanding debt. Thus if $P_0 = 80$ percent and $P_1 = 40$ percent, net benefit expressed as a fraction of outstanding loans is 34.2 percent.

In East Asia in 1997 the international lenders in fact rushed to get out all at once. Thus, total annualized capital inflow to five East Asian countries (interbank plus bank lending to non-banks plus net bond issuance) in the three-quarters ending 1997·III was $54 billion falling to an outflow of $31 billion in the last quarter of 1997 (BIS, 1998, p. 122). Presumably the new information that came to light on the shakiness of many East Asian banking systems in mid-1997 (on this see chapter 14) meant that P_1 (the probability of default after new loans are made) did not increase very much, if at all. Contagion factors were also probably at work (section 14.6).

23.7 Some Debt Reform Proposals

The objective of a plethora of debt reform proposals can be understood with reference to equation (23.4) which shows how the DSR changes with the rate of interest, the trade deficit, the amount of annual amortization, and the rate of growth of exports. Debt reform proposals target one or some combination of these variables. For example, IMF loans conditional on structural adjustment and devaluation by a debtor country could raise the rate of growth of export earnings (notice that lifting of trade-protectionist measures by the importing nations has never been seriously considered at the official level because of the political roadblocks in the General Agreement on Tariffs and Trade (GATT).

Hundreds of rescheduling agreements aimed at reducing immediate debt-service problems have featured rescheduling of interest and annual amortization (in equation (23.4) di and dA are negative). A few debtor countries have unilaterally limited debt-service payments to levels said to be manageable given the level of export earnings.[8]

The policy of "benign arrears" (Cline, 1988) is one of making a virtue out of necessity. The commercial banks, multilateral agencies, and bilateral donors should allow arrears to accumulate without pressing the debtor for hurried repayment. Even without being adopted as a formal policy, arrears are an important source of debt relief: in the period 1985–90 arrears grew by almost $60 billion (reaching $80 billion) and this was only $5 billion less than the aggregate relief given by rescheduling (World Bank, 1990). Debt–equity swaps reduce annual debt service and are "an attractive way to reduce the external debt of the developing countries" (Balassa, 1988). In a debt–equity swap an international bank converts a loan to a company into equity. The company thereby reduces its debt service obligations and the bank diversifies its portfolio.[9]

A couple of interesting but untried schemes include repayment of some debt in local currency (thereby effectively reducing i and A as in equation (23.4) interest and principal is repaid in foreign currency). Under a tax-credits-for-debt swap (Dooley and Helpman, 1989) a creditor bank would sell debt back to the debtor country in exchange for tax credits that could later be resold. The main advantage of this scheme is that debt outstanding would be reduced without the need for banks to take losses. The main disadvantage is that the loss of tax revenue would worsen fiscal deficits.

The essence of the Baker plan (1985–8) was to buy time for debtor countries to reduce their trade deficits and to raise their rates of export growth. $30 billion was directed to 15 major debtor countries over a three-year period as new loans – even though the commercial banks were, to say the least, reluctant to extend them. In exchange, the debtors agreed to implement structural reforms. The Baker plan is regarded as being a failure, as is American international debt policy (Makin, 1989).

Debt forgiveness was a stated objective of the next American initiative – the Brady plan (1989). This was the first official recognition by the USA that debt forgiveness would have to be incorporated in debt reform if default by the major debtor nations was to be avoided.[10] The "test case" was Mexico. It was agreed between the Mexican government and 500 creditor banks that the banks could choose to swap old loans for new bonds that carried either a discount or lower interest rates. Alternatively, a bank could make new loans. Although much trumpeted at the time, a United Nations analysis of it concluded that little had been achieved. Net interest payments abroad were cut by about 10 percent but this was achieved by rescheduling rather than by debt forgiveness. Indeed, although

$7 billion of old debt to banks was exchanged for discount bonds, about the same amount was added to debt owed to official sources and in new bank loans (money that was used to collateralize the discount bonds).

There are several reasons for the failure of the Brady plan to make a significant contribution to relieving the "debt problem": the banks had different interests between themselves, and so called for an array of policies rather than support- ing a single design (Bartolini and Dixit, 1988); some banks held out hope of eventually being repaid in full, especially if most other banks wrote down the value of their loans, i.e. a free-rider problem existed; many banks were simply disinclined to give much away; few banks opted to put more money into Mexico – which meant that Mexico was unable to fund a larger loans-for-bonds swap. But, perhaps above all else, the Brady plan did not tackle the problem of attract- ing flight capital back to Mexico. It is little wonder, therefore, that the bankers did not have much confidence in the Brady plan when Mexicans themselves had so little monetary resources.

23.7.1 The free-rider issue

The free-rider problem is central to debt forgiveness because it helps to explain why banks have been so reluctant to write down the face value of loans in ex- change for discount bonds. The issue can be understood using figure 23.4 which is due to Claessens et al. (1991).

As the face value of debt increases, at some stage its burden becomes so great that doubts begin to arise whether it can be repaid on time or in full. On the secondary market "old" debt trades at a discount, in some actual cases at rates as high as 90 percent. In figure 23.4 the market and face values of debt are equal on the 45° line but, once the face value of debt becomes greater than $OQ, old debt begins to be discounted: e.g. at P the discount is MN/MP (notice that to

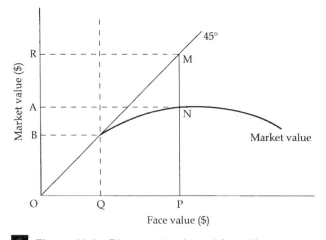

Figure 23.4 Discounted debt and free-riders

the right of Q the discount is an increasing function of the face value of debt). The face value of debt may have become greater than $OQ due to "the lenders' trap" (see above), to faulty expectations on the part of bank loan officers, to "over-generous" bilateral and/or multilateral aid or to changed conditions in a debtor country's economic circumstances that make repayment more difficult (i.e. the market value schedule in figure 23.4 has been shifted downward from some previous higher level).

Since $AB is the market value of $QP debt, banks should be willing to sell debt with this face value for the sum $AB. However, there is a *free-rider problem*. An individual bank would be better off not selling (a degraded) asset as part of a debt-reduction scheme because the discount on the face value of remaining "old" debt will decline. For example, the average discount on $QP debt is AB/QP whereas the discount falls to zero on the remaining $OQ debt. With the free-rider problem, banks are willing to sell debt only at the discount expected *after* the face value of the debt has been reduced, not at the current average market discount. In the circumstances envisaged in figure 23.4 (where the discount on remaining debt falls to zero), banks would be willing to sell $QP debt only for $BR – which is much more than the current market value of the debt.

Two consequences follow from the above argument: (i) since not much debt gets sold off, debt remains as a burden on a debtor country; and (ii) debt reduction is expensive because those banks that do sell old debt for discount bonds (e.g. as in the Brady plan schemes negotiated for Mexico, the Philippines, Costa Rica, and Venezuela) are compensated generously in relation to the current market value of the debt. Thus, there is a need to get around the free-rider problem. One suggestion that has attracted attention is to press all the creditor banks of a debtor country to participate in an international debt facility (IDF).

23.8 An International Debt Facility

An IDF is a scheme through which developing country debt may be forgiven, i.e. loans exchanged for discount bonds. An early advocate was Kenen (1983) who proposed the setting up of an international organization that would sell bonds guaranteed by the member countries, mainly the industrial countries. The key feature of the scheme was the write-down of the value of the creditors' assets (the loans) in recognition of the near impossibility of the debtors' servicing the debt on the original terms. One of the main barriers to implementation of the proposal, as Kenen said, was to induce the borrowers, the guarantor nations, the IMF and thousands of international banks "to sit down and settle this thing. If they could, it would be a good trick." Almost twenty years later the trick had not been pulled off.

More recently, interest has renewed in an IDF (Corden, 1988; Dooley, 1988b) as the realization has deepened that debt forgiveness needs to be a part of the solution to the debt problem. In these schemes the IDF would buy debt from banks at a discount in exchange for bonds guaranteed by the owners of the facility. So the banks exchange debt, subject to default risk, for lower-valued bonds with no (or very low) default risk. The banks also gain from the *market price effect* as the market price of their remaining loans increases – due to a reduction in default risk caused by the debt forgiveness. But the banks also accept lower-valued bonds for their bank debt. Don't they, therefore, lose here? Not necessarily – the debtor may be incapable of ever repaying its debts at face value.[11]

How then does the debtor country gain? Its debt may be written down, but if it was anyway incapable of repaying in full, there is no gain from the debt forgiveness (strictly, if the forgiveness reduces debt to the maximum level that the country could repay).[12] However, a debtor country may gain from the *ceiling effect*: the probability of repayment in full may be very low, but it is not necessarily zero (e.g. an unforeseen improvement in the country's terms of trade could occur). Thus, the debtor gains if it turns out that it could have repaid an amount greater than the ceiling but, in fact, has only to repay up to the ceiling.

The IDF scheme incorporates the transfer of default risk from the banks to the guarantor governments and, according to Corden, this could be an "overwhelming obstacle" to the establishment of an IDF. If the debtor nations default or even fail to make interest payments, the guarantor governments would be required to make good their guarantees. There are no direct pecuniary benefits to the guarantor governments. However, industrial countries may well gain from the external economies that the IDF may generate. For example, the health of their banking systems may well improve as the quality of bank assets recovers; as the debt burden is reduced developing country economic growth and import capacity may increase, creating exports and jobs for the industrial countries; and, on a broader plain, industrial countries have an interest, political and humanitarian, in a prosperous world economy. (Vines and Muscatelli (1989) model economic interactions between industrial countries and developing countries, in particular showing how developed country income depends upon developing country imports.)

But the various proposals for an IDF suffer from a major handicap: they are not time consistent. Whatever covenants may be issued by a debtor nation to adjust its economy and finances so as to be able to service the remaining debt, as time passes default on interest or principal may be preferred to adjustment.

NOTES

1 It is usual in the national income accounting identities to define saving as S – which we do here. Later we will revert to our use of S as the exchange rate. The context in which S is used will be clear.

2 Equation (23.1) is derived as, by definition, aggregate national expenditure on goods and services is $E = C + I + G + X - M$ and the disposition of national income is $Y = C + S + T + R_F$. In equilibrium $E = Y$.

3 Stymne (1989) considers that the maximum sustainable debt–income ratio for sub-saharan African countries is in the range 150–180 percent.

4 It is the foreign real rate of interest and not the nominal rate because, if inflation is occurring in the creditor countries, i will increase via the Fisher effect (defined in section 3.4) and, assuming that purchasing power parity holds, a developing country's exchange rate S will be falling at the same rate as the creditor's rate of inflation. The

rise in i and the fall in S simply offset each other, leaving the debtor country still needing to grow at a rate at least as fast as the foreign real interest rate. Put another way, the creditor country's rate of inflation p should be subtracted from both sides of equation (23.7), which again shows that the rate of real economic growth must equal the real interest rate charged on loans.

5   Quoted by *The Economist*, August, 12 1989, p. 16.
6   Virtually all borrowing by developing countries is denominated in a foreign currency, usually the US dollar.
7   Rojas-Suarez (1990) has pointed to the continuation of capital flight even after capital inflow from foreign banks has all dried up. She argues that debt–equity swaps can be used to reduce capital flight further.
8   For a description of the case of Peru see Ugarteche (1988).
9   Examples of debt–equity conversions in Brazil are Chase Manhattan's $200 million investment in the Autolatina SA car company and Manufacturers Hanover's $80 million investment in Companhia Suzano de Papel & Celulose. It has been estimated that conversions could reduce Brazil's $66 billion bank debt (as of 1988) by $19 billion by 1994 (*Wall Street Journal*, September, 9 1988).
10 Greene (1989b), referring to sub-Saharan African countries, argues that debt forgiveness is the only viable strategy given the size of their debt burdens and prospects for economic progress.
11 That an international debt facility has been proposed by the Chairman American Express bank is, perhaps, indicative of the gains that bankers see for their banks (Robinson, 1988).
12 Corden (1988) notes a moral hazard problem related to the determination of the amount of debt forgiven. For the debtor country the more debt forgiven the better. By making "default noises" it can influence the IDF to set a low ceiling even though the ceiling should really have been higher.

24

International Monetary Reform

There is a growing dissatisfaction with the rather *ad hoc* international monetary system (IMS) of floating exchange rates in existence since the early 1970s. At the heart of the desire to move to a new form of IMS is the belief that the exchange rate volatility that has been such a feature of the recent float has had a deleterious effect on trade flows and on the ability of governments to pursue non-inflationary macroeconomic policies.

Since 1973 the IMS has, generally speaking, been characterized by a system of some form of flexible exchange rates. It is tempting to suggest that the adoption of this system was the outcome of the persuasive powers of academic economists on the political decision-making process. More realistically, however, the previous IMS, the Bretton Woods system, was abandoned because of its inherent inflationary bias and lack of effective adjustment mechanism. The marked volatility of exchange rates was noted not long into the floating rate regime (see, for example, McKinnon 1976), and it has been reiterated more recently on several occasions (see Frenkel and Mussa, 1980; IMF, 1984; Dornbusch and Frankel, 1987; MacDonald, 1992a).

In this final chapter we examine the issue of international financial stability against this background of exchange rate volatility. In section 24.1 we discuss some general features displayed by international monetary systems. Section 24.2 lays out some theoretical considerations relevant to the construction of a viable IMS. Section 24.3 outlines the DM and Yen currency blocs. In section 24.4 we outline why exchange rate volatility is often viewed as undesirable and then go on to discuss some commonly cited advantages of flexible exchange rates. We then concentrate on two of the most widely canvassed solutions to the problem of international financial stability: the McKinnon and the target zone proposals. The chapter closes with some concluding comments.

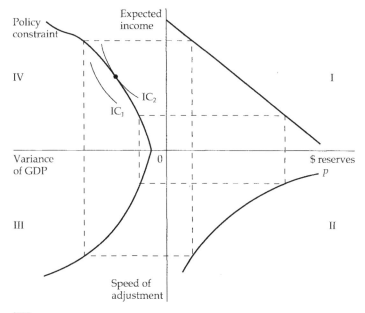

Figure 24.1 Optimal reserves and speed of adjustment

24.1 Financing or Adjustment?

An appropriate mix has to be found between the financing and adjustment of (above the line) balance of payments deficits. The greater is financing the less is the need for adjustment. But what is the appropriate mix for a country? The answer depends upon the policy-makers' objectives (we take the policymaker to be the "representative citizen") and the constraints that they face. Clark (1970) provides a neat model which frames the problem. In figure 24.1 segment I shows the relationship between expected income and the level of foreign exchange reserves – it is negative because reserves absorb resources that otherwise could have been invested in real capital. Segment II shows the trade-off between reserves and the speed of adjustment: adjustment has to be quick if reserves are small.[1] In segment III the variance (a measure of instability) of gross domestic product (GDP) increases with the speed of adjustment (this presupposes some degree of price rigidity and/or factor immobility between sectors). In segment IV the policy constraint between expected income and the variance of income is constructed from the functions in the other three segments – as can be seen by following the broken lines. Also shown is the policy-maker's indifference curve preferences. Satisfaction increases as higher indifference curves are reached by moving upward in segment IV.

A lower cost of reserves – e.g. if special drawing rights (SDRs) are allocated freely rather than reserves having to be earned through balance of payments

Table 24.1 Exchange rate regimes

Exchange rate	Reserve asset	Capital account
I Fixed	A gold	1 Fully open
II Adjustable parity	B SDR	2 Dual
III Crawling peg	C $, other currencies	3 Controlled
IV Managed float	D ECU	
V Free float		

Source: Based on Cooper, 1987

surpluses – shifts the function in segment I upward, swings the policy-maker's constraint clockwise in segment IV and leads to a preference for more reserves and a slower speed of adjustment. If a country's domestic economy becomes more flexible owing to, say, an increase in price flexibility, the function in segment III pivots anticlockwise and the policy constraint function pivots clockwise. The policymaker moves to a higher indifference curve, reserve holding falls and the speed of adjustment rises. Support for flexible exchange rates among economists in the 1960s and 1970s may have been based on the belief that the policy constraint function was more favorable (i.e. swung further clockwise) than it in fact was.

24.1.1 Choosing an international monetary system

Table 24.1 shows the IMS menu. A global monetary system results from agreement implicit or explicit on rules by the nations that form that system. If leading nations face similar constraints – and have policymakers with similar preferences – agreement on the broad outline of a system is facilitated. For example, if rapid adjustment is believed to be desirable countries may choose to float exchange rates and agree not to interfere with the adjustment mechanism – leaving changes in the exchange rate to give immediate price adjustment signals. Alternatively, the members may fix the exchange rate and allow the balance of payments automatically to adjust the money supply – as was approximated by the international gold standard. Both of these automatic regimes require "hands-off" rules of the game. If rapid adjustment is seen by policy-makers to be undesirable foreign exchange reserves are needed to support the exchange rate during the period when monetary and fiscal policies are being used to smooth adjustment.

Using the notation of table 24.1 the international gold standard was I,A,1; the original Bretton Woods system was II,A,3; what the Bretton Woods system became in the 1960s – the dollar standard – was II,C,3 (see chapter 17); the current "dollar standard on the booze" is IV,C,1; and theoretically the European monetary system (EMS) was I,D,1. The McKinnon proposal discussed later is I,C,1 and the target zone proposal (also discussed later) IV,C,1. Incidentally, the formerly centrally planned economies are in the process of joining the IMS and their best advice may be for IV,C,3 (see chapter 22). As the high inflation Latin American countries strived to join the IMS in the last decade the best advice was for either I,C,2 or 3 or III,C,2 or 3 (see section 21.3).

But international agreement on a monetary system is hard to achieve as is witnessed by the failure of the International Monetary Fund's (IMF's) Committee of Twenty during 1972–4 to find a blue print for the replacement of the Bretton Woods Accord. According to Williamson (1977) selfish national interests were too prominent: America had given up on "benign neglect" and wanted a system that strongly encouraged nations in balance of payments surplus to adjust; the Europeans, especially the French, wanted symmetry between themselves and the USA – which could be achieved by replacing the dollar with the SDR as the principal reserve asset. Both of these groups were against the developing countries' proposal for the SDR-aid link which only directly benefited developing countries and was seen as confusing the criteria governing the creation of international liquidity – should more SDRs be created because of the needs of international trade or because developing countries deserved more foreign aid?

In general, distributional factors do influence the choice of international monetary regime. Seigniorage is an economic rent gained by the issuer of a money whose monetary value is greater than its commodity value (i.e. cost of production). It was sometimes argued that under the dollar standard the USA gained seigniorage from the issue of dollars held by foreign central banks. However, this is probably untrue because interest is paid on these dollar deposits. The basis of the SDR-aid link proposal was that, as the cost of issuing SDRs is next to nothing, seigniorage is great and it would be fair to distribute it to poor countries. However, it is not true that rich countries reap most of the seigniorage just because under the IMF's quota arrangements (which govern the distribution of SDRs) they receive most of the SDRs. If, on average, recipients of SDRs hold them in foreign exchange reserves, SDRs are not used to increase domestic consumption – they are merely used as a liquidity reserve.

Aside from seigniorage, the issuer of an international money such as the dollar – or sterling in an earlier period – has been accused of benefiting from the support that its currency enjoys from being held by foreign central banks as a reserve asset. This should appreciate the currency and have a beneficial terms of trade effect on the issuer. Against this the issuer bears a cost as its traded goods sector shrinks – a variety of "Dutch disease". Another criticism of an IMS based on a national currency is that the issuer gets to set economic policy for the monetary area as a whole. In the 1970s western Europe broke away from US economic hegemony by floating exchange rates against the US dollar. In the 1990s, in the EMS, the antidote to the deutschmark zone is the creation of a European central bank (in which all European Community (EC) members have a say) and the euro. At the level of the global international monetary system, the two main reform proposals (discussed below) also aim to replace the uncertain and waning hegemony of the USA with cooperation between the main international players.

In the next section we discuss the matter of choosing an international monetary regime in a more formal framework.

◆ 24.2 Designing an International Monetary System

The designers of an explicit IMS need to ensure that it is internally consistent. In particular, their most important consideration is that institutional structures and/or practices allow for the solution of three factors: national balance of payments, the pattern of exchange rates and the relative and absolute levels of national money supplies. Inconsistency implies that at least one member of the system is dissatisfied with the outcome for its balance of payments/exchange rate/money supply and takes steps to move to a preferred position, so upsetting the international equilibrium.

These matters can be explained by supposing that n countries, each with its own currency and central bank, form a monetary union by fixing exchange rates between themselves. Examples of such monetary unions are the formation of the international gold standard in the nineteenth century, the Bretton Woods system the EMS, and the euro area.

It turns out that in an IMS of n countries only $n - 1$ balance of payments can be independently determined. That is, a maximum of $n - 1$ countries can independently set balance of payments targets (or, what amounts to the same thing, targets for changes in their net international indebtedness); the nth country has to accept the outcome or else the system is inconsistent.

For an n-country monetary union we can write

$$S_1 \Delta F_1 + S_2 \Delta F_2 + \ldots + S_{n-1} \Delta F_{n-1} + \Delta F_n = 0 \tag{24.1}$$

where the ΔF_i is the balance of payments of country i measured as the domestic currency value of the change in its foreign exchange reserves. It is true that in a world of n countries the world's balance of payments sums to zero (as one country's surplus is another's deficit).[2] As each country has its own currency, the latter statement has meaning only if each $\Delta F_i (i = 1, \ldots, n - 1)$ is converted into a common currency. The common currency is one of the currencies of the system – designated as the nth currency. Thus, ΔF_i is multiplied by S_i, where S_i here has the interpretation of the nth currency price of currency i.

Accordingly, if $n - 1$ countries each set a target for their balance of payments (by setting both an exchange rate S_i and the domestic currency value of ΔF_i). H_n – country n's high-powered money base (see chapter 8) – is determined as a residual. For the system to be consistent (i.e. sum to zero) the nth country must not try to set an independent target for its balance of payments, ΔF_n. Nor must the nth country intervene in the foreign exchange market in an effort to set any of the exchange rates $S_1, \ldots, S_{n-1}$ that have been chosen by the other members of the system. (It might be tempted to do so if, for example, the nth country's government thought that ΔF_n was too large and negative and so tried a devaluation of its currency – i.e. increasing the values of S_i.) Such a policy is the stuff of competitive devaluations, trade wars and use of foreign exchange controls – sure signs that the IMS has become inconsistent.

Equation (24.1) helps to crystallize the issues in the debate in the late 1960s and early 1970s over the break-up of the Bretton Woods system. One view is that the USA was the nth country and practised "benign neglect," leaving ΔF_n to be set as a residual. But the USA, tiring of its large payments deficits, in 1971 set out to devalue the dollar. It succeeded in breaking up the existing IMS because other countries would not accept the new values for their exchange rates. Another view – the "European view" – is that the USA independently set a target for the rate of monetary growth and that this, willynilly, determined the change in US foreign exchange reserves.[3] The other members of the system had to accept the consequent increase in their foreign exchange reserves and increases in their domestic money supplies (at least to the extent that sterilization was limited in effect).

The logic of equation (24.1) is then that:

1 $n - 1$ countries are free to choose their exchange rates and balance of payments, and the nth country must forgo both a balance of payments and an exchange rate policy; or
2 if exchange rates are fixed, and the nth country independently determines its rate of domestic credit expansion, the other members of the currency zone must allow their balance of payments to be determined by the nth country; or
3 if neither of these alternatives is acceptable the system is inconsistent and it will ultimately collapse.
4 To head off collapse the members must agree to cooperate politically on setting desirable and consistent levels of national money supplies, balance of payments, and exchange rates.

Since 1973 major trading nations such as Japan, the USA, and the EU have adopted floating exchange rates. If each S_i were truly free to find its market-clearing value the IMS would again be consistent. However, exchange rates have not been left entirely free to float and the resulting inconsistency has revealed itself in international periodic political conflict over foreign currency values and the size of balance of payments deficits, one country accusing another of having an "undervalued" currency, an over-large payments surplus, or an overly large fiscal deficit. Resolution of the inconsistencies is now regularly attempted, apparently without much success, through international cooperation, e.g. in the Group of seven industrial countries or bilaterally, on matters such as the level of exchange rates, interest rates and level of imports by one country from another (see chapter 6 for a further discussion of the policy coordination issue).

Indeed, at this juncture, the industrial countries, afraid of the rigours that they would face in a consistent clean-float – but unstable – exchange rate system, have to choose between a newly designed automatic and consistent IMS and blundering along with the present inconsistent system, trying only to modify its worst excesses through international cooperation.

24.2.1 More on exchange rates and consistency

Exchange rates with the nth currency – the numeraire – are determined using a particular version of the monetary model discussed in chapter 9 (the particular application is from Salin, 1982):

$$S_{i,n} = f(M_i, M_n, k_i) \tag{24.2}$$

where $S_{i,n}$ is the ith country's exchange rate with the numeraire currency; the Ms are the money supplies of the ith and nth countries (which in the long run determine exchange rates); and k is a factor which allows the exchange rate to diverge from PPP in the short run (due perhaps to factors disturbing the real exchange rate or to intervention in foreign exchange markets by central banks). Taking S_i as fixed, for a given M_n, long-run M_i is determined. If the money supplies are correctly determined for the given S_i but k_i is not equal to zero, balance of payments disequilibria will have to be financed.

The final part of the monetary union to which we must pay attention is the money supply of the zone as a whole. $M_{z,n}$ measures this in terms of the currency of the nth country – the numeraire currency. Thus:

$$M_{z,n} = \sum_{i=1}^{n-1} \left(\frac{1}{S_{i,n}} M_i \right) + M_n \tag{24.3}$$

In this model there are n equations (i.e. equation (24.2) written for $n-1$ countries plus the equation for the zone's money stock). Moreover, there are $2n$ variables:

$$
\begin{aligned}
\text{national money stocks} &= n \\
+ \text{ exchange rates} &= n - 1 \\
+ \text{ zone's money stock} &= M_{z,n} \\
\hline
\text{Total} &= 2n
\end{aligned}
$$

For the system to be determinate we need as many endogenous variables as we have equations so, of the $2n$ variables, n of them must be set exogenously.

Any of several IMSs may be chosen to solve the system. These are as follows:

1 *Floating exchange rates*: each of the n countries sets its own money stock, leaving $n-1$ exchange rates plus the zone's money stock endogenous.
2 *Rigidly fixed exchange rates*, i.e. a monetary union: here $n-1$ exchange rates are fixed against the nth currency, which means that one more equation must be made exogenous. The alternatives are as follows.
   (a) The nth-country fixes its money supply. Thus, $n-1$ money supplies become endogenous as is the money stock of the zone.
   (b) Again $n-1$ exchange rates are determined exogenously but the quantity of money for the monetary zone as a whole, $M_{z,n}$, is agreed upon, then

the *n* national money supplies become endogenous. There are two broad possibilities here:

   (i)   Agreement on the zone's aggregate money supply is through international cooperation between independent central banks – this is effectively the system that the EU has tried to operate with the EMS.

   (ii) A single central bank is established for the zone and is left to run the zone's monetary policy. This is the Delors "solution" for the EU.

3 *An n + 1 variable is introduced*: this was gold under the gold standard. Then the $n - 1$ exchange rates and the price of gold are exogenous and the *n* money supplies become endogenous. A suggestion by McKinnon (1979) is that a monetary zone with $n - 1$ fixed exchange rates could aim to stabilize the zone's wholesale price index as the $(n + 1)$th variable. Stabilization of the price of an "outside asset" is said to provide a "nominal anchor" for the system. As long as the supply of this outside asset is fairly rigid, growth of the money supply of the zone as a whole will be constrained and so, presumably, will the rate of inflation. Targeting a specific price index achieves the same result directly.

From this menu the members of the international community have to select an IMS. The gold standard solution was abandoned mainly because it imposed upon the members of the system a discipline that was too rigid and rigorous. A variant of a commodity-based IMS is to use a basket of commodities rather than just gold (an idea due to Graham, 1937) and this found support even as recently as 1992.[4] However, the scheme is too farfetched: it would entail the holding of commodity stockpiles and open market operations would in effect be accomplished in commodity markets. It is far more sensible for central banks to target the price level and to accommodate monetary policy to this end rather than to get involved in commodity market intervention.[5]

A global fixed exchange rate zone on the lines of the Bretton Woods system is non-viable today simply because no one country can be found with sufficient international respect to lead the system: to which the members of the zone would be willing to tie their exchange rates and monetary conditions. In the meantime the international community struggles on with volatile floating exchange rates between major trading blocks. In the next section we discuss aspects of two regional monetary zones – the yen and the DM. In section 24.4 we discuss some currently fashionable proposals for the reform of the IMS.

 ## 24.3 Yen and DM Currency Blocs

24.3.1 A Japanese yen currency bloc?

As Japan's is the second largest economy in the world, some commentators have asked whether a Japanese currency bloc has emerged? Historically the development of currency blocs – where a currency is used as an international store of value, unit of account, and an exchange rate peg (such as the sterling dollar and franc areas) – has rested on high levels of international trade with the key currency country.

With respect to the idea of an East Asian trading bloc Frankel (1993) estimated a gravity model of intra-regional trade for various East Asian country groupings. (In a gravity model a trading bloc exists if intra-bloc trade is greater than can be explained by fundamental factors such as levels of GNP, per capita income, and geographic proximity.) Perhaps the most striking finding is that the strongest statistical support is for a trading bloc based on the Association of Pacific Economic Cooperation grouping – which includes both the USA and Canada, rather than any strictly East Asian grouping. This is not a sign of the emergence of a yen bloc.

The existence of a yen bloc has also been assessed by measuring the elasticity of a given East Asian country's dollar exchange rate to changes in the yen–dollar rate (BIS, 1997). Thus,

$$\ln X/\$_t - \ln X/\$_{t-1} = \alpha + \beta(\ln \text{yen}/\$_t - \ln \text{yen}/\$_{t-1}) \qquad (24.4)$$

where X is an East Asian currency. A low value for the measured elasticity, β, means that changes in the yen/dollar exchange rate have little effect on currency X's exchange rate with the dollar. In other words, X is not strongly pegged to the yen. Across seven East Asian currencies during the 1994–7 period the *highest* elasticity was 0.2, which amounts to pretty strong evidence against the existence of a yen bloc – as the pegs (which were in fact against currency baskets rather than to a single currency) were more against the dollar rather than the yen. This finding is supported by Frankel (1993) who finds evidence that East Asian interest rates are influenced more by New York than Tokyo rates.

One may speculate as to other reasons why a yen bloc has not yet emerged despite the huge weight of the Japanese economy in East Asia. Tavlas and Ozeki (1992) argue that Japanese financial markets remain narrow, thin, and restricted which discourages the use of the yen as an international store of value. And, along with Iwami (1995) and McKinnon (1999), they argue that as most of Japan's exports are to dollar area countries and a large proportion of its imports are denominated in dollars, the use of the yen as an international unit of account has not been encouraged.

24.3.2 A German mark currency bloc?

It is widely recognized that by stages the European Monetary System (EMS) became a DM bloc (Ungerer et al., 1990). The phase of "trial and orientation", 1979–83, experienced strongly diverging economic conditions and tensions in the EMS – leading to seven exchange rate realignments and the marginalization of the official ECU (which was supposed to have been the monetary focal point). During the "phase of consolidation", 1983–7, the DM emerged as the anchor currency and common economic policies began to be organized around it. In the "phase of reorientation," 1987–89, there was questioning of the asymmetrical operation of the EMS (with Germany determining monetary conditions for the zone) and discussion of the need for commonly-defined polices.

Anecdotal evidence that Germany emerged as the dominant player was the tendency for some central banks to adjust short-term interest rates within hours of changes by the Bundesbank. This accords with evidence suggesting that foreign exchange intervention to support intra-EMS parities was predominantly undertaken by non-German members, and that intervention was systematically sterilized in Germany but much less commonly so by the other EMS countries. Similar supporting evidence is found in Giovazzi and Giovannini (1989) and Ungerer et al. (1990). Furthermore, MacDonald and Taylor (1990), and Artis and Taylor (1988a, 1988b), find econometric evidence of convergence of economic and monetary conditions in the EMS – something that is expected in a pegged exchange rate system with a dominant player (see chapter 17 on the dominance of the USA in the dollar area).

Finally, using the same methodology as equation (23.4), the BIS (1997) finds β elasticities in the order of 0.9 or more for the French and Belgian francs, Dutch guilder, Danish krone, and Spanish peseta -- indicating that when the DM/$ rate changed, they each moved with the DM rather than the dollar.

DM standard on the booze? Like the USA, as leader of a currency bloc it became Germany's responsibility to manage its monetary conditions with some respect for the preferences of other countries. Failure to do so would set a dilemma for other members: either follow the German lead or break free from the DM by leaving the EMS or at least devaluing within it. However, following the reunification of Germany in 1990, the German budget deficit, and nominal and real interest rates, increased sharply and was the underlying cause of the currency crises of September 1992–August 1993. With attractive nominal and real interest rates and expected DM appreciation, money began to flow on a massive scale into Germany. To support their currencies against the DM, interest rates in other countries had to be raised just at a time when they were in or near recession. The British and Italians chose, on September 16 and 17 respectively, to suspend EMS membership. Spain devalued the peseta, Ireland raised overnight interest rates to 1000 percent to protect the punt, and in the week following France spent $10 billion – over half of its foreign exchange reserves – to maintain the franc's parity with the DM. Prime Minister John Major vowed that Britain would not rejoin the EMS until it had been "made to work for the benefit of all its members." Indeed, the replacement of the DM by the euro in 1999 can be viewed as a move to introduce symmetric governance over monetary conditions in the EU as central banks from each euro member country sit on the board of the European central bank.

 ## 24.4 The Costs and Benefits of Flexible Exchange Rates

As we have seen, one way of solving equation (23.3) is to have an IMS characterized by a system of floating exchange rates.[6] As we have emphasized previously, one of the key features of the recent floating experience has been the volatility of exchange rates. The implications of such volatility for the operation of the IMS is the subject matter of this section. The discussion here is related to that in chapter 18 where the benefits of a common currency were considered. The focus is different since we are concerned with how countries, or trading blocks that have already formed a monetary union, may best preserve their trading relations with other countries and with other trading blocks. Ultimately, of course, trading relations with the latter could take the form of some kind of monetary union.

What, then, are the implications of exchange rate volatility for the operation of the IMS? As we have indicated, the volatility of exchange rates, although great on a number of measures, is no greater than the volatility of other asset prices. The key question, then, concerns whether such price movements are consistent with informational efficiency in the respective markets. With respect to the foreign exchange market, the asset approach to the exchange rate (see chapters 9–13) would explain the volatile movement of exchange rates as the outcome of rational forward-looking expectations. On the basis of this view, volatile expectations simply reflect the volatility of underlying policies. Indeed, the fact that exchange rates approximate random-walk processes has led many researchers to conclude that the foreign exchange market is efficient. A fairer assessment of the evidence on foreign exchange market efficiency would be to say that the evidence is inconclusive (see chapters 12 and 13). However, even if it could be proved that the foreign exchange market was informationally efficient, it may not be socially efficient. *In fact it is the social inefficiency of floating exchange rates which is at the heart of the recent international financial stability debate.*

The social inefficiency of floating exchange rates is usually illustrated in two ways. First, it is true that exchange rates are more volatile than the prices of goods (as represented in indexes such as the consumer price index). This has meant that as nominal exchange rates change, so to do real rates. In the short run, with goods' prices effectively fixed, large changes in nominal rates result in large changes in real rates. Such changes may result in allocations of goods and services which are not justified in terms of underlying factors and, indeed, it may result in costly changes in the production base (e.g. UK sterling in the early 1980s and the US dollar in the mid-1980s). Second, the uncertainty which volatile nominal and real exchange rates can impart into the trading behavior of importers and exporters may have a deleterious effect on trade flows and may, indeed, lead to the sovereign states introducing impediments to international trade.

The first cost, outlined above, is perhaps the least controversial in terms of its empirical credentials, whilst the second has limited empirical support (e.g. see De Grauwe, 1988). Consider an example of the former in a little more detail. The world price of oil rose sharply in 1979 and this coincided with a period in which the UK was emerging as a major oil producer. Forward-looking agents expected an improvement in the UK's current account and brought the expected appreciation that this entailed forward into the current exchange rate. Given that the UK authorities were at the time pursuing a disinflationary policy (reflected in relatively high interest rates) the sterling exchange rate sharply appreciated. This resulted in around one-fifth of the UK's industrial base being wiped out (see MacDonald (1988b) for a further discussion). It may be argued that this reduction in manufacturing was warranted given the increased production of oil. Whatever the merits of this argument, there can be no doubt that the speed at which the adjustment took place was undesirable from the point of view of the unemployment, particularly of the labor force, that ensued. A better policy mix is therefore desirable to cope with this type of shock.

Studies which have sought to determine the effects that exchange rate volatility has had on trade flows have not indicated a strong and clear relationship (see MacDonald (1988b) for a discussion). Although this may in some measure merely reflect the relative lack of sophistication of the econometric methods used, such studies (which effectively regress the trade balance on some measure of exchange rate volatility) may not fully capture the deleterious effect on trade of exchange rate volatility because, by definition, they cannot capture trade that has not taken place but otherwise would have in the absence of such volatility. However, Krugman (1989) has forcefully argued that exchange rate volatility has not much affected trade flows because companies engaged in international trade have attempted to keep the foreign currency price of their goods relatively stable in order to maintain their market share; in this sense the current account has been decoupled from the real exchange rate.

A proponent of flexible rates (i.e. Friedman, 1953) would argue that exchange rate volatility, and the riskiness it may impart into international trade, would not, in any case, be a real problem because of the existence of forward and futures markets for the purpose of hedging foreign exchange risk. Indeed, one of the salient features of the recent floating experience, encouraged no doubt by the rapid degree of financial deregulation throughout the period, has been the development (in terms of the number of currencies traded, the number of markets, and the volume of trading) of such markets. However, Kindleberger (1985) has forcefully argued that firms wishing to invest in physical plant or human capital cannot hedge all of the potential exchange rate risk. Why does this apparent paradox arise?

The paradox arises because a manufacturer considering investing in a particular country, to produce some internationally traded commodity, would ideally like to off-load all of the potential future risks, contingent on different states of nature, connected with his investment decision. However, because the transaction costs and moral hazard associated with long-lived futures contracts are so great, futures markets for commodities are generally incomplete. As we have indicated, a manufacturer can easily hedge for relatively short periods of time, but this in no way covers him from longer-term exchange risk, which may be so great under a floating regime that the investment is never made. This argument, however, perhaps overemphasizes the riskiness of foreign investment. Exchange rate volatility is usually regarded as a relatively short-term phenomenon and it tends, as we have argued in chapter 13, to be unforecastable. However, in the longer term exchange rates tend to exhibit much clearer trends and it may be possible for the foreign exchange department of, say, a multinational firm to make reasonably accurate forecasts of the longer-run exchange rate based on the fundamental determinants of exchange rates.

The above discussion has centred on what many perceive as the costs of a floating rate system. As we have indicated, such costs stem from the *volatility* of exchange rates rather than the flexibility of exchange rates *per se*. Many commentators would argue (see, for example, Williamson, 1988) that although excessive exchange rate volatility may be undesirable, for the reasons we have just given, some form of exchange rate flexibility is essential because flexible rates provide a number of useful social functions.

The first social function that a flexible rate provides arises because it enables a country better to adjust to real shocks. Thus, say, a change in preferences, and consequently spending patterns, necessitates a permanent change in real exchange rates. If exchange rates are fixed, all of the adjustment will be thrown onto wages and prices. In a world in which such prices are sticky, adjustment may be slow and painful in terms of its consequences for unemployment. In such circumstances it may therefore be preferable to allow the nominal exchange rate to adjust in order to facilitate a corresponding real change. The fact that the majority of goods entering international trade are imperfect substitutes (see Isard, 1977, Kravis and Lipsey, 1978) would be another reason why a country may want to retain an element of exchange rate flexibility. Thus differences in spending patterns and the imperfect substitutability of goods are both factors which imply that world goods markets are less than perfectly integrated and may therefore require real exchange rate adjustment to facilitate current account adjustment. This kind of argument also spills over to the growth context. For example, and as Dornbusch (1988) has emphasized, real exchange rates in the postwar period have been trending. If nominal exchange rates are to be fixed, then real exchange rate trends will be accomplished by divergent money wage trends.

A second advantage of a flexible rate arises when countries have different propensities to inflate. A flexible exchange rate, by depreciating at a rate equal to the inflation differential, would allow countries to pursue these varying objectives without cumulative payments imbalances arising. Such inflation differentials may arise even when countries have equal productivity growth rates (if, say, they have different inflation tax objectives). In a world of productivity growth, differential inflation rates can occur even when countries do not pursue deliberate inflation tax policies. This may be thought of as a reworking of the Balassa–Samuelson biased productivity argument (set out in section 7.4). For example, consider two countries, A and B, which have a target of zero inflation for their tradeables goods prices (as we shall see this is most relevant from the perspective of the McKinnon proposal) and their overall consumer price level is a weighted average (with weights equal to 0.5) of the prices of traded and non-traded goods. If both countries experience the same (zero) rate of productivity growth in their non-traded sector but A has a productivity growth rate of 6 percent relative to 3 percent in B, then their inflation rates will differ: the inflation rate will be 3 percent in A and 1.5 percent in B.

A third useful advantage of flexible rates arises in a world in which countries put different weights on recession relative to inflation as their primary objective. Thus, in a recessionary environment one country may wish to have an interest rate objective which differs from that pursued in other countries. In a world of high (perhaps perfect) capital mobility the country can only have a relatively lax monetary policy if its currency can depreciate sufficiently to engender the expectation of a future appreciation.

A final useful function of a flexible exchange rate arises in circumstances where a currency is subject to short-lived speculative attacks. In such circumstances, the authorities may prefer to let the exchange rate take up the pressure, rather than throwing the burden of adjustment onto interest rates and/or international reserves.

 ## 24.5 Alternative Plans for the Reform of the International Monetary System

In this section we consider two of the most widely discussed proposals for reforming the IMS, namely the McKinnon plan and the Miller–Williamson target zone proposal.

24.5.1 The McKinnon plan

The McKinnon plan centers around three currencies, each of which are seen as the key currencies for three major trading blocks in the world economy: the US dollar (the North American bloc), the German mark (the EC bloc), and the Japanese yen (the Asian bloc). The plan involves the cooperation of the USA, Germany, and Japan – the Group of three countries – in forming a new international monetary standard based – in the long run at least – on fixed exchange rates. Because it would eliminate exchange rate volatility, the move to such a standard would, it is argued, greatly increase commodity trade and make financial flows more efficient. In many ways, the plan is entirely analogous to the arguments in favor of a money-using economy at the national level. We now present a brief discussion of the details of this plan, indicate how it differs from other international monetary regimes and mention some criticisms of the proposal.

The ultimate, long-term, objective of the McKinnon plan is for the prices of internationally traded goods (as measured by, say, producer or wholesale price indexes) for the three currency blocs to be the same when expressed in any of the three currencies: i.e. some form of absolute PPP is regarded as the long-run anchor to the system. Once exchange rates are so aligned, the central banks of the Group of three countries should monitor the behavior of the "common" internationally traded goods price and collectively alter monetary aggregates to ensure this alignment; commodity arbitrage, it is argued, would be supportive of this objective (given that exchange rates were expected to be fixed indefinitely). The central banks would use their own producer price indexes as their target for monetary expansion but ultimately McKinnon has a common international producer price index as the preferred target. The latter would be priced in each country using a common set of representative weights for the industrial economies.

The McKinnon plan recognizes that in the short run the objective of PPP is not feasible and proposes that the Group of three currencies should set their currencies within (narrow) bands and coordinate monetary policy to ensure that the currencies stay within the bands. For example, if the US dollar fell to the bottom of its band the US Federal Reserve would tighten monetary policy whilst such a policy was being loosened in Japan and Germany. The policy would take the form of changes in relative interest rates and they would occur on a continuous (daily) basis. Assuming that private sector agents have confidence in the system, it is argued that such adjustments would only need to be small. If, however, turbulence in the foreign exchange market did develop as a result of currencies moving to the limits of their bands, the interest rate changes are to be backed up by symmetric unsterilized intervention.

The main criticism of the McKinnon plan is that in its attempt to eliminate exchange rate volatility it eliminates *all* exchange rate flexibility. As we have indicated in the previous section, there are circumstances, particularly when countries face real shocks, in which some degree of exchange rate flexibility may be desirable. The McKinnon response to this criticism would be to assert that real exchange rate movements have little or no effect on the current account deficit; the deficit is determined by the government's fiscal deficit. Some support for this view may be adduced from Krugman's (1989) analysis, referred to above, that exchange rate volatility has resulted in current accounts becoming decoupled from the exchange rates because of the pricing behavior of firms. However, the Krugman thesis is not an argument against volatility *per se*; rather it is an argument for reducing volatility to enable exchange rate movements to fulfil their proper social functions.

McKinnon's view that current account imbalances are driven largely by public/private sector imbalances is reflected in statements like: "[the US] trade deficit of $150 billion to $200 billion a year merely reflects the savings–investment in the American economy created by the coincidentally equally large US fiscal deficit". This is effectively a restatement of the New Cambridge view of the determinants of the current account. The assertion that changes in the budget deficit are reflected on a one-for-one basis on the trade account relies on the restrictive condition that the marginal propensity to import multiplied by the income–expenditure multiplier be unity. For most Group of seven countries this condition seems unlikely to be met. Hence for most countries the real exchange rate will be a valuable extra instrument for policy purposes.

The McKinnon plan may also be criticized from the perspective of its view of exchange rate determination. McKinnon's exchange rate model seems to be rooted in the currency substitution view of the determination of the exchange rate, of which he was an early advocate (see McKinnon, 1982b, and section 9.5). In McKinnon (1988), emphasis is placed on exchange rate volatility being the outcome of money (M1) demand disturbances. On this view, central banks can offset such shifts by intervention. However, even if central banks could estimate a stable money demand function (a task which has been made difficult by financial deregulation), it is not clear that all exchange rate movements are driven by monetary movements: they may be driven by other kinds of portfolio disturbances

– substitution between bonds – or by real shocks. Therefore it may be difficult, if not impossible, for central banks to discern the source of a shock and even if they could they may not want to attenuate all exchange rate movements, for reasons given earlier.

24.5.2 The extended target zone proposal

An alternative to the McKinnon plan is the extended target zone proposal (TZP) which has its origins in the crawling peg of Williamson (1983b) and is developed fully in Edison et al. (1987). This proposal is in agreement with the McKinnon approach regarding the social costs of excessive exchange rate volatility but differs fundamentally from that view in its advocacy of *some* exchange rate flexibility. In particular, exchange rate flexibility is deemed to be desirable for the reasons noted above. The TZP involves a complete set of policy coordination rules to be followed by the main Group of seven industrial countries. The first part of the proposal may be motivated around the following equation:

$$\hat{y}^* = g + \gamma \hat{p}_{t-1} + \varphi d \qquad 0 < \gamma < 1, \ \varphi > 0 \tag{24.5}$$

It is proposed that each country should have, as an intermediate target, an endogenous target rate of growth for nominal income, $\hat{y}^*$, which is equal to the sum of the (estimated) growth of production potential, g, plus some fraction of the past rate of inflation, $\hat{p}_{t-1}$ (the latter term allows implementation of a gradualist deflation strategy) and the deflationary gap d. In addition to the nominal income growth target, each country would have a target for the real effective exchange rate that would ensure internal and external balance in the medium run. It is this second target which gives rise to the label "TZP".[7] These twin country targets, which from an aggregate perspective consist of $2n - 1$ targets, are to be achieved by three basic assignment rules (which should in principle be sufficient to satisfy the $2n - 1$ targets).

First, domestic fiscal policy (i.e. the fiscal policy of any one nation) is to be used, in standard Keynesian fashion, to achieve the national target for income growth. Second, interest rate differentials between countries are to be used to prevent exchange rates moving by more than around 10 percent of their target levels. It is envisaged that such movements could be reinforced by sterilized or non-sterilized intervention. Third, and in common with McKinnon, the average (absolute) level of world interest rates would be revised up or down in response to deviations of aggregate income growth from the aggregate target level. This rule aims to ensure that aggregate monetary policy should be changed in response to the joint needs of the participating countries. It has been referred to by Williamson (1988) as "McKinnon without the monetarism."

It is worth noting that the proponents of the TZP do not necessarily envisage an immediate move to the full-blown plan. Rather, an initial adoption of the target zone component would be a useful first step and, indeed, is seen as pushing the system towards coordination in the other areas. It is further worth noting that assignment rules need not be followed in an inflexible and rigid manner and should instead be interpreted as policy guidelines (see, for example, Williamson, 1988). This is seen as important in order that the proposal be politically acceptable and, additionally, because actual events may require some flexibility.

The TZP has much in common with the McKinnon proposal. Both proposals assign the average level of interest rates to the control of global inflation. Also, both plans emphasize multilateral cooperation with respect to the stabilitzation of exchange rates, although both have different targets. As we have indicated, in the former system exchange rates are free to move around within bands whilst with the latter the targets for exchange rates are to be fixed. Proponents of the TZP argue that it is superior to the McKinnon plan because it allows exchange rates to satisfy all of its supposed key social functions.

The TZP has been criticized in a number of ways (see, for example, Boughton, 1987, 1989). First, it is not entirely clear that the real exchange rate is the optimal external target. This is because the relationship between the real exchange rate and the current balance is unclear in circumstances where there are important public and private sector imbalances in the domestic economy (the USA in the 1980s and 1990s being a case in point). It may therefore be best to target the current account directly and use an appropriate mix of policies to achieve the target. This leads on to the second criticism: what is the appropriate macroeconomic policy instrument for achieving external balance? There are in fact at least two reasons why one might want to reverse the TZP assignment of fiscal policy to the internal objective and monetary policy to the external objective. In terms of comparative advantage, it might be argued that the opposite pairing of instruments with objectives would be more appropriate. Thus, Bryant et al. (1988) have indicated that monetary policy has relatively little impact on the current account even in the medium to long run. The reverse pairing may also have institutional appeal since political and institutional constraints in some countries may make the use of fiscal policy for demand management purposes somewhat difficult. Boughton (1987) has therefore forcefully argued for the reverse assignment.

A third criticism of TZP relates to the width of the exchange rate bands. Krugman (1989), for example, has argued that the proposed bands are too narrow. The narrowness of the bands will be important in circumstances where the credibility of the system is at issue. For example, if the TZP is seen as credible by market operators they will very nearly fix the rate. If the rate is, say, near the top of the band, agents will believe that the rate has more room to go down than up, and vice versa when the rate is at the bottom of the band. This kind of reasoning implies that exchange rates will be strongly (too strongly) stabilized and will fail to fulfil their socially desirable functions. Conversely, a loss of credibility quickly pushes the exchange rate past the edge of the exchange rate band. Thus, to Krugman, target zones produce the temptation to try to sustain the wrong exchange rate and the risk of a speculative attack on the target that an unsustainable fixed rate presents.

Krugman's favored reform of the IMS involves a return to a system of fixed but adjustable exchange rates. In working toward this ultimate objective, currencies should be allowed to move within very wide zones. This, it is argued, should simultaneously attenuate wild speculative movements whilst not tying rates down within a narrow, unsustainable, band. Additionally, countries should pursue "sensible" macroeconomic policies (i.e. policies which are designed to complement macro-policies pursued in other countries). It is envisaged that, as policies become more stable, exchange rates will also become more stable and this should allow the underlying equilibrium exchange rates to become more discernible. At this stage it is envisaged that a new international monetary regime could be instigated based on an adjustable peg exchange rate system.

The extended TZP, and the alternative suggested by Boughton, have been evaluated by Currie and Wren-Lewis (1989). The evaluation utilized the National Institute's Global Econometric Model (GEM) and compared the performance of the two assignments relative to each other and relative to the actual historical performance of the Group of three countries over the period 1975–86. In sum they found that both schemes improved welfare compared with the historical base but the gains corresponding to the TZP were generally of a greater magnitude than for the alternative assignment. One of the reasons for the superior performance of the former scheme was the finding that fiscal policy had a comparative advantage over monetary policy in the control of national aggregate demand. However, Currie and Wren-Lewis qualify this conclusion by noting that the historical period examined may underestimate the importance of the current account as an indicator of policy because of the abnormal US deficit.

NOTES

1 The function P in figure 24.1 is drawn for a given "probability of reserve exhaustion". The latter is exogenous to the model being chosen by the policymakers, who must face the (political) consequences of running out of reserves and having speedy adjustments forced on them. A lower probability shifts the P function to the right (away from the origin).

2 The exception to this will be in circumstances where the supply of outside assets to the IMS (such as gold and SDRs) is changing. If this is the case the sum in (24.1) need not equal zero.

3 It was pointed in section 8.2 (figure 8.3) on the monetary approach to the balance of payments that, with a fixed money demand function, the rate of domestic credit expansion determines the rate of dishoarding and, in turn, the latter determines the balance of payments and change in foreign exchange reserves.

4 See *The Economist*, February 22, 1992, p. 12.

5 For a discussion of the so-called commodity reserve currency schemes, see Hallwood (1986).

6 This section and the next draw on MacDonald (1992a).

7 The title suggests similarities with the target zone literature considered in chapter 15. There are important deferences, however. Thus, the target zone literature is concerned with explaining the theoretical determinants of a *nominal* exchange rate within a target zone, whereas the TZP is about targeting real exchange rates in order to achieve policy cooperation.

Bibliography

Abuaf, N. and Jorion, P. (1990): Purchasing Power Parity in the Long Run. *The Journal of Finance*, 45, 157–73.

Adler, M. and Lehmann, B. (1983): Deviations from Purchasing Power Parity in the Long-Run. *Journal of Finance*, 38, 1471–83.

Agenor, P-R. (1990a): Stabilization Policies in Developing Countries with a Parallel Market for Foreign Exchange: A Formal Framework. IMF, WP/90/16.

Agenor, P-R. (1990b): Exchange Restrictions and Devaluation Crises. IMF, WP/90/84.

Agenor, P-R. (1992): Parallel Currency Markets in Developing Countries: Theory, Evidence, and Policy Implications. Princeton University *Essays in International Finance*, 188.

Agenor, P-R.; Bhandari, J. S., and Flood, R. P. (1992): Speculative Attacks and Models of Balance of Payments Crises. *IMF Staff Papers*, 39 (2), 357–94.

Alexander, S. S. (1951): Devaluation Versus Import Restrictions as a Means for Improving Foreign Trade Balances. *IMF Staff Papers*, April, 379–96.

Alexander, S. S. (1952): Effects of a Devaluation on a Trade Balance. *IMF Staff Papers*, 263–78.

Alexander, S. S. (1961): Devaluation versus Import Restrictions as a Means for Improving Foreign Trade Balances. *IMF Staff Papers*, 379–96.

Aliber, R. Z. (1973a): National Preferences and the Scope for International Monetary Reform. Princeton University *Essays in International Finance*, 101.

Aliber, R. Z. (1973b): The Interest Rate Parity Theorem: A Reinterpretation. *Journal of Political Economy*, 81, Nov.–Dec., 1451–9.

Aliber, R. Z. (1987): *The Reconstruction of International Monetary Arrangements*. New York: St. Martin's Press.

Allen, H. (1990): Chartism in the Foreign Exchange Market. Unpublished PhD thesis, University of London.

Allen, H. and Taylor, M. P. (1990): Charts, Noise and Fundamentals in the Foreign Exchange Market. *Economic Journal*, 100, supplement, 49–59.

Allen, P. R. (1976): *Organization and Administration of a Monetary Union. Princeton Studies in International Finance*, No. 38.

Allen, P. R. and Kenen, P. B. (1978): *The Balance of Payments, Exchange Rates and Economic Policy*. Centre of Planning and Economic Research, Athens.

Allen, P. R. and Kenen, P. B. (1980): *Asset Markets, Exchange Rates, and Economic Integration: A Synthesis*. Cambridge: Cambridge University Press.

Allen, R. R. and Stein, J. L. (1989): The Dynamics of the Real Exchange Rate Capital Intensity, and Foreign Debt. University of Connecticut, Working Paper.

Allen, P. R. and Stein, J. L. (1991): The Real Exchange Rate: Can it be Explained and is it a Basis for Policy? *The AMEX Bank Review*, 4, 105–19.

Alogoskoufis, G. S. (1992): Monetary Accommodation, Exchange Rate Regimes and Inflation Persistence. *Economic Journal*, 102, 461–80.

Alogoskoufis, G. S. and Smith, R. (1991): The Phillips Curve, The Persistence of Inflation, and the Lucas Critique: Evidence from Exchange Rate Regimes. *American Economic Review*, 81(5), 1254–75.

Alpert, M. and Raiffa, H. (1982): A Progress Report on the Training of Probability Assessors. In D. Kahneman, P. Slovic, and A. Tversky (eds.), *Judgement Under Uncertainty: Heuristics and Biases*. Cambridge: Cambridge University Press.

Andreassen, P. and Kraus, S. (1988): Judgmental Prediction by Extrapolation. Mimeo, Harvard University.

Angell, J. W. (1926): *The Theory of International Prices*. Cambridge, MA: Harvard University Press.

Anthony, M. and MacDonald, R. (1998): On the Mean-Reverting Properties of Target Zone Exchange Rates: Some Evidence from the ERM, *European Economic Review*, 42, 1493–1523.

Anthony, M. and MacDonald, R. (1999): 'The Width of the Band and Exchange Rate Mean-Reversion: Some Further ERM-based Results', *Journal of International Money and Finance*, 18, 411–28.

Argy, V. (1981): *The Postwar International Monetary Crisis*. London: Allen and Unwin.

Argy, V. and Porter, M. G. (1972): The Forward Exchange Market and the Effects of Domestic and External Disturbances under Alternative Exchange Rate Systems. *IMF Staff Papers*, 19, 503–27.

Argy, V. and Salop, J. (1979): Price and Output Effects of Monetary and Fiscal Policy under Flexible Exchange Rates. *IMF Staff Papers*, 26, 103–24.

Artis, M. J. and Currie, D. A. (1981): Monetary Targets and the Exchange Rate: A Case for Conditional Targets. In W. Eltis and P. Sinclair, *The Money Supply and the Exchange Rate*. Oxford.

Artis, M. J. and Taylor, M. P. (1988a): Exchange Rates, Interest Rates, Capital Controls and the European Monetary System: Assessing the Track Record. In Giavazzi et al. (eds.), 1988, 185–206.

Artis, M. J. and Taylor, M. P. (1988b): Exchange Rates and the EMS: Assessing the Track Record. CEPR Discussion Paper, No. 250.

Artus, J. R. (1975): The 1967 Devaluation of the Pound Sterling. *IMF Staff Papers*, November, 595–640.

Artus, J. R. (1976): Exchange Rate Stability and Managed Floating: the Experience of the Federal Republic of Germany. *IMF Staff Papers*, 312–33.

Aubrey, H. G. (1969): Behind the Veil of International Money. Princeton *Essays in International Finance*, 71.

Backus, D. (1984): Empirical Models of the Exchange Rate: Separating the Wheat from the Chaff. *Canadian Journal of Economics*, 17, 824–46.

Baillie, R. T., Lippens, R. E., and McMahon, D. C. (1983): Testing Rational Expectations and Efficiency in the Foreign Exchange Market. *Econometrica*, 51, 553–64.

Baillie, R. T. and Selover, D. D. (1987): Cointegration and Models of Exchange Rate Determination. *International Journal of Forecasting*, 3(1), 43–51.

Balassa, B. (1964): The Purchasing Power Parity Doctrine: A Reappraisal. *Journal of Political Economy*, 72, 584–96.

Balassa, B. (1978): Export Incentives and Economic Performance in Developing Countries. *Weltwirschaftliches Archiv*, Band, 114, 24–60.

Balassa, B. (1982): *Adjustment Incentives and Development Strategies in Sub-Sahara Africa, 1973–78*. World Bank, Development Research Department, Report DRD41.

Balassa, B. (1988): The Debt Problem of Developing Countries and Proposed Solutions. In Elliott and Williamson, 1988, 149–67.

Banerjee, A., et al. (1986): Exploring Equilibrium Relationships in Econometrics Through Static Models: Some Monte Carlo Evidence. *Oxford Bulletin of Economics and Statistics*, 48, 253–77.

Banerjee, A., et al. (1993): *Co-Integration, Error Correction, and the Econometric Analysis of Non-Stationary Data*. Oxford: Oxford University Press.

Barro, R. (1989): *Modern Business Cycle Theory*. Cambridge, MA: Harvard University Press.

Barro, R. J. (1974): Are Government Bonds, Net Wealth? *Journal of Political Economy*, 82, 1095–117.

Bartolini, L. and Dixit, A. (1988): Market Valuation of Liquid Debt and Implications for Conflicts Among Creditors. IMF, WP/90/88.

Baumol, W. J. (1957): Speculation, Profitability and Stability. *Review of Economics and Statistics*, 263–71.

Bayoumi, T. (1994): A Formal Model of Optimum Currency Areas. *IMF Staff Papers*, 41(4), 537–54.

Bayoumi, T. and Eichengreen, B. (1992): Shocking Aspects of European Monetary Unification. NBER Working Paper 3949.

Bayoumi, T. and Eichengreen, B. (1994): One Money or Many? Analyzing the Prospects for Monetary Unification in Various Parts of the World. *Princeton Studies in International Finance*, 76.

Bayoumi, T. and Eichengreen, B. (1995): Restraining Yourself: The Implications of Fiscal rules for Economic Stabilization. *IMF Staff Papers*, 42(1), 32–48.

Bayoumi, T. and MacDonald, R. (1995): Consumption, Income and International Capital Market Integration. *IMF Staff Papers*, 42, 552–76.

Bayoumi, T. and MacDonald, R. (1998): Deviations of Exchange Rates from Purchasing Power Parity: A Story Featuring Two Monetary Unions. IMF Working Paper 98.

Bayoumi, T. and Masson, P. R. (1995): Fiscal Flows in the United States and Canada: Lesson for Monetary Union in Europe. *European Economic Review*, 39, 253–74.

Bayoumi, T. and Prasad, E. (1997): Currency Unions, Economic Fluctuations, and Adjustment; Some New Empirical Evidence. *IMF Staff Papers*, 44(1), 36–58.

Baumol, W. and Benhabib, J. (1989): Chaos: Significance, Mechanism and Economic Applications. *Journal of Economic Perspectives*, 3(1), 92–111.

Baumol, W. J. and Quandt, R. E. (1985): Chaos Models and their Implications for Forecasting. *Eastern Economic Journal*, 11, 3–15.

Baxter, M. (1994): Real Exchange Rates and Real Interest Rate Differentials: Have We Missed the Business Cycle Relationship? *Journal of Monetary Economics*, 33, 5–37.

Baxter, M. and Stockman, A. C. (1989): Business Cycles and the Exchange Rate Regime: Some International Evidence. *Journal of Monetary Economics*, 23, 377–400.

Bean, D. (1976): International Reserve Flows and Money Market Equilibrium, the Japanese Case. In Johnson and Frenkel (eds.), 1976.

Bec, F., Ben Salem, M., and MacDonald, R. (1999): Real Exchange Rates and Real Interest Rates: A Nonlinear Perspective, mimeo, University of Strathclyde.

Begg, D. K. H. (1982): *The Rational Expectations Revolution in Macroeconomics*. Oxford: Philip Allan.

Begg, D. K. H., Halpern, L. and Wyplosz, C. (1999): *Monetary and Exchange Rate Policies, EMU and Central and Eastern Europe.* East-West Institute, New York.

Bell, G. (1973): *The Eurodollar Market and the International Financial System.* New York: Wiley.

Benassay-Quere, A., Larribeau, S., and MacDonald, R. (1999): Do Individuals Use Different Models to Forecast Exchange Rates? *Royal Bank of Scotland,* Discussion Paper 10.

Bergesten, C. F. and Cline, W. R. (1985): *The US–Japan Economic Problem.* Institute for International Economics, October.

Bertola, G. and Caballero, R. J. (1992): Target Zones and Realignments. *American Economic Review,* 82, 520–36.

Bertola, G. and Svensson, L. E. O. (1993): Stochastic Devaluation Risk and the Empirical Fit of Target-Zone Models. *Review of Economic Studies,* 60, 689–712.

Beveridge, S., and Nelson, C. R. (1981): A New Approach to the Decomposition of Economic Time Series Into Permanent and Transitory Components, with Particular Attention to the Measurement of Business Cycles. *Journal of Monetary Economics,* 7, 151–74.

Bhandhari, J. S., Driskell, R. and Frenkel, J. A. (1984): Capital Mobility and Exchange Rate Overshooting. *European Economic Review,* 24, 309–20.

Bhandari, J. and Putnam B. (eds.) (1983): *Economic Interdependence and Flexible Exchange Rates.* Cambridge, MA: MIT Press.

Bigman, D. and Taya, T. (eds.) (1980): *The Functioning of Floating Exchange Rates.* Ballinger.

Bilson, J. F. O. (1978): Rational Expectations and the Exchange Rate. In Johnson and Frenkel (eds.), 1978.

Bilson, J. F. O. (1981): The Speculative Efficiency Hypothesis. *Journal of Business,* 54, 435–51.

Bilson, J. F. O. and Frenkel, J. A. (1979): *Dynamic Adjustment and the Demand for International Reserves.* National Bureau of Economic Research, Working Paper, 407.

Bird, G. (ed.) (1991): *Recent Developments in the International Monetary System.* London: Academic Press.

BIS (Bank for International Settlements), *Annual Report,* various years, Basel.

Bisignano, J. and Hoover, K. (1983): Some Suggested Improvements to a Simple Portfolio Balance Model of Exchange Rate Determination with Special Reference to the US Dollar/Canadian Dollar Rate. *Weltwirtschaftliches Archiv,* 19–38.

Black, J. (1959): Savings and Investment Approach to Devaluation. *Economic Journal.*

Black, S. (1989): Transactions Costs and Vehicle Currencies. IMF, WP/89/96.

Black, S. W. (1976): Exchange Policies for Less Developed countries in a World of Floating Rates. Princeton *Essays in International Finance,* 119.

Blake, D., Beenstock, M., and Brasse, V. (1986): The Performance of UK Forecasters. *Economic Journal,* 96, 986–99.

Blanchard, O. (1982): Credibility and Gradualism. Unpublished manuscript, Harvard University.

Blanchard, O. J. and Fischer, S. (1989): *Lectures on Macroeconomics.* Cambridge, MA: MIT Press.

Blanchard, O. and Quah, D. (1989): The Dynamic Effects of Aggregate Demand and Supply Disturbances. *American Economic Review,* 79, 655–73.

Blanchard, O. J. and Watson, M. (1982): Bubbles, Rational Expectations and Financial Markets. In P. Wachtel (ed.), *Crises in the Economic and Financial Structure,* Lexington, MA: Lexington Books.

Blanco, H. and Garber, P. M. (1986): Recurrent Devaluation and Speculative Attacks on the Mexican Peso. *Journal of Political Economy,* 94(1), 149–68.

Blejer, M. I. and Ize, A. (1989): Adjustment Uncertainty, Confidence, and Growth: Latin America After the Debt Crisis. IMF, WP/89/105.

Bloomfield, A. I. (1959): Monetary Policy Under the International Gold Standard: 1880–1914. Reprinted Arno Press, New York, 1978.

Bomhoff, E. S. and Korteweg, P. (1983): Exchange Rate Variability and Monetary Policy Under Rational Expectations: Some Euro-American Experiences 1973–79. *Journal of Monetary Economics*, 11, 169–206.

Boothe, P. and Glassman, D. (1987): The Statistical Distribution of Exchange Rates: Empirical Evidence and Economic Implications. *Journal of International Economics*, 22, 297–319.

Bordo, M. D. (1984): The Gold Standard: the Traditional Approach. In M. D. Bordo and A. J. Schwartz, *A Retrospective on the Classical Gold Standard, 1821–1931*, Chicago: University of Chicago Press, 23–113.

Bordo, M. D. and Eichengreen, B. (1993): *A Retrospective on the Bretton Woods System*. National Bureau of Economic Research.

Bordo, M. D. and Kydland, F. E. (1992): The Gold Standard as a Rule. Federal Reserve Bank of Cleveland, Working Paper 9205.

Bordo, M. D. and MacDonald (1997): Violations of the 'Rules of the Game' and the Credibility of the Classical Gold Standard, 1880–1914, NBER Working Paper No. 6115.

Borensztein, E. (1989): Debt Overhang, Credit Rationing and Investment. IMF, WP/89/74.

Boughton, J. (1987): Eclectic Approaches to Policy Coordination, mimeo.

Boughton, J. (1989): Policy Assignment Strategies with Somewhat Flexible Exchange Rates. In M. Miller et al., 1989.

Branson, W. H. (1968): *Financial Capital Flows in the US Balance of Payments*. Amsterdam: North-Holland.

Branson, W. H. (1969): The Minimum Covered Interest Differential Needed for International Arbitrage Activity. *Journal of Political Economy*, 77, 1028–35.

Branson, W. H. (1975a): Stocks and Flows in International Monetary Analysis. In A. Ando et al., 1975, 27–50.

Branson, W. H. (1975b): Monetarist and Keynesian Models of the Transmission of Inflation. *American Economic Review*, 65, 115–19.

Branson, W. H. (1975c): Comment on Whitman. *Brookings Papers on Economic Activity*, 537–41.

Branson, W. H. (1977): Asset Markets and Relative Prices in Exchange Rate Determination. *Sozial Wissenschaftliche Annalen*, Band 1.

Branson, W. H. (1983): Macroeconomic Determinants of Real Exchange Risk. In R. J. Herring (ed.), *Managing Foreign Exchange Risk*, Cambridge, 33–74.

Branson, W. H. and Buiter, W. H. (1983): Monetary and Fiscal Policy with Flexible Exchange Rates. In Bhandari and Putnam (eds.), 1983.

Branson W. H. and Haltunen, H. (1979): Asset Market Determinants of Exchange Rates: Initial Empirical and Policy Results. In Martin and Smith (eds.).

Branson W. H., Haltunen, H. and Masson, P. (1977): Exchange Rates in the Short Run. *European Economic Review*, 10, 395–402.

Branson, W. H. and Katseli-Papaefstratiou (1981): Exchange Rate Policy for Developing Countries. In Grassman and Lundberg (eds.), 1981, 391–419.

Branson, W. H. and Rotemberg, J. (1980): International Adjustment with Wage Rigidity. *European Economic Review*, 309–41.

Brasse, V. (1983): The Inaccuracy of Exchange Rate Forecasting Devices in the UK. CUBS *Economic Review*.

Brett, E. A. (1983): *International Money and Capitalist Crises*. London: Heineman.

Breuer, J. B. (1994): An Assessment of the Evidence on Purchasing Power Parity. In John Williamson (ed.), *Estimating Equilibrium Exchange Rates*. Washington: Institute for International Economics, 245–77.

Brown, W. A. (1940): *The International Gold Standard Reinterpreted 1914–34.* NBER.

Brunner, K. and Meltzer, A. (eds.) (1976): *Public Policies in Open Economies.* Carnegie–Rochester Conference Series, 9.

Brunner, K. and Meltzer, A. H. (eds.) (1979): *Policies for Employment, Prices and Exchange Rates.* Carnegie–Rochester Conference Series on Public Policy.

Brunner, K. and Meltzer, A. H. (1982): *Economic Policy in a World of Change.* Carnegie–Rochester Conference Series on Public Policy, 17, Amsterdam: North Holland.

Bruno, M. and Sachs, J. (1985): *Economics of Worldwide Stagflation.* Harvard University Press.

Bryant, R. C. (1987): *International Financial Intermediation.* The Brookings Institution, Washington D. C.

Bryant, R. C., Currie, D. A., Frenkel, J. A., Masson, P. R., and Portes, R. (1989): *Macroeconomic Policies in an Interdependent World.* Brookings Institution.

Bryant, R. D., Henderson, D., Holtham, G., Hooper, P., and Symansky, S. A. (1988): *Empirical Macroeconomics for Interdependent Economies.* Brookings Institution, Washington D.C.

Buckley, P. J. and Artisien, P. (1987): Policy Issues of Intra-EC Direct Investment: British, French and German Multinationals in Greece, Portugal and Spain, with Special Reference to Employment Effects. *Journal of Common Market Studies,* 26(2), 207–30.

Buffie, E. F. (1984): Financial Repression, the New Structuralists, and Stabilization Policy in Semi-Industrial Economies. *Journal of Development Economics,* 14(3), 451–82.

Buffie, E. F. and Krause, A. S. (1989): Mexico 1958–1986: From Stabilizing Development to the Debt Crisis. In Sachs, 1989, 141–68.

Buiter, W. H. and Marston, R. C. (1985): *International Economic Policy Coordination.* Cambridge University Press.

Buiter, W. H. and Miller, M. (1981): Monetary Policy and International Competitiveness: The Problem of Adjustment. *Oxford Economic Papers,* 33, 143–75.

Buiter, W. H. and Tobin, J. (1974): Debt Neutrality: A Brief Review of Doctrine and Evidence. In G. M. Von Furstenberg, (ed.), *Social Security versus Private Savings,* Cambridge.

Cairncross, A. and Eichengreen, B. (1983): *Sterling in Decline.* Oxford: Blackwell.

Calomiris, C. (1998): Communication. Listserv, eh.res@eh.net. March.

Calvo, G. A. and Frenkel, J. A. (1991): From Centrally-Planned to Market Economies: The Road from CPE to PCPE. *IMF Staff Papers,* 38(2), 268–99.

Campbell, J. Y. and Clarida, R. (1987a): The Term Structure of Euromarket Interest Rates: An Empirical Investigation. *Journal of Monetary Economics,* 19, 25–44.

Campbell, J. Y. and Clarida, R. H. (1987): The Dollar and Real Interest Rates. *Carnegie–Rochester Conference Series on Public Policy,* 27, 103–40.

Campbell, J. Y. and Perron, P. (1991): Pitfalls and Opportunities: What Macroeconomists Should Know About Unit Roots. In O. J. Blanchard and S. Fisher (eds.), *NBER Economic Manual,* Cambridge, MA.

Campbell, J. Y. and Mankiw, G. (1989): Consumption, Income and Interest Rates: Reinterpreting the Time Series Evidence. *NBER Macroeconomics Annual 1989,* ed. O. J. Blanchard and S. Fischer. Cambridge, MA: MIT Press.

Canova, F. and Ito, T. (1988): On Time Series Properties of Time-varying Risk Premium in the Yen/Dollar Exchange Market. NBER Working Paper No. 2678.

Cantwell, J. (1987): The Reorganization of European Industries After Integration: Selected Evidence on the Role of Multinational Enterprize Activities. *Journal of Common Market Studies,* 26(2), December, 127–51.

Canzoneri, M. B. and Gray, J. (1985): Monetary Policy Games and the Consequences of Non-Cooperative Policies. *International Economic Review,* 26, 547–64.

Canzoneri, M. B. and Minford, P. (1986): When International Policy Coordination Matters: An Empirical Analysis. *International Economic Review,* 26: 547–64.

Canzoneri, M. B., Cumby, R. E., and Diba, B. (1996): Relative Productivity and the Real Exchange Rate in the Long Run: Evidence for a Panel of OECD Countries. *CEPR Discussion Paper No. 1464.*

Caporale, G. M. (1993): Is Europe an Optimal Currency Area? Symmetric versus Asymmetric Shocks to the EC. *National Institute of Economic Research.*

Cardoso, E. A. and Fishlow, A. (1989): The Macroeconomics of the Brazilian External Debt. In Sachs (ed.), 1989, 81–99.

Carli, G. (1971): Eurodollars: A Paper Pyramid? Banca Nazionale del Lavoro *Quarterly Review*, June, 95–109.

Carr, J. and Darby, M. (1981): The Role of Money Supply Shocks in the Short Run Demand for Money. *Journal of Monetary Economics*, 8, 183–99.

Cassel, G. (1928): *Foreign Investments.* Lectures of the Harris Foundation, University of Chicago Press.

Caves, D. and Feige, E. (1980): Efficient Foreign Exchange Markets and the Monetary Approach to Exchange Rate Determination. *American Economic Review*, 70(1), 120–34.

Chadha, B. and Prasad, E. (1997): Real Exchange Rate Fluctuations and the Business Cycle. *International Monetary Fund, Staff Papers*, 44(3), 328–55.

Cheung, Y. W. and Lai, K. S. (1993): Long-Run Purchasing Power Parity During the Recent Float. *Journal of International Economics*, 34, 181–92.

Chinn, M. (1997): Sectoral Productivity, Government Spending and Real Exchange Rates: Empirical Evidence for OECD Countries. Chapter 7, this volume.

Chinn, M. and Johnston, L. (1996): Real Exchange Rate Level, Productivity and Demand Shocks: Evidence from a Panel of 14 Countries. *NBER* Discussion paper No. 5709.

Chinn M. and Meese, R. (1995): Banking on Currency Forecasts: How Predictable is the Change in Money? *Journal of International Economics*, 38, 161–78.

Chionis, D. and MacDonald, R. (1997): Some Tests of Market Microstructure Hypotheses in the Foreign Exchange Market. *Journal of Multinational Financial Managment*, 7, 203–29.

Choudhry, T., McNown, R. and Wallace, M. (1991): Purchasing Power Parity and the Canadian Float in the 1950s. *Review of Economics and Statistics*, 73, 558–63.

Chrystal, A. (1984): On the Theory of International Money. In Black and Dorrance (eds.), 1984, 77–92.

Chrystal, A. (1987): Changing Perceptions of International Money and International Reserves in the World Economy. In Aliber (ed.), 19xx, 127–50.

Claassen, E. M. and Salin, P. (eds.) (1976): *Recent Issues in International Monetary Economics.*

Claessens, S., Diwan, I., Froot, K., and Krugman, P. (1991): Market Based Debt Reduction for Developing Countries. World Bank, *Policy and Research Series*, No. 16.

Clarida, R. and Gali, J. (1995): Sources of Real Exchange Rate Fluctuations: How Important are Nominal Shocks? *Carnegie–Rochester Series on Public Policy*, 41, 1–56.

Clark, P. B. (1970): Optimal International Reserves and the Speed of Adjustment. *Journal of Political Economy.*

Clark, P. B. and MacDonald, R. (1998): Exchange Rates and Economic Fundamentals: A Methodological Comparison of BEERs and FEERs. IMF Working Paper 98/00 (Washington: International Monetary Fund, March 1998).

Clark, T. A. (1984): Violations of the Gold Points. *Journal of Political Economy*, 92(5), 791–823.

Classen, E-M. and Peree, E. (1988): Discussion. In F. Giavazzi et al. (eds.), 1988, 206–10.

Cline, W. R. (1983): Economic Stabilization in Developing Countries: Theory and Stylized Facts. In Williamson, 1983.

Cline, W. R. (1984): *International Debt: Systematic Risk and Policy Response*. Cambridge, MA: MIT Press.

Cline, W. R. (1988): Comment. In Elliott and Williamson, 1988, 175–82.

Clinton, K. (1988): Transaction Costs and Covered Interest Arbitrage: Theory and Evidence. *Journal of Political Economy*, 96, 358–70.

Cochrane, J. H. (1986): How Big is the Random Walk in GNP? *Journal of Political Economy*, 96, 893–920.

Cochrane, J. H. (1990): Univariate vs. Multivariate Forecasts of GNP Growth and Stock Returns. NBER Working Paper No. 3427.

Collier, P. and Gunning, J. W. (1992): Aid and Exchange Rate Adjustment in African Trade Liberalizations. *The Economic Journal*, 102(413), 925–39.

Commission of the EEC (1982): *Bulletin of the European Communities*, 4, 16.

Connolly, M. B. (ed.) (1982): *The International Monetary System: Choices for the Future*. New York: Praeger.

Connolly, M. B. (1983): Optimal Currency Pegs for Latin America. *Journal of Money, Credit and Banking*, 15(1), 56–72.

Connolly, M. B. and Taylor, D. (1976): Testing the Monetary Approach to Devaluation in Developing Countries. *Journal of Political Economy*, 849–59.

Cooper, R. N. (1968): *The Economics of Interdependence*. New York: McGraw-Hill.

Cooper, R. N. (1969a): *International Finance*. Harmondsworth: Penguin Books.

Cooper, R. N. (1969b): Macroeconomic Policy Adjustments in Interdependent Economies. *Quarterly Journal of Economics*, 83, 1–24.

Cooper, R. N. (1982): The Gold Standard: Historical Facts and Future Prospects. *Brookings Papers on Economic Activity*, 1, 1–45.

Cooper, R. N. (1987): *The International Monetary System: Essays in World Economics*. Cambridge, MA: MIT Press.

Cooper, R. N. (1991): Comment. In Williamson, 1991, 310–14.

Cooper, R. N. (1992): Fettered to Gold? Economic Policy in the Interwar Period. *Journal of Economic Literature*, 30(4), 2120–28.

Copeland, L. (1984): The Pound Sterling/US Dollar Exchange Rate and the News. *Economics Letters*, 15, 109–13.

Copeland, T. E. and Weston, J. F. (1988): *Financial Theory and Corporate Policy*. Reading, MA: Addison-Wesley.

Coppock, D. J. (1980): Some Thoughts on the Monetary Approach to Balance of Payments Theory. *The Manchester School*, 186–208.

Corbo V. and de Melo, J. (1987): Lessons from the Southern Cone Policy Reforms. *Research Observer*, 2(2), 111–42.

Corden, W. M. (1977): *Inflation Exchange Rates and the World Economy*. Oxford: Oxford University Press.

Corden, W. M. (1985): On Transmission and Coordination Under Flexible Exchange Rates. In Buiter and Marston, 1985.

Corden, W. M. (1988): An International Debt Facility. *IMF Staff Papers*, 35(3), 401–21.

Corden, W. M. (1993): Comment. In Bordo and Eichengreen, 1993.

Corden, W. M. and Neary, J. P. (1982): Booming Sector and De-industrialization in a Small Open Economy. *The Economic Journal*, 92, December, 825–48.

Cornell, B. (1983): Money Supply Announcements, Interest Rates: Another View. *Journal of International Money and Finance*, 201–8.

Cornell, B. and Reinganum, M. R. (1981): Forward and Futures Prices: Evidence from the Foreign Exchange Markets. *Journal of Finance*, 36(4), 1035–46.

Cosandier, P. A. and Laing, B. R. (1981): Interest Rate Parity Tests: Switzerland and Some Major Western Countries. *Journal of Banking and Finance*, 5, 187–200.

Cottarelli, C. and Blejer, M. I. (1992): Forced Savings and Repressed Inflation in the Soviet Union, 1986–1990. *IMF Staff Papers*, 39(2), 256–86.

Coughlin, C. C. and Koedijk, K. (1990): What Do We Know About the Long-Run Real Exchange Rate? *St. Louis Federal Reserve Bank Review*, 72, 36–48.

Crockett, A. (1997): The Theory and Practice of Financial Stability. Princeton University *Essays in International Finance*, 203.

Cross, R. and Laidler, D. E. W. (1976): Inflation, Excess Demand and Expectations in Fixed Exchange Rate Open Economies: some Preliminary Empirical Results. In Parkin and Zis, 1976.

Crowder, W. J. (1994): Foreign Exchange Market Efficiency and Common Stochastic Trends. *Journal of International Money and Finance*, 13, 551–64.

Cuddington, J. T. (1986): Capital Flight Estimates, Issues and Explanations. *Princeton Studies in International Finance*, 58.

Cumby, R. E. and Huizinga, J. (1990): The Predictability of Real Exchange Rate Changes in the Short Run and in the Long Run. NBER Working Paper No. 3468.

Cumby, R. E. and Obstfeld, M. (1981): Exchange Rate Expectations and Nominal Interest Rates: A Test of the Fisher Hypothesis. *Journal of Finance*, 36, 697–703.

Cumby, R. E. and Obstfeld, M. (1984): International Interest-Rate Linkages Under Flexible Exchange Rates: A Review of Recent Evidence. In J. F. O. Bilson and R. C. Marston (eds.), *Exchange Rate Theory and Practice*, 1984.

Cumby, R. E. and van Wijnbergen, S. (1989): Recurrent Devaluation and Speculative Attacks on the Mexican Peso. *Journal of Political Economy*, 94, 148–66.

Currie, D. A. (1976): Some Criticisms of the Monetary Analysis of Balance of Payments Correction. *Economic Journal*, 86.

Currie, D. A. (1990): International Policy Coordination. In D. T. Llewellyn and C. Milner (eds.), *Current Issues in International Monetary Economics*. London: Macmillan.

Currie, D. A. (1992): European Monetary Union: Institutional Structure and Economic Performance. *Economic Journal*, 102(411), March, 248–64.

Currie, D. A. and Wren-Lewis, S. (1989): A Comparison of Alternative Regimes for International Macropolicy Coordination. In M. Miller, B. Eichengreen and R. Portes (eds.), 1989.

Currie, D. A., Hughes Hallett, A. and Holtham, G. (1989): The Theory and Practice of International Policy Coordination: Does Coordination Pay? In R. Bryant et al., (eds.), 1989.

Currie, D. A., Levine, P. and Vidalis, N. (1987): International Cooperation and Reputation in an Empirical Two-bloc Model. In R. Bryant and R. Portes (eds.), *Global Macroeconomics: Policy Conflict and Cooperation*. London: Macmillan.

Cushman, D. (2000): The Failure of the Monetary Exchange Rate Model for the Canadian–US Dollar, forthcoming in *Canadian Journal of Economics*.

Cushman, D. and Zha, T. (1997): Identifying Monetary Policy in a Small Open Economy Under Flexible Exchange Rates, *Journal of Monetary Economics*, 39, 433–48.

Cushman, D., Lee, S. and Thorgeirsson, T. (1996): Maximum Likelihood Estimation of Cointegration in Exchange Rate Models for 7 Inflationary OECD Countries. *Journal of International Money and Finance*, 15, 337–68.

Cutler, D., Poterba, J. and Summers, L. (1990): Speculative Dynamics. NBER Working Paper No. 3242.

Da Cuhna, N. and Polak, E. (1967): Constrained Minimisation of Vector-valued Criteria in Finite Dimensional Spaces. *Journal of Mathematical Analysis and Applications*, 19, 103–24.

Dale, W. B. (1983): Financing and Adjustment of Payments Imbalances. In Williamson, 1983.

Danker, D. J., Haas, R. H., Henderson, D. W., Symansky, S. A., and Tyron, R. W. (1985): Small Empirical Models of Exchange Market Intervention: Applications to Germany, Japan, and Canada. Federal Reserve Staff Paper No. 135.

Darby, M. R. (1980): Does Purchasing Power Parity Work? NBER Working Paper, No. 607.

Darby, M. R. (1983): Sterilisation and Monetary Control: Concepts Issues and a Reduced Form Test. In M. R. Darby and J. R. Lothian, 1983.

Darby, M. R. (1987): The Current Account Deficit, Capital Account Surplus and National Investment and Saving. US Department of the Treasury, May.

Darby, M. R. and Lothian, J. R. (1983): *The International Transmission of Inflation*. Chicago: Chicago University Press.

Davidson, J. (1985): Econometric Modelling of the Sterling Effective Exchange Rate. *Review of Economic Studies*, 211, 231–40.

De Bruyne, G. (1979): Pareto Optimality of Non-cooperative Equilibrium in a Time Dependent Multiperiod Game. *European Economic Review*, 12, 243–60.

De Grauwe, P. (1983): What are the Scope and Limits of Fruitful Intervention Monetary Cooperation in the 1980s? In Furstenberg, 1983, 375–408.

De Grauwe, P. (1988): Exchange Rate Volatility and the Slow Pace of International Trade. *IMF Staff Papers*, 35(1), 63–84.

De Grauwe, P. (1992): *The Economics of Monetary Integration*. Oxford: Oxford University Press.

De Grauwe, P. (1996): *International Money: Post-War Trends and Theories*. 2nd edition. Oxford: Clarendon Press.

De Grauwe, P. and Dewachter, H. (1990): A Chaotic Model of the Exchange Rate. CEPR Discussion Paper No. 466.

De Jong, E. (1991): *Exchange Rate Determination and Optimal Economic Policy under Various Exchange Rate Regimes*. Berlin: Springer-Verlag.

De Long J. B., et al. (1990): Noise Trader Risk in Financial Markets. *Journal of Political Economy*, 98, 703–38.

De Vries, M. G. (1985): The IMF: 40 Years of Challenge and Change. *Finance and Development*, September.

De Vries, R. and Porzecanski, A. C. (1983): Comments. In Wiliamson, 1983.

Deaton, A. (1992): *The Consumption Function*. Cambridge: Cambridge University Press.

DeGregorio, J. and Wolf, H. (1994): Terms of Trade, Productivity and the Real Exchange Rate. NBER Working Paper No. 4807.

Delgado, F. A. (1991): Hysteresis, Menu Costs and Pricing with Random Exchange Rates. *Journal of Monetary Economics*, 28, 461–84.

Dellas, H. (1986): A Real Model of the World Business Cycle. *Journal of International Money and Finance*, 5, 381–94.

Dellas, H. (1989): Currency Switch and the Choice of an International Reserve Currency. IMF, WP/89/27.

Delors Committee Report (1989): *Report on Economic and Monetary Union in the European Community*. European Commission.

Demirguc-Kunt, A. and Detragiache, E. (1998): The Determinants of Banking Crises in Developing and Developed Countries. *IMF Staff Papers*, 45(1), 81–109.

DeRosa, D. A. (1990): Protection and Export Performance in sub-Saharan Africa. IMF, WP/90/83.

Despres, E., Kindleberger, C. P. and Salant, W. S. (1966): The Dollar and World Liquidity – A Minority View. *The Economist*, 5 February.

Devaney, R. (1989): *An Introduction to Chaotic Dynamical Systems*. Menlo Park: Benjamin–Cummings Publishing Company.

Diaz-Alejandro, C. (1963): A Note on the Impact of Devaluation and the Redistribution Effect. *Journal of Political Economy*, December.

Diaz Alejandro, C. (1985): Good-Bye Financial Repression, Hello Financial Crash. *Journal of Development Economics*, 19(1), 1–24.

Dickey, D. and Fuller, W. A. (1979): Distribution of the Estimators for Autoregressive Time Series with a Unit Root. *Journal of American Statistical Society*, 74, 427–31.

Diebold, F. X., Husted, S. and Rush, M. (1991): Real Exchange Rates Under the Gold Standard. *Journal of Political Economy*, 99(6), 1252–71.

Dixit, A. K. (1989): Hysteresis, Import Penetration, and Exchange Rate Pass Through. *Quarterly Journal of Economics*, 104, 205–28.

Dominguez, K. M. (1986): Are Foreign Exchange Forecasts Rational? New Evidence from Survey Data. *Economics Letters*, 21(3), 277–81.

Dominguez, K. M. and Kenen, P. (1991): On the Need to Allow for the Possibility that Governments Mean What They Say – Interpreting the Target-Zone Model of Exchange Rate Behaviour in the Light of EMS Experience. NBER, WP 3670.

Domowitz, I. and Hakkio, C. (1985): Conditional Variance and the Risk Premium in the Foreign Exchange Market. *Journal of International Economics*, 19, 47–66.

Donovan, D. J. (1981): Real Responses Associated with Exchange Rate Action in Selected Upper Credit Tranche Stabilization Programmes. *IMF Staff Papers*, 28, 698–727.

Dooley, M. P. (1988a): Capital Flight. *IMF Staff Papers*, 35(3), 423–36.

Dooley, M. P. (1988b): Buy-Backs and Market Valuation of External Debt. *IMF Staff Papers*, 35(2), 215–29.

Dooley, M. P. and Helpman, E. (1989): Tax Credits for Debt Reduction. IMF, WP/89/64.

Dooley, M. P. and Isard, P. (1974): The Portfolio Balance Model of Exchange Rates. *International Finance Discussion Papers*, 141.

Dooley, M. P. and Isard, P. (1980): Capital Controls, Political Risk and Deviations from Interest Parity. *Journal of Political Economy*, 88, 370–84.

Dooley, M. P. and Isard, P. (1982): A Portfolio-Balance Rational Expectations Model of the Dollar-Mark Exchange Rate. *Journal of International Economics*, 12, 257–76.

Dooley, M. P. and Shafer, J. (1976): Analysis of Short-run Exchange Rate Behaviour: March 1973–September 1975. *International Finance Discussion Papers*, No. 76.

Dooley, M. and Shafer, J. (1983): Analysis of Short-run Exchange Rate Behaviour: March 1973–November 1981. In D. Bigman and T. Taya (eds.), *Exchange Rate and Trade Instability*, Cambridge, MA: Ballinger, 187–209.

Dooley, M., Frankel, J. and Mathieson, D. J. (1987): International Capital Mobility: What do Saving-Investment Correlations Tell US? *IMF Staff Papers*, 34(3), 503–30.

Doornik, J. and Hansen, H. (1994): A Practical Test of Multivariate Normality. Unpublished paper, Oxford: Nuffield College.

Dornbusch, R. (1973): Devaluation, Money and Non-Traded Goods. *American Economic Review*, 63, 871–80.

Dornbusch, R. (1976a): Expectations and Exchange Rate Dynamics. *Journal of Political Economy*, 84, 1161–76.

Dornbusch, R. (1976b): Exchange Rate Expectations and Monetary Policy. *Journal of International Economics*, 6, 231–44.

Dornbusch, R. (1980a): Evidence to the Treasury and Civil Service Committee. *Memoranda on Monetary Policy*, HC770, HMSO.

Dornbusch, R. (1980b): Exchange Rate Economics: Where do we Stand? *Brookings Papers on Economic Activity*, 1, 143–94.

Dornbusch, R. (1982): Flexible Exchange Rates and Interdependence. *IMF Staff Papers*, 30, 3–30.

Dornbusch, R. (1983): Comments. In G. M. Furstenberg (ed.), 1983.

Dornbusch, R. (1984): External Debt, Budget Deficits and Disequilibrium Exchange Rates. *NBER*, Working Paper, No. 1336.

Dornbusch, R. (1985): External Debt, Budget Deficits and Disequilibrium Exchange Rates. In Smith and Cuddington (eds.), 1985.

Dornbusch, R. (1988): Doubts About the McKinnon Standard. *Journal of Economic Perspectives*, 2, 105–12.

Dornbusch, R. (1987): Exchange Rates and Prices. *American Economic Review*, 77, 93–106.

Dornbusch, R. and Fisher, S. (1980): Exchange Rates and the Current Account. *American Economic Review*, 70, 960–71.

Dornbusch, R. and Frankel, J. (1987): The Flexible Exchange Rate System: Experience and Alternatives. In S. Borner (ed.), 1987, 151–97.

Dornbusch, R. and de Pablo, J. C. (1989): Debt and Macroeconomic Instability in Argentina. In Sachs, 1989, 37–56.

Dornbusch, R., Levich, R. and Frenkel, J. (eds.) (1979): *International Economic Policy, Theory and Evidence.* Johns Hopkins Press.

Dornbusch, R., Makin, J. H. and Zlowe, D. (1989a): *Alternative Solutions to Developing Country Debt Problems.* American Enterprise Institute for Public Policy Research, Washington D.C.

Dornbusch, R. et al. (1983): The Black Market for Dollars in Brazil. *Quarterly Journal of Economics*, February, 25–40.

Driskell, R. A. and Sheffrin, S. M. (1981): On the Mark: Comment. *American Economic Review*, 71, 1068.

Driver, R. and Wren-Lewis, S. (1998): FEERs: A Sensitivity Analysis. In R. MacDonald and J. Stein, *Equilibrium Exchange Rates*, Boston, Kluwer, 135–62.

Dufey, G. and Giddy, I. H. (1978): *The International Money Market.* Englewood Cliffs, NJ: Prentice Hall.

Dumas, B. (1992): Dynamic Equilibrium and the Real Exchange Rate in a Spatially Separated World. *Review of Financial Studies*, 5, 153–80.

Dunaway, S. V. (1988): A Model of the US Current Account. IMF, WP/88/77.

Eaton, J. (1987): Public Debt Guarantees and Private Capital Flight. *World Bank Economic Review*, 1(3), 377–95.

Edison, H. J. (1985): Purchasing Power Parity: A Quantitative Reassessment of the 1920s Experience. *Journal of International Money and Finance*, 4, 361–72.

Edison, H. J. (1987): Purchasing Power Parity in the Long Run: A Test of the Dollar/Pound Exchange Rate (1890–1978). *Journal of Money, Credit and Banking*, 19, 376–87.

Edison, H. J. and Pauls, B. (1993): A Re-Assessment of the Relationship Between Real Exchange Rates and Real Interest Rates: 1974–90. *Journal of Monetary Economics*, 31, 165–87.

Edison, H. and Kaminsky, G. (1991): Target Zones, Intervention, and Exchange Rate Volatility: France 1979–90. Federal Reserve Board of Governors, WP.

Edison, H. J. and Melick, W. R. (1995): Alternative Approaches to Real Exchange Rates and Real Interest Rates: Three Up and Three Down. Board of Governors of the Federal Reserve System, *International Finance Papers* No. 518.

Edison, H., Miller, M. and Williamson, J. (1987): On Evaluating and Extending the Target Zone Proposal. *Journal of Policy Modeling*, 9, 199–224.

Edwards R. and Hallwood, C. P. (1980): The Determination of Optimum Buffer Stock Intervention Rules. *Quarterly Journal of Economics*, February, 151–66.

Edwards, R. D. and Magee, J. (1966): *Technical Analysis of Stock Trends.* Boston: John Magee.

Edwards, S. (1982): Exchange Rates, Market Efficiency and New Information. *Economics Letters*, 9, 377–82.

Edwards, S. (1983): Exchange Rates and "News": A Multi-Currency Approach. *Journal of International Money and Finance*, 3, 211–24.

Edwards, S. (1984): The Order of Liberalization in the External Sector in Developing Countries. Princeton University, *Essays in International Finance*, 154.

Edwards, S. (1985): Stabilization and Liberalization: Chile 1973–83. *Economic Development and Cultural Change*, 33, 223–54.

Edwards, S. (1989): *Real Exchange Rates, Devaluation and Adjustment: Exchange Rate Policy in Developing Countries.* Cambridge, MA: MIT Press.

Edwards, S. and Edwards, A. J. (1987): Monetarism and Liberalization: The Chilean Experiment. Cambridge MA: Ballinger Publishing Co.

Edwards, S. and Montiel, P. (1989): Devaluation and the Macroeconomic Consequences of Postponed Adjustment in Developing Countries. IMF, WP/89/11.

Eichengreen, B. (1985): International Policy Coordination in Historical Perspective. In Buiter and Marston, 1985.

Eichengreen, B. (1990): *Elusive Stability: Essays in the History of International Finance.* Cambridge: Cambridge University Press.

Eichengreen, B. (1992): *Golden Fetters: The Gold Standard and the Great Depression, 1919–1939.* Oxford and New York: Oxford University Press.

Eichengreen, B. (1999): *Toward a New International Financial Architecture: A Practical Post-Asia Agenda.* Institute for International Economics, Washington, D.C.

Eichengreen, B. and Flandreau, M. (1996): Blocs, Zones and Bands: International Monetary History in Light of Recent Theoretical Developments. *Scottish Journal of Political Economy*, 43(4), 398–418.

Eichengreen, B., Rose, A. and Wyplosz, C. (1995): Exchange Market Mayhem: the Antecedents and Aftermath of Speculative Attacks. *Economic Policy*, 251–96.

Eichengreen, B., Watson, M. W. and Grossman, R. S. (1985): Bank Rate Policy Under the Inter-war Gold Standard: A Dynamic Probit Model. *Economic Journal*, 95, 725–45.

Einzig, P. (1937): *World Finance 1935–1937.* New York: Macmillan.

Einzig, P. (1970): *A Textbook of Foreign Exchange.* London: Macmillan.

Elliott, K. A. and Williamson, J. (1988): *World Economic Problems.* Institute for International Economics, Washington, D.C.

Ellis, J. G. (1981): Eurobanks and the Interbank Market. *Bank of England Quarterly Bulletin*, September, 351–64.

Enders, W. (1988): ARIMA and Cointegration Tests of PPP Under Fixed and Flexible Exchange Rates. *Review of Economics and Statistics*, August, 504–8.

Engel, C. (1993): Real Exchange Rates and Relative Prices: An Empirical Investigation. *Journal of Monetary Economics*, 32, 35–50.

Engel, C. (1995): The Forward Discount Anomaly and the Risk Premium: A Survey of Recent Evidence. *Journal of Empirical Finance*, 3, 123–91.

Engel, C. (1996): Long-Run PPP May Not Hold After All. *National Bureau of Economics Working Paper*, No. 5646.

Engel, C. and Frankel, J. A. (1984): Why Interest Rates React to Monetary Announcements: an Explanation from the Foreign Exchange Market. *Journal of Monetary Economics*, 13(1), 31–46.

Engel, C. and Rogers, J. H. (1996): How Wide is the Border? *American Economic Review*, 86, 1112–25.

Engel, C., Hendrickson, M. K. and Rogers, J. H. (1997): Intranational, Intracontinental, and Intraplanetary PPP. *Journal of the Japanese and International Economies*, 11, 480–501.

Engel, R. (1982): Autoregressive Conditional Heteroscedasticity with Estimates of the Variance of the United Kingdom Rate of Inflation. *Econometrica*, 50, 987–1007.

Engel, R. and Granger, C. W. J. (1987): Cointegration and Error Correction: Representation, Estimation and Testing. *Econometrica*, 55, 251–76.

Espinosa, M. and Hunter, W. C. (1994): Financial Repression and Economic Development. Federal Reserve Bank of Atlanta, *Economic Review*, 79(5), 1–11.

European Economy (1990): *One Market, One Money: An evaluation of the potential benefits and costs of forming an economic and monetary union.* Commission for the European Communities, Directorate-General for Economic and Financial Affairs, No. 44, October.

Evans, G. (1986): A Test for Speculative Bubbles in the Sterling–Dollar Exchange Rate: 1981–84. *American Economic Review*, 76, 621–36.

Evans, G. (1989): A Measure of the U.S. Output Gap. *Economics Letters* 29, 285–89.

Falvey, R. and Kim, C. D. (1992): Timing and Sequencing in Trade Liberalization. *The Economic Journal*, 102(413), 908–24.

Fama, E. F. (1970): Efficient Capital Markets: A Review of Theory and Empirical Work. *Journal of Finance*, 25, 383–417.

Fama, E. F. (1976): *Foundations of Finance.* New York: Basic Books.

Fama, E. F. (1984): Forward and Spot Exchange Rates. *Journal of Monetary Economics*, 14, 319–28.

Fama, E. F. and Farber, A. (1979): Money, Bonds and Foreign Exchange. *American Economic Review*, 69, 269–82.

Fama, E. F. and French, K. R. (1988): Permanent and Temporary Components of Stock Prices. *Journal of Political Economy*, 96, 246–73.

Fama E. F. and Jensen, M. (1983): Separation of Ownership and Control. *Journal of Law and Economics*, 26, 301–26.

Faruqee, H. (1995): Long-Run Determinants of the Real Exchange Rate: A Stock-Flow Perspective. *IMF Staff Papers*, 42, 80–107.

Faruqee, H., Isard, P. and Masson, P. R. (1998): A Macroeconomic Balance Framework for Estimating Equilibrium Exchange Rates.

Feeny, M. (1989): Charting the Foreign Exchange Markets. In C. Dunis and M. Feeny (eds.), *Exchange Rate Forecasting*, Cambridge: Woodhead-Faulkner.

Feige, E. L. and Pierce, D. K. (1976): Economically Rational Expectations: Are Innovations in the Rate of Inflation Independent of Innovations in Measures of Monetary and Fiscal Policy? *Journal of Political Economy*, 84, 499–522.

Feldstein, M. (1986): The Budget Deficit and the Dollar. NBER, Working Paper No. 1898, Cambridge, MA, April.

Feldstein, M. and Horioka, C. (1980): Domestic Saving and International Capital Flows. *Economic Journal*, 90, 314–29.

Fisher, E. O'N. and Park, J. Y. (1991): Testing Purchasing Power Parity under the Null Hypothesis of Co-integration. *Economic Journal*, 101, 1476–84.

Fleming, J. M. (1962): Domestic Financial Policies under Fixed and Floating Exchange Rates. *IMF Staff Papers*, 369–79.

Flood, M. D. (1991): Microstructure Theory and the Foreign Exchange Market. *FRB of St Louis Review*, November, 52–70.

Flood, R. P. (1981): Explanations of Exchange Rate Volatility and other Empirical Regularities in Some Popular Models of the Foreign Exchange Market. *Carnegie–Rochester Series on Public Policy*, 15, 219–50.

Flood, R. P. and Garber, P. M. (1980): A Pitfall in the Estimation of Models with Rational Expectations. *Journal of Monetary Economics*, 6, 433–5.

Flood, R. P. and Garber, P. (1982): Collapsing Exchange Rate Regimes, manuscript, *Board of Governors of the Federal Reserve.*

Flood, R. P. and Garber, P. (1984): Collapsing Exchange Rate Regimes: Some Linear Examples. *Journal of International Economics*, 17, 1–13.

Flood, R. P. and Marion, N. P. (1980): The Transmission of Disturbances under Alternative Exchange Rate Regimes with Optimal Indexing. *NBER*, Working Paper 500.

Flood, R. P. and Marion, N. P. (1996): Speculative Attacks, Fundamentals and Self-fulfilling Prophecies. *NBER WP 5789*.

Flood, R. P. and Marion, N. P. (1997): Perspectives on the Recent Currency Crises Literature. IMF mimeo.

Flood, R. P. and Rose, A. K. (1995): Fixing Exchange Rates: A Virtual Quest for Fundamentals. *Journal of Monetary Economics*, 36, 3–37.

Flood, R. and Rose, A. K. (1999): Understanding Exchange Rate Volatility without the Contrivance of Macroeconomics. *Economic Journal*, forthcoming.

Flood, R. P., Bhandari, J. S. and Horne, J. P. (1989): Evolution of Exchange Rate Regimes. *IMF Staff Papers*, 36(4), 810–35.

Flood, R. P., Rose, A. K. and Mathieson, D. J. (1991): An Empirical Exploration of Exchange Rate Target Zones. Carnegie–Rochester Series on Public Policy, 35, 7–65.

Frankel, J. A. (1979a): On the Mark: A Theory of Floating Exchange Rates Based on Real Interest Differences. *American Economic Review*, 69, 610–22.

Frankel, J. A. (1979b): Tests of Rational Expectations in the Foreign Exchange Market. *Southern Economic Journal*, 1083–101.

Frankel, J. A. (1981): On the Mark: Comment. *American Economic Review*, 71, 1075–82.

Frankel, J. A. (1982a): A Test of Perfect Substitutability in the Forward Exchange Market. *Southern Economic Journal*, 406–16.

Frankel, J. A. (1982b): The Mystery of the Multiplying Marks: A Modification of the Monetary Model. *Review of Economics and Statistics*.

Frankel, J. A. (1982c): In Search of the Exchange Risk Premium: A Six-Currency Test Assuming Mean-Variance Optimization. *Journal of International Money and Finance*, 1, 255–74.

Frankel, J. A. (1983): Monetary and Portfolio Balance Models of Exchange Rate Determination. In Bhandari and Putnam (eds.), 1983.

Frankel, J. A. (1985): Six Possible Meanings of "Overvaluation": The 1981–85 Dollar. Princeton University *Essays in International Finance*, 159.

Frankel, J. A. (1989): International Nominal Targeting: A Proposal for Overcoming Obstacles to Coordination, mimeo.

Frankel, J. A. (1993): Is Japan Creating a Yen Bloc in East Asia and the Pacific? Centre for International and Development Economics Research, WP C93-007, University of California, Berkeley.

Frankel, J. A. (1993): Quantifying International Capital Mobility in the 1980s. Chapter 2 of *On Exchange Rates*. Cambridge, MA: MIT Press.

Frankel, J. A. (1994): *On Exchange Rates*. Cambridge, MA: MIT Press, 41–76.

Frankel, J. A. (1995): A Panel Project on Purchasing Power Parity: Mean Reversion Within and Between Countries. NBER Working Paper No. 5006 (Cambridge, MA: National Bureau of Economic Research, February).

Frankel, J. A. and Froot, K. (1986): Under the US Dollar in the Eighties: The Expectations of Chartists and Fundamentalists. *Economic Record*, Special Issue, 24–38.

Frankel, J. A. and Froot, K. (1987): Using Survey Data to Test Some Standard Propositions Regarding Exchange Rate Expectations. *American Economic Review*, 77(1), 133–53.

Frankel, J. A. and Froot, K. (1989): Interpreting Tests of Forward Discount Bias Using Survey Data on Exchange Rate Expectations. *Quarterly Journal of Economics*, 104, 89–96.

Frankel, J. A. and Froot, K. (1990): Chartists and Fundamentalists, and the Demand for Dollars. In Courakis and Taylor (eds.), 1990.

Frankel, J. A. and MacArthur, A. T. (1988): Political vs. Currency Premia in International Real Interest Differentials: A Study of Forward Rates for 24 Countries. *European Economic Review*, 32(4), 1083–1112.

Frankel, J. A. and Rockett, K. E. (1988): International Macroeconomic Policy Coordination When Policy Makers do Not Agree on the True Model. *American Economic Review*, 78, 318–40.

Frankel, J. A. and Rose, A. K. (1995): A Survey of Empirical Research on Nominal Exchange Rates. In E. Grossman and K. Rogoff (eds.), *The Handbook of International Economics*, Vol. 3. Amsterdam: North-Holland.

Fratianni, M. and Wakeman, L. M. (1982): The Law of One Price in the Eurocurrency Market. *Journal of International Money and Finance*, 1, 307–23.

Frenkel, J. A. (1976a): A Monetary Approach to the Exchange Rate: Doctrinal Aspects and Empirical Evidence. *Scandinavian Journal of Economics*, 200–24.

Frenkel, J. A. (1976b): International Reserves: Pegged Exchange Rates and Managed Float. In Brunner and Meltzer, 1976.

Frenkel, J. A. (1978): Purchasing Power Parity Doctrinal Perspectives and Evidence from the 1920s. *Journal of International Economics*, 8, 169–91.

Frenkel, J. A. (1980a): The Demand for International Reserves under Pegged and Flexible Exchange Rate Regimes. In Bigman and Taya (eds.), 1980.

Frenkel J. A. (1980b): Exchange Rates, Prices and Money: Lessons from the 1920's. *American Economic Association*, Papers and Proceedings, 235–42.

Frenkel, J. A. (1981a): The Collapse of Purchasing Power Parity During the 1970s. *European Economic Review*, 16, 145–65.

Frenkel, J. A. (1981b): Flexible Exchange Rates, Prices and the Role of the 'News': Lessons from the 1970s. *Journal of Political Economy*, 89, 665–705.

Frenkel, J. A. (ed.) (1984): *Exchange Rates and International Macroeconomics*, NBER.

Frenkel, J. A. and Levich, R. M. (1975): Covered Interest Arbitrage: Unexploited Profits? *Journal of Political Economy*, 83, 325–38.

Frenkel, J. A. and Levich, R. M. (1977): Transaction Costs and Interest Arbitrage: Tranquil versus Turbulent Periods. *Journal of Political Economy*, 85, 1209–24.

Frenkel, J. A. and Mussa, M. L. (1980): The Efficiency of Foreign Exchange Markets and Measures of Turbulence. *American Economic Review*, 70, 374–81.

Frenkel, J. and Mussa, M. L. (1985): Asset Markets, Exchange Rates, and the Balance of Payments. Chapter 14 in E. Grossman and K. Rogoff (eds.), *Handbook of International Economics*, Vol. 3. Amsterdam: North-Holland.

Frenkel, J. and Mussa, M. L. (1986): Exchange Rates and the Balance of Payments. In R. Jones and P. Kenen, *Handbook of International Economics*, vol. 2. Amsterdam: North Holland.

Frenkel, J. A. and Razin, A. (1980): Stochastic Prices and Tests of Efficiency of Foreign Exchange Markets. *Economic Letters*, 6, 165–70.

Frenkel, J. A. and Razin, A. (1988): *Fiscal Policies and the World Economy*. Cambridge, MA: MIT Press.

Frenkel, J. A. and Rodriguez, L. (1981): Exchange Rate Dynamics and the Overshooting of Hypothesis. *IMF Staff Papers*, 1–30.

Friedman, M. (1953): The Case for Flexible Exchange Rates. In *Essays in Positive Economics*. Chicago: University of Chicago Press, 157–203.

Friedman, M. (1969): The Eurodollar Market: Some First Principles. *Morgan Guaranty Survey*, October, 4–14.

Friedman, M. (1990): Bimetallism Revisited. *Journal of Economic Perspectives*, 4(4), 85–104.

Friedman, W. and Clostermann, J. (1997): Determinants of the Real-Mark Exchange Rate, mimeo, Deutsche Baundesbank.

Friedman, M. and Schwartz, A. J. (1963): *A Monetary History of the United States, 1867–1960*. New Jersey: Princeton University Press.

Froot, K. A. and Ito, T. (1988): On the Consistency of Short-run and Long-run Exchange Rate Expectations. NBER Working Paper, No. 2577.

Froot, K. A. and Rogoff, K. (1985): Perspectives on PPP and Long-Run Real Exchange Rates. In. R. W. Jones and P. B. Kenen, *Handbook of International Economics*, Vol. 3, Amsterdam: North Holland, 679–747.

Fry, M. (1978): Money and Capital or Financial Deepening in Economic Development. *Journal of Money Credit and Banking*, 10(4).

Fry, M. (1988): *Money, Interest and Banking in Economic Development*. Baltimore: Johns Hopkins Press.

Fry, M. (1989): Financial Development: Theories and Recent Experience. *Oxford Review of Economic Policy*, 5(4), 13–28.

Fuller, W. A. (1976): *Introduction to Statistical Time Series*. New York: Wiley.

Furstenburg, G. M. (1983): *International Money and Credit: The Policy Roles*. IMF, Washington, D.C.

Gagnon, J. (1996): Net Foreign Assets and Equilibrium Exchange Rates: Panel Evidence. International Finance Discussion Papers, No. 574.

Gallarotti, G. M. (1995): *The Anatomy of an International Monetary Regime: The Classical Gold Standard, 1880–1914*. Oxford: Oxford University Press.

Garber, P. (1998): Speculative Currency Attacks – A Historical Perspective. Deutsche Bank Research, June, 83–93.

Gelb, A. (1989): A Cross-Section Analysis of Financial Polices, Efficiency and Growth. World Bank Development Report background paper.

Genberg, H. (1976): Aspects of the Monetary Approach to Balance of Payments Theory: An Empirical Study of Sweden. In Johnson and Frankel, 1976.

Genberg, H. (1977): The Concept and Measurement of the World Price Level and Rate of Inflation. *Journal of Monetary Economics*, 3, 231–52.

Genberg, H. (1978): Purchasing Power Parity Under Fixed and Flexible Exchange Rates. *Journal of International Economics*, 8, 247–76.

Genberg, H. and Kierzkowski, H. (1979): Impact and Long Run Effects of Economic Disturbances in a Dynamic Exchange Rate Determination. *Weltwirtschaftliches Archive*, 605–27.

Genberg, H. and Swoboda, A. K. (1993): The Provision of Liquidity in the Bretton Woods System. In Bordo and Eichengreen, 1993, 269–306.

Ghosh, A. (1991): Accounting for Real Exchange Rate Movements in the Short-run and in the Long-run, mimeo, New Jersey: Princeton University.

Ghosh, A. R. and Masson, P. (1988): International Policy Coordination in a World with Model Uncertainty. *International Monetary Fund Staff Papers*, 35, 230–58.

Giavazzi, F. and Giovannini, A. (1989): *Limiting Exchange Rate Flexibility: The European Monetary System*. Cambridge, MA: MIT Press.

Giavazzi, F., Micossi, S. and Miller, M. (eds.) (1988): *The European Monetary System*. Cambridge: Cambridge University Press.

Giovannini, A. (1993): Bretton Woods and Its Precursors: Rules versus Discretion in the History of the International Monetary System. In M. Bordo and B. Eichengreen, *A Retrospective on the Bretton Woods System*, Chicago: University of Chicago Press, 109–53.

Giovannini, A. and Jorion, P. (1987): Interest Rates and Risk Premia in the Stock Market and in the Foreign Exchange Markets. *Journal of International Money and Finance*, 6, 234–46.

Girton, L. and Roper, D. (1977): A Monetary Model of Exchange Market Pressure Applied to the Postwar Canadian Experience. *American Economic Review*, 67, 537–48.

Girton, L. and Roper, D. (1981): Theory and Implications of Currency Substitution. *Journal of Money Credit and Banking*, 13, 12–30.

Glen, J. D. (1992): Real Exchange Rates in the Short, Medium and Long Run. *Journal of International Economics*, 33, 147–66.

Godfrey, L. G. (1998): *Misspecification Tests in Econometrics*. Cambridge: Cambridge University Press.

Goldberg, L. S. (1992): Exchange Rate Unification: Understanding the Russian Reforms. Department of Economics, New York University, mimeo.

Goldstein, H. N. and Haynes, S. E. (1984): A Critical Appraisal of McKinnon's World Money Supply Hypothesis. *American Economic Review*, 74, 217–24.

Goldstein, M. and Khan, M. S. (1985): Income and Price Effects in Foreign Trade. Chapter 20 in *Handbook of International Economics*, Vol. 2, ed. Ronald W. Jones and Peter B. Kenen. Amsterdam: Elsevier, 1041–5.

Gonzales Arrieta, G. M. (1988): Interest Rates, Savings and Growth in LDCs: An Assessment of Recent Empirical Research. *World Development*, 16(5), May, 589–605.

Gonzalo, J. and Granger, C. W. J. (1995): Estimation of Common Long-Memory Components in Cointegrated Systems. *Journal of Business Economics and Statistics*, 13, 27–35.

Goodhart, C. A. E. (1972): *The Business of Banking, 1891–1914*. Aldershot: Gower.

Goodhart, C. A. E. (1988): The Foreign Exchange Market: The Random Walk with a Dragging Anchor. *Economica*, 55, 437–60.

Goodhart, C. A. E. (1991): *Money, Information and Uncertainty*, second edition. Cambridge, MA: MIT Press.

Graham, B. (1937): *Storage and Stability: A Modern Ever-Normal Granary*. New York: McGraw Hill.

Granger, C. W. J. and Newbold, P. (1974): *Forecasting Economic Time Series*. New York: Academic Press.

Granger, C. W. J. and Terasvirta, T. (1993): *Modelling Non-Linear Economic Relationships*. Oxford: Oxford University Press.

Grassman, S. and Lundberg, E. (eds.) (1981): *The World Economic Order: Past & Prospects*. Macmillan: London.

Grauer, F. R., Litzenberger, R. and Stehle, R. (1976): Sharing Rules and Equilibrium in an International Capital Market Under Uncertainty. *Journal of Financial Economics*, 3, 233–56.

Gray, W. G. and Linn, J. F. (1988): Improving Public Finance for Development. *Finance and Development*, 25(3), September, 2–5.

Green, R. H. (1983): Political-economic Adjustment and IMF Conditionality: Tanzania 1974–81. In Williamson, 1983a.

Greene, J. (1989a): The Effects of Fund-Supported Adjustment Programmes in African Countries, 1973–86. IMF, WP/89/38.

Greene, J. (1989b): The External Debt Problem of sub-Saharan Africa. IMF, WP/89/23.

Gregory, A. and McCurdy, T. (1984): Testing the Unbiasedness in the Forward Foreign Exchange Market. *Journal of International Money and Finance*, 3, 357–68.

Grilli, V. and Kaminsky, G. (1991): Nominal Exchange Rate Regimes and the Real Exchange Rate: Evidence from the United States and Great Britain, 1885–1986. *Journal of Monetary Economics*, 27, 191–212.

Grossman, R. H. and Stiglitz, J. E. (1980): Information and Competitive Price Systems. *American Economic Review*, 66, 246–53.

Grubel, H. G. (1968): Internationally Diversified Portfolios. *American Economic Review*, December, 1299–1314.

Gruben, W. C. and McComb, R. (1997): Liberalization, Privatization and Crash: Mexico's Banking System in the 1990s. Federal Reserve Bank of Dallas, *Economic Review*, first quarter, 21–30.

Guitian, M. (1981): Fund Conditionality and the International Adjustment Process. *Finance and Development*, 18(2), 14–17.

Guitian, M. (1976): The Balance of Payments as a Monetary Phenomenon, Empirical Evidence, Spain 1955–71. In Johnson and Frenkel (eds.), 1976.

Gweke, J. and Feige, E. (1979): Some Joint Tests of Markets for Forward Exchange. *Review of Economics and Statistics*, 334–41.

Gylfason, T. (1987): Does Exchange Rate Policy Matter? *European Economic Review*, 30, 23–36.

Gylfason, T. and Radetzki, M. (1991): Does Devaluation Make Sense in the Least Developed Countries? *Economic Development and Cultural Change*, 40(1), 1–25.

Haberler, G. (1949): The Market for Foreign Exchange and the Stability of the Balance of Payments. *Kyklos*, 3, 193–218.

Haberler, G. (1972): Prospects for the Dollar Standard. *Lloyds Bank Review*, 105, 1–17.

Hacche, G. and Townend, J. (1981): Exchange Rates and Monetary Policy: Modelling Sterling's Effective Exchange Rate. In Eltis and Sinclair (eds.), 1981.

Haggan, V. and Ozaki, T. (1981): Modelling Nonlinear Random Vibrations Using an Amplitude-Dependent Autoregressive Time Series Model. *Biometrika*, 68, 189–96.

Hakkio, C. S. (1981): Expectations and the Forward Exchange Rate. *International Economic Review*, 22, 663–787.

Hakkio, C. S. (1984): A Reexamination of Purchasing Power Parity. *Journal of International Economics*, 17, 265–77.

Hakkio, C. S. and Rush, M. (1989): Market Efficiency and Cointegration: An Application to the Sterling and Deutschemark Exchange Rates. *Journal of International Money and Finance*, 8, 75–88.

Hall, R. E. (1978): Stochastic Implications of the Lifecycle – Permanent Income Hypothesis: Theory and Evidence. *Journal of Political Economy*, 86, 971–87.

Hallwood, C. P. (1980): Oil Prices and Third World Debt. National Westminster Bank *Quarterly Review*, November, 34–42.

Hallwood, C. P. (1986): External Economy Arguments for Commodity Stockpiling. *Bulletin of Economic Research*, 38(1), 25–41.

Hallwood, C. P. and MacDonald, R. (1997a): On Equilibrium Exchange Rates in the Visegrad Four: Theory and Evidence. *Journal of Transforming Economies and Societies*, 4(4), 64–73.

Hallwood, C. P. and MacDonald, R. (1997b): Recent Nominal and Real Exchange Rate Experience in a Transitional Economy: the Case of Albania. Paper submitted to the European Commission ACE 94–0714–R.

Hallwood, C. P. and Sinclair, S. W. (1981): *Oil, Debt and Development: OPEC in the Third World*. London: Allen and Unwin.

Hallwood, C. P., Kemp, A. G. and Wood, P. (1983): The Benefits of North Sea Oil. *Energy Policy*, June, 119–30.

Hallwood, C. P., MacDonald, R. and Marsh, I. W. (1996): Credibility and Fundamentals: Were The Classical and Inter-war Gold Standards Well-Behaved Target Zones? In T. Bayoumi, B. Eichengreen, and M. Taylor, *Modern Perspectives on the Gold Standard*. Cambridge: Cambridge University Press.

Hallwood, C. P., MacDonald, R. and Marsh, I. W. (1997): Crash! Expectational Aspects of the UK's and the USA's Departures from the Inter-war Gold Standard. *Explorations in Economic History*, 34, 174–94.

Hallwood, C. P., MacDonald, R. and Marsh, I. W. (1998): Realignment Expectations and the US Dollar, 1890–97: Was There a "Peso Problem"? ESRC, Global Economic Institutions, No. 42, July.

Hallwood, C. P., MacDonald, R. and Marsh, I. W. (1999): Did Impending War in Europe Really Destroy the Gold Bloc? Mimeo. Paper given at Centre for Economic Policy Research, May 15.

Halm, G. N. (1968): International Financial Intermediation: Deficits Benign and Malignant. Princeton University *Essays in International Finance*, 68.

Halpern, L. and Wyplosz, C. (1997): Equilibrium Exchange Rates in Transition Economies. IMF *Staff Papers*, 44(4), 430–61.

Hamada, K. (1979): Macroeconomic Strategy and Coordination Under Alternative Exchange Rates. In Dornbusch and Frenkel, 1979.

Hansen, B. E. (1990): A Powerful Simple Test for Cointegration Using Cochrane–Orcutt, mimeo, University of Rochester.

Hansen, B. E. (1992): Tests for Parameter Instability in Regression with I(1) Processes. *Journal of Business and Economic Statistics*, 10, 321–35.

Hansen, L. P. (1982): Large Sample Properties of Generalized Method of Moments Estimators. *Journal of Political Economy*, 88, 829–53.

Hansen, L. P. and Richard, S. (1984): A General Approach for Deducting Testable Restrictions Implied by Asset Pricing Models, mimeo.

Hansen, L. P. and Singleton, K. (1982): Generalized Instrumental Variables Estimation of Nonlinear Rational Expectations Models. *Econometrica*, 50, 1269–86.

Hansen, L. P. and Hodrick, R. J. (1980): Forward Exchange Rates as Optimal Predictors of Future Spot Rates: An Economic Analysis. *Journal of Political Economy*, 88, 829–53.

Hansen, L. P. and Hodrick, R. J. (1983): Risk Averse Speculation in the Forward Exchange Market: an Econometric Analysis of Linear Models. In J. A. Frenkel (ed.), *Exchange Rates and International Macroeconomics*, Chicago, IL: Chicago University Press.

Hanson, J. and de Melo, J. (1983): The Uruguayan Experience with Liberalization and Stabilization, 1974–81. *Journal of InterAmerican Studies and World Affairs*, 447–508.

Hardy, D. C. (1992): Soft Budget Constraints, Firm Commitments, and the Social Safety Net. *IMF Staff Papers*, 39(2), 310–29.

Hausman, J. A. (1978): Specification Tests in Econometrics. *Econometrica*, 46, 1251–72.

Hawtrey, R. G. (1919): *Currency and Credit*. London: Longman.

Haynes, S. E. and Stone, J. A. (1981): On the Mark: Comment. *American Economic Review*, 71, 1060–7.

Heckscher, E. F. (1916): Vaxelkursens Grundval vid Pappersmyntfot. *Ekonomisk Tidskrift*, 18, 309–312.

Heckscher, E. F. (1930): *Sweden's Monetary History, 1914–25*. In the Scandinavian volume of the *Economic and Social History of the World War*, New Haven, CT.

Heller, H. R. (1976): International Reserves and Worldwide Inflation. *IMF Staff Papers*, 61–87.

Heller, H. R. (1978): Determinants of Exchange Rate Practices. *Journal of Money Credit and Banking*, 10(3), 308–21.

Heller, P. (1989): Aging, Savings, and Pensions in the Group of Seven Countries: 1980–2025. IMF, WP/89/13.

Heller, P., Boevenberg, L., Catsambas, T., Che, K. and Shome, P. (1988): The Implications of Fund-Supported Adjustment Programmes for Poverty: Experiences in Selected Countries. *IMF Occasional Paper*, No. 58, May.

Hewson, J. (1976): Credit Creation in the Eurocurrency Markets – Is there a Case For Control? In Kasper (ed.), 1976.

Hewson, J. and Sakakibara, E. (1975a): *The Eurocurrency Markets and their Implications.* Lexington, MA: Lexington Books.

Hewson, J. and Sakakibara, E. (1975b): Eurodollar Deposit Multiplier: A Portfolio Approach. *IMF Staff Papers,* July.

Hodrick, R. J. (1978): An Empirical Analysis of the Monetary Approach to the Determination of the Exchange Rate. In Johnson and Frenkel (eds.), 1978.

Hodrick, R. J. (1987): *The Empirical Evidence on the Efficiency of Forward and Futures Markets.* London: Harwood.

Hodrick, R. J. and Srivastava, S. (1986): The Covariation of Risk Premiums and Expected Future Spot Rates. *Journal of International Money and Finance,* 5, S5–S22.

Hoffman, D. L. and Schlagenhauf, D. E. (1983): Rational Expectations and Monetary Models of Exchange Rate Determination: An Empirical Examination. *Journal of Monetary Economics,* 11, 247–60.

Hogan, W. and Pierce, I. (1980): The Incredible Eurodollar: A Fable for Our Time. *The Banker,* June, 35–48.

Hogan, W. P. and Pierce, I. (1982): *The Incredible Eurodollar.* London: Allen and Unwin.

Hogg, R. L. (1987): Chapter 9, in R. T. Griffiths (ed.) (1987), *The Netherlands and the Gold Standard, 1931–36.* Amsterdam: Neha.

Holtham, G. and Hughes Hallett, A. (1987): Optimum Policy Design in Interdependent Economies. In R. Bryant and R. Portes (eds.), *Global Macroeconomics: Policy, Conflict and Cooperation.* London: Macmilan.

Hooper, P. and Mann, C. (1989): The Emergence and Persistence of the US External Imbalance, 1980–87. *Princeton Studies in International Finance,* 65.

Hooper, P. and Morton, J. (1983): Fluctuations in the Dollar: a Model of Nominal and Real Exchange Rate Determination. *Journal of International Money and Finance,* 1, 39–56.

Honkapohja, S. and Pikkarainen, P. (1992): Country Characteristics and Choice of Exchange Rate Regime. CERP Discussion Paper, December, 744.

Horne, J., Kremers, J. and Masson, P. R. (1989): Net Foreign Assets and International Adjustment in the United States, Japan, and the Federal Republic of Germany. IMF, WP/89/22.

Houthakker, H. S. and Magee, S. P. (1969): Income and Price Elasticities in World Trade. *Review of Economics and Statistics,* 51, 111–25.

Hsieh D. (1982): The Determination of the Real Exchange Rate: The Productivity Approach. *Journal of International Economics,* 12, 355–62.

Hsieh, D. (1984): Tests of Rational Expectations and no Risk Premium in Forward Exchange Markets. *Journal of International Economics,* 17, 173–84.

Hsieh, D. (1989): Testing for Non-linear Dependence in Daily Foreign Exchange Rates. *Journal of Business,* 62(3), 25–43.

Huang, R. D. (1981): The Monetary Approach to the Exchange Rate in an Efficient Foreign Exchange Market: Tests Based on Volatility. *Journal of Finance,* 36(1), 31–41.

Hughes Hallett, A. (1986): International Policy Design and the Sustainability of Policy Bargains. *Journal of Economic Dynamics and Control,* 10, 467–94.

Hughes Hallett, A. (1987): Optimal Policy Design in Interdependent Economies. In C. Carraro and D. Saktore (eds.), *Developments in Control Theory for Economic Analysis.* Netherlands: Kluwer Academic Publishers.

Hughes Hallett, A. (1989): Macroeconomic Interdependence and the Coordination of Economic Policy. In D. Greenway (ed.), *Current Issues in Macroeconomics.* New York: Macmillan.

Hughes Hallett, A., Holtham, G. and Hutson, G. (1989): Exchange Rate Targetting as Surrogate International Cooperation. In M. Miller, B. Eichengreen, and R. Portes (eds.), *Blueprints for Exchange Rate Management.* London: Academic Press, 239–78.

Huizinga, J. (1987): An Empirical Investigation of the Long-Run Behaviour of Real Exchange Rates. Carnegie Rochester Conference Series on Public Policy, 27, 149–214.

Hume, D. (1753): Of the Balance of Trade. *Essays Moral, Political and Literary.*

Husted, S. and MacDonald, R. (1997): Monetary-Based Models of the Exchange Rate: A Panel Perspective. *Journal of International Financial Markets, Institutions and Money,* forthcoming.

Husted, S. and MacDonald R. (1998): The Monetary Model Redux, mimeo.

IMF (1983a): *Survey,* 27 June.

IMF (1983b) *Survey,* 7 November.

IMF (1983c): *Interest Rate Policies in Developing Countries,* Occasional Paper No. 22, Washington, D.C.

IMF (1984): Exchange Rate Variability and World Trade. *Occasional Paper,* No. 28, Washington, D.C.

IMF (1998), *World Economic Outlook,* Washington, D.C.

Isard, J. C. (1978): Exchange Rate Determination: A Survey of Popular Views and Recent Models. Princeton University *Essays in International Finance,* 42.

Isard, P. (1977): How Far Can we Push the Law of One Price? *American Economic Review,* 67(5), 942–8.

Isard, P. (1980): Expected and Unexpected Changes in Exchange Rates: the Roles of Relative Price Levels, Balance of Payments Factors, Interest Rates and Risk. *International Finance Discussion Papers.*

Isard, P. (1987): Lessons from Empirical Models of Exchange Rates. *IMF Staff Papers,* 34(1), 1–28.

Ishii, N. W., McKibben, W. J. and Sachs, J. (1985): The Economic Policy Mix, Policy Cooperation and Protectionism: Some Aspects of Macroeconomic Interdependence among the United States, Japan and other OECD countries. *Journal of Policy Modelling,* 7, 533–72.

Ishiyama, Y. (1975): The Theory of Optimum Currency Areas: a Survey. *IMF Staff Papers,* 22, 344–83.

Ito, T. (1988): Foreign Exchange Rate Expectations: Micro Survey Data. NBER Working Paper Series, No. 22679.

Ito, T. (1990): Foreign Exchange Rate Expectations: Micro Survey Data. *American Economic Review,* 80, 434–9.

Ito, T., Lyons, R. K. and Melvin, M. T. (1998): Is there Private Information in the Foreign Exchange Market? The Tokyo Experiment. *Journal of Finance,* 53, 1111–30.

Iwami, T. (1995): *Japan in the International Financial System.* New York: St. Martin's Press.

Jacquillat, B. and Solnik, B. H. (1978): Multinationals are Poor Tools for Diversification. *Journal of Portfolio Management,* Winter, 8–12.

Jensen, M. and Meckling, W. (1976): Theory of the Firm: Managerial Behaviour, Agency Costs and Capital Structure. *Journal of Financial Economics,* 3, 305–60.

Johansen, S. (1988): Statistical Analysis of Cointegration Vectors. *Journal of Economic Dynamics and Control,* 12, 231–54.

Johansen, S. (1989): Estimation and Hypothesis Testing of Cointegration Vectors in Gaussian Vector Autoregressive Models, mimeo, *Institute of Mathematical Statistics,* Copenhagen; forthcoming *Econometrica.*

Johansen, S. (1995): *Likelihood-based Inference in Cointegrated Vector Autoregressive Models.* Oxford: Oxford University Press.

Johansen, S. and Juselius, K. (1990): Maximum Likelihood Estimation and Inference on Cointegration – With Applications to the Demand for Money. *Oxford Bulletin of Economics and Statistics,* 52, 169–210.

Johansen, S. and Juselius, K. (1992): Testing Structural Hypothesis in a Multivariate Cointegration Analysis of the PPP and the UIP for the UK. *Journal of Econometrics*, 53, 211–44.

Johnson, H. G. (1961): *International Trade and Economic Growth: Studies in Pure Theory*. London: Allen and Unwin.

Johnson, H. G. (1970): The Case for Flexible Exchange Rates, 1969. In Hack, 1970.

Johnson, H. G. (1976): Elasticity, Absorption, Keynesian Multiplier, Keynesian Policy and Monetary Approaches to Devaluation Theory: A Simple Geometric Exposition. *American Economic Review*.

Johnson, H. G. (1977): The Monetary Approach to the Balance of Payments: A Nontechnical Guide. *Journal of International Economics*, 7, 251–68.

Johnson, H. G. and Frenkel, J. A. (eds.) (1976): *The Monetary Approach to the Balance of Payments*. London: Allen and Unwin.

Johnson, H. G. and Frenkel, J. A. (eds.) (1978): *The Economics of Exchange Rates*. Reading, MA. Addison-Wesley.

Johnson, O. and Salop, J. (1980): Distributional Aspects of Stabilization Programmes in Developing Countries. *IMF Staff Papers*, 1–23.

Johnson, H. G. and Swoboda, A. K. (1976): *International Trade and Money*. Chicago, IL: Chicago University Press.

Johnston, R. B. and Brekk, O. P. (1989): Monetary Control Procedures and Financial Reform: Approaches, Issues and Recent Experience in Developing Countries. IMF, WP/89/48.

Jorion, P. (1989): Asset Allocation With Hedged and Unhedged Foreign Stocks and Bonds. *Journal of Portfolio Management*, Summer, 49–54.

Jorion, P. and Sweeney, R. (1996): Mean Reversion in Real Exchange Rates: Evidence and Implications for Forecasting. *Journal of International Economics*, 40, 215–32.

Junz, H. B. and Rhomberg, R. R. (1973): Price Competitiveness in Export Trade Among Industrial Countries. *American Economic Review*, May.

Juselius, K. (1995): Do Purchasing Power Parity and Uncovered Interest Parity Hold in the Long-Run? An Example of Likelihood Inference in a Multivariate Time Series Model. *Journal of Econometrics*, 69, 211–40.

Juselius, K. (1999): Models and Relations in Economics and Econometrics. *Journal of Economic Methodology*, 6(2), 259–90.

Kahkonen, J. (1987): Liberalization Policies and Welfare in a Financially Repressed Economy. *IMF Staff Papers*, 34(3), September, 531–45.

Kaldor, N. (1970): The New Monetarism. *Lloyds Bank Review*, July, 1–18.

Kamin, S. B. (1988): *Devaluation, External Balance and Macroeconomic Performance. Princeton Studies in International Finance*, No. 62, August.

Kaminsky, G. L., Lizando, S. and Reinhart, C. M. (1998): Leading Indicators of Currency Crises. *IMF Staff Papers*, 45(1), 1–48.

Kaminsky, G. L. and Peruga, R. (1988): Risk Premium and the Foreign Exchange Market, mimeo, University of California, San Diego.

Kaminsky, G. L. and Reinhart, C. M. (1998): Financial Crises in Asia and Latin America: Then and Now. *American Economic Review Papers and Proceedings*, 88(2), May, 444–8.

Kapstein, E. B. (1991): Supervising International Banks: Origins and Implications of the Basle Accord. Princeton University *Essays in International Finance*, 185.

Karapatakis, A. G. (1992): *Financial Liberalization and Inflation in a Small Open Economy: Theory and Evidence from Cyprus*. University of Connecticut, PhD thesis.

Kasper, W. (ed.) (1976): *International Money – Experiments and Experience*. Dept. of Economics, Australian National University.

Kawai, M. and Ohara, H. (1997): Nonstationarity of Real Exchange Rates in the G7 Countries: Are They Cointegrated with Real Variables? *Journal of Japanese and International Economies*, 11, 523–47.

Kearney, C. P. and MacDonald, R. (1986): Intervention and Sterilisation under Floating Exchange Rates: The UK 1973–83. *European Economic Review*, 30, 345–64.

Kearney, C. P. and MacDonald, R. (1988): Asset Markets, the Current Account and Exchange Rate Determination: An Empirical Analysis of the Sterling/Dollar Exchange Rate, 1973–1983. *Australian Economic Papers*, December, 213–32.

Kearney, C. P. and MacDonald, R. (1990): Rational Expectations, Bubbles and Monetary Models of the Exchange Rate: The Australian/US dollar rate During The Recent Float. *Australian Economic Papers*, June, 1–20.

Kearney C. P. and MacDonald, R. (1991): Efficiency in the Forward Foreign Exchange Market: Weekly Tests of the Australian/US Dollar Exchange Market, January 1984–March 1987. *Economic Record*, 67, 237–42.

Kenen, P. B. (1969): Theory of Optimum Currency Areas: An Eclectic View. In Mundell and Swoboda, 1969.

Kenen, P. B. (1983): Quoted in *The Wall Street Journal*, 8 February.

Kenen, P. B. (1985): *The International Economy*. Englewood Cliffs, NJ: Prentice-Hall.

Kenen, P. B. (1988): Reflections on the EMS Experience. In Giavazzi, et al. (eds.), 1988, 388–93.

Kenen, P. B. (1991): From EMS to EMU and Beyond. *The Bosman Lecture*, Tilburg University, April.

Khan, M. S. and Haque, N. U. (1985): Foreign Borrowing and Capital Flight: A Formal Analysis. *IMF Staff Papers*, 32, 606–28.

Kim, Y. (1990): Purchasing Power Parity in the Long-Run: A Cointegration Approach. *Journal of Money, Credit and Banking*, 22, 491–503.

Kincaid, G. R. (1983): Korean's Major Adjustment Effort. *Finance and Development*, 20(4), 20–3.

Kindleberger, C. P. (1965): Balance of Payments Deficits and the International Market for Liquidity. Princeton University *Essays in International Finance*, 46.

Kindleberger, C. P. (ed.) (1970): *The International Corporation: A Symposium*. Cambridge, MA: MIT Press.

Kindleberger, C. P. (1985): The Dollar Yesterday, Today and Tomorrow. Banca Nazionale del Lavoro *Quarterly Review*, 2, 295–308.

Kindleberger, C. P. (1986): *The World in Depression 1929–39*. Berkeley, CA: University of California Press.

King, D. T., Putnam, B. H. and Wilford, D. S. (1977): A Currency Portfolio Approach to Exchange Rate Determination: Exchange Rate Stability and the Independence of Monetary Policy. In *The Monetary Approach to the Balance of Payments*, New York: Praeger.

Kissinger, H. (1994): *Diplomacy*. New York: Simon and Schuster.

Klein, M. and Marion, N. (1994): Explaining the Duration of Exchange Rate Pegs. *NBER Working Paper*, No. 4651.

Klopstock, F. H. (1968): The Eurodollar Market: Some Unresolved Issues. Princeton University *Essays in International Finance*, 65.

Koedijk, K. and Schotman, P. (1990): How to Beat a Random Walk: an Empirical Model of Real Exchange Rates. *Journal of International Economics*, 29, 311–31.

Kohsaka, A. (1984): High Interest Rate Policy Under Financial Repression. *Developing Economies*, 22(4), 419–52.

Korajczyk, R. A. (1985): The Pricing of Forward Contracts for Foreign Exchange. *Journal of Political Economy*, 346–68.

Kouretas, G. (1997): Identifying Linear Restrictions on the Monetary Exchange Rate Model and the Uncovered Interest Parity: Cointegration for the Canadian–US Dollar. *Canadian Journal of Economics*, 30, 875–90.

Kouri, P. (1977): International Investment and Interest Rate Linkages Under Flexible Exchange Rates. In R. Aliber (ed.), *The Political Economy of Monetary Reform*. London: Macmillan.

Kouri, P. and Porter, M. G. (1974): International Capital Flows and Portfolio Equilibrium. *Journal of Political Economy*, 82, 443–67.

Krasker, W. S. (1980): The Peso Problem in Testing the Efficiency of Forward Exchange Markets. *Journal of Monetary Economics*, 6, 269–76.

Kravis, I. B. (1978): *International Comparisons of Real Product and Purchasing Power*. Baltimore: Johns Hopkins Press.

Kravis, I. and Lipsey, R. (1978): Price Behaviour in the Light of Balance of Payments Theory. *Journal of International Economics*, 8(2), 193–246.

Kravis, I. B. and Lipsey, R. E. (1983): *Towards an Explanation of National Price Levels*. Princeton Studies in International Finance 52, November.

Kreinin, M. E. and Officer, L. H. (1978): The Monetary Approach to the Balance of Payments: A Survey. *Princeton Studies in International Finance*, 43, Princeton, NJ: Princeton University International Finance Section.

Kremers, J. M. (1989a): External Imbalances and Fiscal Policy in the Group of Three Countries: The Role of Stock-Flow Dynamics. IMF, WP/89/81.

Kremers, J. M. (1989b): Gaining Policy Credibility in the EMS: The Case of Ireland. IMF, WP/89/36.

Kremers, J. and Lane, T. D. (1991): Economic and Monetary Aggergation and the Demand for Money in the EMS. *IMF Staff Papers*, 37, 777–805.

Krugman, P. (1978): Purchasing Power Parity and Exchange Rates: Another Look at the Evidence. *Journal of International Economics*, 8, 397–407.

Krugman, P. (1979): A Model of Balance of Payments Crises. *Journal of Money Credit and Banking*, 11, 311–25.

Krugman, P. (1988): Target Zones and Exchange Rate Dynamics. NBER Working Paper No. 2481, Cambridge, MA.

Krugman, P. (1989): *Exchange Rate Instability*. Cambridge, MA: MIT Press.

Krugman, P. (1991a): Has the Adjustment Process Worked? Policy Analyses in International Economics, 34, Institute for International Economics.

Krugman, P. (1991b): *Geography and Trade*. Cambridge, MA: MIT Press.

Krugman, P. (1991c): Target Zones and Exchange Rate Dynamics. *Quarterly Journal of Economics*, 106(3), 669–82.

Krugman, P. and Taylor, L. (1978): Contractionary Effects of Devaluation. *Journal of International Economics*, 8, 445–56.

Kugler, P. and Carlos, L. (1993): Multivariate Cointegration Analysis and the Long-Run Validity of PPP. *Review of Economics and Statistics*, 75, 180–4.

Kydland, F. E. and Prescott, E. C. (1977): Rules Rather than Discretion: The Inconsistency of Optimal Plans. *Journal of Political Economy*, 77, 473–91.

La Cour, L. and MacDonald, R. (1998): Modelling the ECU against the US Dollar: A Structural Monetary Approach. Royal Bank of Scotland Discussion Paper No. 2.

Laidler, D. (1992): *The Demand for Money*. New York: HarperCollins.

Laidler, D. and Nobay, A. R. (1976): International Aspects of Inflation: A Survey. In Claassen and Salin (eds.), 1976.

Laidler, D. and Parkin, J. M. (1975): Inflation: A Survey. *Economic Journal*, 85, 741–809.

Laney, L. O., Radcliffe, C. D. and Willett, T. D. (1984): Currency Substitution: A Comment. *Southern Economic Journal*, 50, 1196–200.

Laskar, D. M. (1983): Short Run Independence of Monetary Policy under a Pegged-Exchange Rates System: An Econometric Approach. *Journal of International Money and Finance*, 1, 57–79.

Laursen, S. and Metzler, L. A. (1950): Flexible Exchange Rates and the Theory of Employment. *Review of Economics and Statistics*, 32(4), 281–99.

Le Fort, G. R. (1988): The Relative Price of Nontraded Goods, Absorption, and Exchange Rate Policy in Chile, 1974–82. *IMF Staff Papers*, 32(2), June, 336–70.

Lee, B. E. (1973): The Eurodollar Multiplier. *Journal of Finance*, 28, 867–74.

Lerner, A. (1944): *The Economics of Control*. New York: Macmillan.

Levich, R. (1978): Further Results on the Efficiency of Markets for Foreign Exchange. In *Managed Exchange Rate Flexibility: the Recent Experience*. Federal Reserve Bank of Boston, 58–80.

Levich R. (1979): On the Efficiency of Markets for Foreign Exchange. In Dornbusch and Frenkel, 246–67.

Leivch, R. (1982): How the Rise of the Dollar took Forecasters by Surprise. *Euromoney*, 98–111.

Levin, A. and Chien-Fu Lin (1992, 1994): Unit Root Tests in Panel Data: Asymptotic and Finite Sample Properties. Unpublished; Washington: Federal Reserve Board of Governors.

Levine, R. (1987a): The Pricing of Forward Exchange Rates. *International Finance*, Discussion Papers, No. 312.

Levine, P. and Currie, D. A. (1987): The Design of Feedback Rules in Linear Stochastic Rational Expectations Models. *Journal of Economic Dynamics and Control*, 11, 1–28.

Levy, E. and Nobay, A. R. (1986): The Speculative Efficiency Hypothesis: A Bivariate Analysis. Supplement to the *Economic Journal*, 96, 109–21.

Lim, J. (1987): The New Structuralist Critique of the Monetarist Theory of Inflation: the Case of the Philippines. *Journal of Development Economics*, 25, 45–61.

Lindberg, H. and Soderlind, P. (1992): Testing the Basic Target Zone Model on Swedish Data. Institute for International Economic Studies, Paper 488, Stockholm.

Lindert, P. H. (1969): *Key Currencies and Gold 1900–1913. Princeton Studies in International Finance*, No. 24.

Lipschitz, L. (1979): Exchange Rate Policy for a Small Developing Country, and the Selection of an Appropriate Standard. IMF *Staff Papers*, 26(3), 423–49.

Lipsey, R. G. and Lancaster, K. J. (1956–7): The General Theory of Second Best. *Review of Economic Studies*, 24, 11–32.

Liu, P. C. and Maddala, G. S. (1992): Rationality of Survey Data and Tests for Market Efficiency in the Foreign Exchange Markets. *Journal International Money and Finance*, 11, 366–81.

Liviatan, N. (1980): *Anti-Inflationary Monetary Policy and the Capital Import Tax*. Warwick Economic Research Paper, No. 171.

Llewellyn, D. T. (1980): *International Financial Integration*. London: Macmillan.

Llewellyn, D. T. (1984): Modelling International Banking Flows: an Analytical Framework. In Black and Dorrance, 1984, 35–76.

Llewellyn, D. T. and Milner, C. (eds.) (1990): *Current Issues in International Monetary Economics*. London: Macmillan.

Lo, A. W. and MacKinley, A. C. (1988): Stock Market Prices Do Not Follow Random Walks: Evidence From a Simple Specification Test. *Review of Financial Studies*, 1, 41–66.

Logue, D. E. and Sweeney, R. J. (1977): White Noise in Imperfect Markets: The Case of the Franc–Dollar Exchange Rate. *Journal of Finance*, 32, 761–8.

Longworth, D. (1981): Testing the Efficiency of the Canadian–US Exchange Market Under the Assumption of No Risk Premium. *Journal of Finance*, 36, 43–9.

Longworth, D., Boothe, P. and Clinton, K. (1983): A Study of the Efficiency of the Foreign Exchange Market. Ottawa, Canada: Bank of Canada.

Loopesko, B. E. (1984): Relationships Among Exchange Rates, Intervention, and Interest Rates: An Empirical Investigation. *Journal of International Money and Finance*, 3, 257–78.

Lothian, J. (1997): Multi-Country Evidence on the Behaviour of Purchasing Power Parity Under the Current Float. *Journal of International Money and Finance*, vol. 16.

Lothian, J. and Taylor, M. (1995): Real Exchange Rate Behaviour: The Recent Float From the Behaviour of the Past Two Centuries. *Journal of Political Economy*, 104, 488–509.

Lucas, R. (1977): Economic Policy Evaluation: A Critique. In *The Phillips Curve and Labour Markets*. Carnegie–Rochester Conference Series on Public Policy, 19–46.

Lucas, R. (1978): Asset Pricing in an Exchange Economy. *Econometrica*, 46, 1429–45

Lucas, R. (1980): Equilibrium in a Pure Currency Economy. *Economic Enquiry*, 18, 203–20.

Lucas, R. (1982): Interest Rates and Currency Prices in a Two-Country World. *Journal of Monetary Economics*, 10, 335–60.

Luce, R. D. and Raiffa, H. (1957): *Games and Decisions*. New York: J Wiley and Sons.

Lutkepohl, H. (1993): *Introduction to Multiple Time Series Analysis*. Berlin: Springer-Verlag.

Lutz, F. A. (1974): The Eurocurrency System. Banca Nazionale Lavoro *Quarterly Review*, 110.

Lyons, R. (1991): Information Intermediation in the Microstructure of the Foreign Exchange Market. *NBER* Working Paper, No. 3889.

Lyons, R. (1996): Optimal Transparency in a Dealer Market with an Application to Foreign Exchange. *Journal of Financial Intermediation*, 5, 225–54.

Lyons, R. (1997): A Simultaneous Trade Model of the Foreign Exchange Hot Potato. *Journal of Financial Economics*, 42, 275–98.

MacDonald, R. (1983a): Some Tests of Rational Expectations Hypothesis in the Foreign Exchange Market. *Scottish Journal of Political Economy*, 30, 235–50.

MacDonald, R. (1983b): Tests of Efficiency and the Impact of News in Three Foreign Exchange Markets. *Bulletin of Economic Research*, 35(2), 123–44.

MacDonald, R. (1984): The Monetary Approach to the Exchange Rate Revisited. *Applied Economics*, 16(5), 771–82.

MacDonald, R. (1985): Do Deviations of the Real Effective Exchange Rate Follow a Random Walk?. *Economic Notes*, 14(1), 63–9.

MacDonald, R. (1985): "News" and the 1920's Experience with Floating Exchange Rates. *Economics Letters*, 17, 379–83.

MacDonald, R. (1985b): Are Deviations from Purchasing Power Parity Efficient? Some Further Answers. *Weltwirtschaftliches Archiv*, 121(4), 638–45.

MacDonald, R. (1987): The Demand for International Reserves Under a Regime of Floating Exchange Rates. *Economics Letters*, 23, 189–92.

MacDonald, R. (1988a): *Floating Exchange Rates: Theories and Evidence*. London: Unwin-Hyman.

MacDonald, R. (1988b): Purchasing Power Parity: Some Long Run Evidence from the Recent Float. The *Economist*, 136, 239–52.

MacDonald, R. (1990a): Are Foreign Exchange Market Forecasters Rational?: Some Survey Based Tests. *The Manchester School of Economic and Social Studies*, 58, 229–41.

MacDonald, R. (1990b): Empirical Studies of Exchange Rate Economics. In Llewellyn and Milner (eds.), 1990.

MacDonald, R. (1991): Exchange Rate Economics and Empirical Perspective. In G. Bird (ed.), 1991.

MacDonald, R. (1992): Floating Exchange Rates. In J. Eatwell, M. Milgate, and P. Newman (eds.), *The New Palgrave Dictionary of Money and Finance*. London: Macmillan.

MacDonald, R. (1992a): International Financial Stability. In J. Eatwell, M. Milgate, and P. Newman (eds.), *The New Palgrave Dictionary of Money and Finance*. London: Macmillan.

MacDonald, R. (1992b): Exchange Rate Survey Data: A Dissagregated G-7 Perspective. *The Manchester School of Economic and Social Studies*, Special Edition, forthcoming.

MacDonald, R. (1993): Long-Run Purchasing Power Parity: Is It for Real? *Review of Economics and Statistics*.

MacDonald, R. (1995a): Long-Run Exchange Rate Modeling: A Survey of the Recent Evidence. *IMF Staff Papers*, 42(3), 437–89.

MacDonald, R. (1995b): Asset Market and Balance of Payments Characteristics: An Eclectic Exchange Rate Model for the Dollar, Mark, and Yen. IMF Working Paper, No. 95/55. Washington: International Monetary Fund.

MacDonald, R. (1995c): Random Walks, Real Exchange Rates and Panel Unit Root Tests. *Economics Letters*.

MacDonald, R. (1997): What Determines Real Exchange Rates?: The Long and The Short of It. IMF Working Paper, No. 95/55. Washington: International Monetary Fund, June 1995. Forthcoming in *Journal of International Financial Markets, Institutions and Money*.

MacDonald, R. (1999a): *Exchange Rate Economics: Theories and Evidence*, second edition. London: Routledge Kegan Paul.

MacDonald, R. (1999b): Exchange Rates: Do Fundamentals Matter? *Economic Journal*, forthcoming.

MacDonald, R. (2000): Expectations Formation and Risk in Three Financial Markets: Surveying what the Surveys Say. *Journal of Economic Surveys*, forthcoming.

MacDonald, R. and Marsh, I. (1992): Forecasting the Exchange Rate: Are Economists Equally Bad, or Are "N" Heads Better Than One?. Mimeo. University of Strathclyde.

MacDonald, R. and Marsh, I. W. (1994): On Long- and Short-Run Purchasing Power Parity. In *Econometric Analysis of Financial Markets*, ed. Jürgen Kaehler and Peter Kugler. Heidelberg: Physica-Verlag, 23–46.

MacDonald, R. and Marsh, I. W. (1997): On Casselian PPP, Cointegration and Exchange Rate Forecasting. *Review of Economics and Statistics*, November.

MacDonald, R. and Marsh, I. W. (1997): A Forward Premium Puzzle and the Power of the Panel, mimeo, University of Strathclyde.

MacDonald, R. and Marsh, I. W. (1999a): *Exchange Rate Modelling*. Amsterdam: Kluwer Academic Press.

MacDonald, R. and Marsh, I. W. (1999b): Currency Spillovers and Tri-Polarity: A Simultaneous Model of the US Dollar, German Mark and Japanese Yen. CEPR Discussion Paper, No. 2210.

MacDonald, R. and McAvinchey, I. D. (1990): Some Specification Tests of Uncovered Interest Parity. *Recherches Economiques de Louvain*, 56, 61–78.

MacDonald, R. and Milbourne, R. (1991): Recent Developments on Monetary Theory. In D. Greenaway, M. Bleaney, and I. Stewart (eds.), *Companion to Contemporary Economic Thought*. London: Routledge.

MacDonald, R. and Moore, M. (1996): Long-Run Purchasing Power Parity and Structural Change. *Economie Appliquee*, 49, 11–48.

MacDonald, R. and Moore, M. (2000): The Spot–Forward Relationship Revisited: An ERM Perspective. *Journal of International Financial Markets, Institutions and Money*, forthcoming.

MacDonald, R. and Swagel, P. (1998): Real Exchange Rates and the Business Cycle. Forthcoming as IMF Working Paper.

MacDonald, R. and Taylor, M. P. (1988): Empirical Exchange Rate Economics: An Expository Survey. In R. MacDonald and M.P. Taylor, 1989a.

MacDonald, R. and Taylor, M. P. (1989a): *Exchange Rates and Open Economy Macroeconomics.* Oxford: Blackwell.

MacDonald, R. and Taylor, M. P. (1989b): International Parity Conditions. *Greek Economic Review*, 11, 257–90.

MacDonald, R. and Taylor, M. P. (1989c): Foreign Exchange Market Efficiency and Cointegration: Some Evidence from the Recent Float. *Economics Letters*, 29, 63–8.

MacDonald, R. and Taylor, M. P. (1989d): The Term Structure of Forward Foreign Exchange Rate Premiums. *The Manchester School of Economic and Social Studies*, 58, 54–65.

MacDonald, R. and Taylor, M. P. (1989e): Economic Analysis of Foreign Exchange Markets: An Expository Survey. In MacDonald and Taylor, 1989a.

MacDonald, R. and Taylor, M. P. (1990a): International Parity Conditions. In A. S. Courakis and M. P. Taylor (eds.), *Policy Issues for Interdependent Economies.* Oxford: Oxford University Press.

MacDonald, R. and Taylor, M. P. (1990b): Exchange Rates, Policy Convergence and the European Monetary System. *Centre for Economic Policy Research*, Discussion Paper 44, London.

MacDonald, R. and Taylor, M. P. (1991a): Testing Efficiency in the Interwar Foreign Exchange Market: A Multiple Time Series Approach. *Weltwirschaftliches Archiv*, Band 127, 500–23.

MacDonald, R. and Taylor, M. P. (1991b): Exchange Rates, Policy Convergence and the European Monetary System. *Review of Economics and Statistics*, 73, 3, 553–8.

MacDonald, R. and Taylor, M. P. (1991c): The Monetary Model of the Exchange Rate: Long Run Relationships and Coefficient Restrictions. *Economics Letters*, 37, 179–85.

MacDonald, R. and Taylor, M. P. (1992): Exchange Rate Economics: a Survey. *IMF Staff Papers*, 1–57.

MacDonald, R. and Taylor, M. P. (1993): The Monetary Approach to the Exchange Rate: Rational Expectations, Long-Run Equilibrium and Forecasting. *IMF Staff Papers*, forthcoming.

MacDonald, R. and Taylor, M. P. (1994): The Monetary Model of the Exchange Rate: Long-Run Relationships, Short-Run Dynamics, and How to Beat a Random Walk. *Journal of International Money and Finance*, 13, 276–90.

MacDonald, R. and Torrance, T. S. (1987): Monetary Policy and the Real Interest Rate: Some UK Evidence. *The Scottish Journal of Political Economy*, 35, 361–71.

MacDonald, R. and Torrance, T. S. (1987): Sterling M3 Surprises and Asset Prices. *Economica*, 54, 505–15.

MacDonald, R. and Torrance, T. S. (1988a): On Risk, Rationality and Excessive Speculation in the Deutschemark–US Dollar Exchange Market: Some Evidence Using Survey Data. *Oxford Bulletin of Economics and Statistics*, 50(2), 1–17.

MacDonald, R. and Torrance, T. S. (1988b): Covered Interest Parity and UK Monetary "News". *Economics Letters*, 26, 53–6.

MacDonald, R. and Torrance, T. S. (1988c): Exchange Rates and the "News": Some Evidence Using UK Survey Data. *The Manchester School*, 56(1), 69–76.

MacDonald, R. and Torrance, T. S. (1988d): Some Survey Based Tests of Uncovered Interest Parity. In R. MacDonald and M. P. Taylor (eds.), 1989a.

MacDonald, R. and Torrance, T. S. (1989): Some Survey Based Tests of Uncovered Interest Parity. In R. MacDonald and M. P. Taylor (eds.), *Exchange Rates and Open Economy Macroeconomics.* Oxford: Blackwell.

MacDonald, R. and Torrance, T. S. (1990): Expectations Formation and Risk in Four Foreign Exchange Markets. *Oxford Economic Papers*, 42, 544–61.

MacDonald, R. and Young, R. (1986): Decision Rules, Expectations and Efficiency in Two Foreign Exchange Markets. *De Economist*, 134, 42–60.

Machlup, F. (1970): Eurodollar Creation: A Mystery Story. Banca Nazionale del Lavoro *Quarterly Review*, 23, 219–60.

Machlup, F. (1971): The Magicians and their Rabbits. *Morgan Guaranty Survey*, May, 3–13.

Magee, S. P. (1976): The Empirical Evidence on the Monetary Approach to the Balance of Payments and Exchange Rates. *American Economic Review P&P*, 66, 163–70.

Magee, S. P. and Rao, R. (1980): Vehicle and Non-Vehicle Currencies in International Trade. *American Economic Review P&P*, 70, 368–73.

Makin, J. H. (1972): Demand and Supply Functions for Stocks of Eurodollar Deposits: an Empirical Study. *The Review of Economics and Statistics*, 54, 381–91.

Makin, J. H. (1989): Developing-Country Debt Problems After Seven Years. In Dornbusch et al., 1989, 9–20.

Mankiw, N. G. and Summers, L. H. (1984): Do Long-term Interest Rates Over-react to Short-term Interest Rates? *Brookings Papers on Economic Activity*, 1, 223–47.

Mark, N. C. (1985): On Time-varying Risk Premia in the Foreign Exchange Market: An Econometric Analysis. *Journal of Monetary Economics*, 16, 3–58.

Mark, N. C. (1990): Real and Nominal Exchange Rates in the Long-Run: An Empirical Investigation. *Journal of International Economics*, 28, 115–36.

Mark, N. C. (1995): Exchange Rates and Fundamentals: Evidence on Long-Horizon Predictability. *American Economic Review*, 85, 201–18.

Mark, N. C. (1997): Fundamentals of the Real Dollar–Pound Rate 1871–1994.

Mark, N. C., Wu, Y. and Hai, W. (1993): Understanding Spot and Forward Rate Regressions, mimeo, Ohio State University.

Markowitz, H. (1959): *Portfolio Selection: Efficient Diversification of Investments*. New York: Wiley.

Marris, S. (1985): Deficits and the Dollar: the World Economy at Risk. Institute for International Economics, December.

Marshall, A. (1923): *Money, Credit and Commerce*. Basingstoke: Macmillan.

Marston, R. C. (1976): Interest Arbitrage in the Eurocurrency Markets. *European Economic Review*, 7, 1–13.

Marston, R. C. (1990): Systematic Movements in Real Exchange Rates in the G-5: Evidence on the Integration of Internal and External Markets. *Journal of Banking and Finance*, 14, 1023–44.

Marston, R. C. (1990): Pricing to Market in Japanese Manufacturing. *Journal of International Economics*, 29, 217–36.

McCloskey, D. N. and Zecher, J. R. (1976): How the Gold Standard Worked, 1880–1913. In J. A. Frenkel and H. G. Johnson (eds.), *The Monetary Approach to the Balance of Payments*. Toronto: University of Toronto Press, 357–85.

McCormack, F. (1979): Covered Interest Arbitrage: Unexploited Profits? *Journal of Political Economy*, 87, 411–17.

McCulloch, J. H. (1975): Operational Aspects of the Siegal Paradox. *Quarterly Journal of Economics*, 98, 170–2.

McKibben, W. J. and Sachs, J. D. (1991): *Global Linkages, Macroeconomic Interdependence and Cooperation in the World Economy*. Washington, D.C.: The Brookings Institute.

McKinnon, R. I. (1963): Optimum Currency Areas. *American Economic Review*, 53, 717–25.

McKinnon, R. I. (1969a): Portfolio Balance and International Payments Adjustment. In Mundell and Swoboda, 1969.

McKinnon, R. I. (1969b): Private and Official International Money: The Case for the Dollar. Princeton University *Essays in International Finance*, 74.

McKinnon, R. I. (1973): *Money, and Capital in Economic Development*. Washington, D.C.: The Brookings Institute.

McKinnon, R. I. (1974): A New Tripartite Monetary Arrangement for a Limping Dollar Standard? Princeton University *Essays in International Finance*, 106.

McKinnon, R. I. (1976): Floating Exchange Rates 1973–4: The Emperor's New Clothes. *Carnegie–Rochester Supplement to the Journal of Monetary Economics*, 3.

McKinnon, R. I. (1979): *Money in International Exchange*. Oxford: Oxford University Press.

McKinnon, R. I. (1981a): Financial Repression and the Liberalization Problem within Less Developed Countries. In Grassman and Lundberg, 1981, 365–86.

McKinnon, R. I. (1981b): The Exchange Rate and Macroeconomic Policy: Changing Postwar Perceptions. *Journal of Economic Literature*, 19, 531–57.

McKinnon, R. I. (1982a): The Order of Liberalization: Lessons from Chile and Argentina. In Brunner and Meltzer, 1982, 159–86.

McKinnon, R. I. (1982b): Currency Substitution and Instability in the World Dollar Standard. *American Economic Review*, 72(3), 320–33.

McKinnon, R. I. (1983): A Programme for International Monetary Stability. Discussion Paper 3, Centre for Economic Policy Research, Stanford University.

McKinnon, R. I. (1984): International Influences on the US Economy: Summary of an Exchange. *American Economic Review*, 74, 1132–4.

McKinnon, R. I. (1988): Monetary and Exchange Rate Policies for International Financial Stability: A Proposal. *Journal of Economic Perspectives*, 2, 83–103.

McKinnon, R. I. (1989): Financial Liberalization and Economic Development: A Reassessment of Interest-rate Policies in Asia and Latin America. *Oxford Review of Economic Policy*, 5(4), 29–54.

McKinnon, R. I. (1991a): *The Order of Economic Liberalization: Financial Control in the Transition to Market Economy*. Johns Hopkins University Press.

McKinnon, R. I. (1991b): Liberalizing Foreign Trade in a Socialist Economy. In J. Williamson, 1991, 96–115.

McKinnon, R. I. (1993): *The Order of Economic Liberalization: Financial Control in Transition to a Market Economy*. Baltimore: London.

McKinnon, R. I. (1999): The East Asian Dollar Standard, Life After Death? Economic Development Institute, World Bank at The Asia Foundation, San Francisco, 1999.

McKinnon, R. I. and Oates, W. (1966): The Implications of International Economic Integration for Monetary, Fiscal and Exchange Rate Policy. Princeton University *Essays in International Finance*, 16.

McKinnon, R. I. and Tan, K-Y. (1983): Currency Substitution and Instability in the World Dollar Standard: A Reply. *American Economic Review*, 73, 474–6.

McKinnon, R. I. et al. (1984): International Influences on the US Economy: Summary of an Exchange. *American Economic Review*, 74, 1132–4.

Meade, J. E. (1951): *The Balance of Payments*. Oxford: Oxford University Press.

Meade, J. E. (1956): *The Theory of Customs Unions*. Amsterdam: North-Holland.

Meese, R. A. (1984): The Out-of-Sample Failure of Empirical Exchange Rate Models: Sampling Error or Misspecification? In J. A. Frenkel (ed.), *Exchange Rates and International Macroeconomics*. Chicago: NBER, 67–109.

Meese, R. A. (1986): Testing for Bubbles in Exchange Markets: A Case of Sparkling Rates. *Journal of Political Economy*, 94, 345–73.

Meese, R. A. and Rogoff, K. (1984): Empirical Exchange Rate Models of the Seventies: Do they Fit Out of Sample? *Journal of International Economics*, 14, 3–24.

Meese, R. A. and Rogoff, K. (1988): Was It Real? The Exchange Rate–Interest Differential Relation Over the Modern Floating-Rate Period. *Journal of Finance*, 43, 933–48.

Meese, R. A. and Rose, A. K. (1990): Non-linear, NonParameter Nonessential Exchange Rate Estimation. *American Economic Review*, May, 80, 192–96.

Melitz, J. (1995): A Suggested Reformulation of the Theory of Optimal Currency Areas. *Open Economies Review*, 6, 281–98.

Mendoza, E. G. (1992): The Effect of Macroeconomic Shocks in a Basic Equilibrium Framework. *IMF Staff Papers*, 39(4), 855–89.

Michael, P., Nobay, A. R. and Peel, D. A. (1997): Transaction Costs and Nonlinear Adjustment in Real Exchange Rates: An Empirical Investigation. *Journal of Political Economy*, 105, 4.

Michaely, M. (1962): *Concentration in International Trade.* Amsterdam: North-Holland.

Michaely, M., Choski, A. and Papageorgiou, D. (1989): The Design of Trade Liberalization. *Finance and Development*, 2–5.

Micossi, S. and Miles-Ferretti, G. M. (1994): Real Exchange Rates and the Prices of Nontradable Goods. IMF Working Paper No. 94/19.

Miller, M. and Weller, P. (1991): Currency Bands, Target Zones and Price Flexibility. *IMF Staff Papers*, 38, 184–215.

Miller, M., Eichengreen, B. and Portes, R. (eds.) (1989): *Blueprints for Exchange Rate Management.* London: Academic Press.

Miller, S. M. (1988b): Are Saving and Investment Cointegrated? *Economics Letters*, 27, 31–4.

Minford, P. (1989): Do Floating Exchange Rates Insulate? In MacDonald and Taylor, 1989a.

Minford, P., Agenor, R. and Nowell, E. (1986): A New Classical Econometric Model of the World Economy. *Economic Modelling*, 3, 154–74.

Minford, P. and Peel, D. A. (1983): *Rational Expectations and the New Macroeconomics.* Oxford: Martin Robertson.

Mizrach, B. (1995): Target Zone Models with Stochastic Realignments: An Econometric Evaluation. *Journal of International Money and Finance* 14(5), 641–57.

Montiel, P. J. and Ostry, J. D. (1991): Macroeconomic Implications of Real Exchange Rate Targeting in Developing Countries. *IMF Staff Papers*, 37(1), 872–900.

Montiel, P. J. and Ostry, J. D. (1992): Real Exchange Rate Targeting Under Capital Controls. *IMF Staff Papers*, 39(1), 58–78.

Moore, M. J. (1993): System of Bilateral Real Exchange Rates. *Applied Economics*, 25, 1161–6.

Morgan-Webb, C. (1934): *The Rise and Fall of the Gold Standard.* New York: Macmillan.

Mundell, R. A. (1961): A Theory of Optimum Currency Areas. *American Economic Review*, 51, 657–65.

Mundell, R. A. (1962): The Appropriate Use of Monetary and Fiscal Policy for Internal and External Balance. *IMF Staff Papers*.

Mundell, R. A. (1963): Capital Mobility and Stabilization Policy under Fixed and Flexible Exchange Rates. *Canadian Journal of Economics and Political Science*, 475–85.

Mundell, R. A. (1968): *International Economics.* New York: Macmillan.

Mundell, R. A. and Swoboda, A. K. (1969): *Monetary Problems in the International Economy.* Chicago: University of Chicago Press.

Mussa, M. (1976): The Exchange Rate, the Balance of Payments and Monetary and Fiscal Policy under a Regime of Controlled Floating. *Scandinavian Journal of Economics*, 78, 229–48.

Mussa, M. (1979a): Empirical Regularities in the Behaviour of Exchange Rates and Theories of the Foreign Exchange Market. In Brunner and Meltzer, 1979, 9–57.

Mussa, M. (1979b): Macroeconomic Interdependence and the Exchange Rate Regime. In Dornbusch et al. (eds.), 1979.

Mussa, M. (1981): The Role of Official Intervention. *Group of Thirty Occasional Papers*, 6.

Mussa, M. (1982): A Model of Exchange Rate Dynamics. *Journal of Political Economy*, 90, 74–104.

Mussa, M. (1984): The Theory of Exchange Rate Determination. In J. F. O. Bilson and R. C. Marston (eds.), *Exchange Rate Theory and Practice*, NBER Conference Report. Chicago: The University of Chicago Press.

Mussa, M. (1986): Nominal Exchange Rate Regimes and the Behaviour of Real Exchange Rates: Evidence and Implications. *Carnegie-Rochester Conference Series on Public Policy*, 26.

Myhram, J. (1976): Experiences of Flexible Exchange Rates in Earlier Periods: Theories, Evidence and a New View. *Scandinavian Journal of Economics*, 78(2), 169–96.

Myint, H. (1971): *Economic Theory and Underdeveloped Countries*. New York: Oxford University Press.

Nerlove, M., Dieblod, F. X., van Beeck, H. and Cheung, Y. (1988): A Multivariate ARCH Model of Foreign Exchange Rate Determination, mimeo, University of California.

Niehans, J. (1968): Monetary and Fiscal Policies in Open Economies Under Fixed Exchange Rates. *Journal of Political Economy*, 68, 893–920.

Niehans, J. (1975): Some Doubts About the Efficiency of Monetary Policy Under Flexible Exchange Rates. *Journal of International Economics*, 5, 275–81.

Niehans, J. (1984): *International Monetary Economics*. Baltimore: Johns Hopkins University Press.

Obstfeld, M. (1982): Can We Sterilize? Theory and Evidence? *American Economic Review P&P*, 72, 45–50.

Obstfeld, M. (1985): Floating Exchange Rates: Experiences and Prospects. *Brookings Papers on Economic Activity*, 2, 369–450.

Obstfeld, M. (1986): Rational and Self-fulfilling Balance of Payments Crises. *American Economic Review*, 76, 72–81.

Obstfeld, M. (1995): International Capital Mobility in the 1990's. In P. B. Kenen (ed.): *Understanding Interdependence: The Macroeconomics of the Open Economy*. Princeton, NJ: Princeton University Press.

Obstfeld, M. and Rogoff, K. (1998): *Foundations of International Macroeconomics*. Cambridge, MA: MIT Press.

Obstfeld, M. and Taylor, A. M. (1997): Nonlinear Aspects of Goods-Market Arbitrage and Adjustment: Hecksher's Commodity Points Revisited. *Journal of Japanese and International Economies*, 11, 441–79.

O'Connell, P. (1996): Market Frictions and Relative Traded Goods Prices. *Journal of International Money and Finance*, forthcoming.

O'Connell, P. (1997): The Overvaluation of Purchasing Power Parity. *Journal of International Economics*, 44, 1–21.

O'Connell, P. and Wei, S-J. (1997): The Bigger They Are the Harder They Fall: How Price Differences Across US Cities are Arbitraged, mimeo.

Officer, L. H. (1976): The Purchasing Power Parity Theory of Exchange Rates: A Review Article. *IMF Staff Papers*, 23, 1–60.

Officer, L. H. (1982): *Purchasing Power Parity and Exchange Rates: Theory, Evidence and Relevance*. Greenwich, CT: JAI Press.

Officer, L. H. (1993): Gold Point Arbitrage and Uncovered Interest Arbitrage Under the 1925–31 Dollar-Sterling Gold Standard. *Explorations in Economic History*, 30(1), 98–127.

Officer, L. H. (1996): *Between the Dollar–Sterling Gold Points*. Cambridge: Cambridge University Press.

Oh, K-Y. (1996): Purchasing Power Parity and Unit Root Test Using Panel Data. *Journal of International Money and Finance*, 15, 405–18.

Ohlin, B. (1967): *Interregional and International Trade*. Cambridge, MA: Harvard University Press.

Okun, A. (1965): The Gap Between Actual and Potential Output. In *The Battle Against Unemployment*, A. Okun (ed.), 13–22, Norton.

Ostry, J. D. (1991): Trade Liberalization in Developing Countries: Initial Trade Distortions and Imported Intermediate Inputs. *IMF Staff Papers*.

Oudiz, G. and Sachs, J. D. (1985): International Policy Coordination in Dynamic Macro-economic Models. In Buiter and Marston, 1985.

Owen, D. and Fallas, O. S. (1989): Unorganized Money Markets and Unproductive Assets in the New Structuralist Critique of Financial Liberalization. *Journal of Development Economics*, 31(3), 341–55.

Papell, D. H. (1997): Searching for Stationarity: Purchasing Power Parity Under the Current Float. *Journal of International Economics*, 43, 211–40.

Papell, D. H. and Theodoris, H. (1997): The Choice of Numeraire Currency in Panel Tests of Purchasing Power Parity, mimeo, University of Houston.

Parkin, M., Richards, L. and Zis, G. (1977): The Determination and Control of the World Money Supply Under Fixed Exchange Rates 1961–71. *Manchester School*, 293–316.

Parkin, J. M. and Zis, G. (eds.) (1976): *Inflation in the World Economy*. Manchester: Manchester University Press.

Patel, J. (1990): Purchasing Power Parity as a Long-Run Relation. *Journal of Applied Econometrics*, 367–79.

Pattison, L. (1976): The International Transmission of Inflation. In Parkin and Zis, 1977.

Pearson Commission (1969): *Partners in Development*. London: Pall Mall Press.

Pedroni, P. (1997): Panel Cointegration: Asymptotic and Finite Sample Properties of Pooled Time Series Tests with an Application to the PPP Hypothesis, mimeo, Indiana University.

Perez-Campanero, J. and Leone, A. M. (1991): Liberalization and Financial Crisis in Uruguay (1974–87). IMF, WP/91/30.

Perron, P. and Vogeslang, T. J. (1992): Nonstationarity and Level Shifts with and Application to Purchasing Power Parity. *Journal of Business and Economic Statistics*, 10, 301–20.

Phillips, P. C. B. (1987): Time Series Regression with a Unit Root. *Econometrica*, 55, 277–301.

Phillips, P. C. B. and Hansen, B. E. (1990): Statistical Inference in Instrumental Variables Regression with I(1) Processes. *Review of Economic Studies*, 57, 99–125.

Phylaktis, K. (1991): The Black Market for Dollars in Chile. *Journal of Development Economics*, 37, 155–72.

Polak, J. J. (1957): Monetary Analysis of Income Formation and Payments Problems. *IMF Staff Papers*, 4, 1–50.

Polak, J. J. (1991b): The Changing Nature of IMF Conditionality. Princeton University *Essays in International Finance*, 184.

Poole, W. (1967): Speculative Prices as Random Walks: An Analysis of Ten Time Series of Flexible Exchange Rates. *Southern Economic Journal*, 33, 4.

Poole, W. (1970): Optimal Choice of Monetary Policy Instruments in a Simple Stochastic Macro Model. *Quarterly Journal of Economics*, 85.

Poterba, J. M. and Summers, L. H. (1988): Mean Reversion in Stock Prices: Evidence and Implications. *Journal of Financial Economics*, 22, 27–59.

Putnam, B. H. and Woodbury, J. R. (1980): Exchange Rate Stability and Monetary Policy. *Review of Business and Economic Research*, 15, 1–10.

Quah, D. (1994): Exploiting Cross-Section Variation for Unit Root Inference in Dynamic Data. *Economics Letter*, 44(1), 9–19.

Rabin, A. A. and Yeager, L. B. (1982): Monetary Approaches to the Balance of Payments and Exchange Rates. Princeton University *Essays in International Finance*, 148.

Radcliffe, L., Warga, A. and Willet, I.D. (1984): Currency Substitution and Instability in the World Dollar Standard: Comment. *American Economic Review*, 74, 1129–31.

Radcliffe Committee (1959): *Report on the Working of the Monetary System*, Cmnd 827. London: HMSO.

Razin, A. and Sadka, E. (1989): Optimal Incentives to Domestic Investment in the Presence of Capital Flight. IMF, WP/89/79.

Ribe, H. and Carvalho, S. (1990): Adjustment and the Poor. *Finance and Development*, 27(3), 15–17.

Richards, A. and Terseman, G. (1995): Growth, Nontradeables and Price Convergence in the Baltics. *IMF Working Paper*, 95/45.

Robinson, J. (1937): The Foreign Exchanges. *Essays on the Theory of Employment.*

Robinson, J. D. (1988): A Comprehensive Agenda for LDC Debt and World Trade Growth. The Amex Bank Review, *Special Papers*, No. 13, March.

Robinson, R. J. and Schmitz, L. (1989): Jamaica: Navigating Through a Troubled Decade. *Finance and Development*, 26(4), December, 30–3.

Rogers, J. H. (1995): Real Shocks and Real Exchange Rates in Really Long-Term Data. Princeton University, *International Finance Discussion Paper*, No. 493.

Rogers, J. H. and Jenkins, M. (1995): Haircuts or Hysteresis? Sources of Movements in Real Exchange Rates. *Journal of International Economics*, 38, 339–60.

Rogoff, K. (1984): On the Effects of Sterilized Intervention: An Analysis of Weekly Data. *Journal of Monetary Economics*, 14, 123–50.

Rogoff, K. (1985): Can International Monetary Policy Coordination be Counter-Productive? *Journal of International Economics*, 18, 199–217.

Rogoff, K. (1992): Traded Goods, Consumption Smoothing and the Random Walk Behaviour of the Real Exchange Rate. NBER Working Paper No. 4119.

Rogoff, K. (1995): The Purchasing Power Parity Puzzle. *Journal of Economic Literature*, 34, 647–668.

Rojas-Suarez, L. (1990): Risk and Capital Flight in Developing Countries. IMF, Working Paper WP/90/64.

Roll, R. (1979): Violations of Purchasing Power Parity and Their Implications for Efficient International Commodity Markets. In M. Sarnat and Szego, G. (eds.), *International Finance and Trade 1*. Cambridge, MA: Ballinger.

Roper, D. (1975): The Role of Expected Value Analysis for Speculative Decisions in the Forward Currency Market. *Quarterly Journal of Economics*, 89, 157–69.

Rose, A. K. and Svensson, L. E. O. (1991): Expected and Predicted Realignments: the FF/DM Exchange Rate During the EMS. Institute for International Economic Studies, Paper 485, Stockholm.

Ross, M. H. (1983): Currency Substitution and Instability in the World Dollar Standard. *American Economic Review*, 73, p. 473.

Ruff, J. (1967): A Dollar-Reserve System as a Transitional Solution. Princeton University *Essays in International Finance*, 57.

Sachs, J. D. (1989): *Developing Country Debt and the World Economy*. Chicago: University of Chicago Press.

Sachs, J. D. and Radelet, S. (1998): The East Asian Financial Crisis. www.hiid.harvard.edu.

Sachs, J. A. and McKibben, W. D. (1985): Macroeconomic Policies in the OECD and LDC External Adjustment. NBER Working Paper No. 1255. Cambridge, MA.

Sachs, J. A., Tornell, A. and Velasco, A. (1996): Financial Crises in Emerging Markets: the Lessons from 1995. *Brookings Papers on Economic Activity*, 16, 147–215.

Salant, W. (1941): Foreign Trade Policy in the Business Cycle. *Public Policy.*

Sali-i-Martin, X. and Sachs, J. (1992): Fiscal Federalism and Optimum Currency Areas: Evidence for Europe from the US. In Canzoneri, M. et al., *Establishing a Central Bank: Issues in Europe and Lessons for the US.* Cambridge: Cambridge University Press, 195–219.

Salin, P. (1982): Lessons from the European Monetary System. In Connolly (ed.), 1982, 175–98.

Salop, J. (1974): Devaluation and the Balance of Trade under Flexible Wages. In G. Horwich and P. Samuelson (eds.), *Essays in Honour of Lloyd O. Metzler.* London: Macmillan.

Salter, W. (1959): Internal and External Balance: The Role of Price and Expenditure Effects. *Economic Record,* August, 226–38.

Samuelson, P. (1964): Theoretical Problems on Trade Problems. *Review of Economics and Statistics,* 46, 145–54.

Sargent, T. (1979): A Note on Maximum Likelihood Estimation of the Rational Expectations Model of the Term Structure. *Journal of Monetary Economics,* 84, 133–43.

Sarte, P. (1994): On the Identification of Structural VARs, unpublished mimeo, University of Rochester.

Savvides, A. (1993): Real Exchange Rate Variability and the Choice of Exchange Rate Regime by Developing Countries. *Journal of International Money and Finance,* 9, 440–54.

Schinasi, G. J. and Swamy, P. A. V. B. (1987): The Out-of-Sample Forecasting Performance of Exchange Rate Models when Coefficients are Allowed to Change. *International Finance Discussion Papers of the Federal Reserve System,* No. 301, Washington, D.C.

Schwartz, A. J. (1987): *Money in Historical Perspective.* Chicago: University of Chicago Press.

Schwert, G. W. (1987): Effects of Model Specification on Tests for Unit Roots in Macroeconomic Data. *Journal of Monetary Economics,* 20, 73–103.

Sercu, P., Uppal, D. and Van Hulle, R. (1995): The Exchange Rate in the Presence of Transaction Costs: Implications for Tests of Purchasing Power Parity. *Journal of Finance,* 50, 1309–19.

Sharpley, J. (1983): Economic Management and IMF Conditionality in Jamaica. In Williamson, 1983.

Shaw, E. S. (1973): *Financial Deepending in Economic Development.* New York: Oxford University Press.

Shiller, R. J. (1981): Do Stock Prices Move too Much to be Justified by Subsequent Changes in Fundamentals? *American Economic Review,* 71, 421–36.

Shiller, R. J. (1990): *Stock Market Volatility.* Cambridge, MA: MIT Press.

Shiller, R. J. and Perron, P. (1985): Testing the Random Walk Hypothesis: Power Versus Frequency of Observation. *Economics Letters,* 18, 381–6.

Siegal, J. (1972): Risk, Interest Rates and the Forward Exchange Rate. *Quarterly Journal of Economics,* 86, 303–9.

Smith, G. W. and Cuddington, J. T. (eds.) (1985): *International Debt and the Developing Countries.* World Bank, Washington, D.C.

Smith, P. and Wickens, M. (1990): Assessing Monetary Shocks and Exchange Rate Variability with a Stylised Econometric Model of the UK. In A. S. Courakis and M. P. Taylor (eds.), *Private Behaviour and Government Policy in Interdependent Economies.* Oxford: Oxford University Press.

Sohmen, E. (1961): *Flexible Exchange Rates.* Chicago: University of Chicago Press.

Sohmen, E. (1967): Fiscal and Monetary Policies under Alternative Exchange Rate Systems. *Quarterly Journal of Economics,* 81, 515–23.

Solnik, B. H. (1974): Why Not Diversify Internationally Rather than Domestically? *Financial Analysts Journal,* July–August, 48–54.

Spinelli, F. (1983): Currency Substitution, Flexible Exchange Rates, and the Case for International Monetary Cooperation. *IMF Staff Papers,* 30, 755–83.

Spitaller, E. (1980): Short Run Effects of Exchange Rate Changes on the Terms of Trade and Trade Balance. *IMF Staff Papers*, 27(2), 320–48.

Spraos, J. (1986): IMF Conditionality: Ineffectual, Inefficient, Mistargeted. Princeton University *Essays in International Finance*, 166.

Stein, J. (1998): The Evolution of the Real Value of the US Dollar Relative to the G7 Currencies. In R. MacDonald and J. Stein (eds.), *Equilibrium Exchange Rates*. Boston: Kluwer.

Stein, J. and Allen, P. R. (1995): Fundamental Determinants of Exchange Rates. Oxford: Oxford University Press.

Stern, R. M. (1973): *The Balance of Payments: Theory and Economic Policy*. London: Macmillan.

Stevenson, A., Muscatelli, A. and Gregory, M. (1988): *Macroeconomic Theory and Stabilization Policy*. Oxford: Phillip Allan.

Stiglitz, J. and Weiss, A. (1981): Credit Rationing in Markets with Imperfect Information. *American Economic Review*, 71, 393–410.

Stock, J. H. (1987): Asymptotic Properties of Least Squares Estimators of Cointegrating Vectors. *Econometrica*, 55, 1035–56.

Stockman, A. (1978): Risk, Information and Forward Exchange Rates. In Johnson and Frenkel (eds.), 1978.

Stockman, A. (1980): A Theory of Exchange Rate Determination. *Journal of Political Economy*, 88, 673–98.

Stockman, A. (1987): The Equilibrium Approach to Exchange Rates. Federal Reserve Bank of Richmond *Economic Review*.

Stockman, A. (1988): Real Exchange Rate Variability Under Pegged and Floating Nominal Exchange Rate Systems: An Equilibrium Theory. *Carnegie–Rochester Conference Series on Public Policy*, 29, 259–94.

Stockman, A. (1994): Sources of Exchange Rate Fluctuations: a Comment. Carnegie-Rochester Conference Series on Public Policy, 41, 57–65.

Stockman, A. (1995): Sources of Real Exchange-Rate Fluctuations: A Comment. *Carnegie–Rochester Conference Series on Public Policy*, 41, 57–65.

Strauss, J. (1995): Real Exchange Rates, PPP and the Relative Price of Nontraded Goods. *Southern Economic Journal*, 61, 991–1005.

Strauss, J. (1996): The Cointegrating Relationship Between Productivity, Real Exchange Rates and Purchasing Power Parity. *Journal of Macroeconomics*, 18, 299–313.

Stymne, J. (1989): Debt Growth and the Prospects for Debt Reduction: The Case of sub-Saharan African Countries. IMF, WP/89/71.

Sumner, S. (1991): The Equilibrium Approach to Discretionary Monetary Policy under an International Gold Standard. *Manchester School*, 59(4), 378–94.

Sundakov, A., Ossowski, R. and Lane, T. D. (1994): Shortages Under Free Prices: The Case of Ukraine in 1992. *IMF Staff Papers*, 41(3), 411–24.

Svensson, L. E. O. (1993): Assessing Target Zone Credibility: Mean Reversion and Devaluation Expectations in the ERM: 1979–1992. *European Economic Review*, 37, 763–802.

Svensson, L. E. O. (1991): The Simplest Test of Target Zone Credibility. *IMF Staff Papers*, 38, 655–65.

Svensson, L. E. O. (1992): An Interpretation of Recent Research on Exchange Rate Target Zones. *Journal of Economic Perspectives*, 6(4), 119–44.

Swan, T. (1955): Longer-run Problems of the Balance of Payments. In *Readings in International Economics*. American Economic Association, London: Allen and Unwin.

Sweeney, R. J. (1986): Beating the Foreign Exchange Market. *Journal of Finance*, 41, 163–82.

Swoboda, A. K. (1968): The eurodollar Market: An Interpretation. Princeton University *Essays in International Finance*, 64.

Swoboda, A. K. (1976): Monetary Policy Under Fixed Exchange Rates: Effectiveness, the speed of Adjustment and Proper Use. In Johnson and Swoboda.

Tait, A. A. (1989): IMF Advice on Fiscal Policy. IMF 89/87.

Tanzi, V. (1987): Fiscal Policy, Growth, and Stabilization Programmes. *Finance and Development*, 87(2), 15–17.

Tanzi, V. (1989): Fiscal Policy and Economic Reconstruction in Latin America. IMF, WP/89/94.

Tanzi, V. (1990): The IMF and Tax Reform. IMF, WP/90/39.

Tanzi, V. (1991): Mobilization of Savings in Eastern European Countries: The Role of the State. In Atkinson and Brunetta, 1991.

Tanzi, V. (1993): The Budget Deficit in Transition: A Cautious Note. *IMF Staff Papers*, 40(3), 697–707.

Taussig, F. W. (1927): *International Trade*. New York: Macmillan.

Tavlas, G. S. (1994): The Theory of Monetary Integration. *Open Economies Review*, 5, 211–30.

Tavlas, G. S. and Ozeki, Y. (1992): The Internationalization of Currencies: An Appraisal of the Japanese Yen. IMF *Occasional Paper*, 90.

Taylor, J. B. (1988): Should the International Monetary System be Based on Fixed of Flexible Exchange Rates? *International Monetary Policy Rules: An Econometric Evaluation*.

Taylor, L. (1983): *Structuralist Macroeconomics*. New York: Basic Books.

Temin, P. (1989): *The Lessons from the Great Depression*. Cambridge, MA: MIT Press.

Tew, B. (1977): *The Evolution of the International Monetary System 1945–77*. Amsterdam: North-Holland.

Tew, B. (1982): *The Evolution of the International Monetary System*. London: Hutchinson.

Throop, A. (1994): A Generalised Incovered Interest Rate Parity Model of Real Exchange Rates. Federal Reserve Bank of San Fransisco, mimeo.

Tinbergen, J. (1952): *On the Theory of Economic Policy*. Amsterdam: North-Holland.

Tirole, J. (1982): On the Possibility of Speculation under Rational Expectations. *Econometrica*, 50, 1163–81.

Tobin, J. (1958): Liquidity Preference as Behaviour Towards Risk. *Review of Economic Studies*, 25(1), 65–86.

Tobin, J. (1967): Commercial Banks as Creators of Money. In Hestor and Tobin, 1967.

Tobin, J. (1969): A General Equilibrium Approach to Monetary Theory. *Journal of Money Credit and Banking*, 1, 15–30.

Tobin, J. and Buiter, W. H. (1976): Long Run Effects of Fiscal and Monetary Policy on Aggregate Demand. In J. L. Stein (ed.), *Monetarism*. Amsterdam: North-Holland.

Tokarick, S. (1995): External Shocks, the Real Exchange Rate, and Tax Policy. *IMF Staff Papers*, 42(1), 49–79.

Tootell, G. M. B. (1992): Purchasing Power Parity Within the United States. *New England Economic Review*. Federal Reserve Bank of Boston, July/August, 15–24.

Triffin, R. (1960): *Gold and the Dollar Crisis*. New Haven: Yale University Press.

Triffin, R. (1969): The Myth and Realities of the So-called Gold Standard. In Cooper, 1969.

Tsay, R. S. (1989): Testing and Modeling Threshold Autoregressive Processes. *Journal of the American Statistical Association*, 84, 231–40.

Tsiang, S. C. (1959): The Theory of Forward Exchange and Effects of Government Intervention on the Forward Exchange Market. *IMF Staff Papers*, 75–106.

Tsiang, S. C. (1961): The Role of Money in Trade Balance Stability: Synthesis of the Elasticity and Absorption Approaches. *American Economic Review*, 912–36.

Tullio, G. and Wolters, J. (1996): Was London the Conductor of the International Orchestra or Just the Triangle Player? An Empirical Analysis of Asymmetries in Interest Rate Behaviour During the Classical Gold Standard, 1876–1913. *Scottish Journal of Political Economy*, 43(4), 419–43.

Ugarteche, O. (1988): Peru: The Foreign Debt and Heterodox Adjustment Policy Under Alan Garcia. In S. Griffith-Jones, 1988, 170–92.

Ungerer, H., Hauvonen, J. J., Lopez-Claros, A. and Mayer, T. (1990): *The EMS: Developments and Perspectives*. IMF, Occasional Paper 73, November, Washington, D.C.

Urich, T. J. and Wachtel, P. (1981): Market Responses to Weekly Money Supply Announcements in the 1970's. *Journal of Finance*, 36, 1063–72.

Van Wijnbergen, S. (1982): Stagflationary Effects of Monetary Stabilization Policies: A Quantitative Analysis of South Korea. *Journal of Development Economics*, 10, 133–69.

Van Wijnbergen, S. (1983a): Credit Policy, Inflation and Growth in a Financially Repressed Economy. *Journal of Development Economics*, 13(3), 45–65.

Van Wijnbergen, S. (1983b): Interest Rate Management in Ldcs. *Journal of Monetary Economics*, 12(3), September, 433–52.

Vaubel, R. (1980): International Shifts in the Demand for Money, their Effects on Exchange Rates and Price Levels and their Implications for the Preannouncements of Monetary Expansion. *Weltwirtschaftliches Archiv*, 116, 1–44.

Villanueva, D. and Mirakhor, A. (1990): Strategies for Financial Reforms. *IMF Staff Papers*, 37(3), 509–36.

Vines, D. and Muscatelli, A. (1989): Macroeconomic Interactions Between North and South. In Bryant et al., 1979, 381–412.

Wadhwani, S. (1984): Are Exchange Rates "Excessively" Volatile? Centre for Labour Economics, Discussion Paper 198, London: London School of Economics.

Weber, A. (1997): Sources of Purchasing Power Disparities between the G3 Economies. *Journal of Japanese and International Economies*, 11, 548–83.

Wei, S-J. and Parsley, D. (1995): Purchasing Power Disparity during the Recent Floating Rate Period: Exchange Rate Volatility, Trade Barriers and Other Culprits. *Quarterly Journal of Economics*.

Weil, G. (1987): The Pegging Practices of Less Developed Countries: A Look at Recent Behaviour. *Eastern Economic Journal*, March, 49–53.

Whitman, M. (1975): Global Monetarism and the Monetary Approach to the Balance of Payments. *Brookings Papers on Economic Activity*, 3, 491–536.

Whitt, J. A. (1992): The Long-Run Behaviour of the Real Exchange Rate: A Reconsideration. *Journal of Money, Credit and Banking*, 24, 72–82.

Williamson, J. (1973): International Liquidity: A Survey. *Economic Journal*, 83, 685–746.

Williamson, J. (1976): Exchange Rate Flexibility and Reserve Use. *Scandinavian Journal of Economics*, 78, 327–39.

Williamson, J. (1977): *The Failure of World Monetary Reform, 1971–74*. New York: New York University Press.

Williamson, J. (1983a): *IMF Conditionality*. Cambridge, MA: MIT Press.

Williamson, J. (1983b): *The Exchange Rate System*. Institute for International Finance, Washington, D.C.

Williamson, J. (1985): *The Exchange Rate System*. Washington, D.C.: Institute for International Economics.

Williamson, J. (1988): Comment on McKinnon's Monetary Rule. *Journal of Economic Perspectives*, 2, 113–19.

Williamson, J. (1991): *Currency Convertibility in Eastern Europe*. Washington, D.C.: Institute for International Economics.

Williamson, J. (1993): Comment. In Bordo and Eichengreen, 1993.

Williamson, J. (1994): *Estimating Equilibrium Exchange Rates.* Washington, D.C.: Institute for International Economics.

Wolff, C. P. (1987): Forward Foreign Exchange Rates, Expected Spot Rates, and Premia: A Signal-Extraction Approach. *Journal of Finance,* 42, 395–406.

Wolff, C. P. (1987): Time-Varying Parameters and the Out-of Sample Forecasting Performance of Structural Exchange Rate Models. *Journals of Business and Economics Statistics,* 5, 87–97.

World Bank (1989a): *World Development Report.* Oxford: Oxford University Press.

World Bank (1989b): *Liberalizing Foreign Trade.* Oxford: Basil Blackwell.

World Bank (1990): *World Debt Tables: Volume I Analysis and Summary.* Washington, D.C., December.

World Bank (1991): *World Development Report: 1991,* Washington, D.C.: World Bank.

Wren-Lewis, S. (1992): On the Analytical Foundations of the Fundamental Equilibrium Exchange Rate. In C. P. Hargreaves (ed.), *Macroeconomic Modelling of the Long Run.* Aldenshot: Edward Elgar.

Wu, Y. (1996): Are Real Exchange Rates Nonstationary? Evidence from a Panel Data Set. *Journal of Money Credit and Banking,* 28, 54–63.

Wyplosz, C. (1993): Comment. In Bordo and Eichengreen, 1993, 150–2.

Yamori, N. (1995): The Relationship Between Domestic Savings and Investment: The Feldstein–Horioka Test Using Japanese Regional Data. *Economic Letters,* 48, 261–366.

Yeager, L. B. (1958): A Rehabilitation of Purchasing Power Parity Theory. *Journal of Political Economy,* 66, 516–30.

Zecher, J. R. (1976): Monetary Equilibrium and International Reserve Flows in Australia. In Johnson and Frenkel (eds.), 1976.

Author Index

Subject Index

hybrid exchange rate model 199–201; inflation as a worldwide phenomenon 173–5; long-term capital mobility 400–1, 402–4; Mundell–Fleming model 220; news and the exchange rate 295–9; portfolio balance model 242–6, 298; PPP 136 (*by method used*: autoregressive model 142–3, cointegration test 144–5, exponentially autoregressive model 143–4, Johansen's method 144, 146, 148, 150, non-linear tests 142–3, unit cost test 137–44, variance ratio test 138); predictions of target zone model 325–6, 341; real exchange rate 147–50 (trends in transition economies 451–3); real interest rate parity 41–2; realignment expectations 348, 351–2; reserve creation in the dollar standard 362; reserve offset coefficient 168–70; risk premium 268–74; speculative attack 311–12, 313; speculative bubbles 206–8; sticky price monetary model 198–200, 299; uncovered interest parity 41

ECU 480

Efficient Markets Hypothesis (EMH) 4, 178–9, 277, 300, 302; as joint hypothesis 4, 253, 256, 257; forward market for foreign exchange 255–9; news approach 294–5; noise trader 4, 177, 278, 299, 300–2; peso effect and regime changes 4; 279; 285; weak, semi- and strong-form efficiency 257, 262, 275; tests of 259 (choice of estimator 261, failure of 288–91, properties of forecasting errors 260–1, rejection of unbiasedness 261)

elasticities approach to the balance of payments 3, 28–31 156; compared with other theories 156–9; J curve 29–30; Marshall–Lerner condition derived 28–9; problems with 44, 64; US elasticities 30

elasticities view of the exchange rate 24, 26, 27, 55; Balassa–Samuelson thesis 130

emerging markets 46, 47, 65. *See also* Asia; developing countries; Latin America

equilibrium real exchange rate 46–9, 129–30, 147–50, 445; Balassa–Samuelson theorem 145–7; faster productivity growth 132–3; transition economies 445–9, 451–3, 453

euro, the 8, 475, 476–9, 481

eurobanks 8, 390–6; Brady plan 467; debt management system 394–6; lenders' trap 466–7; money multiplier 393–4, 407

eurobonds 404–7; used in empirical test of covered interest parity 39

European central bank 8, 475

European currency snake 7

European Monetary System (EMS) 6, 7, 8, 367, 377, 383, 387, 476; as DM bloc 480–1; target zone 322, 325, 326, 328, 337, 346

European Union 7, 96, 98, 99, 354; case for two speed 384. *See also* monetary union

ex ante PPP 37–8

exchange market pressure model 6, 196, 312, 332–4

exchange rate forecasting xvii, 1, 5, 23, 35 250–5, 274; bubbles 206–8; can beat a random walk 203–6; can't beat a random walk 201; deterministic chaos 287–8; efficient markets hypothesis 255–9; expectational failures 280–94; forward premium as an optimal predictor 261–3; news 294–300; noise traders 300–2; peso effects 278–80; risk premium 263–8, 268–74. *See also* econometric tests; efficient market hypothesis

exchange rate mechanism (of the EMS) 112, 141

exchange rate theories 3, 4, 5; augmented fundamentals model 215–17; currency substitution 193–6; exchange market pressure model 332–4; flexible price monetary approach 179–85, 213–15; general equilibrium monetary model 213–15; hybrid model 199–200; Mundell–Fleming model 68–72, 74, 75, 80–3, 84; portfolio balance model 226–42; purchasing power parity sticky price model (overshooting) 84, 188–93, 201 212; target zones 321–32; *and*

Made in the USA
Lexington, KY
07 September 2014